FIVE HUNDRED YEARS
OF CHAUCER CRITICISM
AND ALLUSION
1357–1900

VOLUME I
CONTAINING
PART 1

PORTRAIT OF CHAUCER, PAINTED BY ORDER OF HIS FRIEND AND PUPIL THOMAS HOCCLEVE

In a MS. Copy of the Latter's 'Regiment of Princes' Written 1412

MS. Harl. 4866. Fol 87 back (British Museum)

FIVE HUNDRED YEARS
OF CHAUCER CRITICISM
AND ALLUSION
1357–1900

By

CAROLINE F. E. SPURGEON

DOCTEUR DE L'UNIVERSITÉ DE PARIS; HON. LITT. D. MICHIGAN;
HILDRED CARLILE PROFESSOR OF ENGLISH LITERATURE IN THE
UNIVERSITY OF LONDON

WITH
TWENTY-FOUR
COLLOTYPE ILLUSTRATIONS
INTRODUCTION, NOTES, APPENDICES
AND GENERAL INDEX

IN
THREE VOLUMES
VOLUME I

New York

RUSSELL & RUSSELL

FIVE HUNDRED YEARS OF CHAUCER
CRITICISM AND ALLUSION: 1357–1900

appeared as Series 48–50, 52–56 of The Chaucer Society publications in 1908–1917. Subsequently, the sections were gathered into three volumes and published in 1925 by Cambridge University Press. The present edition is published by Russell & Russell, Inc., in 1960 by arrangement with Cambridge University Press.

PRINTED IN THE U. S. A.

CONTENTS

LIST OF ILLUSTRATIONS

Vol. I

PART I

FOREWORD.

THE collection of this body of Chaucer references and allusions was begun nearly twenty-three years ago. For various reasons it has taken a long time to get the whole completed and printed (a six-years' interval, for example, during and after the war), and in any case it is clearly not, as Sir Thomas Browne would say, a work which a man, or a woman either, can do 'standing upon one legge.'

The idea of collecting a body of opinion on Chaucer was Dr. Furnivall's, and as early as 1888 he appealed in the *Academy* for a volunteer to undertake it. It was not, however, until 1901, when he met me, then an unwary as well as an eager student, that he succeeded in persuading anyone to undertake a task which was far heavier than either he or I then suspected.

It has now been done very much more fully than Dr. Furnivall at first suggested, and up to 1800 the references, as far as I have found them, are given fairly completely; from 1800 to 1867 the most important or interesting ones are selected, while from 1868, the date of the foundation of the Chaucer Society, to 1900, only the chief editions of the poet and a few notable or typical criticisms are included. This gradual thinning out was found necessary for reasons of sheer bulk of material.

An Appendix (A) contains additional English and Latin references, and two Appendices (B and C) give French and German ones. Further, a few copies of a " Supplement," containing some 900 additional allusions between 1868 and 1900, have been printed and placed in the chief public libraries.

The greatest care has been taken to guard against inaccuracies or misprints, as a compilation of this kind only justifies its existence in so far as it can approach to accuracy. But no large collection of detail is ever free from errors, and I

v

can hardly hope that this is an exception. I shall be most grateful, therefore, if readers who discover mistakes will kindly tell me of them, and if those who know of important allusions to Chaucer not here included, will be so good as to send me the references.

No one can be more conscious than I am of how much better this work could be done, or indeed of how much better even I myself could do it were I to begin all over again. But faulty and incomplete as it is, I hope that in various ways it may be of use to students, and that it may perhaps serve as a humble but solid brick in the future building of a history of English poetics and poetical taste.

It only remains for me to thank all those who, throughout these years, have so generously helped me in sending me references, in searching for references and in copying and collating. To name them all individually would be too lengthy, but I must specially refer to Professor Churton Collins, who, during one fruitful evening, first started me on various lines of investigation, to Dr. Paget Toynbee, who has sent me many references, to Professor Hyder E. Rollins, who most generously handed over to me a valuable collection of *Troilus* allusions, and to M. J. J. Jusserand, who gave me several suggestions in connection with French criticism.

Among others who have helped in various ways, I desire to record, with much gratitude, the names of Miss Evelyn Fox, Major J. J. Munro, Mrs. H. C. Tait, and, above all, Mr. Arundell Esdaile of the British Museum, who is responsible for the Index, and without whose expert and invaluable help in recent years these volumes would, I fear, still be unfinished.

There is, however, one name and personality above all others to whom I owe, not only the suggestion of the work, but also for nine years constant stimulus, help and inspiration. All Chaucer students know Dr. Furnivall—I speak of him in the present, for his spirit still lives in the work which is being done—and they all owe him a debt. But no one of them owes him more than I do for encouragement, inspiration and generous and unsparing aid of every kind.

I cannot help wishing that in the Elysian Fields, or wherever he may be, he could just have a look at the finished work which he initiated and so greatly desired to see accomplished; for, if he at all resembles what he was on earth, I know that these volumes, even with their many imperfections, would give him pleasure.

Caroline F. E. Spurgeon.

New York,
  December, 1923.

INTRODUCTION.

THIS record of the changing attitude of Englishmen during five centuries towards one of their greatest poets furnishes food for thought of many kinds; literary, artistic and philosophical.

The aim of this Introduction is first to sum up, briefly and in a concise form, the actual results which the following documents furnish, and secondly to suggest, very tentatively, a few of the problems which these collected facts raise, and upon which they may help to throw some light.

Viewing the matter first of all from what is here our chief concern, namely, as a contribution towards the history of literary criticism, it will be discussed under the following headings :—

§ 1. An outline of the fluctuations of the literary reputation of Chaucer during the last five hundred years.

§ 2. An examination of the criticisms and allusions themselves, roughly grouped and sorted.

§ 3. The various classes of qualities ascribed to Chaucer.

§ 4. The evolution of Chaucer biography.

§ 5. A note on some Chaucer lovers and workers of whom we get glimpses throughout the centuries.

A few notes will then be made on more abstract or philosophical questions, and we shall consider our material to some extent as a contribution towards the history of poetics in England, more especially in connection with the following points :—

§ 6. The change or curve of literary taste and fashion.

§ 7. The birth and growth of criticism itself as an art.

§ 8. The gradual evolution of new senses in the race.

§ 9. The evolution of scholarship and accuracy in literary matters.

§ 1. An Outline History of Chaucer Criticism.

Broadly speaking, from 1400 to the present day, Chaucer's reputation may be said to pass through six fairly well marked stages :—

(1) Enthusiastic and reverential praise by his contemporaries and immediate successors, which lasts to the end of the fifteenth century.

(2) The universal acknowledgment of his genius by the Scottish poets of the fifteenth and early sixteenth centuries, this admiration noticeably taking the form of imitation; whereas in England at this period Chaucer is admired rather more as a social reformer and as an exposer of vice and folly, than as a literary artist.

(3) The critical attitude, which begins towards the end of the sixteenth century with the Elizabethans. Chaucer still holds his place as prince of English poets; Sidney praises him, Spenser looks to him as master. Now, however, begins to creep in that general belief which clung so persistently to the minds of all writers of the seventeenth and eighteenth centuries; that Chaucer was obsolete, that his language was very difficult to understand, his style rough and unpolished, and his versification imperfect.

(4) During the seventeenth century this belief gains so much ground that Chaucer's language is said to be an unknown tongue; the knowledge of his versification entirely disappears; for eighty-five years (1602–87) no edition of his works is published, and his reputation altogether touches its lowest point.

(5) Dryden's *Fables* in 1700 inaugurate what may be called the period of 'modernizations.' This is a time of ever-increasing interest in and admiration for Chaucer, combined with the fixed belief that in order to make him intelligible or possible to modern readers his writings must be 'refined'; that is, diluted and translated into current English. This phase may be said to have continued up to 1841, when the last ambitious 'modernization' was published, but it was co-existent with and largely overlapped the sixth and present period of—

(6) Scholarly study and appreciation, dating from the publication of Tyrwhitt's edition of the *Canterbury Tales* in 1775. Tyrwhitt made possible to the general reader the rational study of Chaucer's own works by editing a careful and scholarly text of his Tales, and for the first time he definitely and clearly stated and proved the true theory of the poet's versification, thus disposing of one of the most serious obstacles to the proper recognition of Chaucer's greatness as a literary craftsman. This work was carried on and practically completed by the labours of the members of the Chaucer Society, founded in 1868, which prepared the way for the final scholarly complete edition of the poet's works brought out by Professor Skeat in 1894.

PERIOD I.—The early praise of the poet, and the estimation in which he was held, are more generally known than the tributes of later years, because portions of the eulogies by Gower, Lydgate, Hoccleve, Caxton, and others, are reprinted many times in various lives of Chaucer and editions of his works.

When we remember that Chaucer could only be read and praise of him be recorded in manuscript by a very limited public, the appreciation which he received from his contemporaries and which has come down to us, is remarkable. If we take into account the printing facilities and the growth of the reading public in Shakespeare's time, and add to that the fact that the dramatist's work could be seen and judged by the unliterary public, there is no comparison between the contemporary appreciation shown of the two poets. That given to Chaucer is undoubtedly greater, and the unquestioned recognition of his position as a great poet is as hearty as it is universal. The earliest literary reference, and it is only a possible one, occurs in one of Gower's French poems, the *Mirour de l'omme* (1376–9), but there is considerable doubt as to whether Gower is here referring to Chaucer's *Troilus* or not (*see* below, p. 4). The next reference is, curiously enough, also to *Troilus*,[1] but here

---

[1] For the early popularity of this poem, *see* pp. lxxvi–lxxvii below.

there is no doubt that Chaucer's work is meant.   It occurs in the *Testament of Love* by Thomas Usk (*c.* 1387, *see* below, p. 8) and refers to a special passage in the poem (*Troilus*, IV, 953–1085).   The discourse between the author and the fair lady who is Love (in imitation of that between Boethius and Philosophy) has been on divine foreknowledge and human freewill, and Love refers to Chaucer in the warmest terms as her own true servant who in wit and clear writing surpasses all other poets.   Next, in point of time, comes the well-known message sent to Chaucer by Venus, in Gower's *Confessio Amantis*, which bears upon the margin of the manuscript the date 1390.   Venus, in taking leave of Gower, sends a greeting to Chaucer, who, she says, is her ' disciple ' and ' poete,' and to whom she is 'above alle othre' 'most holde,' and she bids him finish his work by making his ' testament of love ' (*see* below, p. 10).

The next certain reference is by Lydgate, and it is from him and another contemporary and survivor, Hoccleve, that Chaucer receives the most constant and whole-hearted admiration in these earlier years.   The praise and estimate of Chaucer left by these two comparatively obscure writers has a value for us which no other can have ; for they alone—of all his critics save Gower—knew the poet personally ; and we can gather from them not only the admiration he excited as an artist, but the personal devotion he inspired as a man.   In the poems of Lydgate, during some forty years (*c.* 1400–1439), we find repeated allusion to and unstinted praise of his ' master Chaucer ' ; praise, which in spite of certain set phrases repeated more than once, we feel comes straight from the heart of the writer.   Mingled with the praise are to be found little personal or characteristic descriptions, which are to many people the most precious things in Lydgate's voluminous writings ; such, for instance, as that in the *Troy Book* (1412–1420), where he thus records his master's kindness, tolerance, and encouragement to younger writers, an amiable trait which from the literary point of view the hapless reader of Lydgate may often find occasion to deplore :—

For he þat was gronde of wel seying
In al hys lyf hyndred no makyng
My maister Chaucer þat founde ful many spot
Hym liste not pinche nor gruche at euery blot
Nor meue hym silf to perturbe his reste
I haue herde telle but seide alweie þe best
Suffring goodly of his gentilnes
Ful many þing embracid with rudnes.

It is in the translation of the *Fall of Princes*, written probably thirty years after Chaucer's death, that there are most references to him, including the well-known passage giving a list of his writings (pp. 37–42 below). However, in the case of Lydgate —most garrulous of poets—the supreme proof of his admiration for Chaucer, greater than praise or than imitation itself, is the fact that he refrains from telling several stories or only tells them in the shortest possible way, because they have already been treated by the older poet. Thus, in translating Deguileville's *Pilgrimage of the Life of Man* [1426], Lydgate gives Chaucer's version of the A.B.C.; and again in the *Fall of Princes* he says :—

Myn Auctour here no lengere lyst soiourne,
    Off this Emperours the Fallys for to wryte,
But in haste he doth his stylë tourne
    To Zenobia hire story for tendyte;
    But, for chaunceer so wel did hym quyte
    In this tragédyes hir pitous fal tentrete,
    I wyl passe ovir Rehersyng but the grete.

Lydgate excels in frequency of reference to Chaucer, and Hoccleve perhaps in fervency. In his *Regement of Princes*, Hoccleve goes so far as to say that England can never again bring forth Chaucer's equal : 'Death myght have stayed her hand,' he cries,

She myghte han taried hir vengeance awhile,
Til that sum man had egal to the be.
Nay, lat be þat ! sche knew wel þat þis yle
May neuer man forth bryngë lyk to the.

He calls him

> The firstë fyndere of our faire langage,

and again :—

> O, maister deere, and fadir reuerent !
> Mi maister Chaucer, flour of eloquence,
> Mirour of fructuous entendëment.

And he goes on to liken him to Aristotle in philosophy, and to Virgil in poetry (below, pp. 21, 22).

So great and whole-hearted was the admiration and devotion given to Chaucer by these two men, his friends and followers, that we cannot doubt they would have been the first to acknowledge it fitting that the principal value of their writings to us —five centuries later—lies in their references to their ' maister Chaucer.'

On the whole, amongst all Chaucer's contemporaries and successors during the fifteenth century, the most discriminating appreciations are those given him by Caxton, and by the unknown author of the *Book of Curtesye*. The remarks of both writers sound curiously modern as to the qualities they specially single out for approval. Chaucer's vivid powers of description, his felicitous use of words, his freedom from long-windedness—in which he differed so markedly from his contemporaries—all are noted by Caxton :—

> He comprehended hys maters in short, quyck and hye sentences, eschewyng prolyxyte, castyng away the chaf of superfluyte, and shewyng the pyked grayn of sentence uttered by crafty and sugred eloquence. . . . [Prohemye to *Canterbury Tales*, 2nd edn. *c.* 1483, below, p. 62.]
>
> He wrytteth no voyde wordes, but alle hys mater is ful of hye and quycke sentence. [Epilogue to the *Book of Fame*, below, p. 61.]

And in the *Book of Curtesye* (*a.* 1477), Chaucer's works are recommended above all others :—

> Redith his werkis / full of plesaunce
> Clere in sentence / in langage excellent
> Briefly to wryte / suche was his suffysan̄ce
> Whateuer to saye / he toke in his entente

> His langage was so fayr and pertynente
> It seemeth vnto mannys heerynge
> Not only the worde / but verely the thynge.

The imaginative power of the poet is here specially noted in a way which is not equalled until Sir Brian Tuke, fifty-five years later, wrote his introduction to Thynne's edition (1532).

One early piece of indirect praise must not pass unnoticed, more especially as it cannot find a place under the ' allusions '; and this is the charming poem of the *Flower and the Leaf*, so long attributed to Chaucer, now generally thought to have been written by a woman, probably about 1475. The authoress was evidently well acquainted with and an admirer of Chaucer's writings, more particularly the *Prologue* to and the *Legend of Good Women*. (*See* Skeat's Chaucer, vol. vii, pp. lxii–lxviii.)

PERIOD II.—Next we come to the enthusiastic and reverent devotion expressed for Chaucer by the Scottish poets of the latter end of the fifteenth and early sixteenth centuries. Henryson, Gawain Douglas, Dunbar and Lyndsay, all speak of him in terms of fervent admiration. Henryson, in 1475, wrote a continuation of *Troilus and Cressida*, called the *Testament of Cresseid*—for a long time included amongst Chaucer's works—in the beginning of which he says he made up the fire, took a drink to comfort his spirits and cut short the winter night, and then leaving all other amusement, he took down a book written by ' worthie Chaucer glorious, of fair Cresseid and worthie Troylus.' Gawain Douglas speaks of Chaucer in the *Palace of Honour* (1501) as ' *a per se*, sans peir in his vulgare,' and later as

> Hevinlie trumpat, horleige and reguleir,
> In eloquence balmy, condit, and diall,
> Mylky fountane, cleir strand, and rose riall,
> Of fresch endite, throw Albion iland braid.

When, later on, in this same Prologue (to the *First Buik of Eneados*, 1513), Douglas finds fault with Chaucer for not following Virgil accurately in his account of Dido (p. 72 below), he does so with great timidity, and a clear consciousness of his own inferiority :

My master Chaucer greitlie Virgile offendit
All thocht I be to bald hyme to repreif.

Dunbar, in his *Lament, or the Makaris*, speaks of ' The noble Chaucer, of makaris flouir '; and in the *Golden Targe* he surpasses all Chaucer's other Scottish followers in his enthusiasm :—

O reverend Chaucere, rose of rethoris all,
As in oure tong ane flour imperiall
That raise in Britane ewir, quho redis rycht,
Thou beris of makaris the tryumph riall;
Thy fresch anamalit termes celicall
This mater coud illumynit haue full brycht :
Was thou noucht of oure Inglisch all the lycht,
Surmounting ewiry tong terrestriall
Alls fer as Mayes morow dois mydnycht ?

Lyndsay, in the *Testament of the Papyngo*, also refers to Chaucer in the usual way. But a more remarkable testimony to the admiration felt, is the wholesale imitation of Chaucer by these Scottish writers. The ideas of their poems, the forms they assumed, whole passages, single lines, turns of phrase and words are borrowed from Chaucer, and suggested by him. James I, if he was the author of the *King's Quair*, was in 1423 the first Scottish imitator, and of all this group, this is perhaps the poem the most completely saturated with the master's spirit.

The Scottish view, then, was one of unstinted admiration, complete comprehension of Chaucer's writings, and hearty acknowledgment of his superiority as artist to every other English or Scottish poet.

In England, in the meantime, printing had been introduced, and we see by the books issued that Chaucer's popularity had not waned, for there was a continual demand for his works. Two editions of his *Canterbury Tales* were published by Caxton; and before the end of the fifteenth century two more followed from the presses of Wynkyn de Worde and Pynson.

In 1532 William Thynne, the first real editor of Chaucer, brought out his edition of the poet's works, which must indeed have been a labour of love. Francis Thynne tells us that his father had a commission from Henry VIII ' to serche all the liberaries of Englande for Chaucers workes, so that oute of all the Abbies of this Realme . . . he was fully furnished with multitude of Bookes.' This ' multitude ' of copies, probably about twenty-five, Thynne collated to the best of his ability.

The dedication to Henry VIII, though signed by Thynne, was written by Sir Brian Tuke, and the following quotation may presumably be taken therefore as expressing the appreciation of both men :—

> I . . . haue taken great delectacyon . . . to rede and here the bokes of that noble & famous clerke Geffray Chaucer, in whose workes is so manyfest . . . suche frutefulnesse in wordes, wel accordynge to the mater and purpose, so swete and plesaunt sentences, suche perfectyon in metre, the composycion so adapted, suche fresshnesse of inuencion, compendyousnesse in narration, such sensible and open style . . . . . . that it is moche to be marueyled, howe in his tyme . . . . suche an excellent poete in our tonge, shulde . . . spryng and aryse.

The literary influence of Chaucer in England in the sixteenth century can be clearly traced even before the publication of Pynson's edition of the ' Works ' in 1526. John Heywood owes a good deal to Chaucer in his *Mery playe betwene the pardoner and the frere* (written probably before 1521), and he incorporates in it two long speeches out of the mouth of Chaucer's Pardoner. Later, in *The Foure P's*, and in a ballad written in 1554, he shows further Chaucerian influence (*see* pp. 80–81 below).

The effect of Pynson's *Chaucer* on the first English poet of the Renaissance was immediate, for Sir Thomas Wyatt's debt to it between 1528 and 1532 is undoubted, and later his study of Thynne's edition is equally clear (*see* below, App. A, *a*. 1542).

The general criticism of Chaucer in England in the early sixteenth century is, from a literary point of view, not quite so satisfactory as in Scotland. There are two things in especial which detract from the value of the remarks we find about him :

(1) That in the greater number of cases where he is praised, Chaucer is not, as he was by Hoccleve or Caxton, placed alone, but he is associated with Gower and Lydgate [1]—sometimes with no apparent difference in the commendation bestowed— whilst one writer at least actually places Lydgate above him. This is Stephen Hawes, who, in his *Pastime of Pleasure* (below, p. 67), begins thus with the usual praise of Gower, Chaucer, and Lydgate :—

> As morall Gower, whose sentencious dewe
> Adowne reflareth with fayre golden beames,
> And after Chaucers, all abroade doth shewe,
> Our vyces to clense, his depared streames
> Kindlynge our hartes, wyth the fiery leames
> Of morall vertue, as is probable
> In all his bokes so swete and profitable.

Hawes goes on to speak in warm terms of the *Book of Fame*, the *Legend of Good Women*, the *Canterbury Tales* and *Troilus*, and the reader is gratified with the discrimination shown, until he discovers that the writer is but leading up to a peroration on Lydgate, who receives a much larger share of praise, ending :—

> O mayster Lydgate, the most dulcet sprynge
> Of famous rethoryke, wyth balade ryall,
> The chefe original of my lernyng.

This enthusiasm somewhat detracts from the value of his remarks on Chaucer.

Hawes, it is true, is in a minority of one in placing Lydgate above Chaucer,[2] but the type of allusion which brackets the three early writers together on equal terms is very common,

---

[1] This habit began quite early, and he was first bracketed with Gower, Lydgate being later added to the list to make it complete, so that by the end of the 15th century it was a well-established formula. Such references are, for example, those by John Walton, 1410 (p. 20 below), James I, 1423 (p. 34), Bokenham, 1443–7 (p. 46), George Ashby, c. 1470 (p. 54), Thomas Feylde, 1509 (p. 70), John Rastell, 1520 (p. 73), Skelton, 1523 (p. 74), etc.

[2] Until 1707, when an unknown writer in an essay on the old English poets and poetry, in the *Muses Mercury*, vol. i, No. 6, pp. 130–1, definitely states that Lydgate's English and his ' numbers ' are more polished than his master's (*see* p. 295 below). This view reappears occasionally later, as in the article on Lydgate in the *Encyclopædia Britannica*, 1780 (*q. v.* below), and in Sharon Turner's *History of England*, 1815 (*q. v.* below).

and shows a certain formalism and convention in the acknowledgment of the genius of the three ' primier poetes of this
nacion,' as Ashby calls them; and shows also, though not so
markedly as in the case of Hawes, a lack of critical faculty.
These shortcomings have to be borne in mind when we are
estimating the early sixteenth century praise of Chaucer in
England. We may compare, for instance, the difference in
critical judgment shown by Douglas and Dunbar in their
respective references to the three poets on pp. 65 and 66
below, and the supremacy unhesitatingly awarded by them to
Chaucer, and the allusion by Hawes following next on p. 66,
which, unlike his later one, is quite representative of the
ordinary English attitude.

(2) The other point which lessens the value of Chaucer
criticism at this time is also indicated in the verse quoted above,
from Hawes's *Pastime of Pleasure,* and that is that Chaucer is
valued primarily as a reformer, as a moralist and satirist who
exposes and rebukes vices and follies. This view is continually
emphasised all through the sixteenth century, and for this
characteristic Chaucer receives praise consistently from a
curious assortment of critics.

He was annexed by the Reformers, not without reason, as a
kind of forerunner and a sharer of their opinions with regard to
Rome, as evidenced by his keen satirical exposure of the religious
orders of his time. There is support for this view in the
Canterbury Tales alone, and more especially in the *Prologue,* but
when in addition Chaucer was credited with the authorship of
Jack Upland, the *Pilgrim's Tale,* and the *Plowman's Tale* (all of
them diatribes against the Church of Rome) one is not surprised
to find him cited as a great religious reformer.

Foxe, writing in 1570, in his enlarged second edition of his
' Book of Martyrs,' expresses the views held on this point by a
certain section of the serious thinkers of the sixteenth century,
when he points out that the bishops, in condemning all English
books that might lead the people to any light of knowledge,
had yet allowed Chaucer to be read, takin his work ' but for
jests or toys,' and not seeing or understanding that he ' albeit . . .

in mirth and covertly ' was upholding the ends of true religion
and was indeed a right Wicklifian.   In this manner God—for
the sake of his people—was pleased to blind the eyes of the
adversary, that through the reading of the poet's books good
might redound to the Church, which, says Foxe, has certainly
been the case, for, ' I am partly informed of certain which
knew the parties, which to them reported that by reading of
Chaucer's works they were brought to the true knowledge of
religion.'   When we remember the popularity of Foxe's book,
and the number of editions it went through, we realize he must
have done a good deal to strengthen this conception of the poet.
(*See* the whole passage, p. 106 below.)

This quaint view of Chaucer, as a theologian, reformer and
moralist, is one which would, of all those here collected, perhaps
have most surprised and amused the poet himself, yet it is held by
certain writers with great persistence from the time that Leland
(his first biographer, *ante* 1550) tells us that Chaucer ' left the
University a devout theologian,' to the sketch of him prepared by
Henry Wharton (*c.* 1687) as an addition to Cave's *Ecclesiastical
Writers,* in which we are told that the poet was scarcely excelled
by any theologian of his time in his zeal for a purer religion.[1]

In addition to this conception of him as a reforming divine,
he is much admired for the energy with which he scourges vice
of all kinds, and he is referred to continually as an unquestioned
authority in such matters.   Thus Ascham, in speaking of gaming,

> Whose horriblenes is so large that it passed the eloquence
> of our *Englishe Homer* to compasse it : yet because I euer
> thought hys sayinges to have as much authoritye as
> eyther *Sophocles* or *Euripedes* in Greke, therefore gladly do
> I remember these verses of hys [and he quotes from the
> Pardoner's Tale, see p. 85 below].

So also Thomas Lodge, in his *Reply to Stephen Gosson* (1579)
says, ' Chaucer in pleasant vain can rebuke sin vncontrold, &
though he be lauish in the letter, his sence is serious '; and
Webbe notes that Chaucer,

---

[1] *See* also below, 1834, R. A. Willmott, *Lives of Sacred Poets.*

by his delightsome vayne, so gulled the eares of men with
his deuises, that . . . without controllment might hee
gyrde at the vices and abuses of all states . . . which he
did so learnedly and pleasantly, that none therefore would
call him into question. For such was his bold spyrit, that
what enormities he saw in any, he would not spare to pay
them home, eyther in playne words, or els in some pretty
and pleasant covert, that the simplest might espy him
(p. 129, below).

Episodes or sayings in his poems are repeatedly quoted by
divines and moralists, or even later by seventeenth-century
Puritans, to point their remarks and support them in the
denunciation of special sins,[1] so that one easily sees how it
came to be generally believed, both by those who looked only
to his moral teaching, and also by those who admired him as
poet, but wished to justify their admiration by grounding it
on morality, that—to quote Francis Beaumont—his ' drift
was to touch all sorts of men, and to discover all vices of that
Age.'
    There were, however, a certain number of writers who held
just the contrary opinion, and considered the poet's works to be
anything but edifying literature. ' Canterbury Tale ' seems
very early to have been used as a term of contempt, meaning
either a story with no truth in it, or a vain and scurrilous tale.
We get three such references, curiously enough, in the same
year, 1549, by Becke, Latimer and Cranmer; Wharton, in
1575, refers to the ' stale tales of Chaucer,' and Proctor (1578),
and Fulke (1579), make similar allusions, while Thomas Drant
(1567), and Sir John Harington (1591), openly condemn
Chaucer, the latter for ' flat scurrilitie.' This is a view which,
as we shall see later, gradually gained ground, although in the
laxer days of the Restoration and earlier eighteenth century
the poet was not condemned for it, and finally it completely
ousted the aspect of Chaucer as a great moral reformer.

---

[1] *See below* Calfhill, 1565, p. 99, Hanmer, 1576, p. 112, Northbrook,
1577, p. 115, Bp. Babington, 1583, Scot, 1584, p. 124, Stowe, 1598, p. 159,
and a letter from a Parliament Officer, 1645–6, p. 224.

PERIOD III.—At the end of the sixteenth century the references to Chaucer become very numerous, and as a whole they are very appreciative. Among the most interesting are those by Sir Philip Sidney (1581?), by Gabriel Harvey (MS. notes *c.* 1585 and 1598), by Webbe and Puttenham in their discourses on poetry, by the unknown writers of *Greene's Vision* (1592) and of the *Returne from Parnassus* (1597), and by Francis Beaumont and Francis Thynne in their respective letters called forth by Speght's edition of Chaucer in 1598.

Francis Beaumont the judge (died 1598) was the father of the dramatist, and he prided himself on being one of those who first urged Speght to edit Chaucer. His letter (p. 145 below) is of particular interest, for in addition to his defence of the two faults of which Chaucer is most commonly accused—obsolete language and coarseness—he reminds Speght that when they were at Cambridge together (at Peterhouse, between 1560 and 1570) there were a group of older scholars there who were well read in Chaucer, and who commended him to the younger men, and it was they who first brought Speght as well as Beaumont himself to be ' in love ' with the poet.

Francis Thynne, the son of William Thynne, the first editor of Chaucer (*see* 1598, below), was another Chaucer enthusiast. He had rather a chequered career, but ended finally by holding a post in the Herald's Office; he was a born antiquary, and, judging from his ' Animadversions,' a somewhat querulous and pedantic but kindly old man, much concerned with small points of detail, intensely proud of his family, of his father's good name and literary work, and of his own office as Lancaster Herald.

He evidently shared his father's love for Chaucer manuscripts, some five and twenty of which he inherited : some of them, he says, were stolen out of his house at Poplar, and some he gave to the parson. In any case he had made preparations for a new edition of the poet, when, in 1598, his acquaintance, Thomas Speght, brought out his new edition of Chaucer's works, and in his preface insinuated that no editor before then had collated manuscripts for his text. This, combined with the fact that he, the hereditary editor of Chaucer, had not been consulted, enraged Thynne, and he at once produced the ' Animad-versions,' in which he snubs Speght for his injustice to William Thynne, his lack of courtesy to himself, Francis Thynne, and his general ignorance, of which he gives detailed specimens.

The most interesting part of Thynne's treatise is the account he gives of his father's cancelled edition (pp. 151, 152 below). But the critical value of Thynne's comments is also consider-able; only in four instances out of fifty is he wrong, and some-times (as on the date of the *Nonne Preestes Tale*, 'Animadver-sions,' pp. 59–62) his notes are admirable, and always show great accuracy and scrupulous care in consulting authorities.

Altogether it would seem as if Francis Thynne, of all the Chaucer scholars up to Tyrwhitt, had been the best equipped to bring out a really correct and critical edition of the poet's text, and we can only regret that he did not carry out his intention to re-edit Chaucer (*see* below, p. 155), and more especially to try to distinguish between his genuine and spurious works; for, with the help of those twenty-five manuscript copies, especially the one inscribed ' examinatur Chaucer,' some invalu-able evidence might have been supplied.

Among criticisms and appreciations of a more literary kind there is one writer at the end of the sixteenth century whose praise is more emphatic than any other, who of all his readers during these five hundred years has been most influenced by Chaucer's language and literary methods, and who, in his turn, has exerted so much influence over others, that he has justly been called the ' poet's poet.' Spenser's admiration for Chaucer began early, and continued to increase up to the time when he made his dying request to be laid near the master he loved and honoured. In the first great poem of the Elizabethan age, Chaucer is mentioned repeatedly, both in the introductory letter, the notes by ' E. K.,' and in the poem itself—where Spenser calls him ' Tityrus ' :—

> The God of shepheards, *Tityrus* is dead,
> Who taught me homely, as I can, to make.
> He, whilst he lived, was the soueraigne head
> Of shepheards all that bene with loue y-take :
> .   .   .   .

(O ! why shouid death on hym such outrage showe ?)
And all hys passing skil with him is fledde,
The fame whereof doth dayly greater growe.

This last line is interesting, and is probably quite true.
Chaucer had as yet no rival in England. We know by Beaumont's letter that at Cambridge twenty or twenty-five years
earlier he was much read and discussed, and in the intellectual
activity of the time, doubtless there was keen interest in the
greatest and first English Poet.

The strong Chaucerian influence shown in the *Shepheardes
Calender* and *Mother Hubberd's Tale* is well known, but the close
resemblance of Spenser's *Daphnaïda* to the *Book of the Duchess*,
has not, until recently, been worked out, showing that Spenser,
not only early, but also comparatively late in his career, is
indebted to Chaucer for general subject-matter, form, incidents,
words and phrases.[1]

Spenser has said some very graceful and beautiful things
about

Dan Chaucer, well of Englishe vndefyled
On Fames eternall bead roll worthie to be fyled,

but his famous apology to his master when he was about to
add an ending to the *Squires Tale*, in the fourth book of the
Faerie Queene, is perhaps the finest tribute ever paid by one
great poet to another.

Then pardon, O most sacred happie spirit,
That I thy labours lost may thus reuiue,
And steale from thee the meede of thy due merit,
That none durst euer whilest thou wast aliue,
And being dead in vaine yet many striue :
Ne dare I like, but through infusion sweete
Of thine owne spirit, which doth in me surviue,
I follow here the footing of thy feete,
That with thy meaning so I may the rather meete.

With Spenser as one of his strongest advocates and
adherents, Chaucer now enters upon his period of storm and

---

[1] *See* note below, p. 119, and especially T. W. Nadal's article on
' Daphnaïda and the Book of the Duchess,' in Publications of Modern
Language Association of America, Dec. 1908.

stress; of misunderstanding, misinterpretation, buffetings of every description, and finally of obloquy and neglect.

We can see from all the references by critics and others at this time that it was already a matter of common opinion that Chaucer's style was rough and unpolished, his language obsolete, and his metre halting.[1] As far as we can judge, his versification was not wholly understood by any one, the secret of it was lost when inflections were lost, no one seems to have been aware of the pronunciation of the final ' e '; with the result that there was a general agreement that the poet's verse was ' harsh ' and ' irregular.' Spenser, his follower and admirer,—himself most musical of poets—when he thinks he is writing in Chaucer's manner produces this sort of verse :—

> But this I wot withall, that we shall ronne
> Into great daunger, like to bee undone,
> Thus wildly to wander in the world's eye
> Withouten pasport or good warrantye.

or

> His breeches were made after the new cut,
> Al Portugese, loose like an emptie gut;
> And his hose broken high above the heeling,
> And his shooes beaten out with traveling,

thus showing plainly in his imitations of Chaucer's versification in *Mother Hubberd's Tale* and *Colin Clouts come home again* that he considers his aim best achieved when he writes irregular lines without the proper number of syllables, distinguished by a lack of harmony and rhythm such as we find nowhere else in Spenser's work.

This attitude both as to language and verse must have begun very early; for, little more than one hundred years after Chaucer's death, Skelton, in *Philip Sparrow*, feels it necessary to repudiate the idea that Chaucer is difficult to understand. His language, he says, was—

---

[1] When we remember that Chaucer was known only through the blackletter texts which mangled his verse, this complete misconception of it is not extraordinary. *See* Wyatt's system of versification built on his reading of Chaucer in Pynson's 1526 edition (below, App. A., *a*. 1542).

> At those days moch commended,
> And now men wold haue amended
> His english, where-at they barke,
> And marre all they warke :
> Chaucer, that famous Clarke,
> His tearmes were not darcke,
> But pleasaunt, easy, and playne ;
> No worde he wrote in vayne.

The various attitudes assumed by critics in discussing Chaucer's limitations are curious and interesting. There were those, who, like Spenser, felt something in themselves respond to Chaucer's touch, who knew he was a true poet and a great one, and looked upon his antique diction, and occasional ruggedness of versification—a fact which had to be conceded—as in themselves worthy of imitation, having proceeded from so great a master.

So we find Spenser not only deliberately composes rough and halting lines in the older poet's honour, but also goes so far in copying Chaucer's words (or rather what he thought were his words) in the *Shepheardes Calender*, that Ben Jonson was well justified in saying that in ' affecting the ancients, Spenser writ no language.'

This is the slavish imitation so strongly condemned by Ascham in *The Scholemaster*, when he says :—

> Some that make *Chaucer* in Englishe and *Petrarch* in *Italian*, their Gods in verses, and yet be not able to make true difference, what is a fault, and what a iust prayse, in those two worthie wittes, will moch mislike this my writyng.   But such men be even like followers of *Chaucer & Petrarke* as one here in England did follow Syr *Tho. More* : who, being most vnlike vnto him in wit and learning, neuertheles in wearing his gowne awrye vpon the one shoulder, as Syr *Tho. More* was wont to doe, would needes be counted like vnto hym.

Next there was the apologetic party—and this was largely in the majority—who, whilst honouring and revering Chaucer, yet deliberately avowed these great faults in him, the while excusing him on the score of his antiquity, and the barbaric age in which he lived.   Such were Sidney and Webbe.

Sidney, in his *Apologie for Poetrie*, says :—

> *Chaucer*, vndoubtedly did excellently in hys *Troylus* and
> *Cresseid*, of whom truly I know not, whether to meruaile
> more, either that he in that mystie time could see so clearly,
> or that wee in this cleare age walke so stumblingly after
> him. Yet had he great wants, fitte to be forgiuen in so
> reuerent antiquitie.

Webbe, in his *Discourse of English Poetrie*, says :—

> Though the manner of hys stile may seem blunt and
> course to many fine English eares at these dayes, yet in
> trueth if it be equally pondered, and with good judgment
> aduised, and confirmed with the time wherein he wrote, a
> man shall perceiue thereby even a true picture or perfect
> shape of a right Poet.

Again, there were those of the new classical school, the
denouncers of ' rude and beggarly riming,' who actually praised
Chaucer for the supposed irregularity of his metre, which they
regarded as an approach to the classical method of quantitative
verse. Gascoigne is one of these who gets curiously near the
truth of Chaucerian versification without actually reaching it.
For he maintains that some natural quality of the words, their
sound, as he puts it, makes the short line right. They are not
equal-syllabled and yet they scan. Thus, writing in 1575,
he says :—

> Our father *Chaucer* hath vsed the same libertie in feete
> and measures that the Latinists do vse : and who so euer
> do peruse and well consider his workes, he shall finde that
> although his lines are not alwayes of one selfe same number
> of Syllables, yet beyng redde by one that hath vnder-
> standing, the longest verse and that which hath most
> Syllables in it, will fall (to the eare) correspondent vnto
> that whiche hath fewest sillables in it : and like wise
> that whiche hath in it fewest syllables, shalbe founde yet
> to consist of woordes that haue suche naturall sounde,
> as may seeme equall in length to a verse which hath many
> moe sillables of lighter accentes.

Lastly there were those—but they were woefully few—who
would not allow these faults in Chaucer at all, and attributed

them, when they did occur, either to lack of intelligence in
the reader or to the negligence of the scribe.

Foremost amongst these was Thomas Speght, who stoutly
upholds syllabic versification, and in his prefatory address to
his second edition of Chaucer, writes :—

> And for his verses, although, in diuers places they may
> seeme to vs to stand of vnequall measures : yet a skilfull
> Reader, that can scan them in their nature, shall find it
> otherwise.   And if a verse here and there fal out a sillable
> shorter or longer than another, I rather aret it to the
> negligence and rape of *Adam Scriuener*, that I may speake
> as *Chaucer* doth, than to any vnconning or ouersight in
> the Author.

PERIOD IV.—The edition of Chaucer's works in which the
foregoing preface is to be found, was published in 1602, and
there was no other edition brought out until 1687—an interval
of eighty-five years.   This speaks for itself.

Even the more hardy spirits who admired Chaucer foresaw
this neglect, and were reconciled to it.   They genuinely believed
that he had had his day, and that he was too antiquated to
endure.   Daniel, in his *Musophilus*, as early as 1599, expresses
this sentiment, and consoles himself by reflecting how long
Chaucer's fame had already lasted :—

> For what hy races hath there come to fall,
>   With low disgrace, quite vanished and past,
> Since *Chaucer* liu'd who yet liues and yet shall,
>   Though (which I grieue to say) but in his last.
>
> Yet what a time hath he wrested from time,
>   And won vpon the mighty waste of daies,
> Vnto th' immortall honor of our clime,
>
> .   .   .   .   .   .
>
> Vnto the sacred Relicks of whose rime
>   We yet are bound in zeale to offer praise?

Even Chaucer's most ardent admirers at this time are forced
to acknowledge that his language is obsolete, although they
maintain that once that difficulty is surmounted, the reader is
well rewarded.

So Henry Peacham, the schoolmaster at Wymondham, says to his *Compleat Gentleman* in 1622 :—

> Of English poets of our owne Nation, esteeme Sir *Geoffrey Chaucer* the father; although the stile for the antiquitie, may distast you, yet as vnder a bitter and rough rinde, there lyeth a delicate kernell of conceit and sweet inuention. . . . In briefe, account him among the best of your English bookes in your librarie.

In spite of all the talk about Chaucer's barbarous style, there was one writer, at least, who, even in the seventeenth century, maintained that he ought to be read easily, and that if not, the fault lay with his readers. This is Sir Aston Cockayne, who in 1658 writes :—

> Our good old *Chaucer* some despise : and why ?
> Because say they he writeth barbarously.
> Blame him not (Ignorants) but your selves, that do
> Not at these years your native language know.

Notwithstanding the sound advice given by these two last-named writers, Chaucer was obviously little read and less understood, although his name continued to have great power. We find a curious illustration of this in John Earle's remark in his *Microcosmographie* (1628), a collection of ' Characters ' such as was dear to seventeenth-century writers, in which he defines the character of a *Vulgar Spirited Man*, as one ' that cries *Chaucer* for his Money aboue all our English Poets, because the voice ha's gone so, and he ha's read none '; thus indicating that Chaucer was still called the greatest of English poets by those only who preferred to follow convention and tradition, rather than to use their own judgment.

By the end of the century Chaucer was frankly looked upon as antiquated and barbaric by the highest authorities in these matters. Waller, in his poem *Of English Verse* (first published 1668), says :—

> Poets that lasting Marble seek,
> Must carve in *Latine* or in *Greek*,
> We write in Sand, our Language grows
> And like the Tide, our work o're flows.

> *Chaucer*, his Sense can only boast,
> The glory of his numbers lost,
> Years have defac'd his matchless strain,
> And yet he did not sing in vain.

Crushing though this estimate may appear, it is complimentary compared with Addison's judgment, delivered some twenty-six years later, to which, however, too much weight must not be given, as the critic was only twenty-one when he wrote it, and was obviously, as Pope remarked later (1728–30, *see* p. 370 below), ignorant of Chaucer. Still, taking it in conjunction with similar remarks by Waller, Howard (1689), Cobb (*a.* 1700), Wesley (1700), Bysshe (1702), Hughes (1707), and others, we may assume it to be the ordinary conventional view taken by most writers, though expressed with unusual force by Addison. These are his lines, in his *Account of the Greatest English Poets* (1694) :—

> Long had our dull Fore-Fathers slept Supine,
> Nor felt the Raptures of the Tuneful Nine;
> Till *Chaucer* first, a merry *Bard*, arose;
> And many a Story told in Rhime and Prose.
> But Age has Rusted what the *Poet* writ,
> Worn out his Language and obscur'd his Wit:
> In vain he jests in his unpolish'd strain
> And tries to make his Readers laugh in vain.[1]

Other writers acknowledge Chaucer's position in former times, but it is taken as understood that he is now quite superseded : so Edward Phillips (Milton's nephew) in 1675 says :—

> True it is that the style of Poetry till Henry the 8th's time, and partly also within his Reign, may very well appear uncouth, strange and unpleasant to those that are affected only with what is familiar and accustom'd to them, not but there were even before those times some that had their Poetical excellencies if well examin'd, and chiefly among the

---

[1] This is perhaps only equalled by the following judgment pronounced by Byron at the still more immature age of nineteen :—
' Chaucer, notwithstanding the praises bestowed upon him, I think obscene and contemptible; he owes his celebrity merely to his antiquity, which he does not deserve so well as Pierce Plowman or Thomas of Ercildoune.' [Nov. 30, 1807.] Moore's *Life of Byron*, 1875, p. 80.

rest, CHAUCER, who through all the neglect of former ag'd Poets still keeps a name, being by some few admir'd for his real worth, to others not unpleasing for his facetious way, which joyn'd with his old *English* intertains them with a kind of Drollery.

Later in the same work he speaks of him as ' the *Prince* and *Coryphæus*, generally so reputed, till this Age, of our *English* Poets, and as much as we triumph over his old fashion'd phrase and obsolete words, one of the first refiners of the *English* language.'

There are numerous other references of this description to Chaucer. Sir Thomas Pope Blount in his *De Re Poetica* (1694) says :—

' This is agreed upon by all hands, that he [Chaucer] was counted the chief of the *English Poets*, not only of his time, but continued to be so esteem'd till this Age,' and so on. It is generally agreed, except by Waller, Cowley and Addison, that with all his shortcomings, Chaucer refined our English, and deserves respect and mention because of his antiquity. So Rymer in the *Short View of Tragedy* tells us :—

They who attempted verse in English, down till *Chaucers* time, made an heavy pudder, and are always miserably put to't for a word to clink. . . . . *Chaucer* found an Herculean labour on his Hands ; And did perform to Admiration. He seizes all Provencal, French or Latin that came in his way, gives them a new garb and livery, and mingles them amongst our English : turns out English, gowty, or super-annuated, to place in their room the foreigners, fit for service, train'd and accustomed to Poetical Discipline.

This, as Professor Ker points out,[1] is ' the passage of literary history summed up in Rymer's Table of Contents in the following remarkable terms : Chaucer *refin'd our English, Which in perfection by* Waller.' [2]

In addition to the recognition of his work as ' refiner,' Chaucer, although no longer looked upon as the greatest, is

---

[1] Dryden's prose works, ed. W. P. Ker, vol. ii, Notes, p. 307.

[2] For a more detailed account of the attitude towards Chaucer as the ' refiner' and remodeller of the English language, *see* pp. lxxiii, lxxiv below.

the first or earliest English poet; priority in point of time is
still granted him, and is by some considered his greatest title to
fame. So Drayton, in his *Epistle to Henry Reynolds* (1627)
alludes to him as :—

> That noble *Chaucer*, in those former times,
> The first inrich'd our *English* with his rimes,
> And was the first of ours, that euer brake,
> Into the *Muses* treasure, and first spake
> In weighty numbers,

And Sir John Denham begins his poem on the death of Cowley
thus :—

> Old *Chaucer*, like the Morning Star,
> To us discovers day from far,
> His light those Mists and Clouds dissolv'd,
> Which our dark Nation long involv'd;
> But he, descending to the shades,
> Darkness again the Age invades.

There are, however, a few bright spots in this somewhat gloomy
outlook.

It is of interest to note that ' the great person ' Strafford
clearly knew the *Canterbury Tales* well and quoted them
readily, as may be seen in his two letters of 1635 and 1637
(App. A. pp. 69, 70).   Doubtless his liking for Chaucer was
known to his friends, and so we find Lord Conway, when
writing to Strafford, also referring to the poet (*ibid.*, p. 70).

There is no doubt that Milton was well acquainted with
Chaucer's writings, although he cannot be said to have left
any record in praise of them, except the well-known invocation
to Melancholy in *Il Penseroso*, to

> . . . call up him that left half told
> The story of *Cambuscan* bold,

and he couples him in this connection with Musæus and
Orpheus.

At the beginning of the poem, when he banishes the
' fancies fond '

> ' as thick and numberless
> As the gay motes that people the Sun Beam '

there is a clear reminiscence of the twelfth line of the *Wife of Bath's Tale*, and he refers to that Tale no less than three times in his *Common-place Book*, where he also quotes with special approval from the *Physiciens Tale* the condemnation of feasts and dances for the young (*see* below, *a* 1674).

About the same time that Milton was writing *Il Penseroso*, another great admirer of Chaucer was preparing a somewhat curious composition in his honour. This was Sir Francis Kynaston, who, in 1635, brought out the first two books of *Troilus and Cressida*, translated into Latin rimed verse. It is a quaint little volume, with the English on one side and the translation on the opposite page. In the preface, which is also in Latin, Kynaston tells us how he daily saw Chaucer coming to be more despised and less known, while clothed in the ancient English tongue; and so he determined to rescue him from this oblivion, and to secure his fame for all ages by turning him into Latin. Fifteen prefatory poems by various writers, ten of which are also in Latin, nearly all agree in saying that Chaucer's fame is almost dead, because few people can understand what he wrote; but that will now be changed, and he will live for ever, and be known throughout the world in the Latin of Kynaston.

This desire to translate Chaucer into Latin was one of the curious outcomes of the belief which was so general in the seventeenth century, and lasted on in many minds during the eighteenth century, that the English language being in a continual state of change had no stability, and that the writings of one age would be quite unintelligible to succeeding generations. (*See* Pope in his *Essay on Criticism*, pp. 310–11, below.) This was the belief which led Bacon to have his English works translated into Latin in order to secure their permanence, 'for,' as he writes in 1623, 'these modern languages will at one time or other play bankrupt with books.' We have seen Waller, in his lines on English verse (1668), expressing the same opinion (*see* also Edward Phillips, 1675), and one writer at any rate went so far as to wish that all our poets, including Shakespeare, had written in Latin instead of in their mother tongue.

This was Dr. William King (1663–1712), best known perhaps as the author of *A Journey to London in the Year 1698*, who remarks in his *Adversaria* :—

> It is pity, that the finest of our English poets, especially the divine Shakespeare, had not communicated their beauties to the world so as to be understood in Latin, whereby Foreigners have sustained so great a loss to this day; when [*sic*] all of them were inexcusable but the most inimitable Shakespeare. I am so far from being envious, and desirous to keep those treasures to ourselves, that I could wish all our most excellent Poets translated into Latin that are not so already.

'This hint of the Doctor's,' continues his editor, John Nichols (writing in 1776), 'was not lost. Among other things, we have seen since not only a Latin translation of Prior's *Solomon* but even of Milton's *Paradise Lost* excellently performed in verse by Mr. Dobson, Fellow of New College, Oxford,' and he goes on to detail other essays of the same nature. (See *Adversaria*, in Original Works of . . . Dr. William King, 1776, vol. i, p. 241, also p. xxix.)

To return to other admirers of Chaucer in the seventeenth century. One of these is mentioned by Pepys in his *Diary*, when on the 14th of June, 1663, he notes an assembly at Sir William Penn's. 'Among the rest,' he writes, 'Sir John Minnes brought many fine expressions of Chaucer, which he doats on mightily, and without doubt he is a fine poet.'

Sir John Minnes was a retired vice-admiral and a controller of the navy, who in business matters was a continual thorn in the side of his subordinate, the Clerk of the Acts, who refers to him more than once as a 'doating fool,' and says he 'would do the king more hurt by his dotage and folly than all the rest can do by their knavery' (*Diary*, March 2, 1667–8). Although apparently quite inefficient and tactless in his office, Minnes had an undoubted reputation as a lover of the fine arts and a wit, for we find Sir William Coventry swearing to Pepys that Minnes was so bad at his work, that he (Coventry) would henceforth be against a wit being employed in business. Minnes published

several books (*e. g. Wit and Drollery*, 1656); Pepys quotes
many of his stories with evident gusto (*e. g.* Oct. 30, 1662), he
alludes to his judgment in pictures (Sept. 28, 1663), and he
records another pleasant evening (Sept. 18, 1665), when having
had news of the defeat of the Dutch, they made merry together,
and Minnes and John Evelyn vied with one another in bouts
of wit, Evelyn on this occasion surpassing Minnes in the latter's
' own manner of genius.'

Thus Minnes may be assumed to have had certain qualifications for judging of Chaucer, and he is an interesting example
of the genuine admiration of and enthusiasm for the poet to
be found in unexpected places, even when his fame was at its
lowest.

Pepys himself had a fondness for Chaucer. In an entry of
Dec. 10, 1663, he tells us he went to his booksellers, and names a
number of books which he looked through before making his
final choice. A Chaucer was among the number, and he was
evidently sorely tempted; but he did not buy it on that occasion, although he must have done so later, for in July of the
following year (1664) we find him going to the binder's about
' the doing of my Chaucer, though they were not full neat
enough for me, but pretty well it is; and thence to the clasp-
maker's to have it clasped and bossed.' The next day he
takes the copy home, well pleased with it, and a month later he
quotes Chaucer: so in addition to having the poet's works
bound and ' clasped and bossed,' he must also have read them.
It was thirty-four years later, when Dryden one day was dining
with him, that Pepys recommended to him the character of
Chaucer's ' Good Parson,' which led Dryden to put it into ' his
English.' (*See* Dryden's letter to Pepys, July 14, 1699, p. 270
below.)

Richard Brathwait, a north-country squire of literary tastes,
who published in 1665 a comment upon two of Chaucer's
Tales, is forced to take a very curious position in order to defend
his favourite. He contends that the substance of what Chaucer
says is so good that the manner of saying it matters comparatively little. In a quaint little Appendix at the end of

his volume, a carping critic is represented as coming forward
and saying

> that he could allow well of Chaucer, if his Language were
> Better. Whereto the Author of these Commentaries
> return'd him this Answer : " Sir, it appears, you prefer
> Speech before the Head piece; Language before Invention;
> whereas Weight of Judgment has ever given Invention
> Priority before Language. And not to leave you dis-
> satisfied, As the Time wherein these Tales were writ, ren-
> dered him incapable of the one; so his Pregnancy of
> Fancy approv'd him incomparable for the other." Which
> Answer still'd this Censor, and justified the Author.

Brathwait is interesting as a survival—far into the seventeenth century—of the Elizabethan attitude towards Chaucer.
As a matter of fact he had written his *Comment* in 1617, and,
for some unknown reason, waited forty-eight years to publish
it, by which time he was an old man of nearly eighty. In the
Appendix, however, written at the time of publication, Brathwait shows that in spite of the change in public opinion as to
Chaucer's merits, he clings faithfully to the tradition of his
youth. He knew the poet's works well and loved them
genuinely; could his life be renewed he tells us ' his Youthful
genius could not bestow his Endeavour on any Author with
more Pleasure nor Complacency to Fancy, than the Illustrations
of Chaucer.' For him Chaucer is still ' the Ancient, Renowned
and Ever Living Poet '; his teaching is sound and moral and
his imagination and wit incomparable, although owing to the
dark age in which he lived his style is often rude and rough.
This view in the early years of the seventeenth century was
common enough; but when Brathwait in 1665 published his
little volume, containing a few whole-hearted words of praise
of him who, so he never doubted, was the greatest of English
Poets, the old man's opinions and literary tastes were quite
behind the times, thoroughly old-fashioned and obsolete. They
differed widely from those held by Waller and Cowley (*see*
Dryden, *Preface to Fables*, 1700, below), and later by Addison;
but they dated back to the days when Edmund Spenser counted

it his greatest honour to call 'Dan Chaucer' master, and his highest aspiration to follow in the 'footing' of his feet.

With Brathwait's little book we may end our account of the very few bright places of Chaucer criticism during the time of gloom and neglect encountered by the old poet in the seventeenth century, and Brathwait himself seems to help to bridge over this dreary interval, by reaching out a hand on the one side to Spenser, and on the other to Dryden, forming thus a link between one of the greatest of English poets and one of the greatest of English critics, who were each distinguished by their appreciation of Geoffrey Chaucer.

PERIOD V.—In 1700 appeared Dryden's volume of *Fables*, which contained the modernized version of several Chaucerian poems, prefixed by Dryden's celebrated dissertation, which is the first detailed and careful criticism of Chaucer, as well as one of the most interesting literary discussions ever written.

He compares Chaucer to Ovid, and actually prefers the English poet, for which, he says, the vulgar judges 'will think me little less than mad.' He notes Chaucer's power of vivid description,—'I see,' he says, 'all the Pilgrims in the *Canterbury Tales*, their Humours, their Features, and the very Dress as distinctly as if I had supp'd with them at the *Tabard* in *Southwark*;'—his good sense: 'He is a perpetual Fountain of good Sense;'—his feeling of proportion: 'He . . . speaks properly on all Subjects: As he knew what to say, so he knows also when to leave off; a continence which is practised by few Writers, and scarcely by any of the Ancients, excepting *Virgil* and *Horace*;'—his truth to Nature: '*Chaucer* follow'd Nature everywhere, but was never so bold to go beyond her;'—his power of characterization: 'He must have been a Man of a most wonderful comprehensive Nature, because, as it has been truly observ'd of him, he has taken into the Compass of his *Canterbury Tales*, the various Manners and Humours of the whole *English* Nation, in his age. Not a single Character has escap'd him. All his Pilgrims are severally distinguish'd from each other; and not only in their Inclinations, but in their very Phisiognomies and Persons.'

Such a discerning criticism as this, coming from such a writer as Dryden, carried with it great weight, and all through the eighteenth century we can trace its influence. Those who knew something of Chaucer, and liked what they knew, had the authority of the great Mr. Dryden to support them in a judgment they might otherwise have hesitated to express. Thus one can feel Elizabeth Elstob [1] (1715) is emboldened by her knowledge of Dryden; and Dart, and later Cibber, are strengthened in their apology for Chaucer's language by the argument that even Dryden did not in some places attempt to alter it (pp. 361, 406 below); while George Sewell (1720), who writes the most sensible and enlightened criticism of Chaucer between Dryden and Warton, is obviously well pleased that he has the greatest modern poet and critic on his side. Some of those who would be naturally inclined to depreciate Chaucer, are a little restrained and often not a little puzzled by Dryden's attitude in the affair.   In a curious dialogue in a coffee-house in hell between Dryden and Chaucer, written by Thomas Brown (*a.* 1704) Chaucer is represented as thanking his successor for the honour he has done him in furbishing up some of his ' old musty Tales,' but he remonstrates strongly with him for his exaggeration in likening him to Ovid.   To this Mr. Dryden, anticipating the methods of Dr. Johnson, thus makes reply : ' Why, sir, I maintain it, and who then dares be so saucy as to oppose me ? '   One feels in truth that the adverse, often contemptuous criticism of the earlier eighteenth century is very greatly weakened by the firm stand taken by Dryden.

With regard to Chaucer's verse, Dryden is not so happy. ' It is,' he says, I confess, ' not Harmonious to us; . . . They who liv'd with him, and some time after him, thought it Musical. . . . There is the rude Sweetness of a *Scotch* Tune in it, which is natural and pleasing, though not perfect.'   Then

---

[1] ' It will not be taken amiss,' she says apologetically, ' by those who value the Judgment of Sir Philip Sydney and Mr. Dryden if I begin with Father Chaucer ' (*see* p. 338 below).

follows Dryden's famous denunciation of Speght's theory, that the fault might possibly lie with the readers :—

> 'Tis true, I cannot go so far as he who publish'd the last Edition of him; for he would make us believe the Fault is in our Ears, and that there were really Ten Syllables in a Verse where we could find but Nine : but this Opinion is not worth confuting; 'tis so gross and obvious an Errour, that common Sense . . . must convince the Reader, that Equality of Numbers, in every Verse which we call *Heroick*, was either not known, or not always practis'd, in *Chaucer's* Age.

In addition to giving his own estimate, Dryden also shows in this preface the general attitude of the age towards Chaucer. There were two objections, he says, raised to this work of modernization, and raised by two parties or classes of people who took entirely opposed views of Chaucer. The first class objected that the subject was unworthy of his pains, because, says Dryden, ' they look on Chaucer as a dry old-fashioned wit —not worth reviving.' Doubtless Waller, had he still been alive, would have endorsed this view. Addison certainly did. Dryden himself cites Cowley :—

> I have often heard the late Earl of *Leicester* say, that Mr. *Cowley* himself was of that opinion; who, having read him over at my Lord's Request, declared he had no Taste of him. I dare not advance my Opinion against the Judgment of so great an Author : But I think it fair, however, to leave the Decision to the Publick. Mr. *Cowley* was too modest to set up for a Dictatour; and being shock'd perhaps with his old Style, never examin'd into the depth of his good Sense.

The other party considered Chaucer should not be modernized ' out of a quite contrary Notion,' says Dryden. ' They suppose there is a certain Veneration due to his old Language; and that it is little else than Profanation and Sacrilege to alter it.' Foremost amongst these, Dryden mentions the Earl of Leicester (who had persuaded Cowley to read Chaucer) ' who valued *Chaucer* as much as Mr. *Cowley* despis'd him.' He had indeed dissuaded Dryden from his intention to modernize the poet; and Dryden had refrained from doing so until after Lord Leicester's death.

Between these two extreme views Dryden himself takes up an intermediate one, of admiration and veneration for Chaucer, combined with a conviction, that in order to perpetuate his memory, he must be translated. ' *Chaucer*, I confess, is a rough Diamond, and must first be polish'd e'er he shines.'

This work of ' polishing ' continued for nearly one hundred and fifty years; all sorts and conditions of writers, from the greatest poets down to the most obscure scribblers—from Dryden, Pope and Wordsworth, to Ogle, Betterton and Lipscomb—tried their hands in turn at it; and when we see the consensus of opinion in England, headed by Dryden himself, as to the complete obsoleteness of Chaucer's language, we are not surprised that so many attempts were made to ' improve ' and modernize it.

There is no question but that the men of the eighteenth century were as firmly convinced as their forefathers that the continual change in the English language was destined to render unintelligible, within a comparatively short period, all writers who chose that medium.[1] Their suggested remedy, however, was not to write in Latin as urged by Bacon or Waller, but the introduction of a mysterious process, reminiscent of the photographic ' dark room,' which they called ' fixing the language.'

Swift's well-known letter to Lord Oxford in 1712 best expresses the views generally held at this time on the subject; he there says that every man can hope to be read with pleasure for a few years only. After that he will need an interpreter; and he urges on the Earl in his function as Lord High Treasurer of Great Britain to lose no time in establishing an academy to fix a standard of speech.[2]

This argument is based on the assumption that the further

---

[1] *See*, for instance, the last paragraph in the quotation from Cibber's *Lives of the Poets*, 1753, p. 407 below.

[2] A Proposal for correcting, improving and ascertaining the English tongue . . . London, 1712, pp. 38, 40–3.

removed we are from a period in time, the less intelligible will become its words and grammar. In one sense this is true, particularly of uncultivated speech. But the formation of a great literature, and the spread of a general knowledge of reading, at once checks this tendency. The great authors are increasingly read and studied, until their words and turns of phrase become familiar, so that language, and more especially the cultured written language, instead of moving on in a straight line, away from its source, tends to revolve about its literature.[1]

One's natural inclination would be to think that Shakespeare, Spenser and Chaucer would have been more intelligible to the men of Queen Anne's time than they are to us, two hundred years later. But this was not the case. What collector of an English anthology would to-day think of excluding Shakespeare's poems on the ground that his language was obsolete ? Yet in 1702, we find Bysshe, in his Preface to *The Art of English Poetry*, saying that the reason ' the Good Shakespeare ' is not so frequently quoted in his book as he otherwise deserves to be, is because, like Chaucer and Spenser, the garb in which he is clothed is so out of fashion that readers of that age have no ear for him (*see* pp. 290–91 below). This is probably one of the works indignantly referred to by Charles Gildon in 1718 (Advertisement to Shakesperiana in *The Complete Art of Poetry*, p. 303) when he writes : ' Finding the inimitable Shakespear rejected by some Modern Collectors for his Obsolete Language, and having lately run over this great Poet, I could not but present the Reader with a Specimen of his Descriptions and Moral Reflections, to shew the Injustice of such an Obloquy.' [2]

What poet of to-day would append a glossary to his verses to explain the following ' obsolete words ' :—' to appal,' ' to carol,' ' certes,' ' deftly,' ' fays,' ' glee,' ' lea,' ' lithe,' ' loathly,'

---

[1] *See* Lounsbury, *Studies in Chaucer*, iii, p. 145–50.

[2] Shakespeare's language being looked upon as obsolete, or at any rate difficult, naturally was a bar to his being read, and probably at no period was he so little known as in the first quarter of the 18th century. Thus we find the Duke of Buckingham, who refers to Falstaff in his poem called ' An Essay on Poetry ' in 1721, adding the following doubtless necessary footnote : ' An admirable Character in a Play of Shakespeare's.'

'sooth' and 'thrall'? Yet these words are all carefully expounded by Thomson in the glossary to his *Castle of Indolence* published in 1748; and Gay, in his notes to *The Shepherd's Week*, in 1714, explains such words as 'doff,' 'don,' 'token,' 'scant,' 'deft,' 'glen' and 'dumps.'

At this time (when imitations of Spenser were so much in vogue) one finds continually glossaries appended to poems explaining what to all readers to-day are perfectly familiar terms. Thus, in notes to 'The Salisbury Ballad' (*see* below, p. 329), published in 1714, we find 'lore,' 'bouncing,' 'twang,' 'bard,' and 'lyre' all carefully annotated and interpreted, and in a contemporary hand in a copy of this same book (in the British Museum), extra notes are made on some of the words not explained by the editor, among which is 'blithe, an old word for cheerfull.' These details are cited to prove what really was the case, that the ignorance of our earlier literature was at this time so great, that words and phrases which are to us to-day perfectly familiar and in ordinary use, were then practically unknown.

No wonder, then, that the English of Chaucer was looked upon as to all intents and purposes a dead language, for the comprehension of which a special and an arduous course of study was necessary. Thus in an essay on the old English poets, written in 1707, we are told that in order to understand Chaucer, his readers will need a knowledge of French and also of Dutch, because 'there is so much of the Saxon or German Tongue in his language' (below, p. 295).

On almost every page which deals in any way with English poetry at this time are to be found remarks of the nature of the following lines addressed by Elijah Fenton to Mr. Southerne, in which he says :—

> *Chaucer* had all that Beauty cou'd inspire,
> And *Surry's* Numbers glow'd with warm Desire :
> Both now are priz'd by few, unknown to most,
> Because the Thoughts are in the Language lost;
> Ev'n *Spencer's* Pearls in muddy Waters lye,
> Rarely discover'd by the Diver's Eye :
> Rich was their Imag'ry, till Time defac'd
> The curious Works, but *Waller* came at last. . . .

Then follows the usual glowing panegyric which the name of Waller invariably aroused. This extract is of interest, as showing that not only Chaucer, and, as we have already seen, Shakespeare, but Surrey and Spenser are looked upon as obsolete in the year 1711.

Thus we find Chaucer's language, and by degrees his very name becoming synonymous with decay. In some verses written on the great actress, Mrs. Oldfield (died 1730), the writer moralizes on the transitoriness of human fame and says :—

> In vain secure of deathless praise,
>   There poets' ashes come,
> Since obsolete grows Chaucer's phrase,
>   And moulders with his tomb.

Pope, in his *Essay on Criticism*, is but carrying this gloomy belief to its melancholy but logical conclusion, when he asserts that the writers of his day would in their turn be as unintelligible to succeeding generations as Chaucer was to his.

> Short is the date, alas ! of modern rhymes,
> And 'tis but just to let them live betimes.
> No longer now that golden age appears,
> When patriarch wits survived a thousand years.
> Now length of fame (our second life) is lost,
> And bare threescore is all ev'n that can boast;
> Our sons their fathers' failing language see,
> And such as Chaucer is shall Dryden be.

It is small wonder then, in view of this state of affairs, that those who cared **for** Chaucer should have done their utmost to translate him into intelligible language whilst yet there was time, and whilst they themselves had still some glimmering of his meaning. Dryden and Pope set the fashion,[1] each in his turn clothing the poet anew, and it was in the dress provided by them that Chaucer was principally known to readers of the eighteenth century.

There is no need to say anything here about these modernizations; they are well known, and they have their own merits.

---

[1] There was one earlier attempt at a modernization, but it was never published; this was Sidnam's version of the first three books of *Troilus and Cressida, c.* 1630. (*See* p. 203 below.)

They were hailed with delight, were universally praised, and for many years were held unquestioningly to be far superior to Chaucer's own poems; most of their admirers appear to think that the more they belittled the originals the greater was the honour which redounded to the modernizers. This is the kind of verse one meets with continually on the subject :—

> Revolving Time had injur'd *Chaucer's* Name,
> And dimm'd the brilliant Lustre of his Fame;
> Deform'd his Language, and his Wit depress'd,
> His serious Sense oft sinking to a Jest;
> Almost a Stranger ev'n to *British* Eyes,
> We scarcely knew him in the rude Disguise :
> But cloath'd by Thee, the banish'd Bard appears
> In all his Glory, and new Honours wears.
> Thus *Ennius* was by *Virgil* chang'd of old;
> He found him Rubbish, and he left him Gold.
>   (*Verses occasioned by reading Mr. Dryden's Fables,*
>   by Jabez Hughes, *c.* 1707.)

These sentiments are expressed over and over again all through the eighteenth century. In the *Gentleman's Magazine* for January 1740 there is a little poem by ' Astrophil,' *In Praise of Chaucer,* which, though giving to Chaucer every recognition, yet ends in the usual way :—

> So true with life his characters agree,
> What e'er is read we almost think we see.
> Such *Chaucer* was, bright mirror of his age
> Tho' length of years has quite obscur'd his page;
> His stile grown obsolete, his numbers rude,
> Scarce read, and but with labour understood.
> Yet by fam'd modern bards new minted o'er,
> His standard wit has oft enrich'd their store;
> Whose *Canterbury Tales* could task impart
> For *Pope's* and *Dryden's* choice refining art;
> And in their graceful polish let us view
> What wealth enrich'd the mind where first they grew.

Later still, in 1781, we find Walpole in a letter to Mason refusing the offer to procure a first edition of Chaucer for a guinea, saying, ' I am too, though a Goth, so modern a Goth that I hate the black letter, and I love Chaucer better in Dryden and Baskerville than in his own language and dress.'

The tendency of the modernizations was to divert people from reading the originals. Chaucer's *name* became better known, but his actual *works* less and less known : only a kind of tradition about them was kept up.

The attitude of the great dictator of letters himself was not favourable to Chaucer, although he at one time contemplated bringing out a new edition of the poet; he rarely mentions him, and when he does, the utterance is not sympathetic, so that we cannot help suspecting him of the fault he imputes to Dryden, who, he says, ' in confidence of his abilities, ventured to write of what he had not examined, and ascribes to Chaucer the first refinement of our numbers.' But Johnson goes on to show that Gower's numbers are quite as smooth, and his rimes as easy as those of Chaucer. The works of Chaucer, he says, which Dryden has modernized,

> require little criticism. The tale of *The Cock* seems hardly worth revival; and the story of *Palamon and Arcite*, containing an action unsuitable to the times in which it is placed, can hardly be suffered to pass without censure of the hyperbolical commendation which Dryden has given it in the general Preface.

For Johnson, in short—and he well represents the dominant eighteenth-century critical attitude—English poetry began with Waller, and earlier writers (with a very qualified exception of Shakespeare) were not worthy serious attention; Chaucer was a Goth, and the greatest praise to which he was entitled was that he might perhaps, with great justice, be styled ' the first of our versifiers who wrote poetically.'

Those who wrote the modernizations at any rate were forced to read the originals, and from them occasionally we get a sensible criticism. We have heard Dryden; and Pope is reported by Spence to have said—

> I read Chaucer still with as much pleasure as almost any of our poets. He is a master of manners, of description, and the first tale-teller in the true and enlivened natural way.

And again he writes—

> Good sense shows itself in every line of the Prologue to
> the Canterbury Tales. . . . Addison's character of Chaucer
> is diametrically opposed to the truth, he blames him for
> want of humour.

In 1739, George Ogle, in his Letter to a Friend (p. 384 below),
prefixed to his modernization of the Clerk of Oxford's tale, which
he calls *Gualtherus and Griselda*, shows that he too, having read
Chaucer, can appreciate his merit.   He quotes Dryden's
criticism with approval, and adds, ' As to the Point of Characterizing, at which CHAUCER was most singularly happy : You can
name no Author even of Antiquity, whether in the Comic or
in the Satiric Way, equal, at least superior, to Him.'   Then he
' throws together ' a few touches taken from his Descriptions
of the Pilgrims.   ' The *Knight*, an old soldier, who, though he
was *worthy* (meaning a man of excessive Bravery) yet was
wise . . . and the *Serjeant at Law ;* Who *seemed* much *busier*
than he *was*.'   So he goes through twenty more of them, showing thorough sympathy and understanding.   Yet it was this
same Mr. Ogle, a sincere admirer of Chaucer's, who, when he
brought out the whole of the *Canterbury Tales* ' modernized by
several hands,' thus rendered the Prologue fit for modern
ears :—

> When April, soft'ning sheds refreshing Show'rs
> And frees, from droughty March the springing Flow'rs,
> *April*, That bathes the teeming womb of Earth
> And gives to Vegetation, kindly Birth !
> When Zephyr breathes the Gale that favours Love,
> And Cherishes the Growth of ev'ry Grove ;
> Zephyr !   That ministers with genial Breeze,
> Bloom to the Shrubs and Verdure to the Trees.
> When youthful Phœbus half his course compleats
> Divides the Ram, and glows with temp'rate Heats ;
> Phœbus !   Our equal Good, the live-long year
> Or should he take or should he quit the Sphere ;
> When Philomel injoys the Coming Spring,
> And feeling her approach, delights to sing.
> Sweet Philomel !   Of all the Birds that fly,
> The Sole, to pass the Night with sleepless Eye.

One is tempted to linger over these modernizations 'by several hands.' They are very fascinating, though not in the way their authors intended; for they seem more curious to us than even the ' barbaric ' relics of Chaucer himself, and their language is far stranger than his.

There is a beautiful and high-sounding poem by Henry Brooke, *Constantia*, or *The Man of Law's Tale*, the opening of which is especially worthy of note. In the original, Chaucer writes thirty-five lines descriptive of the ills of poverty, but Henry Brooke transmutes these into one hundred and sixty-eight lines on the same topic.

We must, however, leave Chaucer in the hands of his merciless interpreters, of whom there were many more (notably Lipscomb, 1792–5, and the last great attempt to modernize him in 1841, to which reference will be made later), and consider very briefly another form of appreciation which was rather popular in the eighteenth century. This consisted of imitation of Chaucer, that is poems or verses written in what was supposed to be his manner.

This ' imitation ' of the older poets—Chaucer, Spenser and Milton—was one of the many ways in which eighteenth-century writers gave expression to their growing interest in the earlier literature of their country, and the number of Spenserian imitations published; good, bad, and worse than indifferent, from the *Castle of Indolence* to Mickle's *Sir Martyn*, is almost incredible until one collects a list of them.[1]

The imitations of Chaucer were comparatively few in quantity, but they make up for this by being fearful and wonderful in quality. The earliest instance of this kind of imitation is in William Bullein's *Dialogue . . against the fever Pestilence*, 1564. Chaucer is here introduced in person, and commends ' his deare Brigham ' for the monument he has erected to him, at the same time he laments the rifling of tombs and spoiling of epitaphs which is so common, and he concludes these remarks in a stanza of what is apparently intended to be Chaucerian verse

---

[1] *See* the list from 1700 to 1775 in *The Beginnings of the English Romantic Movement*, by William Lyon Phelps, 1893, Appendix I.

(*see* below, p. 99). In the seventeenth century we find several imitations. There are some verses in Chaucer's style among the dedicatory poems to Kynaston's *Troilus* in 1635, and a similar poem by the same author, Francis James, in 1638. These, combined with the jargon Cartwright puts into the mouth of the antiquary, Moth, in his play of *The Ordinary* (c. 1634, *see* below, p. 206), are interesting as showing the strange conception of Chaucer's language which was current among seventeenth-century scholars.

Two satiric pieces in Chaucer's style, one of them probably by Sir John Minnes, were published in the Musarum Deliciae in 1655, and in the next year an imitation of the tale of Sir Thopas appeared in a collection called *Choyce Drollery*.

In the eighteenth century the recipe for this class of composition was, as Professor Lounsbury points out,[1] quite simple, and consisted of three main ingredients; the story must be obscene, the language ungrammatical, and the verse rugged. The first was not always insisted on—though it made it more complete—but the last two were absolutely indispensable.

There is no doubt that Dryden's modernizations and his praise of Chaucer gave a great impetus to this kind of poetic exercise, of which Prior's two imitations are typical examples, published in 1712; about which time there seems to have been a curious outburst of interest in Chaucer. In 1711, Pope brought out his *Temple of Fame*, largely based on the elder poet's work; in 1712, in addition to Prior's imitations, Betterton and Cobb both published their modernizations, and a tract called the *Parliament of Birds* appeared; in 1713 Gay produced his comedy called *The Wife of Bath*, with Chaucer as the principal character; while all this time at Oxford, as we can tell from Hearne's diaries, there was among scholars much interest in and talk about Chaucer, for Urry was working hard at his edition of the poet, and collecting all the manuscripts and printed copies on which he could lay hands.

The greater number of the ' imitations ' are to be found in

---

[1] *Studies in Chaucer*, vol. iii, p. 121.

the first half of the eighteenth century; [1] we may note Gay's
Answer to the Sompner's Prologue, Fenton's *Tale devised in the
plesaunt manere of gentil Maister Jeoffrey Chaucer,* both published in Lintott's Miscellany in 1717, and William Thompson's
In Chaucer's Boure (c. 1745).

The Rev. Thomas Warton, at one time Professor of Poetry at
Oxford, but best known as the father of two eminent sons,
published in 1747 a less crude caricature of Chaucer's style than
any of the above, in his paraphrase of some verses in Leviticus
in the manner of the *Parlement of Foules;* and in the same
year Mason, the friend of Gray, shows best perhaps all the
peculiarities of bad grammar, unknown words, and halting
verse which to the eighteenth century represented Chaucer's
' homely rhyme.' Here are some of the lines he puts into
Chaucer's mouth when mourning the death of Pope, in the
Musæus (for the whole extract *see* p. 393 below) :—

> For syn the daies whereas my lyre ben strongen,
> And deftly many a mery laie I songen,
> Old Time, which alle things don maliciously,
> Gnawen with rusty tooth continually,
> Gnattrid my lines, that they all cancrid ben,
> Till at the last thou smoothen 'hem hast again;
> Sithence full semely gliden my rymes rude.

Comment here seems needless, unless it be to remark that,
if Chaucer's lines resembled these, they certainly required
smoothing.

Now we may turn to the more grateful task of tracing the
gradual revival in the eighteenth century of genuine appreciation
of Chaucer, based on knowledge of his work. This change
naturally was brought about by scholars, not by poets and men
of letters, for the study and understanding of Chaucer in the
original was in the eighteenth century confined to scholars, and
to extremely few of these. We can see the interest he aroused
in Hearne, and we may regret that Dean Atterbury did not

---

[1] Whether the imitations which were called out by the Chatterton-
Rowley discussion at the end of the century were supposed to be in
Chaucer's or in Rowley's language is not quite clear. *See,* for instance,
pp. 465, 466 below, 1782, John Baynes and E. B. Greene.

fix on him instead of on Urry to edit the poet's works.   Morell, in 1737, as a result of really reading and studying Chaucer, came to the conclusion that he had ' been wretchedly abused, miswrote and mismetred by all his editors,' and he shows that he had a glimmering, partly suggested to him by Urry, that to sound the final ' e ' might make a great difference to the alleged roughness of his verse.   Morell also incidentally gives us a clue to the reason why the rational study of Chaucer was so long delayed : which was that it was not thought quite a dignified or weighty subject worthy of the whole attention of scholars.   It was suitable enough for an amusement or hobby, but not for a serious occupation.   ' This then has been my amusement for some time,' he says at the end of the preface to his unfinished edition of the *Canterbury Tales*, ' and I hope with no great detriment to the more severe and decent studies required by my place and character.   I believe many a leisure hour might have been spent worse.'

There are two writers, both scholars, and curiously enough, both women, who must be noted in the early eighteenth century as showing some real knowledge, and consequently genuine appreciation of Chaucer.   Elizabeth Elstob, the earlier of these, was a born scholar and linguist, whose love for learning helped her to overcome incredible difficulties in the days when it was considered almost indecent for a woman to occupy her mind with such studies as Anglo-Saxon; in 1715 she published the first attempt at an Old English grammar, written in English,[1] with the following significant title :—

The Rudiments of Grammar for the English-Saxon Tongue, first given in English : with an Apology for the study of Northern Antiquities.   Being very useful toward the understanding our ancient English Poets, and other Writers.

In her preface she takes occasion to point out more fully that a knowledge of the Saxon Tongue, by which she means Old

---

[1] The first Old English grammar was in Latin by George Hickes, Oxford, 1689, republished and enlarged later under the title *Thesaurus Grammaticocriticus,* 1705.   Elizabeth Elstob was Hickes's niece.

and Middle English, is necessary or at least useful to the right understanding of the older English Poets, such as Chaucer.

Elizabeth Cooper was the second of these writers, and was one of the very earliest people to try to revive a knowledge of the older English poets, of whose work she in 1737 published Specimens,—' from the Saxons to the Reign of King Charles II,' so runs the title page. As a matter of fact the complete project of the ' Muses Library ' was from lack of support not carried out, but the first volume, the only one published, has a number of well-chosen poetical extracts ranging from *Piers Plowman* to Daniel.

Her preface is very interesting, showing on the subject of the older literature a combination of accurate and first-hand knowledge with critical independence and judgment not to be met elsewhere at that time. ' Very Few,' she says, ' of these great Men [Chaucer, Barclay, Skelton, Surrey, Sackville, Spenser, Lord Brook, Donne, Corbet, Carew, etc.] are generally known to the present Age : And tho' *Chaucer* and *Spencer* are ever nam'd with much Respect, not many are intimately acquainted with their Beauties ' (below, p. 379) ; and then, after praising Chaucer in terms which show that she, at any rate, has read him, she selects as a specimen of his work the unhackneyed and yet highly characteristic Prologue to the *Pardoner's Tale.*

The first writer, however, who really attacked the question with authority combined with knowledge and insight, was Thomas Warton. As early as 1754 he held a brief for Chaucer, and in his *Observations on the Faerie Queene*, wrote a most acute and discriminating account of him, in which he pointed out that it was the modernizations which had stood in the way of Chaucer himself being read, and had brought about a general ignorance of the original (*see* p. 409 below). ' Chaucer,' he says, ' seems to be regarded rather as an old poet, than as a good one, and that he wrote English verses four hundred years ago seems more frequently to be urged in his commendation, than that he wrote four hundred years ago with taste and judgment.[1] . . . When I

---

[1] Compare Sewell's remarks in 1720 : ' they who speak of him rather pay a blind Veneration to his Antiquity than his intrinsic Worth.'

sate down to read Chaucer with the curiosity of knowing how
the first English poet wrote, I left him with the satisfaction of
having found what later and more refin'd ages could hardly
equal in true humour, pathos, or sublimity.'

Warton's enlightened view of Chaucer is displayed very
much more fully in his *History of English Poetry* in 1774, but
by that time the tide of opinion was beginning to turn. Gray,
in his notes on metre (*c.* 1760), repudiates the idea that Chaucer
had no ear, and definitely asserts, what had been suggested
first by Speght, and later by Urry and Morell, that if the poet's
verse appeared irregular, the fault lay not with the writer but the
reader. He instances the sounding of initial and final syllables,
especially the genitive singular, and nominative plural of nouns,
and he is the first, we believe, clearly to point out how much the
change in the accentuation of words must affect our reading of
the older poets : ' we undoubtedly destroy,' he says, ' a great
part of the music of their versification by laying the accent of
words where nobody then laid it.'

Gray's notes were not published till 1814, otherwise we
might think that Tyrwhitt owed something to them.

Bishop Hurd, in his *Letters on Chivalry and Romance* (1762),
again shows that Chaucer himself is being read, when he calls
attention to what is evidently to him a surprising fact, that in
so early an age when chivalry still flourished, Chaucer in *Sir
Thopas* actually detected the absurdity of the old romances,
and was making fun of them. In the same year (1762) Warton
issued a second edition of his *Observations*, in which he slightly
alters his remarks on Chaucer. In 1754 he had emphasized the
fact that it was Chaucer who ' first gave the English nation in
its own language an idea of *Humour,*' he now points out that the
poet ' abounds not only in strokes of humour, which is commonly
supposed to be his sole talent, but of pathos and sublimity.'
This remark, perhaps more than anything else, shows that a
new era is dawning for Chaucer.

That which is most surprising in looking back over the great
mass of Chaucer criticism, up to this date, is that even his most
ardent admirers do not seem to have had a complete conception

of what Chaucer really was, nor wherein lay his great strength as a poet.

The characteristics which most attract us to him to-day, in addition to his delightful humour, are his simplicity, his tenderness, his wisdom, toleration and broad-mindedness, his close knowledge of human nature, and his almost constant felicity of expression. Yet, with curiously few exceptions, from the middle of the sixteenth to the end of the eighteenth century, not one of these qualities seems to be remarked in Chaucer. All his early admirers understood and praised his verse, but, as we have seen, in later years that found no supporter. Spenser, Dryden and Pope, as well as Caxton, the author of the *Book of Curtesye*, and William Thynne, note Chaucer's true poetical strength, his imagination and power of expression. Otherwise, he is looked upon for the most part as a comic poet chiefly remarkable for the scurrility of his verses. This is a view which, as we have seen, began to creep in at the end of the sixteenth century; it was for this that men like Drant or Harrington openly condemned him, while others, less stern, merely laughed at his ' merie tales,' and looked on his outspokenness as sufficient reason that they should outvie him in this respect; so we find the unknown author of *Greene's Vision* making Chaucer cite his own practice in order to reassure Greene, who is reproaching himself for the wanton writings of his youth (*see* pp. 137–38 below). This attitude of tolerant amusement rapidly gained ground in the seventeenth and earlier eighteenth centuries,[1] and if his coarseness is not insisted on, he is at best a good, jolly story teller; as Warton says, ' strokes of humour ' are ' commonly supposd to be his sole talent.'

> Old *Chaucer* shall, for his facetious style,
> Be read, and prais'd by warlike *Britains*, while
> The Sea enriches, and defends their Isle,

writes John Evelyn in 1685. Chaucer was a merry wit, but a rough one, for even his humour, the only quality granted him, was not recognized to be the most light and delicate ever

---

[1] *See*, for instance, Rowlands 1602, Smith 1656, Philips 1675, Evelyn 1685, Addison 1694, Cobb *a.* 1700, Gay 1712, Draper 1713 and Harte 1727.

possessed by an Englishman, but rather quaint and coarse, fit only for a barbarous age. This point is emphasized here, for it must be remembered that it was the general and common attitude existing side by side with the new and intellectual interest which we have seen scholars were beginning to take in his work. Moreover it is one which, with a certain class of writers—men who did not read Chaucer, but yet thought it correct to refer to him—increases all through the first three quarters of the eighteenth century. It is well summed up in the following lines in an Elegy called *Woodstock Park*, published anonymously in 1761 :—

> Old Chaucer, who in rough unequal verse,
> Sung quaint allusion and facetious tale ;
> And ever as his jests he would rehearse,
> Loud peals of laughter echoed through the vale.
>
> .   .   .   .
>
> What though succeeding poets, as they [their ?] sire,
> Revere his memory and approve his wit ;
> Though Spenser's elegance and Dryden's fire
> His name to ages far remote transmit ;
> His tuneless numbers hardly now survive
> As ruins of a dark and Gothic age ;
> And all his blithesome tales their praise derive
> From Pope's immortal song and Prior's page.

This poem, which was published the year before the second edition of Warton's *Observations*, illustrates better perhaps than could anything else the startling change in Chaucer criticism which was inaugurated immediately afterwards by the work of scholars like Warton and Tyrwhitt.

PERIOD VI.—It is with the publication of Tyrwhitt's edition of the *Canterbury Tales* in 1775, that we enter upon the sixth and present period of Chaucer criticism ; it is entirely owing to the work of this great, but little known, scholar that the sane and rational study of the poet's work was, for the first time since the early sixteenth century, made possible for Englishmen. Not only did Tyrwhitt edit the first good text of the *Canterbury Tales*, but in his prefatory essay he definitely and clearly disposed for ever of the persistently erroneous view which was held of Chaucer's versification (*see* pp. 442–45 below). His text of the 'Tales' was almost immediately pirated by Bell for his edition of the English poets (1782); it was also used by Anderson in his English poets (1795), and other reprints of it in the nineteenth century were numerous, so it thus became easily accessible to every would-be reader.

With Tyrwhitt's monumental work as a starting-point and basis, we can trace in this period very clearly the history, first of the gradual disappearance of certain persistent and long-cherished beliefs about Chaucer founded upon ignorance either of his language, or his work, or of both; and the substitution for these of sane, sound and scholarly appreciation, not only of the wisdom, the humour and the imagination of the poet, but also of his supreme technical and artistic skill.[1]

The distinctly eighteenth-century ideas which gradually dispersed like mist before the sunlight, may for convenience be summarized as follows :—

As regards *manner* :—

(1) That Chaucer's language was barbarous and difficult.

(2) That he had no ear for metre, and wrote rough and irregular lines.

(3) That these shortcomings were not wholly his fault, but a necessary result of the rude age in which he wrote, when poetry was in its infancy.

(4) That therefore the only possible way to read him was in a 'modernization.'

As regards *matter* :—

(5) That he was principally a 'facetious' or roughly comic poet, chiefly delighting in coarse tales, and lacking seriousness and dignity.

These beliefs were not by any means swept away at one breath, as they might have been by a careful reading of Tyrwhitt's text and preface. Convictions so firmly rooted in men's minds cannot be disposed of in a moment. For example, we

---

[1] For an early example of the effect of Tyrwhitt's work on the ordinary reviewer or hack writer, *see* below, p. 488, Philip Neve, 1789.

find the idea that Chaucer's verse is rough and that he is difficult to read and understand is one that lasts on with curious persistence.   In the article on Lydgate in the second edition of the *Encyclopædia Britannica* (1778–83) it is stated that Lydgate's versification is much more harmonious than Chaucer's. This assertion is repeated in subsequent editions of the Encyclopædia up to 1842, and we hear echoes of this view from time to time in the nineteenth century, as in Sharon Turner's *History of England* (1815), or in Burrowes's *Modern Encyclopædia* (1837).

Anna Seward, who in 1792 writes of Chaucer's 'obsolete, coarse and inharmonious diction,' maintains this attitude in her letters to Scott and others later on.   She comments, in 1806, on the 'insane partiality' of Godwin for the poetic powers of Chaucer, whose compositions, she says, 'have so little good which is not translation, and so much that is tedious, unnatural, conceited and obscure.'   Richard Wharton, in 1804, speaks of his 'hobbling cadences and obsolete phrases'; in 1807 'Peter Pindar' (Dr. John Wolcot) writes just as did Hughes and Cobb a century earlier,

> Though obsolete, alas ! thy line,
> And doomed in cold neglect to shine,

and Byron, in *Hints from Horace* (1811), takes the usual eighteenth century view when he says that our forefathers, who did not trouble about the classics,

> Were satisfied with Chaucer and old Ben;
> The jokes and numbers suited to their taste
> Were quaint and careless, anything but chaste.

Lord Thurlow, who, unlike Byron, much admired Chaucer, yet speaks of his 'homely rhyme' (1813); 'quaint and rough,' a writer in the *Gentleman's Magazine* (May 1818) calls it; 'antiquated' and 'outworn' says Horace Smith in 1825, and in the following year, Hazlitt, in reporting the conversation which took place at one of Lamb's Wednesdays on 'Persons one would wish to have seen,' says that all the company were in favour of Chaucer, except William Ayrton, the musician, 'who said something about the ruggedness of the metre.'

Consequently, the idea tends to be developed about this time which is baldly stated by Berington in 1814 (below, Part II, p. 61), that the chief merit and interest of Chaucer is not as a poet but as a historian of manners, and that his works are not merely ' effusions of a poetical imagination ' but ' they are pregnant with instruction of a higher order. They are an essential portion of the authentic history of his country ' (see end of article in *The Retrospective Review*, 1824 below, Part II, p. 155).

Nott's views, in 1815, on Chaucer's versification are worth noting, for they are not careless remarks made on insufficient knowledge, but are the result of close study of the text. He examines Tyrwhitt's ' system respecting Chaucer's versification,' and objects to it. He does not believe in the sounding of the final ' e ' feminine; he maintains that Chaucer's lines are not intended for iambic decasyllables, although unintentionally such lines occur, but that his principle of versification is rhythmical and not metrical, and that he ' designed his lines to be read with a cæsura and rhythmical cadence.' Southey, in 1807, had partly anticipated this view, and later, in 1833, having been reinforced by the views of Farmer and Nott, he is more emphatic on the point and says he believes Chaucer to have written his verses on the same principle on which Coleridge wrote his *Christabel*.

Isaac D'Israeli, as late as 1841, completely routs Tyrwhitt's theory of Chaucer's versification and asserts, that the poet makes his words long or short, dissyllabic or trisyllabic at his pleasure. ' It is evident,' he continues, ' that Chaucer trusted his cadences to his ear, and his verse is therefore usually rhythmical and accidentally metrical.' He also doubts if anything but the Canterbury Tales (made accessible by Tyrwhitt) will ever be read, for the difficulties are too great. Readers will be appalled by having to face ' a massive tome dark with the Gothic type, whose obsolete words and difficult phrases, and for us, uncadenced metre, are to be conned by a glossary as obsolete as the text, to be perpetually referred to, to the interruption of all poetry and all patience.'

It was in this same year (1841), just one hundred years after

Ogle's venture, that the last important attempt was made to modernize Chaucer.   This was a small volume called ' The Poems of Geoffrey Chaucer Modernized,' which is chiefly remarkable for the worthlessness of its contents and the eminence of its contributors, many of whom, one is tempted to think, ought to have known better.

It was edited by Richard Hengist Horne, who says he thinks the project was set on foot by Wordsworth, who promised to contribute, assisted by Leigh Hunt, Miss Barrett, Robert Bell, Monckton Milnes, Leonhard Schmitz and Horne himself.   For the second volume (which, happily, never appeared), it was intended to ask for the help of Tennyson, Talfourd, Browning, Bulwer, Mr. and Mrs. Cowden Clarke, and Mary Howitt; and we are told that every one who was invited to take part in the project agreed cordially, with the sole exception of Landor, who at once saw the folly of the attempt, and expressed his views on it with great decision.   His first reply to Mr. Horne's application was that he believed ' as many people read Chaucer (meaning in the original) as were fit to read him.'   Horne misunderstood this remark, and so Landor wrote again to explain his views more fully, expressing himself very characteristically as follows :—' Indeed, I *do* admire him, or rather love him,' adding, ' Pardon me if I say I would rather see Chaucer quite alone, in the dew of his sunny morning, than with twenty clever gentlefolks about him, arranging his shoe-strings and buttoning his doublet.   I like even his *language*.   I will have no hand in breaking his dun but rich painted glass to put in (if clearer) much thinner panes.'   ' And thus,' commented Horne, —when he published part of this correspondence in 1877—' with the true but narrow devotion of the best men on the black-letter side, and their resistance to all attempts to melt the obsolete language and form it into modern moulds . . . the Homer of English poetry continues unread except by very few.'

The introduction to the ' Modernizations ' is interesting. We see that in 1841 the state of Chaucer's language was looked upon as being as hopelessly unintelligible as in the days of Pope; and that the reader must, among other qualifications, be ' learned in the black letter ' (whatever that may be) in order to hope to understand him. We also learn that in 1841 everything had been done for Chaucer's works in the collation of texts and the writing of notes and glossaries that could be wished for; which causes us to wonder what the Chaucer Society has since found to do. Horne's criticisms of earlier translations, as well as some of his own renderings of Chaucer's text, are quite worth study, and indeed the whole book is a curiosity of literature.[1] Its chief interest from our point of view consists in the proof it gives of the growth during the past eighty years, not only of general knowledge of Chaucer and familiarity with his language, but of English scholarship generally. This is made clear at once when we reflect how impossible it would be for a group of writers of intelligence and even genius to-day, of the same standing as these contributors, to attempt a similar production.

We find also the distaste for Chaucer experienced by Cowley, lasting far on into the nineteenth century, especially in some of the Reviews. A reviewer of Godwin's ' Life,' in 1804, asserts that the idea that Chaucer in the ' uncouth and antiquated style of the original ' could ever give the pleasure he does in the ' finely-turned versification ' of Dryden and Pope, is one ' which could be entertained for a moment only by the blindest enthusiasm.'

A writer in the *Gentleman's Magazine* for October 1818, while giving Chaucer some appreciation, yet at the same time denounces the poet in all the old familiar terms, speaks of his ' rough phraseology,' the ' harshness and lameness of his numbers,' his ribaldry and coarseness, and concludes by saying

---

[1] *See* Lounsbury's *Studies in Chaucer*, vol. iii, pp. 213–29, where an amusing account of this book is given, and some of the most flagrant mistakes and blunders in it are noted. Such are, for instance, the ascription to Wordsworth of a quotation from Drayton which is printed on the title page; or the entire misunderstanding of many of Chaucer's words; or such grotesque renderings as that of Chaucer's description of the poor Clerk of Oxford :
' Full threadbare was his overest courtepy,'
which in Horne's version becomes
' His uppermost short coat was a bare thread.'

that not ' all the hyperbolical praises of the illustrious Dryden [can] prove that he was gifted with one spark of the sublime spirit of the Grecian Bard.'

The view of Chaucer as a coarse and comic poet unfit for study by serious people also persists, and a delightful example of it is the case of the Rev. Henry Richman, who, in his youth, had written a sequel to the *Canterbury Tales*, of which his friends could never obtain a sight; for, says one of them, ' he always declined permitting . . . [them] to peruse it, upon this principle, that the levity of such compositions was inconsistent with the decorum of the clerical character ' (*see* below, *c.* 1810). The severely moral view of Chaucer's sins is also taken by an anonymous writer, who, in 1841, published an abridgment of Dryden's version of the character of the good parson, as well as the Parson's Prologue and Tale.   In alluding to the ' ribaldry and pollution ' to be found in other parts of Chaucer's writings and to his [spurious ?] Retractation at the end of the *Canterbury Tales*, the editor of this pamphlet concludes, ' an author should never forget, that . . . his works, if calculated to corrupt, may still be doing their mischief, and . . . his crimes may thus be extended . . . through centuries.'   This forms a curious contrast to the estimate of Chaucer's outlook and influence as expressed later, for instance, by Ruskin and Alfred Austin. For what Ruskin says in *Fors Clavigera*, see p. lxiv below; and the then poet laureate, when speaking on the occasion of Chaucer's quincentenary, said that ' poets like Chaucer were themselves ministers of God,' and that ' he was an exponent of the purest and the most permanent elements of Christianity.'

The latest expression of the older view we meet with is in 1878, when in a *History of English Humour*, by A. G. K. L'Estrange, the surprising statement is made that although no doubt at the time he wrote he was thought witty, that ' scarcely any part of Chaucer's writings would raise a laugh at the present day, though they might a blush.'

But it is not only among unknown reviewers and odd writers that we find a distaste for Chaucer in the first half of the nineteenth century.   Byron's condemnation is well known :

' Chaucer, notwithstanding the praises heaped upon him, I think obscene and contemptible' (1807), and John Galt, the novelist, writes in 1812 : ' I have never been able to bring myself to entertain any feeling approximating to respect for Chaucer, Gower, Lydgate, and the other tribe of rhymers before Henry VIII,' for which remark we are glad to see he was severely chastised in the *Quarterly* of September of the same year. The poet Moore found Chaucer unreadable (1819), so did Lord Lansdowne, and Sir Kenelm Digby, in 1844, calls him ' impious and obscene.'

Cardinal Wiseman, who showed some appreciation of him as a poet, nevertheless regrets (1855) that in his work, as well as in that of Spenser's, ' every rich description of natural beauty is connected with wantonness, voluptuousness, and debauchery.'

It was this ' foul and false accusation' (Leigh Hunt's *Correspondence*, 1862, vol. ii., p. 264) which roused Leigh Hunt to write in defence of these two poets one of his last articles published in Fraser's Magazine four months after his death (December 1859).

A remnant of the survival of the predominating eighteenth century idea that Chaucer was a ' comic ' poet, and thus un-dignified, may have affected Matthew Arnold's criticism of him in 1880.[1] He classes Chaucer, quite rightly, below Homer, Dante and Shakespeare, but he does so not because he did not equal them in genius, but because he lacked seriousness.

The uncritical attitude towards Chaucer, and real ignorance about him, his life and work, is to be found in unexpected places long after ample materials were published which would have made, one would have thought, such mis-statements impossible. Emerson, who read Chaucer with delight in early youth (c. 1820), and continually refers to him with appreciation, yet reveals the vague knowledge of facts and dates which is reminiscent of sixteenth century writers. In his essay on Shakespeare (1848) he says, ' Chaucer is a huge borrower : [He] . . . drew con-

---

[1] Introduction to *The English Poets*, edited by T. H. Ward, London, 1880, reprinted in *Essays in Criticism*, 2nd series.

tinually, *through Lydgate and Caxton*, from Guido di Colonna.' Professor Minto, in his article (1876) on the poet in the ninth edition of the *Encyclopædia Britannica*, says that Chaucer's father was in the expedition of 1359 instead of that of 1338; he declares the *Court of Love* to be genuine, dating it about 100 years before it was written, and invents a statement that James I in the *Kingis Quhair* attributes it to Chaucer.

And in the *Cornhill* for March 1877, we find no less a critic than Leslie Stephen attributing to Chaucer a large number of spurious poems, and saying in a note on the *Court of Love* :— ' The Chaucer critics reject this poem, but as we are not writing a critical paper, we cannot afford to forgo so much good material.'

The main trend, however, of nineteenth-century opinion and knowledge has been very markedly in the contrary direction to these cases we have cited, which are really survivals. We find (with the exception of Byron) all the greatest men of letters of the early nineteenth century reading Chaucer and delighting in him.

Scott is very appreciative; he points out that Chaucer is sometimes much better than his modernizer Dryden; he has a charming reference to him in *Woodstock* ; his mind is clearly stored with reminiscences of him, he quotes him in several of his novels, and (in 1817) he urges the intending reader not to be put off by apparent difficulties of obsolete spelling and the like.

Blake has left us a wonderful and luminous criticism of the Canterbury Tales (1809), in some ways anticipating Carlyle in thought. He points out that Chaucer has, in his pilgrims, pictured for all time the eternal classes of men, eternal principles, changing in outward details, but in essentials remaining the same, the Hero, the Knave, the Apostle, and so on, for ' every age is a Canterbury Pilgrimage, we all pass on, each sustaining one or other of these characters; nor can a child be born, who is not one of these characters of Chaucer.'

He was one of the few authors Wordsworth read constantly, and one of the still fewer to whom he felt and admitted himself inferior; that fine critic, Dorothy, read him with ' exquisite

delight'; Southey repeatedly praises him, and speaks enthusi-
astically of 'his versatility of talents,' 'in which only Ariosto
has approached, and only Shakespeare equalled him'; Thomas
Campbell, in 1819, appreciates the 'pathetic beauty' of *Troilus*,
'a story of vast length and almost desolate simplicity,' and the
vivid characterization of the Canterbury Tales, and Coleridge,
as early as 1804, planned an Essay on his genius and writings,
while thirty years later he says, 'I take increasing delight in
Chaucer. His manly cheerfulness is especially delicious to
me in my old age. How exquisitely tender he is, and yet how
perfectly free from the least touch of sickly melancholy or
morbid drooping.'

Lamb's references (13 in all, from 1797 to 1827) are slight,
but sufficient to show his knowledge and love. He compares
Coleridge's poem of 'The Raven' to Chaucer, and he points
out the radiance of the 'almost Chaucer-like painting' in
Keats's *Eve of St. Agnes.* He clearly revels and delights in his
'foolish stories,' the 'darling things . . . old Chaucer sings,'
he treasures his 'black letter' Speght, he marvels at the
'comprehensiveness of genius' in the Pilgrims' portraits, and
compares the thought underlying the poet's comedy with
Hogarth's handling of his themes.

He suggests to Haydon for a picture the subject of Chaucer
beating a Franciscan friar in Fleet Street, and we are not surprised that it was Lamb, sooner than any one else apparently,
who appreciated to the full Blake's brilliant description of the
Pilgrims, 'the finest criticism he had ever read of Chaucer's
poem,' 'mystical and full of vision.' How entirely we can
sympathise with his trouble over the review of Godwin's ill-
proportioned and pompous 'Life' (1803); little wonder that
although he sat down to it 'for three or four days successively'
he could not produce anything which would satisfy both
Godwin and himself.

Landor, as we have seen, thoroughly appreciated Chaucer,
and in an unpublished prose fragment, written probably about
1861, he says: 'There is no poet excepting Homer whom I
have studied so attentively as Chaucer. They are the ablest
of their respective countries.' In other writings he places

him next Shakespeare and Milton, and prefers him to Spenser. Shelley speaks of him with understanding and reverence, and Hazlitt, who writes on him the first appreciative literary criticism of any length since Dryden, ranks him with Spenser as one of the four greatest English poets. Miss Mitford, as early as 1815, writes : ' Two or three of Chaucer's Canterbury Tales, and some select passages from his other productions, are worth all the age of Queen Anne . . . ever produced '; De Quincey says he is ' a poet worth five hundred of Homer,' and Mrs. Browning (despite the modernizations) has written of him some of the most charmingly discriminating praise ever penned : Peacock, Edward Fitzgerald and George Meredith have all recorded their admiration; we are told that Tennyson enjoyed reading Chaucer aloud more than any poet except Shakespeare and Milton; while the enthusiasm of the Pre-Raphaelite group for Chaucer was so great, that in addition to painting scenes from his life and poems, they saw a physical likeness to him in the people they admired. This resemblance they said was noticeable in Rossetti, Morris and R. W. Dixon.

Ruskin was reading and quoting Chaucer with appreciation for forty years (1849–1889); and he refers one hundred and eight times to the poet or his works (*Index* to the *Complete Works*, ed. Cook and Wedderburn). A few of these references are printed here, and a larger selection (between 1869 and 1889) in the *Supplement to Five Hundred Years of Chaucer Criticism* (*see Foreword*, also footnote p. lxix below). His remarks, as one would expect, are acute and unusual, as when in *The Harbours of England* (1856), he notes Chaucer's aversion to the sea and everything connected with it.

Ruskin is among those who place Chaucer very high as a theologian and teacher; in *Fors Clavigera* (letter 61, January 1876) he says he is ' one of the men who have taught the purest theological truth,' and he chooses him together with Moses, David, Hesiod, Virgil, Dante and St. John as one of the seven authors of ' standard theological writings ' whose lives and works are to be specially edited for the St. George's schools; a scheme which was, however, not carried out.

He is also one of the few people who express surprise or vexation at the pre-eminent position given to the *Canterbury Tales* (letter to Dr. Furnivall, December 15, 1873, unpublished), and he deliberately excludes them from his planned edition for St. George's library, while he includes, ' be they authentic or not, the *Dream* and the fragment of the translation of the *Romance of the Rose.*' (*Fors*, ut sup.) He was particularly attracted to the *Dream* (the *Isle of Ladies*), and, as he had told Dr. Furnivall (letter of Dec. 15, 1873), about the year 1869, he had prepared an edition of it for press ' (not at all as a fine example of Chaucer, but as one about which I had much to say) —with long notes, and hunting down of words—and no doubt at all expressed of the genuineness.' ' Had this come out,' he adds, ' I should never have got over it in literary dis-reputation.'

However, in spite of the demonstration that it was not Chaucer's, he remained constant in his predilection for the *Dream* as well as for the authentic minor poems, and he definitely set himself to work mainly on them and on the ethics and temper of them.

Perhaps, however, the most constant and enthusiastic lover of Chaucer in the early nineteenth century was Leigh Hunt. He came to him comparatively late (' Chaucer, who has since been one of my best friends, I was not acquainted with at school, nor till long afterwards,' *Autobiography*, 1860, p. 79), but for nearly half a century (1812–59) Hunt shows increasing knowledge of and admiration for Chaucer. So numerous are his references to him both in prose and verse that a large bundle of them has been put aside, and only a small selection (43) are here printed, as otherwise they would have thrown out of proportion the mass of nineteenth-century criticism.

Hunt genuinely loves Chaucer, he reads him constantly and carefully, and, in spite of Lockhart's scathing snub in *Blackwood* (*see* below, 1817, Z.) his praise is discriminating as well as enthusiastic.

He is as daring and independent in his judgment of Chaucer's poetic powers as he is of those of Keats. As early as 1816, he classes him with Dryden, Spenser, Milton, Ariosto and Shake-

speare as one of the great masters of modern versification, and
some years later (1820) he maintains that Chaucer's verse is
' touched with a finer sense of music even than Dryden's.'

He constantly recurs to this theme in his critical writings
and points out that Chaucer is scarcely known at all, that he is
considered ' a rude sort of poet,' that his versification has never
had justice done it, and that the ' sweet and delicate gravity
of its music ' is as ' unlike the crabbed and unintentional stuff
it is supposed to be as possible.'

He considers Chaucer has ' the strongest imagination of real
life, beyond any writers but Homer, Dante and Shakespeare,
and in comic painting inferior to none.'   Hunt's appreciation
of Chaucer's ' comic genius ' is given in full in *Wit and Humour*
(1846) and the three characteristic qualities of it which he
selects reveal his close understanding of it.

And through all these years, Hunt proves his admiration in
the most practical way, by making every effort to get Chaucer
better known, to bring his work to the notice of the ordinary
reader and to induce him to go to the original for himself.   He
writes about him and quotes him constantly, he gives copious
extracts from his poems in modern spelling in a series of numbers
of the *London Journal* (1835), and he modernizes several of the
Tales.   His views on the function of modernizations are
thoroughly sound (see specially the Preface to *Death and the
Ruffians*, 1855).   Modernizations, he says, should be little more
than a change of spelling, ' for every alteration of Chaucer is
an injury,' and their only excuse is that they 'may act as
incitements towards acquaintance with the great original.'

Hunt's love of Chaucer deserves emphasis, for it is especially
interesting historically because of his influence on Keats.

Hunt and Keats first met probably in the early summer of
1816; they immediately became friends and read and talked
together, leaving, as Hunt records, ' no imaginative pleasure '
untouched or unenjoyed.   It is practically certain that they
talked about Chaucer, and that Keats was led to read far
more than the non-Chaucerian *Floure and Lefe* which so took
his fancy and from which he chose the motto for *Sleep and*

Poetry, written probably during his first intimacy with Hunt in the autumn of 1816. It was in the following February that he wrote the sonnet in Cowden Clarke's Chaucer, and a few months later he began *Endymion* with the prayer that he 'might stammer where old Chaucer used to sing.' By the end of the next year (1818) he is the proud possessor of a 'black letter Chaucer' of his own; all through 1819 it is obvious from his letters that he is reading it, and the result of his study is to be seen in the *Eve of St. Mark* at which he was working at intervals during that year. Its narrative method and metre are clearly suggested by Chaucer, as well as the pseudo old English which is surely an echo of him rather than of Chatterton as has generally been assumed. That this is so is even more clearly seen in the additional sixteen lines in the Woodhouse transcript (found in 1913) beginning

> Gif ye wol stonden hardie wight—
> Amiddes of the blacke night—
> Righte in the churche porch, pardie
> Ye wol behold a companie,

in which Keats deliberately tries to reproduce the style and vocabulary of Chaucer.

Thus we have a series of links which form one of the most interesting bits of literary history in the nineteenth century.

Leigh Hunt's immense admiration for Chaucer undoubtedly stimulated, if it did not start, Keats's serious study of him; this study profoundly affected the wonderful fragment of the *Eve of St. Mark*, which, with *La Belle Dame*, were the poems which kindled the enthusiasm of the Pre-Raphaelite group and gave to William Morris his immediate impulse in romantic story telling. As Sir Sidney Colvin points out (Life of Keats p. 438), the opening of the *Eve of St. Mark*, reminiscent of the movement of Chaucer's verse and anticipating the very cadences of Morris, forms a direct bridge or stepping stone between the two great poets. It was in 1855 that Morris with Burne-Jones at Oxford was for the first time reading and rejoicing in the older narrative poet whom later he definitely took as his master. For not since the days of Elizabeth had

Chaucer so directly inspired a great English singer as he did him who prayed :—

> Would that I
> Had but some portion of that mastery
> That from the rose-hung lanes of woody Kent
> Through these five hundred years such songs have sent
> To us, who, meshed within this smoky net
> Of unrejoicing labour, love them yet.
> And thou, O Master !   Yea, my Master still
> Whatever feet have scaled Parnassus' hill
> Since like thy measures, clear and sweet and strong,
> Thames' stream scarce fettered drave the dace along
> Unto the bastioned bridge, his only chain—
> O Master, pardon me if yet in vain
> Thou art my Master, and I fail to bring
> Before men's eyes the image of the thing
> My heart is filled with : thou whose dreamy eyes
> Beheld the flush to Cressid's cheek arise,
> As Troilus rode up the praising street,
> As clearly as they saw thy townsmen meet
> Those whom in vineyards of Poictou withstood
> The glistening horror of the steel-topped wood.

The changed attitude of the important Reviews towards Chaucer in the early nineteenth century is worthy of notice ; he is constantly put next to Shakespeare, and sometimes compared to Goethe ; the *Quarterly* is almost uniformly favourable to him, and often enthusiastic.   Thus in the volume of May 1809, Chaucer is placed next below Shakespeare and Milton ; in July 1814 he is called ' a star of the first magnitude,' and it is urged that it is a disgrace that the *Canterbury Tales* should be the only portion of his works edited with ability ; while in the *Edinburgh* for July 1830 he is said to be in manner and expression the most Homeric of our poets.

All this appreciation, however, though very enthusiastic, was largely uncritical, and based on an incomplete knowledge of Chaucer's real work, and it was not until the appearance in 1862 (in the United States) of Professor Child's masterly and exhaustive essay on the use of the final ' e ' in the Harleian manuscript 7334, followed in 1868 by the foundation of the

Chaucer Society by Dr. Furnivall, that the scholarly and critical work was inaugurated, which is one of the literary glories of the nineteenth century.

Professor Child furnished the money which enabled the Chaucer Society to start work, and so it is to him that Dr. Furnivall dedicates its first great publication, the Six-Text print of the *Canterbury Tales* [1] (see 1868–77, below).

The work of Chaucer scholars in England and America during the last fifty years has been so great that to write any detailed account of it would demand more space than can here be given. Some record of it will be found in the following pages, and a still fuller record in the *Supplement*.[2] These speak for themselves. Certain landmarks in the work can, however, be indicated.

The Chaucer Society, which was established ' to do honour to Chaucer, and to let lovers and students of him see how far the best unprinted manuscripts of his works differed from the printed texts,' has achieved results of four kinds :—

(1) The printing of all the best Chaucer manuscripts.
(2) The establishment of the chronology of Chaucer's works, including the arrangement of the *Canterbury Tales*.
(3) The final settlement of the Chaucer Canon.
(4) The discovery of many hitherto unknown facts about Chaucer's life and family.

---

[1] That is the six best and oldest MSS. of the *Canterbury Tales*, printed in parallel columns so as to make the different readings at once apparent.

[2] *Five Hundred Years of Chaucer Criticism and Allusion: A Supplement, containing additional entries*, 1868–1900 ; London, privately printed, 1920.

As the work of collecting these Chaucer allusions proceeded, it became clear that it would be impossible, for reasons of mere bulk of matter, to deal so comprehensively with the last generation as with those up to 1800, or even up to 1867. A break therefore is made at the latter date, and after the foundation of the Chaucer Society only the chief editions of the poet are included and a few important or typical criticisms.

As, however, a considerable number of allusions for this period, about 900 in all, had already been collected and were in type, a few copies of this matter were printed off and have been placed in the principal libraries.

A complete list of the publications of the Chaucer Society down to 1907 is given in *Chaucer, a bibliographical manual*, by E. P. Hammond, 1908, pp. 523–41.

(1) The first attempt to print a single manuscript was made by Thomas Wright, who in 1848–51 edited for the Percy Society the *Canterbury Tales* from the Harleian 7334, with additions and collations from the Lansdowne MS. Later the printing of all the best Chaucer MSS. was carried through by the indefatigable energy of Dr. Furnivall; this made possible the edition of the poems published at Boston in 1880 by Mr. Gilman, and finally resulted in the first complete, accurate, and critical edition of Chaucer's works, which was edited by Professor Skeat in 1894–7.

All through the nineteenth century, from Southey onwards (*see* below, 1812), we find repeated desire expressed for a complete critical text of Chaucer's works, culminating with the statement in the long and well-informed article in the *Edinburgh Review* for July 1870, that it is a national reproach to be still without one.

Skeat's great six-volume edition, based on the careful collation of the seven best manuscripts, was therefore received with enthusiasm, and widely reviewed. After its publication and of that of the smaller reprint of the text (Student's Edition) in 1895, there is a noticeable increase in the general knowledge and study of Chaucer. This tendency was quickened by the appearance, in 1896, of William Morris's Kelmscott Chaucer, illustrated by Burne-Jones,[1] which aroused considerable interest and comment.

The impetus given to the reading of Chaucer by the work of the Chaucer Society is clearly seen in the increase of editions of his works published between 1851 and 1910. For various reasons it is difficult to be certain of getting these numbers absolutely complete, but the table below is approximately correct and shows the result of this impetus pictorially.

Between 1801 and 1850 there appeared seven editions of Chaucer's complete works (in the original text). Between 1851 and 1900 nine new editions came out, as well as one German translation. Only three editions of the *Canterbury Tales* were

---

[1] Or by drawings suggested by Burne-Jones. See *The Nation*, 1903, I, pp. 313–14.

TABLE OF EDITIONS OF CHAUCER'S WORKS FROM 1801 TO 1910.

	NUMBER OF EDITIONS PUBLISHED.		
	(1801-1850)	(1851 1900)	(1901-1910)
Complete Works (original text)	7	9 (+ 1 German)	2
Complete Works (modernised)	1	—	—
Canterbury Tales (original text)	3 (+ 1 re-issue)	9 (+ 2 re-issues : 1 French and 1 German)	2 (+ 1 French and 1 German)
Canterbury Tales (modernised, paraphrased, or 'retold')	4 (+ 1 unpublished)	12	13
Selected or single poems (original text)	9 (+ 1 French and 1 German)	67 (+ 1 French and 1 German)	32 (+ 1 re-issue and 1 Dutch)
Selected or single poems (modernised, paraphrased, or 'retold')	3	1	6

published in the first half of the nineteenth century, as compared with nine editions in the second half. Nine editions of selected or single poems (in the original text) came out between 1801 and 1850, whereas there were sixty-seven of these between 1851 and 1900. And this increase of figures still continues, for between 1901 and 1910 there appeared two new editions of Chaucer's complete works, two editions of the *Canterbury Tales* as well as one French and one German translation, and thirty-two editions of selected or single poems.[1]

(2) The first serious attempt to fix the chronological order of Chaucer's works was largely due to a man who had never even seen a Chaucer manuscript, or heard of the Chaucer Society, Professor ten Brink, who, in 1870, astounded English scholars by the publication of his *Chaucer Studien,* in which he for the first time threw a real light on the distinction between genuine and spurious in the poet's works, and also on their true order of succession. Although some of these questions are in

---

[1] The Clarendon Press, Oxford, report that Chaucer's poetical works have a larger sale than those of either Pope or Dryden, so that he is now the most 'popular' author of the three.

dispute still, the chronology is for the most part now fairly well established.

Mr. Bradshaw, at Cambridge, had been working at the same problem independently for some years previously, but had not printed any account of his results. To him, however, is due the solution of the puzzle as to the right order and structure of the ' Tales.'

(3) To the final settlement of the genuine poems many scholars have contributed, notably ten Brink, Bradshaw, Furnivall, Koch, and Skeat, and these results have been summed up in such books as Koch's *Chronology of Chaucer Writings*, Chaucer Society, 1890; Pollard's *Chaucer* in ' Literature Primers,' 2nd edition, 1903; Skeat's *Complete Works of Chaucer*, 1894, introductions to vols. i and vi; Skeat's *Chaucer Canon*, 1900; and Tatlock's *Development and Chronology of Chaucer's Works*, Chaucer Society, 1907.

(4) Of the life records of Chaucer, some few were printed by Godwin in 1803, and still more by Sir Harris Nicolas in 1843, but to Dr. Furnivall almost alone are due the discoveries along this line, not only on account of his own extensive researches, but because of the way he stimulated others, notably Mr. Selby, Mr. Bond and Mr. Kirk, to undertake the work; so that in 1900 it was possible to publish the completed volume of the *Life Records of Chaucer*, a fitting commemoration of the poet's quincentenary.

So the work goes on, and our poet has come to his own at last; and the heart of Francis Thynne would rejoice to see how ' Chawcer's Woorkes, by much conference and many judg-mentes ' have at length obtained ' their true perfectione and glory '; for after long years of neglect and misinterpretations, we of to-day are fortunate enough to have the old poet's verses as he wrote them, and to be able to read them for ourselves, even without a knowledge of ' the black letter '; and we can picture Chaucer himself smiling on us benignly as he says,

> Be glad, thou reder, and thy sorwe of-caste,
> Al open am I; passe in and hy the faste !

§ 2. EXAMINATION AND CLASSIFICATION OF THE VARIOUS TYPES OF CHAUCER REFERENCES.

The allusions to Chaucer, from his death up to 1800, fall for the most part fairly easily into certain definite types, which it may be useful very briefly to summarize.

(1) **A dedicatory notice to Chaucer** of some one of the following kinds :—

(a) *The acknowledgment of indebtedness to Chaucer as first and greatest of English poets.*

This is the earliest and most common for the first 150 years after his death. It is specially found among Chaucer's contemporaries and immediate successors, and among poets of the ' Chaucerian school ' both in England and Scotland. Lydgate is the stock example of this sort of reference; he writes at great length on the subject, bewailing his own inferiority and the irreparable loss he has sustained in the death of the master. With Lydgate we must class Hoccleve (1412), and the references by Scogan (*c.* 1407), Walton (1410), James I. (1423), Bokeman (1443–7), Shirley (*c.* 1450), Ashby (*c.* 1470), Dunbar (1503), Hawes (1503–4), and many others. Late examples are Gascoigne (1576), Spenser (1579 and 1590–6), and Drayton (1627), which latter acknowledges Chaucer as the earliest but no longer as the greatest of English poets.

(b) *A reference to Chaucer in company with Gower and Lydgate.*

These, with two or three exceptions, are formal from the first and soon crystallize into a kind of stock phrase. Such are Bokenam (1443–7), Unknown (*c.* 1450), Ashby (*c.* 1470), Unknown (*c.* 1500), Douglas (1501), Hawes (1503–4), Feylde (1509), Rastell (1520), Skelton (1523), Lindsay (1530), Forrest (*c.* 1545), Harvey (1577), Lawson (1581), Meres (1598), Bodenham (1600), and Freeman, who in 1614 is the last we have found mentioning these three poets and these alone.

(c) *A reference to Chaucer in company with other poets.*

These are so very common that it is unnecessary to enumerate them. The earliest here is that by Bradshaw (1513), who

classes Chaucer with Lydgate, Barkley and Skelton; while in
some verses in 1561 he is classed with Homer, Virgil and Ovid.
Churchyard (1568) puts him with ' Peers Plowman, Surrey and
Lord Vaus,' and with Sir Thomas More, Surrey, Sidney, and
later Spenser, Drayton, Shakespeare and Jonson he is often
bracketed, while, in the eighteenth century Milton, Cowley
and Dryden are added.

> (d) *An apostrophe by a poet or writer expressing the desire to
> have the genius or ' muse ' of Chaucer, or to call up his
> spirit ; or an assertion that Chaucer's soul is revived in
> the later writer.*

This is not to be found among the very early references,
for the respect and veneration of the poet's first admirers were
so great that none of them would have dared even to suggest
or hope that a portion of his power might descend to them.
Lydgate compares himself deprecatingly with his master, but
never dreams of aspiring to his 'muse,' so great is the distance
between them ; compare also the humility of the last stanza of
George Ashby's *Active policy of a Prince* (*c.* 1470) below.   It is in
the Elizabethan age, when Chaucer was still much admired, but
not so deeply venerated, that we first find this class of allusion,
and it is practically non-existent after 1650.   Such are Stanihurst (1582), Churchyard (1587), Spenser (1590–6), Harvey
(1592), Davies (1594), Haxby (1636), E. G. (1646), while Milton's
well-known reference in *Il Penseroso* (1632), is of this nature.

(2) **A quotation from Chaucer's works** (or what were taken
to be his works), or a reference to one of his characters, or to
incidents in his poems :—

> (a) *As a matter of literary interest.*
> (b) *To enforce some moral point, taking Chaucer either as
> standing for morality or against it.*
> (c) *As an authority or precedent for sundry things.*

In the first subdivision (a) Lydgate leads the way, for he
quotes from Chaucer and refers to his stories continually.[1]
There are a fair number in the fifteenth and sixteenth centuries,

---

[1] There is a possibility that the earliest reference of this class is that to
Troilus in the *Gest hystoriale* (*a.* 1400), but this is doubtful.

but this class of reference is far more numerous in the first half of the seventeenth century.   Indeed, in the following references there are close on twice as many of this nature between 1600–50 as there are during the whole of the eighteenth century.   Men like Camden, Selden, Burton, Ben Jonson, Strafford, Milton and Joseph Hall, quote Chaucer (some of them repeatedly) in a way which shows they know him well, whereas in the eighteenth century not only is there no general writer (that is excepting language and Chaucer specialists such as Morrell or Tyrwhitt, or literary historians like Thomas Warton and Robert Henry), who cites him with this familiar knowledge, but even when referred to, he is misquoted by those who ought to know better.

Thus Addison quotes with approval as being Chaucer's the sixteenth-century poem *The Remedy of Love* (printed by Thynne), and Horace Walpole in his first reference (1742) adds a note which looks as if he did not know Chaucer's *Wife of Bath*,[1] while in a letter in 1789 he quotes two well-known lines in the *Prologue*, as being Spenser's.   In a note below is given a list of references up to 1800 where Chaucer is quoted as a matter of literary interest.[2]

---

[1] Ten Brink (*History of Eng. Lit.*, vol. ii, p. 126) possibly on the ground of this allusion and the *New Wife of Bath* 1785, &c., suggests that the name of ' Wife of Bath ' had been a sort of proverb before Chaucer immortalised it.

[2] *Gest hystoriale* (a. 1400)? Lydgate (1400–30), Ed. 2nd Duke of York (1406–13), Scogan (c. 1407), Hoccleve (1421), Unknown (1440 ?), Norton (c. 1477), John de Irlandia (1490), Hawes (1506), Skelton (1507), Feylde (1509), Margaret Roper (1535), Layton (1535), Unknown (1536), Wyatt (a. 1542), Lyndsay (1548), Unknown (1549), Baldwin (1561), Calfhill (1565), Drant (1567), B. G. (1569), Gascoigne (1575), Kirke (1579), Howell (1581), Ferne (1586), Spenser (1590–6), Greene (1592), Nash (1592, 1599), Peele (a. 1596), Breton (1597), Hall (1598), Spenser (1599), Stowe, Thynne (1600), Unknown (c. 1600), Rowlands (1602), Scoloker (1604), Camden (1605, 1616), Walkington (1607), Thynne (a. 1608), Wybarne (1609), Beaumont (1610), Ἀποδημουντόφιλος (1611), Selden, William F. (1612) Peacham (1615), Fletcher (c. 1615), Burton (1621–52), B. Jonson (1625, 1629, 1632, a. 1637, 1641), Drayton (1627), Nash (1633), Cartwright (c. 1634), Fletcher (1634), Strafford (1635, 1637), Marmion (1641), Milton (1641, a. 1674), Hall, Kynaston (1642), Cavendish (1645), A Parliament Officer (1645–6), Selden (1646), Plume (1649), Cleveland (a. 1658), Jones (1659), à Wood (1661–6), Gayton (1663), Whitelock (a. 1675), Coles (1676), Aubrey (1683–4), Unknown (1696), Wanley (1701), Addison (1711), Pope (1711, 1712, 1725), Johnson (1712), Gay (1715), Oldys (1725), Unknown (1732), Walpole (1742, 1789), Carter (1753), Chatterton (a. 1770), Strutt (1775–6), Rogers (1782), Unknown (1785), Ritson (1796).

(a) *Poems and characters which are most popular and most frequently quoted.*

An investigation of this point shows that up to 1700 *Troilus and Cressida* is by far the most popular, the most generally known and the most often quoted of Chaucer's poems. If at any time during the sixteenth or seventeenth centuries it had been proposed to translate Chaucer's representative work into French, as has recently been done, *Troilus*, and not the *Canterbury Tales*, would assuredly have been chosen. It is the first poem to be mentioned by a contemporary writer; and if the allusions by Gower (1376–9) and in the *Gest hystoriale* (*a.* 1400) are to Chaucer's poem, we have three very early references to it by name. Unquestionably up to 1700 it is on the whole looked upon as Chaucer's representative and greatest poem; [1] Henryson (1475) wrote a sequel to it, Berthelet (1532) refers to it as Chaucer's ' moste speciall warke,' it is obviously the poem Sidney knew best, and he singles it out as Chaucer's masterpiece, it gave its name to the form of verse in which it is written, so that as we now speak of the ' Spenserian stanza,' the Elizabethan critics wrote of ' Troilus verse,' [2] and in the *Returne from Parnassus* (1597) where Chaucer and Skakespeare are parodied and imitated, it is the *Troilus* and *Venus and Adonis* which are chosen for the purpose, as being probably the best-known work of each writer. In Chapman's (?) *Sir Gyles Goosecappe* (1606) we find direct imitation of the first three books of the poem, a little later (*c.* 1630) it is being modernized by an admirer, the first of Chaucer's poems to be subjected to this process, and in 1634 another enthusiast turns it into Latin verse, presumably because he considered it the poem of Chaucer's best worth preserving.

Up to 1700 the number of references to *Troilus* are more than double those made to the *Canterbury Tales* (as a whole), and they are over three times as many as those to the General Prologue. This marked preference for the love poem may be

---

[1] See Feylde (1509), Hawes (1516), Lyndsay (1548), Gascoigne (1575).
[2] See James VI (1584), below.

compared with the numerous references to Shakespeare's *Venus and Adonis* up to 1650. When we remember that the plays had the advantage of being known to the non-reading public, it is significant to find that with the exception of *Hamlet* and *Henry IV* there are, up to 1650, more allusions to the *Venus and Adonis* than to any other single work of Shakespeare's.[1] The preference for *Troilus* in the earlier centuries is not to be wondered at, the wonder rather is that during the last hundred and fifty years it has dropped so much out of the knowledge of the general reader. For it is the first great tragic novel,[2] rich in variety of character, and throbbing with humanity and passion, it stands out from among all the other poems of its author in dignity and beauty, and it brings out the strength of Chaucer's imagination more than even the dramatic monologues of the *Wife of Bath* and the *Pardoner.*

This priority of reference as regards *Troilus* continues up to 1750, although during the latter fifty years the allusions are more perfunctory and show little direct knowledge (which is the case as regards all Chaucer's work), but there is at the same time an increase in the references to the General Prologue and the separate Tales, owing chiefly to Dryden, who gave a great ' lift ' to the *Canterbury Tales* by devoting, as he did, practically all his criticism and eulogy to them, and only mentioning *Troilus* in passing as an amplified translation. After 1750, however, a marked change is shown, and from that time on the *Canterbury Tales* easily come first, while *Troilus* sinks to the fifth place. This must be largely owing to the fact that *Troilus* was not modernized, and that Chaucer himself in the original was not read. Still there is no question that from 1750 onwards, aided naturally much by Tyrwhitt's edition, the

---

[1] As computed by Mr. Munro (editor of the *Shakespere Allusion-Book,* 1909), *Hamlet* (the most popular of the plays) is alluded to 58 times, the much-loved Falstaff 32 times, and the play of *Henry IV* 38 times; as compared with 44 references to the *Venus and Adonis.* During the same years we find 2 references to *As You Like It,* 6 to *Henry V,* 5 to *Lear,* and 4 to *Antony and Cleopatra* and *Twelfth Night* respectively. See *ibid.* vol. ii, pp. 540–1.

[2] See W. P. Ker in the *Quarterly Review,* April 1895, below.

Canterbury Tales became the most popular and the recognized representative work of Chaucer, completely putting all the others in the shade.

As regards the separate Tales, only one shows any marked change in favour, and this is the *Nun's Priest's*. Up to 1700, and more especially in the seventeenth century, it was very popular, being quoted nearly as often as the General Prologue, the *Knight's Tale* and the *Wife of Bath's Prologue*, while between 1700 and 1800 we find only four references to it, and two of these belittle it. Dr. Johnson (1779) remarks that it was not worth revival by Dryden, while an annotator of Dryden's *Fables* (c. 1785 ?) scratches it all out, saying that it is so foolish, if not worse, that it adds little to Chaucer's reputation that he was the author of it (below, p. 481).

In the estimation of the proportionate number of references given in the tables below, there are included only references or quotations which are made as a matter of literary interest, or to illustrate a point, or where a poem is specially picked out for praise or blame. Hence the following are not counted :— Prologues, epilogues or headlines to Chaucer's works, such as those by Shirley and Caxton, lists of Chaucer's works, as given by Leland, Bale or Hearne, or a detailed account of the whole of Chaucer's work, such as Francis Thynne's *Animadversions* (1598) or Dryden's preface; and, in the eighteenth century, general literary criticism or histories of literature, such as that by Hearne, the Wartons, Tyrwhitt, etc., where every poem is mentioned many times, or notes to Shakespeare's plays, as this latter would give an undue proportion to *Troilus and Cressida* and the *Knight's Tale*. The numerous references to spurious poems are naturally omitted, as also are quotations which are so incorrect as to make it doubtful from what poem they are taken.

TABLE OF THE RELATIVE POPULARITY OF CHAUCER'S POEMS AT DIFFERENT TIMES.

(i)
Order up to 1700.

	Approximate No. of refs.
Troilus	115
Cant. Tales (as a whole) . . .	53
General Prol. C. T.	33
Nonne Preestes T. .	26
Knight's T. . . .	23
W. of Bath's Prol. .	20
H. of Fame . . .	18
Clerke's T. . . .	17
Sir Thopas . . .	16
Marchant's T. ⎱ W. of Bath's T. ⎰ ·	15
Squieres T. . ⎱ Rom. of Rose ⎬ . Legend . . ⎰	13
Pardoneres T. . .	12
Astrolabe . . .	8

(ii)
Order up to 1750.

Troilus . . .	124
Cant. Tales . . .	59
Genl. Prol. C. T. .	42
Knight's T. . .	29
Nonne Preestes T. .	26
W. of Bath's Prol. .	25
House of Fame .	24
Clerke's T. . . .	18
Marchant's T. ⎱ Rom. of Rose ⎬ . Sir Thopas . ⎰	17
Squieres T. . . .	13
Pardoneres T. . .	12
Astrolabe . . .	8

(iii)
Order from 1750 *to* 1800.

Cant. Tales . . .	19
General Prol. C. T.	11

	Approximate No. of refs.
Knight's T. . .	10
Squieres T. . . .	8
W. of Bath's Prol. ⎱ Troilus . . . ⎬ House of Fame ⎰	5
Sir Thopas . . ⎱ Nonne Preestes T. ⎰	4
Pardoneres T. ⎱ Rom. of Rose ⎰ ·	2

(iv)
Order from 1700 *to* 1800

Cant. Tales . . .	24
General Prol. C. T.	17
Knight's T. . . .	16
Troilus	13
H. of Fame . . .	11
W. of Bath's Prol. .	10
Squieres T. . . .	8
Rom. of Rose . .	6
Sir Thopas . . ⎱ Nonne Preestes T. ⎰	4
Pardoneres T. . .	2

(v)
Order from the beginning up to 1800.

Troilus . . .	129
Cant. Tales . . .	78
Genl. Prol. C. T. .	50
Knight's T. . . .	39
W. of Bath's Prol. ⎱ Nonne Preestes T. ⎰	30
House of Fame .	29
Sir Thopas ⎱ . . Squieres T. ⎰ . .	24
Clerkes T. . . .	20
Rom. of Rose . .	19
Marchantes T. . .	18
Pardoneres T. . .	14
Astrolabe . . .	9

(b) *Chaucer quoted to enforce some moral point, in which he is ranged either on the side of morality or against it.*

This type of reference becomes, as we have seen (*see* above, pp. xix–xxi), very common about the middle to the end of the sixteenth century. Thus Sir John Elyot points out what **a** discord there is between *Troilus* and the New Testament (1533), while Ascham (1544), John Northbrooke (1577) and Bishop Babington (1583) quote the *Pardoneres Tale* in condemnation of gaming and card-playing. Becke, Cranmer and Latimer refer to ' Canterbury tales ' as light and trifling reading upon which people waste much time, while, on the other hand, Foxe maintains that Chaucer's works have been the means of bringing many to the true knowledge of religion. Some writers, like Sir John Harrington, condemn Chaucer for ' flat scurrilitie,' whilst others not only emphasise the value of his satire against Rome (see Foxe, Scot and Harsnet), but even maintain, as does Prynne (1633), who surely cannot have read the poet very exhaustively, that his subjects are all ' serious, sacred and divine.'

Later, at the end of the seventeenth century, Milton and Aubrey both quote Chaucer with approval as to methods of education.

(c) *As an authority or precedent for sundry things.*

For instance John Bossewell, in his *Workes of Armorie,* (1572), quotes Chaucer as authority for a definition of generosity, for an allusion to gentle birth, for the name of the inventor of the game of chess, and the preciousness of the daisy ; in the *Returne from Parnassus* (1597) he is quoted for his ' vayn ' *i.e.* style ; Hakluyt (1598) quotes him as authority for the voyages and exploits of our nobles and Knights in the fourteenth century ; Milton (1641) cites him as a precedent for mis-spelling foreign names ; Hawkins (1776) and Burney (1782) for evidence as to the musical instruments and love of music in his time, and many later writers (*e. g.* Robert Henry 1781, Strutt 1799) for light thrown on contemporary customs, dress and habits.

(3) **Biographies, or short references to the Poet's life.**
These are examined under § 4.

(4) **Notices of Chaucer in connection with language and style.**
These must be noted under a separate heading, although

they do not, as a rule, stand alone; that is (with the exception of (e)) they more generally occur in the course of a life or account of the poet.

They are mainly of the following kinds :—

(a) *Those which state that he refined and improved the language.*
(b) *Those which assert he corrupted it.*
(c) *Those which say he is difficult to understand and obsolete, and that his versification is rough and irregular.*
(d) *Those which refute this, or try to excuse it.*
(e) *Remarks, prefaces or verses in connection with translations and modernizations of Chaucer.*

(a) As Tyrwhitt points out in his introductory essay (1775, below) the language of Chaucer has undergone two entirely opposite judgments : (a) and (b) above. His earlier admirers, Lydgate ('the ffyrste in any age that amended our language,') Hoccleve ('the firste fyndere of our faire language,') Caxton, Skelton, the Scotch poets, Sir Brian Tuke, and others at intervals up to Spenser (1590–6), who has immortalized him as 'well of Englishe undefyled,' all agree that he first showed of what English was capable, and in the matter of style set up a high standard for his followers and imitators.

An interesting early example of this view is in the jilted lovers' reply to the scorn or 'flyting' letter of his mistress (MS. Bodl. Rawl. poet. 36, *c.* 1470), where he says satirically :—

> To me ye haue sent a letter of derision
> Werfore I thanke you as I fynde cause,
> The ynglysch of Chaucere was nat in youre mynd,
> Ne tullyus termys wyth so gret elloquence,
> But ye as vncurtes and crabbed of leynde
> Rolled hem on a hepe it semyth by the sentens.

A little later, however, to this view is added the assertion or implication, that Chaucer definitely and deliberately set himself the task of refining and polishing our language. Indeed some writers would make out that to accomplish this was his dearest wish, and that he expressed himself in verse merely as a means to this end, to which he devoted himself with untiring patience.

Leland, in his mythical account of the poet, as retold by Bale (published 1619), first fully emphasizes this point of view.

Following in the footsteps of his master Gower, who took ' wonderful pains to polish the English tongue,' Leland tells us that Chaucer had one distinct aim in his studies, which was to render the English speech as polished as possible in all respects,' and he thought ' that no stone should be left unturned by himself in order to reach the farthest goal of success.' To this end he chose to express himself in poetry, because of the scope it gives for ornaments of speech and grace of style, and he also translated from French and Latin into English. ' Nor did he cease from his labours until he had carried our language to that height of purity, of eloquence, of conciseness and beauty, that it can justly be reckoned among the thoroughly polished languages of the world.' This is the point of view, more or less exaggerated, which is repeated constantly by later writers, from many of whom it would be assumed that the ' refining ' of the English tongue was the one thing for which Chaucer lived and worked. Speght (1598), for instance, says ' Chaucer had alwaies an earnest desire to enrich and beautifie our English tongue, which in those days was verie rude and barren '; and the tenor of Rymer's remarks (1692) is to the effect that Chaucer found himself faced with the herculean task of remodelling the language, which he immediately and with great energy set himself to do, the process of which described in detail resembles nothing so much as the recipe for making a pudding.[1]

---

[1] As late as 1879 we find Dr. Weisse (in *Origin, progress and destiny of the English Language and Literature*, New York, 1879), definitely stating that Chaucer, ' after rendering himself master of the situation as to Anglo-Saxon, French and Latin, resolved to bring some order out of this confusion,' so he immediately and as it were by a stroke of the pen, ' dropped the thirty-four senseless inflections of the Anglo-Saxon definite article,' replacing them by ' the,' and introducing ' a ' as an indefinite article, he swept away all inflections of adjectives, largely reduced the changes in the personal and possessive pronouns, reduced twenty-three inflections of the demonstrative pronoun to two, dropped all inflections in nouns, substituting the particles ' of,' ' from,' etc., to denote the various cases, and adopted the French rule of forming the plural of nouns by adding an ' s ' to the singular. This was a fair achievement for one man single-handed to accomplish.

(b) Next we come to the opposite statement, that Chaucer corrupted the language.

The writer who appeared definitely to start this view (although it was indicated earlier, see *e. g.* Chapman 1598) was Richard Verstegan (or Rowlands), the antiquary and old English scholar. In his *Restitution of Decayed Intelligence* (1605) he says that he does not agree with those who call Chaucer the first illuminator of the English tongue, because ' he was a great mingler of English with French, unto which language by lyke, for that he was descended of French or rather Wallon race, he caryed a great affection.'

Verstegan was looked upon as a great authority in antiquarian matters, and all through the seventeenth and eighteenth centuries his remark is quoted with respect, and its truth accepted as unquestioned, although there is a difference of opinion as to whether introducing French terms was a corruption of English or not. So, for instance, Tooke (1647), Fuller (1662), and Rymer (1692) defend Chaucer against this accusation, while Dr. Johnson (1755) points out that Gower uses the French words of which Chaucer is charged as being the importer. But more often it is assumed as true that the French words were a corruption, and it is repeated with approval, as by Phillips (1658), Lewis (1737), Oldys (1738) and Percy (1765); or, as in the case of Skinner, it is expanded and emphasized. In the Latin preface to his *Etymological Dictionary* (1671) Skinner writes :—' Chaucer having by the worst sort of example brought in whole cart-loads of words into our speech from . . . France, despoiled it, already too much adulterated by the victory of the Normans, of almost all its native grace and elegance.' This kind of assertion in an authoritative work of reference naturally increased the general belief in Chaucer's wickedness in this respect.

In addition to Chaucer having imported French words wholesale into the language, it was for nearly a century generally assumed that he had also borrowed largely from the Provençal; although this is generally held to be to his credit rather than the reverse. Rymer seems to have started this belief in 1692, and Dryden quoted Rymer's remark with approval, which gave it general currency.   In the sketches of a history of English poetry drawn up by both Pope [1] and Gray [2] it is laid down that Chaucer imitated the Provençal writers, and Warburton and Warton both endorse this, the latter stating that 'Chaucer formed a style by naturalizing words from the Provencial.' [3]   Tyrwhitt (1775) finally put an end to this theory by asserting that he could find no phrase or word in Chaucer which appeared to have been taken from south of the Loire, and he even doubted whether Chaucer had any acquaintance with the poets of Provence.

(c) and (d) have been dealt with fully in the earlier part of this introduction.   Of (c)—the assertion that Chaucer is obsolete and his versification rough—the most noteworthy early references are Ashton (1546), Wilson (1553), Puttenham (1584), Covell (1595), Marston (1598), Daniel (1599 and 1646), Jonson (a. 1637), Waller (1668), Phillips (1675), Dryden (1679 and 1700), Howard (1689), Addison (1694), and Blount (1694). Later on, right up to the third quarter of the eighteenth century, this class of reference becomes increasingly common. Of (d)—the refutation of or excuse made for this assertion— we may note Skelton (a. 1508), Webbe (1586), Sidney (1595), Gascoigne (1575), Beaumont (1597), Speght (1602), Peacham (1622), Cockayne (1658), and Brathwait (1665).

(e) Verses and prose writing in connection with translations and modernizations are fairly well marked and easy to find, beginning with the preface and verses before Kynaston's Latin translation (1634); after the publication of Dryden's Fables there are a great number (see the years 1700, 1706, 1707); and again after Pope's and the many other modernizations all through the eighteenth century.

(5) **References to a 'Canterbury Tale,'** meaning a fictitious and utterly improbable tale, or a scurrilous story.

---

[1] Ruffhead's *Life of Pope*, 1769, pp. 424–5; see also p. 377 below.

[2] Letter to Warton, April 15, 1770, see p. 436 below.

[3] *History of English Poetry*, by Thomas Warton, 1774, vol. i, p. 344.

The earliest references we have found of this description are those in the year 1547, when Latimer, Cranmer and Becke all allude to ' Canterbury Tales ' in the sense either of profane histories or ' fables or trifles.'

We do not meet it again (though doubtless it was an ordinary expression, and there are many examples of it) until 1575, when Turberville uses it, and at the same time explains exactly what he means by it, *viz.* : ' a verie olde woman's fable,' and in the same year Wharton speaks of ' olde bables, or stale tales of Chaucer.'

The expression then becomes fairly common, and we find it under Proctor (1578), Fulke (1579), Lyly (1580), who alternates it with ' an Æsop's Fable,' Stanihurst (1582), Dekker (1605), who in 1625 uses a ' Kentish Tale ' in the same sense, Chapman (?) (1606), Wither (1621), Unknown (1630), and in *A Fraction in the Assembly* (1648) the same meaning is implied, though the actual expression is not used. The Elizabethan meaning evidently took root in America, for Dean Stanley, writing in 1855 (see below), says that Americans have been accustomed from their earliest years to hear a marvellous story followed by the exclamation, " What a Canterbury ! " It was still in use in England in the eighteenth century, meaning a long-winded tale, for Steele (1709) twice uses it in this connection; also unknown writers in 1737, 1753 and 1795, the last in the sense of a ' cock and bull ' story.

(6) **References relating to Westminster and Chaucer's Tomb.**

These are to be found in three connections; of which (a) and (b) are very common.

(a) *In speaking of poets or others buried near Chaucer*, as for instance, Spenser, Drayton, Cowley, Dryden, Robert Hall (*see* below Vallans, 1615).

(b) *In any general account of the tombs at Westminster.*

(c) *In connection with the curious custom of using Chaucer's tomb as a meeting place for the payment of money.*

See below 1566, 1585 and 1596, Order by the Court of

Requests to pay money at Chaucer's tomb, and *c.* 1833, Haslewood.

(7) **Titles of pamphlets or books or plays taken from or
connected with Chaucer,** such as :—

1566. Palamon and Arcite (a play, now lost), by Richard
Edwards.

1590. The Cobler of Canterburie.

1597. The Northern Mothers Blessing. The way of Thrift,
written nine years before the death of G. Chaucer.
By S. J.

1603. The Pleasant Comodie of Patient Grissil, by Thomas
Dekker.

1617. Chaucer's incensed Ghost (a poem), by Richard
Brathwait.

1623. Chaucer new painted, by William Painter.

1630. The Tincker of Turvey [running title is ' Canterburie Tales '].

1641. A Canterbury Tale, Translated out of Chaucer's
old English Into our now vsuall Language. . . .
by Alexander Brome.

1672. Chaucer's Ghoast, Or a Piece of Antiquity.

1700 and 1778. The New Wife of Beath (a poem).

1701. Chaucer's Whims.

1709. The Court of Love. A Tale from Chaucer [a poem],
by Arthur Maynwaring.

1711. The Temple of Fame : A Vision, by Alexander
Pope.

1712. Parliament of Birds.

1713. The Wife of Bath, a comedy, by John Gay.

1716. Brown Bread and Honour, A Tale moderniz'd from
an Ancient Manuscript of Chaucer.

1717. The Court of Love. A Vision from Chaucer (a
poem), by Alexander S. Catcott.

1717. A Tale Devised in the plesaunt manere of gentil
Maister Jeoffrey Chaucer, by Elijah Fenton.

1727. A Tale of Chaucer. Lately found in an old Manuscript, by Alexander Pope.

1747. Hereafter in English Metre ensueth a Paraphrase on the Holie Book entitled Leviticus, Chap. xi, vers. 13, etc. Fashioned after the Maniere of Maister Geoffery Chaucer in his Assemblie of Foules (a poem), by Thomas Warton.

a. 1758. A Fragment of Chaucer, by J. H., Esq.

1797–8. Canterbury Tales, by Harriet and Sophia Lee.

1802. Canterbury Tales, by Nathan Drake.

(8) **Notes to books.**

Such, for instance, as to works of Spenser, Shakespeare, Dryden, or the Scottish poets; or illustrative passages in dictionaries, grammars, etc.

(9) **A vision of poets, in which Chaucer appears.**

There are a fair number of these, both in prose and verse, such as Douglas (1501), Skelton (1523), Bullein (1564), Greene's Vision (1592), Foulface (1593), Dekker (1607), Webster (1624), Holland (1656), Unknown (1656), Unknown (*c.* 1669), Phillips (1673), Unknown (1700), Brown (*a.* 1704), Croxall (1715), Unknown (1730 and 1738), Clarke (*c.* 1740), Mason (1747), Warton (1749), Lloyd (1751), Craven (1778), Hayley (1782).

(10) **Prefatory matter in verse and prose, prologues to plays, epigrams and epitaphs.**

(11) **References to Chaucer's Works in Wills, and in catalogues of libraries or sales.**

These are interesting, and throw incidentally some light on how much Chaucer was read and valued at certain times. The earliest bequest of any of his works to be found in a will is in that of John Brinchele, 1420, who leaves to John Broune the book in English called Boecius de Consolacione Philosophie, and to William Holgrave one of his executors, 6s. 8d., his best bow, and his book called the Tales of Canterbury.

In 1450 Sir Thomas Cumberworth leaves to his niece Anne his 'boke of the talys of Cantyrbury' and in 1471 Dame Elizabeth Brune bequeaths to one fortunate legatee her copy of the *Canterbury Tales*, together with a gilt cup, a sparver (baldachin) of silk, a diall of gold, two horses in her stable, and one double harp.

In 1509 the Countess of Richmond details among her legacies ' a booke of velom of Canterbury Tales in Englische,' and in 1568 Henry Payne leaves, in one bequest, his Chaucer ' written in vellum and illumyned in gold ' together with his best gelding.

The earliest library catalogue among the following references, in which a work of Chaucer's appears, is John Paston's (*c.* 1482), in which a ' Boke of Troylus ' is entered as having been lent to a friend and apparently not returned.

Among other early private library catalogues in which Chaucer's works are mentioned is that of William Cavendish, 1540; of Sir William More, 1556; of Henry Fairfax, *a.* 1665, and of Prince Rupert, 1677.

(12) Textual Comments on Chaucer.

These often take the form of copying out portions of his works and annotating them. Among the most interesting of these are Walter Stevin's emendations to Chaucer's *Astrolabe* (*c.* 1555), Gabriel Harvey's notes on Chaucer's learning and nature descriptions (*c.* 1585), Bryan Twyne's extracts (1608–44), Samuel Butler's use of Chaucer's characters to illustrate his points (*c.* 1667), Elias Ashmole's marginal notes in his Chaucer MS. (*a.* 1692); while Brathwait's Comments in 1665 are a printed example of the same kind of exercise.

(13) MS. additions to Chaucer's text in the MS. copies.

These are generally merely headings or end lines to the poems, they are nearly all early, and a great number will be found from about 1420–1500, practically all by unknown scribes, except in the case of John Shirley, who contributes a good many (principally placed *c.* 1445–50), of which the most important are his metrical prologue to Boethius and his prose introduction to the *Knight's Tale* (*a.* 1456).

(14) **References in connection with certain places and certain people.**

These are to be found in histories, guide books, etc., in connection with places like Woodstock or Oxfordshire, and people such as Wicklif and John of Gaunt.

(15) **Bibliographical references.**

These are comparatively rare until we come to the nineteenth century, but among earlier ones may be noted part of Thynne's *Animadversions* 1598, some of Stow's notes 1600, the letters of Hearne and Bagford 1708–9, the diaries of Hearne 1709–15, and the Typographical Antiquities by Ames and Herbert 1749 and 1785.

(16) **References that stand alone, because of some peculiar interest.**

These often come under one or other of the above headings, but they deserve to be picked out because of some special light they throw on Chaucer's reputation. Such, for instance, is the statute of 1542–3 for the abolishing of forbidden books, Chaucer's being among those excepted; or Wilson's remark in his *Arte of Rhetorique* (1553), that ' the fine Courtier will talke nothing but Chaucer.' John Earle's interesting remark in 1628, the letter of the Parliament Officer in 1645–6, Brathwait's 'Comments' (1665), Addison's criticism (1694), the references by Pepys (1663–4), Gay's comedy (1713), Mr. Brome's letter (1733), and others, are referred to in the earlier part of this introduction. The references by Miss Carter (1774), Miss Seward (1792), Miss Mitford (1815), and Byron (1807), also deserve special notice.

(17) **References that are really literary criticism.**

By this is meant references that are not merely textual annotations or general repetition of common opinion (such as Sir T. Pope Blount 1694, Giles Jacob 1720, John Dart 1721, John Entick 1736, William Thompson 1745, *Biographica Britannica* 1747, or Theophilus Cibber 1753), but original criticism, showing first-hand knowledge, and contributing something fresh to the body of critical work on Chaucer. Of these we will merely give a list (up to 1800), as this question as already been dealt with.

	1400–30	John Lydgate.
	1412	Thomas Hoccleve.
	1475	Robert Henryson.
	a. 1477	*Book of Curtesye,* stanza 49.
Early appreciation by English and Scottish writers.	c. 1483	William Caxton.
	1501 and 1513 }	Gavin Douglas.
	1503	William Dunbar.
	1507	John Skelton.
	1532	Sir Brian Tuke.

	1544, 1552, 1563–8 }	Roger Ascham.
	1553	Thomas Wilson.
Elizabethan criticism, which, with the exception of Spenser, Beaumont and Speght, consists chiefly of investigation of metre and language.	1555	Robert Braham.
	1575	George Gascoigne.
	1579, 1590–6 }	Edmund Spenser.
	1581	Sir Philip Sidney.
	1584–8	George Puttenham.
	1586	William Webbe.
	1597	Francis Beaumont.
	1602	Thomas Speght.

17th-century criticism. With the very great exception of Dryden, who writes the first literary criticism in the modern sense of the term, there is otherwise little of original worth, for Brathwait, whose 'Comment' was written in 1617 (see p. xxxvi above), is really a survival from the Elizabethans.	1622	Henry Peacham.
	1665	Richard Brathwait.
	1675	Edward Phillips.
	1692	Thomas Rymer.
	1700	John Dryden.

Eighteenth-century criti-cism.	1720	George Sewell.
	1728–30	Alexander Pope.
	1737	Thomas Morell.
	1737	Elizabeth Cooper.
	1739	George Ogle.
	1751	John Upton.
	1754, 1762, 1774	} Thomas Warton.
	1755	Samuel Johnson (very little).
	1760–1	Thomas Gray.
	1762	Richard Hurd.
	1775	Thomas Tyrwhitt.

The above seventeen types will be found roughly to account for all the references up to 1800. Allusions in letters are not separately classed, because they are of so many various kinds, bibliographical (as Hearne and Bagford), a quotation as a matter of literary interest (as Margaret Roper (1535) or Horace Walpole (1789)), or critical. Records of Chaucer in his life-time also are not separately specified, as they all fall between 1357–99, and therefore are very easily found.

There is one class of reference that one would have expected to be fairly common, and that is the inclusion of passages from Chaucer in books of poetical selections or extracts. Such, however, is not the case, for upon examination of these up to 1800, there seems, with one exception, to have been a curious shyness about including Chaucer in any of them. The single exception is, however, rather interesting. Tottell's *Songes and Sonnettes*, published in 1557, is the first poetical miscellany in English,[1] and among the poems by 'Uncertain Authours' is included Chaucer's 'Truth' ('Flee fro the prees'). The editor of Tottell heads it 'To leade a vertuous and honest life,' and prints it with some curious variations from the usual text.

---

[1] Though this title ought, strictly speaking, to be given to Thynne's edition of 'Chaucer' in 1532, *q. v.* below, p. 78.

In the later collections, such as the *Paradise of Dainty Devices* (1578), the *Gorgeous Gallery of Gallant Inventions* (1578), or *England's Helicon* (1600), there was no question of including any but practically contemporary poets. But John Bodenham, the editor of *Belvedére* (1600), seems to have had a desire to include extracts from Chaucer and the older poets, which was not carried out. *Belvedére* is a collection of single ten-syllable lines or couplets from a number of poets arranged under various subject headings, such as Life, Death, Hope, Learning, etc., a method very popular later on, especially in the eighteenth century. The reasons for the non-inclusion of Chaucer, Gower and Lydgate were apparently two; first, because of the irregularity of their verse, ' it was not knowne how their forme would agree with these of ten syllables only,' and secondly, because ' the Gentleman who was the cause of this collection ' absolutely refused to include them. Notwithstanding this, Bodenham had hopes that in the next edition (which never appeared) they might be added.

Naturally, in the seventeenth century, there would be no question of including Chaucer in a poetical miscellany, and therefore no excuse was needed for the omission, but in 1702 we find Edward Bysshe apologizing for the non-inclusion of Chaucer and Spenser in his *Art of English Poetry*, which is a collection of a similar nature to Bodenham's, though not limited to single or ten-syllable lines. The reason he gives for the omission is that ' the garb in which they are cloath'd . . . is now become so out of fashion, that the readers of our age have no ear for them.'

In another book of the same sort which he published twelve years later (*The British Parnassus ; or, a compleat Common-place-Book of English Poetry*, 1714), which consists of fresh extracts gathered from 83 instead of from 43 different poets, as in the earlier collection, although there are long quotations from Dryden's modernizations of Chaucer, and some from Pope's, and Spenser is added to the list of poets, there are no quotations from Chaucer in the original.

Charles Gildon, who in 1718 published the *Complete Art of*

Poetry, shows a great advance on Bysshe in the matter of appreciation of the older poets, for he makes a point of quoting much from both Spenser and Shakespeare (see his Preface), but all his extracts from Chaucer are from Dryden's versions.

Elizabeth Cooper (1737) is the first editor after Tottell who includes an extract from Chaucer in the original in a Poetical Miscellany, but her good example is not followed.

Although there was evidently at one time an intention to include Chaucer among Dr. Johnson's poets (see letter from Edward Dilly to Boswell, 1777, below), this was not carried out. In 1781 a book of extracts was published, stating in the title that they were selected from ' Chaucer to Churchill,' but this must have been merely for the sake of alliteration, for there are no Chaucer extracts in the book; and in 1787, when Henry Headley published *Select Beauties of Ancient English Poetry*, he deliberately omitted Chaucer, as well as Shakespeare, Jonson and Milton, because, as he says, though they are ' familiar to us in conversation,' they are nevertheless ' not universally either read or understood.'

§ 3. QUALITIES ATTRIBUTED TO CHAUCER.

In examining the qualities ascribed to Chaucer as a poet, one is struck by a rather curious fact which applies more especially to the first three hundred and fifty years of criticism, and this is that certain epithets have a distinct and well-marked vogue; during a definite time they are used repeatedly, and evidently represent the leading characteristic of the poet in the minds of his critics; they then completely fall out of fashion, to be replaced by some other leading and quite different quality.

Thus, for instance, to note in their chronological order the most salient of these :—

(1) Chaucer is *golden tonged, eloquent, ' ornate,'* for about the first 150 years after his death (1400–1550). This view was started by Lydgate, who again and again dwells on the rhetorical powers of his master ' the noble rethor Poete of breteine ' who

' made firste to distille and reyne the golde dewe droppis of speeche and eloquence into our tounge.' This quality is emphasized by Walton (1410), Hoccleve (1412), ' flour of eloquence,' James I (1423), ' Shirley ' (*c.* 1450), the author of the *Book of Curtesye* (*a.* 1477), Caxton (*a.* 1479 and *c.* 1483), John de Irlandia (1490), Dunbar (1503), Hawes (1503–4), Feylde (1509), Douglas (1513), Skelton (1523), Unknown (1525 and 1561), B. G. (1569).   By the middle of the sixteenth century Chaucer's verse and language were becoming difficult to understand, so that he was no longer thought of as ' golden tongued ' ; and this class of praise drops with such completeness, that it is something of the nature of a shock to find as late as 1602 and 1609 the expression ' golden pen ' (1602, Nixon, below, and 1609, Heale).   The first one is accounted for when one finds that the *Christian Navy* is merely a reprint (with title and a few words altered) of a poem published in 1569, which is itself, with these two last exceptions, the very latest reference we have found to the ' golden eloquence ' of Chaucer.

When his most ardent admirer can no longer assert that he has a flowing and melodious style, the quality which comes in to replace this is that—

(2) *He is a moral poet.*   This is a view held by a certain class of critic almost exclusively in the sixteenth century, although there are isolated examples earlier and later.   Lydgate, who ascribes most qualities to Chaucer except imagination and humour, of neither of which he was very well qualified to judge, notes that ' in vertu he set al his entent ydelnesse and vices for to flee ' ; but the first definite allusion to Chaucer's use of satire with a clear moral purpose is that made by Hawes in 1506 ; and he is followed by Foxe (1570), Lodge (1579), Webbe (1586), and Prynne (1633).   This quality is also implied in many other references where sayings and stories of Chaucer's are quoted which condemn some particular sin.   Such are Ascham (1544), Northbrooke (1577), Babington (1583), Scot (1584), and Harsnet (1603).

Side by side with this view, and often coupled with it,

there goes another attribute which is very general, and peculiarly Elizabethan. This is that—

(3) *He is a learned poet*, prevalent from about 1530 to 1660. Sir Brian Tuke first draws attention to it in his preface to Thynne's edition of the poet in 1532, but it is not till the third quarter of the century that it becomes the favourite attribute. G. B. in 1569 speaks of 'learned Chaucer'; Foxe, in 1570, couples Chaucer with Linacre and Pace in commendation of his 'studie and lernyng'; Holinshed, in 1577, lays special stress on his exquisite learning 'in all sciences'; Spenser (1579) prays that on him 'some little drops' might flow ' of that spring was in his learned hedde,' and Puttenham (1584–88) singles out Chaucer to be commended above Gower, Lydgate and Harding ' for the much learning appeareth to be in him above any of the rest.' This view is strongly emphasized by Gabriel Harvey in his curious and hitherto unpublished MS. notes (*c.* 1585), where he says that Chaucer and Lydgate were 'much better learned than oure moderne poets,' and sums up his remarks on them in the following characteristic sentence : 'Other commend Chawcer and Lidgate for their witt, pleasant veine, varietie of poetical discourse, and all humanitie. I specially note *their Astronomie, philosophie,* and other parts of *profound or cunning art.* Wherein few of their time were more exactly learned. It is not sufficient for poets to be superficial humanists : but they must be exquisite artists, and curious uniuersal schollers.' Churchyard (1587) speaks of Chaucer's 'learned tales,' the author of the *Cobler of Caunterburie* (1590) praises his 'conceited learning,' the first epithet used by Hakluyt (1598) is 'learned,' and Francis Thynne (1598) refers to the love his father had for Chaucer's 'lernynge,' Harsnet (1603) and Stowe (1603) allude to him as a learned writer rather than as a poet, and it is significant that Speght calls his edition of 1598, the 'Workes of our Antient and lerned English Poet.' That Speght does this of set purpose, is evident from his preface of 1602, where he says that it would be a good piece of work for some industrious scholar to look up and note all Chaucer's classical authorities,

'which would,' he adds, 'so grace this auncient Poet, that whereas divers have thought him vnlearned, and his writings meere trifles, it should appeare, that besides the knowledge of sundrie tongues, he was a man of great reading, and deep judgement.'

Selden also (1612) specially notes Chaucer's learning and wit, asking how many of the poet's readers suspect his knowledge 'transcending the common Rode' in his use, for instance, of 'Dulcarnon' in *Troilus and Cressida*.

Freeman (1614) again dwells on the same point, coupling Chaucer in this respect with Lydgate and Gower, who, he affirms, 'equal'd all the Sages of these, their owne, of former Ages.' Webster (1624) classes Chaucer, Gower, Lydgate, More and Sidney together as 'five famous scholars and poets of this our kingdom,' and 'five learn'd poets'; and 'learned' is the adjective selected for Chaucer by Basse in his well-known epitaph on Shakespeare (c. 1622). Other similar references are Unknown (1622), E. G. (1646), Leigh (1656), Howard (1689), Hatton (1708).

But on the whole (in the following extracts, with the sole exception of Robert Henry 1781), to the men of the later seventeenth and the eighteenth centuries, Chaucer was no longer a learned poet, and on the very rare occasions when that adjective is used it is more in the sense of repeating a commonplace which was at one time, but is no longer, generally believed; see, for instance, Grainger's account in the *Biographical History of England*, 1769, below. The quality to which 'learned' gave place, and which may fairly be called the dominant characteristic from about 1670 to 1760, is that—

(4) *He is a jovial, facetious, merry poet.*

These qualities of 'merry' or 'jovial' are applied to Chaucer with two rather different meanings—

(a) really pleasant, lively, amusing;

(b) one who delights in a broad jest, and tells coarse stories.

The first meaning (with the exception of the discriminating criticism in the *Boke of Curtesye* 1477) is found mostly from about 1570 to 1600, as in Robinson (1574) and Spenser (1579), who both speak of Chaucer's 'merry tales'; Puttenham (1584) speaks of his 'pleasant wit,' Webbe (1586) of his 'delightsome vayne,' in which he wrote 'learnedly and pleasantly,' unfolding 'pleasant and delightsome matters of mirth'; in the *Cobler of Caunterburie* his wit and pleasantness are dwelt on, and Beaumont (1597) says Chaucer is 'the verie life itself of all mirth and pleasant writing.'

We occasionally find the term 'witty' applied to Chaucer, and his 'wit' is often alluded to. It is, however, difficult to know exactly what was meant by 'wit' and 'witty,' particularly at the end of the sixteenth and in the early seventeenth centuries. We know that 'wit,' which originally meant simply the intellect or understanding, first acquired its secondary and more restricted meaning somewhere about this time, and that a little later the adjective 'witty' passed from the signification of 'skilful' or 'wise' to that of ingenious and quick in a certain imaginative quality of seizing resemblances between two apparently different things. Early in the seventeenth century 'wit' appears often [1] as an equivalent for the Italian 'ingegno,' and indeed is used by Jonson as synonymous with 'ingenuity.' [2] Hobbes tells us in the *Leviathan* (1651) that wit had become a synonym for 'fancy,' and in his *Answer to Davenant's Discourse upon Gondibert* (1650), he defines the function of 'fancy' to be the furnishing of the ornaments of poetry, whereas 'judgment' supplies the 'strength and structure.' His distinction between the two was adopted by later seventeenth and eighteenth century critics, and wit came to mean a quickness of mind in seeing unexpected resemblances.[3] Dryden and Addison both say that to the resemblance of ideas

---

[1] But not always; thus in Glapthorne's *Wit in a Constable*, 1639, 'witty' appears to be used in the sense of 'knowing,' 'clever,' the reverse of stupid.

[2] *Every Man out of His Humour*, III, iii. For the whole question of the change of meaning in 'wit' at this time, see *Critical Essays of the 17th Century*, Oxford, 1908; Introduction by Prof. Spingarn, pp. xxvii-xxxi.

[3] Locke, *Human Understanding*, 1690, book ii, chap. xi, § 2. Temple, *Miscellanea*, 2nd part, p. 318; and Addison, *Spectator*, No. 62.

should be added the sensation of surprise and delight, and so we can see how the particular meaning now attached to the adjective ' witty ' gradually crept in.[1]

So that when Stevins (*c.* 1555) and Bullein (1564) speak of ' wittie Chaucer ' we have to remember that they mean ' possessed of wisdom or understanding,' [2] in which sense it falls in under ' learned,' the characteristic epithet of the time, and when Puttenham (1584) and Thynne (1600) speak of his ' pleasant ' and ' flowing wit,' they mean intellect or understanding.   But when William Barker, in his prefatory verses to Kynaston (1635), alludes to ' up start verse-wrights ' first stealing Chaucer's ' wit ' and then pronouncing him dull, something of the new meaning of ' ingenium ' is included,[3] and Gayton (1654) in saying Chaucer writes ' wittily ' certainly means with ingenuity, while Addison (in 1694) probably interprets the word much as he did in the *Spectator* (No. 62). Sewell (1718), in describing Chaucer's satire, says it is severe, but it is ' the Severity of a Court Poet; much wit and more good manners.'   Here we have completely reached the modern meaning, and it is the only time in the following references (up to 1800) that we can be certain it is applied to Chaucer; for Walpole, in writing to George Montagu in 1768, though he probably had Chaucer's wit in his mind, is not speaking directly of him.

Adjectives such as ' merry ' or ' jovial,' in their second

---

[1] There was, however, a good deal of variation in the meaning attached to ' wit ' by different 17th and 18th century writers.   Thus, in addition to the meanings given it by Jonson and Hobbes, Dryden uses it at one time as a synonym for ' imagination ' (Letter to Sir Robt. Howard, prefaced to *Annus Mirabilus*, 1666), and at another he defines it as ' a propriety of words and thoughts adapted to the subject ' (*Essays*, ed. Ker, vol. i, p. 190); whereas Dennis uses it almost to mean ' reason ' (*Miscellanies in Verse and Prose*, 1693, preface).

[2] Cf. Spenser's use of ' wittily ' in the *F. Q.*, ii, c. 9—
' All artes, all science, all Philosophy,
And all that in the world was ay thought wittily '
and Marlowe in *Tamb.*, Pt. I, Act ii, sc. 4 : ' Are you the witty King of Persia ? '   Also Shakespeare in *Richard III*, iv, ii, 42.

[3] Note Walkington in *The Optick Glasse of Humours*, below, 1607, translates ' wit ' by ' ingenium.'

meaning of delighting in a broad jest or coarse story, begin
to be used about 1575, and for the following hundred years we
find this signification occasionally.   Towards the end of the
seventeenth century it becomes more common, and for the first
sixty years of the eighteenth century something of this nature
is the characteristic epithet.   ' Joking,' ' jocound,' ' sprightly,'
' gleeful,' ' blithe,' ' merry,' ' gay,' ' frolic,' ' facetious,' are
among the adjectives used quite constantly in speaking of
Chaucer or his work at this time; and one annotator (towards
the end of the eighteenth century) goes so far as to compare
Chaucer, as regards this tendency to jocoseness, with Charles II
' who could hardly sustain his gravity long enough to make a
speech from the throne ' (see *c.* 1785, below).

The fact is that in spite of the growing admiration for the
antique and ' Gothic ' in the eighteenth century, there was at
the same time a tendency to think what was old very ludicrous.
That this was so is clearly shown in the attitude towards the
other great poet whose language was generally considered
obsolete.   We can see that Chaucer's love of a jest and his
sense of fun might give reason to superficial readers to think
there was little else than the comic in him, but when we find
that the ' ludicrous element ' in Spenser is what most strikes
many of his admirers at this time, we realize that the older
turns of phrase and so-called ' simplicity of diction ' were to
the eighteenth-century reader really funny in themselves.
Shenstone, whose *School-Mistress* (1742) is, next to the *Castle
of Indolence,* one of the best of the many Spenserian imitations,
writes to Mr. Graves, in June 1742, that he could not at first
read Spenser, but that later ' Pope's Alley made me consider
him ludicrously; and in that light, I think, one may read him
with pleasure.   I am now . . . from trifling and laughing at
him, really in love with him.' [1]   Thomson, in the *Advertisement*
to the *Castle of Indolence* (1748) says that as the poem is written
in the manner of Spenser, ' the obsolete words and a simplicity
of diction in some of the lines, which borders on the ludicrous,'

---

[1] Shenstone's Works, 1769, vol. iii, p. 66.

are necessary in order to make the imitation more perfect. And William Mickle, another imitator, writes, in his preface to *Sir Martyn* (1778), that 'some reasons perhaps may be expected for having adopted the manner of Spenser,' and he will only say that the 'fulness and wantonness of description, the quaint simplicity, and above all, the ludicrous, of which the antique phraseology and manner of Spenser are so happily and peculiarly susceptible' are what attracted him to it.

In the light of these remarks, it is not surprising that Chaucer was thought of chiefly as a very good joke, and that Joseph Warton, in his essay on Pope (1782) found it necessary to draw attention to the common though mistaken notion that Chaucer's excellence and 'vein of poetry' lay chiefly in his manner of treating light and ridiculous subjects; Warton attributes the mistake to the accidental fact that Dryden and Pope had modernized principally the gay and ludicrous poems; and he assures those who look into Chaucer that they will soon be convinced of this prevailing prejudice, and will find his comic vein . . . to be only like one of mercury, imperceptibly mingled with a mine of gold.'

This attitude towards the poet did in fact gradually change at the end of the century, and after the publication of Tyrwhitt's work, which brought about a gradually increasing knowledge of Chaucer, we can find no special quality ascribed to the poet at any particular period.

Such general adjectives as ' venerable,' ' ancient,' or ' celebrated,' have not been noted. These are particularly common in the eighteenth century when he was least known, as they were safe and non-committal terms.

It will be noticed that the characteristic qualities attributed to Chaucer from 1400 to 1800, are those in which the critics or men of letters of the time were themselves more specially interested.

In the fifteenth and earlier sixteenth centuries, when the language was still crude and unsettled, and good writing was very scarce, the desire for ease of expression was strong and the appreciation of it great. Later, the closely allied

Reformation and Renaissance brought with them an overmaster-
ing interest in ethics, morality, and learning, and so ' moral '
and ' learned ' go side by side throughout the Elizabethan age.
Then, when the overladen exuberance of the Renaissance
literature had brought about a reaction in favour of ' clearness ' and ' wit,' as Chaucer was certainly not ' clear ' to the
readers of the seventeenth century, they searched for his
' wit '; and to men who delighted in the Restoration drama,
this seems mostly to be found in his broadest stories.

So it is, that here as elsewhere, what men seek for, that
generally do they find.

§ 4. THE EVOLUTION OF CHAUCER BIOGRAPHY.

*List of the Chief Lives or Biographical Accounts of Chaucer up
to 1900.*

DATE.	AUTHOR.	TITLE OF WORK.
[c. 1545]	John Leland	[in] Commentarii de Scriptoribus Britannicis, [first printed by] A. Hall, Oxford, 1709, pp. 419–26 [in Latin].
1548	John Bale	[in] Illustrium Maioris Britanniæ Scriptorum . . . *Summarium* [1st edn.] fol. 198 and *b* [in Latin].
1557–9	,, ,,	[in] Scriptorum Illustrium maioris Brytanniæ . . . *Summarium* Basilæ . . . [2nd edn.] vol. i, pp. 525–7 [in Latin].
1598	Thomas Speght (aided by John Stow)	[prefixed to] The Workes of our Antient and lerned English Poet Geffrey Chaucer, newly printed. Londini, Impensis Geo. Bishop, anno 1598.
1602	Thomas Speght (aided by Francis Thynne)	[in 2nd edn. of] The Workes of . . . Geffrey Chaucer.

DATE.	AUTHOR.	TITLE OF WORK.
[*a.* 1616]	John Pits	[in] Relationes Historicæ de Rebus Anglicis, Parisiis, 1619, pp. 572–5 [in Latin].
1655	Thomas Fuller	[in] The Church-History of Britain, book iv, pp. 151–2.
1662	,, ,,	[in] The History of the Worthies of England, pp. 337–8.
1660	William Winstanley	[in] England's Worthies . . . 1600, pp. 91–8.
1675	Edward Phillips	[in] Theatrum Poetarum, or a Compleat Collection of the Poets . . . pp. 50–1.
[*c.* 1687]	[Henry Wharton]	[printed in Appendix to vol. ii of] Scriptorum Ecclesiasticorum Historia Literaria, by William Cave, 1740–3, Notæ MSS. & Accessiones Anonymi, &c., pp. 13–15; [in Latin].
1687	William Winstanley	[in] The Lives of the most Famous English Poets, pp. 23–32 [altered and enlarged from the earlier 'Life' in 1660].
1694	Sir Thomas Pope Blount	[in] De Re Poetica . . . [Part 2.] Characters and Censures, pp. 41–4.
1700	John Dryden	[slight account in] Preface to Fables Ancient and Modern . . .
1701	Jeremy Collier	[in] The Great Historical, Geographical, Genealogical and Poetical Dictionary . ., vol. i, sign Bbb 2.
1709	Thomas Hearne	A Letter to Mr. Bagford, containing some Remarks upon Geffry Chaucer . . [in] Robert of Gloucester's Chronicle, Transcrib'd . . by Thomas Hearne, 1724, vol. ii, App. iv, pp. 596–606.

DATE.	AUTHOR.	TITLE OF WORK.
1720	Giles Jacob	[in] An Historical Account of the Lives and Writings of our most Considerable English Poets [being the 2nd vol. of the Poetical Register, 1719], pp. 26–30.
1721	John Dart (corrected by William Thomas)	[prefixed to] The Works of Geoffrey Chaucer. . . . By John Urry, . . London, Printed for Bernard Lintot . . sign a 1—f 2.
1748	Unknown	[in] Biographia Britannica : or, the Lives of the most eminent Persons who have flourished in Great Britain and Ireland . . 6 vols., 1747–63; vol. ii, 1748, pp. 1293–1308.
1748	Thomas Tanner	[in] Bibliotheca Britannico-Hibernica, pp. 166–70; [in Latin].
1753	Theophilus Cibber [or Robert Shiels [1]]	[in] The Lives of the Poets of Great Britain and Ireland . . vol. i, pp. 1–17.
1774	Thomas Warton	[a very slight account in] The History of English Poetry, vol. i, pp. 341–2.
1775	Thomas Tyrwhitt	[a short abstract of historical passages in life, prefixed to] The Canterbury Tales of Chaucer, vol. i, pp. xxiv–xxxvi.
1803	William Godwin	The Life of Geoffrey Chaucer . . 2 vols.

[1] See *Life of Johnson*, by James Boswell, April 10, 1776, ed. G. Birkbeck Hill, 1887, vol. iii, pp. 29–30; also *Six Essays on Johnson* by Walter Raleigh, Oxford, 1910, p. 120, *note.*

DATE.	AUTHOR.	TITLE OF WORK.
1810	Henry J. Todd	Illustrations of the Lives and Writings of Gower and Chaucer, collected from authentic documents.
1844	Sir Nicholas Harris Nicolas	The Life of Chaucer [prefixed to] Chaucer's poetical works, Aldine edn. of British poets, vol. 47.
1876	W. Minto	[Article 'Chaucer' in] Encyclopædia Britannica [ninth edition].
1880	A. W. Ward	Chaucer [in the English Men of Letters Series].
1880	Arthur Gilman	[prefixed to] The Poetical Works of Geffrey Chaucer . . ed. by Arthur Gilman . . Boston, 1880, vol. i, pp. xix–lvi.
1887	John W. Hales	[Article in] The Dictionary of National Biography.
1887	Henry Morley	[in] English Writers, vol. v, pp. 83–347.
1892	Thomas R. Lounsbury	The Life of Chaucer [in] Studies in Chaucer, vol. i, chap. i.
1893	Alfred W. Pollard	Chaucer [in Literature Primers].
1894	Walter W. Skeat	[in] The Complete Works of Geoffrey Chaucer, ed. . . by the Rev. Walter W. Skeat . . Oxford, 1894, vol. i, pp. ix–lxi.
1900	[edited by] W. D. Selby F. J. Furnivall E. A. Bond R. E. G. Kirk	Life Records of Chaucer . . . comprising all known records relating to Geoffrey Chaucer. (Chaucer Society.)

The first life of the poet, the first attempt made to record any facts about him, is the sketch written in Latin by Leland the antiquary. Leland, as we know, was armed with a commission from Henry VIII to search all likely places throughout the land—castles, monasteries, colleges, etc.—for records of the past; and after spending six years in this search, and another six in endeavouring to put his materials in order, his mind gave way early in 1547, and he died in 1552. Some of his information, doubtless, was correct and of great value, but if his other biographies resemble that of Chaucer they must be more remarkable for fertility of imagination than for accuracy of fact.

These biographies were never printed till 1709, but Leland's manuscript collections were freely used by later writers, and in the case of Chaucer, all the information was incorporated by Bale in his life in 1557–9, and again by Pits in the life published in 1619; and it formed the starting-point of the following legends about Chaucer, some of which have survived until quite recent years.

(i) That Chaucer was born of a noble family.

(ii) That he studied at Oxford.

(iii) That he was taught there by John Some and the friar Nicolas.

(iv) That he left the University ' an acute logican, a delightful orator, an elegant poet, a profound philosopher, an able mathematician . . . [and] a devout theologian.'

(v) That he admired and imitated Gower, looking up to him as master.

(vi) That he had a sister married to William Pole, Duke of Suffolk, who ' passed her life in great splendour at Ewelme.'

(vii) That he had a house at Woodstock, adjoining the palace of the King.

(viii) That he lived in France during the last years of Richard II.

(ix) That he was highly esteemed by (and personally known to) Henry IV and Henry V.

Leland also gives a list of Chaucer's works, 'which,' he says, 'at the present day are read everywhere.' In this all his principal writings are included, as well as the ten following spurious works : *Piers Plowman's Tale, The Testament of Cresseid, The Flower of Courtesy* (which he notes is rejected by many as spurious), *The Assembly of Ladies, The Complaint of the Black Knight, A Praise of Women, The Testament of Love, Lamentation of Mary Magdalen, The Remedy of Love,* and *The Letter of Cupid.*

John Bale (1495–1563), the violent reformer, writer of morality plays, and later Bishop of Ossory, who for many years was a friend of Leland, and, like him, was desirous of saving old chronicles and 'noble antiquities,' was about the same time collecting material for his Lives of Illustrious British Writers, the first edition of which appeared in 1548. His account of Chaucer is very short and vague; he evidently knew little about him, and that little was largely incorrect. Thus he states that he was a knight ('eques auratus'), and that it is said that he lived until the year 1450, under Henry VI. For the rest, he was chiefly remarkable for his good manners and for the graceful eloquence of his English, and was considered to have been the renovator of the English tongue. Before the appearance of the second edition of his work in 1557–9, however, Bale had come across Leland's MSS., and incorporated in his enlarged account of the poet most of Leland's mistakes, reproducing them largely word for word, and adding a few more on his own account. Thus, although he does not in this edition give 1450 as the date of Chaucer's death, he says he was living in 1402, because of the last verse of the (spurious) *Letter of Cupid.*

The next biography is that prefixed by Speght to his edition of the poet's works in 1598. This is the first life written in English, and it is much the most careful and the fullest biography that had so far appeared. It represented a good deal of search among public records, and some real facts were contributed to what was known of the poet's life; such as Chaucer's titles of 'armiger,' 'scutifer' and 'valettus,' the

grant to him of the custody of the lands and body of Edmund
Staplegate of Kent, his controllership of the port of London,
his employment abroad, and the gifts and pensions received
by him from Richard II and Henry IV. These researches
were, as we know from himself, the work of the antiquary
Stow, who handed over his materials to Speght (see *Survey of
London*, 1598, below). In addition, however, to Stow's contributions, Speght relies much on Leland and Bale, and quotes
from them, adding also the following fictions of his own :—

(i) Chaucer was born in London, because of his words in
the (spurious) *Testament of Love.*

(ii) He went to Cambridge, as well as to Oxford, because
of his remarks in the (spurious) *Court of Love.*

(iii) He suggests that Chaucer got into political trouble in
Richard II's reign, and ' kept himselfe much out of
the way in Holland, Zeland and France, where he
wrote most of his bookes ' (also founded on the
Testament of Love).

(iv) He suggests Chaucer's journey to Italy in 1368, when
he may have met Petrarch.

Speght also printed a family pedigree of the poet, made
out by Glover, the Somerset Herald, in which, for the first time
Chaucer is represented as marrying a daughter of Sir Payne
Roet (sister of John of Gaunt's third wife) and having Thomas
Chaucer as his son. Some further records about ' Chaucers,'
possibly forbears of the poet, were contributed by Francis
Thynne in his criticism of Speght's edition: a ' John ' and an
' Elias ' Chaucer, as well as a Ralph le Chaucer living in King
John's time, had been found. ' But,' says Thynne, in closing
this section of his remarks, ' what shall wee stande uppon the
Antiquyte and gentry of Chaucer, when the rolle of Battle
Abbaye affirmeth hym to come in with the Conqueror ' [1]
(*Animadversions*, 1598, pub. Chaucer Soc., 1875, p. 14 and

---

[1] This, which at first was thought to be incorrect, is true, and the
reference is to be found in Harl. MS. 53 and Lambeth MS. 6.

note 2). This additional information, which was very popular
with succeeding biographers, was embodied by Speght in his
second edition of 1602.

In 1619 was published the *Relationes Historicæ de Rebus
Anglicis,* by John Pits, whose life of Chaucer (in Latin) is, like
that of Bale, founded upon Leland, with some amplifications
and additional inaccuracies. He expanded Leland and Bale's
remarks about the poet's noble birth to the assertion that both
he and his father were Knights; ' patrem habuit Equestris
ordinis virum, & ipse tandem auratus factus est Eques.'

The belief in Chaucer's knighthood, probably started by
Bale's statement in 1548, was evidently quite general throughout the latter half of the sixteenth century, for we find him
constantly called ' Sir ' (cf. Unknown, *c.* 1560, Legh 1562,
Whetstone 1576 and 1578, *A poore knight his Pallace of private
pleasures* 1579, in which Chaucer is referred to as ' The cheefest
of all Englishmen, and yet hee was a knight,' Greene 1590,
The Cobler of Caunterburie 1590, Greene's *Vision* 1592). Pits
also positively states that Chaucer was born at Woodstock,
here again merely crystallizing what was by this time a
recognized tradition; see Camden in his *Britannia* (1586,
below).

Leland's life, as reproduced and embellished by Bale and
Pits in Latin, and Speght's life in English, to which Stow and
Francis Thynne contributed, were the only authorities on the
facts connected with Chaucer all through the seventeenth
century. Dryden, in the few remarks he makes on Chaucer's
life in his Preface to the Fables (1700), simply repeats the
mistakes of these earlier biographers. Other lives of him
which appeared during this time (see list, p. cii above) were
also repetitions of the facts and inaccuracies recorded by
these writers, with occasionally some added fictions. Thus
Edward Phillips asserts that Chaucer ' flourished ' during the
reigns of Henry IV, Henry V and part of Henry VI (*i. e.* 1399–
c. 1440), and that, as well as being knight, he was Poet Laureate.

This is naturally all repeated by subsequent biographers
(*e. g.* Sir Thomas Pope Blount, 1694), and it was doubtless on

the strength of Phillips's information that Jeremy Collier positively asserted in his Dictionary (1701) that 1440 was the date of the poet's death.

Early in the eighteenth century, the antiquary Thomas Hearne was making notes and collecting information about Chaucer's life, as may be seen from his diary of 1709, and the results—which are not great—are summed up in his letter to Bagford of the same year, where he points out that Leland is probably mistaken in saying Chaucer was of noble birth, whereas in all likelihood, his father, though wealthy, was only a merchant (which was suggested by Speght), and he adds that he is sure much information relating to the poet would be found by a careful inspection of the records, which task he has not himself time to undertake. Failing these, however, many of Hearne's other conjectures are based on the *Testament of Love* and the *Plowman's Tale.* The spurious poems, especially these two and the *Court of Love,* have been an unfailing quarry up to quite recent years for deductions about the poet's life, and they were made full use of by the writers (John Dart, corrected by William Thomas) of the account of Chaucer prefixed to Urry's edition of 1721.

This was the most elaborate life of the poet which had yet appeared, and was not merely a re-statement of Leland and Speght, but it contained many fresh assertions mostly founded on the above poems; such, for instance, as that Chaucer composed the *Court of Love* when he was a student at Cambridge, aged eighteen; and a very definite account was given of his collision with the court party in his later years, his forced exile in Zealand, and his imprisonment in the Tower, all founded on remarks in the *Testament of Love.* Dart, however, on the other hand, suggested that John Chaucer was the poet's father, first mentioned the Scrope and Grosvenor dispute, and Chaucer's testimony there (see 1386, below), doubted Chaucer ever having been poet laureate, and rejected his authorship of the *Plowman's Tale* and *Jack Upland.*

The life in the Biographia Britannica, 1748, is very detailed and careful, in that it is based on all the old authorities, Leland,

Bale, Pits, Speght, Hearne and Urry, but there is no original work in it, and the same mistakes are repeated.

Tyrwhitt, in his introductory matter to the *Canterbury Tales* (1775), wisely refrained from writing any life of Chaucer at all, for he says after searching for materials, he found he could add few facts to those already published, and ' he was not disposed, either to repeat the comments and inventions, by which former biographers have endeavoured to supply the deficiency of facts, or to substitute any of his own for the same laudable purpose.' He contented himself, therefore, with pointing out the untrustworthiness of Leland's information, as well as the lack of proof for other commonly accepted facts (such as Chaucer's connection with Donnington Castle), and with printing a short abstract of the historical passages in the life of the poet, consisting of the few records published by Speght and Rymer. He also notes one or two points which may possibly be inferred from the *Testament of Love* (that he was a Londoner) and the *Court of Love* (that he was at Cambridge). He is careful, however, to deduce nothing further from the poems,[1] and gives a warning against ' supposing allusions which Chaucer never intended, or arguing from pieces which he never wrote, as if they were his.'

This warning was, unhappily, not taken to heart by the poet's next biographer, William Godwin, Shelley's father-in-law, who, in 1803, brought out Chaucer's life in two large volumes.

His method was the exact antithesis of the procedure of the scholarly and cautious Tyrwhitt, and, except for the fact that he found and printed some fresh official records about Chaucer, his Life, though entertaining, is absolutely worthless.

Godwin snubs Tyrwhitt for casting so much doubt on Leland, and for not having made any exertions to discover facts as to the history of the poet, and compares his own indefatigable search of the records. The fresh information thus acquired did not, however, enable him to write a life any more

---

[1] The possible political troubles at the end of Chaucer's life are referred to only in a note.

correct than those which had preceded his; on the contrary it forced him to evolve theories whereby the newly discovered and rather troublesome dates might be made to fit in with preconceived facts, largely derived from the *Testament of Love*. For instance, it was in the beginning of 1384 that the political disturbances in London took place which were supposed to have caused Chaucer's flight abroad. But Godwin found by the records that in November 1384 Chaucer was still at his post as Controller of the Customs, for he then applied for leave of absence for one month. This was very awkward, and all Godwin could do was to transport him abroad in November (nine months after the riots which were the supposed cause of his flight) and to extend his month's holiday into an exile of two years. The exile is described in great detail; Chaucer, we are told, doubtless took his wife with him, that is if she were still living, for 'although prudence would have dictated their separation, yet Chaucer was too deeply pervaded with the human and domestic affections to be able to consent to such a measure.' The whole book is written in this style, and as regards Chaucer, it is a tissue of baseless conjecture from beginning to end. In addition to this, it contains a mass of entirely irrelevant information, for Godwin held that ' the full and complete life of a poet, would include an extensive survey of the manners, the opinions, the arts and the literature of the age in which the poet lived.'

Acting on this principle, the chapters are built up something as follows:—It is not improbable that Chaucer was brought up in the Roman Catholic faith, so thirteen pages are devoted to the Church in England in the fourteenth century; he possibly studied in the Inner Temple, therefore twelve pages are given to an account of civil and canon and feudal law of the English constitution, the early writers on English law, modes of pleading and so on.[1]

---

[1] The following paragraph, with which this section on law closes, sufficiently indicates the style of the whole book :—' It may be amusing to the fancy of a reader of Chaucer's works, to represent to himself the

No wonder Mrs. Godwin confidentially asked Charles Lamb whether he did not think there was rather too much fancy in the work.[1]

In 1844 Sir Nicholas Harris Nicolas published his memoir, prefixed to the Aldine edition of Chaucer's works, which really is the first life of Chaucer produced on modern methods of research and accuracy. Nicolas uses Godwin's documents, but prints many more records which finally demonstrated that the story in the *Testament of Love* could not be regarded as auto-biographic.

They showed that during the time Chaucer was supposed to be in exile, he was living in London and personally receiving his pension half-yearly, that he was holding his offices in the Customs from 1382 to 1386, and that in August 1386, instead of being imprisoned in the Tower, he was a member of parliament as Knight of the shire for the County of Kent.

Although in soundness and accuracy this work is a great advance, yet Nicolas makes a few mistakes, such as the ' eleven months ' of Chaucer's stay in Italy, his disbelief in Chaucer's knowledge of Italian, and his acceptation as genuine of *The Cuckoo and the Nightingale, The Flower and the Leaf* and the *Testament of Love.* For in spite of the evidence of the newly discovered records, which proved it could not be autobio-graphical, the faith of critics in Chaucer's authorship of the

young poet, accoutred in the robes of a lawyer, examining a witness fixing upon him the keenness of his eye, addressing himself with anxiety and expectation to a jury, or exercising the subtlety of his wit and judgment in the development of one of those quirks by which a client was to be rescued from the rigour of strict and unfavouring justice. Perhaps Chaucer, in the course of his legal life, saved a thief from the gallows, and gave him a new chance of becoming a decent and useful member of society : perhaps by his penetration he discerned and demon-strated that innocence, which to a less able pleader would never have been evident, and which a less able pleader would never have succeeded in restoring triumphant to its place in the community and its fair fame.' (Godwin's *Life of Chaucer,* vol. i, chap. xviii, pp. 369–70.)

[1] See Lamb's letter to Godwin, Nov. 10, 1803, below. The book was, on the whole, condemned by the reviewers. See below, *Gentle-man's Magazine,* Dec. 1803; Scott, in the *Edinburgh Review,* Jan. 1804, is very severe, and *Blackwood's* reviewer in 1821 dismisses it as being ' contemptible in criticism.'

Testament of Love remained unshaken until William Hertzberg, who translated the *Canterbury Tales* into German in 1866, pointed out the proofs against its being by Chaucer at all,[1] while in 1867, John Payne Collier in England independently came to the same conclusion. But this did not prevent later writers of Chaucer's life detailing his flight, exile and imprisonment as actual occurrences,[2] sometimes shifting the date of these to between the years 1386–88 so as not to clash quite so much with the records.

After the foundation of the Chaucer Society, however, in 1868, Dr. Furnivall and others set to work at the records, whence a number of interesting facts have been extracted, enabling us now at any rate to say very definitely what is *not* true in earlier Chaucer biographies.

Mr. Bond's discovery in 1873, of a page of the household accounts of Lionel, third son of Edward III, from which it is certain that between 1356–59 Chaucer was attached to the household of that prince, and most probably (judging from the value of the articles recorded as given him) in the position of a page, makes the hitherto generally stated date of 1328 for the poet's birth an impossible one; and 1340, for which there is supporting evidence, is now the generally accepted one.

In 1894 Professor Skeat published his life of the poet, prefixed to his edition of Chaucer's collected works, which embodies all discoveries made up to then, more especially Dr. Furnivall's important finds in the public record office, published in the *Athenæum* during the years 1873, 1874; and in 1900 the complete Life Records of Chaucer appeared, containing some fresh information, and comprising all known records relating to the poet.

---

[1] *Geoffrey Chaucer's Canterbury-Geschichten*, uebersetzt von Wilhelm Hertzberg, Hildburghausen, 1866.   Einleitung, pp. 34–37.

[2] See, for instance, *Origin . . . of the English Language and Literature*, by John Weisse, N. York, 1879, pp. 269–70.

§ 5. A NOTE ON SOME CHAUCER LOVERS AND WORKERS
THROUGHOUT THE CENTURIES.

In the following pages we get many peeps at students of
Chaucer ; men who during these five hundred years have
loved him and have been content to spend much time in the
generally unremunerative labour of studying and editing his
works, and in collecting information about him. Sometimes
we actually see them at work—Caxton in his Westminster
printing office, Brian Tuke 'tarying for the tyde at Greenwich,' Urry in his college rooms at Oxford, or Tyrwhitt in the
British Museum,—sometimes only the result of their labours
is visible.

Foremost among this gallant band comes—

(1) **John Shirley** (1366 ?–1456), translator and transcriber,
who possibly knew Chaucer personally, and most certainly
loved and admired him, for he busied himself in writing out
copies of the poems,[1] to which he added various pieces of
information,[2] and sometimes of exhortation to the reader (see
c. 1450, *a.* 1456, below).

We know little about Shirley, beyond the lines recorded as
being on his monument in the Church of S. Bartholomew the
Less,[3] among which are the following :—

> ' His Pen reporteth
> His Lives Occupation,'

to which Stowe adds that he was ' a great Traveller in divers
Countries, and amongst other his Labours painfully collected

---

[1] The MSS. we owe to Shirley are the Sion College MS. (contains of
Chaucer only an inserted copy of the ABC), Trin. Coll. Cam. R. 3. 20,
Addit. 16165, Ashmole 59, Harl. 78 (4 leaves only). The Harl. 7333
and 2251 are not in Shirley's hand. For full details on Shirley's MSS.
see E. P. Hammond in *Chaucer, a bibliographical manual*, N. York,
1908, pp. 515–17.

[2] It is on Shirley's authority that the following works are ascribed
to Chaucer :—the ABC, the Complaint to Pity, Complaint of Mars,
Anelida, Lines to Adam, Fortune, Truth, Gentilnesse, Lak of Stedfast-
nesse, Complaint of Venus, and Complaint to his Empty Purse.

[3] Stowe's *Survey of London*, ed. Strype, 1720, bk. iii, pp. 232–3.

the Works of *Geffrey Chaucer, John Lidgate,* and other learned
Writers, which works he wrote in sundry volumes to remain
for Posterity.'

Next we encounter—

(2) **William Caxton** (1422 ?–1491), whose love and admiration are expressed with so much warmth and charm in his Prohemye to the *Canterbury Tales ;* where we catch a glimpse of
him with care and pride printing the Tales from his own MS.
copy (1st ed. 1477–8), which had been brought to him, and
which he supposed to be very true and correct. But soon after
one of the purchasers of a copy of this first edition pays him a
visit, and points out that the printed version differs considerably from the book as Geoffrey Chaucer had written it. To
this Caxton mildly answers that he had set up the type according
to his own MS. copy, which he had followed faithfully. His
visitor replies that his father possesses a copy of the *Canterbury
Tales* which he much loves, and which is true to Chaucer's
original, and that if Caxton would print it again, he would
get him this actual book for a copy, although he knew that
his father would be loth to part with it. To this suggestion
Caxton gladly agrees, and sets to work at once to print the
whole book over again (2nd ed. 1484 ?), humbly apologizing
the while to the shade of Chaucer for the mistake he in his
ignorance had made of printing his book other than he
wrote it.

Caxton was not content with printing Chaucer, but he
further tried to perpetuate his memory by erecting a pillar
near his tomb to support a tablet on which was written Surigo's
Latin epitaph (see *a.* 1479, below), at the end of which there
were four lines, possibly by Caxton himself.[1]

The next worker is—

(3) **William Thynne** (d. 1546), Chief Clerk of the Kitchen
to Henry VIII, and the holder of many other offices, who
combined the faithful and apparently successful discharge of

---

[1] See Caxton's *Epilogue to Boethius, a.* 1479, below, also Blade's
Life and Typography of Caxton, 1861, vol. ii, p. 67.

many duties in the King's household with an enthusiastic devotion to Chaucer and study of his works. In 1532 he published his edition of the poet, and sixty-six years later, his son Francis Thynne, in the course of his rather querulous letter of criticism to Speght on his edition of 1598 (see 1598, below), affords us a delightful glimpse of his father at work on Chaucer. The elder Thynne was commissioned by Henry **VIII**, with whom he was a great favourite, to search all the libraries and monasteries of England for Chaucer's works; which he did with such success that he was ' fully furnished with multitude of Bookes, amongst which was one copy which was marked " Examinatur Chaucer." ' All these copies he carefully collated, so that although four of Chaucer's pieces had been issued together by Pynson in 1526, yet Thynne's may fairly claim to be the first attempt at a collected edition of the ' Works,' and Thynne himself is the first real editor of Chaucer, for he produced a better text of the *Canterbury Tales* than had been given before, as well as printing for the first time Chaucer's part of the *Romaunt of the Rose*, his *Legende of Good Women, Boece, Book of the Duchess, Pity, Astrolabe*, and *Lack of Stedfastness.*

His son further tells us that he included (or perhaps intended to include?) the (spurious) *Pilgrim's Tale*, which gave such offence to Wolsey and the Bishops, that they brought pressure on the King to insist that Chaucer must be newly printed, and the *Pilgrim's Tale* omitted. This was done, but in the second edition of 1542 Thynne managed to get the (spurious) *Plowman's Tale* (an equally strong invective against the clergy) inserted; although it was sanctioned with great difficulty.[1]

William Thynne must have been a good hater of Romanism and the priests, and Wolsey, his ' old enymye,' owed him a

---

[1] This story of Francis Thynne's about the cancelled edition has been discredited, as the *Pilgrim's Tale* is not to be found in any edition of Thynne's Chaucer, nor has any one-columned edition of Thynne's come down to us. See on the whole question, Thynne's *Animadversions*, ed. F. J. Furnivall, Chaucer Soc., 1875, pp. xli, xlii, and 75, 76.

grudge for many reasons, so Francis Thynne tells us, but mostly because Thynne had protected Skelton, and helped him to publish *Colin Clout*, most of which was written at Thynne's house at Erith in Kent.

Thynne dedicates his edition in his name to Henry VIII, but it is practically certain that this preface was written by Sir Brian Tuke, then Postmaster, and so a colleague of Thynne's in the Royal Household.   Leland refers to a preface by Tuke, and in a copy of Thynne's Chaucer (1532) in Clare College, Cambridge, Sir Brian Tuke has written in his own hand : ' This preface I sir Bryan Tuke knight wrot at the request of Mr. Clarke of the Kechyn then being tarying for the tyde at Grenewich.' [1]

(4) **John Stowe** (1525 ?–1605), chronicler and antiquarian by choice, and tailor by profession, is entitled to a place among Chaucer students and editors, although the service he rendered the poet is a doubtful one.   His own account of his claim to the position is that Chaucer's works were ' corrected and twice increased through mine owne painefull labours, in the raigne of Queene Elizabeth, to wit in the yeare 1561, and again beauti- fied with noates, by me collected out of diuers Recordes and Monumentes, which I deliuered to my loving friende Thomas Speight ' for his edition of 1597.

The modern view of Stowe's work does not quite agree with this.   He is principally famed for having assigned more spurious poems to Chaucer than any one else has ever successfully done, and it has been indeed—as Tyrwhitt prophesied in 1775 —' a work of time to sift accurately the heap of rubbish which was added ' by him to the edition of 1561.   Not only did he for the first time in 1561 publish a number of poems as Chaucer's which are not his (see list 1532, below), but by reprinting all that was in Thynne's edition of 1532 (which was really a miscellany, see note to 1532, Thynne, below), and altering the title to ' The workes of Geffrey Chaucer, newlie printed, with

---

[1] See **Mr. Bradshaw** in Thynne's *Animadversions,* Chaucer Soc., **p. xxvi.**

diuers addicions, whiche were neuer in print before,' he practically claimed for Chaucer the whole of Thynne's volume.

On the other hand, we owe to him the first print of Chaucer's
words to Adam, and three other short pieces, and there is no
doubt that he furnished a good deal of matter to Speght for
use in his life of the poet. He seems to have been a cheery,
lively man, a hard worker, and a great favourite with men of
letters. He was a member of the old Society of Antiquaries,
founded about 1559, and among his colleagues and friends were
Walter Cope, Joseph Holland, Francis Tate, and Francis Thynne.
He was always desperately poor, and consequently carried on
his researches with great difficulty; for his was not then, any
more than it is now, the kind of work which brings in money.
In 1598 he writes of his *Summarie of Englyshe Chronicles,*
'It hath cost me many a weary mile's travel, many a hard-
earned penny and pound, and many a cold winter night's
study.' He could not afford to ride in order to make his
enquiries, but was forced to go on foot. We realize how sharp
was the pressure of poverty, when as an old man, probably
upwards of seventy-seven, after years of hard work at the
chronicles of London and other records of value, we find that
in acknowledgment of his services a grateful government
granted him a license to beg and collect voluntary contributions
in the streets.

Of

(5) **Thomas Speght** (fl. 1600), the next editor of Chaucer,
we know very little, except that he was possibly a Yorkshire-
man, and certainly a graduate of Cambridge, a schoolmaster,
and a lover of Chaucer. It was at college that he first came to
know and love Chaucer (see above, p. xxii, and Beaumont's
letter to Speght, 1597, below). Speght had evidently long
studied Chaucer's works and annotated them (see his preface,
1598, below), and in 1598, when his first edition of the poet
appeared, he added a good deal of extra matter, and wrote the
fullest and most correct life of the poet which had yet appeared
(see p. cvi above).

Francis Thynne was preparing notes for a full commentary

on Chaucer's works when Speght anticipated him, and so Thynne contented himself with writing his long letter, minutely criticizing Speght's production, and correcting many of his mistakes. All these remarks Speght took in good part, and embodied them, with grateful acknowledgment, in his next edition of 1602. He also had much help from Stowe, who put his notes at Speght's disposal.

We must pass over Sir Francis Kynaston (1587–1642), the seventeenth-century littérateur, poet and scholar, who was called more Geoffreyan than Chaucer himself; [1] the founder of the Musæum Minervæ, that curious academy of learning, designed to give a lengthy course of instruction to intending travellers; whose fervent admiration of Chaucer took the unusual form of translating his *Troilus* into Latin verse, and copiously annotating it, both in English and Latin.

(6) **John Urry** (1666–1715) is the next editor of Chaucer, and also the worst. As a man he seems to have been a sturdy, honest scholar with a sense of humour, and a certain charm of style (see his sketch of a preface, 1714 below), of staunch loyalist principles, unlike his uncle Sir John Urry the soldier, who seemed unable to make up his mind on which side to fight. Our Urry bore arms against Monmouth in the Rebellion, and refused to take the oath of supremacy to William III, though this cost him his studentship at Christ Church. Dr. Atterbury, the Dean of Christ Church, persuaded him, much against his inclination, to prepare a new edition of Chaucer, his sole qualification apparently being that he came of a Scottish family, so that his familiarity with the northern tongue enabled him to read Chaucer more easily than an Englishman. [2] He carried through the task with a will, and collected together from many sources a good number of MSS. and printed copies of Chaucer for the purpose. We catch glimpses of him in Hearne's diary from the year 1711 to February 17$\frac{14}{15}$, working in the Bodleian, examining the Junius MSS., collecting Chaucer editions and

---

[1] See Strode's verses, 1635, below.
[2] See Timothy Thomas's Preface to Urry's *Chaucer*, 1721, below.

MSS., over which the two friends often pored together in the evenings. In an interesting letter to Lord Harley (1712, see below), Urry describes his method of work, and expresses the belief, after close study of the *Canterbury Tales*, that ' Chaucer made them exact metre, but the transcribers have much injured them.' He adds that he hopes, by collating many MSS. and printed editions, to be able to ' restore him to his feet again.'

In March 17$\frac{14}{15}$, however, Urry died very suddenly of a fever, leaving his Chaucer unfinished. He appears to have completely prepared the text after a curious fashion of his own, which was to lengthen or shorten Chaucer's words, or to add an extra word, whenever he thought the verse would be improved by it, without giving to the reader any indication whatever of his alterations (see below 1721 Thomas). It seems that he originally had the intention of enclosing these additions within hooks [   ] (the reverse process from that of ' slashing Bentley '), but this ' just, useful and necessary ' design, as Timothy Thomas calls it, was for some unknown reason not carried out. Consequently the edition, as regards text, is quite the worst ever issued. It was taken in hand, after Urry's death, by the authorities of Christ Church and Urry's executor, William Brome, and Bernard Lintot the bookseller, and, after many vicissitudes, it was published in two enormous folios in 1721; the preface and glossary being added by Timothy Thomas, and the life of Chaucer by John Dart.

The edition was divided between the College, Brome and Lintot, in equal shares, the proceeds for the College being devoted to the building of Peckwater Quadrangle. It does not, however, appear to have been in great demand, for twelve years later we find poor Mr. Brome complaining that he cannot sell his copies, ' which lie upon hand, so that I am like to be a great sufferer ' (p. 375 below). Lintot, being in the way of business, was better able to sell his, and the College authorities had adopted a simple and effective method of disposing of theirs, which was to oblige all scholars upon entrance to buy a copy. The picture of the young fox-hunting squires of Christ Church being forced willy-nilly to carry off their Chaucer folios is a delightful one; and it may perhaps account for the number of copies of Urry's Chaucer to be found in the old country houses of England.

(7) **Thomas Tyrwhitt** (1730–86) is the next, and up to this date by far the greatest Chaucer scholar and editor. Considering the importance of Tyrwhitt's work, there is curiously little known about him. He was a man of good family and ample means, educated at Eton and Oxford, where he was elected to a fellowship at Merton College in 1755; he was appointed Deputy Secretary at War in 1756, and he was Clerk of the House of Commons from 1762 to 1768, in which latter year he resigned the position, preferring to that ' post of honour a private station devoted to learned ease.' Later he did good work for a year or two as a trustee of the British Museum.

He was a well-known classical scholar, editor and annotator, a Shakespeare critic, and the only eighteenth-century writer who on sound linguistic grounds was able to expose the Chatterton forgeries; he was indeed reputed to have a knowledge of nearly every European tongue. He seems to have been quiet and reserved, not strong in health, a born student; from his earliest years he loved books, ' for,' as one writes who knew him, ' he never was a boy.' He was quietly benevolent and generous to those less well off than himself,[1] and is reported to have given away as much as £2,000 in one year. He worked for sheer love of the work, indifferent to fame or recognition. The letter he writes on the occasion of the pirating of his Chaucer text by Bell (June 12, 1783) is indicative of his character. It is dignified and restrained, and not without a dry sense of humour. A friend had told him that in Bell's edition of the English poets (1782–3) his text of the *Canterbury Tales* and his notes had just been annexed and printed. Tyrwhitt replies that it is true, but he finds he can do nothing, for as his book has not been entered at Stationers' Hall he has no legal right over it. ' But even if I had,' he continues, ' would you advise me to go to law for a property unattended by any profit ?

---

[1] See the letter from the Bishop of St. Davids in Nichol's *Literary Anecdotes*, vol. ix, pp. 756–7.

A certain philosopher, when his gouty shoes were stolen, only wished that they might fit the thief as well as they fitted himself; and for my own part I shall be contented, if my book shall prove just as lucrative to Mr. Bell as it has been to me.'

Tyrwhitt got nothing for his work in money, and, until long after his death, very little in fame or recognition. What led him to undertake the editing of the *Canterbury Tales* we do not know, but he was admirably fitted for the task; he possessed what was at that time a probably unique knowledge of the literature of the Middle Ages and of the English language of the fourteenth and fifteenth centuries, and he had the finest literary taste combined with sound independent judgment and critical insight. Probably it was the desire to do this special piece of work which made him anxious to give up the Clerkship of the House of Commons, so that he might have all his time for literary research.

In 1771 and the following year we get a glimpse of him collating Chaucer texts at the British Museum. The Rev. Thomas Morell, the friend of Hogarth and Handel, a cheerful, musical and an improvident scholar, had himself designed an edition of the *Canterbury Tales*, and had, in 1737, actually published a modernization of the *Prologue* and *Knight's Tale*. Morell, like Tyrwhitt, found that editing Chaucer was not remunerative, but, on the contrary, rather expensive, and so he was obliged to put the remainder of his Chaucer work on one side. One day, however, in the summer of 1771, he writes to Mr. West, that he had happened to see in the Museum a 'gentleman collating Chaucer.' This reminded him of his work which had lain by him unfinished for forty years, ' which,' he adds rather pathetically, ' being unwilling to lose, I intend to continue ere long, some way to reassume the work, and hope to get the start of him, as there is one volume already printed.' The ' gentleman ' was undoubtedly Tyrwhitt, for Richard Gough, in writing to Mr. Tyson in the following January (1772), says that ' Mr. Tyrwhitt (late Clerk of the House of Commons) applies himself *totis viribus* to Chaucer in the Museum, where is a copy of Urry's edition, with infinite collations by Bishop Tanner. Mr.

Tyrwhitt conceals his design from his most intimate friends; but much is suspected and expected from his leisure and application.'

Morell did not ' get the start ' of the worker in the Museum, and the first four volumes of Tyrwhitt's fine edition appeared a little more than three years later. There is no need to describe it here, it is generally acknowledged to be not only one of the best editions of a great English classic, but also the first to be done in the scholarly and conscientious way which is now thought necessary.

In the light of the immense advance in the knowledge of our own language during the last fifty years, it is easy now to point out where Tyrwhitt makes mistakes; but when we remember that in the eighteenth century practically nothing was known about Middle English, and that Tyrwhitt had to discover it all for himself, his book stands out as a monument of learning and critical acumen, and to it all subsequent editors of Chaucer owe an incalculable debt.

It would be impossible here to mention all the Chaucer scholars of the nineteenth century, for the study of our first great poet has been taken up with enthusiasm, not only in England, but also in Germany and America, where such excellent work has been done by Lounsbury, Kittridge, Koch, Lowes, Tatlock, and many others. In France, also, of late years, interest has awakened in Chaucer, and a great impetus was given to the French study and appreciation of our first and most Gallic poet, by the admirable translation of the *Canterbury Tales* in 1908, to which all the best-known English scholars in France contributed, under the editorship of M. Émile Legouis. So much has been done, and so many and able have been the workers, that a book itself might be written on them and their labours. F. J. Child, ten Brink and Skeat are names that will be remembered as long as Chaucer is read; but there is one figure which stands out above the rest, one name and personality which older Chaucer students of to-day will not easily forget. Dr. F. J. Furnivall, in 1868, from a sheer love of our early literature, founded the Chaucer Society, and, since then, not only carried through herculean tasks himself, but stimulated, helped, advised and encouraged two whole generations of workers in this field.

Somehow, one cannot help thinking that, of all the great and distinguished men who have so freely given of their time and labour to our old poet, no one of them would have been more congenial to Chaucer himself, with no one would he have talked more readily or laughed more heartily than with this latter-day ' Clerk of Cauntebrigge ' ' that unto rowing haddè longe y-go,' [1] this happy octogenarian who almost to the end was young and vigorous, who loved the river and the green fields, and youth and good fellowship, and who

> . . . not for place or pay,
> But all for the fame of the English wrought in the
> English way.[2]

§ 6. THE CHANGE AND FLUCTUATION OF LITERARY TASTE AND FASHION.

In the foregoing notes we have pointed out how the mass of critical material here printed illustrates and throws light on the change of attitude towards Chaucer himself throughout these five hundred years, the change to be discerned in an ever-shifting multitude of separate minds turned towards one fixed central point. It is, however, impossible to survey a great body of critical opinion such as is to be found in the following pages, without certain problems connected with the philosophy of taste, and the doctrine of evolution generally, rising to one's mind. It is not proposed seriously to investigate the problems, or to attempt any solution of them here, but it may be of interest perhaps just to indicate a few of them, such as those discussed in this and the three following sections.

As we watch this vast company of writers passing before Chaucer, and leaving on record their opinion of him, it is curious to reflect that the criticism Chaucer has received throughout

---

[1] See Skeat's poem, ' In Honorem F. J. F.' (A.D. 1900), in *An English Miscellany*, Oxford, 1901, a quotation from which fitly closes our main series of allusions.

[2] G[eorge] S[aintsbury] to F. J. F., p. 1, *ibid.*

these five centuries in reality forms a measurement of judgment —not of him—but of his critics.   Just as we trace the development of the mind of an individual by studying his opinions and works at different periods of his life, so it would seem that in looking at this ever-shifting procession of critics we can trace the development of the mind and spirit of the nation to which they belong.   We know that as individuals our taste changes and fluctuates from youth to age; the favourite authors of our youth are not, as a rule, the favourites of middle age, or, if they are, we like them for other qualities, they make another appeal to us.   Similarly, we can here watch the taste of a nation changing and fluctuating; Chaucer is now liked for one quality, now for another, while at times different ideals and interests so predominate that he makes no appeal to it at all.

Chaucer undoubtedly suffered from change in language quite as much as from change in taste, but even making due allowance for this, there is no question that had the average men of letters and critics of the later seventeenth and earlier eighteenth centuries been able to read and scan his work with perfect ease, they would yet not have seen in him what is seen by the average literary reader of to-day.   Cowley would probably still have had 'no taste of him,' and Addison would have thought his 'wit' out of date.   They had different ideals before them, with which Chaucer did not fit in.   It is for precisely this reason that we no longer have 'a taste of' Waller, who, to the later seventeenth century, was the most important figure in English letters.

We are so accustomed to this change of taste that we accept as a natural condition of evolution, as a necessary sign of growth, in nations as in individuals, this continual fluctuation, of which not the least curious quality is that, although we are intellectually conscious of its existence, we are as incapable of realizing it as we are of realizing that our physical bodies are composed of whirling and ever-changing atoms.

We all of us, individually and collectively, at any given time, trained and guided as we are by the best thought of our age, are inclined to feel that the way we regard an author, a classic, for instance, like Chaucer, is the truest and only possible way he can be regarded. We of to-day are sure that we appreciate to the full all his special qualities, and that his position in the history of our literature has been once and for all established. It may be so, but the experience of the past does not confirm it. Cowley, Addison, Dr. Johnson, and a host of minor critics, all probably felt exactly as we do; they never doubted that their taste was true, their attitude the only sane one, and that Chaucer's position, in spite of Dryden's curious fancy for him, was quite certainly and definitely settled.

To-day, with the record of the opinion of five centuries before us, we can see that the verdict of the most competent critic cannot be wholly trusted until Time has set his seal on it, and that much allowance must always be made, as Hazlitt would have said, ' for the wind,' that is, for the prevailing bias of the age, the standards, ideals and fashions, change in which constitutes change in taste.

Some further light may be thrown on the evolution of critical taste and method when we are able to compare over an appreciable space of time the critical attitude of a nation towards more than one great poet of its own race. This is only to-day beginning to be possible. If, for instance, we compare the movement of critical opinion and research on Shakespeare with that on Chaucer, it is clear that there is a certain similarity, which would appear to indicate the existence of a definite rhythm in the evolution of taste and critical method, as there is a rhythm in all life. The investigation in the future will be complicated by the fact that there will be two rhythms to follow, (1) that of the development of the nation itself and of its critical powers, and (2) that of the evolution of its attitude towards any one given poet. Owing, however, to the literary barrenness of the fifteenth century in England, the development of the first was not at the outset sufficiently rapid to make any great difference in the treatment of Chaucer and Shakespeare.

Thus, in the case of each of these poets there is a period of early praise and personal appreciation, love for the man, with an unquestioned recognition of his position as a great artist.

This is followed by a more critical attitude, which, in Shakespeare's case, for various fairly obvious reasons, comes about much sooner after his death than it does with Chaucer. Then follows, for both poets, a time of effort to make their rough and unpolished works more acceptable to modern taste; Shaksperian revision and 'improvement' began as early as 1662 (when Davenant produced his blend of *Measure for Measure* and *Much Ado*), though it did not continue so late into the nineteenth century as is the case with Chaucer.

At the same time it is in the eighteenth century that the gradual revival of real first-hand knowledge and appreciation of both poets began, critical and scholarly investigation was started, stupendous work on Shakespeare's text was done by the great succession of eighteenth-century editors, and Tyrwhitt brought out his monumental edition of the *Canterbury Tales*.

In the later period of 'romantic' criticism for both poets, which began at the end of the eighteenth century and went on all through the nineteenth century, we find in the case of Chaucer that this romantic, psychological and often ethical appreciation is followed and accompanied from the eighteen sixties onwards with very close textual work and specialised investigation of his language and versification. This closer and specialised investigation of Shakespeare has yet to come; it is, possibly, just beginning. It is in fact probable that investigators to-day, three hundred years after Shakespeare's death, may be about to do for his text something analogous to what Tyrwhitt, three hundred and seventy-five years after Chaucer's death, did for him when he disposed of the persistently erroneous view of his versification and proved that he was a far greater artist and a far more finished literary craftsman than had up to that time been suspected.

It is not suggested that Shakespeare's supreme technical skill has in modern times ever been in doubt, but he has been believed to be very careless, and the text of his plays to be very corrupt, and it has been taken for granted that the quarto editions were very carelessly printed and not to be trusted. Mr. Pollard, Mr. Dover Wilson and other workers are to-day taking us back, not only to close investigation of Elizabethan book-production and of the Quartos in particular, but also in part to the reconstruction of Shakespeare's manuscript, and as a result they show us that passages which to modern eyes appear corrupt and ungrammatical in punctuation are in reality most delicately and sensitively pointed as an indication of how they are to be *said*, and that lines written by some one apparently devoid of the most elementary sense of rhythm, can, in the light of the study of contemporary manuscripts, be easily accounted for and reconstructed.

In addition to this dawning likeness in what might be called critical approach, there are other parallels in the works and qualities of both poets most appreciated at certain times. Such, for instance, is the early preference for the love poems, Chaucer's *Troilus*, and in Shakespeare's case the *Venus and Adonis* and *Romeo and Juliet* (*see* The Shakespere Allusion book, vol. i, p. xxiii, vol. ii, p. 540). It is clear that the works of a poet most prized by contemporaries or immediate successors are by no means those which later generations will put first.

A striking illustration of this is the lack of contemporary appreciation of *Antony and Cleopatra*, which to-day most lovers of Shakespeare would place among the very greatest and most poetical of his plays. There is a noticeable absence of the borrowing of phrases from it by other authors, and up to 1700 only fifteen references to it have been found compared with ninety-five to *Hamlet*, eighty to Falstaff and sixty-one each to *Romeo and Juliet* and *Venus and Adonis*.

Indeed, as Mr. Munro suggests (*Shakespere Allusions*, vol. i, p. xxiv), the cause of the neglect of *Antony* may be the secret of the Elizabethan attitude towards Shakespeare the dramatist, and may show us better than anything else the qualities they most prized and those they ignored. In the same way, as we have seen (p. lxxvii above), it is not until after 1750 that the *Canterbury Tales* takes the first place among Chaucer's works.

It is clear then that taste does change, but if we ask what it is that causes it to change, there is no satisfactory answer to be given.

There are certain influences, foreign literatures, canons of criticism, indicated in every history of the subject, which we can plainly see do much to bring about this change. But all these ' causes ' only push the question one step further back. These influences, taken singly or together, do not explain why taste is in a state of continual flux and changes with each generation. This flux is as mysterious as life itself; it is in truth the fundamental characteristic of life, and it is because taste is a living thing, because it is the capacity for discernment of what is good, that it must inevitably change.

Granting this, then, we see that in Chaucer's case the change in critical attitude accounts for much. We no longer have a definite body of poetic rules and ideals to which all poets, however alien in kind, must conform or be condemned; and that class of criticism is extinct, which is so admirably exemplified in Miss Jenkyns's remark on the author of the *Pickwick Papers*, ' Doubtless, a young man, who might do very well if he would take Dr. Johnson for a model.'

Our demands are different and our tests are different. To-day we prize Chaucer above all because he is a great artist, we delight in his simplicity, his freshness, his humanity, his humour, but it is possible that these may not be the only or even the principal reasons why he is liked three hundred years hence. If, as would seem to be the case, the common consciousness of a people becomes enriched with time and experience, enabling them to see ever more and more in the work of a great poet, the lovers of Chaucer three centuries hence will be capable of seeing more in him and will be able to come actually nearer to him than can those who love him to-day.

Three directions may be indicated in which this enrichment of consciousness is here seen. They are all exactly parallel with what takes place in the growth and development of the individual personality. The first is the development of self-consciousness, of the art of criticism itself; the second is the development of a new sense, and the third is intellectual development, as seen in accuracy and trained scholarship.

§ 7. THE BIRTH AND GROWTH OF CRITICISM AS AN ART.

We know that in nations, as in individuals, the critical faculty develops late, for criticism is a self-conscious art, and cannot exist in the intellectual childhood of a race. England, as compared with France and Italy, was backward in this art, for the northern races mature less quickly, and it is only necessary to cast a glance over the tributes to Chaucer during the first 150 years after his death, to realize why England was late in producing criticism. Chaucer is praised mainly for two reasons, because he settled or established the language, and because he was our first, and by far our greatest poet. We lacked, until later than either France or Italy, a single form of standard speech, and, with one exception, we also lacked good writers. Thus no criticism was for us possible until the pre-eminence of Chaucer's work had helped to establish the dialect of London as the standard English speech, and until we possessed a certain body of literary work, both in prose and verse, which could be analyzed, commented on and compared.

We have here under our hand, and can easily trace as we turn over the pages, the gradual change in the conception of criticism. It begins with bare classification of the external and obvious, and the analysis of form, or, it is concerned only with the ethics of the matter : next it searches for the establishment of an outside fixed standard, by the degree of conformity to which it judges a work, and it delights in the manufacture of receipts for poetry. With Dryden comes the dawn of the conception of organic life and growth in matters literary—' for we have our Lineal Descents and Clans, as well as other Families '—in the eighteenth century the reaction to the judgment by fixed standard, and finally the gradual realization that æsthetic is not fixed, but relative, varying from age to age, and from country to country, and that criticism, even as poetry, is a creative art, whose true function lies in interpretation, in painting to the intellect what already ' lies painted to the heart

and imagination.' [1] From this point of view the remarks on
Chaucer by Ascham (1544), Gascoigne (1575), Nash (1592),
Waller (1668), Dryden (1700), Johnson (1755), Warton (1774),
Blake (1809), and Hazlitt (1817–18) would in themselves, if
rightly read, form a short illustrated History of English
Criticism.

Besides the new idea of the function of criticism and the
change in the standard in critical judgment, we find here what
is really a rather startling illustration of the curiously slow
growth of any sort of critical power in the modern sense of the
word.

If we examine the comments on Chaucer which have any
pretension to be called literary or æsthetic criticism (see list,
p. xc above), we see that up to the middle of the sixteenth
century they consist purely of praise of a very simple and vague
kind, the vagueness and general nature of the remarks being
their most striking feature. Elizabethan criticism is either
a very elementary analysis of Chaucer's metre and language,
or a tribute of admiration, or a defence of the poet against
certain shortcomings with which he is charged. The sixteenth-
century criticisms are good illustrations of how completely
literature was treated as an external phenomenon; the work
was tested ' in vacuo,' [2] the critic was concerned with its unity,
regularity, harmony and so on, but never with its relation to
the mind that created it, or to the age in which it was written.
Of the change in this respect which gradually took place in the
seventeenth century, we cannot here judge, for of seventeenth-
century Chaucerian criticism there is practically none, until
in the last year of the century, quite suddenly, and as it were
without any preparation, we find the first æsthetic criticism of
his work, which is in many respects the finest, sanest and most
illuminating essay ever written concerning Chaucer's merits
and position as a poet.

---

[1] Carlyle, ' State of German Literature,' 1827, *Miscellaneous Essays*,
1899, vol. i, p. 61.

[2] See Professor Spingarn in Introduction to *Critical Essays of the 17th
Century*, 1908, vol. i, pp. xxvii–viii.

Nothing more astonishingly brings out Dryden's greatness as a critic, his freedom, breadth, acuteness, courage, and extraordinary independence of view, than does his treatment of Chaucer. Not only is he the first writer to give us real criticism in the modern sense of the word, but in an age which despised Chaucer, and frankly looked upon him as barbarous and obsolete,[1] Dryden calmly compares him with Ovid, and maintains that the English poet is the more classical of the two. In this surprising and ever refreshing piece of criticism, Dryden makes use, for the first time as applied to Chaucer, of the comparative and historical methods, both of which were new in English criticism. Before this time the mention of a date or of the fact that Chaucer is our first poet is the only evidence that a rudimentary historical sense existed. There is no attempt really to compare one writer with another, unless the simile ' our English Homer ' is to be described as such. Dryden also shows the way to the study of poetry by definite illustration, quotation and comparison. This method was practically unknown in England until Rymer wrote his preface to Rapin in 1674, before which date, as has been pointed out,[2] ' scarcely a line of English verse had been quoted for the purpose of critical analysis or discussion.' Unfortunately, Rymer in discussing the heroic poets of England, passes Chaucer over, because in his time the English language was ' not capable of any Heroick character.'

After Dryden, criticism as an art stood still for more than a hundred years, or, indeed, it may more accurately be said to have gone back. This is well illustrated by the Chaucer criticism of the eighteenth century. George Sewell, in 1720, shows acuteness in his remarks, putting his finger on the weak points in contemporary Chaucer criticism, and he gives two concrete

---

[1] The general and most lenient attitude towards Chaucer at this time is well represented by Edward Phillips (1675), who says that Chaucer ' through all the neglect of former ag'd Poets still keeps a name, being by some few admir'd for his real worth, to others not unpleasing for his facetious way, which joyn'd with his old English intertains them with a kind of Drollery.'

[2] Introduction to *Critical Essays of the 17th Century,* ed. Spingarn, vol. i, p. lxv.

illustrations of the statement he makes as to Dryden's debt to Chaucer. George Ogle (1739) also uses concrete illustrations, and attempts some comparison of qualities with the classical poets. Apart from these, which only stand out because other criticisms are so inadequate, there is nothing of real critical worth about Chaucer until we come to the revival in the third quarter of the century, which shows itself so strongly in the love for the literature of the past. Thomas Warton, first in his observations on Spenser (1754 and 1762), and later and more fully in his *History of English Poetry* (1774–78); Gray, in his notes on Chaucerian metre (1760–1), and Tyrwhitt, in his edition of the *Canterbury Tales* (1775), mark a new departure in interpretative, philological and metrical criticism. Warton is followed by Scott, Blake, Coleridge, Hazlitt, and the early nineteenth-century reviewers, but it was to be nearly ninety years before any worthy successor of Tyrwhitt again applied himself to the text of Chaucer.

It is a fact worth noting, that the earliest literary critic, and the earliest philologist in England (in the modern sense of the terms), were alike in their love for Chaucer, and each of them has left as a monument to him, a work which was not even approached in merit for a century after its appearance.

§ 8. THE EVOLUTION OF NEW SENSES.

In addition to the evolution in taste, in critical standard, and critical faculty, we would seem also to have evolved new senses.

An obvious instance of this is the feeling for nature, the development of which is so recent a feature of our literature. Why should this sense, more especially the appreciation of wild scenery, have lain practically dormant until the third quarter of the eighteenth century ? Why should mountains and moors until then have been found ' sad,' ' frightful ' and ' horrid ' ? [1] ' Who *can* like the Highlands ? ' replied Dr. Johnson to an incautious inquiry from a Southerner as to how he had liked the

---

[1] *See* a letter from Mason to Walpole, 1773, Walpole's *Letters,* ed. Cunningham, vol. v, p. 501, *note,* or *Life of John Buncle,* by Thomas Amory, 1756, vol. i, p. 291; ii, p. 97, or Hutchinson's *Excursion to the Lakes,* 1773, pp. 11, 17.

North. An Englishman, describing in 1740 the beautiful road
which runs along the south-eastern shore of Loch Ness, calls the
rugged mountains ' those hideous productions of nature '; [1] the
poet Gray, when crossing Perthshire early in September (1765),
when the heather must have been a blaze of purple, describes
it as ' a weird and dismal heath, fit for an assembly of witches '; [2]
and a little later (1775) we find the citizens of Edinburgh being
urged to plant trees near the town so as to purify the air ' and
dispel those putrid and noxious vapours which are frequently
wafted from the Highlands.' [3] Twenty-three years later Wordsworth and Coleridge were writing the Lyrical Ballads.

A similar problem as regards the evolution of a sense meets
us in respect of the subtle and well-nigh indefinable quality,
which we now call humour.

This faculty, which surely must be distinctively human, for
the animals have it not, and the gods perchance transcend it,[4]
this consciousness of human life in relation to its eternal
environment, this quick recognition of incongruity and contrast
seen in the light of a larger wisdom; this power of inverting the
relative values of things both small and great, because of an
instinct that from some point outside they would be seen to be
neither small nor great, but only deeply significant—this is a
quality which, in its literary expression, is peculiarly English.
Wit we cede to France, and philosophy to Germany, but in
humour we stand supreme.

It is an interesting, although an obviously natural fact that
seriousness and humour constantly go together; it is the most
serious nations in Europe—England and Spain—who have on
the whole been the most humorous. For humour implies
belief, deep feeling, tenderness; and the dissonances of life

[1] *Letters from a Gentleman in the North of Scotland*, London, 1754,
vol. ii, p. 339.

[2] Gray's *Works*, ed. Gosse, vol. iii, p. 214.

[3] Topham's *Letters from Edinburgh*, 1776, pp. 231, 233.

[4] ' A sense of humour is dependent on a condition of partial knowledge.
Complete knowledge or complete ignorance are fatal to it. A Mrs.
Gamp is not humorous to a Betsy Prig, for both are on the same level.
Neither could be humorous to a Power, who knows everything and can be
surprised at nothing and to whom no one thing is more incongruous than
another.'—W. H. Mallock.

stand out more apparent to eyes which have been used 'to look on man's mortality.' [1]

That the quality of humour existed in full measure in fourteenth-century England we know by reading Chaucer's Prologue, but we are forced to ask whether it was less common than now, only to be found here and there among men of genius. If it was as general and as well recognised as it is to-day, by what name was it called? The faculty, it would seem, is of late growth, in the race as in the individual, savages and children possess it very slightly and in a very elementary form. Possibly it is only yet in the germ. One thing is certain, that in Chaucer's time, and for long after, it was not called ' humour,' for it is evident that no glimmering of the modern meaning of that word was known until the very end of the seventeenth century. It is perhaps the most important of a number of words—such as ' wit,' ' fancy,' ' taste '—which have so extended their meaning as to be new creations. These all came into being in their literary sense, as qualities of the mind, during the seventeenth and eighteenth centuries, and brought about practically a new terminology in criticism.

' Humour,' which is literally ' moisture,' was first used in mediæval physiology as a term for one of the chief fluids of the body (blood, phlegm, choler and melancholy),[2] and so by extension in the later sixteenth century in England it came to mean the special singularity of disposition or character which distinguishes a man from his fellows. Shakespeare employs it in this sense, while Ben Jonson's use of it is characteristic.[3]

---

[1] See *The Evolution of Humour*, by S. J. Butcher, in *Harper's Magazine*, May 1890, vol. 80, p. 906: also *The Humorous in Literature*, by J. H. Shorthouse, in *Literary Remains*, 1905, vol. ii, pp. 248–280.

[2] So used by Chaucer, for example, in the *Nonne Preestes Tale*, ll. 4113–4128.

[3] Thus, in the Induction to *Every Man out of his Humour*, Jonson, after explaining the medical notion of a humour, continues—

' It may by metaphor apply itself
Unto the general disposition :
As when some one peculiar quality
Doth so possess a man, that it doth draw
All his effects, his spirits, and his powers,
In their confluctions, all to run one way
This may be truly said to be a Humour.'

Dryden, when expounding humour in his *Essay of Dramatic Poesy* (1668), does not seem conscious of any but the Jonsonian meaning, but there is no doubt that Shaftesbury, in his Essay on *The Freedom of Wit and Humour* (1709), gave it another interpretation, and looked upon it as an alternative to Wit. The fresh extension of meaning, from *humours* meaning singular traits of character, to *humour* a special and subtle quality of mind, seems to have taken place somewhere between these two dates.

Sir William Temple, in his *Essay of Poetry* (1692), certainly has something of the modern signification in his mind when he speaks of ' a vein, natural, perhaps to our country, and which with us is called humour—a word peculiar to our language too, and hard to be expressed in another; nor is it, that I know of, found in any foreign writers, unless it be Molière. Shakespeare was the first that opened this vein upon our stage.'

Congreve, in his letter to Dennis (1695),[1] and the Swiss, Bèat de Muralt, who visited England at the end of the seventeenth century, both speak of it as a universally recognized quality possessed by the English. ' They have what they call *Humour*, and pretend 'tis all their own . . . it seems they mean by it a certain Fruitfulness of Imagination, which for the most part tends to overthrow the Ideas of things, turning Virtue into Ridicule, and making Vice agreeable.' [2]

Whether Temple were responsible for the belief or no, it is certain that not only English but also French writers of the eighteenth century generally spoke of ' humour ' as something specially English, both as regards the quality and the word

---

[1] Letter from Congreve to Dennis, Concerning Humour in Comedy, July 10, 1695 [in] Letters upon several occasions, published by Mr. Dennis, London, 1696, pp. 80–96. Congreve gives the Jonsonian meaning to humour, with a slight indication of the wider extension in the use of the adjective ' humorously.'

[2] Letters describing the character and customs of the English and French, by Bèat de Muralt (Eng. Trans., 1726), p. 28.

denoting it.[1] This claim was disputed by some writers; thus
Swift, while agreeing with Temple that the word was peculiar
to English, points out that the quality is to be found in other
nations, and cites Cervantes in proof of this.[2] Voltaire goes a
step further and maintains that neither the quality nor the word
was the exclusive possession of English literature.[3] Addison,
as early as 1711, points out very clearly [4] the difference between
True and False Humour, and shows that a great deal was
called ' humorous' which did not deserve the name. Indeed there
was much uncertainty in the use of the term throughout the
eighteenth century, and even later. There is no question that
although by some (*e.g.* Addison and Swift) the greatness of
humour was recognized, yet in many minds the meaning of the
word was degraded, and it was connected to some extent with
' buffoonery' or ' facetiousness,' and even with holding up
something or some one as an object of ridicule. This was

---

[1] See *Idée de la Poèsie Anglaise,* by Abbé Yart, Paris, 1749, i, pp. 195
and 214; also *Pensées et fragments inédits de Montesquieu,* Bordeaux,
1901, ii, pp. 8, 14–16; also *Nouvelles Littéraires, &c., de France et
d'Angleterre,* Lettre xxii, 1752, pp. 2, 3; and as late as 1800, Madame de
Staël's *De la Littérature,* chap. xiv, *De la Plaisanterie Anglaise.* For the
whole subject of the development of humour, see an article by Benedetto
Croce in the *Journal of Comparative Literature,* N. York, 1903, i, 222;
also *Études d'histoire littéraire,* par F. Baldensperger, Paris, 1907, pp.
176–227; *Molière et Shakespeare,* par Paul Stapfer, Paris 1887, ch. vi
and vii; and *Critical Essays of the 17th Century,* ed. J. E. Spingarn,
Oxford, 1908, Introduction, pp. ix–lxiii.

[2] *The Intelligencer,* 1698, No. 3.

[3] Letter to the Abbé d'Olivet, Aug. 20, 1761, Œuvres de Voltaire, ed.
Moland, Paris, 1883, xli, 405. ' Ils [les Anglais] ont un terme pour
signifier cette plaisanterie, ce vrai comique, cette gaieté, cette urbanité,
ces saillies qui échappent à un homme sans qu'il s'en doute; et ils rendent
cette idée par le mot humeur, *humour,* qu'ils prononcent *yumor*; et ils
croient qu'ils ont seuls cette humeur; que les autres nations n'ont point
de terme pour exprimer ce caractère d'esprit. Cependant c'est un ancien
mot de notre langue, employé en ce sens dans plusieurs comédies de
Corneille.' A passage illustrating Corneille's use of ' humeur' is quoted
by Génin in *Récreations Philologiques,* i, p. 213–6, (*Suite du Menteur*
(1643), III, i), but the meaning there seems to be ' original,' ' eccentric,'
' something of a character,' rather than our modern sense of the term.
See Corneille's *Lexique ;* ' humeur,' and note. Voltaire's definition of
' esprit' (wit) in his *Dictionnaire philosophique* is worth noting, as it seems
to include certain qualities which we consider essentially characteristic of
' humour.'

[4] *The Spectator,* No. 35, April 10, 1711.

obviously the meaning which Goldsmith had in his mind when he deliberately placed humour below wit; [1] while as late as 1805, Sydney Smith evidently takes it to mean little more than ' agreeable raillery and facetious remark.' [2]

It is not until nearly fifty years later (1851) that we find Thackeray giving a definition of the term that satisfies the modern mind.[3]

There can be no question, then, that although the quality itself is to be found as far back as Chaucer, the people as a whole possessed it only in an elementary and gross form, and were far less susceptible to it than they are to-day. ' Nothing,' says Goethe, ' is more significant of men's character than what they find laughable.' George Eliot, in quoting this remark, observes that it would perhaps have been more accurate to say ' culture ' instead of ' character.' [4] It is most certain that, as men evolve, as they grow in refinement, in quickness and delicacy of perception, in sensitiveness and in sympathy, their conception of what is humorous must grow proportionately.

It is only necessary to stray a little in the by-paths, more especially of sixteenth- and seventeenth-century literature, to realize that in no one quality of mind is the growth of the race more marked and apparent than in this conception. We may briefly illustrate this point by the history of Chaucer criticism. In Chaucer we have a poet whose distinguishing quality of mind is a subtle, shifting, delicate and all-pervading humour, to which full justice has not perhaps even yet been done [5]; yet through all these years of critical remark there is until the eighteenth century no reference to the quality as we know it,

---

[1] ' Wit raises human nature above its level ; humour acts a contrary part and equally depresses it. To expect exalted humour is a contradiction in terms . . when a thing is *humorously* described . . we compare the absurdity of the character represented with our own, and triumph in our own conscious superiority.' *An Enquiry into the Present State of Polite Learning in Europe*, 1759, pp. 155, 156.

[2] *Elementary Sketches of Moral Philosophy*, by Sydney Smith, 1854, Lecture xi, p. 144.

[3] In the opening paragraphs of *The English Humourists of the 18th Century.*

[4] German Wit, Heinrich Heine, *Westminster Review*, 1856.

[5] See the excellent remarks on this by Prof. Saintsbury in the *Cambridge History of English Literature*, vol. ii, 1908, chap. vii.

which he so amply possessed.   There is a certain recognition
among some earlier writers of his ' pleasant vayne and wit,'
and his ' delightsome mirth ' (see p. xcvii above), by which is
probably meant his relish of a good story, his sly sense of fun,
and the general atmosphere of good-humour which pervades
his work, but there is no hint of appreciation of that deeper
and more delicate quality alone deserving the name of
' humour,' which is insight, sympathy and tender seriousness,
all brought into play upon the ever-present sense of the incongruous, and of the inconsistent in character and life.   Of all
this, as far as we can judge, they are unconscious.

The first mention we find of the word ' humour ' as applied
to Chaucer is in some verses by John Gay in 1712, where he
speaks of Prior entertaining the admiring reader with ' Chaucer's
Humour ' ; but we cannot be certain of the exact meaning here
attached to the word, although if we may judge from the coarse
and vulgar comedy which Gay in some sense founded on the
Canterbury pilgrims, what he was most aware of in Chaucer
was facetiousness, jokes and general jollity.   In 1715 John
Hughes clearly employs the word in the older Jonsonian sense
of the predominating characteristic, but it would seem as if
Pope, in 1728, when censuring Addison, was using the word
with some approach to its modern meaning.   So, surely, was
Elizabeth Cooper (1737), when she says that Chaucer ' blended
the acutest Raillery, with the most insinuating Humour.'

It is Thomas Warton who, in 1754, first uses the term in
what we can be quite sure is something near the modern sense ;
moreover he lays considerable emphasis on the fact that Chaucer
was the first English writer to possess it.   After Warton, the
idea began very gradually to creep in that a sense of humour
was one of the qualities of the poet.   Bishop Percy (1765), in
his remarks on Sir Thopas, and Charles Burney (1782), who
speaks of Chaucer's ' wit and humour,' are cases in point.[1]   It
is not, however, until well on in the nineteenth century, not
indeed until Leigh Hunt wrote on it in 1846, that Chaucer's
humour seems to have met with any adequate recognition.

---

[1] It is worth noting that although Gray seems to use the word in its
modern sense in speaking of Lydgate, he does not apply it at all to
Chaucer (see 1760–1, Gray).

§ 9. THE EVOLUTION OF SCHOLARSHIP AND ACCURACY IN LITERARY MATTERS.

The development along this line is here more conspicuous than perhaps anything else. It is so obvious that it is only necessary to give one or two illustrations in point. Consider, for instance, the history of Chaucer biography. The fertility of invention, the touching and unquestioning faith in the printed word, the unhesitating belief of later biographers in all the utterances of their predecessors, and the extraordinary blindness to contradiction and inaccuracy in statements of fact, these are characteristics which undergo little change up to the eighteenth century. Thus we know that Leland was as an antiquary quite justly much revered both by his contemporaries and succeeding generations, and the main body of his work was for full three hundred years accepted as authoritative. Much of his historical and topographical work was certainly most valuable, and proves him to have been painstaking and laborious, and he appears to have set before himself the very highest ideals as to research and accuracy; [1] indeed his name became almost synonymous with a passionate love of truth.[2]

Yet his life of Chaucer, which we have already examined, shows gross ignorance, carelessness and inaccuracy; statements are authoritatively made without any hesitation, which we know now could not have had any foundation in fact.

We can understand that owing to scarcity of books and libraries, and difficulties of access to public records, it was not

---

[1] See Leland's 'New Year's Gift,' in *The Itinerary of John Leland*, ed. L. Toulmin Smith, 1907, vol. i, pp. xxxviii–xli.

[2] Bale refers to this in his 'Kynge Johan' (ed. J. P. Collier, Camden Society 1838, ll. 2163–4), written probably when Leland was insane, when he makes Verity say, opposing a supposed lie of the Romanist, Polydore Virgil,

'Yes! therefore, Leylonde, out of thy slumbre awake,
And wytnesse a trewthe for thyne owne contrayes sake.'

easily within the power even of scholars to verify their facts, and it does not surprise us to find that so careful a critic as Dryden takes on trust all the assertions of earlier biographers, or accepts unquestioningly Chaucer's authorship of the *Plowman's Tale* and even confuses it with the *Vision of Piers Plowman*, until lately thought to be by Langland. What remains a puzzle is the apparent lack of perception of obvious errors and inconsistencies within these narratives themselves. For instance Leland represents Chaucer as highly esteemed by Henry IV and his son (Henry V), and yet, although the generally accepted date for Chaucer's death was 1400, Tyrwhitt is, so far as we know, the first writer to point out that Leland evidently considered Chaucer as living at least 20 years later than he really did. Far from noticing this blunder, succeeding historians only made it more definite, and we find Giles Jacob in 1720, in his *Lives of the English Poets*, stating that Chaucer was Poet Laureate in the reigns of Henry IV and Henry V, and that he died in 1400. The fact that the reigns of these two kings extend from 1399–1422 seems to escape the notice, not only of the writer of these ' Lives,' but also of his readers.

Another point well illustrated here is the slender equipment thought necessary by the best authorities for the editing of a great classic. We know that as late as the eighteenth century men of letters, though as a rule possessed of wide general knowledge and interests, entirely lacked the training and specialization in any one branch of study which to-day seems so essential. They attempted, and carried through single-handed, tasks, such as Gibbon's History and Johnson's Dictionary, which to-day would afford life-long employment to a small army of specialists.

Plenty of courage and a Scottish extraction, although good qualifications in their way, would not to a modern Dean of Christ Church seem sufficient grounds upon which to persuade a man to undertake a critical edition of Chaucer. Yet Dr. Atterbury appears to have urged this task on John Urry mainly for these two reasons. As we know, Dr. Johnson himself seriously contemplated editing Chaucer with full critical

apparatus of notes and linguistic remarks, and although better
equipped than Urry, his qualifications for the task were not
striking. The fact is that critical scholarship and minute
and searching investigation were at this time practically unknown, and therefore were not regarded as necessary. Goldsmith, in addition to his imaginative work, produced with
equal ease and confidence histories of England, of Rome, of
Greece, and of the Earth and Animated Nature; and Johnson,
when writing his ' Lives,' could not be troubled to make many
researches or to do much reading for the purpose,[1] preferring to
trust to his sound common-sense and wide general knowledge.
This lack of thoroughness and scholarly accuracy may be
forgiven in Johnson or Goldsmith, and the more easily when we
realize the general lowness of standard in this respect which is
so marked in the work of the smaller writers and commentators
in connection with Chaucer criticism until the middle of the
nineteenth century. A study of these brings home to us what
strides ordinary scholarship has made during the last hundred
years, and how changed are our ideals and requirements in
this connection. The modernizations of Chaucer in 1841 have
already been cited as a good illustration of this (see p. lix
above); we will add only one more. In 1795 the Rev. William
Lipscomb, a scholar of Corpus Christi, who had carried off a
Chancellor's prize at Oxford, was private tutor and chaplain
to the Duke of Cleveland, and a constant contributor to the
Gentleman's Magazine, published a complete modernization of
the Canterbury Tales; in the preface he states that the Life of
Chaucer he reprints is ' taken from the valuable edition of his
original works published by Mr. Tyrwhitt.' Not only is the ' Life'
which Lipscomb prints taken wholesale from the *Biographia
Britannica* for 1747, but remarks in it are diametrically
opposed in important particulars (as regards language, etc.)

---

[1] For instance, in writing of Congreve, Johnson says, ' Of his plays
I cannot speak distinctly; for since I inspected them many years have
passed, but what remains in my memory is . . .' and a critical account
follows. A nineteenth-century writer, even of the same eminence as
Johnson, would have re-read the plays.

to what Tyrwhitt says in his essay.[1] But this is not all. Lipscomb, who apparently much admired Chaucer, had undertaken to reprint all existing modernizations of the Tales, and to supply omissions by his own renderings. One would therefore not unnaturally assume that before publication he would make himself familiar with the literature of the subject. He does not, however, thus trammel himself. He reprints the versions of Ogle, Betterton, Dryden, Pope, Brooke, Markland, Grosvenor and Boyse, which appear in Ogle's edition of 1741, but he supplies his own version of the Nun's Priest's Tale, for, as he tells us in a naïve Postscript,[2] he did not know, until the book was finished, of the existence of a version by Dryden. Comment is superfluous, except to add that Lipscomb got some excellent reviews.

Our material has been considered from various points of view, and these notes must now end. Each reader will, however, find other aspects from which it may be regarded, and other problems upon which it may possibly throw a ray of light.

The collection itself must in one sense remain unique. Of no other great English poet will it be possible, for a century and a half to come, to collect a continuous record of the critical opinion of his countrymen during five hundred years. Indeed there is only one other European poet,—greater even than Chaucer—the fluctuations of whose fame can be followed during these special centuries, which bridge over the time of transition from the Middle Ages to the Renaissance, and from the Renaissance to the modern world.

Dante and Chaucer,—seer and humanist—could the body of opinion on these two poets throughout the centuries be

---

[1] Tyrwhitt wrote no ' life ' of Chaucer, only an ' abstract of historical passages.'

[2] ' I have barely time here, the Tales being already almost all printed off, to apologize to the Reader for having inserted my own translation of the Nun's Priest's Tale, instead of that of Dryden : but the fact was, I did not know that Dryden's version existed; . . . having never till very lately, strange as it may seem, seen the volume of Dryden's Fables, in which it may be found.' Postscript, vol. i, p. xi.

studied together, it would light up a good deal of literary history. In many ways, as is natural, there is resemblance between their fortunes, although the Englishman never encountered anything like the discredit and even abuse which in the eighteenth century fell to Dante's lot.[1] Now, however, each poet rests secure in his appointed niche in the great ' Hous of Fame,' and the history of their reputation seems but a fulfilment of the half bitter, half triumphant words of Spenser :—

> For deeds doe die, how ever noblie donne,
> And thoughts of men do as themselves decay ;
> But wise wordes, taught in numbers for to runne,
> Recorded by the Muses, live for ay ;
> Ne may with storming showers be washt away,
> Ne bitter-breathing windes with harmfull blast,
> Nor age, nor envie, shall them ever wast.

---

[1] See the remarks on Dante by Lord Chesterfield, who writes to his son that the poet is not worth the pains necessary to understand him ; Goldsmith, who regards him as little better than a barbarian, who owed ' most of his reputation to the obscurity of the times in which he lived ' ; Horace Walpole, who characterizes him as ' extravagant, absurd, disgusting, in short, a Methodist parson in Bedlam ' ; Thomas Warton, who is shocked by his ' disgusting fooleries ' ; and above all Voltaire, who scarce can find words to express his contempt. For all these, and the whole question of Dante criticism in England, see *Dante in English Literature from Chaucer to Cary*, by Dr. Paget Toynbee, 1909.

1

FIVE HUNDRED YEARS OF CHAUCER CRITICISM AND ALLUSION.

[THE following entries, pp. 1–14 (with the exception of 1376–9, 1390, Gower, and
c. 1387 Usk), are references to Geoffrey Chaucer contained in documents in the Public
Record Office, the City of London Town-Clerk's Office, Guildhall, etc., as compiled and
edited by Mr. R. E. G. Kirk, in *Life-Records of Chaucer*, part iv, Chaucer soc. 1900; the
numbers which follow, within round brackets, refer to pages in Mr. Kirk's book. Only
direct references to Geoffrey Chaucer are noted. The full titles of the works of the three
authorities who have previously printed some of these records (given below within round
brackets as Rymer, Godwin, and Nicolas), are respectively, *Foedera*, etc., by Thomas
Rymer, 20 vols., 1704–32; *The Life of Geoffrey Chaucer*, by William Godwin, 2 vols., 1803;
and *The Life of Chaucer*, by Sir Nicholas Harris Nicolas, 1845, prefixed to Chaucer's poetical
works, Aldine edn. of British poets, vol. 47.]

1357, April to Dec. *Payments to and for Geoffrey Chaucer, then in the
household of the Duchess of Clarence,* Addit. MS. 18,632; ff. 2, 101,
fly leaves (Kirk, 152–3. See also *Life-Records of Chaucer,* III, ed
E. A. Bond, pp. 105–13, and *New Facts in the Life of Chaucer,* by
E. A. Bond, in the *Fortnightly Review,* Aug. 15, 1866, No. xxxi).

1359, Nov. 3 to Nov. 7, 1360. *Account of William de Farle, Keeper
of the Wardrobe of the King's Household, containing the entry of
Edward III.'s contribution towards the ransom of Chaucer after he
was taken prisoner by the French.* Exchequer Q. R. Wardrobe and
Household Accounts, $\frac{393}{11}$ ff. 69, 70 (Kirk, 153–5).

1360 [Oct. 9 to 30?]. *A payment to Chaucer, by order of Lionel, earl
of Ulster, of nine shillings for bearing letters to England from
Calais and returning.* Exchequer Accounts $\frac{314}{?}$.

> [This entry, only discovered by M. Delachenal in 1909 (*Histoire de Charles V.*,
> Paris, 1909, vol. ii, p. 241, *n.* 1), and therefore not in Kirk's *Life-Records*, occurs in an
> account of the Earl of Ulster's expenses at Calais at the time of the treaty of peace,
> and runs :]

> Expense domini Comitis Vltonie apud Caleys existentis
> ibidem ad tractatum et redeundo in Angliam, facte per manus
> Andree de Budeston, anno xxxiiij^{to} . . .
>
> Datum Galfrido Chaucer per preceptum domini eundo cum
> literis in Angliam iij roiales precio ixs.

> [See *A new Chaucer Item,* by O. F. Emerson in *Modern Language Notes,* Jan.,
> 1911, vol. xxvi, pp. 19–21; and, for a more correct statement and a print of the
> document, *The new Chaucer Item,* by S. Moore, in *Modern Language Notes,* March,
> 1912, vol. xxvii, pp. 79–81.]

1367, June 20. *The King grants an annuity of 20 marks to Geoffrey
Chaucer, his beloved yeoman.* Patent Roll, 41 Edw. III., p. 1, m.
13 (Kirk, 160. Rymer, vol. vi, p. 567. Godwin, App. v).

" **Nov. 6.** *The first half-yearly payment of Geoffrey Chaucer's annuity.* Issue Roll, Mich.,[2] 42 Edw. III., m. 9 (Kirk, 160, and
Nicolas, note B).

CHAUCER CRITICISM.

[This annuity from the King, of 20 marks yearly, continues to be paid, half-yearly, with some irregularities, down to February 1389. See *Life Records*, ed. Kirk, pp. xix, 161, 170, 175, 179-82, 188, 192-4, 196, 198, 200, 213, 216, 221, 223, 224, 228, 231, 233-5, 237-8, 240, 242, 245-6, 249, 251, 255, 258, 266, 271-4.]

[1368, Dec.]   *Schedule of names of the Household of Edward III., for whom Robes for Christmas were to be provided, including . . . Geoffrey Chaucer among the Esquires.* Exchequer Q. R. Wardrobe and Household Accounts, $\frac{396}{10}$ (Kirk, 162, 165. For date, see p. 162, note 2).

1369, June 27.   *Counter-roll of the Comptroller of the King's Household, furnishing, among other matters, the names of the members of the Household who received money for their Summer Robes. Chaucer is among the " scutiferi."* Exchequer Q. R. Wardrobe and Household Accounts, $\frac{396}{11}$ (Kirk, 171).

   ,,   **Sept. 1.**   *Writ of Privy Seal to Henry de Snayth, clerk, Keeper of the Wardrobe, directing him to issue divers lengths of black cloth to the members of the King's Household for their Mourning at the funeral of Queen Philippa. Chaucer receives 3 ells of black cloth, short.* Exchequer Q. R. Wardrobe and Household Accounts, $\frac{396}{2}$ (Kirk, 172-4).

   ,,   *Extract from the enrolled Account of Henry de Wakefield, Keeper of the Wardrobe of the King's Household; containing the advances of money made—at the commencement of the war in France—to certain members of the Household, including Chaucer, on account of their wages and expenses at various times in the year 43 Edw. III.* Exchequer L. T. R. Enrolled Accounts, Wardrobe, Roll 4, m. 21 (Kirk, 175-6).

1370, June 20.   *Chaucer, going to parts beyond the seas, has letters of protection till Michaelmas.* Patent Roll, 44 Edw. III., p. 2, m. 20 (Kirk, 180. Godwin, App. vii).

1372, Nov. 12.   *Commission appointing James Provan, John de Mari, and Geoffrey Chaucer, as envoys to treat with the Duke, Citizens, and Merchants of Genoa, for the purpose of choosing some port in England where the Genoese may form a commercial establishment.* French Roll, 46 Edw. III., m. 8 (Kirk, 181-2. Rymer, vol. vi, p. 755. Godwin, App. viii).

   ,,   **Dec. 1.**   *Payment to Chaucer of £66 13s. 4d. for his expenses in his mission to foreign parts on the King's secret affairs.* Issue Roll, Mich., 47 Edw. III., m. 13 (Kirk, 182-3. Nicolas, note D).

1373, May 23.   *Chaucer's account of receipts and expenses for his journeys to Genoa and Florence, from Dec. 1, 1372, to May 23, 1373.* Exchequer L. T. R. Foreign Accounts, 47 Edw. III., forula C (Kirk, 183-4. *See also* F. J. Mather in *The Nation*, Oct. 8, 1896, p. 267).

   ,,   **June 27.**   *Account of the Keeper of the Wardrobe of the King's Household, from June 27, 1371, to June 27, 1373, containing particulars of the Winter and Summer Robes delivered to members of the Household, including Chaucer, as a " scutifer" of the King's Chamber.* Exchequer Q. R. Household and Wardrobe Accounts, $\frac{14}{1}$ (Kirk, 185-6).

1373, Sept. 29. *Extract from the Account of the Sheriffs of London and Middlesex, showing Chaucer's discharge from the £10 received by him at the commencement of the war.* Pipe Roll, 47 Edw. III. (Kirk, 186–7).

„ **Nov. 11.** *Writ to the Treasurer, Barons, and Chamberlains of the Exchequer to pay Chaucer for his journeys to Genoa and Florence.* Exchequer Q. R. Memoranda Roll, Mich., 48 Edw. III., *Brevia*, m. 14 (Kirk, 187–8).

1374, Jan. 20. *Enrolment of a Writ of Privy Seal directed to the Treasurer and Barons of the Exchequer, by which the repayment of the sums advanced by the King to Chaucer and others is remitted* [see Entry 2 under 1369]. Exchequer Q. R. Memoranda Roll 48 Edw. III., *Brevia*, Hilary, m. 3 (Kirk, 188–9).

1374, Feb. 4. *Payment to Geoffrey Chaucer, the King's Esquire, of £25 6s. 8d., for his wages and expenses in going to Genoa and Florence.* Issue Roll, Mich., 48 Edw. III., m. 20 (Kirk, 189. Nicolas, note E).

„ **April 23.** *King Edward III. grants Chaucer a pitcher of wine daily, to be received in the port of London at the hands of the King's Butler.* Patent Roll, 48 Edw. III., part 1, m. 20 (Kirk, 189, 190. Rymer, vol. vii, p. 35. Godwin, App. ix).

„ **May 10.** *Chaucer obtains a lease from the Mayor, Aldermen, and Commonalty of the City of London of all the "mansion" above the gate of Aldgate.* City of London Records, Letter Book G, fol. 321 (Kirk, 190, 191. For a translation of this document see H. T. Riley's *Memorials of London and London Life*, ed. 1868, pp. 377–8; also App. to *Trial Forewords to Parallel text edition of Chaucer's minor poems*, by F. J. Furnivall, Chaucer Soc., 1871, p. i).

„ **June 8.** *Chaucer is appointed Comptroller of the Custom and Subsidy of Wools, Hides, and Wool-fells in the Port of London.* Patent Roll, 48 Edw. III., p. 1, m. 7 (Kirk, 191. Rymer, vol. vii, p. 38. Godwin, App. x).

„ **June 8 and 12.** *Chaucer is appointed Comptroller of the Custom and Subsidy of Wools, etc., and also Comptroller of the Petty Customs of Wines, etc., in the Port of London; and he appears in the Court of Exchequer to take his oath.* Exchequer Q. R. Memoranda Roll, Trin., 48 Edw. III., *Recorda*, m. 1 d (Kirk, 191–2).

„ **June 13.** *Grant by John of Gaunt, Duke of Lancaster, to Geoffrey Chaucer of £10 a year for life, for his own and his wife's services.* Duchy of Lancaster Registers, No. 13, fol. 90 (Kirk, 192).

> [There are a few more entries in the Duchy of Lancaster Registers of the payment of this annuity, but few of the Duke's accounts have been preserved, so all the payments cannot be traced. *See* Kirk, pp. xxiv, 193, 212, 223, 226.]

„ **July 6.** *Five half-yearly payments of Phillipa Chaucer's annuity paid all at once to Chaucer himself, together with two half-yearly payments of his own annuity.* Issue Roll, Easter, 48 Edw. III., m. 12 (Kirk, 192–3).

[This is the first payment made to Chaucer of his wife's annuity of 10 marks for life, granted her on Sept. 12, 1366, by Edward III., as "domicella" of the Queen's Chamber, and paid, with some irregularities, from June 1367, to June 1387; *see* Kirk, pp. xix, 158. Other payments to Chaucer of his wife's annuity are on Jan. 24, Oct. 20, 1375; May 31, Nov. 27, 1376; Feb. 1, May 24, 1381; Nov. 11, 1382; April 30, Oct. 18, 1384; April 24, Nov. 3, 1385; Oct. 20, 1386; and June 18, 1387. Kirk, pp. 192-3, 196, 198-9, 200, 229, 231, 240-1, 246-7, 249, 251-2, 255-6, 266, 271.]

1375, July 26. *Accounts of John de Bernes and Nicholas de Brembre, Collectors of Customs and Subsidies, under the survey of Chaucer, from Feb.* 26, 1374, *to July* 26, 1375. Exchequer, L. T. R., Enrolled Accounts, Customs, Roll 8, m. 62 (Kirk, 194-5).

[Similar entries occur on Nov. 15, 1375, Oct. 15, 1376, Aug. 24, 1377, Sept. 29, 1378, 79, 80, 81, 82, 83, 84, 85, 86, and Jan. 20, 1387, when Chaucer was succeeded in the Comptrollership of the Customs by Adam Yerdeley. Kirk, pp. 197, 199, 211, 220, 222, 228, 233-4, 238, 243, 248. 253, 263, 268.

In these same documents payments are made to Chaucer, on Aug. 24, 1377, of £8 11s. 4d. (his wages as Controller being £10 a year), on Sept. 29, 1378, of £10 19s. 6d., on Sept. 29, 1379, 80, 81, 82, 83, 84, 86, of £10.]

1375, Nov. 8. *Chaucer, as "Scutifer Regis," gets a grant of the custody of the lands and person of Edmund Staplegate, of Kent, aged 18, who afterwards paid Chaucer £104 for his wardship and marriage.* Patent Roll, 49 Edw. III., p. 2, m. 8 (Kirk, 196-7. Godwin, App. xi).

„ **Dec. 28.** *Grant to Chaucer of the wardship of the heir of John Solys, a tenant of the heir of Thomas de Ponynges, tenant of the King in chief.* Patent Roll, 49 Edw. III., p. 2, m. 4 (Kirk, 198).

1376, July 12. *Chaucer obtains a grant of the price of wool forfeited by John Kent, of London, who had exported it to Dordrecht without paying custom.* Patent Roll, 50 Edw. III., p. 1, m. 5 (Kirk, 199. Godwin, App. xii).

„ **Dec. 23.** *Payment to Chaucer, going on the King's secret affairs in the company of Sir John de Burlee, of £6 13s. 4d.* Issue Roll, Mich., 51 Edw. III., m. 25 (Kirk, 201. Nicolas, note G).

1376-9. Gower, John. *Mirour de l'omme,* Cambr. univ. lib., MS. Add. 3035, ll. 5249-60. (Works of John Gower, ed. G. C. Macaulay, 1899-1902, vol. i, p. 64.)

[Somnolent, one of the Children of Sloth, is bored by church-going; he does not think of his prayers.]

.   .   .   ainz bass la teste
Mettra tout seuf sur l'eschamelle,
Et dort, et songe en sa cervelle
Qu'il est au bout de la tonelle,
U qu'il oït chanter la geste
De Troylus et de la belle
Creseide, et ensi se concelle
A dieu d'y faire sa requeste.

[There is considerable doubt as to whether this reference is to Chaucer's *Troilus* or not. For evidence that it is, see J. S. P. Tatlock in *Modern Philology*, 1903, vol. i, pp. 317-24, also his *Development and Chronology of Chaucer's Works*, Chaucer Soc. 1907, particularly pp. 15-34, 220-5.

On the other hand, neither Dr. Macaulay, the editor of Gower, nor many other Chaucer students, accept Prof. Tatlock's identification of Gower's *geste* with Chaucer's poem. It upsets the generally received scheme of Chaucer's chronology, and is moreover contradicted by Prof. J. L. Lowes's admirable suggestion that the A. in st. 25, bk. i of the *Troilus*—'Right as our firste letter is now an A,' is Anne of Bohemia, crowned Queen of England on Jan. 14, 1382, about whom Chaucer had written in the *Parliament of Foules;* see Publications of the Modern Language Association, 1908, vol. xxiii, no. xiii, pp. 285–306.]

1377, Feb. 12.   *Letters of Protection are granted to Chaucer, to last till Sept. 29, he being about to go abroad in the King's service.*   French Roll, 51 Edw. III., m. 7 Kirk, 201. Godwin, App. xiii).

1377, Feb. 17.   *Payments to Sir Thomas Percy and Geoffrey Chaucer, sent to Flanders on the King's secret affairs, on account of their expenses.*   Issue Roll, Mich., 51 Edw. III., m. 29 (Kirk, 201–2. Nicolas, note H).

„   **Feb. 17, June 26.**   *Chaucer's enrolled Account for his two journeys to Paris, Montreuil, and elsewhere.*   Exchequer, L. T. R., Foreign Accounts, 3 Ric. II., forula D, dorse (Kirk, 202–3).

[*See* entry under Froissart, 1410, p. 20 below.]

„   **April 11.**   *The King gives Chaucer a reward for his services in several voyages abroad.*   Issue Roll, Easter, 51 Edw. III., m. 2 (Kirk, 205. Nicolas, note I).

„   **April 28.**   *Letters of Protection are again granted to Chaucer, to last till Aug. 1, he being about to go abroad in the King's service.*   French Roll, 51 Edw. III., m. 5 (Kirk, 205. Godwin, App. xiv).

„   **April 30.**   *Payment on account to Chaucer, sent to France on the King's secret affairs.*   Issue Roll, Easter, 51 Edw. III., m. 6 (Kirk, 205–6. Nicolas, note I).

„   **April.**   *The Earl of Salisbury and others, including Chaucer, are sent on an embassy to France.*   John Stowe's *Annales of England,* 1592, p. 431 [*q. v.* below, p. 136].

„   **June 22.**   *The new King grants Chaucer the office of Controller of the Customs.*   Patent Roll, 1 Ric. II., p. 1, m. 27 (Kirk, 206).

„   **July 9.**   *Petition of Edmund . . . Staplegate . . . in which he says that he had paid Chaucer (Geffray Chausyer) for his wardship and marriage* £104. Close Roll, 1 Ric. II., m. 45 (Kirk, 207–8. Godwin, App. xv).

„   **July 26.**   *Extracts from the Account of Richard de Beverlee, showing the payments to Chaucer for his robes as "scutifer Regis," and for his wine pension, from Nov. 25, 1376, to this date.*   Exchequer Q. R. Wardrobe and Household Accounts, $\frac{3.9.2}{9}$ (Kirk, 209–10).

„   **Sept 29—Sept. 29, 1378.**   *Chaucer is charged with a balance of* 18s. 9d. *for wages in the King's Household overpaid.*   Pipe Roll, 1 Ric. II. (Kirk, 212–3).

1378, Mar. 9.   *Chaucer becomes surety for Sir William Beauchamp.*   Fine Roll, 1 Ric. II., p. 2, m. 11 (Kirk, 213).

„   **Mar. 23.**   *The King confirms his grandfather's grant to Chaucer of an annuity of 20 marks, because he has retained him in his service; with a reference to a later grant to John Scalby on May* 1, 1388. Patent Roll, 1 Ric. II., p. 5, m. 27 (Kirk, 213).

1378, April 18. *Chaucer has a grant under the Privy Seal of 20 marks a year in lieu of his daily pitcher of wine.* Warrants (Chancery), Series I, Writs of Privy Seal, 1 Ric. II., file 456, No. 339 (Kirk, 214. Nicolas, note K).

„ **April 18.** *Enrolment of the letters patent of the same grant; with a reference to a later grant to John Scalby on May 1, 1388.* Patent Roll, 1 Ric. II., p. 5, m. 6 (Kirk, 215).

„ **May 10.** *Letters of Protection for Chaucer, going abroad on the King's service.* French Roll, 1 Ric. II., p. 2, m. 6 (Kirk, 215).

„ **May 21.** *Chaucer has the King's letters of attorney, for John Gower and Richard Forester, during his absence abroad.* French Roll, 1 Ric. II., p. 2, m. 6 (Kirk, 216. Nicolas, note M).

„ **May 28.** *Payments to John of Gaunt for his army serving in the King's wars; and to Sir Edward de Berkeley and Geoffrey Chaucer, sent to the Lord of Milan and [Sir] John Hawkwood, in Lombardy, for assistance in the said wars.* Issue Roll, Easter, 1 Ric. II., m. 14, 16 (Kirk, 217).

„ **Sept. 19.** *Chaucer's enrolled Account for his journey to Lombardy, from May 28 to this date.* Exchequer L. T. R., Foreign Accounts, 3 Ric. II., forula D., dorse (Kirk, 218–9).

„ **Sept. 29—Sept. 29, 1379.** *The Sheriffs of London pay the 18s. 9d. charged on Chaucer (see under Sept. 29, 1377); and Chaucer is charged with moneys advanced to him for his journeys to Flanders and France on the King's affairs.* Pipe Roll, 2 Ric. II. (Kirk, 219).

1380, Feb. 26. *Two Writs to the Exchequer for payment of Chaucer's expenses on his journeys to France and Italy (see under Sept. 19, 1380).* Exchequer Q. R. Memoranda Roll, Easter, 3 Ric. II., m. 9 (Kirk, 338).

„ **May 1.** *Deed of Release by Cecily Chaumpaigne to Geoffrey Chaucer in respect of her "raptus."* Close Roll, 3 Ric. II., m. 9 d. (Kirk, 225–6).

„ **June 30 and July 2.** *Deeds of Release by Richard Goodchild and John Grove to Chaucer, and by Cecily Chaumpaigne to them, with a bond by John Grove to her for £10.* City of London Records, Pleas and Memoranda, A. 23, m. 5 d. (Kirk, 226–7).

1381, March 6. *Gift of £22 by the King to Chaucer, as compensation for his wages and expenses in going to France in the time of Edward III. to treat of a peace, and again to negotiate a marriage between Richard II. and a French Princess.* Issue Roll, Mich., 4 Ric. II., m. 21 (Kirk, 230. Nicolas, note R).

[*See also* entries under Feb. 17, 1377, and Sept. 29, 1378—Sept. 29, 1379. *See* below, 1410, for a reference to this in Froissart.]

„ **June 19.** *Release by Geoffrey Chaucer, son of John Chaucer, Vintner, of London, to Henry Herbury, of a tenement in St. Martin's in the Vintry, extending from Thames Street to the Water of Walbrook, which had belonged to his father.* Husting Roll, 110. No. 8 (Kirk, 232–3).

1381, Nov. 28.   *Payment to Brembre and Philippot of £20 each, and to Chaucer of 10 marks, for their diligence in collecting the Customs and Subsidies.*   Issue Roll, Mich., 5 Ric. II., m. 10 (Kirk, 235).

[See *Notes and Queries*, 3 S., 1865, viii, p. 367. Similar rewards are made on Dec. 10, 1382; Feb. 11, Dec 9, 1384; Dec. 11, 1385; Nov. 28, 1386. Kirk, pp. 241, 245, 250, 256, 267. In the entry on the Issue Roll for Dec. 9, 1384 (Kirk, p. 250), the name is given as PHilippo CHAUCEr, but this is an evident error for *Galfrido;* see W D. Selby in the *Athenæum*, April 14, 1888, p. 468.]

1382, April 20.   *Grant to Chaucer of the office of Controller of the Petty Custom in the Port of London, during the King's pleasure.*   Patent Roll, 5 Ric. II., p. 2, m. 21; and Chancery Warrants, series I, file 1565 (Kirk, 236).

„   **May 8.**   *Grant to Chaucer of the office of Controller of the Petty Custom in the Port of London, with "the other part" of the "Coket" seal.*   Patent Roll, 5 Ric. II., p. 2, m. 15 (Kirk, 237. Godwin. App. xvii).

„   **Sept. 29.**   *Account of John Organ and Walter Sibill, Collectors of [Petty] Customs, under the survey of John Hyde and Geoffrey Chaucer, successively Comptrollers, for the year preceding.*   Enrolled Accounts, Customs, Roll 14, m. 39 (Kirk, 239).

[Similar entries occur of the Petty Customs Accounts under the survey of Chaucer, on Sept. 29—Dec. 5, 1382, Dec. 5, 1382, Sept. 29, 1383, July 3, 1384, Sept. 29, 1385, Sept. 29, 1386 (when a house was hired for collecting and depositing the Customs), and finally under the survey of Chaucer and his successor, Henry Gysores, on March 15, 1387. Kirk, pp. 239, 241, 244, 247, 254, 263, 269. Chaucer was superseded in the office of Controller of Petty Customs (and also of the Customs) in Dec. 1386.]

1384, Nov. 25.   *Licence to Chaucer to be absent from his office of Controller of Customs for one month, provided he appoint a sufficient deputy.*   Close Roll, 8 Ric. II., m. 31 (Kirk, 250. Godwin, App. xviii, who gives it incorrectly as m. 30).

[1385, Feb.]   *Petition of Chaucer to the King for leave to appoint a permanent deputy at the Wool-quay of London; with a note of the King's assent.*   Warrants, Chancery, series I, file 1401 (Kirk, 251).

[*See* W. D. Selby in the *Athenæum*, Jan. 28, 1888, p. 116.]

1385, Feb. 17.   *Licence to Chaucer to appoint a deputy in his office of Controller, as long as he holds it.*   Patent Roll, 8 Ric. II., p. 2, m. 31 (Kirk, 251. Godwin, App. xix).

„   **Oct. 12.**   *Association of Chaucer with the Warden of the Cinque Ports and others as one of the Justices of the Peace for the County of Kent.*   Patent Roll, 9 Ric. II., p. 1, m. 30 d (Kirk, 254).

1386, June 28.   *Commission of the Peace to Simon de Burley, Warden of the Cinque Ports, and others, including Geoffrey Chaucer, for the County of Kent.*   Patent Roll, 10 Ric. II., p. 1, m. 47 d (Kirk, 259–61).

„   **Aug. 8.**   *Writ to the Sheriff of Kent for the election of two Knights of the Shire, and of Citizens and Burgesses of the Cities and Boroughs, to attend Parliament on 1st October, for the consideration of important matters concerning the defence of the Kingdom and of* *the Church of England; with the Return of Geoffrey Chaucer as one of the Knights.* Writs and Returns of Members of Parliament, Chancery, 10 Ric. II., (Kirk, 261–2).

1386, Oct. 5. *Lease to Richard Forster of the dwelling above Aldgate.* City of London Records, Letter Book H, fol. 204 b (Kirk, 264).

[There is no reference to Chaucer or his previous lease in this document, which was discovered by Prof. J. W. Hales; see *Academy*, Dec. 6, 1879, p. 410, and his *Folia Litteraria*, 1893, p. 87.]

„ **Oct. 15.** *Testimony given by Geoffrey Chaucer, Esquire, in the Court of Chivalry, in the dispute as to the right to bear certain arms between Sir Richard le Scrope and Sir Robert Grosvenor, before Sir John de Derwentwater, in the Refectory of Westminster Abbey.* Chancery Miscellaneous Rolls, ed. Nicolas, bundle 10, no. 2 (Kirk, 264. Godwin, App. i. Nicolas, pp. 29–31).

„ **Nov. 28.** *Precept [to the Sheriff of Kent] for payment of the expenses of Chaucer and his colleague as Knights of the Shire in Parliament, viz. £24 9s. for 61 days.* Close Roll, 10 Ric. II., m. 16 d (Kirk, 267).

„ **Dec. 4 and 14.** *Appointments of successors to Chaucer in the Controllership of the Customs and Petty Customs.* Patent Roll, 10 Ric. II., p. 1, m. 10 and 4 (Kirk, 268).

[*c.* 1387.] **Usk,** Thomas. *The Testament of Love,* bk. iii, ch. iv. No MS. copy known. First printed in Chaucer's works, ed. W. Thynne, 1532, bk. iii, fol. ccclix *b.* (Chaucerian and other pieces, ed. W. W. Skeat, 1897, p. 123, ll. 248 *et seq.*; also The Development and Chronology of Chaucer's Works, by John S. P. Tatlock, Chaucer Soc., 1907, pp. 21–3.)

(Q*u*od L*o*ue) I shall tel the this lesson to lerne / myne owne trewe seruaunt / the noble philosophical poete / in Englissh whiche evermore him besyeth and trauayleth right sore my name to encrease / . . . . trewly his better ne his pere in schole of my rules coude I neuer fynde : He (q*u*od she), in a treatise t*ha*t he made of my seruant Troylus / hath this mater touched / and at the ful this questyon assoyled. Certaynly. his noble sayinges can I not amende : In goodnes of gentyl manlyche speche / without any maner of nycite of storieres ymagynacion in wytte and in good reason of sentence he passeth al other makers. In the boke of Troylus / the answere to thy questyon mayste thou lerne.

[For the prose paraphrase by Usk of the House of Fame, ll. 269–359, see Chaucerian and other pieces, ed. W. W. Skeat, Oxford, 1897, pp. xxvi–vii, 54, 55.]

1387, May 16. *Commission to William Rikhill, Geoffrey Chaucer, and others, to inquire as to the abduction of Isabella, daughter and heir of William atte Halle, out of the custody of Thomas Kershill, at Chislehurst, Kent.* Patent Roll, 10 Ric. II., p. 2, m. 2 d (Kirk, 270).

APPOINTMENT OF CHAUCER AS CLERK OF THE WORKS AT WESTMINSTER PALACE

1389, July 12. *Appointment of Chaucer as Clerk of the Works at Westminster Palace, the Tower of London, and elsewhere, during his good behaviour; with power to impress workmen, to purvey materials and carriage, to pursue absconding workmen, to arrest contrary people, to make inquisition as to materials embezzled, and to sell the branches and bark of trees felled for timber; his wages being 2s. a day.* Patent Roll, 13 Ric. II., p. 1, m. 31 (Kirk, 274–6). Godwin, App. xxi).

1389, July 12. *Account of Roger Elmham, Clerk of the Works, to this date, when he gave up the office to Chaucer as his successor, who is charged with the " dead stock " belonging to it.* Foreign Accounts, 11 Ric. II., forula K (Kirk, 276–7).

[„   **c. July 12.**] *Warrant by Chaucer, as Clerk of the Works, to the Lord Chancellor, for the issue of commissions to Hugh Swayn, Thomas Segham, and Peter Cook to purvey materials and press workmen for the King's Works.* Public Record Office Museum (Kirk, 277–8).

[See also *Athenæum*, Jan. 28, 1888, p. 116.]

„   **July 14.** *Appointment of Hugh Swayne, as Purveyor of the King's Works at Westminster Palace, Shene, Kennington, and other places, on the nomination of Chaucer.* Patent Roll, 13 Ric. II., p. 1, m. 29 (Kirk, 278).

„   **July 14 and 22.** *Two payments to Chaucer, as Clerk of the Works, for expenses at Westminster, the Tower, and elsewhere.* Issue Roll, Easter, 12 Ric. II., m. 13.

[Chaucer held the office of Clerk of the Works from July 12, 1389, to June 17, 1391. These payments continue at intervals, 25 in all, on the following dates— Oct. 7, Nov. 23, Dec. 1, 14, 24, 1389; Mar. 3, 4, June 4, 15, 17, 25, July 9, 19, Oct. 28, Dec. 6, 7, 1390; Feb. 23, Mar. 20, April 20, Dec. 16, 1391; Mar. 4, July 13, 1392, on which last-named date a final payment of arrears due as Clerk of the Works was made to Chaucer by the King.] (Kirk, 278–80, 286–7, 289–90, 297, 314–5, also Introd. pp. xxxvi–xxxix, xlii–xliv.)

„   **Oct. 12.** *Appointments of Peter Cook at Eltham, Thomas Segham at Berkhampstead, and William Suthwerk at the Tower, as Purveyors to the Works under Chaucer, at his instance.* (See above, under [c. July 12].) Patent Roll, 13 Ric. II., p. 1, m. 8 (Kirk, 281–2).

„   **Nov. 10.** *Indenture between Roger Elmham, late Clerk of the Works, and Chaucer, as to the delivery of "dead store" to the latter.* Exchequer Accounts, etc., Works, ⁴⁴₃², No. 2. A file of parchment documents, subsidiary to the Accounts of Roger Elmham, Clerk of the Works, 11–13 Ric. II. Among them is the above Indenture, (Kirk, 282–3).

1390, March 12. *Commission to Sir Richard Stury and others, including Chaucer, to survey the walls, ditches, sewers, bridges, etc., on the coast of the Thames, between Greenwich and Woolwich, etc.* . . . . Originalia Roll, 13 Ric. II., m. 30 (Kirk, 282–3).

„   **April 19.** *Mandate to the Exchequer to allow to Chaucer, in his account, the wages of Hugh Swayn, Purveyor for the King's Works.* Exchequer Q. R. Memoranda Roll, Hilary, 14 Ric. II., *Brevia* roll 21 (Kirk, 285).

1390, July 1. *Mandate to the Exchequer to allow Chaucer his costs for the scaffolds made for the King and Queen at the jousts in Smithfield, in May last.* Exchequer Q. R. Memoranda Roll, Hilary, 14 Ric. II., *Brevia,* roll 19 d (Kirk, 287).

[Another writ on this subject was dated Oct. 4th; *see* Kirk, pp. 305, 311.]

„ **July 12.** *Appointment of Chaucer to repair St. George's Chapel, Windsor, and to take masons, carpenters, and other workmen wherever found, except in Church lands, for that purpose, for the term of three years; and of William Hannay, Controller of the Works at Westminster, to counter-roll Chaucer's expenses.* Patent Roll, 14 Ric. II., p. 1, m. 33 (Kirk, 287–9. Godwin, App. xxii).

„ **Oct. 15.** *Commission to certain Justices to inquire what felons assaulted and robbed Geoffrey Chaucer, at Hatcham, of a horse worth £10, goods worth 100s., and £20 6s. 8d. in money, and by whose procurement.* Patent Roll, 14 Ric. II., p. 1, m. 17 d (**Kirk,** 339).

„ **Oct. 18.** *Mandate to the Exchequer to allow to Chaucer, in his account, the arrears due to Henry de Yeveley on his grant of 12d a day from 7th March,* 1378, *"during the King's Works."* Exchequer Q. R. Memoranda Roll, Hilary, 14 Ric. II., *Brevia,* roll 22 (Kirk, 289).

[1390.] **Gower,** John. *Confessio Amantis* [first version]. Leave-taking of Venus. Lib. octavus, ll. 2941–57. (Works of John Gower, ed. G. C. Macaulay, 1899–1902, vol. iii, 1901, p. 466; for date and MSS. *see* introd., vol. ii).

> And gret wel Chaucer whan ye mete,
> As mi disciple and mi poete :
> For in the floures of his youthe
> In sondri wise, as he wel couthe,
> Of Ditees and of Songes glade,
> The whiche he for mi sake made,
> The lond fulfild is oueral :
> Whereof to him in special
> Aboue alle othre I am most holde
> For thi now in hise daies olde
> Thow schalt him telle this message,
> That he vpon his latere age,
> To sette an ende of alle his werk
> As he which is myn owne clerk,
> Do make his testament of loue,
> As thou hast do thi schrifte aboue
> So that mi Court it mai recorde.

[This passage does not occur in any later versions of the Confessio. For the whole literature on the subject of the supposed quarrel between Gower and Chaucer, see *Chaucer, a bibliographical manual*, by E. P. Hammond, N. York, 1908, pp. 278–9.
It is interesting to know that the 'Confessio' was translated into Portuguese, soon

after it was written, by Robert Payn, Canon of Lisbon Cathedral, and then into Spanish (Castilian) prose by 'Juan de Cuenca, natural de Huete,' in 1400, whose version is MS. g ii 19, in the Library of the Escorial, Madrid.   The Chaucer greeting (Gower's Works, iii, 466 *n*, bk. viii, ll. 2941-56 ff.) runs thus : "Saluda de mi parte a caucer, mi disciplo e mi poeta ; quando con el topares, el qual por mi en la su mancibia fiso toda su diligencia para componer y escreuir desyres e cantares de diversas maneras de los quales toda la tierra es llena ; por la qual cosa en especial le soy mucho tenido mas que a ninguno de los otros. Por ende dile que le enbio desir que tal esta en su postrimera hedad, por dar fyn a todas sus obras, se travaje de faser su testamento de amor, asi como tu has fecho agora en tu confision."— *Gower's Works*, ed. Macaulay, ii, clxvii-viii. As the Queen of Portugal was Henry IV's sister, the presence of Robert Payn and other Englishmen in Portugal is easily understood. *See* History . . . . of Henry IV by J. H. Wylie, vol. ii, 1894, p. 329 *et seq.*]

1390–1. *Chaucer is appointed Sub-Forester of the Forest of North Petherton, by the Earl of March* (Kirk, 291). *History and Antiquities of the County of Somerset*, 1791, by John Collinson, vol. iii, pp. 54–74. *See also* W. D. Selby in the *Athenæum*, Nov. 20, 1886, pp. 672–3, also *Life Records of Chaucer*, III, pp. 117–23.

[Chaucer was re-appointed to this post in 21 Ric. II. [1397–8] by Alianor, Countess of March ; *see* the authorities as above.]

1391, Jan. 6. *Writ discharging Chaucer, Clerk of the King's Works, from the repayment of the £20 of which he had been robbed near to the "fowle Ok" on Sept. 3, 1390.* Exchequer Q. R. Memoranda Roll, Hilary, 14 Ric. II., *Brevia*, roll 20 (Kirk, 292, and *Life Records*, I, p. 12).

[1391, c. Jan. 20.] *Bill for a Commission to John Elmhurst, as Deputy and Purveyor to Chaucer, Clerk of the Works, to take materials and workmen for the Palace of Westminster, and the Tower of London.* Warrants, Chancery, series I, file 1660 (Kirk, 292–3).

„ **Jan. 22.** *Appointment of John Elmhurst as Purveyor of the Works at Westminster and the Tower, under Chaucer.* . . . Patent Roll, 14 Ric. II., p. 2, m. 34 (Kirk, 293).

„ **Feb. 7.** *Mandate to the Exchequer, to allow to Chaucer, in his account, the wages of Richard Swift, Master Carpenter and "Dispositor" of the King s Works.* Exchequer Q. R. Memoranda Roll, Hilary, 14 Ric. II., *Brevia*, roll 24 d (Kirk, 293–4).

„ **Feb. 23.** *Loan by the Exchequer to Richard Gille, merchant of London, of £533 2s., part of which, £114, he repaid to Chaucer on 6th April.* Issue Roll, Mich., 14 Ric. II., m. 22 (Kirk, 294).

„ **April 6.** *Moneys assigned to Chaucer as Clerk of the Works ; and entry of a loan by him of £66 13s. 4d. to the Exchequer, for which he received a tally.* Receipt Roll, Easter, 14 Ric. II. (Kirk, 294–5).

„ **April 12.** *Enrolment of the Indictment in the King's Bench of Richard Brerelay and others, for the robbery of Chaucer at Westminster on 6th Sept., 1390, etc.* Coram Rege Roll, Easter, 14 Ric. II., Rex, roll 1 (Kirk, 295).

[There are three further entries concerning this robbery (*see above* under Jan. 6, 1391) on April 16 and May 31–June 22 ; (2) *see* the whole of *Life Records of Chaucer*, I, and IV, pp. 295–9.]

1391, July 8.   *Chaucer's Account as Clerk of the Works at St. George's Chapel, Windsor, from July 12, 1390, to this date.* Exchequer L. T. R. Foreign Accounts, 14 Ric. II., forula C (Kirk, 309, 310).

„   **July 12.**   *Indenture between Chaucer and Gedney as to the delivery of certain quantities of stone for the Works in Windsor Castle.* Exchequer Accounts, Works, $\frac{502}{10}$ (Kirk, 310).

„   **Oct.**   *A File of sixteen documents subsidiary to Chaucer's Account as Clerk of the Works, referring to repairs and works at Westminster, the Tower, Windsor, and elsewhere; and consisting of Writs, Indentures and Receipts between June 1389 and October 1391.* Exchequer Accounts, etc., Works, $\frac{502}{10}$ (Kirk, 310–13 ; *see also* Trial-Forewords to parallel-text edition of Chaucer's minor poems, by F. J. Furnivall, Chaucer Soc., 1871, p. 132).

„   **Nov. 12.**   *Mandate to the Exchequer to account with Chaucer as Clerk of the Works, and to pay whatever is due to him.* Exchequer Q. R. Memoranda Roll, Mich., 15 Ric. II., *Brevia*, roll 31 d (Kirk, 313).

1393, Jan. 9.   *Gift of £10, by the King to Chaucer, as a reward for his good service during the "present" year.* Issue Roll, Mich., 16 Ric. II., m. 12 (Kirk, 315).

„   **May 22.**   *Repayment to Chaucer of £66 13s. 4d., lent by him for the King's Works* (see entry under April 6, 1391). Issue Roll, Easter, 16 Ric. II., m. 9 (Kirk, 316).

1394, Feb. 28.   *Grant by the King to Chaucer of an annuity of £20.* Patent Roll, 17 Ric. II., p. 2, m. 35 (Kirk, 316. Godwin, App. xxii).

[There are seventeen payments in all of this annuity on the following dates : Dec. 10, 1394 ; April [loan of £10], June 25 [loan of £10], Sept. 9 [loan of 26s. 8d.], Nov. 27, 1395 ; Mar. 1, Dec. 25, 1396 [loan of £10] ; July 2, Aug. 9 [two loans of 100s. each], Oct. 26, 1397 ; June 4, July 24, 31, Aug. 23, Oct. 28, 1398 [loan of £10] ; Feb. 21, June 5, 1400 ; Kirk, 316–22, 326, 331. There are also two repayments by Chaucer, one of a loan of £10, repaid May 28, 1395, and one of 26s. 8d., repaid March 1, 1396 ; Kirk, 317, 319, 342.]

1395–6.   *Payment of money to Geoffrey Chaucer for Henry, Earl of Derby, at London, by the Clerk of the Earl's Great Wardrobe.* Duchy of Lancaster Accounts (various), 1/5 (Kirk, 342).

[See *History of Henry IV.*, by J. H. Wylie, App.]

1396, April 6.   *Deed by Gregory Ballard, appointing Chaucer and others as his attorneys, to take seisin for him of certain lands in Kent, of which he had been enfeoffed by the Archbishop of York.* Close Roll, 19 Ric. II., m. 8 d (Kirk, 319–20).

1398, May 20.   *Action of Debt in the Common Pleas by Isabella, widow and administratrix of Walter Bukholt, Esquire, against Geoffrey Chaucer, Esquire, for £14 1s. 11d.; and against John Goodale of Milleford, for £12 8s. The Sheriff of Middlesex returns that they have nothing [in his bailwick], and he is ordered to arrest them.* De Banco Roll, Easter, 21 Ric. II., m. 368 d (Kirk, 321, and note 1, 322 ; *see also* the *Athenæum*, Sept. 13, 1879, p. 338).

1398, May 4. *Royal protection for Chaucer, who has been appointed by the King to attend to many urgent affairs, but fears to be hindered by plaints or suits; to last for two years.* Patent Roll, 21 Ric. II., p. 3, m. 26 (Kirk, 322. Rymer, vol. viii, p. 39. Godwin, App. xxiv).

„ **June 12—July 4.** *Action of Debt by Isabella Bukholt against Chaucer and Goodale. The Sheriff returns that they have not been found, and it is ordered that they be arrested.* De Banco Roll, Trin., 21–22 Ric. II., m. 431 d (Kirk, 324).

„ **Oct. 9—Nov. 28.** *Action of Debt by Isabella Bukholt against Chaucer and Goodale. The Sheriff returns that they have not been found, and he is ordered to put them in exigent, till they are outlawed, if not found.* De Banco Roll, Mich., 22 Ric. II., m. 228 (Kirk, 324).

[Kirk states that no later entry of this action has been found, therefore we may take it for granted that it did not come to a trial.]

[1398,] Oct. 13. *Petition by Chaucer to the King, asking for the grant of a butt of wine yearly to be received in the Port of London, by the hands of the Chief Butler.* Warrants, Chancery, series I, file 1394 (Kirk, 325).

[*See also* W. D. Selby in the *Athenæum*, Jan. 28, 1888, p. 116.]

1398, Oct. 13. *Grant to Chaucer of a butt of wine yearly, as above.* Patent Roll, 22 Ric. II., p. 1, m. 5 (Kirk, 325. Rymer, vol. viii, p. 51).

„ **Oct. 15.** *Another grant of the same, with the addition of words, making the Chief Butler's deputy responsible.* Patent Roll, 22 Ric. II., p. 1, m. 8 (Kirk, 325. Godwin, App. xxv).

1399, Oct. 13. *Grant by Henry IV. to Chaucer, for good service rendered to the new King, of an annuity of 40 marks, in addition to the £20 given him by Richard II.* Patent Roll, 1 Hen. IV., p. 5, m. 12 (Kirk, 327. Godwin, App. xxvi).

[*See* note 1 on p. 327 of *Life Records* where Kirk states that Chaucer does not appear to have received any benefit from this grant, as there are no payments of this annuity on the Issue Rolls; but he continued to receive Richard II.'s annuity. *See above* under Feb. 28, 1394. It may be noted that the last day of Richard's reign was Sept. 29, 1399.]

„ **Oct. 18.** *Confirmation by Henry IV. to Chaucer of Richard II.'s two patents of 20 marks and a butt of wine yearly (see above under Feb. 28, 1394, Oct. 13, 1398), he having accidentally lost the original patents.* Patent Roll, 1 Hen. IV., p. 1, m. 18 (Kirk, 327–8. Rymer, vol. viii, p. 94. Godwin, App. xxvii).

„ **Oct. 21.** *Inspeximus and confirmation of the preceding confirmation.* Patent Roll, 1 Hen. IV., p. 1, m. 8 (Kirk, 328).

„ **Dec. 24.** *Lease by the Warden of St. Marys Chapel in Westminster Abbey, to Chaucer, of a tenement situate in the garden of the Chapel for 53 years, at the yearly rent of 53s. 4d.; terminable* *at Chaucer's death. The lessee covenants to repair, and not to sublet, nor to harbour any one having claims against the Abbey, without the Warden's licence.* Muniments of Westminster Abbey (Kirk, 329–30. Godwin, App. xxviii).

[*a.* **1400.**] **Unknown.** *The Gest hystoriale of the destruction of Troy* Unique MS., Hunterian museum, Glasgow, bk. xix, fol. 124 *b*, ll. 8051–4 (ed. G. A. Panton and David Donaldson, E. E. T. soc., 1869 and 1874, pp. 261–2).

> The sorow of Troilus for Breisaid his loue.
>
> .   .   .   .
>
> No lengur of thies lou*er*s list me to carpe,
> Ne of the feynit fate of þat faire lady ;
> Who-so wilnes to wit of þaire wo fir,
> Turne hym to Troilus, & talke þere ynoghe !

[It is doubtful whether this allusion 'Turne hym to Troilus and talke þere ynoghe' refers to Chaucer's Troilus, but there is a possibility that it may do so. The whole Gest is an amplified englishing of Guido de Colonna's *Historia Trojana* (c. 1381–82), and the corresponding passage in Guido runs :—" Cedo, Troile, quæ te tam juvenilis errare Coegit Credulitas, ut Briseidæ lacrimis crederes deceptivis et ejus blanditiis " ; and in what precedes and follows, the English book follows Guido pretty closely ; so that it seems likely that the passage is suggested by him.]

[**1400.**] **Lydgate,** John. *The Serpent of Deuision, Wherein is conteined the true History or Mappe of Romes ouerthrowe . . . . . Whereunto is annexed the Tragedye of Gorboduc . . . . . At London. Printed by Edward Allde for John Perrin, . . .* 1590. sign. c. iij *b* c. iv.

[Describing the death of Cæsar] . . . so that touching the manner of his tragedy : I may conclude with ye flower of Poets in our English tung, and the first that euer elumined our language with flowers of rethorick eloquence : I mean famous and worthy *Chaucer*, which compendiously wrought the death of this mightye Emperour, saying thus

> With Bodkins was *Cæsar Julius*
> Murdred at *Rome* of Brutus Crassus
> When many a Region he had brought full lowe,
> Lo ! who may trust Fortune any throw.

> > [A very free summary of Monkes Tale ll. 3863-5, 3885-98, 3912-15.]

The conclusion. Thus by the large writings and golden vollums of that woorthye Chaucer, the froward Dame of Chaunce hath no respect of persons.

[This tract was previously printed under the title "The Damage and Destruccyon in Realmes, first by me Peter Treuerys," *c.* 1520, then by Owen Rogers, 1559. In Gorboduc, ed. L. Toulmin Smith (Englische sprach. u. lit. denkmäler, ed K. Vollmöller, vol. i) 1883, pp. xx–ii, an extract with part of the Chaucer reference is given from Lord Calthorpe's Yelverton MSS., vol. 35, ff. 146 *b*–156 ; the tract will be found mentioned in Report II, Roy. Com. Hist. MSS., vol. i, 1871, p. 42. *See* Miss Toulmin Smith for date, authorship, editions, etc.]

[*c.* **1400.**] **Lydgate,** John. *The Chorle and the bird.* Last stanza. MS. Harl. 116, fol. 152. (Lydgate's minor poems, ed. J. O. Halliwell, 1840, Percy soc., vol. ii, p. 193.)

> Go gentill quayer, and Recommaunde me
> Vnto my maistir with humble affectioun
> Beseke hym lowly of mercy and pite
> Of thy rude makyng to haue compassioun
> And as touching thy translacioun
> Oute of frensh / hough euer the englisshe be
> Al thing is saide undir correctioun
> With supportacioun of your benignite.

[*c.* **1401.**] **Lydgate,** John. *The floure of curtesye,* stanzas 34–5 ; no MS. copy known; first printed in Chaucer's works, ed. W. Thynne, 1532, sign. D dd. ii *b,* or fol. cclxxxiiii *b,* and in J. Stowe's 1561 edn. of Chaucer, fol. ccxlix, who first attributed it to Lydgate (Chaucerian and other pieces, ed. W. W. Skeat, 1897, p. 273 ; for date and authorship, *see* ibid., introduction, p. xlv).

(34)

> Euer as I can supprise in myn herte
> Alway with feare betwyxt drede and shame
> Leste oute of lose, any worde asterte
> In this metre, to make it seme lame,
> Chaucer is deed that had suche a name
> Of fayre makyng that [was] without wene
> Fayrest in our tonge, as the Laurer grene.

(35)

> We may assay forto countrefete
> His gay style but it wyl not be ;
> The welle is drie, with the lycoure swete
> Both of Clye and of Caliope.

.　.　.　.　.　.　.

[**1402–3.**] **Lydgate,** John. *The complaint of the Black Knight,* MS. Fairfax 16, ff. 20 *b,* 30, [used by Krausser]; Add. 16165, ff. 190 *b,* 200 *b.* ; Arch. Selden, B 24, fol. 120. (Ed. Émil Krausser, 1896, pp. 54–5.)

(53)

> What shal I say of yonge Piramus?
> Of trwe Tristram for al his high renovne?

Of Achilles or of Antonyus?
Of Arcite or of him Palamovne?
What was the ende of her passioun?
But after sorowe dethe and then her graue.
Lo her the guerdon that [thes] louers haue!

. . . .

(55)

Of Thebes eke [loo] the fals Arcite,
And Demophon eke for his slouthe,
They had her lust and al that myght delyte,
For al her falshede and [hir] grete vntrouthe.

[At the end of Arch. Selden (c. 1488, *q.v.*, below p. 63) occur these words: "Here endith the maying and disport of Chaucere," and under this title the Complaint was printed by Chepman and Myllar, 1508 (*q. v.* p. 70). Dart reprinted it also as Chaucer's in 1718 (*q. v.* below). For authorship and date see Chaucerian and other pieces, ed. W. W. Skeat, 1897, introduction, pp. xliii–v; he reprints the Complaint from W. Thynne's edn. of 1532, pp. 245–65, Chaucer references, pp. 256–7.]

[c. 1403. Clanvowe, Sir Thomas?] *The Cuckow and the Nightingale* MSS. in B. M., Bodleian, Camb. Univ. library (Chaucerian and other pieces, ed. W. W. Skeat, 1897, p. 347; for authorship, date, details of MSS. and early printed edns. see *ibid.*, pp. lvii–lxi).

[first line]   The god of love, a! *benedicite!*
How mighty and how greet a lord is he!

[quoted from Knight's Tale, ll. 1785–6].

[For the argument that this poem is by Sir John Clanvowe, and was written before 1391, see G. L. Kittredge in Mod. Philology, Chicago, vol. i, pp. 13–18.]

[c. 1403?] Lydgate, John. *Here begynneth a breue compiled tretyse callyd by the Auctor thereof Curia Sapiencie.* MS. Trin. Coll. Cambr. R. 3. 21. 377; printed by Caxton [1481?] under title *De Curia Sapientiæ* (of which a few verses only are extant among the Caxton fragments in the B. M., pr. mk. IB 55003); and by Wynkyn de Worde, 1510, as *The courte of sapyence.* Proheme, stanzas 7, 8, 9, sign. a ii, f. i b.

(7)

But netheles as tasted bytternesse   [sign. a. ii]
All swete thynge maketh be more precyous
So shall my boke extende the goodlynesse
Of other auctoures whiche ben gloryous
And make theyr wrytynge delycyous
I symple shall extoll theyr soueraynte
And my rudenes shall shewe theyr subtylyte.

(8)

Gower chaucers erthly goddes two
Of thyrste of eloquent delycacye

With all your successours fewe or moo
Fragraunt in speche / experte in poetrye
You ne yet them in no poynt I enuye
Exyled as ferre I am from your glorye
As nyght from daye / or deth from vyctorye.

(9)

I you honour / blysse / loue / and gloryfye

  .   .   .   .   .

Who so thynketh my wrytynge dull & blont [sign. f. 1 b]
And wolde conceyue the colours purperate
Of Rethoryke go he to triasunt
And to Galfryde the poete laureate
To Januens a clerke of grete astate
Within the fyrst parte of his gramer boke
Of this mater there groundely may he loke.

[The extract here given is from the 1510 edn. The allusion to ‘Galfryde the poete laureate,’ refers most probably to Galfridus de Vinosalvo, also called ‘Galfridus Anglicus.’ *See* below, p. 49. *See* The Temple of Glas, ed. J. Schick, E. E. T. soc., notes, pp. 77–8.
Dr. H. N. MacCracken will not allow that this poem is by Lydgate; see his Lydgate Canon, Philological society Transactions 1908, p. xxxi.]

[1403 ?] **Lydgate**, John.   *The Temple of Glas.* MS. Tanner, 346, ff. 76–97. 1400–20. ll. 102–10 (direct reference to Chaucer), ll. 75–6, 137–42, 184–5, 405–6, 409–10 (indirect references). (Ed. J. Schick, E. E. T. soc., extra series lx, 1891, pp. 3–7, 17.)

[ll. 75-6]

There was [also] Grisildis innocence
And al hir mekenes, & hir pacience.

  .   .   .   .   .   .

[ll. 102-10]

There saugh I also þe soror of Palamoun,
That he in prison felt, & al þe smert,
And hov þat he, þurugh vnto his hert,
Was hurt vnwarli þurugh castyng of an eyȝe
Of faire fressh, þe ȝung[e] Emelie,
And al þe strife bitwene him & his broþir,
And hou þat one fauȝt eke with þat oþir
Wiþ-in þe groue, til þei bi Theseus
Acordid were, as Chaucer telliþ us.

  .   .   .   .   .   .

[ll. 137-142]

And vppermore depeint men myȝt[e] se,
Hov with hir ring, goodli Canace

CHAUCER CRITICISM.

Of euere foule þe ledne & þe song
Coud vndirstond, as she welk hem among;
And hou hir broþir so oft holpen was
In his myschefe bi þe stede of bras.

.   .   .   .

[ll. 184–5]   For it ne sit vnto fressh[e] May
Forto be coupled to oold[e] Ianuari—

.   .   .   .

[ll. 405–6]   Grisild[e] was assaied at[te] ful,
That turned aftir to hir encrese of Ioye;

.   .   .   .

[ll. 409–10]   Also þe turment þere coude no man akoye
Of Dorigene, flour of al Britayne.

[1406–13]. Edward, 2nd duke of York. *Here begynneth . . . . the Book of Huntyng the which is clepyd Mayster of the Game.* MS. Cott. Vesp. B. xii, f. 12 *b*. (The Master of the Game, ed. Wm. A. and F. Baillie-Grohman, 1904, p. 3.)

The Prologe [to King Henry IV].

. . . . þough I vnworþi be I am Maister of this game wiþ þat noble prince your fadere oure aldere souereyne and liege lord forsaid. And for I ne wold þat his hunters ne yours þat now be or shuld come here aftir weren vnknowe in þe profite-nesse of þis art for þi shall I leue this symple memorial ffor as Chaucer saiþ in this prologe of the xxv good wymmen. Be wryteng haue men of ymages passed for writyng is þe keye of alle good remembraunce.

[Prologue to Legend of Good Women, ll. 25–6.]

[c. 1407.] Scogan, Henry. *A moral balade made by Henry Scogane squyer*) [addressed to Henry IV's sons], stanzas 9, 13, 17. MS. Ashmole 59, ff. 26–27. Printed by Caxton [1478?], Caxton frag-ments, no. 1 [B.M. pr. mk. IB 55016], and by W. Thynne in Chaucer's works, 1532, ff. 380–1. (Chaucerian and other pieces, ed. W. W. Skeat, 1897, pp. 239–40 ; Parallel text of Chaucer's minor poems, ed. F. J. Furnivall, Chaucer soc. [1871], pp. 427, 430.)

(9)

[fol. 26]   My maistre Chaucier / god his soule haue /
þat in his langage / was so curyous
He saide þat þe fader / nowe dede and grave /
Beqwaþe no-thing / his vertue with his hous /
Vn-to his sone /

(13)

[fol. 26 b]

By avncetrye þus may yee no-thing clayme
As þat my maistre Chaucier doþe expresse
But tempore‖ thinge / þat man may hurte & mayme
þane is gode stocke / of vertuous noblesse.
. . . . . herke howe my maistre seyde
[*Here follow the three verses of Gentilesse.*]

(17)

[fol. 27]

Loo here þis noble Poete of Brettayne
Howe hyely he in vertuous sentence
þe lesse in youþe / of vertue / can compleyne
Wherfore I prey yowe / dooþe youre diligence

[Scogan quotes Chaucer's poem Gentilesse in full, as it is given in Ashmole MS. 59, fol. 27.]

1409, May 20. *The seal of Geoffrey Chaucer used by Thomas Chaucer at this date.* Ancient Deeds, DS. 79 (Life-Records of Chaucer, ed. Kirk, 1900, p. 433, and Archæologia, 1852, vol. xxxiv, p. 42).

[1409–11 ?] Lydgate, John. *The Life of our Lady.* Cotton MS. App. viii, No. i; Harl. MS. 629, fol. 43 b–44. Printed by Caxton 1484 (?) [B. M. and Bodl.], as *A comendacion of chauceres,* cap. xxxiiij, sign. e 7 b. Printed by Robert Redman, 1531, sign. N iv b. O i. ; table of chapters, sign. a 2 b.

[This poem will also be found in Harl. MSS. 3862; 3952; 4011, No. 7; 5272, No. 1. *See* p. 53, below, for another version of the first 7 lines.]

¶ A commendacioun of Chaucers. [Harl. 629. fol. 43 b–44]

And eke my **master Chauceris** nowe is graue
    The noble **rethor Poete** of breteine
That worthy was the laurer to haue
Of peetrie [*sic*] and the **palme** atteine
That made firste to distille and reyne
The **golde dewe droppis** of speche and eloquence
In-to oure **tounge** thourȝ his excellence
¶ And founde the flourys first of rethoryk
Oure **rude speche** oonly to enlumyne
That in oure **tunge** was neue*r* noon him like
For as the **sunne** dothe in **heuen** shyne
In **mydday** speere dovn̅ to vs by-lyne   [fol. 44]
In whos p*r*esence noo **sterre** may appere
Riȝt so his **ditees** withoute any peere
¶ Eny makyng with his liȝt disteine
In **sothfastnesse** who-so taketh **heede**
Wherfor noo **wondre** thouȝ myn **herte** pleyne
Vpon̅ his **dethe** and for sorowe **blede**
For **wante** of him nowe in my greet[e] nede

That shulde **allas conveie** and directe
And w*ith* his supporte **amende** and corecte
¶ The wronge **tracys** of my **rude penne**
Ther as y **erre** and goo nouȝt **lyne** riȝt
But for that he ne may me not **kenne**
I can no more but witħ alle my myȝt
With alle myne **herte** and myne inward siȝt
Praye for him that nowe lietħ in cheste
To **god** above to ȝiue his **soule** good **reste**
¶ And as y can forthe y wil p*ro*cede
Sithen of his **helpe** ther may noo socour bee
And thourȝ my **penne** ay **quakyng** for drede
Neither to . Cloie . ne to . Caliope
Me liste not **calle** for to **helpe** me
Ne to no **muse** my pointel for to **guye**
But leue alle this and **seie** to Marie
O clene **castel** and the chaste **toure**
Of the **hooly goost modir** and **virgine**
Be thou my **helpe** &c. . . .

1410. Froissart, Sir John. *Here begynneth the first volum of Sir Johan Froyssart: of the cronycles of Englande . . . . translated . . . . into . . . . englysshe . . . . by John Bourchier knight lorde Berners.* Imprinted . . by Richarde Pynson . . M.D. xxiii, cap. cccxiv, fol. cxcvi, col. i. (Tudor trans. ser., ed. W. E. Henley, 5 vols. 1901–2, vol. ii, p. 459; Globe edn., ed. G. C. Macaulay, 1895, p. 205.)

. . . . and than about lent [1377] there was a secrete treatie deuysed to be bytwene the two kynges [of France and England] at Moutrell by the see. And so were sent by the kynge of Englande to Calais sir Rycharde Dangle Rycharde Stan Geffray Chaucer.

[This is printed here because of its interest, although it is not an English reference; *see* App. B. 1386–88, Froissart, and *cf.* also above 1377, p. 5, and below 1592, p. 136.]

1410. Walton, John (of Osney). *Liber boeti de Consolatione philosophi de latino in Angliam, 1410, per Capellanum Joannem* [fol. 1 *b*], Roy. MS. 18 A. xiii, fol. 2 and *b*. (Chaucer's works, ed. W. W. Skeat, 1894, vol. ii, p. xvii, and Athenæum, Dec. 28, 1895, p. 902.)

To Chaucer that is floure of rethoryk
In englisshe tong and excellent poete
This wot I wel no thing may I do lyk
Thogh so that I of makynge entyrmete.

And Gower that so craftily doth trete
As in his book of moralitee
Thogh I to theym in makyng am unmete
ȝit most I shewe it forth that is in me.

[Only a few verses are given by Skeat, but the Chaucer reference is among them. T. Hearne (Robert of Gloucester's Chronicle, ed. T. Hearne, 1724, vol. ii, p. 708) in a letter to John Bagford, 1708, states that he saw an edition of 1525, of this translation, but we can find no further trace of it. *See* below, under 1708, p. 296.]

1412. Hoccleve, Thomas. *The Regement of Princes.* MS. Harl. 4866 [Beggar and Hoccleve], fol. 34, ll. 1863-9. [Lament for Chaucer], ff. 35 *b*-36, ll. 1958-74. [Regement for Henry V. when Prince of Wales—Proem], ff. 37-37 *b*, ll. 2077-2107. [§ 14] De consilio habendo in omni*bus* factis, ff. 87 *b*-88, ll. 4978-98. (Works, Part III. The Regement of Princes, ed. F. J. Furnivall, E. E. T. soc., extra ser. lxxii. 1897, pp. 68, 71, 75-6, 179-80. *See also* extracts reprinted in The Dunbar Anthology, 1401-1508, ed. E. Arber, 1901, pp. 80-3.)

¶ " What schal I callë þe ? what is þi name ? " [fol. 34]

· · · · · ·

"Hoccleuë, sone ? "   "I-wis, fadir, þat same."
" Sone, I haue herd, or this, men speke of þe ;
þou were aqueynted with Caucher, pardee—
God haue his soulë best of any wyg͡ht !—
Sone, I wole holdë þe þat I haue hyg͡ht."

· · · · ·

¶ " O, maist*er* deere, and fadir reu*er*ent !   [fol. 36]
Mi maist*er* Chaucer, flour of eloquence,
Mirour of fructuous entendëment,
O, vniu*er*sel fadir in science !
Allas ! þat þou thyn excellent prudence,
In þi bed mortel mightist naght by-qwethe ;
What eiled deth ? allas ! whi wolde he sle the ?

¶ " O deth ! þou didest naght harme singuleer,
In slaghtere of him ; but al þis land it smertith
But nathëlees, yit hast þou no power
His namë sle ; his hy v*er*tu astertith
Vnslayn fro þe, which ay vs lyfly hertyth,
With bookës of his ornat éndytyng,
That is to al þis land enlumynyng.

· · · · · · · ·

Mi derë maistir—god his soulë quyte!—   [fol. 87]
 And fadir, Chaucer, fayn wolde han me taght;
 But I was dul, and lernèd lite or naght.

¶ Allas! my worthi maister honorable,
 This landës verray tresor and richesse,
Deth, bi thi deth, hath harme irreparable
 Vnto vs doon; hir vengeable duresse
 Despoilèd hath þis land of þe swetnesse
  Of rethorik; for vn-to Tullius
  Was neuer man so lyk a-mongës vs.

¶ Also, who was hier in philosophie
 To Aristotle, in our tonge, but thow?
The steppës of virgile in poesie
 Thow filwedist eeke, men wot wel y-now.
    .   .   .   .

¶ She [Death] myghte han taried hir vengeance awhile,
 Til that sum man had egal to thè be.
Nay, lat be þat! sche knew wel þat þis yle
 May neuer man forth bryngë lyk to the,
 And hir officë needës do mot she;
  God bad hir so, I truste as for thi beste;
  O maister, maister, god þi soule reste!
    .   .   .   .

¶ The firstë fyndere of our faire langáge,   [fol. 87b]
 Hath seyde in caas sembláble, & othir moo,
So hyly wel, þat it is my dotáge
 ffor to expresse or touche any of thoo.
 Alasse! my fadir fro the worlde is goo—
  My worthi maister Chaucer, hym I mene—
  Be þou aduóket for hym, heuenes quene!

¶ As þou wel knowest, o blissid virgyne,
 With louyng hert, and hye deuocïoun
In þyne honour he wroot ful many a lyne;
 O now þine helpe & þi promocïoun,
 To god þi sonë make a mocïoun,
  How he þi seruaunt was, maydén marie,
  And lat his louë floure and fructifie.

¶ Al-þogh his lyfe be queynt, þe résemblaunce
 Of him haþ in me so fressh lyflynesse,

þat, to putte othir men in rémembraunce
Of his persóne, I haue heere his lyknesse
Do makë, to þis ende in sothfastnesse,
þat þei þat haue of him lest þought & mynde,
By þis peynturë may ageyn him fynde.

[Grass-green
background,
black hood
and gown,
gray hair,
hazel eyes,
red lips,
paleish face
and hands;
black beads
and penner
on red
strings.]

[In the MS. Chaucer's carefully-drawn and coloured likeness is in the right margin
of this last verse, with his finger pointing at 'lyknesse' (4th line). At the top of
the much commoner full-length figure in the left margin of the MS. Reg. 17. D. 6,
is "¶ Chaucers yn age." There was another drawing of Chaucer in MS. Cott. Otho
A. 18, but the Chaucer part is now burnt.]

[1412-20.] **Lydgate**, John. *The hystorye, sege and dystruccyon of
Troye.* MS. Cott. Aug. 4, ff. 48 *b*, 72, 90 *b*, 91, 153 ; Arundel MS.
99 ; Roy MS. 18. D. ii ; Printed (with above title) by Richard
Pynson, 1513. 2nd bk., c. xv, fol. I 4 *b* ; 3rd bk. c. xxii, N 5 ;
cxxv, Q 5 *b*–Q 6 ; 5th bk. c. xxxvii, Dd. 3 *b* (ed. Henry Bergen,
E. E. T. soc. 1906–1910, pp. 278, 279, 410, 515, 516–17, 873).

And ouermore to tellen of Cryseyde   [Cott. Aug. 4,
Mi penne stumbleþ for longe or he deyde   fol 48 *b*, col. i]
My maister Chaucer dide his dilligence
To discryve þe gret excellence
Of hir bewte and þat so maisterly
To take on me it were but hiȝe foly

.   .   .   .

Gret cause haue I & mater to compleyne
On antropos & vp-on hir envie
þat brak þe þrede & madë for to dye
Noble galfridë poete of breteyne
Amonge de englisch þat made first to reyne
þe gold dewe-dropis of rethorik so fyne
Oure rude langage only tenlwmyne
To god I pray þat he his soulë haue

.   .   .   .   .   .

And Chaucer now allas is nat alyue   [fol. 72, col. i]
Me to reformë or to be my rede
For lak of whom slouȝer is my spede
þe noble Rethor that alle dide excelle
For in makyng he drank of þe welle
Vndir pernaso þat þe musis kepe
On whiche hil I myȝt neuer slepe

.   .   .   .   .

[Of the Woe of Troylus & Cressid.]

It woldë me ful longë occupie   [fol. 90 b, col. i]
Of euery þinge to makë mencioun
And tarie me in my translacioun
Ȝif I shuldë in her wo procede
But me semeth þat it is no nede
Sith my maister chauncer her-a-forn
In þis mater so wel hath hym born
In his boke of troylus and Cryseyde
Whiche he madë longe or þat he deyde

.   .   .   .   .   .

þe hool story Chauncer kan ȝow telle   [col. ii]
Ȝif þat ȝe liste no man bet alyue
Nor þe processe halfe so wel discryue
For he owre englishë gilt with his sawes
Rude and boistous firste be oldë dawes
þat was ful fer from al perfeccioun
And but of litel reputacioun
Til þat he cam & þoruȝ his poetrie
Gan oure tongë firste to magnifie
And adourne it with his elloquence
To whom honour laude & reuerence
þoruȝ-oute þis londë ȝouë be & songe
So þat þe laurer of oure englishe tonge
Be to hym ȝouë for his excellence
Riȝt a whilom by ful hiȝe sentence
Perpetuelly for a memorial

Of Colum*p*na by the cardynal   [fol. 91]
To petrak frau*n*ceis was ȝouen i*n* ytaille
þat þe report neu*er*e after faille
Nor þe honour dirked of his name
To be registred in þe house of fame
Amongë oþer in þe hiȝeste sete
My maister galfride as for chefe poete
þat eu*er*e was ȝit in oure langage
þe name of who*m* shal passe*n* in noo*n* age
But eu*er* ylyche w*ith*-oute eclipsinge shyne
And for my part I wil neu*er* fyne
So as I can hym to magnifie
In my writyngë pleinly til I dye
And god I praye his soulë bring i*n* Ioie.

·   ·   ·   :   ·   ·   ·

For he þat was gronde of wel seying   [fol. 153, col. i]
In al hys lyf hyndred no makyng
My maist*er* Chau*c*er þat fou*n*de ful many spot
Hym liste not pinche nor gruche at eu*er*y blot
Nor meue hy*m* silf to p*er*turbe his reste
I haue herde telle but seide alweie þe best
Suffring goodly of his gentilnes
Ful many þing enbracid w*ith* rudnes
And ȝif I shal shortly hym discryve
Was neu*er* noon to þis day alyue
To reckne allë boþë ȝonge & olde
þat worþi was his ynkhorn for to holde
And in þis lond ȝif þer any be
In borwe or tou*n* village or cite
þat ko*n*nyng haþ his tracis for to swe
Wher he go brood or be shet in mwe
To hym I makë a direcciou*n*
Of þis boke to han inspecciou*n*

[*See* below, Appendix A, 1412–20, for fuller references. *See also* Chaucer's Troylus and Cryseyde and Boccaccio's Filostrato, ed. W. M. Rossetti, Chaucer soc., pp. x, xi, where a reference is given from the Arundel MS. 99, fol. 96, col. 2, and 96 *b* (corresponds to Cott. Aug. 4, fol. 90 *b*, col. 1). A modernised version by Thomas Heywood was printed by Thomas Purfoot in 1614 under title The life and death of Hector (*q. v.* below, p. 189). Chaucer references are on pp. 102, 183, 185 (wrongly paged 183), 317. *See also* under *c.* 1440, Unknown, below, p. 44, for a note on Lydgate's praise of Chaucer.]

1420. Brinchele, John. *Will.* July 4, 1420. (Commissary Court of London, More, fol. lxiiij *b*.)

Ego, Johannes Brynchele, Ciuis & Cissor London*ie* . . . .
Item relaxo et condono Johanni Broun*e* totum illud debitu*m,*

in quo michi tene*tur* de meio bonis p*ro* prijs.   Et volo q*uo*d ha*b*eat illum libru*m* vocatum Boecius de Consolatione Ph*iloso*ph*i*e in latinis, quem h*ab*ui p*ro* vadio Alterius libri Anglia*m*, vocati Boecius de Consolac*ione* Ph*iloso*ph*i*e.   Item lego David Fyvyan, Rectori ec*cles*ie Sancti Benedicti Fynke Su*pra*dict*i*, vt sit Supe*r*uisor p*re*sent*is* test*amenti* mei, vj s' viij d, et vnu*m* libru*m* in Anglicis voca*tum* Boecium de Consolacione Ph*ilo*soph*i*e.   Item lego Will*elm*o Holg*ra*ve, vt sit vnus executo*rum* meor*um*, vj s' viij d, et optimu*m* Arcu*m* meu*m*, et libru*m* meu*m* vocatu*m* Talys of Caun*ter*bury. . . . . [Will proved] xiij k*a*len*darum* Septemb*ris*, Anno d*o*m*in*i M¹CCCC^{mo}xx^{mo}.

[This earliest bequest of Chaucer's *Canterbury Tales* and *Boece*, is quoted in notes, p. 136, to Fifty earliest English wills in the Court of Probate, London; copied and ed. by F. J. Furnivall for the E. E. T. soc. 1882.]

[*c.* 1420.] **Unknown.** *Headline* to *The Former Age.* Camb. Univ. lib. MS. I i. 3, 21, fol. 52 *b.* (Parallel-text of Chaucer's minor poems, ed. F. J. Furnivall, Chaucer soc. [1871], p. 174.)

Chaw*c*er vp-on this fyfte me*tur* of the second book.

[This, and the following headlines, are given merely as examples, and do not profess to be exhaustive.]

[*c.* 1420.] **Unknown.** *Headline* to *Sir Thopas's end link,* in MSS, Ellesmere (fol. 157) and Hengwrt (fol. 215). (Six-text Canterbury Tales, ed. F. J. Furnivall, Chaucer soc., 1871-8, p. 199, parts i–iii.)

[Ellesmere] ¶ Heere the Host' stynteth Chaucer / of his tale of Thopas.

[Hengwrt] ¶ Here the hoost / stynteth Chaucer of his tale of Thopas / and biddeth hym / telle another tale.

[*c.* 1420.] **Unknown.** *Colophon* to *Cooks Tale.* MS. Hengwrt, fol. 57 *b.* (Six-text Canterbury Tales, ed. F. J. Furnivall, Chaucer soc., 1871-8, parts i–iii, p. 128.)

Of this Cokes tale maked Chaucer na moore.

[1420-22.] **Lydgate,** John. *Siege of Thebes.* Prologue. MS. Arundel 119, ff. 1–3 *b.* The thirde parte, ff. 75–7. Chaucer's works, ed. J. Stowe, 1561, ff. 356–77 *b.* (Ed. A. Erdmann, E. E. T. and Chaucer soc. Prologue, pp. 1–7, practically the whole of it, also pp. 128-9.)

WHan bri3te phebus / passëd was þe ram   [fol. 1]
    Myd of Aprille / *and* in-to bolë cam,
And Satourn) old / wi*th* his frosty face
In virgynë / taken had his place,

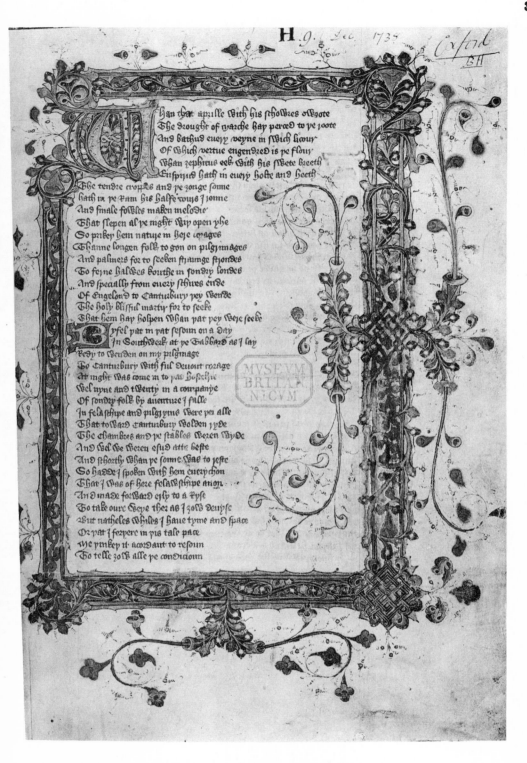

3

PROLOGUE TO THE ' CANTERBURY TALES '
ONE OF THE OLDEST MANUSCRIPTS, VERY BEAUTIFULLY WRITTEN
MS. Harleian 7334, Leaf 1 (British Museum)

Malencolik / *and* slowgh of mociou*n*,
And was also / in thoposiciou*n*
Of lucina / the monë moyst and pale,
That¹ many Shour / fro heuene made avale;
whan Aurora / was in þe morowe red,
And Iubiter / in the Crabbës Hed
Hath take his paleys / and his mansiou*n*;
The lusty tyme / and Ioly fressh Sesou*n*
whan that Flora / the noble myghty que*n*e,
The soyl hath clad / in newë tendre grene,
with her flourës / craftyly ymeynt¹,
Braunch *and* bough / wiþ red *and* whit depeynt,
Fletinge þe bawme / on hillis *and* on valys :
The tyme in soth / whan Canterbury talys
Complet¹ and told² / at¹ many sondry stage
Of estatis // in the pilgrimage,
Euerich man / lik to his degrè,
Some of desport¹ / some of moralitè,
Some of knyghthode / loue and gentillesse,
And some also of *p*arfit¹ holynesse,
And some also in soth / of Ribaudye
To makë laughter² / in þe companye,
(Ech admitted / for non̄ wold other greve)
Lich as the Cook / þe millere and the Reve
Aquytte hem-silf / shortly to conclude,
Boystously / in her teermës Rude,
whan þei hadde / wel dronken of the bolle,
And ek also / with his pyllëd nolle
The pardowner / beerdlees al his Chyn,   [fol. 1 *b*]
Glasy-Eyed / and face of Cherubyn,
Tellyng¹ a tale / to angre with the frere,
As opynly // the storie kan ʒow lere,
word for word / with euery circu*m*stau*n*ce,
Echon ywrite / and put¹ in remembrau*n*ce
By hym þat¹ was / ʒif I shal not¹ feyne,
Floure of Poetës / thorghout¹ al breteyne,
Which sothly haddë / most¹ of excellence
In rethorike / and in eloquence
(Rede his making¹ / who list¹ the trouthë fynde)
Which neuer shal / appallen in my mynde,
But¹ alwey fressh / ben in my memorye :
To whom be ʒouë / pris / honure / *and* glorye

Of wel seyinge / firstᵗ in oure language,
Chief Registrer / of þis pilgrimage,
Al þatᵗ was tolde / forȝeting' noght at al,
Feynëd talis / nor þing' Historial,
With many prouerbe / diuers *and* vnkoutħ,
Be rehersaile / of his Sugrid moutħ,
Of eche thyng' / keping' in substaunce
The sentence hool / with-outë variance,
Voyding' the Chaf / sothly for to seyn,
Enlumynyng' / þe trewë pikëd greyn
Be crafty writinge / of his sawës swete,
Fro the tymë / thatᵗ thei deden mete
First the pylgrimes / sothly euerichoñ,
At the Tabbard / assembled on be oñ,
And fro suthwerk / shortly forto seye,
To Canterbury / ridyng' on her weie,
Tellynge a tale / as I rehercë can,
Licħ as the hoste / assignëd euery man.
None so hardy / his biddyng' disobeye.   [fol. 2]
    And this whilë / thatᵗ the pilgrymes leye
Atᵗ Canterbury / wel loggëd on and all,
I notᵗ in sotħ / whatᵗ I may itᵗ call,
Hap / or fortune / in Conclusioun,
Thatᵗ me byfil / to entren into touñ,
The holy seyntᵗ / pleynly to visite
Aftere siknesse / my vowës to aquyte,
In a Cope of blak / *and* notᵗ of grene,
On a palfrey / slender / long' / and lene,
wiþ rusty brydel / mad natᵗ for þe sale,
My man to-forn / with a voidë male ;
whicħ of Fortunë / took' myn Inne anoñ
Wher þe pylgrymes / were loggëd euerichōñ,
The samë tyme / Her gouernour, the hostᵗ,
Stonding in halleᶜ ful of wynde *and* bostᵗ,
Licħ to a man / wonder sterne *and* fers,
Which spak to me / and seide anoñ, " daun Pers,
Daun Domynyk / Dan Godfrey / or Clementᵗ,
ȝe be welcom / newly into kentᵗ,
Thogh ȝoure bridel / haue neiþer boos ne belle ;
Besechinge ȝou / þat ȝe wil me telle
Firstᵗ ȝoure name / and of what contrè
With-outë morë · shorte-ly thatᵗ ȝe be,

That¹ loke so pale / al deuoyde of blood,
Vpon ʒoure hede / a wonder thred-bar hood,
Wel araïed / for to ridë latë."
  I answerde / 'my namë was Lydgate,
Monk of Bery / nyʒ fyfty ʒere of age,
Come to this toune / to do my pilgrimage,
As I haue hight¹ / I haue therof no shame.'
"Daun Iohn," quod he / " wel brokë ʒe ʒoure name!
Thogh ʒe be soul / beth right¹ glad *and* light!   [fol. 2 b]
Preiyng¹ ʒou / soupë with vs to-nyght¹,
And ʒe shal hauë / mad at ʒoure devis,
A gret¹ puddyng¹ / or a rounde hagys,
A Franchëmole / a tansey / or a froyse.
To ben a Monk / Sclender is ʒoure koyse;
ʒe han be seke / I dar myñ hede assure,
Or latë fed / in a feynt pasture.
Lift¹ vp ʒoure hed / be glad, tak no sorowe!
And ʒe shal hom ridë with vs to-morowe!
I seyë, whan ʒe rested han ʒour' fille,
Aftere soper / Slepe wil do noñ ille.
Wrappe wel ʒoure hede / *with* clothës rounde aboute!
Strong¹ notty ale / wol makë ʒou to route.
Tak a pylow / þat¹ ʒe lye not¹ lowe!
ʒif nedë be / Sparë not¹ to blowe!
To holdë wynde / be myñ opynyoun
Wil engendre / Collikes passioun
And makë men to greuen / on her roppys,
whan thei han filled / her mawës *and* her croppys.
But¹ toward¹ nyght¹ / ete some fenel Rede,
Annys / Comyn / or coriandre sede!
And lik as I / pouer haue / *and* myght¹,
I Chargë ʒow / rise not¹ at¹ Mydnyght,
Thogh it¹ so be / the moonë shynë cler.
I wol my-silf / be ʒoure Orloger
To-morow erly / whan I se my tyme,
For we wol forþ / parcel a-forë Pryme,
A company / pardè / Shal do ʒou good.
What¹! look vp, Monk / for, by kokkis blood,
Thow shalt¹ be mery / who so þat sey nay.
For to-morowe, anoon / as it¹ is day,
And that¹ it¹ gynne / in þe Est¹ to dawe,   [fol. 3]
Thow shalt¹ be boundë / to a newë lawe,

Att goyng oute of Canterbury toune,
And leyn a-sidë / thy professioun.
Thow shalt not chesë / nor þi-silf withdrawe,
ȝif eny myrth / be founden in thy mawe,
Lyk the custom / of this Compenye ;
For non so proude / that dar me denye,
Knyght nor knauë / Chanon / prest / ne nonne,
To telle a talë / pleynly as thei konne,
Whan I assigne / and se tyme opportune.
And for that we / our purpoos wil contune,
We wil homward / the samë custome vse,
And thow shalt not / platly the excuse.
Be now wel war / Stody wel to-nyght !
But, for al this ·/ be of hertë liȝt !
Thy wit shal be / þe Sharper *and* the bett."

   And we anon / were to Soper set,
And seruëd wel / vnto oure plesaunce ;
And sone after / be good gouernaunce
Vnto bed goth euery maner wight.
And touarde morowe / anoñ as it was light,
Euery Pilgryme / bothë bet *and* wors,
As bad oure hostë / toke a-noñ his hors,
Whan the sonnë / roos in the est ful clyere,
Fully in purpoos / to come to dynere
Vnto Osspryng / and brekë þer our faste.

   And whan we weren / from Canterbury paste
Noght the space / of a bowë draught,
Our hoost in hast / haþ my bridel rauht,
And to me seide // as it were in game,
" Come forth, daun Iohn / be ȝour Cristene name,
And lat vs make / some manere myrth or play !   [fol. 3 *b*]
Shet ȝoure portoos / a twenty deuelway !
It is no disport / so to patere *and* seie.
It wol make ȝoure lippës / wonder dreye.
Tel some tale / and make ther-of a Iape !
For be my Rouncy / thow shalt not eskape.
But preche not / of noñ holynesse !
Gynne some tale / of myrth or of gladnesse,
And noddë not / with thyn heuy bekke !
Telle vs some thyng / that draweþ to effecte
Only of Ioyë ! / make no lenger lette ! "
   And whan I saugh / it woldë be no bette,

I obeyëd / vnto his biddynge,
So as the lawë / me bonde in al thinge;
And as I coudë / with a palë cheere,
My tale I gan / anoñ / as ȝe shal here.

Explicit¹ Prologus.

The thirde part, ff. 75–76.

¶ And ȝit¹, allas! / bothen eve and morowe,
O thyng¹ ther was / that¹ doubled al her sorowe,
That Old Creon / fader of fellonye,
Ne woldë suffre, thorgh his Tyrannye,
The dedë bodies / be buryed nowther brente,
But¹ with beestis and houndys to be rente.
he made hem all / vpon an hepe be leyde.
wherof the wymmen trist¹ *and* evyl apeyde,
For verray dool, as it was no wonder,
her hertys felt¹ almost ryve a-sonder.
¶ And as my mayster Chaucer⁹ list¹ endite,
Al clad in blak / with her wymples whyte,
With gret¹ honour / and duë reuerence,   [fol. 75 b]
In the temple / of the goddesse Clemence
They abood the space / of fourtënyght¹,
Tyl Theseus / the noble worthy knyght¹,
Duk of Athenys / with his Chyvalrye
Repeyrëd hom / out¹ of Femynye,
And with hym ladde / ful feir vpon to sene,
Thorgh his manhod / ypolita the quene,
And her suster / called Emelye.
and whan thies wommen / gonnë first espye
This worthy Duk / as he cam rydynge,
Kyng¹ Adrastus /, hem alle conveyinge,
The wommen brouht¹ vnto his presence,
which hym bysought¹ / to ȝive hem audience.
And all attonys swownyng *in* the place,
Ful humblely / preiden hym of grace
To rewe on hem / her harmys to redresse.
But¹ ȝif ȝe list¹ / to se the gentyllesse
Of Theseus / how he hath hym borñ,
ȝif ȝe remembre / ȝe han herde it¹ to forñ
wel rehersyd / at Depforth in the vale,
In the begynnyng¹ / of the knyghtys tale:

¶ First how that he / whan he herd hem speke,
For verray routhë felt his hertë / breke ;
And her sorowys / whan he gan aduerte,
From his courser / doun anoñ he sterte,
Hem confortyng in ful good entente,
And in his Armys he hem all vp hente.
The knyghtys tale / reherseth euery del
Fro poynt to poynt / ʒif ʒe lookë wel.
And how this Duk / with-oute more abood,   [fol. 76]
The samë day / toward Thebës rood,
Ful lik in soth / a worthy conquerour,
And in his hoost / of Chyualrye the flour.
And fynally, to spekyn of thys thing,
with old Creon / that was of Thebës kyng,
how that he faught / and slough hym lik a knyght,
And all his host / putte vnto the flyght.

[*c.* **1420-30.**] **Unknown.** *Colophon* to *Parson's Tale.* MSS. Ellesmere, fol. 236 *b* ; Addit. 5140, fol. 357 *b* ; Harl. 1758, fol. 231 ; Petworth, fol. 307 *b.* (Six-text Canterbury Tales, ed. F. J. Furnivall, Chaucer soc. 1871–8, parts v–viii, p. 685.)

[Ellesmere] ¶ Heere is ended the book / of the tales of Caunterbury / compiled by Geffrey Chaucer / of whos soule Ihesu crist / haue mercy Amen.

[Addit.] Explicit narracio Rectoris et ultima inter narraciones huius libri de quibus composuit Chaucer / cuius anime propicietur Deus / AMEN.

[Harl.] ¶ Here / endeth the / book / of / the / tales / of Caunterburye /. Compyled bi Geffroye / Chaucers /. Of / whos / soule / Ihesu crist / haue mercye / ¶ AmeN quod Cornhylle.

[Petworth] Here endeþ þe boke of þe talys of Canterbury compiled by Geffray Chawcer on whoos soule Ihesu crist haue mercy // AmeN //

[*c.* **1420-30.**] **Unknown.** *Headline* to *Sir Thopas.* MSS. Ellesmere, fol. 155 *b* ; Hengwrt, fol. 213 *b* ; Cambridge Univ. lib. Gg. 4. 27, fol. 323 ; Corpus, fol. 215 ; Petworth, fol. 224. (Six-text Canterbury Tales, ed. F. J. Furnivall, Chaucer soc. 1871–8, parts i–iii, p. 191.)

[Ellesmere]   Heere bigynneth Chaucers tale of Thopas.
[Hengwrt]   Heere bigynneth Chaucers tale of Thopas.
[Cambridge] Heere begynnyth Chaucers tale of sere Thopas.
[Corpus]   Here bygynneth þe tale of Chaucer of sire Thopas.
[Petworth] Here bygynneþ þe tale of chaucere by Sire Thopace.

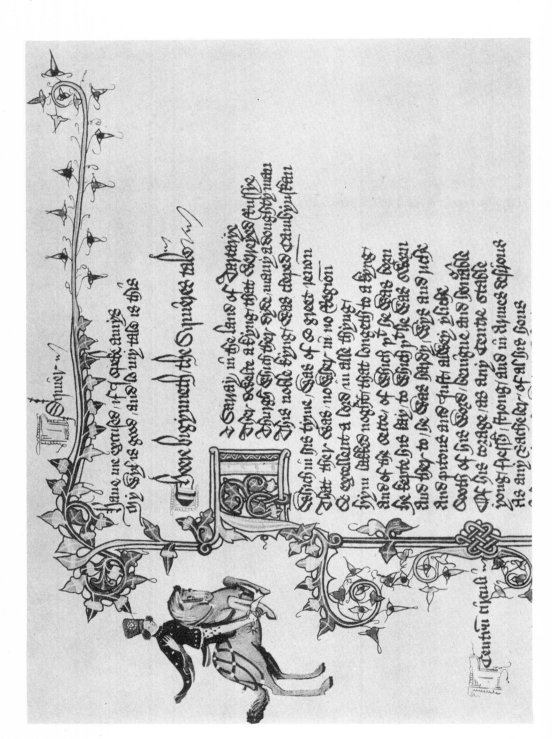

[**1420-30.**] **Unknown.** *Headlines and colophons to Tale of Melibeus.*
MSS. Ellesmere, ff. 157 *b*, 171 ; Hengwrt, ff. 216, 234 *b* ; Corpus,
fol. 217 *b* [headline only]; Lansdowne, 851, ff. 192, 206 ; Harl.
1758, fol. 182 [col. only] ; Petworth, fol. 246 *b* [col. only]. (Six-
text Canterbury Tales, ed. F. J. Furnivall, Chaucer soc. 1871-8,
part iv, pp. 201, 252.)

[Ellesmere] ¶ Heere bigynneth Chaucers tale of Melibee.
            ¶ Heere is ended Chaucers tale of Melibee / and
            of Dame Prudence.
[Hengwrt] ¶ Heere bigynneth Chaucers tale of Melibeus.
            ¶ Here is endid / Chaucers tale / of Melibe.
[Corpus]   Here bygynneþ Chauceres tale of⸍ Melibe and
            his wyf⸍ Prudence and his doughter Sapience.
[Lansdowne] Hic incipit fabula de Mellybeo *per* Chaucer.
            Explicit⸍ Fabula Galfridi Chaucer / de Melibeo.
            Milite
[Harl. 1758] Here / endith Chaucers / tale / of⸍ Melibe / And
            Prudence.
[Petworth] ¶ Here endeþ chaucers tale of melebye.

[*c.* **1420-35.**] **Unknown.** *Headline to Prioress's end link.* MSS. Ellesmere, fol. 155 ; Hengwrt, fol. 213 ; Cambridge Univ. lib. Gg. 4. 27,
fol. 322 *b* ; and side-note in Lansdowne 851, fol. 189. (Six-text
Canterbury Tales, ed. F. J. Furnivall, Chaucer soc. 1871-8, parts
i-iii, p. 190.)

[Ellesmere] Bihoold the murye wordes of the Hoost⸍ to
            Chaucer.
[Hengwrt] Bihoold the myrie talkyng / of the Hoost /. to
            Chaucer.
[Cambridge] Byhold the myrie talkynge of the Hoost⸍ to
            Chaucer.
[Lansdowne] Byhold the myrie talkynge of the Hoost⸍ to
            Chaucer.

1421-2. Hoccleve, Thomas. [*Dialogus cum Amico.*] MS. Durham iii,
9, fol. 23 *b*. (Hoccleve's works, ed. F. J. Furnivall, E. E. T. soc.
vol. i, The minor poems, 1892, p. 135, ll. 694-7.)

       The wyf of Bathe, take I for auctrice
       þat wommen han no ioie ne deyntee
       þat men sholde vp-on hem putte any vice ;
       I woot wel so / or lyk⸍ to þat, seith shee.
CHAUCER CRITICISM.

[*c.* 1421-5.] **Lydgate**, John. *Horse, Goose, Sheep.* Incip*it* Dis*putacio*
inter Equu*m* Aucam, & Ouem. MS. Harl. 699, fol. 68. (Political,
religious and love poems, ed. F. J. Furnivall, E. E. T. soc., 2nd edn.
1903, p. 18.)

> ¶ The hardy prikeris / vpon hors[ë] bak
>> Be sent to-forn) / what ground is best to take,
>> In that ordynaunce, that ther be no lak
>>> Bi providance / the feelde / whan thei shal make,
>>> An hors wole weepë / for his maistir sake :
>>>> Chaunser remembrith / the swerd, the ryng, the glas,
>>>> Presented wern) / vpon a stede of bras.

1423. James I., King of Scotland. *The Kingis Quair.* Unique MS.
Arch. Selden B. 24. (Ed. W. W. Skeat, Scott. text soc. 1884, p. 48.)

> Vnto [the] Impnis of my maister*is* dere,
>> Gowere and chaucere, that oñ the steppis satt
> Of rethorike, quhill thai were lyvand here,
>> Superlatiue as poetis laureate
>> In moralitee and eloqueñce ornate,
>>> I reco*m*mend my buk In lynis sevin,
>>> And eke thair saulis vn-to the blisse of heviñ. Ameñ.

[For general resemblance of this poem to Chaucer's work, *see also ibid.* Introd. pp.
xxiii–xxxii, xxxvii, and notes, pp. 57–96; and English Poets, ed. T. H. Ward,
2nd edn. 1883, vol. i. pp. 129–31.]

[*c.* 1425.] **Unknown.** *Colophon at end of Chaucer's Parliament of
Foules.* MS. Camb. Univ. lib. Gg. 4. 27, fol. 490 *b.* (Parallel text
of Chaucer's minor poems, ed. F. J. Furnivall, Chaucer soc. [1871],
p. 98.)

Explicit' p*ar*liamentu*m* Auiu*m* In die s*an*cti Valentini tentu*m*
secund*um* Galfridu*m* Chaucer.   Deo gracias.

[1426.] **Lydgate**, John. *The Pilgrimage of the Life of Man.* [Translated
by Lydgate from the French of Diguileville.] MS. Cott. Vitel.
Cxiii, ff. 256 *b*-7. (Ed. F. J. Furnivall, E. E. T. soc. 1901, part ii,
pp. 527, 528, ll. 19751–89.)

> And touchynge the translacioun
> Off thys noble Orysoun,
> Whylom (yiff I shal nat feyne)
> The noble poete off Breteyne,
> My mayster Chaucer, in hys tyme,
> Affter the Frenche he dyde yt ryme,
> Word by word, as in substaunce,
> Ryght as yt ys ymad in Fraunce,
> fful devoutly, in sentence,
> In worshepe, and in reuerence

Off that noble hevenly quene,
Bothe moder and a maydë clene.

And sythe, he dyde yt vndertake,
ffor to translate yt ffor hyr sake,
I pray thys [Quene] that ys the beste,
ffor to brynge hys soule at reste,
That he may, thorgh hir prayere,
Aboue the sterrys bryht and clere,
Off hyr mercy and hyr grace
Apere afforn hyr sonys fface,
Wyth seyntys eu*ere*, for A memórye,
Eternally to regne in glorye.

And ffor memoyre off that poete,
Wyth al hys rethorykës swete,
That was the ffyrste in any age
That amendede our langage;
Therfore, as I am bou*n*de off dette,
In thys book I wyl hym sette,
And ympen thys Orysoñ
Affter hys translac*i*on,
My purpós to détermyne,
That yt shal énlwmyne
Thys lytyl book, Rud off makyng,
Wyth som clause off hys wrytyng.

And as he made thys Orysou*n*
Off ful devout entenc*i*ou*n*,
And by maner off a prayere,
Ryht so I wyl yt settyn here,
That men may knowe and pleynly se
Off Our lady the .A. b. c.

[Here follows Chaucer's A B C Prayer to the Virgin.]

[c. **1430 ?**] **Lydgate**, John. *Nowe foloweþe here þe maner of a bille by wey of supplicacou*n *putte to þe kyng holding his noble feest of Christmasse in þe Castel of Hertford, as in a disguysing of þe Rude vpplandische people compleyning on hir wyues, with þe boystous aunswere of hir wyues, deuysed by lydegate.* MS. Trin. Coll. Cambridge, R. 3. 20. ff. 45–6. (Printed by E. P. Hammond [in] Anglia, vol. xxii, Halle, 1899, pp. 371–2.)

[The wives answer]

And for oure partye þe worthy wyff of Bathe
Cane shewe statutes moo þan six or seuen

howe wyves make hir housbandes wynne heven

.　　.　　.　　.　　.　　.　　.　　.

þer pacyence was buryed long agoo
Gresyldes story recordeþe pleinly soo.

[The editress states that she is unable to fix a probable or even approximate date
for this ' disguising'.]

[1430.] Lydgate, John.　*The Prohemy of a marriage betwix an olde
man and a yonge wife*, etc.　MS. Harl. 372, fol. 45.　(Lydgate's
minor poems, ed. J. O. Halliwell, 1840, Percy soc., vol. ii, p. 28.)

Remembre wele / on olde Ianuary
Which maister Chaunceres / ful seriously descryueth
And on fressh May / and how Iustyne did vary,
Fro placebo / but yet þe olde man wyueth
þus sone he wexeth blynde / & þan onthryueth
Fro worldly joye / for he sued bad doctryne ;
Think on Damyan / Pluto & Proserpyne.

[Dr. H. N. MacCracken considers this poem is far more likely to be by Hoccleve
than by Lydgate. *See* his Lydgate Canon, Philological soc. Trans. 1908, p. xliv.]

[1430.] Lydgate, John.　*This world is a thurghefare ful of woo*,
MS. Harl. 2251, fol. 249 (old no. 275 *b*).　(Lydgate's minor poems,
ed. J. O. Halliwell, 1840, Percy soc., vol. ii, p. 128.)

O, ye maysters, that cast shal yowre looke
Vpon this dyte made in wordis playne,
Remembre sothly that I the Refreyd tooke,
Of hym that was in makynge souerayne,
My mayster Chaucier, chief poete of Bretayne,
Whiche in his tragedyes made full yore agoo,
Declared trewly and list nat for to seyne,
How this world is a thurghfare ful of woo.

[1430.] Unknown.　*Headlines*, etc., in MS. Addit. 35,286, the best
Ashburnham MS. of the Canterbury Tales, ff. 166, 168 *b*, 188.

Here bigynneth Chaucers tale of syr Topas.
Here bigynneth Chaucers tale of Melibee and prudence.
Here endeth Chaucers tale of Melibee and prudence.

1430. Lydgate, John.　*Fall of Princes*.　MSS. Harl. 1766, ff. 8, 8 *b*, 9,
9 *b*, 26, 26 *b*, 101, 190, and 262, and Harl. 4203, ff. 78 *b*, col. 2. 140 *b*,
col. 1.
　　[1] *Here begynneth the boke of Johan Bochas discryuing the fall
of princes. . . . Translated in to Englysshe by John̄ Lydgate.* [col.]
Imprinted at London in flete strete by **Richarde Pynson**. . . . 1527.

[2] *A Treatise . . . shewing . . the falles of . . . Princes . . . First. compyled in Latin by the excellent Clerke Bocacius . . . and . . . translated . . . by Dan John Lidgate . . .* [col.] Imprinted at London . . . by Richard Tottel 1554.

[3] *The tragedies, gathered by John Bochass, of all such Princes as fell from theyr estates. . . . Translated into Englysh by John Lydgate. . . .* Imprinted at London, by John Wayland . . . [1558]

[For convenience of identification, references to all three editions are given, numbered respectively 1, 2, 3.]

Harl. 1766, fol.	8–9 *b*	(1) A ii–iii	(2) A ii–iii	(3) A ii–ii *b*	
„ „ „	26–26 *b*	(1) viii *b*–ix	(2) viii *b*–ix	(3) viii–*b*	
„ „ „	101	(1) xlvii	(2) xlvi	(3) xliii *b*	
„ 4203 „	78 *b*	(1)	(2) xc [only in this edn.]		
„ „ „	140	(1) clxiiii–*b*	(2) clxiiii *b*	(3) cliiii	
„ 1766 „	190	(1) clxxx	(2) clxxx	(3) sign aa iii *b*	
„ „ „	262	(1)	(2) ccxvii [only in this edn.]		

My mayster Chaunceer / with his fressh comodyes,   [Harl. 1776
    Is ded, Allas / Cheef Poete of breteyne,   fol. 8.]
That whylom made / ful pitous tragedyes :
    The Fal of Prynces / he did also compleyne
    As he that was / of makyng¹ souereyne ;
        Whoom al this lond / shulde of ryght preferre,
        Sith of your language / he was the lodesterre.

. . . .

[Then, after mentioning 'Senek in Rome . . And Tullius . . Fraunceys Petrark . . And John Bochas,' and their works of 'materys lamentable,' Lydgate goes on]

And semblably / as I haue toold to-fforn,   [fol. 8 *b*]
    my mayster Chaunceer / did his besynesse
And in his dayës / hath so wel hym born,
    Out of our tounge / tauoyden al Rudnesse,
    And to Reffourme it / with Colours of swetnesse
        Wherfore let vs / yiue hym lawde and glorye
        And putte his name / with Poetys in memorye.

Off whoos labour / to makë mencïonᵓ,
    Wheer-thorugh he shulde / of ryght comendyd be,
In yowthe he madë / a translacïonᵓ
    Off a book / which callyd is Trophe
    In lombard tounge / as men may Rede and see,
        And in Our Vulgar / longe or that he deyde,
        Gaff it the name / of Troylus and Creseyde,

Which for to Redë / louers hem delyte,
They ha[n] ther-Inne / so greet Deuocïoŋ
And this Poete / hym-sylff also to quyte,
Off Boeces book / the consolacïoŋ
made in his tyme / an hool translacïoŋ
 And to his sone / that Callyd was 'lowys,'
 he made a tretees / ful noble and of greet prys

Vpon thastrelabre / in ful notable fourme
Sette hem in Ordre / with ther dyuisïoŋs,
mennys wittes / taplyen and confourme,
To Vndirstonde / be ful expert Resoŋs,
Be Domeffying / of sondry mansyoŋs,
 The Roote Out sought / at the assendent
 To-fforn or he gaff / ony Iugëment.

He wrot also / ful many a day agone,
Dante in ynglyssh [1] / hym-sylff so doth expresse,
The pitous story / of Ceix and Alcyone
And the Deth of blaunchë / the Duchesse ;
And notably / [he] did his besynesse
 By greet auys / his wittës to dyspose
 To translate / the Romaunce of the Rose.

Thus in Vertu / he set al his entent /
ydelnesse and vices / for to Flee.
Off foulys also / he wrot the parlement /
Ther-Inne remembryng / of Royal Egles thre
how in ther Choys / they felte aduersite
 To-for naturë / proffryd the bataylle,
 Ech for his party / yiff it wolde auaylle.

He dyd also / his dilligence / and peyne   [fol. 9]
In Our Vulgar / to translate and endyte
Orygen / vpon the mawdeleyne ;

[1] [This statement by Lydgate, which is repeated by Bale ('Dantem Italum transtulit,' *see* below, App. A. 1557-9), Speght (in his list of Chaucer's works in his 1598 edn. fol. ci.), Laurence Humphrey, 1582 below, p. 122, Edward Leigh 1656, pp. 232-3, and others, has given rise to considerable discussion as to whether Chaucer did or did not translate any part of Dante (*see* Studies in Chaucer, by T. R. Lounsbury, vol. i, p. 425, vol. ii, pp. 236-7). Prof. Skeat holds that under this name Lydgate is referring to the 'House of Fame' which shows marked Dante influence (Minor Poems of Chaucer, pp. lxx-lxxi, *see also* an article by A. Rambeau, in Englische Studien, 1880, vol. iii, p. 209, 'Chaucer's House of Fame in seinem Verhältniss zu Dante's Divina Commedia'). Dr. Paget Toynbee does not agree that this refers to the House of Fame, as Lydgate was ignorant of Italian, *see* Dante in English Literature, 1909, pp. 1-2.]

And of the lyon / a book he did wryte.
Off Anneleyda / and of fals Arcyte
 he made a compleynt / doolful and pytous,
 And of the brochë / which that Vulcanus

At thebes wrought / ful dyuers of nature,
Ouyde wryteth / whoo therof hadde a sight /
For hyħ desir / he shuldë nat endure
 But he it hadde / neuir be glad nor lyght /
 And yif he hadde it / Onys in his myght /
  lych as my mayster / seith and wryt in dede
  It to conserue / he shulde ay leue in drede.

This poete wrot / at Request of the quene,
 A legendë / of parfight hoolynesse
Off goode women / to Fynden out nyntene
 That did excelle / in bounte and fayrnesse,
 But for his labour / and his besynesse
  Was inportable / his wittes to encoumbre,
  In al this world / to Fynde so greet a noumbre.

He made the book / of Cauntirbury talys
 Whan the pylgrymës / Rood on pylgrymage
Thorugh-out kent / by hillës and by Valys,
 And al the storyes / toold in ther passage,
 Endyted hem / ful wel in our language,
  Somme of knyghthood / and somme of gentillesse,
  And somme of loue / and somme of parfightnesse,

And somme also / of greet moralyte,
 Somme of dispoort / includyng greet sentence.
In prose he wrot / the tale of mellybe
 And of his wyff / that callyd was prudence,
 And of Grysyldes / parfight pacience,
  And how the monk / of storyes newe and Olde,
  Pitous tragedyes / by the weyë tolde.

This seide Poete / my mayster, in his Dayes,
 Made and compyled / ful many a fressh Dyte,
Compleyntës, ballades / Roundelles, Virrelayes
 Ful delytable / to heryn and to se,
 For which, men shulde / of ryght and equite,
  Sith he of ynglyssh / in makyng was the beste
  Prey vn-to god / to yeue his soule good Reste.

And this Poetys / I make of mencïon)   [fol. 9 *b*]
 Wer, be Old tyme / had in greet deynte,
With kynges, Prynces / in eu*er*y Regïon)
 Gretly *p*referryd / afftir ther degre,
 For lordys haddë / plesaunce for to se,
  To studye among / and to Caste ther lookys
  At good leyser / vpon wysë bookys.

. . . .   [fol. 26, at foot]

But yif ye lyst / haue cleer inspeccïon)
 Off this stoory / vpon eu*er*y syde,
 Redith the legende / of martyrs of Cupyde
  which that Chauncer / in Ordre as they stood,
  Compyled of women / that wer callyd good.

TOwchyng the stoory / of Kyng Pandyon)   [fol. 26 *b*]
 And of his goodly / fayrë Doughtre tweyne,
How Thereus / fals of Condicïon),
 hem to Dysceyue / did his besy peyne,
 They bothe namyd / of bewte sou*er*eyne,
  Goodly progne / and yong[e] phylomene,
  Bothe Innocentys / and of Entent ful Clene.

Ther pitous Fate / in hopë to expresse,
 It wer to me but a presumpcïon),
Sith that Chauncer / dyd his besynesse
 In his legende / as made is mencyon),
 Ther martirdam / and ther passyon)
  For to Rehersen hem / and dyd his besy peyne
  As Cheef Poetë / Callyd of breteyne.

Off goodë women / a book he did wryte,
 The nou*m*bre vncomplet / fully of nyntene,
And ther the stoory / he pleynly did endyte
 Off Tereus of progne / and phylomene
 wher ye may seen / ther legende, thus I mene,
  Doth hem worshepe / and forth ther lyff doth shewe
  For a Cleer merour / be Cause ther be so fewe,

I wyl passe ouir / and speke of hem no more,
 And vn-to Cadmus / forth my stylë dresse.
  . . . .

TOwchyng lucrece / Exaumple of wyffly trouthe,   [fol. 101]
    How yongë Tarquyn / hire falsly did Oppresse,
And afftir that / which was a greet[e] Routhe
    How she hire sylff / slowh for heuynesse
    It nedith nat / Rehersyn the processe,
        Sith that Chaunceer / Cheef Poete of breteyne
        Wrot of hire lyff / a legende souereyne.

Ek othir stooryes / which he wroot in his lyue
    Ful notably / with euery Circumstaunce,
And ther Fatys / did pitously descryue,
    Lyk as they Fyl / put hem in Remembraunce.
    Wherfore / yiff I shulde my penne auaunce
        Afftir his makyng / to putte hem in memórye,
        Men wolde deme it / presumpcioṅ and veynglorye.

FOr as a sterre / in presence of the sonne
    Lesith his fresshnesse / and his Cleer[e] lyght,
So my Rudnessë / vndir skyës donne,
    Daryth ful lowë / and hath lost his syght
    To be comparyd / ageyn the beemys bryght
        Off this Poete / wherfore it wer but veyn ;
        Thyng seid by hym / to wryte it newe ageyn.

        .   .   .   .

Dant In ytaylle . Virgyle in Romë towṅ),   [Harl. 4203, fol. 78 b.,
    Petrak in Florence . hadde al hys plesance,   col. 2]
And prudent Chauseer . in brutys Albyoṅ),
    lik hys desyr . fondᵗ vertuous suffysance.
    Fredam of lordshype . weyed in ther ballance
        Be cause they flouryd . in wysdam & science ;
        Support of prynces . fonde hem ther dyspence.

In this trouble . dreedful & odyous   [fol. 140 b, col. 1]
    As is rehersyd . in ordyr ye may reede,
The noble knyght . Paulus Lucious
    Exiled was . of malis & hatereede,
    Folwyng vpon . the grete horrible dede,
        The pitous detħ . & the hateful cas
        Of gret Antonye . & Cleopatras.

The tragedyë . of these ilkë tweyne
    For me, as now . shal be set a-syde,
Cause Chaucer . cheef poyet of bretaygne,

In hys book . the legende of Cupyde,
Seying ther hertys . coudë not devyde.
  Remembryng . there . as oon they dide endure,
  So wer they buryed . in oon sepulture.

Thyng onys seid . be labour of chauceer
Were presumpcion) . me to make ageyn),
Whos makyng was . so notable & enteer'
  Ryght compendious . & notable in certeyn),
  Which to reherse . the labour were in veyn),
    Bochas remembryng . how Cleópatras
    Causyd Antonye . that he destroyed was.

Hyr auarice . was so Importable,   [col. 2]
  He supprysed . with hyr gret fayrnesse,
Folwyng ther lustys . foul & habomynable,
  She desyryng . to haue the Emperesse,
  And he, allas . of froward wylfulnese
    To plesyn hyr . vnhappily began)
    To werreyë . the gret Octauyan).

.   .   .   .   .   .

Myn Auctour here / no lengere lyst soiourne,   [Harl. 1776,
  Off this Emperours / the Fallys for to wryte,   fol. 190]
But in haste / he doth his stylë tourne
  To Zenobia / hire story for tendyte ;
  But, for chaunceer / so wel did hym quyte
    In this tragédyes / hir pitous fal tentrete,
    I wyl passe ovir / Rehersyng but the grete.

In his book / of Cauntirbury talys,
  This souereyn Poete / of brutys Albyon),
Thorough pylgrymes toold / by hillys and by valys,
  Whereof Zenobia / is made mencyon)
  Off hire noblesse / and of hire hyh Renon)
    In a tragedye / Compendyously told al
    Hir marcyal prowesse / and hire pitous fal.

I nevir was aqueynted / with virgyle   [fol. 262]
  nor with sugryd Dytees / of Omer,
nor Dares frygius / with his goldene style,
  nor with Ovyde / in Poetrye moost entieer,
  nor with the souereyn balladys of Chaunceer,
    which, among alle / that euere wer Rad or songe,
    Excellyd al othir / in our Englyssh tonge.

.   .   .   .

As the gold-tressyd / bryght[e] somyr sonne
  Passith othir sterrys / with his beemys clere,
And as Lucynya / Chaseth skyës donne,
  The frosty nyghtes / whan Esperus doth appere,
  Ryght so my[1] mayster / had[dë] neuir pere,   [1] MS. my may
    I mene Chaunceer / in stooryes that he tolde,
    And he also wrot / tragedyës Olde.
The Fal of Prynces / gan pitously compleyne
  As Petrark did / and also Iohn̄ bochas,
Laureat Fraunceys / Poetys bothë tweyne,
  Toold how Prynces / for theer greet trespace,
  wer ouirthrowe / Rehersyng al the caas
    As Chaunceer did / in the monkys tale . . . .

[The two references from Harl. 4203 are wanting in the earlier and better MS. Harl.
1766. *See* below, p. 219, 1641, Wits Recreation, where the first verse is given.]

[*c.* **1430–40.**] **Shirley**, John. *Headlines* to *Fortune.* MSS. Camb.
  Univ. lib. Ii. 3. 21, fol. 53; Fairfax 16, fol. 191; and Shirley's two
  MSS., Ashmole 59, fol. 37, and Trin. Coll. Camb. R. 3. 20, fol.
  142. (Parallel text of Chaucer's minor poems, ed. F. J. Furnivall,
  Chaucer soc. [1871], pp. 440–1.)

[Ii. 3. 21] Cau*ser* / Balades de vilage sanz pein*ture.*

[Ashmole] ¶ Here foloweþe nowe a compleynte of þe
Pleintyff[t] ageinst[t] agenst [*sic*] fortune translated[t] oute of
ffrenshe into Englisshe by þat famous Rethorissyen⟩ / Geffrey
Chaucier /

[Trin. Coll.] and[t] here filoweþe a balade made by Chaucier
of[t] þe louer / and[t] of[t] Dame ffortune.

[Fairfax] ¶ Balade de vilage saunz Peynture. Par Chaucer.

[*c.* **1430–40.**] **Unknown.** Fairfax MS. 16. *See* below, Appendix A.

1434–57. Gascoigne, Thomas. *Dictionarium Theologicum.* MS. 117,
  118, Lincoln Coll. Oxford, pars secunda, p. 377.

[Gascoigne, after mentioning Chaucer's regrets for some of
his writings, expressed just before his death, adds these words]:
" Fuit idem Chawserus pater Thome Chawserus [*sic*] armigeri,
qui Thomas sepelitur in Nuhelm [Ewelme] juxta Oxoniam."

[This extract is printed by Prof. J. W. Hales in his article on 'Geoffrey and Thomas
Chaucer,' in *Athenæum*, March 31, 1888, pp. 404–5. It does not occur in Loci e libro
veritatum, passages selected from Gascoigne's theological dictionary, ed. J. E.
Thorold-Rogers, 1881. This is the earliest assertion that Thomas Chaucer was the
poet's son. For the whole question see *Life Records of Chaucer*, Chaucer soc., 1900,
part iv, pp. li–lvii; also *Chaucer a bibliographical manual*, by E. P. Hammond,
N. York, 1908, pp. 47–8.]

1439. Lydgate, John. *The glorious lyfe and passion of seint Albon . . . and . . . saint Amaphabel.* MSS. Trin. Coll. Camb. 39 ; Lincoln 57, etc. Sign. a ii. of the edn. pr. in 1534 at the request of Robert Catton. [Unique copy in the B. M., pr. mk. C. 34. g. 17.] (ed. C. Horstmann 1882, p. 11.)

> The golden trompet of the house of fame,
> With full swyfte wyngës of the pegasee
> Hath [blowe ?] full farre the knyghtly mannes name,
> Borne in Verolame, a famous olde citie.

[*c.* **1440.**] **Unknown.** *Note* to Lydgate's Troy Book in MS. Roy. 18 D. ii fol. 88 [ink, 87 pencil] *b.* col. i at foot. Of the worshipful recommendacyoñ that the monke of Bury þat translate þis boke gaue Chaucere, þe chef poete off Breteyne.

> Sythe my Maystare chaucer here aforne.

[*See* above, p. 25, for this reference of Lydgate's to Chaucer.]

[*c.* **1440.**] **Unknown.** *Headline* to *general prologue to Canterbury Tales.* Harl. 1758, fol. 1. (Six-text Canterbury tales, ed. F. J. Furnivall, Chaucer soc. 1871–8, pts. i–iii, p. 1.)

> hEre begynneth the book of tales of Caunterburye . compiled by Geffraie Chaucers . of Brytayne chef poete.

[**1440 ?**] **Unknown.** *The Tale of Colkelbie Sow.* Bannatyne MS. [1566]. Printed for the Hunterian club [ed. James Barclay Murdoch], 1896, vol. iv, p. 1048. (Early popular poetry of Scotland, ed. David Laing (revised W. C. Hazlitt 1895), vol. i, p. 210.)

> Twenty-four chikkynis of þame scho hes
> .   .   .   .   .   .
> The first wes the samyn Chantecleir to luke
> Off quhome Chaucer treitis in to his buke,
> And his lady Partlot sister and wyfe
> Quhilk wes no lyse in detis of þat lyfe.

[Robert Pitcairn, in his introduction to Early popular poetry of Scotland, ed. by David Laing (vol. i, pp. 179–81), says "that from the Prohemium the poem appears to have been written during the era of Minstrelsy, although from internal evidence posterior to Chaucer," and he therefore assigns it to "some time previous to the middle of the 15th century, since it seems to have been very popular considerably anterior to the age of Douglas and Dunbar."]

[*c.* **1440.**] **Unknown.** *The Chaunces of the Dyse.* MS. Fairfax 16, ff. 152, 153 *b* (supplementary vol. to Minor Poems of Lydgate, ed. MacCracken, E. E. T. soc., in preparation).

> Of olde stories taken ye grete hede   [fol. 152]
> That ye ne had moo bokes is gret skathe
> For your talent ys gretely set to rede

Ye kan by rote the wifes lyfe of Bathe
He myght wel sey ful erlych and to rathè
Chosen he had that machched with yow were
Sure of a shrewe myght he ben with out fere.

. . . .

Creseyde is here in worde bothe thought and dede [fol. 153 b]
Fil neuer dise sith god was bore so trewe

. . . .

Ye leue youre olde and taken newe and newe.

[This poem has one stanza for every possible throw, and, like Ragman Roll, the stanza was given as a 'fortune' to the thrower. It is quoted by Stowe as being by Chaucer, *q.v.*, p. 159 below.]

[*c.* 1440.] **Unknown.** *A Rebuke to Lydgate.* MS. Fairfax 16, fol. 326 *a* (supplementary vol. to Minor Poems of Lydgate, ed. H. N. MacCracken, E. E. T. soc., in preparation).

So wolde god that my symple connyng [15]
  Ware sufficiaunt this goodly flour to prayse
For as to me ys noŋ so ryche a thyng
  That able were this flour to counterpayse
O noble chaucer passyd beŋ thy dayse
Off poetrye ynamyd worthyest [20]
  And of makyng᾿ in alle othir days the best

  Now thou art go thyñ helpe I may not haue
    Wherfor to god I pray right specially
  Syth thou art dede and buryde in thy graue
    That oŋ thy sowle hym lyst to haue mercy [25]
  And to the monke of bury now speke I
For thy connyng᾿ ys syche and eke thy grace
After chaucer to occupye his place.

[*c.* 1440.] **Unknown.** *Head lines and end lines* [in] Addit. MS. 34,360, ff. 21 *b*, 49, 53.

[fol. 21 b] Balade that Chauncier made, [with an 'Envoy' of six lines, beginning :] So hath myn hert caught in remembraunce.

. . . .

[fol. 49] [Chaucer's Complaint to Pity, headed, as in Harl. 78, fol. 80,] And now here folwith A Complaynt of Pite made by Geffray Chauncier the Aureat Poete that euer was founde in oure vulgar to fore his dayes.

. . . .

[fol. 53] Explicit Pyte dan Chaucer lauture.

[*See* Two British Museum MSS. by E. P. Hammond [in] Anglia, vol. xxviii, 1905, pp. 1–28.]

[*c.* **1440.**] **Unknown.** *A Greeting on New Year's morning.* Lambeth MS. 306, fol. 136. (Political, religious and love poems, ed. F. J. Furnivall, E. E. T. soc. [new edn. 1903], p. 66, l. 19.)

> palaman gafe his herte to emely.

[This refers most probably to Chaucer's *Knight's Tale*, rather than to Boccaccio. Such, at least, is Dr. Furnivall's opinion.]

[**1443-7 ?**] **Bokenam,** Osbern. *The Lewys of Seyntys.* Translated into Englys be a Doctour of Dyuynite clepyd Osbern Bokenam, Frer Austyn of the Conuent of Stokclare. Unique MS. Arundel 327. *Vita Sanctae Margaretae*, ll. 170-8. (Reprinted for Roxb. club 1835, p. 13. O. Bokenam's Legenden, ed. Carl Horstmann 1883, pp. 11, 12.)

> . . as Homer / Ouyde or ellys Virgyle
>
> Or Galfryd of Ynglond / I wolde cōpyle
>
> A clere descripcyoūn / ful expressely
>
> Of alle hyr feturys / euene by & by
>
> But sekyr I lakke both eloquens
>
> And ku*n*nyng / swych maters to dilate
>
> For I dwellyd neu*e*re / w^t the fresh rethoryens
>
> Gower / Chauncers / ner wyth lytgate.
>
> Wych lyuyth yet / lest he deyed late.

[Galfryde of Ynglond in Prol. l. 83 is Galfridus de Vinosalvo. *See* The temple of glas, ed. J. Schick, E. E. T. soc. 1891, notes, p. 78; and *cf.* above, p. 17 [*c.* 1403?] Lydgate, Court of Sapyence, note.]

[*c.* **1444. Lydgate,** John.] *Poem on the truce of* 1444. MS. Harl. 2255, fol. 132. (Political poems and songs, ed. Thomas Wright, 1861, vol. ii, p. 216.)

> Comou*n* *Astrologeer* as folk expert weel knowe
>
> To kepe the howrys and tydis of the nyght,
>
> Sumtyme hih and sumtyme he syngith lowe
>
> *Dam pertelot* sit wi*th* hire brood dou*n* right
>
> The *ffox* comyth neer with oute Candellyght
>
> To trete of pees, menyng no treson,
>
> To avoyde al gile and ffraude he hath be hight
>
> Alle go we stille the *Cok* hath lowe shoon.

[Each verse ends with the same refrain, and the first three verses (the above is the fourth) of the poem point out that 'specche is but fooly and sugryd elloquence' and that silence is good. Reminiscences of the *Nonne Preestes Tale* run all through the first four verses.]

[*c.* **1445 ?** **De la Pole,** William, Duke of Suffolk ?] *See* below, Appendix A.

[*c.* **1445 ?**] **Shirley,** John. *Sidenote to Chaucer's A. B. C.* in MS. Sion Coll., Arc. 2. 23, fol. 79. (Odd texts of Chaucer's minor poems, ed. F. J. Furnivall, Chaucer soc. 1868-80, p. 66.)

> ¶ Chauc[er] ¶ Deuotissima oracio [ad] Mariam . p*ro* om*n*i ten[tacione] tribulaci*one* necess[itate] angustia.

[*c.* **1445.**] **Unknown,** and **Shirley,** John. *Headline* to *Lack of Stedfastness.* MSS. Harl. 7333, fol. 147 *b*, and Shirley's Trin. Coll. Camb. R. 3. 20, *b* of 10th fol. from end. (Parallel-text of Chaucer's minor poems, ed. F. J. Furnivall, Chaucer soc. [1871], p. 434.) *See* below, App. A.

[Harl.] This balade made Geffrey Chaunciers the Laureat Poete Of¹ Albion and sent it to his souerain lorde kynge Richarde the secounde þane being / in his Castel of / Windesore /.

[Cambridge] ¶ Balade Royal made by · oure laureal poete of Albyon · in hees laste yeeres /.

[*c.* **1445.**] **Unknown.** *Headline* to *Marriage or Bukton.* MS. Fairfax 16, fol. 193 *b*, and in Julian Notary's edn. *q.v.* (1499–1502, p. 65) sign. B iii. (Parallel-text of Chaucer's minor poems, ed. F. J. Furnivall, Chaucer soc. [1871], p. 424.)

[Fairfax] ¶ Lenvoy de Chaucer A Bukton. /
[Notary] Here foloweth the counceyll of Chaucer touchyng Maryag &c. whiche was sente te [*sic*] Bucketon &c.

[*c.* **1445.**] **Unknown.** *Headline* to *Envoy to Scogan.* MSS. Camb. Univ. lib. Gg. 4. 27, fol. 7 *b* ; Fairfax 16, fol. 192 *b* ; Pepys 2006, p. 385, hand E. (Parallel-text of Chaucer's minor poems, ed. F. J. Furnivall, Chaucer soc. [1871], p. 421.)

[Cambridge] Litera directa de Scogon per .G. C.
[Fairfax]   ¶ Lenuoy de Chaucer A Scogan./
[Pepys]   ¶ Lenuoie de Chaucer' A Scogan).

1448–9. Metham, John, of Norwich. *Amoryus and Cleopes.* Unique MS. Quaritch [since sold], Epilogue, [fol. 57 *?*.] (Political, religious and love poems, ed. F. J. Furnivall, E. E. T. soc. [new edn. 1903], pp. 306–7.)

And yff I *the* trwthe schuld here wryght,
As gret a style I schuld make in eue*r*y dregre,
As Chauncerys, off qwene Eleyne or Cresseyd, doht e*n*dyht,[so]
Or off Polyxchene, Grysyld, or Penelope.

.   .   .   .

My mastyr Chau*n*cerys, I mene, *that* longe dyd endur*e*
In practyk off rymyng ; qwerffor*e* proffoundëly
W*ith* many p*r*oue*r*bys, hys bokys be rymyd naturelly.

[*c.* **1450.**] **Burgh,** Benedict. *See* below, Appendix **A.**

[*c.* **1450.**] **Shirley,** John. *Headline* and *marginal note* to *Gentilesse.* Shirley's MSS. Ashmole 59, fol. 27 ; Trin. Coll. Camb. R. 3. 20*b* of fol. 9 from end ; Harl. 7333, fol. 147 *b*, col. 2. (Parallel-text of

Chaucer's minor poems, ed. F. J. Furnivall, Chaucer soc. [1871], p. 428.)

[Ashmole, marginal note] Geffrey Chaucier made þeos thre balades nexst þat followen //

[Cambridge] ¶ Balade by Chaucier.

[Harl.] ¶ Moral balade of / Chaucier /

[*c.* **1450**.] **Shirley,** John. *Headline to the Compleynt of Venus.* Shirley's MSS. Trin. Coll. Camb. R. 3. 20, fol. 139 ; and Ashmole 59, fol. 43 *b.* (Parallel-text of Chaucer's minor poems, ed. F. J. Furnivall, Chaucer soc. [1871], p. 412.)

[Trin. Coll.] And̛ filowing begynneþe · a balade translated̛ out̛ of̛ frensħe in to englissħe /by Chaucier Geffrey þe frensħe made . *sir* . Otes de Grauntsoɱe · knigħt · Sauosyen /

[Ashmole] Here begynneþe a balade made by þat worþy Knigħt of Sauoye in frenshe calde *sir* Otes Graunsoɱ . translated by . Chauciers //

[*c.* **1450**.] **Shirley,** John. *Headline to Stanza* in Ellesmere Lydgate MS. *See below,* App. A.

[*c.* **1450**.] **Shirley,** John. *Headline to Truth.* Shirley's MS. Trin. Coll. Camb. R. 3. 20 [2 copies], p. 144, and 9th fol. from end. (Parallel-text of Chaucer's minor poems, ed. F. J. Furnivall, Chaucer soc. [1871], p. 409.) *See* note below in App. A. under [*c.* 1450] Shirley.

¶ Balade þat Chaucier made on his deetħ bedde.

[*c.* **1450**.] **Shirley,** John. *Headline to Adam Scrivener.* Shirley's MS. Trin. Coll. Camb. R. 3. 20, 4th fol. from end. *Cf.* J. Stowe's edn. 1561, fol. ccclv *b,* col. 1. (Parallel-text of Chaucer's minor poems, ed. F. J. Furnivall, Chaucer soc. [1871], p. 177.)

[Trin. Coll.] ¶ Chauciers wordes · a . Geffrey vn to Adame his owen scryueyne.

[Stowe] Chaucers woordes vnto his owne Scriuener.

[*See* below, 1614, Ben Jonson, p. 189, for a reference to Adam Scrivener.]

[*c.* **1450**.] **Shirley,** John (?). *Headline to The Compleynt of Mars.* MS. Trin. Coll. Camb. R. 3. 20, fol. 130. (Parallel-text of Chaucer's minor poems, ed. F. J. Furnivall, Chaucer soc. [1871], p. 100.)

¶ Loo yee louers gladeþe and̛ comforteþe you . of̛ þallyánce etrayted̛ bytwene / þe hardy and̛ furyous Mars . þe god̛ of̛ armes / and̛ Venus þe double goddesse of̛ loue made by . Geffrey Chaucier . at þe comandement of̛ þe renōmed̛ and̛ excellent Prynce my lord̛ þe Duc Ioħn of̛ Lancastre.

[**1450**.] **Shirley,** John. *Heading and headline to* þe *Cronycle made by Chaucier.* MS. Ashmole 59, fol. 38 *b.* (Odd texts of Chaucer's minor poems, ed. F. J. Furnivall, Chaucer soc. 1868–80, app. p. vi.)

þe Cronycle made by Chaucier.

¶ Here nowe folowe þe names of¹ þe nyene worshipfullest¹
Ladyes þat in alle cronycles . and storyal bokes haue beo
foundeñ of trouþe of¹ constaunce and vertuous or reproched
womanhode . by Chaucier¹.

[*c.* **1450.**] **Shirley,** John. *Verses* in praise of Chaucer, in his metrical
prologue to Boethius de Consolacione Philosophiæ ; running title,
etc., and praise of Chaucer at the end of Boethius. Add. MS.
16,165, ff. 2, 4, 5 *b*–6, 8–12, 14 *b*–16, 21 *b*–22, 25 *b*–26, 33 *b*–36, 94.

þe prologe of the Kalendere of þis litell booke.   [fol. 2]

.   .   .   .

And for to put hit in youre mynde
First þus by ordre shul ye fynde
Of Boece þe hole translacyoun
And Phylosofyes consolacyoun
Laboured by Geffrey Chaucier   [fol. 2 *b*]
Whiche in oure volgare had neuere ys pere
Of eloquencyale Retorryke
In Englisshe was neuer noon him lyke
Gyff him þe prys and seyþe þerhoo
For neuer knewe ye such na moo. . . .

And þus endeþe . . . Boece . . . translated¹ by þe moral and
famous Chaucyer which first enlumyned þis lande with retoryen
and eloquent langage of oure rude englisshe modere tonge . . .

[*a.* **1450.**] **Unknown.** *The Tale of Beryn.* *See* below, Appendix A.

[*c.* **1450** ?] **Unknown.** *Poem. How a Louer Prayseth hys Lady.* MS.
Fairfax 16, fol. 309. (Temple of Glas, by J. Lydgate, ed. J. Schick,
E. E. T. soc., extra series lx, 1891, pp. cxliii, 78.)

Cum oñ Iulius, with su*m* of thy flouris ;
Englesshe geffrey¹ with al thy colourys,
That wrote so wel to pope Innocent ;
And mayster Chauser, sours and fundement
On englysshe tunge swetely to endyte
Thy soule god haue with virgynes white
Moral gower, lydgate, rether and poete
Ouide stase lucan of batylls grete
Wher art thou boece symach*us* and Guido
Virgil barnard Austyn and Varro
Archytressy melbeely and Aleyne
They knouwe me not my al is in veyne.

¹ [' Englesshe geffrey ' is Galfridus de Vinosalvo. *See* above, p. 17, note.]
CHAUCER CRITICISM.

[*c.* **1450.**] **Unknown.** *Headline* to *Purse.* MSS. Fairfax 16, fol. 193 ; Shirley's Harl. 7333, fol. 147 *b* ; and in French, Pepys 2006, p. 388, hand E. (Parallel-text of Chaucer's minor poems, ed. F. J. Furnivall, Chaucer soc. [1871], pp. 448–9.)

[Fairfax] The complaynt of Chaucer to his Purse.
[Harl.]   ¶ A supplicacion to Kyng Richard by chaucier.
[Pepys]   ¶ La Compleint de Chaucer' A sa Bourse Voide.

[*c.* **1450.**] **Unknown.** *Headlines* to *Proverbs.* MSS. Fairfax 16, fol. 195 *b* ; Harl. 7578, fol. 20. (Parallel-text of Chaucer's minor poems, ed. F. J. Furnivall, Chaucer soc. [1871], p. 432.)

[Fairfax] Prouerbe of Chaucer'.
[Harl.]   Prouerbe of Chaucers.

[Dr. Furnivall, p. 431, adds [Quod Chaucer] to the Answers, at Mr. Bradshaw's suggestion.]

[*c.* **1450.**] **Unknown.** *Headline* to *the Compleynte to Pite.* MSS. Harl. 78, fol. 8 ; Phillipps, Cheltenham, 9053, p. 91. (Parallel-text of Chaucer's minor poems, ed. F. J. Furnivall, Chaucer soc. [1871] p. 41, and note p. 49 ; More odd texts of Chaucer's minor poems, 1886, p. 11 ; Odd texts of Chaucer's minor poems, 1868–80, App., p. ii note.)

[Harl.] þe balade . of . Pytee . By Chauciers.
[Phillipps] And now here folwith A complaynt' of' pite made by Geffray Chaucier the Aureat' Poete that' eu*er* was founde in oure vulgar to fore his dayes.

[*c.* **1450.**] **Unknown.** *Colophon* to *Balade of Pite.* Phillipps MS., Cheltenham, 9053, p. 99. (More odd texts of Chaucer's minor poems, ed. F. J. Furnivall, Chaucer soc. 1886, p. 50.)

Explicit Pyte
dan Chaucer Lauceire (?).

[*c.* **1450.**] **Unknown.** *Latin headings and colophons* to MS. Egerton 2726 (Haistwell MS. of Cant. Tales, the H. A. of Tyrwhitt's edn.), ff. 180, 180 *b*, 197, 270 *b*.

[Fol. 1 in a late 16th or early 17th century hand, " Gaulfridus Chaucer " ; fol. 271, late 18th or early 19th century hand, in red ink, " here endith the Canterbury Tales compiled by Geffrey Chaucer, of whose soule Ihesu Crist haue mercy. Amen."]

1450.] **Unknown.** *Spurious links in the Canterbury Tales.*

[These links, or additional lines joining up the Tales, are given here, although they do not refer to Chaucer by name. Still, being of the nature of an addition to, and imitation of his work, they may be-termed references. With the exception of the first two extracts, which are not elsewhere printed, the text is not given.]

Four lines of a spurious Prologue to Sir Thopas, with some changes in the Prologue to Melibeus following, in MS. Trin.

Coll. Camb. R. 3 3, fol. 87, 87 *b*. [The true Prologue to Sir Thopas is not found in this MS.]

Hiere endeth the Manciples tale.
A Prolog and a tale tolde be Master Chaucer.

Whan Chaucers

be oure oost was praide.   To telle a tale he is na
withsaid.   But beningly
and with gode chere.   Began his tale
and saide as folwith hiere.

[fol. 87 *b*]   Listeneth lordinges in good entent . . .

[ll. 1–30 only : ending]

There any Ram shal stonde &ce.

[then follow 'Verba Hospitis,' *i. e.* prologue to Melibeus,
50 lines, including 2 lines (not in Skeat) at the end :]

Wich anon in profe I wol telle in this presence
Of Melibe & his wif & there douzter Sapience.

[also in place of Skeat, ll. 7–8, MS. has :]

Whi so quod I whi wolt thou lat me
That I may nat telle at my liberte.

[then at the end the rubric :]

Anothir   tale   in   prose ⎫
    tolde be mastir Chaucer ⎬
of Melibe and Prudence. ⎭

[followed by the Tale on fol. 88.]

Four additional lines at the end of the Cook's Tale in MS. Rawl.
poetry 141, fol. 29.

And thus w^t horedom & bryberye
To geder thei vsed till thei honged hye.
ffor who so euel byeth shal make a sory sale
And thus I make an ende of my tale.

Twelve additional lines at the end of the Cook's Tale in MS.
Bodley 686, printed in Chaucer's works, edn. of 1687, *q. v.* below,
p. 260.

Four lines between Cook's Tale and Gamelyn in MS. Lansdowne
851, printed in Canterbury Tales, ed. T. Wright, 1847, vol. i,
p. 175, also in App. A. of Six Text Canterbury Tales, ed.
Furnivall, 1868, part I.

Two lines between Cook's Tale and Gamelyn in MSS. Royal 18, C. ii, Sloane 1685, Barlow, Hatton, Laud 739, Camb. Univ. Libr. Mm. ii. 5, Petworth, Egerton 2863, Hodson-Ashburnham, printed in App. A. to Six Text Canterbury Tales, ed. Furnivall 1868, part I.

Sixteen lines between Merchant's Tale and W. of Bath in MSS. Barlow, Laud 739, Royal 18, C. ii, printed by Tyrwhitt in his edn. of the Canterbury Tales, 1775–8, vol. iv, note to l. 5583, also in Canterbury Tales, ed. T. Wright, 1847, vol. i, pp. 245–6 note, also in Chaucer, a bibliographical manual, by E. P. Hammond, N. York, 1908, p. 297.

Six lines between the Franklin's and Doctor's Tale in MS. Harl. 7335, printed by Tyrwhitt in his edn. of the Canterbury Tales, 1775–8, vol. ii, pp. 162–3, see also his Introd. Discourse, § xxviii, and his note on l. 11929; also printed by T. Wright in his edn. of the Canterbury Tales, 1847, vol. ii, pp. 245–6.

Fourteen lines between Canon's Yeoman's Tale and Doctor's Tale in MSS. Arch. Selden, B 14, Royal 17, D. xv, Royal 18 C. ii, Rawl. poet. 149, Petworth, Camb. Univ. Libr. Mm. ii. 5, Hatton, Sloane 1685, Barlow, Egerton 2863, Laud 739, printed in separate issue of the Petworth MS. Chaucer soc. 1875.

Sixteen lines between Canon's Yeoman's Tale and Doctor's Tale (different from above) in MS. Lansdowne 851, fol. 169, printed in separate issue of this MS., Chaucer soc., part V, 1875, also by T. Wright in Canterbury Tales, 1847, vol. ii, p. 245 note.

Twelve lines between Pardoner and Shipman's Tale in MSS. Harl. 1758, Rawl. poet. 149, Petworth, Camb. Univ. Libr. Mm. 25 and I i. 3. 26, Hatton, Sloane 1685, Barlow, Laud 739, Royal 18, C. ii, Egerton 2863, printed by Skeat in his edn. of the Canterbury Tales, Chaucer's works, vol. iv, 1894, p. 164 note; also the various MSS. readings in Specimens of . . . Moveable Prologues, prefixed to the Six Text Chaucer, ed. Furnivall, Chaucer soc. 1868, part I.

Six lines between Pardoner and Shipman's Tale (quite different from above) in MS. Lansdowne 851, fol. 180 *b*, printed in the separate issue of this MS., Chaucer soc., part V, 1875.

Eight lines ending Squire's Tale in MSS. Arch. Selden B 14 and Lansdowne 851, printed in the separate issue of Lansdowne MS., Chaucer soc., part iv, 1874, also by T. Wright, in his edn. of the Canterbury Tales, 1847, vol. ii, p. 157 and vol. i, p. 246 note.

Four lines introducing the Wife of Bath in MS. Lansdowne 851, printed in the Six Text Canterbury Tales, ed. Furnivall, 1868, also in separate issue of Lansdowne MS., Chaucer soc., part IV, 1874.

[*c.* **1450.**] **Unknown.** *Two stanzas* linking Hoccleve's poem, No. vi, "Item de beata virgine" to the Canterbury Tales, and turning it into the ploughman's tale, in MS. Christ Church CLII, fol. 228 *b*, [printed in] A New Ploughman's Tale: Thomas Hoccleve's Legend of the Virgin and her Sleeveless Garment, with a spurious link, ed. by A. Beatty, Chaucer soc. 1902, p. 12.

[There is no mention of Chaucer in this 'link,' but it is an attempt by an unknown writer to fit Hoccleve's poem into the scheme of Chaucer's Canterbury Tales, as it represents the host calling upon the Ploughman to tell his tale, and the latter's reply.]

[*c.* **1450.**] **Unknown.** *Account of Lydgate* [in] MS. Harl. 4826, fol. 2. (printed in The ancient poem of Guillaume de Guileville, entitled Le Pelerinage de l'homme . . . 1858, Introd. pp. viii–ix).

John Lidgat, borne at Lidgat in Suffolke, . . . Hee was a great Ornament of ye English Toung, Imitating therein our Chaucer. To this end hee vsed to reade Dante ye Italian, Alan ye French Poet, and such like, w*h*ich hee diligently translated into English. . . .

1451. Cumberworth, Sir Thomas. *Will,* see Appendix A.

[**1450–60**?] **Unknown.** *Stanza* in *praise of Chaucer* at end of Parliament of Foules. MSS. Harl. 7333, fol. 132, col. 4; Trin. Coll. Camb. R. 3. 19, fol. 24 *b* (slightly varying from each other. Parallel-text of Chaucer's minor poems, ed. F. J. Furnivall, Chaucer soc. [1871], pp. 98–9).

[Harl. 7333]   Maister gefferey Chauucers þat now litħ gr*au*e

þe noble Rethor poete . of grete bretayne

þat worthi . was the laurer to have

Of poyetry . And þe palme atain

þ*a*t furst made to stiħ & to rain

þe gold dew Dropes . of speche in eloquen*c*e

In to englisħ tonge / þorow his excellens.

[A version of Lydgate's lines in the Life of our Lady, 1409–11 *q. v.* above, p. 19. This stanza is also given in Chaucerian and other pieces, ed. W. W. Skeat, 1897, p. 450.]

[**1450–60**?] **Unknown.** *Unto my Lady the Flower of Womanhood.* Lambeth MS. 306, fol. 138. (Political, Religious and Love Poems . . . ed. F. J. Furnivall, E. E. T. soc. [2nd edn. 1903], p. 72.)

Go litiħ bill, with all humblis,

Vnto my lady, of woman hede þe floure

and saie hire howe newe troilus lithe in distreȝ

All onely for hire sake.

[*a.* **1456.**] **Shirley,** John. *The Prologue of the Knyghtes tale.* MS. Harl. 7333, fol. 37, col. 1. (Prose introduction to Chaucer's Knight's Tale.)

O yee so noble and worthi pryncis and princesse, oþer estatis or degrees, what-euer yee beo, þat haue disposicione or ple-

saunce to rede or here þe stories of old tymis passed, to kepe
yow frome ydelnesse and slowthe, in escheuing oþer folies
þat might be cause of more harome filowyng, vowcheth sauf,
I be-seche yowe to fynde yowe occupacioun in þe reding
here of þe tales of Caunterburye wiche beon compilid in þis
boke˙ filowing First foundid, ymagenid and made boþe for
disporte and leornyng of all þoo that beon gentile of birthe or
of condicions by þe laureal and moste famous poete þat euer was
to-fore him as in þemvelisshing of oure rude moders englisshe
tonge, clepid Chaucyer a Gaufrede of whos soule god for his
mercy have pitee of his grace.   Amen.

[For Stow's reference to Shirley's collecting Chaucer's works, *see* below, 1603, p. 174.]

[c. 1460-70.] Unknown. *Headlines and end lines* in Sloane MS.
1686 (Canterbury Tales), ff. 243 b-244, 247 b.

Here endith the Prioresse tale   [fol. 243 b]
And here begynneth Chauncer the prolog¹ of¹ sir Thopas.
When seide was this tale, euery man
As sobre was / as wonder was to see
Tille at oure Oost / iape to be-gañ
And than at erst / he loked vpon me   .i. Chauncer.
And seid thus : .   .   .   .

.   .   .   .   .   .

A tale of Chauncer.

[Headline
fol. 244]   Here endith Chauncer the prolog¹ of sir Thopas
And here begynneth his tale

.   .   .   .

[Headline of fol. 247 b]   Prolog off Chauncer.

Pleasith you to here the Tale of Maister Chauncer.
Chauncer   A yong man whilom called Melibe.

.   .   .   .   .   .

[c. 1470.] Ashby, George. *Active policy of a Prince* (prologue). MS.
Camb. Univ. lib. Mm. iv. 42, ff. 2 b-3. (George Ashby's poems,
ed. M. Bateson, E. E. T. soc. extra series, lxxvi, 1899, pp. 13-14.)

(1)
Maisters Gower, Chauucer & Lydgate,
    Primier poetes of this nacion,
Embelysshing oure englisshe tendure algate
    Firste finders to oure consolacioñ
    Off fresshe, douce englisshe and formacioñ
        Of newe balades, not vsed before
        By whome we all may haue lernyng and lore.

(2)

Alas ! saufe godd*es* wille, & his plesaunce,
 That ever ye shulde dye & chaunge this lyffe,
Vntyl tyme / that by youre wise pourueunce (*sic*)
 Ye had lafte to vs / sum remembratife
 Of a personne, lerned & Inuentif,
  Disposed aftur youre condicioñ,
  Of fressħe makyng to oure Instruccioñ.

(3)

But sithe we all be dedly and mortal,
 And no man may eschewe this egressioñ,
I beseche almygħty god eternal
 To pardoñ you all youre transgressioñ
 That ye may dwelle in heuenly mansioñ,
  In recompense of many a scripture
  That ye haue englisshede without lesure.

(4)

So I, George Assħby, not comp*a*risoñ
 Making to youre excellent enditing
Witħ rigħt humble p*r*ayer & orisoñ,
 Pray god that by you I may haue lernyng,
 And, as a blynde man in the wey blondryng,
  As I can, I shall now lerne and practise
  Not as a master but as a p[r]entise.

[c. **1470.**] **Unknown.** *Poem* [in] MS. Bodl. Rawl. poet. 36, fol. 4. (Supplementary vol. to Minor Poems of Lydgate, ed. H. N. Mac-Cracken, E. E. T. soc., in preparation.)

[The poem is a jilted lover's reply to the 'scorn,' or flyting letter of his mistress, which latter is also in verse, and immediately precedes this piece.]

[l. 9]   To me ye haue sent a lett*er* of derision
[10]   Werfore I thanke you as I fynde cause,
   The ynglysch of Chaucere was nat in youre mynd.
   Ne tullyus termys wyth so gret elloquence
   But ye as vucurtes and Crabbed of leynde
[15]   Rolled hem on a hepe it semyth by the sentens.

1471. Bruyn, Elizabeth. *Will* of Dame Elizabeth Brune in South Ockendon church, Essex (Excerpts from ancient wills, by H. W. King; transactions Essex archæol. soc., 1884, new series, vol. ii, pp. 56–7).

I will that Robert Walsall have the boke called Can*t*erbury tales, and one gilt cup w*t* ye coueryng, and one spa*r*uer of silke, and a diall of gold, and ij hors in my stable, and j double harp*e*.

1475. Henryson, Robert. *The Testament of Cresseid.* Compylit be M. Robert Herysone, Sculemai-ster in Dunfermeling. Imprentit at Edinburgh be Henry Charteris MDXciii, [sign. A ii and *b*]. Stanzas 6, 7, 9, and 10. (Chaucerian and other pieces, ed. W. W. Skeat, 1897, pp. 328–9.)

¶ I mend the fyre and beikit me about
   Than tuik ane drink my spreitis to comfort
And armit me weill fra the cauld thairout
   To cut the winter nicht & mak it schort.
   I tuik ane Quair, & left all vther sport.
     Writtin be worthie Chaucer glorious
     Of fair Cresseid, & worthie Troylus.

¶ And thair I fand efter that Diomeid
   Ressauit had that Lady bricht of hew.
How Troilus neir out of wit abraid,
   And weipit soir with visage paill of hew,

   .   .   .   .

¶ Of his distres me neidis nocht reheirs,
   For worthie Chauceir in the samin buik
In gudelie termis, & in Ioly veirs
   Compylit hes his cairis, quha will luik.

   .   .   .   .

¶ Quha wait gif all þ*t* Chauceir wrait was trew   [sign. A. ii. *b*]
Nor I wait nocht gif this narratioun
Be authoreist or fenȝeit of the new
   Be sum Poeit, throw his Inuentioun
   Maid to report the Lamentatioun
     And wofull end of this lustie Creisseid,
     And quhat distres scho thoillit, & quhat deid.

[No early MS. copy is known; first printed by W. Thynne, in his edn. of Chaucer's works, 1532, and long thought to be by Chaucer. Speght printed it as his in 1598, and was remonstrated with by Francis Thynne, *see* below, p. 155, and for full information as to editions and authenticity, see *Chaucer, a bibliographical manual*, by E. P. Hammond, N. York, 1908, p. 457.]

[*a.* **1477.**] **Unknown.** *The Book of Curtesye,* printed by William Caxton, 1477–8, fol. 163 *b.* (Ed. F. J. Furnivall, E. E. T. soc., 1868, pp. 34–5. Dr. Furnivall also printed 2 MS. copies of the same treatise, Oriel MS. 79, and Balliol MS. 354.)

(48)

O fader and founder of ornate eloquence
That enlumened hast alle our bretayne
To soone we loste / thy laureate scyence
  O lusty lyquour / of that fulsom fontayne
  O cursid deth / why hast thow þᵗ poete slayne
    I mene fader chaucer / maister galfryde
    Alas the whyle / that euer he from vs dyde.

(49)

Redith his werkis / ful of plesaunce
Clere in sentence / in langage excellent
Briefly to wryte / suche was his suffysañce
  Whateuer to saye / he toke in his entente
  His langage was so fayr and pertynente
    It semeth vnto mannys heerynge
    Not only the worde / but verely the thynge.

(50)

Redeth my chylde / redeth his bookes alle
Refuseth none / they ben expedyente
Sentence or langage / or bothe fynde ye shalle
  Ful delectable / for that good fader mente
  Of al his purpose / and his hole entente
    How to plese in euery audyence
    And in our tunge / was welle of eloquence.

[Speght quotes the first of the above three verses in Chaucer's Works, 1598, sign. c ii, stating he ' found them in a book of *Iohn Stowes* called Little John.']

[*c.* **1477.**] **Norton,** Thomas. *The Ordinall of Alchimy.* MSS. Harl. 853, No. 4, fol. 40 *b,* Ashmole 57, p. 50. First printed (in Latin) in Michael Maier's Tripus Aureus, 1618, p. 120, (in English) in Elias Ashmole's Theatrum Chemicum, 1652, cap. iii, p. 42 (*cf.* below 1577, Dr. John Dee, p. 114, and Ashmole, p. 227).

Hir name [a stone] is magnesia, fewe people hir knowe,
She is founde in hye places as well as in lowe
Plato knewe her propertie, and called hir by hir name,
and Chauser rehearseth how Titanos is the same.

In the Canon his tale, saynge what is thuse,
but quid ignotum p*er* magis ignotius
that is to saye, what maie this be,
but unknowe by more unknowne named is she.

[This extract is given from the Harl. MS. *c.* 1600-20.]

[1477-8. Parlement of Foules, Gentilesse, Truth, Fortune, Envoy to Scogan. No title-page, date, or place of publication.]

[Printed by William Caxton, imperfect, two copies only known, B. M. and Camb. Univ. library. For description by Mr. Bradshaw of the Cambridge copy *see* Trial forewords to Parallel text of Chaucer's minor poems, ed. F. J. Furnivall, Chaucer soc. [1871], pp. 116-18. *See also* Life of Caxton by William Blades, 1861-3, vol. ii, pp. 61-3; Index to early printed books by R. Proctor, 1898, etc., no. 9629. Gentilesse is here printed as part of Scogan's Moral ballad, *c.* 1407, *q. v.* above, pp. 18-19. The copy mentioned by Blades and other bibliographers as being at the Grammar-school of St. Albans, is the one now in the B. M.]

[1477-8. Anelida and Arcite, compleynt of chaucer vnto his empty purse. No title-page, date, or place of publication.] (A facsimile reprint was issued in 1905, by the Camb. Univ. press.)

[Printed by William Caxton, small 4o., unique copy, Camb.Univ. lib. For description *see* Trial forewords to Parallel text of Chaucer's minor poems, ed. F. J. Furnivall, Chaucer soc. [1871], p. 118. *See also* Life of Caxton by William Blades, 1861-3, vol. ii, pp. 64-6.]

[1477-8. Canterbury Tales. No title page or colophon, printed by William Caxton.]

[Two copies in B. M., also several in other libraries. *See* for description Life of Caxton, by William Blades, 1861-3, vol. ii, pp. 45-7; also Index to early printed books by R. Proctor, 1898, etc., no. 9626.]

[a. 1479]. Boethius de consolacione Philosophie .... [colophon.] Geffrey Chaucer hath translated .... I William Caxton have done my deuoir to enprinte it. [No date or place of publication.]

[For description *see* Life of Caxton by William Blades, 1861-3, vol. ii, pp. 66-71; and Index to early printed books, by R. Proctor, 1898, etc., no. 9630.]

[a. 1479.] Caxton, William. *Epilogue* to *Boethius de Consolacione Philosophie*, fol. 93 *b*. (Reprinted in Life of Caxton, by William Blades, 1861-3, vol. i, pp. 151-2; *cf. also* vol. ii, pp. 66-71.)

. . . the worshipful fader & first foun*d*eur & embelissher of ornate eloquence in our englissh. I mene Maister Geffry Chaucer hath translated this sayd werke oute of latyn in to oure vsual and moder tongue . . . wherein in myne oppynyon he hath deseruid a perpetuell lawde and thanke of al this noble Royame of Englond . . . .

And furthermore I desire & require you that of your charite ye wold praye for the soule of the sayd worshipful mañ Geffrey Chaucer first translatour of this sayd boke into englissh

& enbelissher in making the sayd langage ornate & fayr . whiche shal endure perpetuelly . and therefore he ought eternelly to be remembird . of whom the body and corps lieth buried in thabbay of west-mestre beside london tofore the chapele of seynte benet . by whos sepulture is wreton on a table hongying on a pylere his Epitaphye maad by a Poete laureat . Whereof the copye foloweth &c. . . .

[Caxton here gives Surigo's epitaph ; the last four lines Blades supposes may be Caxton's own ; for these see next entry, below, p. 60.

For the whole question of Chaucer's burial-place and tomb, and his re-interment by Brigham in 1555 or 1556, *see* Berthelet, 1532 ; Brigham, 1556 ; Bullein, 1564 ; Foxe, 1570 ; Camden, 1600 ; Stowe, 1600 ; Weever, 1631 ; Ashmole, 1652 ; Dart, 1723 ; below, pp. 78, 94, 98, 107, 163, 165, 204, 227, 363, also M. H. Bloxam in Archæological Journal, 1881, vol. xxxviii, p. 361, Athenæum, Aug. 9, 1902, p. 189 (art. by J. W. Hales), Aug. 30, 1902, p. 288, Oct. 25, 1902, p. 552 (Mrs. C. C. Stopes), and *Chaucer, a bibliographical manual*, by E. P. Hammond, N. York, 1908, pp. 44–7.]

[*a.* **1479.**] **Surigo,** Stephen (lic. doct. of Milan). *Latin epitaph on Chaucer*, printed by Caxton at end of Boethius de Consolacione philosophie, fol. 94 and 94 *b*. (Life of Caxton by William Blades, 1861–3, vol. i, p. 152 ; and Chaucer's works, ed. W. Thynne, 1532, fol. 383.)

Epitaphium Galfridi Chaucer. per
poetam laureatum Stephanum surigonum
Mediolanensem in decretis licenciatum

Pyerides muse, si possunt numina fletus
    Fundere . diuinas atque rigare genas,
Galfridi vatis chaucer crudelia fata
    Plangite . sit lacrimis abstinuisse nephas
Vos coluit viuens . at vos celebrate sepultum
    Reddatur merito gracia digna viro
Grande decus vobis . est docti musa maronis
    Qua didicit melius lingua latina loqui
Grande nouumque decus Chaucer . famamque parauit
    Heu quantum fuerat prisca britanna rudis
Reddidit insignem maternis versibus . vt iam
    Aurea splendescat . ferrea facta prius
Hunc latuisse virum nil . si tot opuscula vertes
    Dixeris . egregiis que decorata modis
Socratis ingenium . vel fontes philosophie
    Quitquid & archani dogmata sacra ferunt
Et quascunque velis tenuit dignissimus artes
    Hic vates . paruo conditus hoc tumulo

Ah laudis q*ua*ntum preclara britannia perdis
Dum rapuit tantu*m* mors odiosa virum
Crudeles parce . crudelia fila sorores
Non tamen extincto corpore . fama perit
Viuet ineternum . viue*n*t dum scripta poete
Viuant eterno tot monimenta die
Si qua bonos tangit pietas . si carmi*n*e dign*us*
Carmina qui cecinit tot cumulata modis
Hec sibi marmoreo scribantur verba sepulchro
Hec maneat laudis sarcina summa sue
Galfridus Chaucer vates . et fama poesis
Materne . hac sacra sum tumulatus humo

Post obitum Caxton voluit te viuere cura
Willelmi. Chaucer clare poeta tuj
Nam tua non solum compressit opuscula formis
Has quoq*ue sed* laudes . iussit hic esse tuas

[This epitaph, though not by an Englishman, is given here because it is so constantly quoted, see, for example, below, p. 87, c. 1545, Leland; p. 78, 1532, Thynne; p. 186, a. 1613, Commaundre; 1598, Speght, Life of Chaucer, sign. c ii b and c iij, and note on p. 59 above.]

1479. Parmenter, John. *Will* dated 17 Aug. 1479. Prerogative Court of Canterbury, Logge, f. 142.

Item lego Walt*er*o Nonne vnu*m* libru*m* vo*catum* Canterbury tales.

[Parmenter was Commissary-General of Diocese of Canterbury.]

[1482 ?] Paston, John. *Catalogue of John Paston's books* [in] The Paston letters. (Ed. Sir John Fenn, 1787, vol. ii, p. 300; ed. James Gairdner, 1872–5, vol. iii, 1875, p. 300.)

The Inventory off Englysshe Boks off John . . . . made the v daye of Novembre, anno regni Regis E. iiij . . . .
2. Item, a Boke of Troylus whyche William Bra . . . . hathe hadde neer x yer and lent it to Dame . . . . Wyngfelde and *ibi ego vidi ;* valet.

[The Catalogue is very imperfect. It is written on a strip of paper about 17 inches long, and has been rolled up, so that some of the names have been nearly obliterated. The exact date is unknown, but it is not earlier than 1474, when "The Game and Play of Chess" (which is mentioned in the catalogue) issued from Caxton's press at Westminster.]

[*c.* 1483. Troylus and Creseyde] . . . . Here endith Troylus as touchyng Cresede. Explicit per Caxton. [No title or date.]

[*See* for description, Life of Caxton, by William Blades, 1861–3, vol. ii, pp. 169–70, and Index to early printed books, by R. Proctor, 1898, etc., no. 9664.]

5

Prologue

Gret chere made our oft to vs euerychon
And to fouper fette he vs anon
He ferued vs wyth vytaylk at the befte
Stronge was the wyne & wel drynke vs lyfte
A femely man our ofte was wyth alle
Forto be a marchal in a lordes halle
A large man he was wyth eyen ftepe
A feyrer burgeys is ther non in chepe
Bold of hys fpeche and wel was y taught
And of manhood lacked he right nought
Eke therto was he right a mery man
And after fouper to pleyen he begon
And fpak of myrthe amonge other thynges
Whan that we hadde made our rekenynges
He fayd thus now lordynges treuly

WOODCUT OF THE PILGRIMS IN THE PROLOGUE
'CANTERBURY TALES' PRINTED BY CAXTON c. 1483
Copy in the British Museum (G. 11586), sign. ciiij.

[*c.* 1483]. **The book of Fame made by Gefferey Chaucer.** [No title, the above is the beginning of the text, sign. a ij. [col.] Emprynted by wylliam Caxton. [No date or place of publication.]

[*See* for description, Life of Caxton, by William Blades, 1861–3, vol. ii, pp. 165–7; and Index to early printed books by R. Proctor, 1898, etc., no. 9662.]

[*c.* 1483]. **Caxton,** William. *Epilogue* to *the Book of Fame.* Emprynted by wylliam Caxton, sign. d 5. (Life of Caxton, by William Blades, 1861–3, vol. ii, pp. 165–7.)

I fynde no more of this werke to fore sayd / For as fer as I can vnderston̄de / This noble man Gefferey Chaucer fynysshyd at the sayd conclusion of the metyng of lesyng and sothsawe / whereas yet they be chekked and maye not departe / whyche werke as me semeth is craftyly made / and dygne to be wreton & knowen / For he towchyth in it ryght grete wysedom & subtyll vnderstondyng / And so in alle hys werkys excellyth in myn oppynyon alle other wryters in our Englyssh / For he wrytteth no voyde wordes / but alle hys mater is ful of hye and quycke sentence / to whom ought to be gyuen laude and preysyng for hys noble makyng and wrytyng / For of hym alle other haue borowed syth and taken / in alle theyr wel sayeng and wrytyng / And I humbly beseche & praye yow / emonge your prayers to remembre hys soule / on whyche and on alle crysten soulis I beseche almyghty god to haue mercy Amen.

[*See* Blades, vol. ii, p. 166, and Chaucer's works, ed. W. W. Skeat, 1894, vol. iii, Notes to House of Fame, p. 287, for accounts of the lines Caxton added at the end of this poem.]

[*c.* 1483? **Canterbury Tales.** . . . No title, date, or pagination.] (Printed by William Caxton, 2nd edn.)

[*See* for description, Life of Caxton, by William Blades, 1861–3, vol. ii, pp. 162–4; and Index to early printed books by R. Proctor, 1898, etc., no. 9661.]

[*c.* 1483 ?]. **Caxton,** William. *Prohemye to Canterbury Tales* (2nd edn.), sign. a ij and a ij *b.* (Life of Caxton, by William Blades, 1861–3, vol. i, pp. 173–4.)

[sign. a ij] ¶ **G**.Rete thanks lawde and honour / ought to be gyuen vnto the clerkes / poetes / and historiographs / that haue wreton many noble bokes of wysedom of the lyues / passion̄s / & myracles of holy sayntes of hystoryes / of noble and famous Actes / and faittes / And of the cronycles sith the begynnyng of the creacion of the world / vnto thys present tyme / by whyche we ben dayly enformed / and haue knowleche of many thynges / of whom we shold not haue

knowen / yf they had not left to vs theyr monumentis wreton /
Emong whom and inespecial to fore alle other we ought to
gyue a synguler laude vnto that noble & grete philosopher
Gefferey chaucer the whiche for his ornate wrytyng in our
tongue maye wel haue the name of a laureate poete/. For to
fore that he by his labour enbelysshyd / ornated and / made
faire our englisshe / in thys Royame was had rude speche &
Incongrue / as yet it appiereth by olde bookes / whyche at thys
day ought not to haue place ne be compared emong ne to his
beauteuous volumes / and aournate [*sic*] writynges / of whom
he made many bokes and treatyces of many a noble historye
as wel in metre as in ryme and prose / and them so craftyly
made / that he comprehended hys maters in short / quyck
and hye sentences / eschewyng prolyxyte / castyng away
the chaf of superfluyte / and shewyng the pyked grayn of
sentence / vttered by crafty and sugred eloquence / of whom
emong all other of hys bokes / I purpose temprynte by the
grace of god the book of the tales of cauntyrburye / in whiche
I fynde many a noble hystorye of euery astate and degre /
Fyrst rehercyng the condicions / and tharraye of eche of
them as properly as possyble is to be sayd / And after theyr
tales whyche ben of noblesse / wysedom / gentylesse / Myrthe /
and also of veray holynesse and vertue / wherin he fynysshyth
thys sayd booke / whyche book I haue dylygently ouersen
and duly examyned to thende that it be made acordyng vnto
his owen makyng / For I fynde many of the sayd bookes /
whyche wryters haue abrydgyd it and many thynges left out /
And in some place haue sette certayn versys / that he neuer
made ne sette in hys booke / of whyche bookes so incorrecte
was one broughte to me vj yere passyd / whyche I supposed
had ben veray true & correcte / And accordyng to the same
[sign. a
ij b] I dyde do emprynte a certayn nombre of them / whyche
anon were sold to many and dyuerse gentyl men / of whom
one gentylman cam to me / and said that this book was
not accordyng in many places vnto the book that Gefferey
chaucer had made / To whom I answerd that I had made
it accordyng to my copye / and by me was nothyng added ne
mynusshyd / Thenne he sayd he knewe a book whyche hys
fader had and moche louyd / that was very trewe / and
accordyng vnto hys owen first book by hym made / and
sayd more yf I wold enprynte it agayn he wold gete me the
same book for a copye / how be it he wyst wel /· that hys

6

Good wyf ther was of beside bathe
And she was somdeel deef & that was scathe
Of cloth makynge had she suche an haunt
She passed them of ypre and of gaunt
In al the parisshe wyf was ther non
That to the offrynge before hyr sholde goon
And yf ther dyd certayn wroth & as she
Than was she oute of al charyte
Her kercheups ful fyn were of grounde
I durste swere they weyed thre pounde
That on a sonday were on hyr hede
Hyr hosyn were of fyne scarlet rede
Ful streyte I tyed and shoos ful moyst and newe
Bolde was her fare fayr and rede of hewe
She was a worthy womman al hyr lyue
Husbondes at the chyrche dore hadde she fyue
Wythoute other companye in youthe
But her of nedyth not to speke as nowthe

WOODCUT OF THE WIFE OF BATH IN THE PROLOGUE
'CANTERBURY TALES' PRINTED BY CAXTON c. 1483
Copy in the British Museum (G. 11586), sign. bv. back.

fader wold not gladly departe fro it / To whom I said / in caas that he coude gete me suche a book trewe and correcte / yet I wold ones endeuoyre me to enprynte it agayn / for to satysfye thauctor / where as to fore by ygnouraunce I erryd in hurtyng and dyffamyng his book in dyuerce places in settyng in some thynges that he neuer sayd ne made / and leuyng out many thynges that he made whyche ben requysite to be sette in it / And thus we fyll at accord / And he ful gentylly gate of hys fader the said book / and delyuerd it to me / by whiche I have corrected my book / as here after alle alonge by thayde of almyghty god shal folowe / whom I humbly beseche to gyue me grace and ayde to achyeue / and accomplysshe / to hys lawde honour and glorye / and that alle ye that shal in thys book rede or heere / wyll of your charyte emong your dedes of mercy / remembre the sowle of the sayd Gefferey chaucer first auctour / and maker of thys book / And also that alle we that shal see and rede therin / may so take and vnderstonde the good and vertuous tales / that it may so prouffyte / vnto the helthe of our sowles / that after thys short and transitorye lyf we may come to euerlastyng lyf in heuen/. Amen.

By Wylliam Caxton.

[*c.* **1488.**] **Unknown.** *Colophons* in MS. Arch. Selden B. 24, ff. 119–20, 129–31, 136–8, 152, 187, 191. (The authorship of the Kingis Quair, by J. T. T. Brown, 1896, pp. 72–5. The colophons below are printed from this book, and not from the MS.)

[fol. 119, p. 72] Flee from the press and duell with suthfastness

.   .   .   .   .

Explicit Chaucer*es* counsailing.

[fol. 119, p. 73] Richt as pou*er*t causith sobirness

.   .   .   .   .

Qu*o*d Chaucere

[Poem by J. Walton in his translation of Boethius de Consolatione. *See* above, p. 20.]

[fol. 119 *b*] Deuise proues and eke humylitee

.   .   .   .   .

[fol. 120] Qu*o*d Chaucere quhen he was ry*gh*t auisit

[Not Chaucer's ; *see* Chaucer's minor poems (vol. i of works), ed. W. W. Skeat, 1894, p. 47.]

[fol. 120 *b*] In May quhan Flora the fresche lusty quene

.   .   .   .   .

[fol. 129 *b*] Here endith the maying and disport of Chaucere.

[Lydgate's Complaint of the Black Knight, 1402–3, p. 16, above, *q. v.*]

[fol. 130]   Moder of God and virgyne undefouled.

. . . . .

[fol. 131 b]   Explicit or*acio* Galfridi Chaucere.
[Hoccleve.]

[fol. 136]   The compleynt of Ven*u*s folowith.

. . . . .

[fol. 137]   Off Gransou*n* the best th*at* makith france
              Qu*o*d Galfridu*s* Chaucere.

[fol. 137 b]   Of hie Emperice and quene celestial.

. . . . .

[fol. 138]   Ete*r*naly abuse all erdly wight.
              Qu*o*d Chaucere.
[Not Chaucer's. *See* Skeat, as above.]

[fol. 138 b, p. 74]   The Lord of loue crie benedicitœ.

. . . . .

[fol. 152]   Here endis the parliament of foulis
              Qu*o*d Galfride Chaucere

. . , . . .

[fol. 187, p. 75]   I proue as wele as by autoritee.

. . . . .

[fol. 191 b]   And thus ended Chaucere the legendis of ladyis.

1490. Irlandia, John de.   *Colophon* at the end of 2nd book of MS. 18. 2. 8, Advocates' library Edin., immediately before Chaucer's poem "Mother of God." At the beginning of the whole work is "Johannis de Irlandia, Opera Theologica, 1490." (*See* Parallel-text of Chaucer's minor poems, ed. F. J. Furnivall, Chaucer soc. [1871] etc., p. 144.)

And sene I haue spokin samekle of this noble and haly virgin I will in the end of þis buk writ ane orisoune þat Galfryde Chauceir maid and prayit to þis lady And tho[t] I be no[t] Eloque*n*t in þis tovng as was þat noble poet I wil writ her twa orisouns in lattin that I maid of þis noble and excellent lady and send furth of parice with a buk that I maid of hir' concepcioun to þi fader of gud mynd The first is of þe gret hono[r] and dignite of þis lady And the second is of hir' noble and haly byrth of hir blist son Ihsus.

[Two Latin Orisons here follow.]

[c. 1492. The boke of the tales of Canterburie . . . . by W. Caxton. Printed by] R. Pynson.

[*See* Index to early printed books, by R. Proctor, 1898, etc., no. 9780.]

7

¶ The tale of the Pardoner

For though my self be a ful vicious man
A moralle tale yet I you telle can
Whiche I am wont for to preche and also wynne
Now holde your pees my tale I wol begynne

¶ Here endyth the prologue
Of the Pardoner

¶ And begynneth the Tale

IN flaundris sumtyme was a companye
Of yonge folke that hauntedyn folye
As ryot hazard Stewys and tauarnys
Where as wyth harpes lutes and gyternes
They daunce and pleye at the dyce both day & nyght
And etyn also & drynkyn aboue her myght
Thorow whiche they doon the deuyl sacrifise

[c. 1492.] Pynson, Richard. *Prohemye* (signed) by Pynson to his edn. of Chaucer's Canterbury tales, sign. a 1 and a i *b.*

[This is really Caxton's 'prohemye' as it is his edition, *see* above, pp. 61-3 ; *see* below, p. 76, 1526, Pynson, where the differences between the two are pointed out ; there is very little variation between the prohemye as given by Pynson in 1492 and in 1526.]

1498. The boke of Chaucer named Caunterbury tales. sign. ·:. iii b.

[col.] Here endyth the boke of the tales of Caunterbury Compiled by Geffray Chaucer / of whoos Soule Criste haue mercy. Emprynted at Westmestre by Wynkin de Word yᵉ yere of our lord .M.CCCC.lxxxxviii.

[*See* Index to early printed books, by R. Proctor, 1898, etc., no. 9710. The edition of the Canterbury Tales of Wynkyn de Worde, 1495, referred to by Ritson in Bibliographia Poetica, p. 20, Lowndes, Ames, Tyrwhitt and others, is almost certainly non-existent, and comes apparently from a misprint in Ames, who follows Bagford, *see* Chaucer, a bibliographical manual, by E. P. Hammond, N. York, 1908, pp. 203, 543.]

[1499–1502.] The Loue and complayntes bytwene Mars and Venus . . . . Here foloweth the counceyll of chaucer touchyng Maryag . . . . Thys in pryntyde in Westmoster inkyng strete. Per me Julianus Notarii.

[Unique copy in Britwell library. *See* under 1445, headline to Marriage or Bukton given from this edn., p. 47 above.]

[c. 1500.] Unknown. *Two mentions of Chaucer's name* in a volume entitled Astronomiæ aphorismi. Sloane MS. 446, ff. 50 *b* and 56.

Chaucer Anglus . . . . . Chaucer.

[c. 1500.] Unknown. *Praise of the Mass,* Rawl. MS. poet. 36, last folio (supplementary vol. to Minor Poems of Lydgate, ed. H. N. Mac-Cracken, E. E. T. soc., in preparation).

Yif⁺ eny crafte be in baled makyng⁺
I reserve hyt to the poetys olde
Chaucers Gower and lydgatys wrytyng⁺
Whych in balade made bokys manyfold⁺.

1501. Douglas, Gavin, Bishop of Dunkeld. *The Palis of Honoure, compyled by Gawyne dowglas* . . . Imprinted at London . . . by Wyllyam Copland [1553 ?] (Poetical works, ed. J. Small, 1874, vol. i, p. 36).

Sa greit aue prees of pepell drew vs neir,
The hundreth part thair names ar not heir,
Ʒit saw I thair of Brutus Albyon,

CHAUCER CRITICISM.

Geffray Chaucier, as *a per se* sans peir

Chauser & other Englyshe and Scottishe poetis. In his vulgare, and morall Johne Goweir.

Lydgait the monk raid musing him allone.

[No MS. is known to exist; J. Small has reprinted Copland's edn.; a facsimile of the Edinburgh edn. of 1579 (very rare) was made for che Bannatyne club, 1827. The two editions vary greatly in language; the extract here given is from that of 1579.]

1503. Dunbar, William. *The Goldyn Targe,* ll. 253–61. (Poems, ed J. Small, 1893, Scott. text soc., vol. ii, p. 10. For numerous MSS. and edns. *see* introduction, pp. cxciv, etc.

[May 1503.]

O reverend Chaucere, rose of rethoris all,
As in oure tong ane flour imperiall
That raise in Britane ewir, quho redis rycht,
Thou beris of makaris the tryumph riall;
Thy fresch anamalit termes celicall
This mater coud illumynit haue full brycht:
Was thou noucht of oure Inglisch all the lycht,
Surmounting ewiry tong terrestriall
Alls fer as Mayes morow dois mydnycht?

O morall Gower, and Ludgate laureate,
Your sugurit lippis and tongis aureate,
Bene to oure eris cause of grete delyte;
Your angel mouthis most mellifluate
Our rude langage has clere illumynate,
And faire our-gilt oure speche, that imperfyte
Stude, or your goldyn pennis schupe to wryte;
This Ile before was bare, and desolate
Off rethorike, or lusty fresch endyte.

[1503–4.] Hawes, Stephen. *Here begynneth the booke called the example of vertu made by Stephyn Hawys . . . the xix yere* [of the reign of Henry VII.] fol. 3 *b.*

O, prudent GOWER! in language pure
    Without corruption, most facundious!
O, noble CHAUCER! euer most sure
    Of fruitful sentence right delicious
O, virtuous LYDGATE! much sententious
    Unto you all, I do me excuse
    Though I your cunning do now use.
        Explicit Prologus.

. . . . . I miss, as I am sure
My Master, CHAUCER ! to take the cure
    Of my pen ; for he was expert
    In eloquent terms subtle and couert.

[3rd stanza from end.]

[A copy of the 1st edn., printed apparently by Wynkyn de Worde *c.* 1512, is in the Pepys library, Cambridge ; of the 2nd edn. of 1530 (by the same printer) one copy is at Britwell and one belonged to Thomas Corser.]

1506. Hawes, Stephen. *The Historie of graunde Amoure and la bell Pucel, called the Pastime of plesure . . . . imprynted by John Wayland*, 1554, cap. xiv, signs. f iii *b*–f iiii *b*. (ed. Thomas Wright, Percy soc., vol. xviii, 1846, p. 53).

A commendation of Gower, Chaucer and Lydgate.

.   .   .   .   .   .

Remembre the, of the trace and daunce
Of poetes olde, wyth all thy purueyaunce.

As moral Gower, whose sentencious dewe
Adowne reflareth, with fayre golden beames
And after Chaucers, all abroade dothe shewe
Our vyces to clense, his depared streames
Kindlyng our hartes, wyth the fiery leames
Of morall vertue, as is probable
In all his bokes, so swete and profitable

The boke of fame, whiche is sentencious
He drewe him selfe, on his owne inuention
And then the tragidies, so piteous
[sign. f. iiii]   Of the nintene ladyes, was his translation
And upon his ymagination
He made also, the tales of Caunterbury
Some vertuous, and some glad and merye

And of Troylus, the piteous doloure
For his ladye Cresyde, full of doublenes
He did bewayle, full well the langoure
Of all his loue, and great vnhappines
And many other bokes doubtles
He did compyle, whose goodly name
In prynted bookes, dothe remayne in **fame**.

And after him, my master Lydgate

[4 verses on Lydgate]

[sign. f. iiii *b*]   Were not these thre greatly to commende
Whiche them applied, such bokes to contriue
Whose famous draughtes, no man can amend
The tyme of slouthe, they did from them driue
After their deathe, for to abide on lyue
In worthy fame, by many a nacion
Their bokes, their actes do make relation.

O master Lydgate, the most dulcet spryng
Of famous rethoryke .   .   .   .

.   .   .   .

[Then follows Hawes's celebrated praise of Lydgate. First printed by Wynkyn de Worde in 1509; a copy of this edn. is at Ham House, Surrey (library of Earl of Dysart); Wayland's, from which the above extract is taken, is the earliest edn. in the B. M. ; Tottell's edn. of 1555 is the one reprinted by the Percy soc.]

1507. Dunbar, William. *Lament for the Makaris*, ll. 49–52. (Poems, ed. J. Small, Scott. text soc., 1893, vol. ii, p. 50. For numerous MSS. and edns. *see* introduction, pp. cxciv, etc.)

He [*i. e.* Time] hes done petuously deuowr,
The noble Chaucer,[1] of makaris flouir
The Monk of Bery, and Gower, all thre ;
Timor Mortis conturbat me.

[1507?] Skelton, John. ¶ *Here after foloweth a litle book of Phillip sparow,* Compyled by mayster Skelton, Poete Laureate. [col.] Imprinted at London . . . . at the sygne of the Lamb, by Abraham Weale [i. e. Veale], ll. 495–512, 612–27, 788–803, sign. B iv*b*, B v, B vii and *b*, C iii and *b*. Veale's edn. (c. 1570 ?) is the latest of the early edns.   Copy in B. M.   Barclay in his *Ship of Foles,* written in 1508, refers to *Philip Sparrow.* (Poetical works, ed. A. Dyce, 1843, vol. i, pp. 66, 69, 70, 75.)

Chaunteclere, owr Cocke,   [l. 495]
Must tel what is of the clocke
By the astrologye
that he hath naturally
Conceyued and caughte
And was neuer taught
By Albumazer
the Astronomer
[sign. B v]   Nor by ptholomy
Prince of Astronomy,
Nor yet by Haly ;
And yet he croweth dayly
And nightly the tydes
that no man abides

[1] Bannatyne MS. *Chawser.*

With partlot his hen
Whome now and then
He plucketh by the hed   [l. 511]

. . . . .

[sign. B vii]   Though I can rede and spel,   [l. 612]
Recount, report, and tell
Of the tales of Caunterbury,
Some sad storyes, some mery.
[sign. B vii b]   As Palamon and Arcet,
Duke Theseus and partelet;
And of the wife of Bath,
Thar worketh much scath
Whan her tale is told
Among huswiues bold
How she controld
Her husbandes as she wold,
And them to dispise
In the homeliest wise
Bring other wiues in thought
Their husbandes to set at naughte.   [l. 627]

. . . .

[sign. C iii]   In Chauser I am sped,   [l. 783]
His tales I haue red :
His mater is delectable
Solacious and commendable;
His englishe wel alowed,
So as it enprowed,
For as it is enployed
There is no englyshe voyd—
At those days moch commended,
And now men wold haue amended
his english, where at they barke,
[sign. C iii b]   And marre all they warke :
Chaucer, that famous Clarke,
His tearmes were not darcke,
But pleasaunt, easy, and playne;
No worde he wrote in vayne.   [l. 803]
    Also Iohn Lydgate
Wryteth after an hyer rate
It is diffuse to fynde
The sentence of his mind.

. . . . . .

1508. Chepman, Walter, and **Myllar,** Andrew. *Here begynnys the mayng or disport of chaucer.* [col.] Heir endis the maying and disport of chaucer.   Imprentit in the south gait of Edinburgh be Walter chepman and Androw myllar the fourth day of aprile the yhere of god .M.cccc and viii yheris, sign. a vij. (Reprinted by Malcolm Laing under the title 'The Knightly tale of Golagrus and Gawane, and other ancient poems.' . . . 1827.)

[The Advocates' library, Edinb. possesses a unique copy of this book, which is really Lydgate's Complaint of the Black Knight, 1402-3 (*q. v.* p. 16), with the title similar to that in MS. Arch. Selden B. 24. *See* c. 1488, p. 63 above. Colophons given from this MS.]

1509. Feylde, Thomas. *Here begynneth a lytel treatyse called the con- trauerse bytwene a louer and a Jaye lately compyled.* [col.] Thus endeth the treatyse of the louer and a Jaye / lately compyled by me Thomas Feylde.   ¶ Imprynted at London in Flete strete at the sygne of the Sonne by Wynkyn de Worde.   The Prologue stanza 3 ; *Amator,* 2 stanzas ; *Graculus,* 1 stanza, sign. a *b,* b iv *b,* c i, c. ii. (Copy belonging to the Duke of Devonshire, Roxb. Club, Reprint, 1818, ed. T. F. Dibdin.)

[Prologue, st. 3.]

[sign. A i b]   ¶ Cancer[1] floure of rethoryke eloquence
Compyled bokes pleasaunt and meruayllous
After hym noble Gower experte in scyence
Wrote moralytyes herde and delycyous
But Lydgate's workes are fruytefull and sentencyous
Who of his bokes hathe redde the fyne
He wyll hym call a famus rethorycyne.

.   .   .   .

Amator.

[sign. B iv b]   ¶ I have serched of late
Many poete laureate—
That dyuers bookes dyde make
[sign. C i]   And storyes regystred
Yet in comparyson
Of my trewe affeccyon
Scarcely can I fynde one
Syth Troylus reygned
¶ That was trewe and faythfull
In loue that is paynfull
Without fraude dysceytefull
Or preuy stryfe—

[1] [Note the spelling *Cancer* for Chaucer.]

Therefore as I fynde
I wyɪl shewe my mynde
Ryghɩ fewe of Gryseldes kynde
Is now lefte on lyue.

Graculus.

[sign. C ii]   ¶ Recorde of Cresyde
Whome Troylus loued
And was sore payned
Canser doth tell
Her loue was fayned
And wortely chaunged.
And gyuen to Dyomede
With grekes to dwelle.

1509. Richmond, Margaret, Countess of. *Will,* with bequest of the Canterbury Tales. (Memoir of Margaret, Countess of Richmond and Derby, by C. H. Cooper, 1874, App. pp. 129, 134.)

These ben the legacies of vs Margarette Countesse of Richmonde and Derbye moder to our souerain lord King Henry the vij^th made at Hatefelde Episcopi the xv day of Februarye the xxiiij^th yere of hys reign . . . .

To John Saynt John . . . . Item a booke of velom of Canterbury tales in Englische.

1513. Bradshaw, Henry. *The Holy Lyfe and History of Saynt Werburge.* Printed by R. Pynson, 1521 (copy in B. M.), sign. S ii. (Reprint of above for Chetham soc., vol. **xv**, ed. Ed. Hawkins, 1848, p. 209 ; ed. Carl Horstmann, E. E. T. soc. 1887, p. 199.)

To all auncient poetes, litell boke, submytte the
Whilom flowyng in eloquence facundious,
And to all other whiche present nowe be :
Fyrst to maister Chaucer and Ludgate sentencious.
Also to preignaunt Barkley nowe beyng religious
To inuentiue Skelton and poet laureate
Praye them all of pardon both erly and late.

1513. Douglas, Gavin, Bishop of Dunkeld. *The xiii Bukes of Eneados of the Famose Poete Virgill Translated . . . bi . . . Mayster Gawin Douglas.—Proloug of the First Buik.* Elphynstoun MS. Edin. (used by Small), first printed 1553, from the press of William Copland. (Poetical works of G. Douglas, ed. J. Small, 1874, vol. ii, pp. 14–17.)

[1513 is known to be the date of composition of Gavin Douglas's Æneid.]

Chausers   Thocht venerable Chaucer, principall poet but peir, [p. 14]
commenda-   Hevinlie trumpat, horleige and reguleir,
cion.

In eloquence balmy, condit, and diall,
Mylky fountane, cleir strand, and rose riall,
Of fresch endite, throw Albion iland braid,
In his legeand of notable ladyis, said
That he culd follow word by word Virgill,
Wisare than I mycht faill in lakar stile;

Chausers fault.

. . . .

I say nocht this of Chaucer for offence,   [p. 16]
Bot till excuse my lawit insuffitience.
For as he standis beneth Virgill in degre,
Ondir him als far I grant myself to be;
And nocht the les into sum place, quha kend it,
My master Chaucer greitlie Virgile offendit.
All thocht I be to bald hyme to repreif,
He was far baldar, certes by his leif,
Saying he followit Virgillis lantern to forne,
Quhen Eneas to Dido was forsworne.

. . . .

Bot sickirlie, of resoun me behuuis   [p. 17]
Excuse Chaucer fra all maner repruuis,
In loifing of thir ladyis lilly quhyte
He set on Virgile and Eneas this wyte;
For he was euer, God wait, wemenis frend.

[This extract is not given in full. Chaucer's lines to which Douglas refers are:—
Glory and honour, Virgil Mantuan,
Be to thy name! and I shal, as I can,
Folow thy lantern, as thou gost biforn
How Eneas to Dido was forsworn.
The Legend of Good Women, ll. 924–7.
The thirteenth book is the continuation of the Æneid by Maphæus Vegius.]

1517. The noble and amerous auncyent hystory of Troylus & Cresyde in the tyme of the syege of Troye . . . . Compyled by Geffraye Chaucer . . . . [Printed by Wynkyn de Worde, *see* next entry.]

1517. Worde, Wynkyn de. *Colophon* to Chaucer's *Troylus and Cressida* printed by him; sign. z vij *b*. B. M. and Camb. Univ. lib.

Thus endeth the treatyse of Troylus the heuy
By Geffraye Chaucer, compyled and done
He prayenge the reders, this mater not deny
Newly correcked [*sic*], in the cyte of London
In Flete strete, at the sygne of the sonne
Inprynted by me, Wynkyn de Worde
The M.ccccc. and xvii. yere of our lorde.

1517. Talbot, Sir Gilbert. *Inventory of the goods* of Sir Gilbert Talbot [taken after his death which occurred on Aug. 16th, 1517]. Roy. Com. Hist. MSS., MSS. in Various Collections, vol. ii, MSS. of Lord Edmund Talbot, p. 308, 1903.

[Among the contents of Sir Gilbert's own chamber are two books :] A boke in paper prynt of the *talys of Caunterbury*, price vs. iiij*d*. A premour, price x*s*.

1519. Erasmus, Desiderius. *Erasmus Iodoco Ionae Erphordiensi.* S.D. sign. V 2, p. 507, in Opus Epistolarum des. Erasmi Roterodami ... anno MDxxix. (The lives of Johan Vitrier .... and John Colet .... translated by J. H. Lupton, 1883, p. 23.)

Habet gens Britannica, qui hoc præstiterunt apud suos, quod Dantes ac Petrarcha apud Italos. Et horum euoluendis scriptis linguam expoliuit [he, Colet] iam tum se præparans ad prae-conium sermonis Euangelici.

[This letter is dated] Idus Iun. Anno M.D.xix.

[Lupton says Gower and Chaucer are probably alluded to in this rather vague description. *See* Lupton's 'Life of Dean Colet,' 1887, pp. 57-8.]

[1520. Rastell, John ?] *Prologue* [to] *Terens in englysh*, sign. A i and b.

The poet.

[sign. a i] The famous renown through the worlde is sprong
Of poetys ornate that vsyd to indyte
Of dyuers matters in theyr moder tong
Some toke vppon them translacions to wryte
Some to compile bokys for theyr delyte
But in our english tong for to speke playn
I rede but of fewe haue take any gret payn.

Except master Gowre which furst began
And of moralite wrote ryght craftely
Than master Chaucer that exellent man
Which wrote as compendious & elygantly
As in any other tong euer dyd any
Ludgate also which adournyd our tong
whose noble famys through the world be sprong.

[sign. a i b] By these men our tong is amplyfyed so
That we therin now translate as well may
As in eny other tongis other can do.

[This address of "The poet" is placed before "The translacyon out of latin into englysh of the furst comedy of tyrens called Andria." No date or place of publication. There is some doubt whether this was printed by Rastell.]

1523. **Skelton,** John. *A ryght delectable Tratyse upon a goodly Garlande or Chapelet of Laurell.* [col.] Imprynted by me Rycharde faukes, 1523, sign. B ii and *b* D ii, D iv *b*. (Skelton's Poetical works, ed. A. Dyce, 1843, vol. i, pp. 377–8, 405.)

[sign. B ii]
And as I thus sadly amonge them auysid
I saw Gower, that first garnisshed our englysshe rude,
And maister Chaucer, that nobly enterprysyd
How that our englysshe myght fresshely be ameude
The monke of Bury then after them ensuyd
Dane John lydgate: theis englysshe poetis thre,
As I ymagenyd repayrid vnto me.

To geder in armes, as brethern, enbrasid;
There apparell farre passynge beyonde that I can tell;
With diamauntes and rubis there tabers were trasid,
None so ryche stones in turkey to sell;
Thei wantid nothynge but the laurell;
And of there bounte they made me godely chere,
In maner and forme as ye shall after here.

Mayster Chaucer to Skelton.

[sign. B ii *b*]
Counter wayng your besy delygence
Of that we beganne in the supplement,
Enforcid ar we you to recompence,
Of all our hooll collage by the agreament,
That we shall brynge you personally present
Of noble Fame before the quenes grace
In whose court poynted is your place.

Poeta Skelton answeryth.

O Noble Chaucer, whos pullisshyd eloquence
Oure englysshe rude so fresshely hath set out,
That bounde ar we with all dew reuerence,
With all our strength that we can brynge about,
To owe to yow our seruyce, and more if we mowte!
But what sholde I say? ye wote what I entende,
Whiche glad am to please, and loth to offende.

. . . .

[sign. D ii] [Reference to Pandar, Troilus and Cresseid.]

. . . .

[sign. D iv *b*]
Forthwith vpon this, as it were in a thought
Gower, Chawcer, Lydgate, theis thre
Be fore remembred, me curteisly brought
In to that place where as they left me,

8

THE PILGRIMS AT THE 'TABARD

PYNSON'S CHAUCER, 1526, sign. A 6.

Where all the sayd poetis sat in there degre.
But when they sawe my lawrell rychely whought [*sic*],
All other besyde were counterfete they thought.

[1525 ?] Unknown. *Here begynneth a lytell treatyse cleped La Conusaunce Damours.* Imprinted by Rycharde Pynson . . . [colophon undated]. Thus endeth la conusaunce damours, sign. c. i. (T. Corser, Collectanea, Chetham soc., part iv, 1869, p. 439, gives the Chaucer reference and particulars of the title, which is wanting in the B.M. copy.)

[Speaking of Troylus and Creseide]

What shulde I herof longer processe make
Theyr great loue is wrytten all at longe
And howe he dyed onely for her sake
Our ornate Chaucer other bokes amonge
In his lyfe dayes dyd vnderfonge
To translate : and that most plesantly
Touchyng the matter of the sayd story.

1526. [Works of Chaucer and others, printed by R. Pynson. No general title-page, but made up of three parts, probably intended to sell separately.]

[Non-Chaucerian pieces distinguished by italics].

[Part I.] **Here beginneth the boke of Troylus and Creseyde, newly printed by a trewe copye,** [the col. sign. K vi, only mentions Pynson's name as printer.]

[Part II.] **Here begynneth the boke of Fame made by Geffray Chaucer: with dyuers other of his workes,** sign. a i [col.], sign. ciij.

The assemble of Foules, sign. c iiij.

La bell dame sauns mercy [by Richard Ros] sign. d ij *b* [col.] e iij *b*.

Ecce bonum consilium Galfredi Chaucer Contra fortunam, sign. e iiij.

Morall prouerbes of Christyne, sign. e iiij.

The complaynt of Mary Magdaleyne, sign. e v–f iii *b*.

The letter of Dydo to Eneas, sign. f iv–f v.

Prouerbes of Lydgate ['I counsayle whatsoeuer thou be'], sign. f v *b*–f vi.

[Part III.] **Here begynneth the boke of Canterbury Tales dilygently and truely corrected and newly printed,** sign. a i [col.], sign. y iii *b*.

[This is the first attempt at a collected edition of Chaucer s works. It was Pynson who first introduced the precedent of mixing up the works of Chaucer with those of others. *See* Introduction, p. xv, by W. W. Skeat to The Works of Chaucer and Others (facsimile reprint of Thynne's edn.), 1905; and also below, under 1532, Thynne, William, pp. 78-9.]

1526. Pynson, Richard.   *Prohemye* [to the Canterbury tales in his edn. of Chaucer's works. *See* above], sign. a i *b*.   *Colophon* to Assemble of Foules, sign. d ij.   *Title* to La bell dame sauns mercy, sign. d ij *b*. *Colophon* to La bell dame and *Title* to Morall proverbes, sign. e iij *b*.

[The 'prohemye' is really Caxton's, c. 1483 (*q. v.* pp. 61–3) with slight variations of spelling and an omission between "wherin he fynysshyth thys sayd booke" and "as here after alle alonge by thayde of almyghty god," where Pynson has inserted the following :]

Whiche boke is dyligently and trewly corrected by a copy of Willyam Caxtons imprintyng according to the true makyng of the sayd Geffray Chaucer.

[On sign. c iij of the Boke of Fame (bound up with the Canterbury tales), Pynson has inserted Caxton's epilogue to the same, c. 1483 (*q. v.* p. 61).]

[sign. d ij]   Thus endeth the assemble of Foules otherwyse called saynt Valentynes day compyled by the famous clerke Geffray Chaucer.

[sign. d ij *b*]   This boke called la bele Dame Sauns mercy was translate out of Frenche in to Englysshe by Geffray Chaucer flour of poetes in our mother tong.

[sign. e iij *b*]   Thus endeth the boke called La bell dame sauns mercy : And here foloweth certayne morall prouerbes of the foresayd Geffray Chaucers doyng.

[Although these 'moral proverbs' are in this colophon wrongly ascribed to Chaucer, they are yet correctly headed 'Morall prouerbes of Christyne' on sign. e iij. *See*, on this point, Chaucer, a bibliographical manual, by E. P. Hammond, N. York, 1908, p. 115.]

1530. Here foloweth the Assemble of foules . . . . compyled by the preclared and famous Clerke Geffray Chaucer Imprynted in london . . . . by me Wynkyn de Worde 1530.

[Unique(?) copy at Britwell. *See* for an account of this book Ames's *Typographical Antiquities*, ed. T. F. Dibdin, 1810–12, vol. ii, pp. 278–80.]

1530. Copland, Robert.   *Robert Coplande boke prynter to new fanglers* and *Lenuoy of R. Coplande boke prynter.*   Verses in Wynkyn de Worde's Assemble of foules [*see* last entry].   (Quoted in a letter of John Billam, 1786, in Ames's Typographical Antiquities, ed. T. F. Dibdin, 1810–12, vol. ii, pp. 279–80.   *See* below, 1786.)

Chaucer is deed the which this pamphlete wrate
So ben his heyres in all suche besynesse
And gone is also the famous clerke Lydgate
And so is yonge Hawes, god theyr soules adresse
Many were the volumes that they made more and les
Theyr bokes ye lay up, tyll that the lether moules
But yet for your myndes this boke I wyll impresse
That is in tytule the parlament of foules

[Envoy addressing the assemble of foules]

> And where thou become so ordre thy language
> That in excuse thy prynter loke thou haue
> Whiche hathe the kepte from ruynous domage
> In snoweswyte paper, thy mater for to saue
> With thylke same langage that Chaucer to the gaue
> In termes olde, of sentence clered newe
> Than methe muche sweter, who can his mynde auewe.

[The first four verses each terminate with a reference to the ' parlament of foules'; the verse quoted here is the second. There are three verses in the envoy. The references are taken from Dibdin's Ames.]

1530. Lindsay, Sir David. *The complaynte and testament of a Popiniay Which lyeth sore wounded and maye not dye.* [col.] Imprynted at London in Fletestrete . . by John Byddell 1538. Incipit Prologus, sign. a i *b*. [Title of later (Scotch) edns., *The testament and complaynt of our souerane lordis Papyngo, Kyng James the Fyft, etc.*] (Poetical works, ed. D. Laing, 1879, vol. i, pp. 61–2 ; *cf*. App., vol. iii, pp. 259–60. Also Works, part ii, the Monarche and other Poems, ed. J. Small, E. E. T. soc. 1866, 2nd edn. 1883, p. 223.)

> Of poetis now in tyll oure vulgar toung,
> For why the bell of retorik is roung
> By Chaucer, Goweir, and Lidgate laureate
> Who dare presume these poetis till impoung
> Whose swete sentence through Albion bene soung.

[Note there is a great difference in the spelling of the earlier and later edns., the first being English, the later ones Scotch.]

1531–2. Gaunte, William. *Will*, with bequest of Canterbury Tales, *see* below, App. A, 1531–2.

1532. Berthelet, Thomas. *To the Reder.* Jo. Gower de confessione Amantis. Imprinted at London in Fletestrete by Thomas Berthelette, sign. aa iij *b*, aa iiij.

And this . . . I maye be bolde to saye, that if we shulde neuer haue sene his [Gower's] counnynge warkes, the whiche . . . wytnesse, what a clerke he was, the wordes of the mooste famous and excellente Geffraye Chauser, that he wrote in the end of his moste speciall warke, that is intitled Troylus and Creseyde, do sufficiently testifye the same, where he sayth :

O morall Gower [etc. Tr. and Cr., Bk. v, ll. 1856–9.]

¶ The whiche noble warke, and many other of the sayde Chausers, that neuer were before imprinted, and those that very fewe men knewe, and fewer hadde them, be nowe of late put forthe together in a fayre volume. [*i. e.* Thynne's edn. *See* next entry.] By the whiche wordes of Chauser, we may also vnderstonde, that he and Gower were bothe of one selfe tyme, both excellently lerned, both great frendes to gether, and bothe a lyke endeuoured them selfe and imployed theyr tyme so wel and so vertuously, that they dyd not onely passe forth their lyfes here ryght honourably ; but also for their so doyng, so longe (of lykelyhode) as letters shal endure and continue, this noble royalme shall be the better, ouer and besyde theyr honest fame and renowme.   .   .   .   .   .   .

[sign. aa iiij] The other [Chaucer] lyeth buryed in the monasterye of Seynt Peters at westmyster in an ile on the south syde of the Churche.

[In the 2nd edn. of 1554 this address is practically unaltered.]

1532. The workes of Geffray Chaucer newly printed, with dyuers workes whiche were neuer in print before. [Blackletter. ed. by William Thynne. col.] Thus endeth the workes of Geffray Chaucer. Printed at London . . T. Godfray . . . 1532.

[The Dedication to Henry VIII, sign. A ij–A iij is by Sir Brian Tuke (*q. v.* pp. 79–80). On the last page, fol. ccclxxxiii, is Surigo's epitaph on Chaucer. Skeat has pointed out (Chaucerian and other Pieces, Oxford, 1897, p. ix), that if the title of Thynne's book is properly read, it will be seen that he did not intend to include as Chaucer's all the works printed in it. He suggests that the title should read ' The workes of . . Chaucer . . with dyuers workes [*of various authors*] whiche were neuer in print before.' So that it was Thynne's intention to print a collection of the works of Chaucer *and other writers;* and it was Stowe, who, in his edn. of 1561, so altered the title as to claim for Chaucer for the first time the authorship of the whole of Thynne's volume.

Besides these works by other writers (see list in note below), Thynne printed for the first time six of Chaucer's genuine works, *viz.:* Rom. of the Rose, ll. 1–1705 ; Legend of Good Women ; Book of the Duchess ; Complaint to Pity ; Lack of Stead-fastness and Astrolabe. For an account of this edn., and the poems contained in it, as well as for later editions, see Chaucer's works, ed. W. W. Skeat, 1894, vol. i, pp. 28 *et seq.* ; also Skeat's introduction to a facsimile reprint of the above, published by A. Moring and H. Frowde, 1905. For a clear account of all editions of Chaucer's ' Works,' from Pynson 1526 up to 1906, *see* Chaucer, a bibliographical manual, by E. P. Hammond, N. York, 1908, pp. 114–149.

For purposes of reference, we append here a list of the various poems which have by his editors been wrongly attributed to Chaucer, and printed as his in the old folio edns., including those 'appended' by Thynne, and which were claimed by later editors. For further information about these spurious poems, see Skeat's Chaucer Canon, 1900, pp. 94–148, also Chaucer, a bibliographical manual, by E. P. Hammond, N. York, 1908, pp. 406–63. Possibly Nos. 21 and 24 have never been actually quoted as Chaucer's, but Skeat thinks it is difficult to be sure of this. At any rate, they occur in ' Chaucer's Works '. This also applies to No. 5. See list of apocryphal pieces in Skeat's edn. of Chaucer's Works, vol. vii, 1897. For an admirable summary of the present position as regards the Chaucer Canon, *see* Chaucer, by E. P. Hammond, pp. 51–69.]

Spurious poems printed by Pynson 1526.

1. La Belie Dame sans Mercy [by Richard Ros ; repr. by Thynne].
2. Morall prouerbs [by Richard Ros].
3. The complaint of Mary Magdaleyn [Reprinted by Thynne. For author-ship see Skeat's Introduction to the Works of Chaucer and others, p. xl–xli].
4. The letter of Dydo to Eneas.
5. Proverbes of Lydgate.

First printed by Thynne [in collected Works] 1532.

6. Eight Goodly Questions [by Lydgate?].
7. Balades: to King Henry V. and to the Knights of the Garter [by Hoccleve].
8. Three sayings [14 lines].
9. The Romaunt of the Rose, ll. 1706 to end.
10. The Testament of Creseyde [by Henrysoun].
11. A Goodly Balade: 'Mother of norture.'
12. The Flower of Courtesy [by Lydgate].
13. The Assembly of Ladies [by a lady].
14. The Complaint of the Black Knight [by Lydgate].
15. A Praise of Women: 'Al tho the lyste of women euyl to speke' [by Lydgate?].
16. The Testament of Loue [by Thomas Usk.]
17. The Remedy of Love.
18. The Letter of Cupid [by Hoccleve].
19. A commendation of Our Lady [by Lydgate].
20. To my Soverayn Lady [by Lydgate].
21. To King Henry IV [by Gower].
22. The Cuckoo and the Nightingale [by Clanvowe].
23. Envoy to Alison.
24. A Moral Balade [by Scogan].
25. Go forth King [by Lydgate?]
26. Balade of Good Counsel [by Lydgate].

Thynne's 2nd edn. 1542.

27. The Plowman's Tale.

First printed by Stowe 1561.

28. A Saying of Dan John [by Lydgate].
29. Yet of the same [by Lydgate].

30. Balade de Bon Consail: "If it befall."
31. A Balade which Chaucer made in the praise or rather dispraise of women for their doubleness [by Lydgate].
32. The Craft of Lovers.
33. A Balade: "Of their nature they greatly them delite."
34. The Ten Commandments of Loue.
35. The Nine Worthy Ladies.
36. A Virelai.
37. A Balade: "In the Season of Feuerere."
38. A Balade: "O Mercifull and merciable."
39. Mercury, Pallas, Venus, Minerua, and Paris.
40. A Balade pleasaunt: "I haue a Ladie."
41. A Balade: "O Mossy Quince."
42. A Balade, warning men to beware of deceitful women [by Lydgate?].
43. A Balade on Chastity.
44. The Court of Loue.

First printed by Speght (1598).

45. Chaucer's Dream; or, 'The Isle of Ladies.'
46. The Flower and the Leaf [by a lady].

Speght's 2nd edn. 1602.

47. Jack Upland [in prose].

First included in 'Chaucer's Works' by Urry 1721.

48. The Cook's Tale of Gamelyn.
49. The Pardoner and Tapster, and The Second Merchant's Tale or Tale of Beryn.

1532. [Tuke, Sir Brian.] *Dedication* to *Henry viii,* prefixed to Chaucer's works, ed. William Thynne, 1532, sign. A ii–A iij (printed in Francis Thynne's Animadversions, ed. F. J. Furnivall, Chaucer soc. 1876, pp. xxiv–vi).

. . . I . . . Wylliam Thynne / . . . moued by a certayne inclynacion & zele / whiche I haue to here of any thyng soundyng to the laude and honour of this your noble realme / haue taken great delectacyon / as the tymes and laysers might suffre / to rede and here the bokes of that noble & famous clerke Geffray Chaucer / in whose workes is so manyfest comprobacion of his excellent lernyng in all kyndes of doctrynes and sciences / suche frutefulnesse in wordes / wel accordynge to the mater and purpose / so swete and plesaunt sentences / suche perfectyon in metre / the composycion so adapted / suche

fresshnesse of inuencion / compendyousnesse in narration /
suche sensyble and open style / lackyng neither maieste ne
mediocrite couenable *in* disposycion / and suche sharpnesse or
quycknesse in *co*nclusyon / that it is moche to be marueyled /
howe in his tyme / wha*n* doutlesse all good letters were layde
a slepe through out th*e* worlde / . . . . suche an excellent poete
in our tonge / shulde, as it were (nature repugnyng) spryng and
aryse : . .

[Only a small portion of this preface is printed—the direct praise of Chaucer—as it is
so easily accessible in Thynne's *Animadversions.* There follows an account of Thynne's
search for and collation of copies of Chaucer's works ; this also is to be found in the
Animadversions. Although written in Thynne's name, the preface really was composed by his friend Sir Brian Tuke. *See* Thynne's Animadversions, ed. Furnivall,
Hindwords, p. xxvi ; *also* Studies in Chaucer, by T. R. Lounsbury, 1892, vol. i, p. 266.]

[1532–5.] Unknown. *The Plowmans tale.* [col.] Printed at London
by Thomas Godfray. Cum priuilegio.

[This is the earliest known print of The Plowman's Tale : there is a unique copy at
Britwell. It was most probably printed by William Thynne's directions, as he was
apparently prevented from including it (as well as the Pilgrim's tale) in his first edn.
of Chaucer, 1532. *See* Francis Thynne's Animadversions, p. 151 below. The tale is
ascribed to Chaucer by Speght (see App. A, under 1598), and, beginning with Thynne's
second edn., 1542, *q. v.* p. 83, is printed with his works and regularly assumed to be by
him, until Dart in the ' Life' prefixed to Urry's edn. of 1721, for the first time doubts
its authenticity. Tyrwhitt finally rejected it. For later single edns. see under 1606
below, p. 177, also Illustrations of . . . Gower and Chaucer, 1810, by Todd, p. xxxix
note, where an edn. by Wyllyam Hyll (1542 ?) is described. *See also* T. Corser, Collectanea, iv, pp. 330–1, and Chaucer, a bibliographical manual, by E. P. Hammond,
N. York, 1908, pp. 444–6.]

1533. Elyot, Sir Thomas. *Pasquyll the Playne*, sign. A iij *b.*

Pasquill [to Gnato] what a gods name haue ye a booke in
youre hand ? A good feloweshyp wherof is it ? Let me se
Nouum stestamentum [*sic*] . . . . . But what is this in youre
bosom ? An other booke . . . Let se, what is here ? Troylus
& Chreseid ? Lorde what discord is bytwene these two bokes.

[There is no copy of the 1st edn. in the B. M., but there is one in the Douce
collection in the Bodleian; the extract here is from the 2nd edn., 1540.

1533. [Heywood, John.] *A mery playe betwene the pardoner and the
frere the curate and neybour Pratte.* Imprynted by Wyllyam Rastell,
1533 [written probably before 1521, see D.N.B., and Facsimile
Reprint, ed. J. S. Farmer 1909] sign. A ii–A iii (ed. F. J. Child,
Four old plays, 1848, pp. 94–5, 97).

[The two following passages are taken, with almost similar word-
ing, direct from Chaucer's Prologue of the Pardoner's Tale, ll. 7–48,
49–60.]

But first ye shall knowe well y*t* I com fro Rome
[36 lines, to] . . . . .
[sign. A ij b] So that he offer pens or els grotes.

But one thynge ye women all I warant you
[16 lines, to]   .   .   .   .   .
Now shall ye se
[sign. A iij] Lo here the popes bull.

[The Pardoner in *The Foure Ps* (printed *c.* 1545, written *c.* 1530), also resembles Chaucer's Pardoner in tone and attitude ; and there is undoubted reminiscence of Chaucer's *Parlement of Foules* in the description of the eagle in the ballad written by Heywood to celebrate the marriage of Queen Mary with Philip of Spain in 1554. The ballad is reprinted in Harleian Miscellany, ed. Park, 1813, vol. x, pp. 255–6.]

1535. Layton, Richard. *Letter to Thomas Cromwell.* (Record Office, *see* Calendar of State Papers, ed. J. Gairdner, vol. ix, no. 42. This extract is given in Henry VIII and the English Monasteries, by F. A. Gasquet, revised edn. 1899, p. 144.)

[Layton writes from Bath abbey] Ye shall herewith receive a book of Our Lady's miracles well able to match the Canterbury Tales. Such a book of dreams as ye neuer saw, which I found in the library.

1535. Roper, Margaret, or **More,** Sir Thomas. *Letter to Lady Alington.* The workes of Sir Thomas More, 1557, p. 1441, col. 2, F. (The Mirrour of vertue . . . . or the Life of Sir Thomas More . . by William Roper, ed. I. Gollancz, the King's classics, 1903, p. 143 ; for MSS. and edns. *see ibid.*, pp. ix–xii.)

In good fayth father quoþ I, I can no ferther goe, but am (as I trowe Cresede saith in Chaucer) comen to Dulcarnon euen at my wittes ende.

[William Roper prefaces this letter by the following note, on p. 117 :—"When Mistress Roper had received this Letter [from Lady Alington], she, at her next repair to her Father in the Tower, showed him this Letter. And what communication was thereupon between her Father and her, ye shall perceive by an Answer here following (as written to the Lady Alington). But whether this answer were written by Sir Thomas More in his Daughter Roper's name, or by herself, it is not certainly known."]

1536. Unknown. *A Remedy for Sedition, wherein are conteyned many thynges concernyng the true and loyall obeysance, that commens owe vnto their prince and soueraygne lorde the kynge.* sign. B i.

Geffrey Chauser sayeth also somewhat in theyr prayse,
  beare it well away, and lawde theyme as ye fynde cause,
    O eterne people vniuste and vntrewe,
    Ay vndiscrete and chaungynge as a fane,
    Delytynge euer in rumours that be newe ;
CHAUCER CRITICISM.

For lyke the mone euer waxe ye and wane :
Your reason halteth, your jugement is lawe,
Your dome is false, your constance euyll preueth,
A full great foole is he that on you leneth.

[An imperfect rendering of Clerkes Tale, ll. 994–1001.]

[1536–40 ?] **Unknown.** *The Pilgrim's Tale,* ff. xxxiii, vi, xlv, ll. 93, 263, 721–4, 739–40 ; from the reprinted Courte of Venus, Douce fragment 92 *b.* (Thynne's Animadversions, ed. F. J. Furnivall, Chaucer soc. 1876, App. I., pp. 79, 84, 97–8.)

for chaucer sathe in the sted of the quen elfe,   [l. 93]
[Ther walketh now the lymytour himself]   [Wyf of Bath, l. 874]

.   .   .   .

ther ministre shold be diligent   [ll. 260–3]
as Christ himselue, to teache vs nought for-gett
[.   .   .   .   .   .   *line left out*]
and first he dyd yt, and after he taght.   [Cant. Tales Gen. Prol.], Parson, ll. 497–8.

.   .   .   .

he sayd he durst not it dis[c]lose   [ll. 721–4]
but bad me reyd the 'romant of the rose,'
the thred leafe, Iust from the end   [ll. 7129–7214 ? or ll. quoted below.]
to the secund page, ther he dyd me send   [ll. 724]

.   .   .   .

he prayd me thes vi stauis for to marke   [ll. 739–40]
whiche be chaucers own hand work [*i. e.* ll. 7165–70]

[With regard to date and authorship of above, see two articles by Mrs. C. C. Stopes in Athenæum, June 24, 1899, pp. 785–6 (The Metrical Psalms and the Court of Venus), and July 1, 1899, p. 38 (The Authorship of the Newe Courte of Venus).]

1540. Cavendish, William. *MS. Catalogue* of his library at North Awbrey near Lincoln, formerly in the possession of John Wilson, of Bromhead, near Sheffield. (Who wrote Cavendish's life of Wolsey ? [by Joseph Hunter] 1812, p. 21.)

Chaucer, Froyssarte Chronicles, a boke of French and English.

[c. 1540.] **Unknown.** *Two MS. verses,* Harleian MS. 4826, fol. 139.

Off worthy Chaucer
here the pickture stood
That much did wryght
and all to doe vs good.

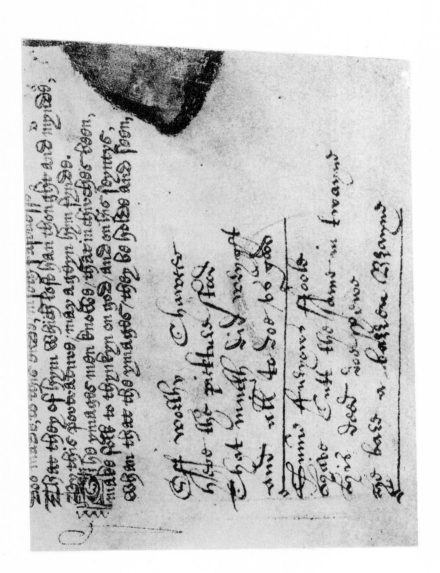

TWO MS VERSES (ABOUT 1540) IN HOCCLEVE'S 'DE REGIMINE PRINCIPIUM'
Harleian MS. 4826, fol. 139.

9

Summe ffuryous ffoole
Have Cutt the same in twayne
His deed doe shewe
He have a barren Brayne.

[Some rightly indignant lover of Chaucer's MS. has written these lines at the foot
of fol. 139, from the margin of which almost all the full-length portrait of Chaucer
has been cut.]

[*c.* 1540.] **Jack by Lande Compyled by the Famous Geoffrey
Chaucer** . . . . . Cum priuilegio Regali. Prynted for Ihon Gough.
[Gonville and Caius Coll. Camb.]   MS. Harl. 6641.
[*See* below, 1570, p. 105, for Foxe's reprint of Jack Upland.]

[*c.* 1540.] **Unknown.** *Tales, and quicke answeres, very mery, and
pleasant to rede.* Unique copy in Huth library. [Reprint called]
Shakespeare's Jest Book, ed. S. W. Singer, 1814, tale 28,
pp. 28–9.

This tale sheweth that dreames sometyme come to passe by
one meane or other.   And he that desyreth to knowe more of
dreames wrytten in our englysshe tonge, let hym rede the tale
of the nounnes preste, that G. Chauser wrote : and for the
skeles howe dreames and sweuens are caused, the begynnynge
of the boke of Fame, the whiche the sayde Chauser compiled
with many an other matter full of wysedome.

1542. Workes of Geffray Chaucer. [Blackletter ed. W. Thynne, 2nd
edn.] W. Bonham, 1542. (*Cf.* Note *under* 1532, Thynne, W.,
pp. 78–9.)

[This 2nd edn. of Thynne's Chaucer often bears different printers' names, Toye,
Kele, Petit, Bonham, Reynes, etc. For this reason it is often confused with the
undated reprint, *see* under 1545 or 1550 below, p. 86, but it is a quite distinct and
rarer edn.]

1542. Unknown. *The Plowman's Tale.* Printed in Thynne's 2nd edn.
of *Chaucer's Works,* as above, fol. cxix, following the *Parson's Tale.*

[This is the first time the *Plowman's Tale* was printed in an edn. of Chaucer's
' Works,' it was first printed separately by Thomas Godfray in folio [1532–5], *q. v.*, p.
80. In the next edn. of Chaucer's ' Works ' (undated, but ascribed to the years 1545
or 1550 *q. v.* p. 86) the *Plowman's Tale* was inserted before the *Parson's*, and the first
line of the prologue to the *Parson's Tale* was altered to suit ; reading "By this the
plowman had his tale ended" instead of *manciple.* The genuine reading was not
restored until Tyrwhitt did so in his edition of 1775. *See* Thynne's Animadversions,
ed. F. J. Furnivall, 1876, pp. 68, 69, 147 ; also for a note of H. Bradshaw's, *ibid.*,
p. 101.]

[*a.* 1542.] **Wyatt**, Sir Thomas (d. 1542). [Satire ii], *Of the Courtiers life
written to Iohn Poins;* [Satire iii], *How to vse the Court and
himselfe therein, written to Syr Fraunces Bryan.* [Printed in] *Songes
and Sonettes written by the* . . . *Lorde Henry Howard* . . . 1557.
[*See* next entry] f. 47 and 48 *b* (Tottell's Miscellany, English
Reprints, ed. E. Arber, 1870, p. 89, ll. 50–1, p. 92, ll. 73–8).

I am not he that can . . . .

· · · · · · · · · ·

[fol. 47]

Praise syr Topas for a noble tale,
And scorne the story that the knight tolde :

. . . .

[fol. 48 b]

In this also se that thou be not idle :
Thy nece, thy cosyn, sister, or thy daughter,
If she bee faire . . . .
If thy better hath her loue besought her :
Auaunce his cause, and he shall helpe thy nede,
It is but loue, turne thou it to a laughter.
But ware I say, so gold thee helpe and spede :
That in this case thou be not so vnwise,
As Pandar was in such a like dede.
For he, the fole of conscience, was so nice :
That he no gaine would haue for all his paine.

[For Chaucer's influence on Wyatt's verse, which was considerable, *see* below, App. A, *a.* 1542.]

[*c.* **1542.**] **Howard,** Henry, Earl of Surrey. *Poem* on the *Death of . . . Sir T[homas] W[yatt].* [First printed in the collection of] *Songes and Sonettes, written by the ryght honorable Lorde Henry Haward late Earle of Surrey, and other.* Apud Richardum Tottel, 1557. [col.] Imprinted at London . . . by Richard Tottel, the fift day of June, An. 1557. [This is known as Tottel's Miscellany, a unique copy of this first edn. is in the Bodleian ; our transcript is from the 2nd edn. [in B. M.], with col. 'Imprinted at London . . . by Richard Tottell the xxxi. day of July, An. 1557,' ff. 16 *b* and 17. (Tottel's Miscellany, English Reprints, ed. E. Arber, 1870, p. 29.)

Of the death of the same sir T.[homas] W.[yatt]

. . . . . .

Of the same.

W. Resteth here, that quick could neuer rest :

. . . . . .

A hand, that taught, what might be said in rime :
That reft Chaucer the glory of his wit :
A mark, the which (unparfited, for time)
Some may approch, but neuer none shal hit.

[There are three known copies of the 2nd edn. of Tottell. *See* an article on Tottel's Miscellany, by W. W. Greg in The Library, April, 1904.]

1542. Leland, John. *Naeniae in mortem Thomae Viati,* ll. 1–8. *See* below, App. A, 1542.

1542–3. *An Acte for thaduauncement of true Religion and for thabbolisshment of the contrarie.* Statute 34 and 35 Henry VIII, chap. i, section v. (Statutes of the Realm, vol. iii, 1817, p. 895.)

[The statute provides for the utter abolishment, etc., of forbidden books.] Provided allso that all bokes in Englishe printed before the yere of our Lorde a thousande fyve hundred

and fourtie intytled the Kings Hieghnes proclamac*i*ons iniunc-
tions, translac*i*ons of the Pater noster, the Aue Maria and the
Crede, the psalters prymers prayer statutes and lawes of the
Realme, Cronycles Canterburye tales, Chaucers bokes Gowers
bokes and stories of mennes lieues, shall not be comprehended
in the prohibic*i*on of this acte . . . .

[1543?] Unknown. *Heading to* **Truth.** MS. Arch. Seld. B 10, fol.
F ii and *b.* (at end of Harding's Chronicle, p. 4 of "the Prouerbes of
Lydgate." More odd texts of Chaucer's minor poems, ed. F. J.
Furnivall, Chaucer soc. 1886, p. 29).

Ecce bonu*m* consiliu*m* galfridi chaucers *co*ntra fortuna*m.*

1544. Ascham, Roger. *Toxophilus.* Londini In ædibus Edouardi
Whytchurch, Book i, sign. E i *b,* E ii *b*–iii, E iv–iv *b,* F ii–ii *b.*
(English Reprints, ed. E. Arber, 1868, pp. 52, 54, 56, 59.)

[sign. E
i b] The Nource of dise and cardes is werisome Ydlenesse,
enemy of vertue, y*e* drowner of youthe, that tarieth in it, and
as Chauser doth saye verie well in the Parsons tale, the greene
path waye to hel, hauinge this thing appropriat vnto it, that
where as other vices haue some cloke of honestie, onely
ydlenes can neyther do wel, nor yet thinke wel.

[Parson's Tale, ll. 710–16?]

. . . .

[sign. E
ii b] Whose horriblenes [speaking of Gaming] is so large that
it passed the eloquence of our *Englishe Homer* [Chaucer] to
compasse it : yet because I euer thought hys sayinges to have
as much authoritye as eyther *Sophocles* or *Euripedes* in Greke,
therefore gladly do I remember these verses of hys :—

Hasardry is very mother of lesinges
And of deceyte and cursed sweringes
[sign. E
iii] Blasphemie of Christ, manslaughter, and waste also,
Of catel of tyme, of other thynges mo.

[Pardoner's Tale, ll. 590–4.]

[Here Ascham inserts a moral disquisition on various clauses
of these verses.]

. . . .

[sign. E
iv] *Cursed sweryng blasphemie of Christe.* These halfe verses
Chaucer in an other place more at large doth well set out, and
verye liuely expresse, sayinge.

Ey bi goddes precious hert and his nayles
And by the blood of Christ that is in Hales

. . . .

Forsweringe, Ire, falsnes and Homicide, etc.

[Pardoner's Tale, ll. 615–7].

[sign. E iv b]   . . . . Two men I herd my selfe, whose sayinges be far more grisely than Chaucers verses. . . .

[sign. F ii]   Yet this I woulde wysche that all great men in Englande had red ouer diligentlye the Pardoners tale in Chaucer, and there they shoulde perceyue and se, howe moche suche games stande with theyr worshyppe, howe great soeuer they be. . . . I wyll make an ende with this saying of Chaucer :

[sign. F ii b]   Lordes might finde them other maner of pleye
Honest ynough to driiue the daye awaye.

[Pardoner's Tale, ll. 627-8.]

1544. Betham, Peter. *The Prefatory Epistle* [to] *The preceptes of Warre*, set forth by James the Erle of Purlilia and translated into Englysh by Peter Betham 1544. [col.] Imprynted at London, in the Olde Jewery, by Edwarde Whytchurche, cum priuilegio ad imprimendum solum. (Title and extract with Chaucer ref. given in Censura Literaria, by Sir S. E. Brydges, vol. vii (iv of new series), 1808, pp. 67–72.)

[p. 69]   Yet lette no man thyncke, that I doo damne all usual termes borowed of other tounges whan I doo well knowe that one tounge is interlaced with an other. But nowe to be shorte, I take them beste Englysshe men, which folowe Chaucer, and other olde wryters, in whyche study the nobles, and gentle men of Englande, are worthye to be praysed, whan they endeuoure to brynge agayne his owne clennes, oure Englysshe toungue, and playnelye to speake wyth our owne termes, as our [f]athers dyd before us . . . .

[There is no copy in B.M., but one in Bodl. and one in Camb. Univ. library.]

[1545 or 1550 ?.] The Workes of Geffray Chaucer . . . Wyllyam Bonham.

[A reprint of Thynne's 2nd edn. 1542, *q. v.* p. 83, in which the Plowman's Tale was inserted before the Parson's, *see* note under 1542, Plowman's Tale, p. 83. Other copies of this edn. bear a different printer's name in the col., Robart Toye, Rycharde Kele, or Thomas Petit. *Cf.* above, pp. 78–9, 1532, Thynne, W.]

[c. 1545.] Forrest, William. *History of Joseph.* Univ. Coll. Oxford MS. 88, fol. 3. (The History of Grisild the Second . . . . . written by William Forrest . . . ed. Rev. W. D. Macray. Roxb. Club, 1875, p. 167.

The Prologe.

.   .   .   .   .

I wote this hathe not the florischinge veyne
    Of *Gowers* phrase, adorned in suche sorte,
Oather of *Chaucers*, that Poete soueraynge

> To aske their counsaylles I came all to shorte :
> *Lydgate* in this gaue me no comforte ;
>   So tell I yowe, before yee doo ytt reade,
>   I cannot them rayse, so longe agoe deade.

["Dated as having been finished April 11, 1569, but said by the author to have been originally written 24 years before." *Cf.* Rox. Club edn. introduction, p. xxi.]

[*c.* **1545.**] **Leland,** John. *Commentarii de Scriptoribus Britannicis.* [MS. Bodl.] [first printed by] Antonius Hall, . . . Oxonii, 1709. Cap. DV, *De Gallofrido Chaucero*, pp. 419-26, cap. CDXCIII, *De Joanne Govero*, p. 416.

[This is the first 'life' of Chaucer. For a print of it, *see* below, App. A *c.* 1545 Leland.]

[*c.* **1545.**] **Leland,** John. *Principum, ac illustrium aliquot & eruditorum in Anglia Virorum, Encomia . . . nunc primum in lucem edita.* Londini, . . . 1589. Encomia illustrium virorum. In laudem Gallofridi Chauceri, Isiaci, p. 79 ; De Gallofrido Chaucero, Equite, p. 80 ; De Gallofrido Chaucero, pp. 93-4. (Reprinted by T. Hearne, in J. Lelandi de Rebus Britannicis Collectanea, 1770, vol. v, pp. 141-2, 152.)

[These three sets of verses are all included (with some variation in the first and third) in the account of Chaucer given by Leland in the Commentarii de Scriptoribus Britannicis. *See* last entry.]

[*c.* **1545.**] **Leland,** John. *Joannes Lelandi antiquarii De Rebus Britannicis Collectanea,* tom. iii [Tanner MS. Bodl.] fol. 48. (Reprinted, with same title by T. Hearne, 1770, vol. iv, p. 49.)

> *Westmonasterii*
> *Distichon ex epitaphio Galfredi Chauceri*
> Galfredus Chaucer, vates & fama poësis
> Maternæ, hac sacra sum tumulatus humo.

[These lines are the last two of Surigo's epitaph, *see* above, 1479, p. 60. The references in *The Itinerary of John Leland* (Tanner MSS. Bodl.), ed. Thomas Hearne, 2nd edn. 1745, are to Thomas and Alice Chaucer : they are vol. ii, p. 7 ; iv, pp. 6, 19 ; vii, pp. 69, 104.]

1546. Ashton, Peter. *Epistle dedicatory* [to] *A shorte treatise vpon the Turkes Chronicles . . . . translated out of Latyne into englysh . . . .* by Peter Ashton. Imprinted at London in Fletestrete . . . . by Edwarde Whitchurche M.D.XL.vi., sign. *vi *b.* (British Bibliographer, ed. Sir S. E. Brydges, 1810-14, vol. ii, 1812, p. 94. Short extract, containing Chaucer reference.)

For truly, throwghe out al this simple and rude translation, I studyed rather to vse the most playn and famylier english speche, then ether Chaucers wordes (which by reason of antiquitie be almost out of vse) or els ink horne termes (as they call them), whiche the common people, for lacke of latin, do not vnderstand.

1548. Bale, John. *Illvstrium Maioris Britanniae Scriptorum.* [1st edn.] fol. 198 and *b* [Life of Chaucer], fol. 202 *b* [John Lydgate], fol. 233 *b* [Thomas Wyat]. (For text of extracts *see* Appendix A, 1548, Bale, and *cf.* 2nd edn. of 1557–9, p. 95 below.)

[1548 ?] Lindsay, Sir David. *The Historie of Ane Nobil and Wailʒeand Squyer, William Meldrum.* [col.] Imprentit at Edinburgh be Henrie Charteris Anno MDxciiii, sign. a ii and a ii *b*. (Poetical works, ed. D. Laing, 1879, vol. i, pp. 159–60 ; also Works, part iii, . . . Squyer . . . Meldrum ed. F. Hall, E. E. T. soc. 1868, pp. 321–2.)

[l. 11]
Poetis thair honour to auance
Hes put thame in rememberance
Sum wryt of preclair Conquerouris,
And sum of vailʒeand Empriouris ;

. . . .

[l. 23]
Sum wryt of deidis amorous ;
As Chauceir wrait of Troilus
How that he luiffit Cressida :
Of Jason and of Medea.

[In the table of contents to The Warkis of . . . Sir Dauid Lyndsay . . . Imprentit . . . be Henrie Charteris, Anno M.DLxxxii, this poem is mentioned as the 'Historie of the Squyer William Meldrum of the Benis, neuer befoir Imprentit,' but it was not included in the Works, and no edn. of that date is now known to exist. Squyer Meldrum occurs again in the table of contents in the 1592 edn. of Lindsay's Works, but is not printed amongst them, yet it seems certain that an edn. was issued previous to 1585, as six copies are mentioned as part of the stock in trade of Robert Gourlay, bookseller of Edinburgh, who died in Sept. of that year. *See* Laing, vol. iii, pp. 278–86.]

1549. Becke, Edmund. *Preface* to Becke's edition of the Bible, fol. 1549, sign. A A vi.

To the most puissant and mighty prince Edwarde the first . .

. . . .

If all magistrates & the nobilitie, wolde wel wey with them selfs the inestimable dignitie, & incomparable goodnes of Gods boke, . . . and wolde also as willingly vouchsafe to suffurate & spare an houre or ii in a day, from theyr worldly busines, emploing it about the reading of this boke, as they have been vsed to do in Cronicles & Canterbury tales, then should they also abandone . . . all blasphemyes, swearing, carding, dysing. . . . Oh what a florishing commune wealth should your grace inioy & haue . . .

[1549 ?] Cranmer, Thomas. *A Sermon concerning the time of Rebellion.* Corp. Christ. coll. MS. Camb. cii, pp. 409–99. (Cranmer's Works, ed. J. E. Cox, Parker soc. 1844–6, vol. ii, 1846, p. 198.)

If we receiue and repute the gospel as a thing most true and godly, why do we not live according to the same ? If we count it as fables and trifles why do we take upon us to give such credit and authority to it?

To what purpose tendeth such dissimulation and hypocrisy? If we take it for a Canterbury tale, why do we not refuse it? Why do we not laugh it out of place, and whistle at it?

[This extract is given from the Parker soc. edition.]

1549. Latimer, Hugh. *The seconde Sermon . . . preached before the Kynges maiestie . . . ye xv. day of March Mcccccxlix.* Imprinted at London by John Daye [1549?]. The second sermon has a different title page to the first, though bound together. *To the Reader,* sign. A iiii. (Seven Sermons before Edward VI. English Reprints, ed. E. Arber, 1869, p. 49. Also Latimer's works, ed. Rev. G. E. Corrie, Parker soc., 1844–5, vol. i, pp. 106–7.)

. . . if good lyfe do not insue and folow upon our readynge to the example of other[s] we myghte as well spende that tyme in reading of prophane hystories, of cantorburye tales, or a fit of Roben Hode.

[1549?] **Unknown.** *Le A. to the Reder,* Envoy to *The goodli history of the moste noble and beautyfull Ladye Lucres of Scene . . . and of her louer Eurialus,* sign. H iij b. (Reprinted in the Hystorie of the most noble knight Plasidas, ed. H. H. Gibbs, Roxb. club, 1873, Preface, p. ix.)

Ther was also the noble Troylus

 Whych all hys lyfe, abode in mortall payne

Delayed by Cresyde whose history is piteous

 Tyll at the last Achylles had hym slayne

Yet other there be whyche in thys carefull chayne

 Of loue haue contynued, all theyr lyfe dayes

Deathe was theyr end, there was non other wayes.

[No date nor printer's name (but possibly W. Copland). A translation of Æneas Sylvius Piccolomini's (afterward Pius II) De duobus amantibus Eurialo et Lucresia, written in 1443. The reference is most probably to Chaucer's version of Troilus and Cressida.]

[1549?] **Unknown.** *The Complaynt of Scotlande.* [Attributed by Murray to an unknown priest of the name of Wedderburn, and by Laing to Robert Wedderburn, Vicar of Dundee; also to Sir James Inglis, and to Sir D. Lindsay] Paris? 1549? [f. 19 b]. Two copies in B. M. (Complaynt of Scotland, ed. J. Leyden, 1801, p. 98,—ed. J. A. H. Murray, E. E. T. soc., 1872–3, part i, p. 63.)

[The shepherds each tell a tale] . . . Sum vas in prose & sum vas in verse sum var storeis and sum var flet taylis. Thir var the namis of them as eftir follouis. the taylis of cantirberrye. Robert le dyabil . . . .

[*See* Murray's edn. for an account of this work; Dr. F. J. Furnivall reprinted in his Captain Cox, ed. for Ballad soc. 1871, the list of books contained in the Complaynt.

In the Grenville copy the foliation ceases at f. 31 recto and commences again as f. 32 on what should be f. 54 recto. The reference here given means f. 19 *b* of the unnumbered leaves; if the foliation were continuous it would be f. 50 *b*.]

[*c.* 1550 ?] **Unknown.** *Extract from Chanon Yemannes Tale*, ll. 1428–71 [in a collection of extracts relating to the philosopher's stone and other alchemical subjects], Sloane MS. 1098, ff. 17 *b*–18.

Lo thus sayeth arnolde of the newe towne

.   .   .   .

when y^t hym lyketh lo this ys hys ende.

Chaucer.

[*c.* 1550 ?] **Unknown.** *Extract from Chanon Yemannes Tale*, ll. 1428–81 [in a collection of extracts similar to above], Sloane MS. 1723, fol. 35.

Jeffray Chawcer.

Lo thus saith Arnolde of the new towne

.   .   .   .

God send euery good man boote of his bale.

finis.

1550. **Coke,** John. *The Debate betwene the Heraldes of Englande and Fraunce,* compyled by Jhon Coke, clarke of the Kynges recognysaunce . . . . MDL. sign. I viii *b.* (Reprinted with Le Débat des Hérauts d' Armes . . . . ed. L. L. Pannier et P. Meyer, soc. des anciens textes Français, 1877, p. 108.)

¶ The names of sum famous Clarkes in Englande of late dayes, and at this present time.

ITEM Syr Heralde what great clarkes & Oratours hath ben of late dayes and be at this daye in England, as Chauser, Gower, Lydgate, Bongay, Grosdon, Payce, Lylly, Lynacre, Tunstall, Latymer, Hoper, Couerdale, with many other.

And albeit the persons of these honourable men, ben to many vnknowen, yet theyr famous workes be common in all the vnyuersities of christendome. So it is euydent that we by reason of thantiquite of our vniuersities haue euermore had and yet haue more famous clarkes then you.

[1550–3 ?] **Turner,** William (Dean of Wells). *Letter to Mr. Fox* concerning his Book of Martyrs : and Some Intelligence of his Knowledge of Bishop Ridley, dated Nov. 26. Harl. MS. 416, fol. 132. (Works of N. Ridley, ed. Rev. H. Christmas, Parker soc., 1841, pp. 490, 94.)

Hoc me valde male habet, quod sanctissimi martyris domini Thorpii liber non sit ea lingua Anglice conscriptus, qua eo tempore quo ipse vixit tunc tota Anglia est usa. Nam talis antiquitatis sum admirator, ut ægerrime feram talis antiquitatis thesauros nobis perire ; quo nomine haud magnam apud me gratiam inierunt qui Petrum Aratorem, Gowerum et Chaucerum, et similis farinæ homines, in hanc turpiter mixtam linguam, neque vero Anglicam neque pure Gallicam, transtulerunt.

[I greatly regret that the book of that most holy martyr Thorp is not edited in the old English which was in general use at the time in which he lived. For so great an admirer am I of antiquity, that I could ill bear treasures of such antiquity to perish from amongst us. On which account I feel no great obligations to those persons, who have translated Piers Plowman. Gower and Chaucer, and authors of a similar stamp, into a mongrel language, neither true English nor pure French.]

[*c.* **1550-57.**] **Bale**, John. [*Entries in Bale's autograph note-book.*] MS. Cod. Seld., supra 64 (No. 3452 in Bernard's Catalogue) Bodl. Library, ff. 50, 59 *b*, 68 *b*, 69, 116, 135, 170 *b*, 211, 212, [printed in] Index Britanniæ Scriptorum . . ed. R. Lane Poole, Oxford, 1902, pp. 74–78, 82, 208, 210, 233, 255, 305.

1552. Ascham, Roger. *A Report and Discourse written by Roger Ascham, of the affaires and state of Germany and the Emperour Charles his court duryng certaine yeares while the sayd Roger was there.* Printed by John Daye [1570?] sign. A iiij. (Works, ed. Rev. Dr. Giles, 1864–5, Library of Old Authors, vol. iii, p. 6.)

Diligence also must be vsed [by an Historian] in kepyng truly the order of tyme: and describyng lyuely, both the site of places and nature of persons not onely for the outward shape of the body: but also for the inward disposition of the mynde, as *Thucidides* doth in many places very trimly, and *Homer* euerywhere, and that alwayes most excellently, which obseruation is chiefly to be marked in hym. And our *Chaucer* doth the same, very praise worthely: marke hym well and conferre hym with any other that writeth of in our tyme in their proudest toung, whosoeuer lyst.

1553. Wilson, Thomas. *The Arte of Rhetorique* . . . . . Book iii, fol. 86 and 86 *b*. (Ed. by G. H. Mair, 1909, p. 162.)

Emong al other lessons, this should first be learned t*h*at we neuer affect any strau*n*ge ynkehorne termes, but so speake as is commonly receiued . . . . Some farre iorneid ientleme*n* at their returne home, like as thei loue to go in forrein apparel, so thei wil pouder their talke w*ith* ouersea la*n*guage. He that cometh lately out of France will talke Fre*n*che English, & neuer blushe at the matter. Another choppes in with Angleso Italiano: the lawyer will store his stomack with the [fol. 86 *b*] pratyng of Pedlers. The Auditour in makyng his accompt and rekenyng, cometh in with sise sould, and cater denere, for vi s iiij d. The fine Courtier wil talke nothyng but Chaucer. The misticall wise menne, and Poeticall Clerkes-will speake nothyng but quaint prouerbes, a*n*d blynd allegories,

delityng muche in their awne darkenesse, especially, when
none can tell what thei dooe saie.

[*c.* 1555.] **Stevins,** Walter. *The conclusions off the astrolabye com-
pylyd by Geffray Chaucer newlye amendyd.* . . . . Sloane MS.
261, ff. 3–4, 30 *b*, 66.

[For an account of this MS. and evidence as to its date, *see* the Introduction to the
Treatise on the Astrolabe, by A. E. Brae, 1870, pp. 6–11.]

[fol. 3]
To the reader

WHEN I happenyd to looke vpon the conclusions of the
astrolabie compiled by Geffray Chawcer, and founde
the same corrupte, and false in so many and sondrie places,
that I doubtede whether the rudenes of the worke weare not a
gretter sclaunder to the authour, then trouble and offence to
the readers ; I dyd not a lytell marvell if a booke shoulde come
oute of his handes so imperfite and indigest, whose other workes
weare not onely reckenyd for the best that euer weare sette
fowrth in oure english tonge : but also weare taken for a manifest argumente of his singuler witte and generalitie in all kindes
of knowledge.   Howebeit, when I called to remembrance that
in his proheme he promised to sette fowrth this worke in fyue
partes, wherof weare neuer extante but these two first partes
onely, it made me belyue that either the worke was neuer
[fol. 3 b] fynisshed of the authoure, or els to haue ben corrupted sens by
some other meanes ; or what other thinge might be the cause
therof I wiste not.   Neuer the lesse vnderstandinge that the
woorke, which before lay as neglected, to the profite of no man
and discourage of many, mighte be tourned to the commoditie
of as manye as herafter showlde happen to trauayle in that parte
of knowledge : I thought it a thinge worth my laboure if I coulde
sette it in better order and frame—which thinge howe I haue
done it, let be theire indifferente iudgemente, which heretofore
haue readen thether settinge forth ; or lyst to compare this and
that together, wherin I confesse that besydes the amendinge
of verie many wordes I haue displaced some conclusions, and
in some places wheare the sentences weare imperfite, I haue
supplied and filled them, as necessitie required.—As for some
conclusions I haue altered them, and some haue I cleane put
[fol. 4] oute for vtterlye false and vntrue : as namelye the conclusion
of direction and retrogradaconn of planetes : and the conclusions to knowe the longitudes of sterres, whether thei be
determinate or indeterminate in the astrolabie.   The conclu-

sion, to knowe with what degree of the zodiacke any planet
ascendeth on the horizonte whether his latitude be north or
sowth; as the meanynge of the same conclusion was most
hardest by reason of the imparfitenes therof so in practise I
fownde him most false, as he shall fynde that lyst to take the
lyke paines. Notwithstandinge this haue I doone, not chal-
lenginge for my selffe, but renuncynge and leauinge to worthie
Chaucer his due praise for this worke, which if it had come
parfite vnto oure handes (no dowbte) woolde haue merited
wonderfull praise. As for me if I haue done any thinge therin
it shall suffice if the louers of wittie Chawcer do accepte my
good will and entente.

Vale.

.   .   .   .

[fol. 90 *b*]   [Upon the first degree of Aries] Albeit y^t in. Chaucers
tyme upon the .12. day of March the sonne entred into the
bedde of Aries: yet in oure tyme y^u shalt finde that the sonne
entreth therin the .10. day of the same moneth.

.   .   .   .

[fol. 66]   Thus endethe the conclusions of the astrolabye composed by
Geoffrey Chawcer.

1555. Braham, Robert. *The pistle to the reader*, [prefixed to] The
  Auncient historie and onely trewe and syncere Cronicle of warres
  betwixte the Grecians and the Troyans . . . translated in to
  englyshe verse by John Lydgate, sign. *B i and *B i *b*. (Prefaces,
  dedications . . . from early English books, by W. C. Hazlitt, 1874,
  pp. 18, 19.)

. . . . And so by these degrees, hath bene at the laste by
ye diligence of John Lydgate a moncke of Burye, brought into
our englyshe tonge: and dygested as maye appere, in verse
whoes trauayle as well in other his doynges as in this hathe
wythout doubte so muche preuayled in this our vulgare language, that hauynge his prayse dewe to his deseruynges, may
worthyly be numbred amongst those that haue chefelye deserued
of our tunge. As the verye perfect disciple and imitator of
the great Chaucer, ye onelye glorye and beauty of the same.
Neuertheles, lyke wyse as it hapned ye same Chaucer to lease
ye prayse of that tyme wherin he wrote beyng then when in
dede al good letters were almost aslepe, so farre was the grose-
nesse and barbarousnesse of that age from the vnderstandinge
of so deuyne a wryter. That if it had not bene in this our
time, wherin all kindes of learnyng (thancked be god) haue as
much floryshed as euer they did by anye former dayes within

this realme, and namelye by the dylygence of one willyam Thime (*sic*) a gentilma*n* who laudably studyouse to y*e* polyshing of so great a Jewell, with ryghte good iudgement trauail, & great paynes causing the same to be perfected and stamped as it is nowe read, y*e* sayde Chaucers workes had vtterly peryshed, or at y*e* lest bin so depraued by corrupcion of copies, [sign. *B 1 *b*] that at the laste, there shoulde no parte of hys meaning haue ben founde in any of them.

1555. Unknown. *The Institucion of a gentleman.* A. . D. . M.D.L.V. Imprinted at London . . . . by Thomas Marshe, sign. a iiii *b*–a v, b ii *b*, g iiii, h vii *b*, h viii.

[sign. a iiii *b*–a v]	Tale of the wyf of Bathe	ll. 1133–76 (a few lines omitted).
[sign. b ii *b*]	Reference to the maunciple's tale	ll. 207–22.
[sign. g iiii]	The reeves prologue	ll. 3903–4.
[sign. h vii *b*]	The pardoners tale	ll. 603–28.
[sign. h viii]	The pardoners tale	ll. 591–602.

[A brief account of the 2nd edn., 1568, of this work will be found in Sir S. E. Brydge's *Restituta*, 1814, vol. i, pp. 536–40; no references to Chaucer are given.]

1556. Brigham, Nicholas. [*Inscription* on Chaucer's Tomb in Westminster Abbey.]

M. S.

QUI FUIT ANGLORUM VATES TER MAXIMUS OLIM
GALFRIDUS CHAUCER CONDITUR HOC TUMULO :
ANNUM SI QUÆRAS DOMINI, SI TEMPORA VITÆ.
ECCE NOTÆ SUBSUNT QUÆ TIBI CUNCTA NOTANT.
25 OCTOBRIS 1400
AERUMNARUM REQUIES MORS.
N. BRIGHAM HOS FECIT MUSARUM NOMINE SUMPTUS
1556.

[*See* p. 186, below, under *a.* 1613, R. Commaundre, who gives this epitaph, down to Octobris 1400, then adds Surigo's two lines, quoted by Leland (*c.* 1545, p. 87); he, however, erroneously puts down the inscription to Hickeman. For the whole question of Chaucer's tomb and re-interment, *see* note under *a.* 1479, Caxton, p. 59 above.]

1556. More, Sir William. *Catalogue of his Books* made by Sir William More, of Losely in Surrey, Aug. 20, 1556, a transcript of which is in *Archæologia*, 1855, vol. xxxvi, pp. 290–2.

[p. 290] Itm. chausore . . . v s.

1557. [Grimoald or **Grimald,** Nicholas, editor ?] *A print of Chaucer's poem on Truth* (Balade de bon conseyl), with interesting variations, in *Songes and Sonettes, written by* . . . *Lorde Henry Haward late Earle of Surrey, and other,* 1st edn., 5 June, 1557 [unique copy in Bodleian], sign. A A i, under 'Uncertain Authors,' and headed 'To leade a vertuous and honest life.' (Tottel's Miscellany, ed. E. Arber, 1870, pp. 194–5.)

CHAUCER'S TOMB IN WESTMINSTER ABBEY

1557–9. Bale, John. *Scriptorum Illustrium maioris Brytanniæ . . .
Catalogus.* [col.] Basileæ, ex officina Ioannis oporini anno Salutis
humanæ M.DLix Mense Februario. 2 vols. [2nd edn.] Further
notices of Chaucer; vol. i, pp. 525–7 [Life of Chaucer, fuller than
in 1st edition]; p. 537 [Thomas Occleve]; p. 586 [John Lydgate];
p. 700 [Radcliffe, R.]; p. 702 [Grimoald, Nicholas]. (For Bale's
whole account of Chaucer, pp. 525–7, *see* below, Appendix A,
1557–9 ; *cf.* also first edn. 1548 above, p. 88.)

[The date 1557 is not on the title-page, but is at the head of sign. a 6.]

[*a.* **1559.**] **Grimoald** or **Grimald,** Nicholas.   *Troilus ex Chaucero
comœdia,* lib. 1.

[No copy of this work is known to exist, the only mention of it is in John Bale's
Scriptorum illustrium maioris Brytanniæ Catalogus, Basle [1557–9], p. 702.]

[*a.* **1559. Radcliffe,** Ralph.]   *De patientia Grisildis.   De Melibœo
Chauceriano.*

[No copies of these two works are known to exist. They are mentioned by John
Bale in his Scriptorum illustrium maioris Brytanniæ Catalogus, Basle [1557–9], p. 700.]

[*c.* **1560 ?**] **Unknown.**   *Heading* to Astrolabe in Sloane MS. 314, fol.
65 *b.*

1391. Sᵣ Jeffery Chawser*es* worke.

[*c.* **1560.**] **Unknown.**   *A fragment of MS.* of 16th century handwriting,
[evidently translated from Leland, as printed by Bale, *see* above,
1557–9] pasted on the fly-leaf of the 2nd edn. of Caxton's Canterbury Tales (printed *c.* 1483) in a copy in B. M. (G. 11,586). It is
stated underneath that the fragment was "cut out from a very
antient binding of this Book."   See Life of Caxton, by W. Blades,
1861–3, vol. ii, pp. 163–4.

Geffery Chaucer Englishman borne of noble parantage, neer
Oxford imployed his studye ther, as a neighbour and well-
willer vnto the same, He was a sharpe Logician, a sweete
Rhetorician, a pure Poett, a graue Philosopher, and a sacred
theologician, He surpassed the Mathematickes in his tyme in ther
art or cemeinge, He studied vnder John Sòmbo, St. Nicholas
Linna of the order of the Carmelites, He had trauailed into
ffraunce, & was expert in that language so well that he made
the Romaunt of the Rosse and a great number of sundry
Bookes, He florished in the yeare 1402.

[**1561.**] **Baldwin,** William.   *Beware the Cat.* [col.] Imprinted at
London at the long Shop adjoyning vnto Saint Mildreds Church in
the Pultrie by Edward Allde, 1584.   The Second Parte.

Chaucers   While I harkned to this broil, laboring to discern
house of
fame   bothe voices and noyces a sunder, I heard such a
mixture as I think was neuer in Chaucers house of
fame, for there was nothing within an hundred mile of me
doon on any side, (for from so far but no further the ayre may
come because of obliquation) but I herd it as wel as if I had

been by it, and could discern all voyces, but by means of noyses understand none.

[There were three impressions of this tract, one in 1561, another in 1570, and the third in 1584, but of the first two only fragments remain ; *see* J. P. Collier's Bibliographical and Critical Account of the rarest books in the English Language, 1865, vol. i, p. 43. Of the last edn. there are now two copies known, one (the Huth copy, now in B.M.) is imperfect, wanting the titlepage ; the other, from which we quote, was in the possession of Professor Edward Dowden ; this copy is perfect, but is cut close, and wants the signatures and headlines.]

1561. The workes of Geffrey Chaucer, newlie printed, with diuers addicions, whiche were neuer in print before : With the siege and destruccion of the worthy Citee of Thebes, compiled by Ihon Lidgate, Monke of Berie. As in the table more plainly doeth appere, 1561. [Blackletter. Generally known as Stowe's edition.]

[This is partly a reprint of Thynne's edn. of 1532, and partly consists of additional matter contributed by John Stowe. There are two issues of it, with different title pages, one with woodcuts in the Prologue to the C. Tales, and one without ; *see* the full account of this edn. given by W. W. Skeat in his edn. of Chaucer's Works, 1894, vol. i, pp. 31-43 ; also by E. P. Hammond, in Chaucer, a bibliographical manual, N. York, 1908, pp. 119-122, and see also the note under 1532, Thynne, above, pp. 78-9.]

1531. Sackville, Thomas, and **Norton,** Thomas. *The Tragedie of Ferrex and Porrex. See* below, App. A, 1561.

1561. Stowe, John. *The workes of Geffrey Chaucer* . . . 1561. Six headlines mentioning Chaucer, ff. 340–48.

1561. Unknown. *A Couplet on Chaucer,* on title page, under the coat-of-arms, in the issue of above edn. without woodcuts. (One in B.M., 83. 1. 5.)

> Vertue florisheth in Chaucer still,
>
> Though death of hym, hath wrought his will.

[This couplet is also printed in Speght's 2nd edn. of Chaucer 1602, after sign ciij *b.*]

1561. Unknown. *Verses* [without heading or signature, among the prefatory matter to] *The firste syxe bokes of the mooste Christian Poet Marcellus Palingenius, called the zodiake of life* . . . . Newly translated . . . by Barnaby Googe. (This extract is given in Censura Literaria by Sir S. E. Brydges, vol. ii, 1806, p. 207, also in Arber's reprint of Googe's Eglogs, &c., 1871, p. 8.)

> If Chaucer nowe shoulde liue,
>
> Whose eloquence deuine,
>
> Hath paste y° poets al that came
>
> Of auncient Brutus lyne,
>
> If Homere here might dwell,
>
> Whose praise the Grekes resounde
>
> If Vergile might his yeares renewe,
>
> If Ouide myght be founde :
>
> All these might well be sure
>
> Theyr matches here to fynde,

So muche dothe England florishe now
With men of Muses kynde.

[The above verses are not in the "firste thre books," translated by B. G. 1560; nor
in the edn. of 1565. *Cf.* the verses on p. 116 below, 1578, Procter.]

1562. Bale, John. *MS. notes* by John Bale, printed by Thomas
Hearne in Johannis de Trokelowe, Annales Edwardi II, ... e
codicibus MSS., nunc primus divulgavit Tho. Hearnius . . 1729.
Appendix iii., pp. 286, 287 ; Notæ MSS. ipsius Joannis Bale,
adjectæ Codici impresso de Scriptoribus, etc. [For extracts, *see*
Appendix A, 1562, Bale.]

1562. Legh, Gerard. *The Accedens of Armory,* sign. C j.

Isidore wryteth, that the planet [Venus] exciteth to loue
wonderfullye, especiallye betwene man and woman. But that
I committe wholy to the iudgement of woorthy Gower, and
of that famous syr Gefferey Chauser, whose workes do yet
remayn as greene, as the Lawrell tree, comparable in euerye
poynt with those, which haue deserued chiefest prayse.

1562. Scott, Alexander. *A ne New ʒeir Gift to the Quene Mary, quhen
scho come first Hame,* 1562, fol. 91 *a,* stanza 16. [Transcribed from
the edn. of the Scottish Text soc.]

For sum ar sene at sermonis seme sa halye,
Singand Sanct Dauidis psalter on þair bukis,
And ar bot biblistis fairsing full þair bellie,
Bakbytand nyᵗbouris, noyand þame in nwikis,
Ruging and raifand vp kirk rentis lyke ruikis ;
As werrie waspis aganis Goddis word makis weir :
Sic Christianis to kis w*ith* Chauceris kuikis
God gife þe grace aganis þis gude new ʒeir.

[The reference to *Chauceris kuikis* is given in Scott's poems, ed. J. Cranstoun,
Scott. text soc. 1896, p. 5 ; poems of A. Scott from the Bannatyne MS., printed for
private circulation 1882, p. 11, and notes pp. 98–9 ; N. and Q. 6th ser., vol. v, 1882,
p. 334, notes by W. W. Skeat and W. E. Buckley. Cranstoun also, p. 5 and notes,
p. 108, quotes from Montgomerie's "The Flyting," *a.* 1584, ll. 112–14 (*q.v.* below, p. 124).
For the reading *Chanteris kuikis, see* Ancient Scottish poems 1770 and 1815, ed. Sir G.
Dalrymple, Lord Hayles, p. 247 ; Poems of A. Scott, ed. D. Laing 1821, p. 9 ; Poems
of A. Scott, modernised, ed. W. Mackean, 1887 ; and Scott's poems, ed. A. Karley
Donald, E. E. T. soc., 1902, p. 6, and notes, pp. 74–5.]

1563–8. Ascham, Roger. *The Scholemaster.* At London. Printed by
Iohn Daye, 1570, [posthumously published] sign. R iiij *b.,* S i and
b. (English Reprints, ed. E. Arber, 1870, pp. 145–6, 8.) [The 2nd
edn., sometimes called the 1st, is dated 1571.]

[sign. R
iiij *b*] Some that make *Chaucer* in Englishe and *Petrarch* in
Italian, their Gods in verses, and yet be not able to make
true difference, what is a fault, and what is a iust prayse, in

[sign.
S i] those two worthie wittes, will moch mislike this my writyng. But such men be euen like followers of *Chaucer* and *Petrarke* as one here in England did folow Syr *Tho. More*: who, being most vnlike vnto him, in wit and learning, neuertheles in wearing his gowne awrye vpon the one shoulder, as Syr *Tho. More* was wont to doe, would needes be counted like vnto hym.

. . . .

[sign.
S i b] And you, that . . . . neuer went farder than the schole of *Petrarke* and *Ariostus* abroad, or els of *Chaucer* at home . . . .

1563. Neville, Alexander. *A dedicatory poem* in *Eglogs, Epytaphes, and Sonettes, newly written by Barnabe Googe,* 1563, 15 Marche. ¶ Imprynted at London, by Thomas Colwell, for Raffe Newbery. Three copies only known, Huth & Britwell libraries and Capel collection Trin. Coll. Camb. (English Reprints, ed. E. Arber, 1871, p. 23).

Alexander Neuyll.

. . . .

Go forward styll to aduaunce thy fame
Life's Race halfe ryghtly ron
Farre easyer tis for to obtain
the Type of true Renowne.
Like Labours haue been recompenst
with an immortall Crowne.
By this doth famous *Chaucer* lyue,
by this a thousande moore
Of later yeares.   By this alone
The old renowmed Stoore
of Auncient Poets lyue . . . .

1564. Bullein, William. *A Dialogue bothe pleasaunte and pietifull, wherein is a goodly regimente against the feuer Pestilence* . . . . *Newly corrected by William Bullein the autour thereof.*—Imprinted at London by Ihon Kingston, Marcii MDL xiiii. [Unique copy of 1st edn. 1564, in Britwell library. In 1573 edn., earliest in B. M., the reference is on pp. 19-20.] (Ed. M. W. Bullen and A. H. Bullen, E. E. T. soc., extra series lii, 1888, pp. 16-17.)

Wittie Chaucer satte in a chaire of gold couered with Roses, writing Prose and Risme, accompanied with the Spirites of many Kynges, Knightes and faire Ladies, whom hee pleasauntly besprinkeled with the sweete water of the welle consecrated unto the Muses ecleped Aganippe ; and as the heauenly spirite commended his deare Brigham for the worthy entombing of his bones, worthy of memorie, in the long slepyng chamber of most famous kinges, Euen so in tragedie he bewailed the sodaine resurrection of many a noble man before their time, in spoylyng of Epitaphes; whereby many haue loste their inheritaunce, &c. And further thus he said lamentynge :—

Couetos men do catch al that thei may haue,
The feeld & the flock, the tombe & the graue,
And as they abuse riches, and their graues that are gone,
The same measure they shall haue euery one,
Yet no burial hurteth holy men though beastes them deuour,
Nor riche graue preuaileth the wicked for all yearthly power.

[*See* above, *a.* 1479, Caxton, p. 59, *also* above, 1556, Brigham, p. 94.]

1565. **Calfhill,** James. *Aunswere to the Treatise of the Crosse* [by John Martiall], fol. 134 *b.* (Ed. R. Gibbings, Parker soc. 1846, pp. 287-8.)

. . . the friers coule must be honored. Ye remember what the hoste in Chawcer sayd to sir Thopas for hys leude ryme : the same do I say to you (bicause I haue to do with your Cantorbury tales) for youre fayre reasons.

> ['No more of this, for goddes dignitee'
> Quod oure hoste, 'for thou makest me
> So wery of thy verray lewednesse
> That, also wisly god my soule blesse,
> Myn eres aken of thy drasty speche.' *Prol. to Melibeus,* ll. 1-5.]

1565. **Googe,** Barnaby. *The Preface to the . . Reader* [in] The Zodiake of Life. *See* below, App. A.

1566. *Decree of the Court of Requests as to the payment of money at Chaucer's tomb.* 7th Feb. 8 Eliz. [1566.]

[*See* below, 1585, p. 128 ; Order by the Court of Requests ; and 1596, Cæsar, p. 143, below.]

1566. **Edwards,** Richard. *Palamon and Arcite,* a play acted before the Queen at Oxford [now lost]. Extract from Wood's MS. (Bodl.?) corrected by Mr. Gough (printed in The Progresses . . . . of Queen Elizabeth, by John Nichols, 1823, vol. i, p. 210).

At night the Queen heard the first part of an English play, named Palamon & Arcyte, made by Mr Richard Edwards, a Gentleman of her Chapel, acted with very great applause in Christ Church Hall.

[*See* below p. 141, 1594, note to Palamon and Arsett.]

1566. **Robinson,** Nicholas (Dean of Bangor). *An account of the performance of Edwards's Palamon and Arcite at Oxford* [*see* above] (printed in The Progresses . . . of Queen Elizabeth, by John Nichols, 1823, vol. i, p. 236).

Dies Aet. die Lunæ . . . . .

Ut superiori nocte, sic et ista Theatrum exornatum fuit splendide, quo publice exhiberetur Fabula Militis (ut Chaucerus nominat) e Latino in Anglicum sermonem translata per *Magistrat*um Edwards et alios ejusdem Collegii alumnos.

1567. Drant, Tho[mas]. [*Address*] *To the Reader*, [prefixed to] *Horace his Arte of Poetrie, pistles and Satyrs Englished* . . . . *by Tho. Drant*, sign. *v *b* and *vi.

     . . . . For good thyngs are hard, and euyl things are easye. But if the settyng out of the wanton tricks of a payre of louers, (as for example let them be cawled Sir Chaunticleare and Dame Partilote) to tell you how their firste combination of loue began . . . . is easye to be vnderstanded and easye to be indyted . . . If onely these be poesis, or be poesis, [*sic*] or haue any comparison to a learned making of poesy :

     Principio me illorum dederis quibus esse poetas
     Excerpam numero :

I take them to be ripe toungued tryfles ; venemouse Allectyues, and sweete vanityes.

1567. H. M. *Prefatory verse* [to] Certaine Tragicall Discourses . . . by Geffraie Fenton . . 1567, sign. *viii. (Ed. R. L. Douglas, Tudor Trans. Series, 1898, p. 13.)

     Floruit antiquo Galfridus tempore Chaucer
     Scripsit & eximio permagna volumina versu
     Et multi viguere viri, quos vnica virtus,
     Nefandos facile effecit tolerare labores.
     Vixerunt : & sola manet, nunc fama Sepultis
     At tua nunc primum, (Galfride) virescere virtus
     Incipit, & teneras cum spe producere plautas.

[1567–1579 ?] Harvey, Gabriel. *Marginal notes* in Quintilian. *See* below, App. A.

1567. Stowe, John. *Epistle Dedicatory* [to the Lord Mayor and Aldermen] [prefixed to] *The Summarie of Englishe Chronicles* [abridged], 1567, sign. a iii *b*. (Stow's Survey of London, ed. C. L. Kingsford, 1908, vol. i, pp. lxxvii–viii.)

[If my book be appreciated] and fruitefullye used to the amendemente of suche grosse erroures [as are to be found in Richard Grafton's books] I shall be encouraged to perfecte that labour that I haue begon, and such worthye workes of auncyent Aucthours that I haue wyth greate peynes gathered together, and partly performed in *M. Chaucer* and other . . .

[1567–8 ?] Howell, Thomas. *Newe Sonets, and pretie Pamphlets.* [Unique copy in the Capell collection, Trin. Coll., Camb.] The britlenesse of thinges mortall, and the trustinesse of Vertue, sign. B iij and *b*. (Howell's poems, in Occasional issues of unique or very rare books, ed. A. B. Grosart, 1879, vol. viii, pp. 121–2.)

[These verses on the moral to be drawn from the story of Troilus and Cressida most probably refer to Chaucer's version of the poem. *Cf.* also the reference in Howell's Devises, 1581, below, p. 120. Howell owed a good deal to Chaucer ; *see* on this point Sir Walter Raleigh's introduction to Howell's Devises, 1906, pp. xi–xiv.]

1567-8. Keeper, John.   *Prefatory Verse* to Newe Sonets, and pretie Pamphlets, by Thomas Howell, sign. A iv.   [*See* last entry.] (Howell's poems, in Occasional issues of unique or very rare books, ed. A. B. Grosart, 1879, vol. viii, p. 115.)

> Ioannes Keper Oxon, ad tho Howell.
>
> Aurea melliflui voluuntur scripta Govveri,
>
> Chaucer; florent acta diserta senis,
>
> Sic quo*que*, Chauterida similis captobis honores,
>
> Pergere si vigilans vt modo pergis aues,
>
> Vt bene capisti, nullos male linque labores,
>
> Gloria sudore est, desidia*que* dolor.
>
> Finis.

[The misprints in this are in the original, as given by Grosart.]

1568. [**Caius,** John, M.D.].   *De Antiquitate Cantabrigiensis Academiæ,* libri duo, London, 1568 [published anonymously, the author being described as 'Londinensis.'   Republished, in 1574, after Caius's death, with his name on the title page.   The references are on pp. 40, 41 of this edition, the only one in the B. M.].   (The works of John Caius, M.D., Cambridge University Press, 1912, pp. 34, 35.)

[p. 40]   Nam ut hic res uniuersas suo complexu contineat, ita hæc uniuersarum scientiarum cognitionem & professionem habeat. Consentit & Hoccleueus, clarissimi Chauceri & Goweri discipulus, in epitome chronicon manuscripta, quam addidit libro quem de regimine principum scripsit ad Henricum sextum :

.   .   .   .

[p. 41]   Sed quia fusior hic Boulus est, proniorquè in rem controuersam de antiquitate Cantebrigiensis Academiæ . . . visum est Ioannis Lydgati (Galfredi Chauceri, nobilissimi olim Poetæ discipuli, omnium poetarum sui temporis in Anglia facilè principis, sicut Baleus scribit etsi tu damnes, ut vanum ut & alios omnes qui a te non stant) proferre testimonium, opus iam ante annos multos Anglico metro formulis excusum, omniquè populo diuulgatum.

[*See* below, p. 104, Thomas Caius, 1570.]

1568. Charteris, Henry.   *Vnto the godlie and christiane reidar, Henrie Charteris, wischis grace* . . . [prefixed to] *The warkis of the famous and vorthie Knicht Schir Dauid Lyndesay* . . Newlie Imprentit be IOHNE SCOT at the expensis of Henrie Charteris . . . . MDLXVIII, [fol. 3, no signatures.]   Two copies of this edn. are known, one at Britwell, and one in Lord Mostyn's library.   (The poetical works of Sir D. Lyndsay, ed. D. Laing, 1879, vol. iii, p. 232; also D. Lyndesay's Works, part v, the minor poems, ed. J. A. H. Murray, E. E. T. soc., 1871, p. 5.)

[Charteris descants on the Clergy's dislike of Lindsay] How cummis it than, that this our Authour being sa plane aganis thame, and as it war professit enemie to thame, culd eschaip thair snairis, quhen vtheris in doing les hes cruellie perischit? Sum will think because his wryting was commounlie mixit with mowis and collourit with craftie consaitis (as Chaucer and vtheris had done befoir) the matter was the mair mitigate.

[This reference is at sign. A 3 in The Warkis of the Famovs and Worthie Knicht, Sir Dauid Lyndesay . . . Imprentit at Edinburgh, be Henrie Charteris, anno MD lxxxxii.]

1568. Churchyard, Thomas. *Verses,* [prefixed to] *Pithy pleasaunt and profitable Workes of maister Skelton, Poete Laureate.* Nowe collected and newly published. Anno 1568, sign. *A iij. (Poetical works of J. Skelton, ed. A. Dyce, 1843, vol. i, p. lxxviii.)

> . . . Peers plowman was full plaine,
> And Chauser's spreet was great
> Earle Surry had a goodly vayne :
> Lord Vaus the marke did beat.

1568. Keeper, John. *Prefatory Verses to the Arbor of Amitie,* by Thomas Howell. (Unique copy in the Bodleian library, sign. A v b. Howell's poems, in Occasional issues of unique or very rare books, ed. A. B. Grosart, 1879, vol. viii, p. 12. *See* British Bibliographer, ed. Sir S. E. Brydges, 1810, vol. i, p. 106.)

> Which wise Minerue in lap hath nurst,
>   and gaue him [Howell] suck so sweete,
> Whom I doe iudge, Apolloes Impe,
>   and eke our *Chaucers* peare :
> What senselesse head of malice mad,
>   will seeke such branch to teare.

1568. Payne, Henry. *The Will of Henry Payne,* of Bury St. Edmunds, co. Suffolk, Esq. June 14, 1568. (The Visitation of Suffolke, made by William Hervey . . . . ed. J. J. Howard, 1866, vol. ii, p. 70.)

[He gave as legacy to Sir Giles Allington, his best gelding and his Chaucer] written in vellum and illumyned in gold.

1568. Unknown. *The Bannatyne MS.* Nine poems falsely attributed to Chaucer, having "quod Chawseir" written at the end of them. (Bannatyne MS., ed. [J. B. Murdoch], Hunterian club, 1896, etc., vol. ii, p. 125 ; iii, 669, 755, 758, 768–9, 798, 804, 822.)

Quhlyome in Grece that nobill regioun [vol. ii, no. xliv, pp. 123–5]

The Song of Troyelus			[„ iii, no. ccxxiv, pp. 668–9]

Schort Epegrammis agains Women		[„ „ „ cclxxviii, p. 755]

Chau-	(This work quha sa sall sie or ried)
ceir.
	quod Chawseir [written in afterwards] [„ „ „ cclxxix, pp. 755 & 8]

Devyce, Proves and eik Humilitie		[„ „. „ cclxxxv, pp. 766–8]

O wicket Weman wilfull and variable	[„ „ „ cclxxxvi, pp. 768–9]

Followis the Lettre of Cupeid		[„ „ „ ccxcvi, pp. 783–98]

All tho that list of wemen evill to speik [„ „ „ ccxcvii, pp. 799–804]

Quat meneth this?			[„ „ „ cccvi, pp. 817–22]

1569. B., G. [Barnabe Googe or William Baldwin?] *A newe Booke called the Shippe of safegarde, wrytten by G. B. anno* 1569. *Imprinted at London by W. Seres,* sign. D vii *b.* (British bibliographer, ed. Sir S. E. Brydges, vol. ii, 1820, pp. 628–9.)

[The writer describes Hypocrisy as]

A rocke but soft and simple to the eie,
	That pleaseth much the minde of worldlye sight,
Whereas disceyte doth closely couered lie,
	Which hindreth men from trauailing aright,
The place is large and riseth some thing hie,
	Upon the top whereof in open sight,
		There stands an Image couered all of stone,
		That there was placed many yeares agone.

Which Image here I would describe to thee,
	But that long since it hath bene painted plaine
By learned Chaucer that gem of Poetrie,
	Who passed the reach of any English braine,
A follie therefore were it here for me,
	To touch that he with pencell once did staine.
		Take here therefore what he therof doth say,
		Writ in the Romance of his Roses gaye.

¶ Another thing was done their write,
	That seemed like an Hypocrite,
And it was cleped Pope holye,

	.	.	.	.	.

[Romance of the Rose, quoted, ll. 413–48.]

Thus hath the golden pen of Chaucer olde,
	The Image plaine descriued to the eie,
Who passing by long since did it beholde,
	And tooke a note therof aduisedly,

Unto his fellowes of that age it tolde,
And left it eke for his posteritie,
That ech man passing by might plainly know,
The perfite substance of that flattring show.

[This book has been attributed to both Googe and Baldwin, the G. standing for the latter's Christian name in Latin. In the Stationers' register, ed. E. Arber, no author is named. The dedication by G. B. is addressed to "his very good sisters Mistresse Phillyp Darell and Mistresse Frances Darell, of the house of Scotneys." As Barnabe Googe was the husband of Mary, dau. of Thomas Darell of Scotney, Kent, and one of her sisters was called Frances, and as Baldwin had apparently no connection with the Darells of Scotney, it seems more probable, in spite of the order of the initials, that Googe, and not Baldwin, was its author. There is a unique copy of this work in the John Rylands library, Manchester; Brydges only prints an extract. *See* below, pp. 171-2, Anthony Nixon, 1602.]

[**c. 1570.**] **Caius**, Thomas. *Vindiciæ Antiquitatis Academiæ Oxoniensis contra Joannem Caium Cantabrigiensem*, p. 333. [First printed by Thomas Hearne, under the above title 1730, vol. ii, pp. 333, 352.]

Producitur Lydgatus, poëta Anglicus, Galfridi olim Chauceri disciplus, qui ex Beda & Alfrido Cantabrum ducem, Partholini regis fratrem, academiæ Cantabrigiensis authorem facit.

[For the whole controversy, *see* the D. N. B. under Thomas Caius; and above, p. 101.]

1570. Lambarde, William. *MS. note* at the beginning of the MS. of Lambarde's Saxon Dictionary, MS. Bodl.

[For complete extract, *see* below, p. 316, 1711, Hearne.]

1570. Foxe, John. *Ecclesiasticall history contaynyng the Actes and Monumentes of thynges passed in euery Kynges tyme in this Realme.* . . . Newly recognised and inlarged by the Author, John Foxe. [2nd edn.] At London, Printed by Iohn Daye . . . 1570, vol. i, sign. ☞ iiij, pp. 341-5, vol, ii, pp. 965-66 (ed. G. Townsend, 1843-9, vol. i, pp. xxii-iii; vol. ii, 1842, pp. 357-63; vol. iv, 1846, pp. 248-50).

[None of these references are in the first edition of 1563, but they appear in full in this, the second edition of 1570, from which they are copied, and are not increased in the latest edition in Foxe's lifetime, that of 1583. This was, as is well known, a very popular work, of which nine editions appeared by 1684; viz. 1563, 1570, 1576, 1583, 1596, 1610, 1632, 1641, 1684.]

[Vol. i. sign. ☞ iiij.] (A Protestation to the whole Church of England.)

To discend now somewhat lower in drawing out the descent of the Church—What a multitude here commeth of faithful witnesses in the time of *Ioh. Wickleffe*, as *Ocliffe*, *Wickleffe*, an. 1376. *W. Thorpe*, *White*, *Puruey*, *Patshall*, *Payne*, *Gower*, *Chauser*, *Gascogne*, *William Swynderby*, *Walter Brute*, *Roger Dexter*, *William Sautry* about the year 1400. *Iohn Badley*, an 1410. *Nicholas Tayler*, *Rich. Wagstaffe*, *Mich. Scriuener*, *W. Smith*, *Iohn Henry*, *W. Parchmenar*, *Roger Goldsmith*, with an Ancresse called *Mathilde* in the Citie of

Leicester, Lord *Cobham*, Syr *Roger Acton* Knight, *Iohn Beuer-
ley* preacher, *Iohn Hus*, *Hierome* of *Prage* Scholemaster, with
a number of faithfull Bohemians and Thaborites not to be told
with whom I might also adioyne *Laurentius Valla*, and
Ioannes Picus the learned Earle of Mirandula.   But what do
I stand upon recitall of names, which almost are infinite.

.   .   .   .

[Vol. i,
p. 341]
For so much as mention is here made of these superstitious
sects of Fryers, and such other beggerly religions, it shall not
seme much impartinent, being moued by the occasion hereof
. . . to annexe . . . a certayne other *auncient* treatise compiled by Geoffray Chawcer by the way of a Dialogue or questions moued in the person of a certaine uplandish and simple
ploughman of the Countrey. which treatise for the same, y°
autor intituled Jack vp land . . .

¶ *A treatise of Geoffrey Chawcer intituled*
Iacke vplande

[Here follows a reprint of Jack Upland.   *See* above, p. 83.]

.   .   .   .

[Vol. ii,
p. 965]
Geffray
Chaucer.
Iohn
Gower.
Moreouer to these two [Linacre & Pace], I thought it not
out of season, to couple also some mention of Geffray
Chaucer, and Iohn Gower: Whiche although beyng much
discrepant from these in course of yeares, yet it may seme not
vnworthy to bee matched with these forenamed persons in com-
mendation of their studie and learnyng . . .

. . . Likewise, as touching the tyme of Chaucer, by hys
owne workes in the end of his first booke of Troylus and
Creseide it is manifest, that he and Gower were both of one
tyme, althoughe it seemeth that Gower was a great deale his
auncient: both notably learned, as the barbarous rudenes of
that tyme did geue, both great frends together, and both in
like kind of studie together occupied, so endeuoryng themselues, and employing their tyme, that they excelling many
other in study and exercise of good letters did passe forth their
lyues here right worshipfully & godly to the worthye fame
and commendation of their name.   Chaucers woorkes bee all
printed in one volume, and therfore knowen to all men.

Chaucer
& Gower
com-
mended
for their
studious
exercise.

This I meruell, to see the idle life of y° priestes and clergye
men of that tyme, seyng these lay persons shewed themselues
in these kynde of liberall studies so industrious & fruitfully
occupied: but muche more I meruell to consider this, how

that the Bishoppes condemnyng and abolishyng al maner of Englishe bookes and treatises, which might bryng the people to any light of knowledge, did yet authorise the woorkes of

Chaucer to remayne still & to be occupyed : Who (no doubt) saw in Religion as much almost, as euen we do now, and vttereth in hys works no lesse, and semeth to be a right Wicleuian, or els was neuer any, and that all his workes almost, if they be throughly aduised will testifie (albeit it bee done in myrth, & couertly) & especially the latter ende of hys thyrd booke of the Testament of loue : for there purely he toucheth the highest matter, that is the Communion. Wherin, excepte a man be altogether blynd, he may espye him at the full. Althoughe in the same booke (as in all other he vseth to do) vnder shadows couertly, as vnder a visoure he suborneth truth, in such sorte, as both priuely she may profite the godly-minded, and yet not be espyed of the craftye aduersarie. And therefore the Byshops, belike, takyng hys workes but for iestes and toyes, in condemnyng other bookes, yet permitted his bookes to be read.

So it pleased God to blinde then the eyes of them, for the Men
brought
to truth
by read-
ing Chau-
cers
workes. more commoditie of his people, to the entent that through the readyng of his treatises, some fruite might redound therof to his Churche, as no doubt, it dyd to many : As also I am partlye informed of certeine, whiche knewe the parties, which to them reported, that by readyng of Chausers workes, they were brought to the true knowledge of Religion. And not vnlike to be true. For to omitte other partes of his volume, whereof some are more fabulous than other, what tale can bee more playnely tolde, then the talke of the ploughman? or what finger can pointe out more directly the Pope with his Prelates to be Antichrist then doth the poore Pellycan reason-
yng agaynst the gredy Griffon? Under whiche *Hypotyposis* or Poesie, who is so blind that seeth not by the Pellicane, the doctrine of Christ, and of the Lollardes to bee defended agaynst the Churche of Rome? Or who is so impudent that can denye that to be true, which the Pellicans there affirmeth in describyng the presumptuous pride of that pretensed Church? Agayne what egge can be more lyke, or figge vnto an other, then ye words, properties, and conditions of that rauenyng Griphe resembleth the true Image, that is, the nature & qualities of that which we call the Churche of Rome,

in euery point and degre? and therfore no great maruell, if that narration was exempted out of the copies of Chaucers workes: whiche notwithstandyng now is restored agayne, and is extant, for euery man to read that is disposed. This Geffray Chauser being borne (as is thought) in Oxfordshire, & dwellyng in Wodstocke, lyeth buried in the Churche of the minster of S. Peter at Westminster, in an Ile on the South side of the sayd Churche, not far from the doore leading to the cloyster, and vpon his graue stone first were written these ii old verses

> Galfridus Chauser vates et fama poesis
> Maternæ, hac sacra sum tumulatus humo.

Afterward, about the yeare of our Lord 1556, one M. Brickam, bestowyng more cost vppon his tumbe, did adde therunto these verses folowyng . . .

[Here follow Brigham's lines, *q. v.* above, p. 94, 1556 ; and *see* above, p. 59.]

[c. 1570.] Rogers, Daniel. *Two Latin Epigrams* on Chaucer's tomb and his poems. MSS. of the Marquis of Hertford. Bk. 2 of Epigrams, leaves unnumbered. (4th Report of the Royal Commission Historical MSS., 1874, App. p. 253, col. 1.)

Tumulus of Geoffrey Chaucer (as follows) :—

> Musarum Phœbique decus, patriæque larisque
> Chaucerum hoc clausit marmore parca brevis ;
> Cui patriis numeris Musas Helicone reduxit
> In patriam et tractus, Albion alma, tuos,
> Mortales acri perstringere suetus aceto ;
> Anglica quo regio vate superba fuit,
> Scilicet, Ausonio laudem quot Horatius orbi,
> Hic patriæ peperit tot monumenta sua [*sic,* for suæ ?].

To Chaucer's poems ; as follows :—

> Quantus erat Tusco Boccacius ore, favebat
> Itala quantum olim lingua suada [*sic*] Petrarche tibi
> Qualis os insurgit Gallo sermone Marottus
> Aptat dum patria [*sic,* for patriæ ?] verba poeta lyræ ;
> Tantus eras Galfride tuis Chaucere Britannis
> Ingenio vates nec minus ore potens
> Anglica quo veneris nunc spirat lingua magistro
> Quas Italio, Gallis, ille vel ille dedit.

1572. Bossewell, John. *Workes of Armorie deuyded into three bookes,*
entituled, the Concordes of Armorie, the Armorie of Honor, and of
Coates and Creastes. In ædibus Richardi Totelli . . . 1572, sign.
C iv, B v *b*–B viii, G iv *b*–G v, R ii *b*, U i–X.

[sign. C iv] The names of the aucthors . . . owt of whiche these
workes are chiefelye collected and amplified . . . Englishe
writers G. Chaucer, Jo. Gower . . . . .

.   .   .   .

[sign. B v *b*] *Sentences concerning generositie,* collected out of sundrye
Aucthors, and firste certayne verses made by G. Chaucer,
teaching what is gentlenes, or who is worthy to be called
gentle.

The firste stocke father of gentlenes,

.   .   .   .

All weare he mitre, crowne, or diademe.

.   .   .   .   .   .   [*Gentilesse*, ll. 1–21.]

[sign. B vi *b*] But nowe yet heare what M. G. Chaucer, oure noble
poete of thys Realme doth write touching gentlenes of birthe,
in hys taile of the wife of Bathe. These are hys woordes.

But for ye speake of suche gentlenesse.

.   .   .   .   .   .   [ll. 1109–64.]

[sign. B vii *b*] M. G. Chaucer, lamenteth in hys second Booke (whiche
hee entituleth the testament of loue) that *Iaphetes* children . . . . .

[Chaucerian and other pieces, I, bk. ii, ch. ii, ll. 105, etc.]

.   .   .   .

[sign. G iv *b*] This game [chess] was first inuented by Athalus, as
Master G. Chaucer reporteth in hys dreame, saying

at the Chesse with me she gan to playe.

[*Book of the Duchesse*, ll. 652–64.]

[sign. R ii *b*] For those, in whose power it is to do good, and doth it
not, the Crowne of honor and worshippe shalbe taken from
them, and (as *Chaucer* sayethe) with shame they shalbe
annulled, & from all dignitie deposed.

.   .   .   .

[sign. U i] *Chaucer* in hys seconde and thirde bokes, entituled, the
Testament of loue, maketh a great processe of them [mar-
guerites] as gemmes very precious, clere, and little . . . . .

[Chaucerian and other pieces, I, bk. iii, ch. i, ll. 35, etc.]

.   .   .   .

[sign. U i *b*] *Chaucer* writeth moche of thys floure [daisy] in many

places of hys workes: and in especially in hys preface to the
legend of good weomen . . . . . [ll. 179–90.]

And the sayd *Chaucer* writeth in a goodly Balade of hys
also of the Daysie, where he calleth it

Daysie of lighte, verie grounde of comforte.

[The other references are quotations from *House of Fame*, ll. 1361–4 ; *Sir Thopas*, ll.
2096–7 ; *Romaunt of the Rose*, ll. 239–46, 1171–86 ; *Knightes Tale*, ll. 975–80, 2140–2.]

1573. Harvey, Gabriel. *The Schollers Looue or Reconcilement of Con-*
traries, fol. 66. (Letter-Book of Gabriel Harvey, 1573–80, ed. from
MS. Sloane 93, by E. J. L. Scott, Camden soc. 1884, p. 134. *See*
also Preface, pp. viii, xv, xvi.)

[Harvey describes his method of reading :]

At Petrarche and Bocace I must have a flynge.
Every idiott swayne
Can commende there veyne.   Chau
Now and then a spare hower is allotted to Gascoyne
                 sage   Gower
And sum time I attende on gentle Master Ascham.
They sownde well enowghe withoute makinge ryme
That iumpe so well in cuntry tunge and tyme.
Would God Inglande cowlde afforde a thowsande sutch and
          better,
On condition my pore selfe knewe never a letter.

[1574.] Robinson, Richard. *The rewarde of Wickednesse* . . . . *Newly*
compiled by Richard Robinson, Seruaunt in housholde to the right
Honorable Earle of Shrowsbury. [col.] Imprinted in London in
Pawles Churche Yarde by William Williamson ; sign. Q 2, *b.*

[sign. P 3 b] Retourning from *Plutos* Kingdome, To noble *Helicon ;*
The place of Infinite Ioye.

.   .   .   .

[sign. Q 2 b] And *Chaucer* for his merie tales, was well esteemed there
And on his head as well ought best, a Laurell garland were,
All these I knewe and many moe, that were to long to name
That for their trauels were rewarde, for euermore with Fame.

[' The Author to the Reader' is dated The xix Maie 1574.]

[1574 ?] Unknown. *Eulogium Chaucerj*. Poem found in MS. in a
black letter Chaucer (1561) ; date of other MS. notes, etc., *c.* 1574,
transcribed by T. A. S., in Notes and Queries, ser. i, 1853, vol. vii.
p. 201.

Geffraye Chaucer, the worthiest flower
Of English Poetrie in all the Bower.
.   .   .   .   .   .   [26 *lines*]
Though for his other parts of grace
Chaucer will liue and shewe his face.

1575. Churchyard, Thomas. *A discourse of vertue, see* below, Appendix A, 1575.

1575. Gascoigne, George. *The delectable history of sundry aduentures passed by Dan Bartholmew of Bath . . . . his first Triumphe. The Posies of George Gascoigne, Esq.* [col.] Imprinted at London by H. M. for Christopher Barker, 1575, sign. E iiij. (Gascoigne's Poems. ed. W. C. Hazlitt, Roxb. library, 1869–70, vol. i, p. 105.)

Thy brother *Troylus* eke, that gemme of gentle deedes
To thinke howe he abused was, alas, my heart it bleedes!
He bet about the bushe, while other caught the birds,
Whome crafty *Cresside* mockt to muche, yet fede him still
    with words.
And god he knoweth, not I, who pluckt hir first-sprong rose,
Since *Lollius* and *Chaucer* both make doubt vpon that glose.

[There are several references to Cresside in Gascoigne's poems ; these are very possibly to Chaucer's poem, but no special reference is made to him, *see* for instance immediately below, The Doale of disdaine.]

1575. Gascoigne, George. *The doale of disdaine,* etc. . . stanzas 5 and 8. The Posies of George Gascoigne Esquire. Weedes, sign. S vi and *b* pp. 283–4. (Gascoigne's Poems, ed. W. C. Hazlitt, Roxb. library, 1869–70, vol. i, pp. 492–3.)

If *Cressydes* name were not so knowen
And written wide on euery wall : [etc.]

.   .   .   .

Thou art as true as is the best
That euer came of Cressedes lyne.

1575. Gascoigne, George. *Certayne Notes of Instruction concerning the making of verse or ryme in English.* Appended to the Posies of George Gascoigne, Esquire. . . . 1575, sign. T ij, T iij *b,* Uij *b.* Reprinted 1587. (Gascoigne's Poems, ed. W. C. Hazlitt, Roxb. library, 1869–70, vol. i, pp. 500, 502, 507.)

[sign. T ij, p. 31] For it is not inough to roll in pleasant woordes nor yet to thunder in *Rym, Ram, Ruff,* by letter (quoth my master *Chaucer*) nor yet to abound in apt vocables, or epythetes.   [From Prologue to Persones tale, l. 43]

.   .   .   .

[sign. T iij *b,* p. 34] Also our father *Chaucer* hath vsed the same libertie in feete and measures that the Latinists do vse : and who so euer do peruse and well consider his workes, he shall finde that although his lines are not alwayes of one selfe same number of Syllables, yet beyng redde by one that hath vnderstanding, the longest verse and that which hath most Syllables in it, will fall (to the eare) correspondent vnto that whiche hath fewest sillables in it : and like wise that whiche hath in it fewest syllables shalbe founde yet to consist of woordes that

haue suche naturall sounde, as may seeme equall in length
to a verse which hath many moe sillables of lighter accentes.

. . . .

[sign. V ij *b*, p. 40]   I had forgotten a notable kinde of ryme, called
ryding rime, and that is suche as our Mayster and Father
Chaucer vsed in his Canterburie tales, and in diuers other
delectable and light enterprises.

[For 'Rym, Ram, Ruff,' *cf.* 1595, Peele, below, p. 142.]

[**1575.**] **Smith,** Richard. *Commendatory Verses to The Posies of George
Gascoigne Esquire.* Corrected, perfected, and augmented by the
Authour [2nd edn.]. Printed at London for Richard Smith, etc.
(Gascoigne's Poems, ed. W. C. Hazlitt, Roxb. library, 1869–70,
vol. i, p. 26.)

The Printer in Commendation of Gascoigne and his workes.

> *Chawcer* by writing purchast fame
> And *Gower* got a worthie name :
> Sweete *Surrey* suckt *Parnassus* springs :
> And *Wiat* wrote of wondrous things :
> Old *Rochfort* clambe the stately Throne,
> Which *Muses* holde, in *Hellicone.*
> Then thither let good *Gascoigne* go,
> For sure his verse deserueth so.

1575. Turbervile, George. *The Booke of Faulconrie or Hawking.* . . .
Imprinted at London, for Christopher Barker, 1575, p. 260, sign.
R ii *b*.

Yet for remedie of this disease.(pin in the Hawkes foote)
some do aduise to open the vain of the leg, a thing not only
friuolous to talke of and a verie olde womans fable or Cantor-
burie tale, but also verie perillous to be put in practise.

[*c.* **1575.**] **Unknown.** *MS. note* 'Gaulfridus Chaucer' on MS. Egerton
2726, fol. i. *See* above, p. 50, *c.* 1450, Unknown.

1575. Wharton, John. *To the Christian Reader Iohn Wharton wisheth
all good giftes of vertue* [Prefatory address to] *A misticall deuise of
the spirituall and godly loue betwene Christ* . . *and the Church.
Firste made by* . . . *Salomon, and now newly set forthe in verse,* by
Jud Smith [*i. e.* the Song of Solomon] . . . . sign. A 2.

For surely (gentle Reader) if thou couit to heare any olde
bables [*sic*], as I may terme them, or stale tales of Chauser, or to
learne howe Acteon came by his horned head: If thy mynde
be fixed to any such metamorphocall toyes, this booke is not
apt nor fit for thy purpose.

[1576.] **A.** F. [Arthur Hall]. *A letter sent by F. A. touchyng the proceedings in a priuate quarell and vnkindnesse, betweene Arthur Hall, and Melchisedech Mallerie . . . With an admonition to the Father of F. A. to him being a Burgesse of the Parliament, for his better behauiour therein,* sign. E iv, E iv *b* and F i. [There are a separate set of signatures for the "Letter" and the "Admonition," our reference is to the latter tract.] (Reprinted in Miscellanea Antiqua Anglicana, or a Select Collection of Curious Tracts, 1816; the two tracts here referred to are dated 1815; pp. 85–6).

[sign. E iv] Now are we come to consider howe to answere the office your trusters put you in, not for any perticular profit, but [sign. E iv b] for the whole common good . . . Will you go to Law of nature, to the Law of God, to the Law of Princes, too ye Law of Confederats : wil not al condemne you if you iugle : I haue found it so. Although in very deede some men accept iuggling for an English word in good part, yet I neuer vnderstoode it in *Chaucer* or olde English, neyther in the conscience of the professors of Charity or well dealing : part the wordes [sign. F i] at your pleasure enter too Ethnickes or too Christianes.

1576. Gascoigne, George. *The Grief of Ioye.* . . . Written to the Queenes moste excellent Matie. Roy. MS. 18, A. 61, fol. 5 *b.* (Gascoigne's Poems, ed. W. C. Hazlitt, Roxb. lib., 1869–70, vol. i, p. 260.)

The first Songe

The greeues or discommodities of lustie yowth.

. . . . . I venter my good will
Yn barreyne verse, to doe the best I can
Lyke Chaucers boye, and Petrarks iorneyman.

But if some Englishe woorde herein seme sweet,
Let Chaucers name exalted be therefore.
Yf any verse doe passe on pleasant feet
The praise thereof, redownd to Petrarks lore.

1576. Hanmer, Meredith. *The Auncient Ecclesiasticall Histories of the First Six Hundred Yeares After Christ . . . . by Eusebius, Socrates, and Euagrius . . . . translated . . . . by Meredith Hanmer,* 1577. The Epistle Dedicatorie, sign. * iij. The Preface vnto the Reader [hist. of Euagrius], p. 408.

Many nowe adayes had rather reade the stories of Kinge Arthur : The monstrous fables of Garagantua : the Pallace of pleasure : the Dial of Princes, ... the Monke of Burie full of good stories : Pierce ploweman, the tales of *Chaucer,* where there is excellent wit, good reading, and good decorum obserued, the life of *Marcus Aurelius* . . . . the Epistles of *Antonie Gwevarra* . . . the pilgremage of Princes . . . Reinard the Fox : *Beuis* of Hampton : the hundred merry tales : *skoggan : Fortunatus* . . . but as for bookes of diuinitie . . . it is the least part of their care.

There is hope the dayes shall neuer be seene when the prophesie of *Chaucer* shall take place, where he sayth

> When fayth fayleth in priestes sawes
>
> .   .   .   .
>
> Than shall the land of Albion
> Be brought to great confusion,

and to the end our wished desire may take effect, let vs hearken what exhortation he geueth vnto the chiefe magistrate, his wordes are these

> Prince desire to be honorable
>
> .   .   .   .   .   .
>
> And wedde thy folke ayen to stedfastnes.
>
> [Lak of Stedfastnesse, ll. 22–8.]

[The first quotation is from sayings printed by Caxton ; Chaucerian and other pieces, ed. W. W. Skeat, 1897, p. 450, ll. 1–6. The dedication is dated 1576, as are the histories of Socrates and Evagrius, each with separate title pages.]

[*c.* **1576.**] **Maitland**, Sir Richard (of Lethington). *On the folye of ane auld manis maryand ane young woman.* MS. in Pepys lib. Cambridge. (Poems of Sir R. Maitland [ed. Joseph Bain], Maitland club, 1830, p. 40.)

> .   .   .   .   For folye is to mary,
>
> Fra tyme that baith thair strenthe and nature faillis ;
>
> And tak ane wyf to bring him selffe in tarye
>
> For fresche Maii, and cauld Januarij,
>
> Agreeis nocht upon ane sang in tune.

[Reference to the *Marchantes Tale*?]

1576. Thynne, Francis. *Another discourse vppon the Philosophers Armes.* MS. Ashmole 766, ff. 85 *b*, 86. Two mentions of Chaucer among a list of alchemists, such as Bacon, Ripley, Norton, etc. (Thynne's Animadversions, ed. F. J. Furnivall, Chaucer soc., 1876, p. 135 ; for date, etc., *see also ibid.*, pp. xlix, 115, 134.)

1576. Whetstone, George. *The Rocke of Regard*, Part i. The Castle of delight ; Cressid's complaint, p. 21, sign. B iij. (Reprinted by J. Payne Collier, 1870 ?)

> [Cressid complains of her age ;]
>
> Or as the horse, in whom disorder growes,
>
> His iadish trickes, againe wil hardly loose ;
>
> So they in youth, which Venus ioyes do proue,
>
> In drouping age, Syr Chaucers iestes will loue.

1577. **Dee,** John, Dr. *Transcript by Dr. John Dee of Thomas Norton's Ordinall of Alchemy.* Ashmole MS. 57 [no pagination].

Authors recited in this booke

> . . . . .
>
> Bacon
> Boetius
> Chauser
> Chanon of Lichfelde
>
> . . . . .

[*See* 1477, Norton, above, p. 57.]

1577. **Harvey,** Gabriel. *Letter Book.* A suttle and trechrous aduantage (poetically imagined) taken at unawares by the 3 fatall sisters to beriue M. Gascoigne of his life . . . . fol. 35, p. 57. (Letter Book of Gabriel Harvey, A.D. 1573–1580, ed. from MS. Sloane 93, by E. J. L. Scott, Camden soc., 1884. *See also* for dates, Preface, pp. viii, xv, xvi.)

[Harvey imagines Gascoigne in Purgatory.]

> This pleasure reape : and shake thou hands
> With auncient cuntrymen of thine :
> Acquayntaunce take of Chaucer first
> And then with Gower and Lydgate dine.

1577. **Holinshed,** Raphael. *The Laste volume of the Chronicles of England, Scotlande, and Irelande, . . . Faithfully gathered and compiled by Raphaell Holinshed.* At London, Imprinted for John Harrison, p. 1163. (Holinshed's Chronicles . . in six volumes, London. 1808, vol. iii, pp. 58, 59.)

But nowe to rehearse what writers of oure English nation liued in the days of this Kyng, [Henry the Fourth]. that renowmed Poete Geffreye Chaucer is worthily named as principall, a man so exquisitely learned in all sciences, that hys matche was not lightly founde anye where in those dayes, and for reducing our Englishe tong to perfect conformitie, hee hath excelled therein all other. He departed this life about the yeare of our Lord 1402. as Bale gathereth, but by other it appeareth, that he deceased the fiue and twentith of October in the yeare 1400, and lyeth buried at Westminster, in the South parte of the great Church there, as by a monumente erected by Nicholas Brigham it doth appeare: John Gower . . . studied not only the common lawes of this Realme, but also other kindes of literature, and grew to greate knowledge in the same, . . . applying his endeuor with Chaucer, to garnish the Englishe tong, in bringing it from a rude unperfectnesse, unto a more apt elegancie : for whereas before those dayes, the learned vsed to write onely in latine or Frenche, and not in Englishe, oure tong remayned very barreyne, rude, and unperfect, but now by the diligent industrie of Chaucer and Gower, it was within a while greately amended, so as it grew not only to be very riche and plentifull in wordes, but also so proper and apt to expresse that which the minde conceyued as any other usuall language. Gower departed this life shortly after the decease of his deere and louing friend Chaucer, to witte, in the yere 1402.

1577. Northbrooke, John. *Spiritus est vicarius Christi in terra. A Treatise wherein Dicing, Dauncing, Vaine plaies . . . . commonly vsed on the Sabboth day, are reprooued, by the authoritie of the worde of God, and auncient Writers.* Imprinted . . . . 1579, pp. 49, 49 *b.* (Ed., same title, by J. P. Collier, Shakespeare soc. 1843, pp. 131–2.)

Youth. Hath any honest man of credite and reputation beene euill thought of, for playing at Dice . . . .

Age. That there hath, and not of the meanest sorte . . . . I will recite to you *Chaucer*, which saieth hereof [of Demetrius] in verses.

Youth. I praye you doe so . . . .

Age. [quotes Pardoners tale, ll. 603–28.]

Youth. This is verie notable : but yet I pray you shewe me, what Chaucers owne opinion is touching Diceplaie :

Age. His opinion is this, in verses also.

[Pardoner's tale, ll. 590–602.]

[Entered at Stationers' Hall, Dec. 2, 1577. The first attack on theatrical representations, six months before Stephen Gosson's. There is another edn., undated, attributed by Collier to 1578, but by other authorities, and in B. M. catalogue given as 1579.]

1578. Harvey, Gabriel. *Gabrielis Harueii Gratulationum Valdinensium Libri Quatuor.* Lib. iv, p. 22.

> Præcones mulierum omnes, scribæque procique
> Hæc in delicijs *Bibliotheca* siet,
> Chaucerusque adsit, Surreius & inclytus adsit ;
> Gascoignoque aliquis sit, Mea Corda, locus.

. . . .

[1578.] Lyly, John. *Evphues. The Anatomy of Wyt.* Imprinted at London for Gabriell Cawood ; no date, sign. D iiij *b.* (Works of John Lyly, ed. R. Warwick Bond, 1902, vol. i, p. 219.)

. . . . though *Aeneas* were to fickle to *Dido*, yet *Troylus* was to faithfull to *Cræssida* . . . .

[See below, Appendix A, [1578], for further notes on Lyly's debt to Chaucer.]

1578. P[rocter], T[homas]. *Preface to Of the knowledge and conducte of warres,* sign. ¶ v.

. . . . Yet amonge so manye bookes, as are written daylie of dreames & fantacies, ... of pleasant meetinges & fables amonge women, of Caunterbury, or courser tales, with diuers iestes, & vaine deuises : in earnest ; there is least labour layd on that arte, wheareby kinges rule . . . .

1578. P[rocter], T[homas]. *In the prayse of the rare beauty, and manifolde vertues of Mistress D. as followeth* in A gorgious Gallery of gallant Inuentions . . . . by T. P. [Thomas Procter]. Imprinted at London for Richard Iones, 1578, sign. H iiij. (Three collections of English Poetry [ed. Sir H. Ellis], Roxb. club, 1844, sign. h iiij.)

If *Chawcer* yet did lyue, whose English tongue did passe,
Who sucked dry *Pernassus* spring, and raste the Juice there was ;
If *Surrey* had not scalde the height of *Ioue* his Throne,
Unto whose head a pillow softe became Mount *Helycon* :
They with their Muses, could not haue pronounst the fame,
Of D. faire Dame, lo, a staming stock, the cheefe of natures
    frame.

[The Roxburgh edition was printed from a copy at Northumberland House. There is also one in the Bodleian library.]

1578. Whetstone, George. *The Right Excellent and famous Historye of Promos and Cassandra.* [col.] Imprinted at London by Richarde Ihones . . . . August 20, 1578. Part I, act i, sc. 3 ; sign. B iii. (Promos and Cassandra *in* Shakespeare's library, ed. J. P. Collier [1843], p. 215.)

La[mia]   .   .   .   .
And can then the force of lawe, or death, thy minde of loue
    bereaue ?
In good faith, no : the wight that once hath tast the fruits of
    loue,
Untill hir dying daye will long, Sir *Chaucers* iests to proue.

1579. Fulke, W. *D. Heskins, D. Sanders, and M. Rastel accounted . . . three pillers and Archpatriarches of the Popish Synagogue,* etc. The Third Booke of Maister Heskins Parleament repealed, by W. Fulke, chap. 34, p. 422.

To shutt vp this Chapter, he flappeth vs in the mouth, with S. Mathewes Masse, testified by Abdias in the diuels name, a disciple of the Apostles (as hee [H.] saith) but one that sawe Christ him selfe, (as M. Harding sayeth) In verie deed a lewd counterfeter of more then Caunterburie tales.

1579. Lodge, Thomas. *A Reply to Stephen Gosson's Schole of abuse. In Defence of Poetry, Musick, and Stage Plays.* Bodl. Malone, Adds. 896, sign. a 6, pp. 1–48. (Works of Lodge [ed. E. W. Gosse], Hunt. club, 1883, vol. i, p. 15.)

> *Chaucer* in pleasant vain can rebuke sin vncontrold; & though he be lauish in the letter his sence is serious.

1579. K[irke], E[dward]. *Letter to Gabriel Harvey,* prefixed to Shepheards Calender. Also *Notes* to Shepheards Calender : Februarie, ff. 7–7 *b* ; March, fol. 10 *b* ; Maye, ff. 21 *b*, 22 ; June, fol. 25 *b* ; Julye, fol. 30 *b* ; September, ff. 39, 39 *b* ; Nouember, fol. 48 ; December, fol. 51. (Works of Spenser, ed. A. B. Grosart, 1882–4, vol. ii, 1882, pp. 19, 20, 72, 74, 90, 142, 144, 147, 163, 185, 221, 223, 270, 282. Works, Globe edn., ed. R. Morris, pp. 441, 450, 451, 453, 462, 463, 466, 469, 475, 476, 483, 485.)

[Tr.&Cr. bk. i, l. 809.] Vncouthe, vnkiste, sayde the olde famous Poete Chaucer, whom for his excellencie and wonderfull skil in making, his scholler Lidgate, a worthy scholler of so excellent a maister, calleth the Loadestarre of our Language [*see* above, 1430, Fall of Princes, p. 37] and whom our Colin clout in his Æglogue calleth Tityrus the God of shepheards, comparing hym to the worthiness of the Roman Tityrus, Virgile. Which prouerbe myne owne good friend Ma. Haruey, as in that good olde Poete it serued well Pandares purpose for the bolstering of his baudy brocage, so very well taketh place in this our new Poete, who for that he is vncouthe (as said Chaucer), is vnkiste, and vnknown to most me*n*, is regarded but of few. But I dout not, so soone as his name shall come into the knowledge of men, and his worthines be sounded in the tromp of fame, but that he shall be not onely kiste, but also beloved of all, embraced of the most, and wondred at of the best. ["From my lodging at London thys 10. of Aprill, 1579."]

[ff. 7–7b] [Glosse to Feb.] *Heardgromes.* Chaucers verse almost whole. [The whole line is :—

> "So loytring liue you little heardgroomes."]

Tityrus. I suppose he meanes Chaucer, whose prayse for pleasaunt tales cannot dye, so long as the memorie of hys name shal liue, and the name of Poetrie shall endure.

This tale of the Oake and the Brese, he telleth as learned of Chaucer, but it is cleane in another kind and rather like to Æsopes fables.

[fol. 25 b] [Glosse to June] *Tityrus.* That by Tityrus is meant Chaucer, hath bene already sufficiently sayde ; and by thys more playne appeareth, that he sayth, he tolde merye tales. Such as be hys Canterburie tales, whom he calleth the God of Poetes for hys excellencie ; . . .

[These are only specimen extracts from the Glosses, but the rest are mainly notes on words. *Cf.* 1595, below, p. 142, Unknown.]

1579. **[Spenser, Edmund.]** *The Shepheardes Calender.* Februarie, fol. iv *b* ; June fol. 24 ; December, fol. 48 *b* and [Envoy] fol. 52. (Works of Spenser, ed. A. B. Grosart, 1882–4, vol. ii, 1882, pp. 63, 156, 273, 289. Globe edn., ed. R. Morris, pp. 449, 464, 484, 486.)

[fol. iv b] *Thenot.*   But shall I tel thee a tale of truth,
Which I cond of *Tityrus* in my youth
Keeping his sheepe on the hills of Kent

.   .   .   .   .   .

[fol. 24] The God of shepheards *Tityrus* is dead,
Who taught me homely, as I can, to make.
He, whilst he lived, was the soueraigne head
Of shepheards all, that bene with loue ytake :
Well couth he wayle his Woes, and lightly slake
The flames, which loue within his heart had bredd
And tell vs mery tales, to keep vs wake,
The while our sheepe about vs safely fedde.

Nowe dead he is, and lyeth wrapt in lead,
(O why should death on hym such outrage showe ?)
And all hys passing skil with him is fledde,
The fame whereof doth dayly greater growe.
But if on me some little drops would flowe
Of that the spring was in his learned hedde
I soone would learne these woods, to wayle my woe
And teache the trees, their trickling teares to shedde.

.   .   .   .   .   .

[fol. 48 b] The gentle shepheard satte beside a springe

.   .   .   .   .   .

That Colin hight which wel could pype and singe
For he of Tityrus his songes did lere.

.   .   .   .   .   .

[Envoy] Goe lyttle Calender, thou hast a free passeporte,
Goe but a lowly gate emongste the meaner sorte

Dare not to match thy pype with Tityrus hys style
Nor with the Pilgrim that the Ploughman playde awhyle,
But followe them farre off, and their high steppes adore
The better please, the worse despise, I aske no more.

[For the influence of Chaucer on Spenser, see specially, Observations on Spenser's Faery Queene, by T. Warton, 1762, sect. 5; On Spenser's use of Archaisms, by G. Wagner, Halle, 1879 ; Quomodo Edmundus Spenserus ad Chaucerum se fingens in eclogis 'The Shepheardes Calender' versum heroicum renovarit, by Émile Legouis, Paris, 1896 ; Introduction to Shepheard's Calender, by C. H. Herford, Macmillan 1897; Studies in Chaucer, by T. R. Lounsbury, N. York, 1892, vol. iii, pp. 43-6, and an article on Daphnaïda and the Book of The Duchess by T. W. Nadal in Publns. of Mod. Lang. Assoc. of America, Dec. 1908, vol. xxiii, No. 4, pp. 646-661.]

1579. A Student in Cambridge [C., J ?]. *A poore Knight his Pallace of priuate pleasures* . . . written by a student in Cambridge, and published by I. C. Gent. Imprinted at London by Richarde Jones, sign. C iij *b.* Of Cupid his Campe. D. of Northumberland's library; unique copy. (Three collections of English Poetry, ed. [Sir Henry Ellis] Roxb. club, 1845, sign. C iij *b*).

Then *Morpheus* sayd, loe where he stands that worthy
   Chauser hight
The cheefest of all Englishmen, and yet hee was a knight.
There *Goure* did stand with cap in hand, and *Skelton* did the
   same,
And *Edwards* hee, who, while he liude, did sit in chaire of
   fame.

1580. Lyly, John. *Euphues and his England.* Imprinted at London for Gabriell Cawood. [Unique copy in Hampstead public library.] Printed by I. R. for Gabriell Cawood, 1597, sign. F ii [earliest edn. in B. M.]. (Works of John Lyly, ed. R. Warwick Bond, 1902, vol. ii, p. 43.)

I can not tell whether it bee a *Caunterbury tale,* or a Fable in
   Aesope . . . .

[*See also* Bond's edition, biographical appendix, vol. i, p. 401, where the editor notes that the expression is used as a synonym for a fable.]

1580. Stowe, John. *The Chronicles of England* . . . [in later edns. *Annales of England*] p. 548, under Hen IV. [There is no Chaucer ref. in the earlier edn., *A Summarie of Englyshe Chronicles,* 1565. The 'Summarie abridged,' quoted above on p. 100, is a distinct work.]

[For the text of this reference *see* p. 164 below, under 1600, *The Annales of England,* pp. 527-8, which is to the same purport as that in this edn., only much more expanded. Below are given all the Chaucer references. Where any change was made in them in the various edns. of this work, the text of the new edition will be found under the year in which it first appeared. In the last edn., revised by Stowe just before his death in 1605, the Chaucer references are identical with those in the 1600 edn.]

1592. *Annales of England,* pp. 431, 517-18. *See* below, p. 136.
1600.   „   „   pp. 437, 458, 527-8. *See* below, p. 164.

1581. Howell, Thomas. *H . His Deuises, for his owne exercise, and his Friends pleasure*, sign. B iij *b.* [Unique copy in the Bodl. library, Malone, 342.] (Occasional issues of unique or very rare books, ed. A. B. Grosart, 1879, vol. viii, p. 178.)

¶ Ruine the rewarde of Vice.

. . . .

Is not the pride of *Helens* prayse bereft?
And *Cresside* staynde, that Troian knight imbrased :
Whose bewties bright but darke defame hath left,
Unto them both through wanton deedes preferred.
As they by dynte of Death their dayes haue ended,
So shall your youth, your pompe, and bewties grace
When nothing else but vertue may take place.

[Howell borrows many phrases from Chaucer in the ' Devises'; *see* Walter Raleigh's introduction to Howell's Devises, Clarendon Press, 1906, pp. xi–xiv, and *see* above p. 100.]

1581. Lawson, John. *Lawsons Orchet, wharin thou shall fynde most pleasaunt fructe of all mannor of sortes. That is to sai, the true acte, fact, or deade, of euery Prince reininge in this lande sens yt was first inhabett, with the yeares of thaire contynuaunce: and the varieite* of the *opinyons of the Historiographers, newly gathyred, and augmented, contynuinge vnto the Conquest.*—1581.—[Then follows a note at the foot of the page] Aº. Dm. 1581. et Regin. Elizab. 23. Jhō. lawson feodary in yᵉ County of Northūb: sent me this booke. [And below it in a modern hand] This is Lord Burghleigh's Handwriting. Lansdowne MSS. 208, ff. 411–411 *b.* (This extract is printed by S. E. Brydges in Restituta, vol. iv, 1814, p. 29.)

[A personal Address from the Author] To the Reader [at the end of the Chronicle is followed by a kind of Dedicatory and explanatory address.]

[fol. 411] To the right honorable lorde Burghley &c. sir William Damsell Knight, and to all his other good maisters off the courte of wairdes and liuereis theire humble seruaunte John lawson, wisheethe healthe, &c.

. . . .

Yet not so contented for more ease to have vnderstande
Thaire travell all, whiche shynde as pearles in dede,
I tooke maister John lydgaite strighte then in my hande,
With whome the reste of my tyme I thought to leede :
Whose wordye praise and everlastynge meade,
[fol. 411 *b*] Thoo he was a monnke at that Abbay late Bury,
Myghte be in equale prase with maister Chawcer truly.

I might thaire reade the greate and actyve chyuelrie ;
Betwene yᵉ Troyaine knightes, and yᵉ Greekes all ;
Chawcer nor Gowere was neuer of more antiquitie
In proise or miter, with theire Englisshe literall,
Thaire ortographia, stile, nor syllapes in especiall :
(Whiche lyghtned my harte the enterpryse for to take)
Than was master lydgaite in the verses he did make.

That tedyous tyme he haithe discouered out at lardge :
In englysshe verse, right plesaunde to the eare ;
Shewinge all the Pamfylie thaire haitered and rage,
Under blossomes of rethoricke, yᵉ style it shoulde not dere :
Off whoose pretence thoo I, maisters, may not come nere :
To attempte suche eloquence in als wightye a matter ;
Made me take on hande yᵉ lyke, to followe at laser.

[**1581** ?] **Sidney**, Sir Philip. *An Apologie for Poetrie, written by the right noble, vertuous, and learned, Sir Phillip Sidney Knight.* Printed for Henry Olney, 1595, sign. B ii *b*, D iii *b*, D iv, G iv, I iv. (English Reprints, ed. E. Arber, 1869, pp. 21, 34, 51, 62.)

[sign. B ii *b*, p. 21] So in the Italian language, the first that made it aspire to be a Treasure-house of Science, were the Poets *Dante*, *Boccace*, and *Petrarch*. So in our English were *Gower* and *Chawcer*.

After whom, encouraged and delighted with theyr excellent fore-going, others haue followed, to beautifie our mother tongue, as wel in the same kinde as in other Arts. . .

. . . .

[sign. D iii *b*, p. 34] See whether wisdome and temperance in *Vlisses* and *Diomedes*, valure in *Achilles*, friendship in *Nisus*, and *Eurialus*,
[sign. D iv] euen to an ignoraunt man, carry not an apparent shyning : and contrarily, the remorse of conscience in *Oedipus*, the soone repenting pride in *Agamemnon*, the selfe-deuouring crueltie in his Father *Atreus*, the violence of ambition in the two *Theban* brothers, the sowre-sweetnes of reuenge in *Medœa*, and to fall lower, the *Terentian Gnato*, and our *Chaucer's* Pandar, so exprest, that we nowe vse their names to signifie their trades. . . . .

. . . .

[sign. G iv, p. 51] Thirdly, that it [Poetry] is the Nurse of abuse, infecting vs with many pestilent desires : with a Syrens sweetnes, drawing the mind to the Serpents tayle of sinfull fancy. And heerein especially, Comedies giue the largest field to erre, as *Chaucer* sayth : howe both in other nations and in ours, before Poets did soften vs, we were full of courage, giuen to martiall exercises ; the pillers of manlyke liberty and not lulled a sleepe in shady idlenes with Poets pastimes.

.   .   .   .

[sign. I iv, p. 62]   *Chaucer,* vndoubtedly did excellently in hys *Troylus* and *Cresseid ;* of whom, truly I know not, whether to meruaile more, either that he in that mistie time, could see so clearely, or that wee in this cleare age, walke so stumblingly after him. Yet had he great wants, fitte to be forgiuen, in so reuerent antiquity.

1582. Humphrey, Laurence. *Iesuitismi pars prima.* Excudebat Henricus Middletonus, impensis G B. 1582. Præfatio, sign. ¶¶¶ 7.

G. Chau- cerus   Oxoniensis fuit Galfridus Chaucerus, propter dicendi gratiam & libertatem quasi alter Dantes aut Petrarcha ; quos ille etiam in linguam nostram transtulit, in quibus Romana Ecclesia tanquam sedes Antichristi describitur & ad viuum exprimitur : Hic multis in locis Fraterculos istos, monachos, missificos, Pontificiorum ceremonias, peregrinationes facunde notauit verum & spiritualem Christi in Sacramento esum agnouit, turpitudinem coactæ virginitatis perstrinxit, libertatem coniugij in Domino commendauit, vt in fabulis Monachi. Fratris, Aratoris & in reliquis legimus.

[For the whole question of Chaucer's translation of Dante, *see* note above, p. 88.]

1582. Stanihurst, Richard. *Thee First Fo[u]re Bookes of Virgil his Æneis ; Translated intoo English heroical verse, by Richard Stanyhurst : wyth oother Poëtical diuises theretoo annexed.* Imprinted at Leiden in Holland by John Pateo, MDLXXXII. Prefatory Address, signs. A ij and A iij. *Epitaph vpon . . . Lord Girald fitz Girald,* p. 106. A copy of 1st edn. is in B. M. (Ed. E. Arber, English scholars library, 1880, pp. 4, 152.)

[Prefatory address] Too Thee Right Honourable my verie loouing Broother thee Lord Baron of Dunsanye.

But oure *Virgil* not content wyth such meigre stuffe, dooth laboure, in telling, as yt were a *Cantorburye tale* . . . .

Too lyke effect *Chauncer* bringeth, in thee fift booke, *Troilus* thus mourning.

Thee owle eeke, which that hight Ascaphylo,
Hath after mee shright al theese nightes two :

And God Mercurye, now of mee woful wreche
Thee soule gyde, and when thee, yt seche.   [ll. 319-22]

[Epitaph] Vpon thee Death of Thee right honourable thee *Lord Girald* fitz Girald, L. Baron of Offalye [died 1580] . . . .

O that I thy prayses could wel decipher in order,
Like *Homer* or *Virgil*, or *Geffray Chauncer* in English :
Then would thy *Stanyhurst* in pen bee liberal holden
Thee poet is barrayn ; for prayse sich matter is offred.

[**1582.**] **Watson,** Thomas. *The Εκατομπαθια, or Passionate Centurie oj Loue.* Sonnet v, prose introduction. London, imprinted by John Wolfe for Gabriell Cawood . . . . in Paules Churchyard, sign. A **3**. (Reprinted for the Spenser soc., 1869, p. 19, and in English Reprints, ed. E. Arber, 1870, p. 41.)

[Sonnet v.] All this Passion (two verses only excepted) is wholly translated out of *Petrarch* where he writeth—

S'amor non è, che dunque è quel ch' isento ?   [Part prima, Sonnet 103.]
Ma s'egli è amor, per Dio que cosa, e quale ?
Se buona, ond' è l'effetto aspro e mortale ?
Se ria, ond' è si dolce ogni tormento ?

Heerein certaine contrarieties, whiche are incident to him that loueth extreemelye, are liuely expressed by a Metaphore. And it may be noted that the Author, in his first halfe verse of this translation varieth from that sense, which *Chaucer* vseth in translating that selfe same : which he doth vpon no other warrant then his owne simple priuate opinion, which yet he will not greatly stand vpon.

If 't bee not loue I feele, what is it then ?
If loue it bee, what kind a thing is loue ?
If good, how chance he hurtes so many men ?
If badd, how happ's that none his hurtes disproue

[Chaucer's version :

If no love is, O god, what fele I so ?
And if love is, what thing and whiche is he ?
If love be good, from whennes comth my wo ?
If it be wikke, a wonder thinketh me,
When every torment and adversitee
That cometh of him, may to me savory thinke ;
For ay thurst I, the more that I it drinke.
       Troilus and Oriseyde, Bk. i, ll. 400-6.]

1583. Babington, Gervase (Bp. of Worcester). *A very fruitfull Exposition of the Commaundements*, pp. 412–13. *Ibid.* 1637, p. 78, [in] The Works of . . . Babington, 1637 (separate pagination for each work.) [In Philip Stubbes Anatomy of Abuses, ed. F. J. Furnivall, New Shakspere soc., 1877–9, pp. 89*–90*, the editor quotes Babington's reference to Chaucer's Pardoneres Tale against the sin of gaming.]

.... Olde *Chaucer* so long agoe set his sentence downe against this exercise, and spares not to display the vertues of it in this maner :   [Here follows the *Pardoneres Tale*, ll. 591–602, 627–8.]

[*a.* **1584. Montgomerie,** Alexander.] *The Flytting betwixt Montgomerie and Polwart.* Newlie corected and ammended, Edinburgh 1629, sign. A 3, A 4. (Montgomerie's Poems, ed. J. Cranstoun, 1887, Scottish Text soc., pp. 63–5. *See also ibid.*, introduction, pp. liii–iv, and Cranstoun's article in D. N. B.)

Montgomerie to Polwart.

[l. 112] Thy scrowes obscure are borrowed fra some buik,
Fra *Lindsay* thou tuik thou'rt *Chaucers* Cuike.

. . . .

Polwart to Montgomerie.

[l. 165] Also I may bee *Chaucers* man
And ʒet thy master not the lesse . . .

[The Flytting was first published in 1621, and the only copy known was in the Harleian library at its dispersal, but all trace of it has since been lost. A portion of the poem was quoted in King James's *Reulis and Cautelis of Scottis Poesie* in 1584, hence it must have been written before that date. *Cf.* above, p. 97, 1562, Alex. Scott.]

1584. James VI, King. *Ane schort Treatise conteining some revlis and Cautelis to be obseruit and eschewit in Scottis Poesie* [in] The Essayes of a Prentise, in the Divine Art of Poesie. 1584. Edinb. library D. e. 2. 57 [the Treatise begins at sign. K]. (Elizabethan Critical Essays, ed. G. Gregory Smith, 1904, vol. i, p. 222, and note pp. 406–7.)

For tragicall materis, complaintis, or testamentis, vse this kynde of verse following, callit *Troilus* verse, as

To thee, Echo, and thow to me agane
In the desert, amangs the wods and wells.

[From ' Echo' by A. Montgomerie.]

1584. Scot, Reginald. *The discouerie of witchcraft.* Book 4, chap. 12, p. 88, book 14, chaps. 1, 2 and 3, pp. 353–59. (Reprint of 1st edn. 1584 ; ed. Brinsley Nicholson, 1886, pp. 69–70, 294–99.)

The censure of G. Chaucer, vpon the knauerie of Incubus.

The twelfe Chapter.

Now will I (after all this long discourse of abhominable cloked knaueries) here conclude with certeine of *G. Chaucers* verses, who as he smelt out the absurdities of poperie so found

he the priests knauerie in this matter of *Incubus* and (as the
time would suffer him) he derided their follie and falshood in
this wise :

    For now the great charitie and praiers

.   .   .   .

    There nis none other Incubus but hee, &c.

Geffr. Chau. in the beginning of the Wife of Baths tale. [ll. 865-880]

.   .   .   .

[p. 853]   Of the art of Alcumystrie . . .

Here I thought it not impertinent to saie somewhat of the
art . . of Alcumystrie . . .; which *Chaucer*, of all other men,
most liuelie deciphereth . . . [In this, and the following two
chapters there are several quotations from the Chanon
Yeoman's Prologue, as well as a prose summary of the tale.]

[1584-88.] Puttenham, George. *The Arte of English Poesie*, 1589, pp.
11, 48-50, 54, 62, 71-3, 120, 177, 187-8, 200. (English Reprints,
ed. E. Arber, 1869, pp. 32, 74-6, 80, 89, 99, 101-2, 157, 221, 232,
246 ; *see also* Elizabethan Critical Essays, ed. G. Gregory Smith,
1904, vol. ii, pp. 17, 62-4, 68, 79, 89, 92-3, 150 ; the two last
references are omitted in this edn.)

And in her Maiesties time that now is are sprong vp
an other crew of Courtly makers, Noble men and Gentlemen
of her Maiesties owne seruauntes, who haue written excellently
well . . . , of which number is first that noble Gentleman,
Edward, Earle of Oxford. *Thomas*, Lord of Bukhurst, when
he was young, *Henry*, Lord Paget, Sir *Philip Sydney*, Sir
Walter Rawleigh, Master *Edward Dyar*, Maister *Fulke
Greuell, Gascon, Britton, Turberuille*, and a great many other
learned Gentlemen. . . . . But of them all particularly this is
myne opinion, that *Chaucer*, with *Gower, Lidgat* and *Harding*
for their antiquitie ought to haue the first place, and *Chaucer*
as the most renowmed of them all, for the much learning
appeareth to be in him aboue any of the rest. And though
many of his bookes be but bare translations out of the Latin
and French, yet are they wel handled, as his bookes of *Troilus*
[p. 50] and *Cresseid*, and the Romant of the Rose, whereof he translated but one halfe, the deuice was *Iohn de Mehunes*, a French
Poet, the Canterbury Tales were *Chaucers* owne inuention
as I suppose, and where he sheweth more the naturall of his
pleasant wit, than in any other of his workes, his similitudes,
comparisons, and all other descriptions are such as can not be

amended.   His meetre Heroicall of *Troilus* and *Cresseid* is very
graue and stately, keeping the staffe of seuen, and the verse of
ten, his other verses of the Canterbury tales be but riding
ryme, neuerthelesse very well becomming the matter of that
pleasaunt pilgrimage in which euery mans part is played with
much decency.   .   .   .   .

[p. 62]   But our auncient rymers, as *Chaucer, Lydgate*, and others,
vsed these *Cesures* either very seldome, or not at all, or
else very licentiously, and many times made their meetres
(they called them riding ryme) of such vnshapely wordes as
would allow no conuenient *Cesure*, and therefore did let their
rymes runne out at length, and neuer stayd till they came to
the end.   .   .   .   .

[p. 120]   Our maker therfore at these dayes shall not follow
Piers plowman, nor *Gower*, nor *Lydgate*, nor yet *Chaucer*, for
their language is now out of vse with vs.

[These are the three longest references to Chaucer, the other allusions are generally
to his verse ; or quotations.   Puttenham mentions Troilus and Criseyde four times,
the C Tales three times, and the Rom. of the Rose and Clerkes Tale once each.   One
of the allusions to Chaucer's ' Cresseida ' however (Arber's reprint, p. 221), and the
quotation which follows, really refers to Henryson's *Complaint of Cresseid*, 1475, and
the quotation is from the opening lines of that poem.]

[*c.* 1585.] **Lambarde**, William. *Dictionarium Angliæ Topographicum
    & Historicum :* An Alphabetical Description of the Chief Places
    in England and Wales . . . . now first published from a Manuscript
    under the Author's own Hand.   London, MDCCXXX, pp. 390–1.

1402,   In the South Part of this Churche [Westminster Abbey]
Eulogium,
Bale Cent.   lyeth *Geffrey Chaucer*, whose Tombe was re-edified in my
Memorie by Mr *Brigham*, and of whome *Leland* sometyme
made this Epitaphe

> *Prædicat algerum merita florentia* Dantem

>   .   .   .   .

> *Cui veneres debet patria lingua suas*
>   [*See* below, App. A, *c.* 1545, Leland.]

. . . And lastly, not farre from *Chaucer* lyeth *Robert Halle*,
slayne by the Lord *Latymer*, as he kneled at Masse, upon a
Strife growen betwene theim in *Fraunce*, for the takinge of
a Prisonner : Thus muche of the Buryed.

[This work was probably written in 1585, as in that year, Lambarde wrote to
Camden saying that he must give up his own work in favour of Camden's ; *see* Cam-
deni et illustrium virorum epistolæ, scriptore Thoma Smitho, 1691, pp. 28–30. *See
also* below, p. 191, 1615, V[allans], W., *The Honourable Prentice.*]

[c. **1585.**] **Harvey,** Gabriel. *MS. notes* in Gabriel Harvey's handwriting, prefixed to his copy of The Surueye of the World, by
Dionise Alexandrine; englished by T. Twine, 1572.   (Gabriel
Harvey's Marginalia, ed. G. C. Moore Smith, Stratford-upon-Avon,
1913, pp. 159–161, 162.)

[These MS. notes deal with astronomy in connexion with Poets, notably Chaucer,
Lydgate and Spenser, but they refer also to foreign writers, and contemporary
Englishmen. They are prefixed to a collection of small Books of Travel bound
together, one of them [The Trauailer, by Ierome Turler] presented by Spenser to
Gabriel Harvey, 1578, most of them having Harvey's name on the title pages. These
books are in the possession of Prof. I. Gollancz.]

Notable *Astronomical descriptions* in Chawcer, and Lidgate;
fine artists in manie kinds, and much better learned than owre
moderne poets.

Chawcers *conclusions of the Astrolabie*, still excellent and
vnempeachable: especially for the Horizon of Oxford.   A
worthie man, that initiated his little sonne Lewis with such
cunning and subtill conclusions: as sensibly and plainly
expressed as he cowld deuise. . . . In the Squiers tale. In the
tale of the Nonnes preist. In the beginning of the seconde
booke of Troilus.

The *Description of the Spring*, in the beginning of the
prologues of Chawcers Canterburie tales.

In the beginning of the Complaint of the Black Knight. In
the beginning of the flo[wre] and the leafe.

In the beginning of Lidgats Storie of Thebes. In the
romant of the Rose: 122.6. In the beginning of the testament
of Creseide, a winterlie springe.

. . . .

The *description of Winter*, in the Frankleins tale. In the
beginning of the flowre of Courtesie: made bie Lidgate.
In the beginning of the assemblie of Ladies. In a ballad 343.

The description of *the hower of the day:* in the Man of
Lawes prologue. In the tale of the Nonnes preist. In the
parsons prologue.

Notable descriptions, and not anie so artificial in Latin, or
Greek.

Eccè etiam personarum rerumque Iconismi.

The artificial description of a *cunning man, or Magician,
or* Astrologer, in the Franklins tale.

Two *cristall stones* artificially sett in the botom of the fresh
well: in the romant of the Rose, 123. The *Natiuitie of
Hypermestre:* in her Legend.

Fowre presents of miraculous vertu: An horse, & a sword;
a glasse & a ring: in the Squiers tale.

The *Natiuitie of Oedipus,* artificially calculated in the first part of Lidgats storie of Thebes : bie the cunningest Astronomers, and philosophers of Thebes.

The *discouerie of the counterfait Alchymist,* in the tale of the Chanons Yeman.

Other commend Chawcer, & Lidgate for their witt, pleasant veine, varietie of poetical discourse, & all humanitie : I specially note *their Astronomie, philosophie,* and other parts of *profound or cunning art.* Wherein few of their time were more exactly learned. It is not sufficient for poets to be superficial humanists : but they must be exquisite artists, and curious uniuersal schollers.

.   .   .   .

Saepe miratus sum, Chaucer*um,* et Lidgatu*m* tantos fuisse in diebus illis astronomos.

[1585–1590 ?] Harvey, Gabriel. *MS. notes* in The Mathematical Iewel. *See* below, App. A.

1585, Nov. 3. *Order by the Court of Requests as to the payment of money at Chaucer's tomb.* Books of Decrees and Orders, Court of Requests, vol. xiv, fol. 29. (Life Records of Chaucer, ed. R. E. G. Kirk, Chaucer soc., 1900, pp. 334–5.)

Michaelmas term 27–28 Eliz., 3rd Nov.

Puttenham *v.* Puttenham.

Order as to £45 received by John Bowyer, Esquire, one of the Queen's [Serjeants-at-]arms, upon a lawful tender thereof by Thomas Colbie, Esquire, on 31st October last, "at the tombe of Jeffrey Chawcer, within the Church of St. Peter in Westm*inster,* betwene the howers of two & fower of the clocke in the after noone of the same," according to a Decree made on the 7th Feb. 8 Eliz. [1566].

[This decree has not been traced. *See* 1596, below, p. 143, Cæsar.]

1586. Camden, William. *Britannia Authore Guilielmo Camdeno,* p. 199. First printed 1586. (Trans., ed. and enlarged by Richard Gough, 1789, vol. i, p. 286.)

Dobuni, Oxfordshire . . . Oppidum ipsum [Woodstock] cùm nihil habeat quod ostentet. Homerum nostrum Anglicum Galfredum Chaucerum alumnum suum fuisse gloriatur. De quo & nostris Poetis Anglicis illud verè asseram, quod de Homero, & Græcis eruditus ille Italus dixit :

Hic ille est, cuius de gurgite sacro
Combibit arcanos vatum omnis turba furores.

Ille enim extra omnem ingenij aleam positus, & Poetastras
nostros longo pòst se interuallo relinquens.

—jam monte potitus
Ridet anhelantem dura ad fastigia turbam.

[For reference in later edn. *see* below, pp. 162–3, 1600.]

1586. Ferne, Sir John. *The Blazon of Gentrie,* etc., p. 202.

The bearer heereof [= Arms of Pressignie], ne none of
his name be English : but bycause it is a french coate I will
give it you in french blazonne : . . . . But if you would
blaze in french of Stratford at Bow, say, that Pressignie
beareth barrewaies sixe peces, per pale counterchanged in
chief . . . . .

[Allusion to Prologue C. Tales, ll. 124–5 ?]

1586. Webbe, William. *A Discourse of English Poetrie,* [only two
copies known, of which one is among the Malone books in the
Bodl. library], sign. C ii *b,* C iii, D iii, E iiii. (English Reprints, ed.
E. Arber, 1871, pp. 31–2, 41, 52 ; Elizabethan Critical Essays, ed.
G. Gregory Smith, 1904, vol. i, pp. 241, 251, 263.)

[sign. C ii *b,* C iii] The first of our English Poets that I haue heard of was Iohn
Gower . . . his freend *Chaucer* . . speaketh of him often-
times in diuers places of hys workes. *Chaucer,* who for that
excellent fame which hee obtayned in his Poetry, was alwayes
accounted the God of English Poets (such a tytle for honours
sake hath beene giuen him), . . . hath left many workes, both
for delight and profitable knowledge, farre exceeding any other
that as yet euer since hys time directed theyr studies that way.
Though the manner of hys stile may seeme blunte and course
to many fine English eares at these dayes, yet in trueth, if it
be equally pondered, and with good judgment aduised, and
confirmed with the time wherein he wrote, a man shall per-
ceiue thereby euen a true picture or perfect shape of a right
Poet. He by his delightsome vayne, so gulled the eares of
men with his deuises, that, although corruption bare such
sway in most matters, that learning and truth might skant bee
admitted to shewe it selfe, yet without controllment, myght
hee gyrde at the vices and abuses of all states, and gawle with
very sharpe and eger inuentions, which he did so learnedly
and pleasantly, that none therefore would call him into
question. For such was his bolde spyrit, that what enormities
he saw in any, he would not spare to pay them home, eyther
in playne words, or els in some prety and pleasant couert,
that the simplest might espy him.

.   .   .   .

^[sign. D iii] Let thinges that are faigned for pleasures sake haue a neer resemblance of the truth. This precept may you perceiue to bee most duelie obserued of *Chawcer :* for who could with more delight prescribe such wholsome counsaile and sage aduise, where he seemeth onelie to respect the profitte of his lessons and instructions? or who coulde with greater wisedome, or more pithie skill, vnfold such pleasant and delightsome matters of mirth, as though they respected nothing but the telling of a merry tale? so that this is the very grounde of right poetrie, to give profitable counsaile, yet so as it must be mingled with delight.

1587. Churchyard, Thomas. *The Worthiness of Wales.* An Introduction for Breaknoke Shiere, sign. H 1 *b.* (Reprint of edn. of 1587, Spenser soc., 1876, p. 62.)

If *Ouids* skill I had, or could like *Homer* write,

Or *Dant* would make thy muses glad, to please ye worlds delite,

Or *Chawser* lent me in these daies, some of his learned tales,

As *Petrarke* did his *Lawra* praise, so would I speake of *Wales.*

1588. Fraunce, Abraham. *The Lawiers Logike . . .* Imprinted by W. How, 1588, fol. 27.

The like absurditie would it bee for a man of our age to affectate such wordes as were quite worne out at heeles and elbowes long before the natiuitie of Geffrey Chawcer.

1589. Greene, Robert. *Menaphon,* sign. F 2 *b.* (Greene's Works, ed. A. B. Grosart, Huth library, 1881–6, vol. vi, 1881–3, p. 86.)

The Reports of the Shepheards.

Whosoeuer *Samela* descanted of that loue, tolde you a *Canterbury* tale.

1589. [Nashe, Thomas.] *To the Gentlemen Students of both Vniuersities.* Introduction to Greene's Menaphon, sign. A 2. (Ed. E. Arber, 1895, pp. 15, 16. Works of Thomas Nashe, ed. R. B. McKerrow, 1904–5, vol. iii, 1905, p. 322.)

. . . Tut saies our English Italians, the finest witts our Climate sends foorth, are but drie braind doltes, in comparison of other countries: whome if you interrupt with *redde rationem,* they will tell you of *Petrache, Tasso, Celiano,* with an infinite number of others; to whome if I should oppose *Chaucer, Lidgate, Gower,* with such like, that liued vnder the tirranie of ignorance, I do think their best louers, would bee much discontented, with the collation of contraries, if I should write ouer al their heads, Haile fellow well met—One thing I am sure of, that each of these three, haue vaunted their meeters, with as much admiration in English as euer the proudest *Ariosto* did his verse in Italian.

[**1589-90 ? Shakespeare,** William ?]   *Titus Andronicus,* II, i, 126-7.

> The emperor's court is like the house of Fame,
> The palace full of tongues, of eyes and ears.

> This is almost certainly a reference to Chaucer's House of Fame. It is true that there is a description of Fama's abode in Ovid (Metam. xii, 39-64), but the expression 'house of fame' is not in Golding's translation. Moreover, the idea of the many tongues, eyes, and ears, is derived, if not direct from Virgil (Aen. iv, 173-83), from the close imitation by Chaucer, whose Fame had 'as fele eyen . . . As fetheres upon foules be'. . . and 'also fele up-stonding eres And tonges' (H. of F. III, 291-2, 299-300). There may be a debt to Peele's *Honour of the Garter,* 1593, which would affect the question of the date of *Titus.* With regard to Shakespeare's authorship of the play, see Dr. M. M. Arnold Schröer, Über Titus Andronicus, Marburg 1891, Fleay's Shakespeare Manual, 1876, p. 44, and H. B. Wheatley in New Shakespere Soc. Transactions, 1874, pp. 126-9. For other possible Chaucer references in Shakespeare, and his indebtedness to Chaucer and knowledge of him, *see* below, Appendix A, 1589, Shakespeare.]

1590. Greene, R[obert].   *Greenes Mourning Garment,* 1616, sign. B 3, Huth library.   (Greene's Works, ed. A. B. Grosart, 1881-6, vol. ix, 1881-3, pp. 130-1.)   [Published originally in 1590, but no copy of this edn. is known; the only edn. that we have been able to trace is one of 1616.]

> The description of the youngest sonne.

Philador . . . . . was courteous to salute all, counting it commendable prodigality that grew from the Bonnet and the Tongue, alluding to this olde verse of *Chaucer.*

> *Mickle grace winnes he*
> *Thats franke of bonnet, tongue and knee.*

1590. Greene, Rob[ert].   *The Royal Exchange. Contayning Sundry Aphorismes of Phylosophie.*   At London, printed by I. Charlewood . . . 1590.   [Unique copy Chetham library.]   (Greene's Works, ed. A. B. Grosart, Huth library, 1881-6, vol. viii, 1881-3, p. 321.)

Olde men, (saith Sir *Ieffrie Chaucer*), are then in their right vaine, when they haue In diebus illis, in theyr mouth; telling what passed long agoe, what warres they haue seene, what charitie, what cheapeness of victuals, alwaies blaming the time present, though neuer so fruitful.

> [This is not in Chaucer, but see the description of Gower and Chaucer in *Greene's Vision,* 1592, xii, p. 209, 'In diebus illis,' hung upon their garments.']

1590. Unknown.   *The Cobler of Caunterburie, or An inuective against Tarltons Newes out of Purgatorie.*   At London, printed by Robert Robinson, 1590.—[2nd edn.] London, Printed by *Nicholas Okes* for *Nathaniel Butter,* 1608, sign. A 3 *b,* B 1 *b,* K 1 *b.* (Ed. Frederic Ouvry, 1862, pp. 2, 3, 6, 76.)

. . . to my booke, wherein are contained the tales that were told in the Barge betweene Billingsgate and Grauesend : imitating herein *old father Chaucer,* who with the like Method

set out his Canterbury tales : but as there must be admitted
no compare betweene a cup of Darby ale, and a dish of durtie
water : So sir *Ieffery Chaucer* is so high aboue my reach, that
I take *Noli altum sapere* for a warning; and onely looke at
him with honour and reuerence . . . .

. . . .

[sign. B 1 *b*] . . . what say you to old father *Chaucer*? how like you
of his *Canterburie* tales? are they not pleasant to delight,
and wittie to instruct, and full of conceited learning to shewe
the excellency of his wit? All men commend *Chaucer* as
the father of English Poets, and said that he shot a shoote
which many have aymed at, but neuer reacht too . . . .

. . . .

[sign. K 1 *b*] Gentlemen . . . at the motion of the Cobler, wee haue
imitated old Father *Chaucer*, hauing in our little Barge, as
he had in his trauell sundry tales . . . .

[Of this work, the author of Greene's Vision [1592, below, pp. 137–8] says, " But
now of late there came foorth a booke called the Cobler of Canterburie, a merrie
worke, and made by some madde fellow, conteining plesant tales, a little tainted
with scurilitie, such reuerend *Chaucer* as your selfe set foorth in your iourney to
Canterbury." Greene's Works, ed. A. B. Grosart, vol. xii, 1881–3, pp. 212–3. A
copy of the first edn. of the Cobler is in the Bodl. library. The references are to the
second edn., which is in the B. M., and varies from the first only very slightly. *Cf.*
1630, The Tincker of Turvey, p. 203, below.]

[*c.* **1590.**] **Unknown.** *Marginal note* in MS. Addit. 24,663, fol. 1.

When Faythe fayleth in prestes sawes ⎫
.   .   .   .   .   ⎬ wrytten by
          be put to grett confusion. ⎭ Jefferae Chawser

[From sayings printed by Caxton, *see* above, p. 113, 1576, Meredith Hanmer.]

1590–6. Spenser, Edmund. *The Faerie Queene* . . . . 1590. *The second
part of the Faerie Queene, containing the fourth, fifth, and sixth
bookes,* 1596 ; book iv, canto 2, p. 28 [should be p. 30]. Two cantos
of Mutabilitie [*i. e.* part of book 7, first printed in] The Faerie
Queene, 1609, book vii, canto 7, p. 359. *Cf. also* book i, canto 1, p.
5 [catalogue of the trees], with the Parliament of Foules, ll. 176, etc.
(Works of Spenser, ed. A. B. Grosart, 1882–4, vols. vii, pp. 70–1 ;
viii, p. 296. Globe edn., ed. R. Morris, 1869, pp. 239, 430.)

[The Squire brings word to Sir Blandamour and Sir Paridell
that two knights and two ladies they have overtaken are :]

[Book iv, canto 2, xxxi] Two of the prowest Knights in Faery lond ;
And those two Ladies their two louers deare,
Courious *Cambell*, and stout *Triamond*,
With *Canacee* and *Cambine* linckt in louely bond.

Whylome as antique stories tellen vs,
        Those two were foes the fellonest on ground,
        And battell made the dreddest daungerous,
        That euer shrilling trumpet did resound ;
        Though now their acts be no where to be found,
        As that renowmed Poet them compyled,
        With warlike numbers and Heroicke sound,
        Dan *Chaucer*, well of Englishe vndefyled,
On Fames eternall beadroll worthie to be fyled.

But wicked Time that all good thoughts doth waste,
        And workes of noblest wits to nought out weare,
        That famous moniment hath quite defaste,
        And robd the world of threasure endlesse deare,
        The which mote haue enriched all vs heare.
        O cursed Eld the cankerworme of writs,
        How may these rimes, so rude as doth appeare,
        Hope to endure, sith workes of heauenly wits
Are quite deuourd, and brought to nought by little bits ?

Then pardon, O most sacred happie spirit,
        That I thy labours lost may thus reuiue,
        And steale from thee the meede of thy due merit,
        That none durst euer whilest thou wast aliue,
        And being dead in vaine yet many striue :
        Ne dare I like, but through infusion sweete
        Of thine owne spirit, which doth in me surviue,
        I follow here the footing of thy feete,
That with thy meaning so I may the rather meete.

        .   .   .   .

[Book vii, So heard it is for any liuing wight,
canto 7,
st. ix]   All her [Dame Nature's] array and vestiments to tell
        That old *Dan Geffrey* (in whose gentle spright
        The pure well head of Poesie did dwell)
        In his *Foules parley* durst not with it mel,
        But it transferd to *Alane*, who he thought
        Had in his *Plaint of kindes* describ'd it well :
        Which who will read set forth so as it ought,
Go seek he out that *Alane* where he may be sought.

1591. Harington, Sir John. *An Apologie of Poetrie.* Prefixed to Orlando Furioso in English heroical verses by John Harington, sign. ¶ vii. (Ancient Critical Essays upon English Poets and Poësy, ed. Joseph Haslewood, 1811-15, vol. ii, 1815, pp. **139–40.**)

> . . . me thinkes I can smile at the finesse of some that will condemne him (*i. e.* Ariosto), & yet not onely allow, but admire our *Chawcer*, who both in words & sence, incurreth far more the reprehen*s*ion of flat scurrilitie, as I could recite many places, not onely in his millers tale, but in the good wife of Bathes tale, & many more, in which onely the decorum he keepes, is that that excuseth it, and maketh it more tolerable.

1591. Lyly, John. *Endimion.* [Character of Sir Tophas, name most probably suggested by Chaucer, *see* Works of John Lyly, ed. R. Warwick Bond, 1902 ; the play is reprinted in vol. iii ; *cf.* notes *ibid.*, pp. 503–4.]

[1591 ?] '**Simon Smel-Knaue** (studient in good-felowship).' *Fearefull and lamentable effects of two dangerous Comets, which shall appeare in the Yeere of our Lord 1591, the 25. of March.* At London, printed by I. C. for John Busbie, sign. C 2. (*See* British Bibliographer, ed. Sir S. E. Brydges, 1810–14, vol. i, p. 375. *Cf.* 1608 The Penniless Parliament, below, p. 183.)

> *Chaucers* bookes shall this yeere, prooue more witty then euer they were : for there shall so many suddayne, or rather sodden wittes steppe abroad, that a Flea shall not friske foorth vnlesse they comment on her.

1591. Spenser, Ed[mund]. *Colin Clouts Come Home Againe.* Printed for William Ponsonbie, 1595, ll. 1–6 [dedication dated 1591]. (Works of Spenser, ed. A. B. Grosart, 1882–4, vol. iv, p. 37, Spenser's Works, Globe edn., ed. R. Morris, 1869, p. 549.)

> The shepheards boy (best knowen by that name)
> That after *Tityrus* first sung his lay,
> Laies of sweet loue, without rebuke or blame,
> Sate (as his custome was) vpon a day,
> Charming his oaten pipe vnto his peres,
> The shepheard swaines that did about him play.

1592. [Harvey, Gabriel.] *Foure Letters, and certaine Sonnets, especially touching Robert Greene* . . . . The Second Letter. *To my louing frend, Maister Christopher Bird of Walden,* pp. 7, 73. (Works of G. Harvey, ed. A. B. Grosart, Huth library, 1884, vol. i, pp. 165, 252.)

> . . . if mother Hubbard in the vaine of *Chawcer*, happen to tel one Canicular tale ; father *Elderton*, and his sonne

Greene, in the vaine of *Skelton* or *Scoggin*, will counterfeit an
hundred dogged Fables, Libles . . . .

. . . .

Sonnet xxii.

L'enuoy : or an Answere to the Gentleman, that drunke to
Chaucer, vpon view of the former Sonnets, and other Cantos,
in honour of certaine Braue men.

Some Tales to tell, would I a Chaucer were :
Yet would I not euen-now an Homer be
Though Spencer me hath often Homer term'd ;
And Monsieur Bodine vow'd as much as he,
Enuy, and Zoilus, two busy wightes,
No petty shade of Homer can appeere,
But he the Diuell, and she his Dam display :

[p. 74] And Furies fell annoy sweete Muses cheere,
Nor Martins I, nor Counter-martins squibb :
Enough a doo, to cleere my simple selfe ;
Momus gainst Heauen ; and Zoilus gainst Earth,
A Quipp for Gibeline ; and whip for Guelph.
Or purge this humour ; or woe-worth the State,
That long endures the one, or other mate.

1592. Nashe, Thomas. *Strange Newes of the intercepting of certaine
Letters* . . . . by Tho. Nashe, The Epistle Dedicatorie, sign. A 2,
A 4, G 3, K 1. (Works of Thomas Nashe, ed. R. B. McKerrow,
1904-5, vol. i, pp. 255, 258, 299, 316-17.)

To the most copious Carminist of our time, &c.

[sign. A2] Gentle M. William, ... I am bolde in steade of new
Wine, to carowse to you a cuppe of newes : Which if your
Worship (according to your wonted CHAUCER*isme*) shall accept
in good part, Ill bee your daily Orator to pray that, &c., &c.
. . . . .

[sign. A4] . . . . . Proceede to cherish thy surpassing carminicall arte
of memorie with full cuppes (as thow dost) let *Chaucer* bee
new scourd against the day of battaile, and *Terence* come but
in nowe and then with the snuffe of a sentence . . . . .

. . . .

[sign. G8] *Homer, and Virgil, two valorous Authors*, yet were they
never knighted, they wrote in Hexameter verses : *Ergo,
Chaucer*, and *Spencer* the *Homer* and *Virgil* of England, were
farre ouerseene that they wrote not all their Poems in Hexa-
miter verses also.

. . . .

[sign. K 1] *Chaucers* authoritie I am certaine, shalbe alleadgd against mee for a many of these balductums [*i. e.* against coining new and Latinised words]. Had *Chaucer* liu'd to this age, I am verily perswaded hee wou'd haue discarded the tone halfe of the harsher sort of them.

They were the Oouse, which ouerflowing barbarisme, withdrawne to her Scottish Northren chanell, had left behind her. Art, like yong grasse in the spring of *Chaucers* florishing, was glad to peepe vp through any slime of corruption, to be beholding to she car'd not whome for apparaile, trauailing in those colde countries.

1592. Nashe, Thomas. *Pierce-Penilesse, his supplication to the Diuell,* sign. D 3 b. (Works of Thomas Nashe, ed. R. B. McKerrow, 1904–5, vol. i, pp. 193, 194.)

The fruits of Poetry   To them that demaund what fruites the Poets of our time bring forth, or wherein they are able to proue themselues necessary to the state. Thus I answere. First and for most, they haue cleansed our language from barbarisme and made the vulgar sort here in *London* . . . . to aspire to a richer puritie of speach . . . . What age will not praise immortal *Sir Philip Sidney* . . . . together with *Sir* english worke *Nicholas Bacon* . . . . and merry sir *Thomas Moore,* for the chiefe pillers of our english speeche? Not so much but *Chaucers* host *Baly* in Southworke, and his wife of Bath he keeps such a stirre with, in his *Canterbury* tales, shalbe talkt of whilst the Bath is vsde, or there be euer a badhouse in Southwork.

1592. Stowe, John. *The Annales of England . . . from the first inhabitation vntill this present yeere* 1592, pp. 431, 517–8. [This is the same book as the Chronicles of England, 1580, only revised and enlarged, *see* above, p. 119, note under 1580, Stowe.]

Chaucer and other sent into France   About the same time the Eale [*sic*] of Salisbury, and *sir Richard Anglisison a* Poyton, the Byshoppe of Saint *Dauids,* the Byshoppe of *Hereford, Geffrey Chaucer,* (the famous Poet of England) and other, were sent into Fraunce to treat a peace, or at the least a truce for two yeere or more, but they coulde not obtayne any longer truce, then for one moneth, which they utterly refused. Whereupon they stayed in Fraunce about these things . . . .

[For this journey of Chaucer's, *see* above, 1377, p. 5 ; 1410, p. 20. For the text of the 2nd reference, pp 517–18, *see* below, p. 164, under 1600, *The Annales of England,* pp. 527–8, where the reference is practically the same.]

1592. Greene, Robert. *A Quip for an vpstart Courtier.* . . . 1592, sign.
D 2. (Works, ed. A. B. Grosart, Huth library, 1881–6, vol. xi,
1881–3, p. 255.)

> . . . for the Sumner it bootes me to say little more against
> him, then *Chaucer* did in his Canterbury tales, who said hee
> was a knaue, briber, and a bawd : but leauing that authority
> although it be authenticall. . . .

[The whole substance of this pamphlet is taken from Francis Thynne's poem,
Pride and Lowlines, *c.* 1568, and the character descriptions in both pieces are much
influenced by Chaucer.]

[1592.] Unknown. *Greenes Vision. Written at the instant of his death.*
Conteyning a penitent passion for the folly of his Pen. Sero sed Serio.
sign. C 1, C 2, C 3, C 4, H 1. (Greene's Works, ed. A. B. Grosart,
Huth library, 1881–6, vol. xii, 1881–3, pp. 208–74.)

[This has hitherto been thought not to be by Greene, but *see* J. Churton Collins in
his edn. of The Plays and Poems of Robert Greene, Oxford, 1905, vol. i, p. 26, note,
who maintains that it is by Greene, and written in 1590. See *ibid.*, pp. 27, 28, for a
full account of the contents of the pamphlet.]

[sign. C 1] The description of sir Geffery *Chaucer.*

> His stature was not very tall,
> Leane he was, his legs were small
> Hosd within a stock of red,
> A buttond bonnet on his head,
> From vnder which did hang I weene
> Siluer haires both bright and sheene,
> His beard was white, trimmed round,
> His countenance blithe and merry found,
> A Sleeuelesse Iacket large and wide,
> With many pleights and skirts side,
> Of water Chamlet did he weare,
> A whittell by his belt he beare,
> His shoes were corned broad before,
> His Inckhorne at his side he wore,
> And in his hand he bore a booke,
> Thus did this auntient Poet looke.

> .   .   .   .

[sign. C 2,
p. 212] Graue Lawreats, the tipes of Englands excellence for Poetry,
and the worlds wonders for your wits, all haile.

> .   .   .   .   ,

[sign. C 3,
p. 215] [Greene blames himself for the writings of his youth ;
Chaucer answers him :] . . . If thou doubtest blame for **thy**

wantonnes, let my selfe suffice for an instaunce, whose Canterburie tales are broad enough before, and written homely and
pleasantly : yet who hath bin more canonised for his workes
than Sir *Geffrey Chaucer* ?

.   .   .   .

[sign. C 4, [Gower on the contrary blames Greene.] . . . Therefore
p. 218]
trust me *John Gowers* opinion is : thou hast applied thy wits
ill, and hast sowed chaffe and shalt reape no haruest.   But my
maister *Chaucer* brings in his workes for an instance, that as
his, so thine shalbe famoused : no it is not a promise to conclude vpon : for men honor his more for the antiquity of the
verse, the english & prose, than for any deepe loue to the
matter : for proofe marke how they weare out of vse.

.   .   .   .

[sign. H 1, [Greene's answer to Chaucer and Gower] . . . Now I per-
pp. 273-4]
ceiue Father *Chaucer*, that I followed too long your pleasant
vaine, in penning such Amorous workes, and that ye same that
I sought after by such trauail, was nothing but smoke.

> [As the whole pamphlet refers to the vision of Chaucer and Gower, and to their
> conversation with the author, only some extracts have been given. *See* above, a note
> under 1590, Cobler of Canterburie, p. 132.]

1593. 'A.' *The Passionate Morrice, a sequel to Tell-Trothes New-Yeares
Gift*, 1593.   Imprinted by Robert Bourne, sign. H 2 b.   Unique copy
Peterborough Cathedral library.   (Ed. F. J. Furnivall, Shakspere
soc., 1876, p. 95.)

Doe yow tearme such dooing iesting ? thought *Honestie* :
if *Chaucers* iapes were such iestes, it was but bad sporte.

1593. Drayton, Michael.   *Idea. The Shepheards Garland, fashioned in
nine Eglogs.*   Imprinted at London for Thomas Woodcocke . . . .
1593, sign. D 3–D 3 b, I 2, pp. 21-2, 60.   (Poems, ed. J. P. Collier,
Roxb. club, 1856, pp. 82, 114-5.   *Cf.* ibid., pp. xvii–xviii, where
this copy is described ; it has on the title-page the autograph of
Robert, Earl of Essex, and a few MS. notes by him ; the copy is
now in the B. M., pr. m. C. 30, e. 21,   *Cf. also* notes, p. 131.)

The Fourth Eglog . . .

Gorbo

.   .   .   .   .   .

Come sit we downe vnder this Hawthorne tree
The morrowes light shall lend us daie enough
And tell a tale of *Gawen* or Sir *Guy*
Of *Robin Hood*, or of good *Clem a Clough*

Or else some Romant vnto vs areed   [* ef MS.]
Which good olde Godfrey * taught thee in thy youth
Of noble Lords and Ladies gentle deede,
Or of thy loue or of thy lasses truth

Eighth Eglog
Motto
Gorbo
Farre in the Country of *Arden*
There wond a knight hight *Cassemen,*
as bold as *Isenbras,*
Fell was he and eger bent,
In battell & in Tournament,
as was the good Sir *Thopas*
He had as antique stories tell
A daughter cleaped *Dowsabelle*
a mayden fayre & free

.   .   .   .   .   .

[In the Eglogs printed in *Poemes lyrick and pastorall* [1605-6], sign. E 8, **the**
'Godfrey' reference is omitted ; the line runs—
By former Shepheards taught thee in thy youth.]

[1593-1601.] Devereux, Robert, 2nd Earl of Essex. *MS. note.* [*See
above* under 1593, Drayton, Michael, for notice of a copy of Drayton's
Idea, which belonged to Essex, and in which he altered 'Godfrey'
to 'Geffrey.']

1593. Foulface, Philip, of Ale-foord, Student in good Felloship
[pseud.]. *Bacchus Bountie . . . .* by Philip Foulface, printed **at**
London for Henry Kyrkham, 1593. (Harleian Miscell., Oldys
and Park, vol. ii, 1809, p. 306. We have been unable to trace the
possessor of this tract. *See* Hazlitt, Handbook, p. 686.)

[In the palace of Bacchus] After these againe came stumbling
in blind Homer, the Grecian poet ; and with him came Aristophanes, Menander, and others ; and along with these came
Virgil, Horace, Ovid, olde father Ennius, Geffery Chaucer,
Lydgate, Anthony Skelton, Will. Elderton, with infinite
mo . . . .

1593. Harvey, Gabriel. *Pierces Supererogation, or A new prayse of an
Old Asse. A Preparatiue to certaine larger Discourses, intituled
Nashes S. Fame,* pp. 145, 173, sign. Ff 1, 2. (Works of G. Harvey,
ed. A B. Grosart, Huth library, 1884, vol. ii, pp. 228, 266, 311.)

. . . . and teach Chaucer to retell a Canterbury Tale.

[p. 173] Come diuine poets and sweet Oratours, the siluer streaming fountaines of flowingest witt and shiningest Art; come Chawcer and Spencer; More and Cheeke; Ascham and Astely; Sidney and Dier.

[sign. Ff. 1–2] Errours escaped in the Printing. With certaine Additions to be inserted . . . . In the *Third booke*, Page 205 [wrongly paged 135] insert . . . . that according to Chawcers English there can be little *adling*, without much *gabbing*, that is, small getting, without greatly lying and cogging.

1593. Peele, George. *The Honour of the Garter, Displaied in a Poeme gratulatorie, to the worthie . . . . earle of Northumberland, Created Knight of that Order and install'd at Windsore. Anno Regni Elizabethæ* 35 . . *Die Junii.* 26 . . . . *Ad Mæcænatem Prologus,* sign. A 4 b. (Peele's Works, ed. A. H. Bullen, 1888, vol. ii, p. 319.)

> Why thither [to heauen] post not all good wits from hence,
> To *Chaucer, Gowre,* and to the fayrest *Phaer*
> That euer ventured on great *Virgils* works?

[There is a good deal of reminiscence of Chaucer's *Hous of Fame* in the poem itself, *cf.* ll. 172–3.]

1594. B., O. *Questions of profitable and pleasant concernings, talked of by two olde Seniors* . . . . Printed by Richard Field . . . . 1594, sign. E 2, H 3 b, I 2 b.

> Their [the catholics'] harmles desire to instruct the ignorant . . . . is laid a sleepe and changed. I remember how they dallied out the matter like *Chaucers* Frier at the first, vnder pretence of spiced holinesse.

[sign. H 3 b] [A young] reueler . . . hieth . . . with his purse in his hand ready drawne, for loosing of time, and that as *Chaucer* saith, tied with a Leeke, that it may not be long in opening.

[sign. I 2 b] I beseech you sir haue you not taken this report out of *Chaucer* his Ianuarie and his May. [Reference to the *Merchantes Tale.*]

[The dedication to . . Robert Devorax [*sic, for* Devereux], Earle of Essex, is signed "Yours [*sic*] honours most bounden O. B."]

[1594.] **Davies**, Sir John. *Orchestra, or A Poeme on Dauncing* . . stanza 128 . . Printed by J. Robarts for N. Ling, 1596, sign. C. 8. (Davies' Works, ed. A. B. Grosart, Fuller's Worthies library, 1869–76, vol. i, p. 229. *See also same*, pp. 172–3.)

> O, that I had Homer's abundant vaine,
> I would hierof another Ilias make;

> Or els the man of Mantua's charmèd braine,
> In whose large throat great Joue the thunder spake.
> O that I could old Gefferie's Muse awake
> Or borrow Colin's fayre heroike stile,
> Or smooth my rimes with Delia's servants' file.

[There is a (unique ?) copy of this edn. in the Bodl. library. This verse does not occur in the 2nd edn. of 1622. The poem was entered for copyright in the Register of the Stationers' Company, under date June 25, 1594, although not published till 1596. *See* Notes and Queries, 3rd S. II, 1862, p. 461.]

1594. Gr[eenwood], P. *Grammatica Anglicana præcipuè quatenus a Latina differt, ad vnicam P. Rami methodum concinnata,* Authore P. G. . . . 1594. [separate title page sign. E 5]. Vocabula Chauceriana quaedam selectiora, et minus vulgaria ipsae Hodie Poetarum deliciæ, vna cum eorum significatis . . . . . . Stellis ac herbis vis est, sed maxima verbis.

[Here follows, sign. E 6–E 8, an explanation of 121 Chaucerian words. The preface is signed P. Gr. ; the book is therefore catalogued in B. M. under Gr., P.]

1594. Unknown. *Palamon and Arsett.*

[A Play mentioned by Philip Henslowe in his diary, possibly Edward's play, 1566 [*q. v.* above, p. 99]. *See* Henslowe's Diary, ed. W. W. Greg, 1904, vol. i, F. 10, l. 21 (p. 19).]

1595. Churchyard, Thomas. *A praise of poetrie,* sign. E 4 *b*, G 1 *b*, part of *A Musicall Consort of Heauenly harmonie . . . called Churchyards Charitie.* Imprinted at London, by Ar. Hatfield for William Holme, 1595, 4to. A copy was in the Huth library ; the title page of A Praise of poetrie is on sign. E 3. (Reprint in Frondes Caducæ, vol. 4, Auchinleck Press, 1817, pp. 28, 38.)

Goore, Chaucer In England liued three great men
and the noble
earle of Surry   Did Poetrie aduance
> And all they with the gift of pen
> Gaue glorious world a glance

> .   .   .   .   .   .

> Our age and former fathers daies
> (Leaue Goore and Chauser out)
> Hath brought foorth heere but few to praise
> Search all our soyle about.

1595. C[ovell], W[illiam]. *Polimanteia, or The meanes lawfull and vnlawfull, to iudge of the fall of a common-wealth . . . . . Whereunto is added, A letter from England to her three daughters, Cambridge, Oxford, Innes of Court . . .* sign. R 2 *b*—R 3 *b*. (Elizabethan England, ed. A. B. Grosart, Occasional issues of unique or rare books, vol. xv, 1881, p. 45.)

Oxford, thow maist extoll thy courte-deare-verse happie *Daniell,* whose sweete refined muse . . . were sufficient

amongst men, to gaine pardon of the sinne to *Rosemond* . . . .
Register your children's petegree in Fames forehead, so may
you fill volumes with *Chauser's* praise, with *Lydgate*, the
Scottish Knight, and such like, whose vnrefined tongues farre
shorte of the excellencie of this age, wrote simplie and purelie
as the times weare. And when base and iniurious trades
. . . . shall haue deuoured them . . . . yet that then such
(if you thinke them worthie) . . . . . . may liue by your
meanes, canonized in learnings catalogue.

[This book was formerly attributed to William Clerke, but in a copy which
belonged to Prof. Dowden, the dedication is signed William Covell, *see* Athenæum,
July 14, 1906, p. 44, col. i.]

1595. P[eele], G[eorge]. *The Old Wiues Tale* . . . Written by G. P.,
sign. E 1 *b* (ed. F. B. Gummere, in Representative English Comedies,
ed. C. M. Gayley, vol. i, 1903, p. 374 and note. Works of G. Peele,
ed. A. H. Bullen, English dramatists, 1888, vol. i, p. 334).

> *Huan[ebango]* Ile nowe set my countenance and to hir in
> prose; it may be this rim ram ruffe is too rude an incounter.
>
> [Prol. Persones Tale, l. 43.]

[*Cf.* above, pp. 110–1, 1575, Gascoigne.]

1595. Unknown, [C., J.?] *Alcilia, Philoparthen's Louing Follie*, 1595,
stanza 48, sign. D 2. Unique copy in Town library, Hamburg.
(Occasional issues of unique or very rare books, ed. A. B. Grosart,
1879, vol. viii, p. 27. *See* introduction for discussion on authorship, etc.)

> Vncouth vnkist our auncient* Poet said,   * Chaucer.
> And he that hides his wants, when he hath need, [Tr. & Cr.
> May after haue his want of wit bewraid,   bk. i. l. 809]
> And faile of his desire, when others speed.
> Then boldly speak : the worst is at first entring,
> Much good successe men misse for lack of ventring.

[*Cf.* above, p. 117, E. K.'s prefatory letter to Shepherd's Calendar, 1579.]

[1595–6 ?] C[arew], R[ichard]. *The Excellencie of the English tongue,*
by R. C. of Anthony Esquire to W. C. Inserted by William
Camden in the 2nd edn. of his Remaines concerning Britaine, 1614,
pp. 43–4. (Elizabethan Critical Essays, ed. G. Gregory Smith,
1904, vol. ii, p. 293).

Adde hereunto, that whatsoeuer grace any other language
carrieth in verse or Prose, in Tropes or Metaphores, in Ecchoes
and Agnominations, they may all bee liuely and exactly
represented in ours: will you haue *Platoes* veine? reade Sir
Thomas Smith, the *Ionicke*? Sir *Thomas Moore*. *Ciceroes*?
Ascham, Varro, Chaucer, Demosthenes? Sir *John Cheeke* (who

in his treatise to the Rebels, hath comprised all the figures of
Rhetorick). Will you reade *Virgill*? take the Earle of Surrey,
Catullus? *Shakespheare* and *Marlows* [printed *Barlows*] frag-
ment, *Ovid*? *Daniell*, *Lucan*? *Spencer*, *Martial*? Sir *John
Davies* and others: will you have all in all for Prose and
verse? Take the miracle of our age, Sir *Philip Sidney.*

[*a.* **1596**?] **Peele,** George. *The Tale of Troy,* by G. Peele, M. of Arts in
Oxford, 1598. Printed by A. H. 1604, ll. 281-87. (Peele's Works,
ed. A. H. Bullen, 1888, vol. ii, p. 255. *See also same,* p. [235].
Introductory note to A Farewell, etc. *See also* A Bibliographical
. . . account of the rarest books in the English Language by J. P.
Collier, 1865, vol. ii, p. 144 *et seq.*)

> So hardy was the true Knight Troilus,
>   And all for loue of the vnconstant Cressed,
> T'encounter with th' unworthy Diomed,
>   But leaue I here of Troilus ought to say,
>   Whose passions for the ranging Cressida,
>   Read as fair England's Chaucer doth vnfold,
>   Would tears exhale from eyes of iron mould.

[This reference is not in the earlier edn. of 1589, appended to Peele's *Farewell to*
. . . *Sir Iohn Norris and Syr Frances Drake.* This 1604 edn. is a tiny volume, one
inch and a half high (48mo); a unique (?) copy exists in private hands. Peele died
about 1597.]

1596. **Cæsar,** Sir Julius. *The Ancient State, Authoritie, and Proceedings of the Court of Requests,* 2 *Octob:* 1596, [Printed] Anno 1597,
p. 140.

Anno 18 Elizab. [1577]

9 Maij. fol. 212. *Memorandum,* that *Mary Puttenham* the
wife of *Richard Puttenham* Esquire, hath this day in open
Court receiued the summe of 13 shil. 8d. due vnto her for the
halfe yeeres paiment of one yeerly annuitie to be taken and
issuing out of the rentes, reuenues, and profites of the said
Richard her husband, by force of a decree heretofore in that
behalf made by her Maiesties Counsell of this Court, the same
being due at the Annunciation of our Lady last past, and
attached and defalked by *Spencer* esquire, one of her Maiesties
Serieants at Armes, by order of this Court, vpon the last day
of Aprill last past, out of such summes of money as were ten-
dered vpon *Chawcers* tombe within the Cathedrall church of
S. *Peter* in Westminster, by *Rob. Cheynie* Citizen of London,
and there paied to the vse of the same *Rich: Puttenham.*

[*Cf.* above, 1566, p. 99, and 1585, p. 128.]

1596. [**Harington,** Sir John.] *Vlysses vpon Aiax.* Written by Miso-diaboles to his friend Philaretes, sign. E 8 *b.*

A pleasant wench of the country (who beside *Chaucers* iest, had a great felicitie in iesting) . . . .

[**1596–7.**] **Shakespeare,** William. *The First Part of King Henry IV,* III, iii, 57.

How now, Dame Partlet the hen !

<small>[The allusion must clearly be to Chaucer's Nonne Preestes Tale, as he first gave the name of 'Pertelote' to the hen. In the Roman de Renart and Reinhart Fuchs, the hen's name is 'Pinte.' *See also* below, App. A, 1589, Shakespeare.]</small>

1597. B[reton], N[icholas]. *The Arbor of Amorous Devices.—In the praise of his Mistresse.* [Unique copy, Capell coll. Cambr.] (Breton's Works, ed. A. B. Grosart, 1879, vol. i, p. 14.)

For Venus was a toy, and onely feignèd fable

And *Cresed* but a *Chawcers* ieast, and *Helen* but a bable.

1597. S., J. *The Northren Mothers Blessing. The way of Thrift, Written nine years before the death of* G. Chaucer. London, Printed by Robert Robinson for Robert Dexter, 1597. [in] Certaine Worthye Manuscript Poems of great Antiquitie Reserued long in the Studie of a Northfolke Gentleman. And now first published by J. S. Imprinted at London for R. D. 1597, sign. E 3. (Ed. H. H. Gibbs, Roxb. club, 1873, bound with *The historie of the most noble knight Plasidas,* p. 162 *a.*)

<small>[There is no allusion whatever to Chaucer in the text. In the B. M. copy, sign. E 2 *b,* there is written in a late 17th or early 18th century hand:—"G. Chaucer was born at Woodstock in Oxfordshire in ye 14th Century, died in 1440." Cf. *The Babees Book,* ed. F. J. Furnivall, E. E. T. soc., 1868, Forewords, pp. lxix–lxxi.]</small>

[**1597.**] **Unknown.** *The Returne from Parnassus.* [Part I.] MS. Rawlinson D 398, act iii, sc. 1 ; act iv, sc. 1. (The pilgrimage to Parnassus with . . . . the return from Parnassus, ed. W. D. Macray, Oxford, 1886, pp. 58, 62–3. For date *see* ibid., p. viii ; *see also* the 2nd part of this play under 1602, below, p. 171. The extracts are given from the modern edn.)

[Gullio wishes Ingenioso to make him verses, which he will himself polish and correct] . . . . make mee them in two or three divers vayns, in Chaucer's, Gower's, and Spencer's and Mr Shakspeare's. . . . .

[pp. 62–3.] [Ingenioso brings his verses] *Gull.* Lett mee heare Chaucer's vaine firste. I love antiquitie, if it be not harshe.

[Ingenioso recites three verses in close imitation of Chaucer's Troilus and Crisyde, bk. ii, ll. 967–73, 1026–27, 1091–2, 1037–43, ending with the lines

With asse's feet and headed like an ape

It cordeth not ; soe were it but a jape.

Gullio thereupon objects to the word *jape* :]

Ingen. Sir, the worde as Chaucer useth it hath noe unhonest meaninge in it, for it signifieth a jeste.

Gull. Tush! Chaucer is a foole, and you are another for defendinge of him.

Ingen. Then you shall heare Spencers veyne.

A gentle pen rides prickinge on the plaine

. . . .

Gull. Stay man! . . . . Let me heare Mr Shakspear's veyne.

Ingen. [Seven lines in imitation of Shakespeare's 'Venus and Adonis.']

Gull. . . . . Ey marry, Sir, these have some life in them! Let this duncified worlde esteeme of Spencer and Chaucer, I'le worshipp sweet Mr Shakspeare, and to honoure him will lay his Venus and Adonis under my pillowe.

[For an account of Chaucer influence on this play, as well as on part II, 1602, *see* Chaucer's Einfluss auf das englische Drama, by O. Ballman, Anglia, xxv, pp. 45-8.]

1597. Beaumont, Francis. *F. B. to his very louing friend T. S.* [Letter to Thomas Speght in] The Workes of . . . . Chaucer [ed. T. Speght], 1598, sign. [a iii *b*–a v].

[sign. a iii *b*] I am sorrie that neither the worthinesse of *Chaucers* owne praise, nor the importunate praiers of diuerse your louing friends can yet mooue you to put into print those good obseruations and collections you haue written of him. For as for the obiections, that in our priuate talke you are wont to say are commonly alledged against him, as first that many of his wordes (as it were with ouerlong lying) are growne too hard and vnpleasant, and next that hee is somewhat too broad in some of his speeches, and that the worke therefore should be the lesse gratious : these are no causes, or no sufficient causes to withhold from *Chaucer* such desert of glorie, as at your pleasure you may bestow vpon him. For first to defend him against the first reproofe. [Beaumont shows that no man can so write in the shifting language of every day,] as that all his wordes may remain currant many yeares. [This even happens among the Latin writers themselues, when Latin was a spoken tongue] . . . .

But yet so pure were *Chaucers* wordes in his owne daies, as *Lidgate* that learned man calleth him *The Loadstarre of the English language:* and so good they are in our daies, as Maister *Spencer* . . . hath adorned his owne stile with that beauty and grauitie, which *Tully* speakes of : [reviving ancient words] and his much frequenting of *Chaucers* antient speeches causeth many to allow farre better of him, then otherwise they would . . .

Touching the inciuilitie *Chaucer* is charged withall; What Romane Poet hath lesse offended this way than hee? [Virgil and Ovid are worse, Plautus and Terence are most to be excused, because they observed decorum] in giuing to their comicall persons such manner of speeches as did best fit their dispositions. And may not the same be saied for *Chaucer?* How much had hee swarued from Decorum, if hee had made his Miller, his Cooke, and his Carpenter, to haue told such honest and good tales, as hee made his Knight, his Squire, his Lawyer, and Scholler tell? . . . .

Chaucers deuise of his Canterburie Pilgrimage is meerely his owne, without following the example of any that euer writ before him. His drift is to touch all sortes of men, and to discouer all vices of that Age, and that he doth in such sort, as he neuer failes to hit euery marke he leuels at . . .

Chaucer [may] bee rightly called, The pith and sinewes of eloquence, and the verie life it selfe of all mirth and pleasant writing : besides one gifte hee hath aboue other Authours, and that is, by the excellencie of his descriptions to possesse his Readers with a stronger imagination of seeing that done before their eyes, which they reade, than any other that euer writ in any tongue. And here I cannot forget to remember vnto you those auncient learned men of our time in Cambridge, whose diligence in reading of his workes them selues, and commending them to others of the younger sorte, did first bring you and mee in loue with him : and one of them at that time was and now is (as you knowe) one of the rarest Schollers of the worlde. The same may bee saide of that worthy man for learning, your good friend in Oxford, who with many other of like excellent iudgement haue euer had *Chaucer* in most high reputation. . . .

From Leicester the last of Iune, Anno 1597.

Your assured and euer louing friend

Francis Beaumont.

[Francis Beaumont, judge, d. 1598, was the father of the dramatist ; he and Speght were both at Peterhouse between 1560–70 ; and he prided himself on being one of those who first urged Speght to edit Chaucer. "The rarest scholler" alluded to is possibly Abp. John Whitgift, who was during those years Fellow of Peterhouse, Master of Trinity College, Regius Professor of Divinity, etc. We have been unable to trace the identity of "your good friend in Oxford." This letter, somewhat expanded, appeared again in Speght's edn. of 1602, though Beaumont died in 1598. *See* below, 1683–4, pp. 256–7, where Aubrey quotes this letter.]

11

FRONTISPIECE (OPPOSITE TITLE-PAGE) TO SPEGHT'S CHAUCER. 1598

1598. The Workes of our Antient and lerned English Poet Geffrey Chaucer, newly printed. [ed. Thomas Speght. Blackletter.]   Londini, Impensis Geor. Bishop, anno 1598.

[Other title pages run, ' London Printed by Adam Islip, at the charges of Bonham Norton, Anno 1598'; or ' London Printed by Adam Islip at the charges of Thomas Wight, Anno 1598.' For second edition *see* below, p. 168.   Bishop's share was transferred to Adams, 14 March, 1610-11 (Arber, iii, 454).]

1598. Speght, Thomas. *The Workes of our Antient and lerned English Poet, Geffrey Chaucer, newly printed.* [*See* also App. A, 1598.]

[On title page]

In this Impression you shall find these Additions :

    1. His Portraiture and Progenie shewed.

    2. His Life collected.

    3. Arguments to euery Booke gathered. [For extracts, *see* App. A, 1598.]

    4. Old and obscure Words explaned.

    5. Authors by him cited, declared.

    6. Difficulties opened.

    7. Two Bookes of his neuer before printed.

Londini, Impensis Geor. Bishop : Anno 1598.

[Preliminary matter]

[Dedication] To . . . Sir Robert Cecil, sign. [a ij.]

To the Readers, sign. [a ii *b*, a iii.]

F. B. to his very louing friend T. S. sign. [a iii *b*–a v] [Francis Beaumont, *q. v.* above, under 1597, pp. 145-6.]

The Reader to Geffrey Chaucer, sign. [a v *b*] [signed H. B., *see* below, pp. 148-9.]

[Portrait of Chaucer after Occleve], sign. [a vi.]

The Life of our learned English Poet, Geffray Chaucer, sign. b i–c iii *b*.

Arguments to euery Tale and Booke, sign. c iii–c vi *b*.   [For some extracts from these, *see* below, Appendix A, 1598.]

The Epistle of William Thinne to King Henry the eight, sign. ¶ i–¶ ii.

A Table of all the names of the workes, contained in this volume, sign. A ii *b*–A iii *b*.

[At end of volume]

The old and obscure words of Chaucer explaned, sign. Aaaa i–Bbbb ii.

The French in Chaucer translated, sign. Bbbb i *b*–Bbbb ii.

Most of the Authours cited by G. Chaucer in his workes, by name declared, sign. Bbbb ii and *b*.

Corrections of some faults and Annotations vpon some places, sign. Bbbb iij–vij *b*.

[*See* note under 1532, Thynne, above, p. 78, also under 1597, Beaumont, pp. 145–6. For a complete reprint of Speght's Life of Chaucer, *see* Chaucer, a bibliographical manual, by E. P. Hammond, N. York, 1908, pp. 19–35.]

[sign. **a** ii *b*–a iii]   To the Readers.

Some few yeers past, I was requested by certaine Gentlemen my neere friends, who loued *Chaucer*, as he well deserueth ; to take a little pains in reuiuing the memorie of so rare a man, as also in doing some reparations on his works, which they iudged to be much decaied by iniurie of time, ignorance of writers, and negligence of Printers. For whose sakes thus much was then by me undertaken, although neuer as yet fully fiñished. [Speght gives a list of the work he has done, much the same as on title page]. As that little which then was done, was done for those priuat friends, so was it neuer my mind that it should be published. But so it fell out of late, that *Chaucers* Works being in the Presse, and three parts thereof alreadie printed, not only these friends did by their Letters sollicit me, but certaine also of the best in the Companie of Stationers hearing of these Collections, came vnto me, and for better or worse, would have something done in this Impression. [Speght then apologises for the faultiness of his additional matter, on the score of its not having been originally intended for publication, and also because he was hurried over it.] . . . . I earnestly entreat al to accept these my endeuours in best part, as wel in regard of mine owne well meaning, as for the desert of oure English Poet himselfe : who in most vnlearned times and greatest ignorance, being much esteemed, cannot in these our daies, wherein Learning and riper iudgement so much flourisheth, but be had in great reuerence, vnlesse it bee of such as for want of wit and learning, were neuer yet able to iudge what wit or Learning meaneth . . . . .

1598. B. H. *The Reader to Geffrey Chaucer.* A short poem in praise of the editor, in Speght's first edn. of Chaucer's works, signed H. B., sign. [a v *b*].

The Reader to Geffrey Chaucer.
Rea[der]

Where hast thow dwelt, good Geffrey, al this while
Unknowne to vs, saue only by thy bookes ?

Chau[cer]

> In haulks and hernes, God wot, and in exile,
> Where none vouchsaf't to yeeld me words or lookes,
> Till one which saw me there, and knew my friends,
> Did bring me forth; such grace sometime God sends.

Rea.

> But who is he that hath thy Books repar'd,
> And added moe, whereby thow art more graced?

Chau.

> The selfe same man who hath no labor spar'd,
> To helpe what time and writers had defaced:
> And made old words, which were vnknown of many
> So plaine, that now they may be known of any.

Rea.

> Well fare his heart: I loue him for thy sake,
> Who for thy sake hath taken all this pains.

Chau.

> Would God I knew some means amends to make,
> That for his toile he might receiue some gains.
> But wot ye what? I knowe his kindnesse such,
> That for my good he thinks no pains too much:
> And more than that; if he had knowne in time,
> He would haue left no fault in prose nor rime.

H. B.

1598. Thynne, Francis. *Animadversions uppon the annotaciouns and corrections of some imperfections of impressiones of Chaucer's Workes . . . 1598,* sett downe by F. Thynne. MS. in the Bridgewater Library. (Ed. F. J. Furnivall, Chaucer soc., 1875 and 1891, pp. 4–75.)

To Master Thomas Speighte
ffrancis Thynn sendethe
greetinge

The Industrye and loue (master Speighte) whiche yo^u haue vsed, and beare, vppon and to oure famous poete Geffrye Chaucer, deseruethe bothe comendati*o*ne and furtherance: the one to recompense yo*u*r trauayle, the other to accomplyshe the duetye, whiche we all beare (or at the leaste, yf we reuerence lernynge or regarde the honor of oure Countrye, sholde beare) to suche a singuler ornamente of oure tonge as the woorkes of Chaucer are: Yet since there is nothinge so fullye perfected, by anye one, whereine som*m*e imp*er*fecti*o*ne maye not bee

founde, (for as the prouerbe is, ' Barnardus,' or as others have,
' Alanus, non videt omnia,') yo^u must be contented to gyue me
leave, in discharge of the duetye and loue which I beare to
Chaucer, (whome I suppose I have as great intereste to adorne
withe my smale skyll as anye other hath, in regarde that the
laborious care of my father made hym most acceptable to the
worlde in correctinge and augmentinge his woorkes,) to enter
into the examinat*i*one of this newe edit*i*one, and that the
[p. 5] rather, because yo^u, with Horace his verse " si quid nouisti
rectius istis, candidus imparti," have willed all others to
further the same, and to accepte yo*ur* labors in good p*ar*te,
whiche, as I most willingly doo, so meanynge but we₦ to the
worke, I ame to lett yo^u vnderstande my conceyte thereof,
whiche before this, yf yo^u woulde have vouchesafed my howse,
or have thoughte me worthy to have byn acqueynted with
these matters (whiche yo^u might we₦ haue donne w*i*thout anye
whatsoeuer dispargement [*sic*] to yo*ur* selfe,) yo^u sholde haue
vnderstoode before the impressione, althoughe this whiche I
here write ys not nowe vppon selfe wi₦ or fonnd conceyte to
wrangle for one asses shadowe, or to seke a knott in a rushe,
but in frendlye sorte to bringe truthe to lighte, a thinge whiche
I wolde desire others to vse towardes mee in whatsoeuer shall
fall oute of my penne.   Wherefore I will here shewe suche
thinges as, in mye opynione, may seme to be touched, not
medlinge withe the seconde editione to one inferior personne
[John Stowe's, 156], above, p. 96] then my fathers editione was.

Fyrste in yo*ur* forespeche to the reader, yo^u saye ' secondly, the texte by written copies corrected ' by whiche worde
' corrected,' I maye seme to gather, that yo^u imagine greate
imperfect*i*one in my fathers editione, whiche peraduenture
maye move others to saye (as some vnadvisedlye have sayed)
that my father had wronged Chaucer :) Wherefore, to stoppe
that gappe, I will answere, that Chaucers woorkes have byn
sithens printed twy*c*e, yf not thrice, and therfore by oure care-
[p. 6] lesse (and for the most p*ar*te vnlerned) printers of Englande,
not so we₦ performed as yt ought to bee : so that, of
necessytye, bothe in matter, myter, and meaninge, yt must
needes gather corrupt*i*one, passinge throughe so manye handes,
as the water dothe, the further it ru*n*nethe from the pure
founteyne.   To enduce me and all others to iudge his edit*i*one
(whiche I thinke yo^u neuer sawe wholye to-gether, beinge fyrst
printed but in one coolume [*sic*] in a page, whereof I will speake

hereafter) was the perfectest : ys the ernest desire and loue
my father hadde to haue Chaucers Woorkes rightlye to
be published. for the performance wherof, my father not onlye
vsed the helpe of that lerned and eloquent kn[i]ghte and anti-
quarye Sir Briane Tuke, but had also made greate serche for
copies to perfecte his woorkes, as apperethe in the ende of the
squiers tale, in his editione printed in the yere 1542 ; but
further had comissione to serche all the liberaries of Englande
for Chaucers Work*es*, so that oute of all the Abbies of this
Realme (whiche reserued anye monumentes thereof) he was
fully furnished with multitude of Bookes. emongest whiche,
one coppye of some part of his woorkes came to his handes
subscribed in diuers places withe " examinatur Chaucer."   By
this Booke, and conferringe manye of the other written copies
to-gether, he deliuered his editione, fullye corrected, as the
amendementes vnder his hande, in the fyrst printed booke that
euer was of his woorkes (beinge stamped by the fyrste impres-
[p. 7] sione that was in England) will well declare, at what tyme he
added manye things whiche were not before printed, as yo[u]
nowe haue donne soome, of whiche I am perswaded (and that
not withoute reasone) the originall came from mee. In whiche
his editione, beinge printed but with one coolume in a syde,
there was the pilgrymes tale, a thinge moore odious to the
[p. 8] Clergye, then the speche of the plowmanne ; that pilgrimes
tale begynnynge in this sorte :

> In Lincolneshyre fast by a fenne,
> Standes a relligious howse who dothe
> yt kenne, &c.[1]

[p. 9] In this tale did Chaucer [that is, the unknown author] most
bitterlye enueye against the pride, state, couetousnes, and
extorcione of the Bysshoppes, their officialls, Archdeacons,
vicars generalls, comissaryes, and other officers of the spirituall
courte. The Inuentione and order whereof (as I haue herde yt
related by some, nowe of good worshippe bothe in courte and
countrye, but then my fathers clerkes,) was, that one comynge
into this relligious howse, walked vpp and doune the churche,
beholdinge goodlye pictures of Bishoppes in the windowes, at
lengthe the manne contynuynge in that contemplatione, not
knowinge what Bishoppes they were, a graue olde manne withe

---

[1] This appears in The Newe Courte of Venus, *see* above, p. 82 [1536–40 ?],
The Pilgrim's Tale.

a longe white hedde and berde, in a large blacke garment girded
vnto hym, came forthe and asked hym, what he iudged
of those pictures in the windowes, who sayed he knewe not
what to make of them, but that they looked lyke vnto our
mitred Bishoppes; to whome the old father replied, "yt
is true, they are lyke, but not the same, for our byshoppes are
farr degenerate from them," and withe that, made a large
discourse of the Bishopps and of their courtes.

This tale, when kinge henrye the eighte had redde, he called
my father unto hym, sayinge, "William Thynne! I dobte this
wiH not be allowed; for I suspecte the Byshoppes wiH call
[p. 10] the in questione for yt". to whome my father, beinge in great
fauore with his prince, (as manye yet lyuinge canne testyfye,)
sayed, "yf y*our* grace be not offended, I hoope to be protected
by yo^u : " wherevppon the kinge bydd hym goo his waye, and
feare not. AH whiche not withstandinge, my father was
called in questi*o*ne by the Byshoppes, and heaued at by
CardinaH Wolseye, his olde enymye, for manye causes, but
mostly for that my father had furthered Skelton to publishe
his 'Collen Cloute' againste the CardinaH, the moste p*ar*te of
whiche Booke was compiled in my fathers howse at Erithe in
Kente.   But for all my fathers frendes, the Cardinalls p*er*-
swadinge auctorytye was so greate withe the kinge, that thoughe
by the kinges fauor my father escaped bodelye daunger, yet
the CardinaH caused the kinge so muche to myslyke of that
tale, that chaucer must be newe printed, and that discourse of
the pilgrymes tale lefte oute [with regard to this supposed
cancelled edn. by Wm. Thynne, *see* note by Mr. Bradshaw in
Thynne's Animadversions, ed. Furnivall, pp. 75-6]; and so
beinge printed agayne, some thynges were forsed to be
omitted, and the plowmans tale (supposed, but vntrulye, to be
made by olde Sir Thomas Wyat, father to hym which was
executed in the firste yere of Quene Marye, and not by Chaucer)
w*i*th much ado p*er*mitted to passe with the reste, in suche
sorte that in one open parliamente (as I haue herde S*i*r JoHne
Thynne reporte, beinge then a member of the howse,) when
talke was had of Bookes to be forbidden, Chaucer had there
for euer byn condempned, had yt not byn that his woorkes had
byn counted but fables.   Whereunto yf yo^u will replye, that
[p. 11] their colde not be any suche pilgrymes tale, because Chaucer in
his prologues makethe not mentione of anye suche personne,
which he wolde haue donne yf yt had byn so : for after that

he had recyted the knighte, the squyer, the squiers yeomane, the prioresse, her noonne, and her thre preistes, the monke, the fryer, the marchant, the Clerke of Oxenforde, seriante at the lawe, franckleyne, haberdassher, goldsmythe, webbe, dyer and tapyster, Cooke, shypmane, doctor of physicke, wyfe of Bathe, parsonne and plowmane, he sayethe at the ende of the plow-mans prologe,

> There was also a Reue, and a millere,
> A Sumpnoure, and a Pardoner,
> A manciple, and myselfe ; there was no mo.

All whiche make xxx persons with Chaucer : Wherefore yf there had byn anye moore, he wolde also haue recyted them in those verses : whereunto I answere, that in the prologes he lefte oute somme of those whiche tolde their tales : as the chanons yomane, because he came after that they were passed out of theyre Inne, and did ouer-take them, as in lyke sorte this pilgrime did or mighte doo, and so afterwardes be one of their companye, as was that chanons yeomane, althoughe Chaucer talke no moore of this pilgrime in his prologe then he doothe of the Chanons yeomane : whiche I dobt not wolde fullye appere, yf the pilgrimes prologe and tale mighte be restored to his former light, they being nowe looste, as manye other of Chaucers tales were before that, as I ame induced to thinke by manye reasons.

But to leave this, I must saye that in those many written Bookes of Chaucer, whiche came to my fathers handes there were manye false copyes, whiche Chaucer shewethe in writinge of Adam Scriuener (as you haue noted) : of whiche written [p. 12] copies there came to me after my fathers deathe some fyue and twentye, whereof some had moore, and some fewer, tales, and some but two, and some three. whiche bookes beinge by me (as one nothinge dobting of this whiche ys nowe donne for Chaucer) partly dispersed aboute xxvj yeres a-goo and partlye stoolen oute of my howse at Popler : I gaue diuers of them to Stephen Batemanne, person of Newington, and to diuers other, whiche beinge copies vnperfecte, and some of them corrected by my fathers hande, yt maye happen soome of them to coome to somme of your frendes handes ; whiche I knowe yf I see agayne : and yf by anye suche written copies you have corrected Chaucer, you maye as well offende as seme to do good.   But I judge the beste, for in dobtes I will not resolue with a settled

iudgeme*n*te althoughe yo^u may iudge this tediouse discourse of
my father a needlesse thinge in setting forthe his diligence in
breaking the yce, and gyuinge lighte to others, who may moore
easeyly p*er*fecte then begyne any thinge, for "facilius est
addere qua*m* Inuenire " : and so to other matters.

[Next Thynne details 15 mistakes made by Speght, of which
the following directly concern Chaucer, viz :—

[pp. 12–13] (1) He states that Richard Chaucer (the poet's grandfather)
was his father.

[pp. 14–15] (2) He says Heralds think Chaucer came of a mean house,
because his armes are mean.—This " ys a slender coniecture ".

[p. 17] (4) He conjectures (from merchants' arms in windows) that
Chaucer's ancestors were merchants.—This has no validity.

[pp. 18–19] (5) He misquotes Gower ; who does not call Chaucer " a
worthye poet " nor " dothe he make hym iudge of his
Workes ". But on the contrary Chaucer submits his works to
Gower in Troilus, book v. This error is Bales' and " yo^u have
swallowed yt ".

[pp. 21–2] (7) He assumes that because in the Temple Records it
is noted that Chaucer beat a Franciscan Friar, that therefore
Gower belonged to the Temple as well as Chaucer ; whereas
Thynne doubts whether Chaucer ever belonged to the Temple.

[p. 22] (8) He says he does not know the name of Chaucer's wife.
Nor does Thynne ; for though some think it was Elizabeth,
a waiting woman to Queen Philippa, who had a grant of
a yearly stipend, he believes this was Chaucer's sister or kins-
woman, who became a nun at S. Helen's, London.

[pp. 27–30] Thynne then details mistakes made by Speght as to the
' Roman de la Rose ' and Chaucer's ' Dreme ' or ' Dethe of
Blaunche the Duchesse '.

[pp. 31–68] He then shows mistakes Speght has made in explaining
Chaucer's old words, and in annotations on, and corrections
of the text of Chaucer.—He then points out six more
mistakes :—

[pp. 68–9] (1) That Speght has wrongly placed the ' Plowman's Tale '
(before the Parson's Tale). Thynne's father put it after the
Parson's Tale (which by Chaucer's own words was the last tale)
because he could not see by any prologues of the other tales
where else to place it. But it ought to " be sett in some other
place before the manciple and persons tale, and not as yt ys in
the last editi*o*ne."]

(2) One other thinge ys, that yt wolde be good that

Chaucer's proper woorkes were distinguyshed from the adulterat, and suche as were not his, as the Testamente of Cressyde, The Letter of Cupide, and the ballade begynnynge 'I haue a layde, where so she bee' &c., whiche Chaucer never composed, as may suffycientlye be proued by the thing*es* them selues.

(3) The thirde matter ys, that in youre epistle dedicatorye [p. 70] to *Sir* Roberte Cecille, yo^u saye, "This Booke, whene yt was first published in printe, was dedicate to Kinge Henrye the eighte". But that is not soo, for the firste dedicatione to that kinge was by mye father, when diuerse of Chaucers woorkes [p. 71] had byn thrise printed before ; whereof two editions were by Willi*a*m Caxtone, the fyrste printer of Englande, who first printed Chaucers tales in one colume in a ragged letter, and after in one colume in a better order ; and the thirde editione was printed, as farre as I remember, by winkine de word or Richarde Pynson, the seconde and thirde printers of Eng-lande, as I take them. Whiche three edit[i]ons beinge verye imperfecte and corrupte, occasioned my father (for the love he oughte to Chawcers lernynge) to seeke the augmente and correcti*o*ne of Chawcer's Woork*es*, w*h*iche he happely fynyshed ; the same beinge, since that tyme, by often printinge muche corrupted. . . .

[Francis Thynne makes two mistakes here. (1) Speght was alluding to the collected edn. of Chaucer's 'Workes' first made by William Thynne, which was the basis of his own edn. Wm. Thynne's dedication is reprinted in all the old editions, 1542 (1550), 1561, 1598, 1602, 1687 and 1721.
(2) Only one edn. of Chaucer's *Works* had been published before the date of Thynne's 1532, and that was Pynson's [*see* note under 1582, Thynne, p. 78]. But many separate works of Chaucer had been published before 1532.]

(4) [Speght, in his catalogue of authors, has omitted many authors ' vouched by chawcer '.

(5) & (6) Speght misreads 'Haroltes' for 'Harlottes'; and [p. 74] 'Minoresse' for 'Moueresse,' both in the 'Romaunt of the Rose']. Thus hoopinge that yo^u wi̵l̵l̵ accepte in good and frendlye [p. 75] parte, these my whatsoeuer conceytes vttered vnto yo^u, (to the ende Chawcer's Woorkes by muche conference and manye iudgments mighte at leng[t]he obteyne their true p*er*fecti*o*ne and glorye,——as I truste they shall yf yt please godde to lende me tyme and leysure to reprinte, correcte, and comente the same, after the manner of the Italians, who haue largelye comented Petrarche ;)—I sett ends to these matt*er*s : comyt-tinge yo^u to god, and me to yo*u*r Curtesye. Clerkenwell Greene, the xvi of december, 1599. Yo*u*r louinge frende,

FRANCIS THYNNE.

1598. Barnfield, Richard. *Poems: In diuers humors.* London. Printed by G. S. for Iohn Iaggard, and are to be solde at his shoppe neere Temple-barre, at the Signe of the Hand and starre, 1598, sign. E 2. Sonnet ii, Against the Dispraysers of Poetrie. (Illustrations of Old English Literature, 1866, ed. J. P. Collier, vol. i, pp. 43–4. *Also* Complete poems of Richard Barnfield, ed. A. B. Grosart, Roxb. club, 1876, p. 189 ; English Scholar's library, No. 14, ed. E. Arber, p. 119.)

> *Chaucer* is dead ; and *Gower* lyes in grave !
> The Earle of *Surrey*, long agoe is gone !
> Sir *Philip Sidneis* soule, the Heauens haue !
> *George Gascoigne* him beforne was tomb'd in stone !
> Yet, tho' their Bodies lye full low in ground,
> (As every thing must dye, that earst was borne)
> Their liuing fame no Fortune can confound ;
> Nor euer shall their labours be forlorne.
> And you, that discommend sweet Poetrie
> (So that the Subject of the same be good,)
> Here may you see your fond simplicitie !
> Sith Kings have fauord it, of royall Blood.
> The King of *Scots* (now liuing), is a Poet ;
> As his *Lepanto* and his *Furies* shoe it !

[These poems are the last of four pamphlets in verse bound and issued together in 1598 ; the title of the first being *The Encomion of Lady Pecunia.* This reference is not in the edn. of 1605.]

1598. Chapman, George. *To the vnderstander,* an address prefixed to *Achilles Shield, translated as the other seuen Bookes of Homer out of his eighteenth booke of Iliades by George Chapman Gent,* sign. B. 2. (Elizabethan critical essays, ed. G. Gregory Smith, 1904, vol. ii, p. 305.)

All tongues haue inricht themselues from their originall . . . with good neighbourly borrowing . . . & why may not ours.

Chaucer (by whom we will needes authorise our true english), had more newe wordes for his time then any man needes to deuise now.

1598. Dallington, Sir Robert. *A Method for Trauell, Shewed by taking the View of France, As it stoode in the yeare of our Lord* 1598. London, printed by Thomas Creede [1606 ?] ? sign. V 4. (The only modern edn. is a French translation, "View of Fraunce," traduit par E. Emérique, 1892, pp. 188–9.)

And as wee may say of our *English*, that it very much Lu Regius differeth from that of *Chaucers* time : so with *Lu* [Louis le Roy] Regius of the French tongue, that within these fiftie yeeres, it is almost growen a new language, and which still

like the French apparell euery yeere altered . . . . But if you
demand the best Authours, for the language it selfe, I thinke,
as *Tuscaine* hath a *Duute* [*sic*] and a *Petrarch*, *Greece* an
Isocrates and a *Demosthenes*, *Rome* a *Cicero* and a *Cæsar*,
we a *Sydney* and a *Chaucer:* so France hath a *Bertas* and a
Romsart [*sic*], in this Kinde most recommendable.

1598. Guilpin, Edward. *Skialetheia, or A shadowe of Truth, in certaine*
Epigrams and Satyres. Satire vi, sign. E i. (Occasional issues of
unique or very rare books, ed. A. B. Grosart, 1878, vol. vi,
Skialetheia, p. 63.)

> . . . . . For in these our times
> Some of Opinions gulls carpe at the riemes
> Of reuerend *Chawcer:* other-some do praise them,
> And vnto heau'n with wonders wings do raise them.
> Some say the mark is out of *Gowers* mouth,
> Others, he's better then a trick of youth.

1598. Hakluyt, Richard. *The Principal Nauigations Voiages Traffiques*
and Discoueries of the English Nation . . . [second edn.] 1598,
vol. i, Preface to the Reader, sign. ** b, A Catalogue of the
Ambassages, sign. ** 4 b, p. 124 (published, MacLehose, Glasgow,
1903, etc., vol. i, pp. liv, 307–8).

[sign. **b] And lastly, our old English father *Ennius*, I meane, the
learned, wittie, and profound *Geoffrey Chaucer*, under the person of his Knight, doeth full iudicially and like a cunning
Cosmographer, make report of the long voiages and woorthy
exploits of our English Nobles, Knights, & Gentlemen, to the
Northern, and to other partes of the world in his dayes.

. . . .

[sign. ** 4b] ¶ The Ambassages, Treatises, Priueledges, Letters, and other
obseruations, depending upon the Voyages of this First Volume.

. . . .

10. Certaine verses of *Geffrey Chaucer*, Concerning the long
Voyages, and valiant exploits of the *English* Knights in his
dayes.   pag. 124.

[At the end of the voyage of Thomas of Woodstocke, Duke
of Gloucester, into Prussia in the yeere 1391].

[p. 124] The verses of Geofrey Chaucer in the Knights Prologues
who *liuing in the yeere* 1402. (*as hee writeth himselfe in his*
Epistle of Cupide) shewed that the English Knights after the
losse of Acon, were wont in his time to trauaile into Prussia
and Lettowe, and other heathen lands, to advance the

Christian faith against Infidels and miscreants, and to seeke honoure by feats of armes.

The English Knights Prologue.

A Knight there was, and that a worthie man, [Hakluyt quotes (in black letter) to 'ayenst another Heathen in Turkie']

The time when Chaucer wrote, is thus mentioned in the end of his letter of Cupide.

Written in the lustie moneth of May
in our Palace, where many a million
of louers true have habitation,
The yeere of grace ioyfull and iocond,
a thousand, foure hundred and second.

[None of these references are in the first edition of 1589.]

1598. [**Hall,** Joseph (Bishop of Norwich).] *Virgidemiarum The Three last Bookes. Of byting Satyres.* Imprinted at London by Richard Bradocke for Robert Dexter, 1598. Lib. 4, Satyre 4, sign. D 1 *b*; Lib. 5, Satyre 2, sign. E 7. [Copy in B. M. is bound with] Virgidemiarum sixe Bookes. First three Bookes of Toothless Satyrs.— London. Printed by Thomas Creede for Robert Dexter, 1597. [The title-page of the 1598 edn. faces sign. F 3 *b*.] (Satires by Joseph Hall with the Illustrations of the late Thomas Warton and Additional Notes by Samuel Weller Singer, 1824, pp. 101, 132.

[sign. D 1]

Till now he waxt a toothlesse Bacheler
He thaw's like Chaucers frosty Ianiuere ;
And sets a Months minde vpon smyling *May*

·   ·   ·   ·   ·   ·   ·

[sign. E 7]

Certes, if *Pity* died at *Chaucers* date,
He liu'd a widdower long behind his mate.

[A reference to the sepulchre of Pity in the *Court of Love* (not by Chaucer), l. 701.]

1598. Marston, John, [*pseud.* W. Kinsayder]. *The Scourge of Villanie, Three Bookes of Satyres.* At London Printed by I. R. and are to be sold by John Buzbie, sign. B 4 and *b*. (The Works of John Marston, ed. J. O. Halliwell, 1856, vol. iii, p. 246.)

To those that seem iudiciall perusers.

Know I hate to affect too much obscuritie, & harshnes, because they profit no sense . . . *Perseus* is crabby, because antient, & his ierkes (being perticulerly giuen to priuate customes of his time) duskie, *Iuuenal* (vpon the like occasion) seemes to our iudgement, gloomie. Yet both of them goe a good seemely pace, not stumbling, shuffling. *Chaucer* is harde euen to our vnderstandings ; who knows not the reason ? Howe much more those old Satyres which expresse themselues in termes, that breathed not long euen in their daies.

[For further traces of Chaucer influence on Marston, *see* Chaucer's Einfluss auf das englische Drama, by O. Ballman, Anglia, xxv, pp. 77–8.]

1598. Meres, Francis. *A Comparatiue discourse of our English Poets,
with the Greeke, Latine, and Italian Poets.* [In] *Palladis Tamia.
Wits Treasvry, Being the second part of Wits Commonwealth,* p. 279.
(English Garner, ed. E. Arber, 1879, vol. ii, p. 94. Elizabethan
critical essays, ed. G. Gregory Smith, 1904, vol. ii, p. 314.)

As *Greece* had three Poets of great antiquity, *Orpheus, Linus*
and *Musæus;* and *Italy,* other three auncient Poets *Liuius
Andronicus, Ennius* and *Plautus:* so hath *England* three
auncient Poets, *Chaucer, Gower* and *Lydgate.*

As *Homer* is reputed the Prince of Greek Poets; and
Petrarch of Italian Poets: so *Chaucer* is accounted the God
of English Poets.

1598. Stowe, John. *A Suruay of London,* 1598, pp. 107, 192, 198,
338–9 [wrongly printed 238], 383 (ed. C. L. Kingsford, Oxford,
1908, vol. i, pp. 143, 241, 253, vol. ii, pp. 62, 110–11.)

[p. 107] Ealdegate Ward [speaking of the shaft set up before
St. Andrew Undershaft] Geffrey Chawcer, writing of a vaine
boaster, hath these wordes, meaning of the said shaft:

Chaucer,
chance
of Dice.

    Right well aloft and high ye beare your heade

.   .   .   .

    That all the streete may heare your body cloke.

.   .   .   .

Chaucer,
fol. 334,
335.

[p. 192] [Stowe quotes 1st stanza of H. Scogan's moral ballad,
then says] Then follow of verse 23 staues, containing a
persuasion from losing of time, follily in lust, & vice, but to
spend the same in vertue and in godlines, as ye may reade in
Geffrey Chawcer his works lately printed.

.   .   .   .

Chaucer,
fol. 334,
335.

[p. 198] *Richarde Chawcer* Vintner gaue lands to that church
[Aldmary], & was there buried 1348. Richard Chaucer father
to Geffrey Chaucer the poet, as may be supposed.

.   .   .   .

[pp. 338–9] For the Inne of the Tabard *Geffrey Chaucer*
Esquire, the most famous Poet of England, in commendation
thereof, in the raigne of E. the 3 writeth thus [Stowe quotes
ll. 19–29 Prologue Cant. Tales].

[p. 383]   The Citie of Westminster.

Geffrey Chaucer the
famous poet of Eng-
land.

. . . . *Geffrey Chaucer* the most famous Poet of
England, also in the Cloyster [of the Abbey],
1400, but since *Nicholas Brigham* Gentleman, raysed a Monument for him in the South crosse Ile of the Church; his
workes were partly published in print by *William Caxton* in

the raigne of *Henry* the sixt : Increased by *William Thinne*
Esquire, in the raigne of *Henry* the eight : Corrected and twice
increased through mine oune painefull labours, in the raigne of
Queene *Elizabeth*, to wit in the yeare 1561, and again beautified
with noates, by me collected out of diuers Recordes and Monumentes, which I deliuered to my louing friende *Thomas Speight*,
and he hauing drawne the same into a good forme and methode,
as also explained the old and obscure wordes, etc., hath
published them in *Anno* 1597.

[The poem here called *Chance of dice*, a MS. of which is in the Bodleian (MS.
Fairfax 16), is anonymous, it is certainly not by Chaucer. *See* above, *c*. 1440, p. 44.]

[**1598–1600.**] **Harvey**, Gabriel. *MS. notes* in his copy of Speght's
Chaucer. *See* below, App. A [1598–1600].

1599. **Daniel**, Sam[uel]. *Musophilus : Containing a generall defence of
learning.* Separate title-page and pagination, but part of the
Poeticall Essayes of Sam. Danyel. Newly corrected and augmented
. . . . 1599, sign. B 3. (Daniel's Complete Works, ed. A. B.
Grosart, 1885–96, vol. i, p. 230.)

But yet in all this interchange of all,
    Virtue we see, with her faire grace, stands fast ;
For what hy races hath there come to fall,
    With low disgrace, quite vanished and past,
Since *Chaucer* liu'd who yet liues and yet shall,
    Though (which I grieue to say) but in his last.

Yet what a time hath he wrested from time,
    And won vpon the mighty waste of daies,
Vnto th' immortall honor of our clime,
    That by his meanes came first adorn'd with Baies,
Vnto the sacred Relicks of whose rime
    We yet are bound in zeale to offer praise ?

And could our liues begotten in this age
    Obtaine but such a blessed hand of yeeres,
And scape the fury of that threatning rage,
    Which in confused clowdes gastly appeares.
Who would not straine his trauailes to ingage,
    When such true glory should succeed his cares ?

But whereas he came planted in the spring,
    And had the Sun, before him, of respect ;
We set in th' autumne, in the withering,
    And sullen season of a cold defect.

[Musophilus was probably also issued separately in 1599, before being bound up
with Poeticall Essayes ; this was a common practice of Daniel's.

1599. Nashe, Thomas.   *Nashes Lenten Stuffe* . . . . sign. D 4, p.23.
(Works of Thomas Nashe, ed. R. B. McKerrow, 1904-5, vol.iii, 1905,
p. 176.)

The prayse of the red Herring.

. . . . had I my topickes by me in stead of my learned
counsell to assist me, I might haps marshall my termes in
better aray, and bestow such costly coquery on this *Marine
magnifico* as you would preferre him before tart and galingale,
which *Chaucer* preheminentest encomionizeth aboue all
iunquetries or confectionaries whatsoeuer.

[1599 ?] Shakespeare, William.   *The Merry Wives of Windsor*, I, iii,
80-1.

> *Pist.* Shall I Sir Pandarus of Troy become,
> And by my side wear steel?

[It is probable that this allusion is to Chaucer's Troilus. For the whole question of
Chaucer references in Shakespeare, *see* below, App. A, 1589, Shakespeare.]

1599. Spenser, Edmund.   *A View of the Present State of Ireland.*
MSS. B. M.. Cambridge, Dublin, etc. (Works of Spenser, ed. A. B.
Grosart, 1882-4, vol. ix, pp. 112, 233.   Spenser's Works, Globe edn.,
ed. R. Morris, 1869, pp. 639, col. 2, and 676, col. 2.)

[p. 639]   *Irenæus.* All these that I have rehearsed unto you, be not
Irish garments, but English ; for the quilted leather Jacke is
old English ; for it was the proper weede of the horseman, as
ye may reade in Chaucer, where he describeth Sir Thopas his
apparrell and armoure, when he went to fight agaynst the
Gyant, in his robe of shecklaton, which shecklaton is that kind
of guilded leather with which they use to embroder theyr Irish
jackes.   And there likewise by all that description ye may see
the very fashion and manner of the Irish horseman most lively
set foorth, his long hose, his shooes of costly cordewayne,
his hacqueton, and his habberjon, with all the rest therto
belonging.

.   .   .   .

[p. 676] For Borh in old Saxon signifyeth a pledge or suretye, and yet
it is soe used with us in some speaches, as Chaucer sayeth,
St. John to *borrowe*, that is for assurance and warrantye.

[Squire's Tale, l. 596.]

1600. [Bodenham, John.]   *Bel-vedére or The Garden of the Muses.*
The Conclusion, p. 235. (Bodenham's Belvedere, reprinted for
Spenser soc., 1875, pp. 235-6.)

In this first Impression, are omitted the Sentences of
Chaucer, Gower, Lidgate and other auncient Poets, because it
CHAUCER CRITICISM.

was not knowne how their forme would agree with these of
ten syllables onely, and that sometime they exceed the compasse herein obserued, hauing none but lineall and couplet
sentences, aboue and beyond which course, the Gentleman who
was the cause of this collection (taking therin no meane
paines him-selfe, besides his friends labour) could not be perswaded, but determinately aimed at this obseruation. Neuerthelesse, if this may enioy but the fauour hee hopes it will,
and the good intent thereof be no way misconstrued : at the
next impression it shall be largely supplyed, with things that
[p. 236] at this present could not be obtained . . . .

[This is a collection of single 10-syllable lines or couplets from a number of poets,
arranged under various subject headings, such as Hope, War, Learning, Life, Death,
&c. A list of the poets from whom they were taken is given in the Address to the
Reader.]

1600. [Breton, Nicholas.] *Pasquils Fooles-cappe*, v. 53. [Unique copy
in the Bodl. library, sign. C 3 *b*.] (Breton's Works, ed. A. B.
Grosart, 1879, vol. i ; Pasquil's Fooles-Cappe, p. 22.)

Shee that   .   .   .   .   .

.   .   .   .   .   .

. . ready is to breake a *Chaucers* ieast.

1600. Butler, Charles (Vicar of Wotton). *Rhetoricæ Libri Duo. Quorum
Prior de Tropis & Figuris, Posterior de Voce & Gestu præcipit : in
vsum scholarum accuratius jam quartò editi.* Oxoniae, 1618, lib. i,
cap. 13, sign. C 5. (The dedication is dated March 1600.)

[Text] Rhythmi genera partim syllabarum suarum numero,
partim variâ sonorum resonantium dispositione distingui
possunt : sed ea (⁴) optimorum poetarum observatio optimè
docebit.

[Note] (⁴) Quales sunt apud nos Homero, Maroni, Ovidio,
cæterisque melioris notæ priscis æquiparandi, D. PHILIPPVS
SIDNEY, EDMVNDVS SPENCER, SAMVEL DANIEL, MICHAEL DRAY-
TON, JOSVAH SYLVESTER, GEORGIVS WITHER, aliique ingenio &
arte florentes, quorum hæc ætas vberrima est : atque inprimis
horum omnium magister, vnicum caligantis sui seculi lumen,
D. GALFRIDVS CHAVCER.

[This 4th edn. of 1618 is the first in B.M. Edn. 1 is of 1600. In the next edition,
London, 1629, the Chaucer reference—sign. E 3 and *b*—is identical.]

1600. Camden, William. *Britannia* [5th edition]. Trinobantes, p.
379. (Trans., ed., and enlarged by Richard Gough, 1789, vol. ii,
p. 8.)

[p. 377
wrongly
paged 277]　Contumulantur in hoc templo (Westminster Abbey)
.   .   .   .

. . . quique minimè tacendus Poëtarum Anglorum princeps Galfredus Chaucer ; & qui ad illum ingenij fælicitate, & diuite Poëseos vena proximè inter Anglicos poëtas accessit Edm. Spencerus.

[This reference first appeared in the 5th edn. of 1600. For reference in the 1st edn. *see* above, under 1586, p. 128. The 6th and last edn., 1607, corrected by the author, contains both references on pp. 266 and 310.]

1600. [**Camden,** William.] *Reges, Reginae, Nobiles, & alij in Ecclesia Collegiata B. Petri Westmonasterij sepulti.* . . . Londini. Excudebat E. Bollifantus MDC, sign. I and *b*, I 2 *b*–I 3.

[sign. I] In Australi plaga Ecclesiæ.

Galfridus Chaucer Poëta celeberrimus, qui primus Anglicam Poësin ita illustrauit, vt Anglicus Homerus habeatur.   Obijt 1400.   Anno vero 1555 Nicholaus Brigham Musarum nomine huius ossa transtulit, & illi nouum tumulum ex marmore, his versibus inscriptis posuit.

[Here follows epitaph, *see* above, p. 94 : Qui fuit Anglorum vates ter maximus olim ; illuminated coat of arms on margin.]

.   .   .   .

[sign. I 1 *b*] Rachael Brigham, filia Nicholai Brigham quadrimula obijt, sita est iuxta Galfridum Chaucerum.   Obijt 1557, 21. Junij.

[With regard to the burial-places of Rachel Brigham and her father Nicholas, *see* Mrs. C. C. Stopes in *Athenæum*, April 28, 1904, p. 541, and Oct. 25, 1902, p. 552.]

[sign. I 2 *b*] Ed^{mun}wardus Spenser Londinensis, Anglicorum Poetarum nostri seculi facilè princeps, quod eius poemata fauentibus Musis victuro genio conscripta comprobant.   Obijt immatura morte anno salutis 1598.   & prope Galfredum Chaucerum conditur qui fælicissimè poesin Anglicis literis primus illustrauit.   In quem hæc scripta sunt Epitaphia

> *Hic prope Chaucerum situs est Spencerius, illi*
> *Proximus ingenio, proximus vt tumulo.*

[sign. I 3]
> *Hic prope Chaucerum Spencere Poeta poetam*
> *Conderis, & versu, quàm tumulo propior.*
> *Anglica te viuo vixit, plausitque Poesis ;*
> *Nunc moritura timet, te moriente, mori.*

[Anne Clifford, Countess of Dorset, caused a monument to be erected to Spenser in 1620, but when it was repaired in 1878 no trace of these Latin lines was found. The change in Spenser's Christian name is added in contemporary MS. in the B.M. copy.]

[c. **1600**.] **Stowe**, John.   *Three MS. notes* in Stowe's hand in MSS.
Addit. 34,360 (formerly Phillipps 9053) ff. 19, 37. (Catalogue
Add. MSS. in B.M., 1888–93; 1894, pp. 318–20, and more odd
texts of Chaucer's minor poems, ed. F. J. Furnivall, Chaucer soc.,
1886, p. 43.)

[fol. 19]   [Heading to Chaucer's ' Complaint to his Purse '] Chaucer.

[Colophon to same poem.]   Thus farr is printed in Chauce[r]
fol. 320 vnder ye name of Tho. Occleeue.

[fol. 37]   [Marginal note to spurious Assembly of Ladies.]   Chausar la
samble des dames.

[*See also* below, *c.* 1640, Browne, William, p. 219.]

1600. Stowe, John.   *The Annales of England,* pp. 437, 458, 527–8.
(The Annales . . . . of England, ed. Edmond Howes, 1614, pp. 276,
288, 326.   *See also* Life Records of Chaucer, iv, ed. R. E. G. Kirk,
Chaucer soc. 1900, p. 206, no. 106.)

[For first reference, p. 437, *see* above, p. 136, *under* 1592, *The
Annales of England,* p. 431, which is the same as here.]

[p. 458]   [Under Richard the second.]

Jeffrey   There were that day beheaded manie, as well Flemings
Chaucer
in the   as Englishmen for no cause, but to fulfill the crueltie
tale of
the   of the rude Commons : for it was a solemne pastime to
Nunnes
Priest.   them, if they could take any that was not sworne to
them, to take from such a one his hoode with their
accustomed clamour, & forth with to behead him . . . .

So hidous was the noyse, a! *benedicite!*

.   .   .   .

As thilke day was maad upon the fox.
[*Nonne Preestes Tale,* ll. 4583–7.]

.   .   .   .   .

[pp. 527–8]   [Under Henry the fourth.]

1400   The famous Poet *Geffrey Chaucer* esquire, the
Geffer. Chaucer
Chiefe Poet   first illuminer of our English language, deceased.
of England.
New elme.   This was a worshipful Gentleman, and of faire
possessions, whose abode was chiefly about Wodstocke, (where
he had a faire manor) and New elme (in Oxford shire)
which also was his, with diuers other manors : he was oft
times imploied by K. *Edward* ye 3. as ambassador into
france, and into other forrain lands : he had to wife the
daughter of *Paine Roete* aliâs *Guian* King at armes, by whom
[p. 528] he had issue *Tho. Chaucer,* who maried *Mawd* daughter
to Sir *Bartholomewe Borwash,* by whom he had issue *Alice*

Chaucer, first maried to Sir *Iohn Philips* Knight, after
to the Earle of Salisbury, and thirdly to *William* Duke of
Suffolke, who at his wiues request founded an hospitall called
Gods house, by yᵉ parish Church of Newelme : which Church
he also builded, in this Church lieth buried *Tho. Chawcer* the
last heire male . . . but our first named *Chaucer* the poet, by
what occasion I know not, was buried at Westminster, his
workes for the most part are extant, first published in print by
William Caxton, sometime a mercer of London, the man that
first brought the Art of printing into this lande, since more
largely collected into one volume by *William boteuil*, aliâs
Thin, Esquier, chiefe Clearke of the Kitchin, and master of
the household to K. *Henry* the 8. vnto whom he dedicated
the fruite of that his labour *Anno Christi* .1540. [*i. e.* 1532
and 1542]. The which volume was since againe, to wit, in
Anno 1560 [pub. 1561, *see* above, p. 86] by viewe of diuers
written copies, corrected by my selfe, the author of this
history, who at that time also corrected and added diuers
workes of the said master *Geffrey Chaucers* neuer before
imprinted, [and againe in the yéere 1597. further increased
with other his workes, as also his life, preferment, issue and
death, collected out of records in the towre and else where by
my selfe, and giuen to *Thomas Spight* to be published, [in
1598] and was performed]. Besides the history of *Oedipus*
and *Iocasta*, with the siege of *Thebes*, translated and made
into English verse, by *Don Iohn Lidgate*, a disciple of the said
Chaucers.

[The above extract is an expanded version of the reference in the first edn. of 1580,
see p. 119 ; and it is identical with that in the edn. of 1592, pp. 517–8 [p. 136, above],
with the exception of the sentence towards the end within square brackets, which is
here added.]

1600. Thynne, Francis. *Emblemes and Epigrams.* Dedication to Sir
Thomas Egerton, Epigrams 21, 38, 51 ; Ellesmere MS., ff. 47,
53 *b*, 57 *b*. (Ed. F. J. Furnivall, E. E. T. soc., 1876, pp. 3, 62,
71, 77.)

[p. 1] [Dedication] to the right honorable his Singuler good Lord,
Sir Thomas Egerton, Knight, Lord Keper of the greate Seale
[p. 3] . . . . Thus, my good Lord, is all dutifull love commend-
inge these my slender poems (which may be equalled with
Sir *Topas* ryme in *Chaucer*) vnto your good likinge . . . .
I humblie take my leaue.

  . . . .

[fol. 47]   (21) Glasses.

The sundrie sort of glasses which art doth put in vse
for our delights, in severall kindes, sweete pleasures doe procure :

.   .   .   .

besides, there is of glasse a temple fair and brighte
which learned Chaucer builded hath with penn of heavenlie
    spright.

.   .   .   .

[fol. 53 *b*]   (38) Spencers Fayrie Queene.
Renowmed Spencer whose heavenlie sprite
ecclipseth the sonne of former poetrie,
in whome the muses harbor with delighte
gracinge thy verse with Immortalitie
Crowning thy fayrie Queene with deitie,
The famous *Chaucer* yealds his Laurell crowne
vnto thy sugred penn for thy renowne.

.   .   .   .

[fol. 57 *b*]   (51) To Humfrie Waldoun.
A foolishe *Cherill* I maye seeme to bee,
that shame not to present vnto thy sight
Sir Topas ridinge rime not meet for thee
Nor Goulding's learned vewe, that famous wight
whose hawtie verse with sugredd words well knitt
bereaves the same of *Chawcers* flowing witt.

[*c.* 1600. **Unknown.**]   *MS. notes* [in] Addit. MS. 10,303, fol. 1 *b*.

[fol. 1 *b*]   [The MS. is lettered at back] Chaucer's Dreame, [title] The
death of Blaunche the Dutchesse of Lancaster, fyrst wyef to Jo :
of Gaunte iiijth sonne to Edwarde the thirde, written by that
honorable Englyshe Poet Geoffrey Chaucer esq^re. [By another
later hand,] no doubte mysse entituled, for this shoulde be
Chaucers dreame, & his dreame, the death of the Duchesse.

[*c.* 1600.] **Unknown.**   *MS. note* [in an early 17th cent. hand] to Shipman's tale, l. 1363.   Hengwrt MS. fol. 206.   (Six-text Canterbury
Tales, ed. F. J Furnivall, Chaucer soc., parts i–iii, 1871–8, p. 180,
col. 2.)

A woman wolld haue her husband to be hardye wyse Ryche
free buxom that is to say gentell . . . . these syxe things a
woman doth desyre as Mr. Chaucer dothe wryte.

[ll. 1363–7]

1600. Vaughan, Sir W[illiam]. *The Golden-groue* . . . . [2nd edn.] 1608, bk. iii, chap. 43, sign. Z 5 *b*.   (British Bibliographer, ed. Sir S. E. Brydges, 1812, vol. ii, p. 272.   A copy of 1st edn. is in the Bodleian, Wood. 743.)

Ieffery Chaucer, the English Poet, was in great account with King Richard the second, who gaue him in reward of his Poems, the Mannour of Newelme in Oxford Shire.

1601. Fitzgeffrey, Charles. *Caroli Fitzgeofridi Affaniæ; sive Epigrammatum. Libri tres; Ejusdem Cenotaphia* . . . . *Oxoniæ, Excudebat Josephus Barnesius* 1601, lib. sign. Dv ; lib. 3, sign. N 2 *b*.   (The poems of the Rev. Charles Fitzgeoffrey, ed. A. B. Grosart, 1881, pp. xix, xx ; trans. p. xxiii.)

AD EDMVNDVM SPENSERVM

[sign. D v]   Nostrum *Maron*[*em*] EDMONDE CHAVCERVM vocas?
Male herclè ! si tu quidpia*m* potes male
Namq*ue* ille noster *Ennius,* sed tu *Maro.*

.   .   .   .

[sign. N 2]   EDMONDO SPENCERO

.   .   .   .   .   .

[sign. N 2 *b*]   *In eiusdem Tumulum*
Chaucere vicinum Westmonast[*erium*]

Spenserus cubat hic *Chaucero* ætate priori
Inferior, tumulo proximus, arte prior.

1601. Holland, Joseph. *Of the Antiquity, and use of Heralds in England,* 28 *Nov*[r] 1601, [in] A Collection of Curious Discourses, Written by Eminent Antiquaries . . . . Now first published by Thomas Hearne, 1720, p. 98.

John of Ghaunt, Duke of Lancaster, married Katharine daughter of Guyon King of Armes in the time of K. Edward the 3. and Geffrey Chaucer her sister.

1601. Winwood, Ralph. *Letter to Sir Thomas Edmondes,* Jan. 12, 1601.   Stowe MSS. 167, vol. ii of Edmondes papers, fol. 226.   (B.M. Cat. Stowe MSS. 1895, vol. i, p. 167.)

[Ralph Winwood, English Resident at Paris, to Edmondes in London]: I am sure you are become a good Chaucerist, and therefore I speake unto yow in his language, and say that yf all the earthe were parchemin scribable, all water inck, and all trees pennes, and so the rest in proportion, yet were there noe meanes fully to declare the contentment which I doe enjoy by the happie tydinges of the late defaist w[ch] those rebells receaved in Ireland, etc.

[This is a reference to Lydgate's "Balade: warning men to beware of deceitful women;" formerly attributed to Chaucer: *see* Chaucerian and other pieces, ed. W. W. Skeat, Chaucer soc. 1897, p. 296, ll. 43–9.   *Cf.* 1645, Cavendish, William, p. 223.]

1602. The Workes of Our Ancient and learned English Poet Geffrey Chaucer, newly Printed [T. Speght's second edn. Blackletter] . . . . London.   Printed by Adam Islip, 1602.

[For full title-page, *see* next entry, and for first edition *see* above, p. 147.]

1602. Speght, Thomas. *The Workes of Our Ancient and learned English Poet, Geffrey Chavcer,* newly Printed [T. Speght's 2nd edn. The following list is on the title-page].

To that which was done in the former Impression [1598] thus much is now added :

1 In the life of Chaucer many things inserted.

2 The whole worke by olde Copies reformed.

3 Sentences and Prouerbes noted.

4 The Signification of the old and obscure words prooued : also Caracters shewing from what Tongue or Dialect they be deriued.

5 The Latine and French, not Englished by Chaucer, translated.

6 The Treatise called *Iacke Vpland* against Friers : and Chaucers A. B. C. called *La Priere de nostre Dame* at this Impression added.

¶ London, Printed by Adam Islip, An. Dom. 1602.

[Additions, which appear for the first time in this, the 2nd edn.]

[A new Dedication] To . . . Sir Robert Cecil.   sign. [a iii.]

[An entirely new address] To the Readers. sign. [a iii *b*–a iv.]

After this booke was last printed, I vnderstood, that M. *Francis Thynn* had a purpose, as indeed he hath when time shall serue, to set out *Chaucer* with a Coment in our tongue . . . Whereupon I purposed not to meddle any further in this work, although some promise made to the contrarie, but to referre all to him ; being a Gentleman for that purpose inferior to none, both in regard of his own skill, as also of those helps left to him by his father.   Yet notwithstanding, *Chaucer* now being printed againe, I was willing not only to helpe some imperfections, but also to adde some things : whereunto he did not only persuade me, but most kindly lent me his helpe and direction.   By this meanes most of his old words are restored : Prouerbes and Sentences marked : Such Notes as were collected, drawne into better order : And the text by old Copies corrected.

But of some things I must aduertise the Reader ; [1st, that Chaucer changes Latin and Greek proper names ; 2nd, that

imitating the Greeks, he uses two negatives ; 3rd, he contracts
the verb with the negative, as, ' I not ' for ' I know not ' ;
4th, that instead of the author, he names some part of his
work, as *Argonauticon* for *Apollonius Rhodius.*]

And for his verses, although in diuers places they may
seeme to vs to stand of vnequall measures : yet a skilfull
Reader, that can scan them in their nature, shall find it otherwise. And if a verse here and there fal out a sillable shorter
or longer than another, I rather aret it to the negligence and
rape of *Adam Scriuener*, that I may speake as *Chaucer* doth,
than to any vnconning or ouersight in the Author : For how
fearfull he was to haue his works miswritten, or his verse
mismeasured, may appeare in the end of his fift booke of
Troylus and Creseide, where he writeth thus :

> And for there is so great diuersitie
> In English, and in writing of our tongue,
> So pray I God, that none miswrite thee,
> Ne thee mismetre for defaut of tongue, &c.

. . . .

It were a labor worth commendation, if some scholler,
that hath skil and leisure, would confer *Chaucer* with those
learned Authors, both in Greek and Latin, from whom he
hath drawn many excellent things ; and at large report such
Hystories, as in his Workes are very frequent, and many of
them hard to be found : which would so grace this auncient
Poet, that whereas diuers haue thought him vnlearned, and
his writings meere trifles, it should appeare, that besides the
knowledge of sundrie tongues, he was a man of great reading,
& deep judgement . . . .

Vpon the picture of Chaucer. [signed] Fran. Thynn. [*q. v.*
below, p. 170] sign. b j.

[Verse] Of the Animadversions vpon Chaucer [unsigned]
sign. b. j. [*q. v.* below, p. 170.]

[Under ' Bookes ' in Chaucer's Life] M. William Thynn in
his first printed booke of Chaucers works with one Columbe
on a side, had a Tale called the Pilgrims tale, which was more
odious to the Clergie, than the speach of the Plowman. The
tale began thus : In Lincolnshire fast by a fenne :
Standeth a religious house who doth it kenne. The
argument of which tale as also the occasion thereof, and

the cause why it was left out of Chaucers works, shall hereafter
be shewed, if God permit, in M. Fran. Thyns Coment vpon
Chaucer: & the Tale it selfe published if possibly it can be
found. sign. c j.

[Couplet on a second title page] sign. c iij *b.*

[The headings to the 'Purse' and its envoy are altered, and
are attributed to Hoccleve instead of to Chaucer as in 1598
edn.] Th. Occleue to his empty purse. fol. 320. Occleue
vnto the King. fol. 320 *b.*

Chaucer's A. B. C. [printed for the first time], fol. 347.

Jack Vpland [not by Chaucer] fol. 348.

[For a summary of the changes in the 'life' of Chaucer in this second edn., *see*
Chaucer, a bibliographical manual, by E. P. Hammond, N. York, 1908, pp. 35, 36;
for other differences between the two edns., *ibid.*, p. 126.]

1602. Thynne, Francis. *Vpon the Picture of Chaucer.* A poem prefixed to the 2nd edn. of Speght's Chaucer, sign. b j. (Thynne's
Animadversions, ed. F. J. Furnivall, Chaucer soc. 1876, pp. cvi–vii.)

Vpon the picture of Chaucer.

What *Pallas* citie owes the heauenly mind
    Of prudent *Socrates,* wise Greeces glorie;
What fame *Arpinas* spreadingly doth find
    By *Tullies* eloquence and oratorie;
    What lasting praise sharpewitted Italie
        By *Tasso's* and by *Petrarkes* penne obtained;
        What fame *Bartas* vnto proud France hath gained,
        By seuen daies world Poetically strained:

What high renowne is purchas'd vnto Spaine,
    Which fresh *Dianaes* verses do distill;
What praise our neighbour Scotland doth retaine,
    By *Gawine Douglas,* in his *Virgill* quill,
    Or other motions by sweet Poets skill,
        The same, and more, faire England challenge may,
        By that rare wit and art thou doest display,
        In verse, which doth *Apolloes* muse bewray.
        Then *Chaucer* liue, for still thy verse shall liue,
        T' unborne Poëts, which life and light will giue.

                                                Fran. Thynn.

1602. Unknown. *Of the Animaduersions vpon Chaucer.* [in] The
Workes . . . of Geffrey Chaucer [T. Speght's 2nd edn.], 1602,
sign. b j.

In reading of the learn'd praise-worthie peine,
The helpefull notes explaining *Chaucers* mind
The Abstruse skill, the artificiall veine ;
By true Annalogie I rightly find,
Speght is the child of *Chaucers* fruitfull breine
Vernishing his workes with life and grace,
Which enuious age would otherwise deface ;
   Then be he lou'd and thanked for the same,
   Since in his loue he hath reuiu'd his name.

1602. [**Day,** John ?]   *The Returne from Pernassvs, or the Scourge of Simony.   Publiquely acted by the Students in Saint John's Colledge in Cambridge* [1602 ? ; first printed] 1606, sign. B 1 *b*, act i. sc. 2. (The Pilgrimage to Parnassus with the return from Parnassus, ed. W. D. Macray, 1886, pp. 84–5 ; or ed. Oliphant Smeaton, Temple Dramatists, 1905, p. 13. *See also* the 1st part of the play [1597, pp. 143–4].)

   But softly may our honour's ashes rest
   That lie by mery *Chaucers* noble chest.

[**Macray,** from a MS. reading, substitutes "Homer's" for "honour's." The preceding lines are in praise of Spenser. For I. Gollancz's views on John Day's authorship, *see* English dramatic literature ed. A. W. Ward, vol. ii. 1899, pp. 640–1, and the introduction to Smeaton's edn., *see* also note under 1597, Part I of this play, above, p. 144.]

1602. Nixon, Anthony. *The Christian Navy.* Wherein is playnely described the perfit course to sayle to the Hauen of eternall happinesse, London, Simon Stafford, 1602, sign. F 4 *b* and G 1. (Transcribed by Dr. Furnivall, in Notes and Queries, series 5, vol. xi, p. 25, 1879.)

Which Image here I would describe to thee,
   But that long since it hath been paynted playne
By learned *Chaucer*, gemme of Poetry,
   Who past the reach of any English brayne :
A folly therefore were it here for me,
   To touch that he did often vse to say,
   Writ in the Romaunt of his Roses gay.

[Here follow ll. 413–48 of the Romaunt of the Rose.]

. . . .

Another thing was done they write.

. . . .

They leesen God and eke his raigne.

. . . .

Thus hath the golden pen of *Chaucer* old,
The Image playne described to the eye,
Who passing by long since, did it behold
And tooke a note thereof aduisedly,
And left the same to his posterity,
That each man passing by, might playnely know
The perfit substance of that flattring show.

[*Cf.* above, 1569. B. G., p. 104. 'The Christian Navy' is merely a reprint of the 'Shippe of Safeguard,' a few lines and words only are altered; the Chaucer references are therefore exactly the same.]

1602. R[owlands], S[amuel]. *Prefatory verses* in *Tis Merrie when Gossips meete*, sign. A 2. (Rowland's works, introduction E. Gosse, notes S. Herrtage, Hunterian club, 1880, vol. i, p. 3.)

Gentlemen.

Chaucer, our famous reuer'nt English *Poet*
When *Canterbury* tales he doth begin,
(Such as haue red his auncient verses know it)
Found store of Guests in *South-warke* at an Inne,
The *Taberd* cal'd, where he himselfe then lay,
And bare them Pilgrimes company next day.

A Kentish iourney they togither tooke,
Towards *Canterbury* marching nine and twentie
Knight, Marchant, Doctor, Miller & Cooke,
Scholler and *Saylor*, with Good-fellowes plentie,
But of blithe Wenches scarcitie he hath
Of all that Crue none but the wife of *Bathe*.
.   .   .   .   S. R.

[*c.* **1602**.] **Davies** [Sir John ?] *Letter* to Sir Robert Cotton. MS. Cott. Julius, c. iii, fol. 133. (Printed in Queen Elizabeth and her times, ed. by Thomas Wright, 1838, vol. ii, p. 493.)

Sweet Robin, for a few sweet words, a client of mine hath presented me with sweet-meates, to what end I know not, except it be as Chaucer speakes

'To make mine English sweet vppon my tongue'

[Prol. to C. Tales, L 265.]

that I may pleade the better for him to-morrow at the Seale.

Notwithstanding, the best vse I can make of it, is to present you with it, especially at this time when you are in physick, that you may sweeten your taste after the Rhewbarb.

[c. 1602.] **Wat.**, Nic. *A MS. stanza* in a mutilated 1602 copy of Chaucer's Works in the possession of Dr. F. J. Furnivall, at the back of his *Ad Galfridum Chaucer* " Progenie" engraving.

[Under the rough full-length portrait on this title-page is the lettering " *The true portraiture of* GEFFREY CHAUCER *the famous English poet, as by* THOMAS OCCLEVE *is described who liued in his time and was his Scholar.*"]

Parnassus Topp, pure streame of Hellicon,
  Grave Lawreat, and thou English Horace, he
(Pearle of Olimp :) whom Muses since each one
  So dearely priz'd, y^t they strove whose shouldst be
    But now thou art gone to him *that* first thee made
    To walke with him in *the* Elizean shade,
    And yet th'art heare, where Poetts are thy Paiges
    And thou a Tutor to surviveing Ages.

                                   Nic°. **Wat.**

1603. Dekker, Thomas. *The Pleasant Comodie of Patient Grissil.*

[For the resemblances in this play to Chaucer's Clerkes Tale, *see* Chaucers Einfluss auf das englische Drama by O. Ballman, in Anglia, vol. xxv, 1902, pp. 66–72.]

1603. H[arsnet], S[amuel]. *Declaration of egregious Popish Impostures,* pp. 137–8.

And *Geoffry Chaucer,* who had his two eyes, wit, and learning in his head, spying that all these brainlesse imaginations, of witchings, possessings . . . were the forgeries . . . of craftie priests . . . writes in good plaine termes of the holy Couent [*sic*] of Friers thus :

  For there as wont to walken was an Elfe

  .   .   .   .

  .   .   .   .

  There nis none other Incubus *but hee.*

                    [Wife of Bath's tale, ll. 873–4, 879–80.]

1603. Holland, Hugh. *Pancharis . . . containing the Preparation of the Loue betweene Owen Tudyr, and the Queene.* Unique copy Bodl. library, sign. A 5, C 2. (Illustrations of Old English literature, ed. J. P. Collier, vol. ii, 1866, pp. 5-6, 34.)

  . . . . *amico Gulielmo Camdeno* . . . .
Cum Nasone tamen ponas (hic namque libellus
Sanctior, ut multis doctior ille modis)
Vel cum Chaucero (nec enim mihi fidus amator
Est minùs, et multo Nympha pudica magis.)

[The courtiers of Queen Katherine (Henry V's wife) do] devise

(So soone as notice of her minde was had)

To entertaine her with some strange disguise,

Done by *Dan Lidgate*, a great learned Munke,

Who then in Poesie bare away the prise ;

For after *Chaucer* had he deeply drunke

Of *Helicon*, as few besides have yet.

1603. Stowe, John. *A Suruay of London* . . . by John Stow . . . increased with diuers rare notes of Antiquitie . . . 1603, p. 377 [not in 1st edn. of 1598]. (Ed. C. L. Kingsford, Oxford, 1908, vol. ii, p. 24.)

This Gentleman (John Shirley) a great traueller in diuers countries amongest other his laboures, painefully collected the workes of Geffrey Chaucer, John Lidgate and other learned writers, which workes hee wrote in sundry volumes to remayne for posterity, I haue seene them, and partly do professe [*sic*] them.

[In the 1st edn. of 1598, p. 306, there is just the mention of Shirley, and no reference to Chaucer. Further additions were made to Stowe's survey by Strype, 1720, *q. v.* below, p. 352. For Shirley *see* above, *a.* 1456, p. 53.]

1604. Harbert, William. *To the Maiestie of King Iames, Monarch of all Britayne. A Prophesie of Cadwallader, last King of the Britaines* . . . sign. H 2. (Poems of W. Harbert, ed. A. B. Grosart, Fuller's Worthies library, vol. i, 1870, p. 92 [p. 248 of whole vol.].)

If *Englands* Load-starre, pride of Poesie   Chaucer, so

Could the firme Centers regiment transpearse :   called by   M. Camden.

And formalize his peerlesse ingeny.

Thy all-surpassing vertues to rehearse,

A Princely matter fitts a princely verse :

Yet were his wit too weake thy [*i. e.* James I's] deeds to praise,

Which brought vs ioyes, in our most mournfull daies.

[1604.] Powel, Gabriel. *Disputationum theologicarum . . de Antichristo . . . Libri II.* . . . 1605 [Epistle dedicatory and title-page to vol. ii dated 1604], p. 32.

Præfatio ad Academ. Oxon.

Geffrey   43. *Galfridus Chaucerus* Anglus, Eques auratus,
Chaucer.   Oxonii diu Literis operam dedit. Multa scripsit, in quibus Monachorum otia, missantium multitudinem, horas non intellectas, reliquias, peregrinationes, ac ceremonias falsè ridet : quinimo Pontificem ipsum Pastorum fatuum & Antichristum apertè denunciat. *Claruit anno Domini* 1402. Chauc. in Aratoris Narratione, & alibi passim.

1604. Sc[oloker], An[thony]. *Diaphantus,* or *the Passions of Loue . . .*
by An. Sc. Gentleman, sign. E 4 *b.* Unique (?) copy in the Douce
coll. Bodl. library. (Ed. R. Wilbraham, Roxb. club, 1818 ; ed. A. B.
Grosart, Occasional issues of unique or very rare books, 1880,
vol. xiii, p. 36.)

> Calls Players fooles, the foole he judgeth wisest,
> Will learne them Action out of *Chaucer's* Pander.

1605. [Camden, William.] *Remaines of a greater worke, concerning
Britaine . . .* London, printed by G. E. for Simon Waterson, 1605,
p. 40, pp. 6, 7. [This last reference is at the end of the volume
after sign. Hh 2.] The 'Epistle Dedicatorie' addressed to Sir
Robert Cotton is signed M. N. *i.e.* William Camden. (Remaines
concerning Britaine, in Library of old authors, with notes by Thomas
Moule, 1870,—a reprint of the 7th edn. of 1674,—pp. 67, 342-4.)

[p. 40]   *Usuall Christian names.*

Alan, is thought by *Iulius Scaliger . . .* to signifie an
hownd in the *Sclauonian* tongue, and *Chaucer* vseth *Aland* in
the same sense.

[pp. 6, 7] *Certaine Poemes or Poesies . . . .* of the English Nation in
former Times.   Verses vpon the death of K. *Richard* the first
penned by one *Gaulfrid . . . .*

> . . . Nihil addere nouerat vltra,
> Ipse fuit quicquid potuit natura, sed istud
> Causa fuit quare rapuisti, res pretiosas
> Eligis, & viles quasi didignata relinquis.

These former verses were mentioned by *Chaucer* our English
Homer in the description of the sodaine stirre & *Panicall*
feare, when *Chanteclere* the Cocke was caried away by Reynold
the Foxe with a relation to the said *Galfride.*

[Here follows a quotation from the Nonne Preestes Tale, ll. 4565-91, followed by
ll. 4537-62.]

[1605.] Dekker, Thomas.⎫ *North-Ward Hoe,* 1607, sign. F 1. Act. iv.
       Webster, John. ⎭
(The dramatic works of Thomas Dekker, London, John Pearson,
vol. iii, 1873, p. 52.)

> *May[bery].* A Commedy, a Canterbury tale smells not halfe
> so sweete as the Commedy I haue for thee old Poet . . . .

1605. James, Thomas. *Catalogus Librorum Bibliothecæ* publicæ *quam
vir ornatissimus Thomas Bodleius Eques Auratus in Academia
Oxoniensi nuper instituit. . . . Auctore Thoma James. . . Oxoniæ*
1605, p. 300.   Libri artium.   Galfredi *Chauceri* opera Anglice.
Lond. 1561. [For the two following Bodleian catalogues *see* below,
1620. Thos. James, p. 193, and 1674, T. Hyde, p. 249.]

[**1605**]. **R.**, R.   *Commendatory lines* prefixed to Bartas his Deuine Weekes & Workes Translated . . . . by Iosuah Syluester, [1605–6] sign. a 6 *b*.   (Works of Joshuah Sylvester, ed. A. B. Grosart, 1880, vol. i, p. 15.)

In Commendation of this worthie Worke.

Foole that I was, I thought in younger times
That all the Muses had their graces sowne
In Chaucers Spencers and sweet Daniels Rimes
(So, good seemes best, where better is vnknowne).

1605. V[**erstegan**], R[ichard], *alias* Richard Rowlands.   *A Restitution of Decayed Intelligence In antiquities Concerning the English nation, By the Studie and trauaile of R. V.*   Printed at Antwerp by Robert Bruney, 1605, chap. 7, pp. 203–4, 211.

Of the Antiquitie and proprietie of the Ancient English
Tovng

Some few ages after [the Conquest] came the poet *Geffrey Chaucer,* who, writing his poesies in English, is of some called the first illuminator of the English toung : of their opinion I am not (though I reuerence *Chaucer* as an excellent poet for his tyme).   He was indeed a great mingler of English with

Chaucer
mingled our
English
toung with
French. French, vnto which language by lyke, for that hee was [p. 204] descended of French or rather wallon race, he caryed a great affection.

Since the tyme of *Chaucer* more Latin & French hath bin mingled with our toung then left out of it.

. . . .

[p. 211]   Buhsomnesse or Bughsomnesse. *Plyablensse* or bowsomnesse, to wit, humbly stooping or bowing doun in signe of obedience. *Chaucer* wrytes it Buxomnesse.

[*See* below, p. 225, 1647, Tooke, and 1655, p. 230, Fuller.]

[**1605–6.**] **Drayton,** Michael.   *Epistle to the Reader,* [in] *Poemes lyrick and pastorall.* . . . . At London, printed by R. B. for N. L. and I. Plasket, n. d., B. M. catalogue [1606 ?], sign. A 4 *b*.   (Poems, ed. J. P. Collier, Roxb. club, 1856, p. 382. *Cf. also* Introduction, p. xlii.)

And would at this time also gladly let thee vnderstand, what I think aboue (*sic*) the rest of the last Ode of the twelue, or if thow wilt Ballad in my Book ; for both the great master of Italian rymes *Petrarch,* & our *Chawcer,* & other of the vper house of the muses, haue thought their Canzons honoured in the title of a Ballade, which for that I labour to meet truely therein with the ould English garb, I hope as able to iustifie as the learned *Colin Clout* his Roundelaye . . . .

1606. Unknown. *The Plough-mans Tale. Shewing by the doctrine and liues of the Romish Clergie, that the Pope is Antichrist, and they his Ministers. Written by Sir Geffrey Chaucer, Knight, amongst his Canterburie tales; and now set out apart from the rest, with a short exposition of the words and matters, for the capacitie and vnderstanding of the simpler sort of Readers.* At London, printed by G. E. for Samuell Macham and Mathew Cooke . . . . 1606. [References to Chaucer in the notes], sign. A 2, note 3, A 2 *b*, headnote, A 3, stanza 3, note 3, G 1 and *b* stanza 46, note 1, H 3 *b*, note 3.

[This is a reprint of the older edns. of 1532-5, 1542, with the addition of notes, 'which,' says Thomas in his preface to Urry's Chaucer, 1721, 'are thought by some to be Mr. Francis Thynne's.' *See* Chaucer, a bibliographical manual, by E. P. Hammond, N. York, 1908, pp. 444-46, *also* above, [1532-5] p. 80.]

1606. Barnes, Barnabe. *Foure Bookes of Offices* . . . . made and deuised by Barnabe Barnes. London, Pr. by George Bishop, etc., 1606. The Second Booke of Offices, sign. H 1 *b*, p. 50.

The best of these which first began to reduce the confused garden of our language into some proportion, were the two laureate knights of their times, *Gower* and his Scholler *Chaucer*, in the times of King *Richard* the second, and King *Henry* the fourth. One *Lydgate* a monke of Edmonsburie, succeeded them in that worke : Most of whose patternes were taken and translated out of Latine, French and Italian, intermingled with some other excellent inuentions of their owne, not including any great matters, tending vnto gouernment and moralitie.

1606. B[axter], N[athaniel]. *Sir Philip Sydneys Ourania* . . . . Written by N. B. London. Printed by Ed. Allde for Edward White, 1606, sign. C 1. (Quoted in T. Corser's Collectanea, Chetham soc. part ii, 1861, p. 220.)

[Endymion] And sang the Song of vniuersal *Pan*

.   .   .   .

A Subject fit for *Sydneys* eloquence,
High *Chaucers* vaine, and *Spencers* influence.

1606. [Chapman, George ?] *Sir Gyles Goosecappe, Knight.* A Comedie presented by the Children of the Chappell. At London, Printed by John Windet for Edward Blunt, 1606, sign. E 2, act iii, sc. 1. (A collection of old English plays, ed. A. H. Bullen, 1884, vol. iii, pp. 46-7.)

Will: Marrie Sir, they are inuited to a greate supper tonight to your Lords house Captaine, the *Lord Furnifall*, and there will bee your great cosen Sir *Gyles Goosecappe*, the Lorde *Tales*, and your vncle Sir *Cutt:* Rudsby, Sir *Cutbert Kingcob.*

Foul[ewether]. The Lord *Tales*, what countriman is hee ?

CHAUCER CRITICISM.

Ia[ck]. A kentish *L*ord Sir, his auncestors came forth off Canterburie.

Foul. Out of Canterburie.

Will. I indeed Sir the best *Tales* in England are your Canterburie *tales* I assure ye.

[There can be no doubt that the source of the plot of *Sir Gyles Goosecappe* is the first three books of Chaucer's *Troilus and Criseyde; see* Kittredge in the Journal of Germanic Philology, vol. ii, 1898, pp. 10–13. He says : ' Pandarus has become *Earl Monford* (Momford), a humorous nobleman. Troilus has become *Clarence*, a poor gentleman allied to Monford in the closest bonds of friendship. Criseyde is now *Eugenia*, a widow, the niece of Monford. Clarence wishes to marry Eugenia and Monford favours his suit. Not only is the correspondence of the stories unmistakable, but the dialogue of the play owes much to Chaucer.' Many interesting parallel passages are then cited, for which *see* below, Appendix A, 1606.

For a discussion of the authorship, and evidences of Chapman having written this play, *see* 'The Authorship of Sir Gyles Goosecappe,' by T. M. Parrott, in Modern Philology, vol. iv, no. i, July 1906, pp. 25–37 ; also for date and authorship, see A. H. Bullen, Old English Plays, vol. iii, introduction and pp. 93–4, F. G. Fleay in Athenæum, June 9, 1883, p. 731, and Biographical Chronicles of the English Drama, vol. i, p. 58, vol. ii, p. 323. Kittredge notes that Chapman uses 'Sir Giles Goosecap' as a synonym for a fool in 'The Gentleman Usher,' II. i.]

1606. W[arner], W[illiam]. *A Continuance of Albions England:* By the first Author, W. W. London. Imprinted by Felix Kingston for George Potter . . . . 1606. [This edn. is not in the B. M. ; *see* Bibliographical catalogue by J. P. Collier, 1865, vol. ii, pp. 483–7 ; Chaucer reference, p. 486.] Albion's England . . . . 1612, p. 331.

To the Reader.

*   *   *   *   *   *

The Musits [*sic*] though themselues they please,

Their Dotage els finds Meede nor Ease :

Vouch't Spencer in that Ranke preferd,

Per Accidens, only interr'd

Nigh Venerable Chaucer, lost,

Had not kinde Brigham reard him cost

Found next the doore Church-outed neere,

And yet a Knight, Arch-Lauriat Heere.

[*See* below, 1850, J. P. Collier.]

1607. C., R. *The Epistle Dedicatorie* [to] *A World of Wonders; see* below, App. A, 1607.

[1607.] Dekker, Thomas. *A Knights Coniuring: Done in earnest: Discouered in Iest,* chap. ix, sign. K 4 and *b.* (Ed. E. E. Rimbault, 1842, Percy soc., vol. v, p. 75.)

Beyond all these places is there a *Groue*, which . . . . is called *The Groue of Bay Trees*, and to this *Consort-Rome*, resort none but the children of *Phœbus* (*Poets* and *Musitions:*) . . . . Full of pleasant Bowers and queint Arboures is all this *Walke.* In one of which, old *Chaucer*, reuerend for prioritie, blythe in cheare, buxsome in his speeches, and benigne in his

hauiour, is circled a round with all the Makers or Poets of his
time their hands leaning on one anothers shoulders, and their
eyes fixt seriously vpon his, whilst their eares are all tied to
his tongue, by the golden chaines of his *Numbers*; for here
(like *Euander's* mother) they spake all in verse : no Attick
eloquence is so sweete : their language is so pleasing to the
goddes, that they vtter their Oracles in none other.

Graue Spencer was no sooner entred into this *Chappell of*
Apollo, but these elder *Fathers of the diuine Furie*, gaue him
a *Lawrer* & sung his *Welcome* : *Chaucer* call'de him his Sonne,
and plac'de him at his right hand. All of them (at a signe
giuen by the whole *Quire* of the *Muses* that brought him
thither) closing vp their lippes in silence, and tuning all their
eares for attention, to heare him sing out the rest of his *Fayrie*
Queenes praises.

1607. [**Middleton**, Thomas.] *The Famelie of Loue* .... 1608, act iii,
sc. 1, sign. D 2 and *b*. [Licensed for printing 1607] quoted by
Thomas Hayward in the British Muse, 1738, vol. ii, pp. 179–80.
(Works, ed. A. H. Bullen, 1885–6, vol. iii, 1885, p. 50.)

Ger[ardine]. Here me exemplify loue's Latine word,
  Together with thy selfe
  As thus ; harts ioynd *Amore* : take *A* from thence
  Then *more* is the perfect morall sence ?
  Plurall in manners, which in thee doe shine
  Saintlike, immortall, spotles and diuine.
  Take *m* away, *ore* in beauties name,
  Craues an eternall Trophee to thy fame
  Lastly take *o*, in *re* stands all my rest :
  Which *I* in *Chaucer* stile do terme a iest.

[For Chaucer's influence on Middleton's plays, *see* Chaucer's Einfluss auf das englische
Drama, by O. Ballmann, Anglia, xxv, pp. 74–6.]

1607. **Niccols**, Richard. *The Cuckow*, p. 46.
[Passing reference to January and May, no mention of Chaucer himself.]

1607. **W[alkington]**, T[homas]. *The Optick Glasse of Hvmors, Or The*
Touchstone of a Golden Temperature ... &c., by T. W., Master of
Artes. Imprinted by Iohn Windet for Martin Clerke [London,]
1607. [same title] Oxford. Printed by W. T. .... [n.d.] cap. ii,
pp. 29, 144.

  .... wee see by experience in trauaile, the rudenesse and
simplicity of the people that are seated farre north ; which no
doubt is intimated by a vulgar speech, when wee say such a
man hath a borrell wit, as if wee said *boreale ingenium* :
whereof that old-english prophet of famous memory (whom
one fondly tearm'd *Albion's* ballad maker, the cunnicatcher of

time; and the second dish for fooles to feede their splenes vpon) G. *Chaucer* tooke notice when in his prologue to the Frankleines tale he sayes

> *But Sirs, because I am a borrell man*
> *At my beginning first I you beseech,*
> *Haue me excus'd of my rude speech.*
>
> [ll. 716–18.]

. . . .

[p. 144] The history is well known of *Cræsus* his dreames, whereof *Pertelot* speakes to *Chaunticleere*, in the merry tale of the Nuns priest.

> *Loe* Cræsus *which was of* Lydia *king,*
> *Met hee not that he sate upon a tree*
> *Which signified that he should hanged be.*
>
> [ll. 318–20.]

Many more be rehearsed in that place which is worthy to be read : wherein the poet shewes himselfe both a Divine, an Historian, a Philosopher and Physician.

[The references here are given from the undated edn. in B. M. Sidney Lee, in Walkington's life in the *D. N. B.*, says it cannot be earlier than 1631, and that the 1607 edn. is the earliest known ; a copy was in the possession of Dr. C. M. Ingleby.]

[1607–9.] **Heywood**, Thomas, } *Fortune by Land, and Sea.* A Tragi-
Rowley, William. Comedy . . . written by Tho. Haywood and William Rowley . . . Printed . . . 1655, act iii, sc. i, p. 22. (reprinted by J. E. Walker, Boston 1899, p. 83, and Heywood's Dramatic Works, printed John Pearson, vol. vi, 1874, p. 393.)

[Reference to *Nonne Preestes Tale.*]

[a. 1608.] **Thynne**, [Francis]. *Of the Antiquity of the Houses of Law,* [in] A Collection of Curious Discourses Written by Eminent Antiquaries . . . . Now first published by Thomas Hearne, 1720, p. 118.

Of the Steward of which Temple [The Temple Law Courts] and Lawyers Chaucer speaketh in the Manciples prologue in the prologues of Chaucer, and diverse Authors mention how the Ribels in 4th of Richard the Second spoiled the Temple and burnt the Lawyers books . .

1608. Twyne, Brian. *Antiquitatis Academiæ Oxoniensis Apologia,* lib. i, p. 27, lib. ii, p. 140.

[p. 27] [Chaucer's name among the] " autores qui Cantabri fabulæ non meminerunt."

. . . .

[lib. ii.
p. 140] Nec dissentit Galfredus Chaucer Oxoniensis poeta laureatus,
in suo ad Ludovicum filium Astrolabio, quod à Mathematicis
Oxoniensibus ob summam perspicuitatem, *Lac puerorum* dici
consuevit.

[**1608-44**?] **Twyne**, Bryan. *Extracts from Chaucer* in vol. 10 of the
collections of B. Twyne, MS. C. C. Coll. Oxford, cclxiii, ff.
120 *b*-125. (Catalogue of Oxford Coll. MSS., by H. Coxe, vol. ii,
1852, p. 113.)

[These are mainly short summaries of the various Canterbury Tales, of which the
following are specimens.]

[fol. 120 *b*]   Out of Chaucer.

A couetous man is called a niggarde and Sr Guy ye bribour
he is his steward. in ye eight quest :

He commendes ye prioresse for her behauior at meate, y^t
she would not let on drap fall from her mouth.   She honoured
ye a b c much, for she had a crowned A in a golden broch,
wth this poesy, Amor uincit omnia.

The frier had his tippet furred and fased wth kniues and
pins to giue wenches.

He saith of ye Frankelen y^t bred and meate did snowe in
his house.

I thinke in ye old time woaman did ride wth spurs : for so
Chaucer saith of ye wife of Bathe.

Of ye strange horse of brasse y^t ye kinge of Arabia sent to
Cambuscan Kinge of Sarra y^t by turninge of a scrue or pin
would fly wth you euery where you would : and ye sworde of
y^t vertue it would pearce thorough any armor neuer so thicke
and ye wounde incurable, it made : but if you stroke y^e
wounde againe wth ye flat side, ye wounde shall close againe.
and a glasse wherein you might see euen ye uery though[t]s of
men : and a ringe, by whose uertue birdes uoices might be
understoode : and thes 2 wer giuen to Canace ye kings
daughter : in ye squires tale.

•   •   •   •   •   •   •   •   •

There is a pretty note in ye friers tale, y^t ye sompner and y^e
diuell goinge about for briberies and preys they met with a
carter driuinge a loade of hay and cursinge his horses because
they were amyred and wished ye diuell had them : ye Sompner
would haue had ye diuell take them away presently : nay saith
ye diuell you shall heare another thinge anone, then when y^e
horses had got out of ye slowe, Christ blesse you saith y^e

Carter, soe saith ye diuell, ye carter speakes one thinge and meanes another.

In ye Sompners tale ye frier commendes glosinge vppon a text, for ye letter kills.

[fol. 121 b] Howe ye angry iudge iudged 3 knights to death : ye one for suspition y^t he had killed another knight : and when y^t knight came home safe, they led ye condemned knight backe to ye iudge againe : but he saide y^t ye one must die because he was condemned : ye other, because he was ye cause of his fellows death : ye thirde because he did fulfill his commaundement : Somp : tale.

In ye sompners tale there is a fine tale of ye diuidinge of a fart amonge a couent of friers : . . . . . .

The scholler of Oxefords tale is how Walter ye Marquesse of Saluce tried ye patience of his wife Grisilde : by takinge away her children and makinge her beleue y^t he would diuorce her and marry a newe : it is taken out of Petrarch.

The second nonnes tale is of ye life and death of St. Cecily : which she deriueth either was cœli lilium : or else from Cœcus because she was ye way to ye blinde by her doctrine : or else from cœlum an λίαν ualde : or else quasi cœlum λαος ye heauen of ye people, because she did shine so much amongest ye rest.

He went as thride bare as an Alchimist : for Chaucer in y^e

[fol. 122] Canons yeomans tale giues 2 reasons howe Alchimists may be knowne : the one by their sent, for they allways stincke of brimstone : another way is by their threadbare apparrell : for they say if they shoulde set forth themselues and be net, so they might be knowne, and euery man would kill them for their science : but indeede ye reason is because they spend all they haue in trienge their art : where you may reade many pretty thinges of Alchimy.

The Pardoner in his prologue to his tale saith y^t whensoeuer he preached, he had alwayes but one them, and y^t was, Radix omnium malorum est cupiditas.

Of ye white win of Lepe of which when you haue dranke 3 drafts, you will thinke your-selfe in Lepe in Spaine. Pardon : tale.

The Pardoners tale is of 3 drunken gluttons y^t went about to kill death, and was killed by it [here follows a summary].

. . . .

The nonnes preist tale is of a cocke and 5 hens which cocke

was beguiled by ye fox who perswaded him to crowe winkinge and then caught him and ran away. Me thinks ye prettiest tale of all.

.   .   .   .

[fol. 122 b] The arrowes of loue : in ye Romant of ye rose of beauty, of simplicity, of fraunchise ye arrowe of company and semblant : loue also had other arrows, of pride, of shame, of vaine hope, of newe thought.

The Romant of ye rose containeth all things appertaininge to loue : what loue is, and howe you must wooe.

He y^t knoweths [*sic MS.*] well ye herbe may safely lay it to his eye. 1 lib : of fame.

Chaucer writes a treatise of fame, and howe ye fame of euery thinge comes to posterity : in his lib: 2 he hath a pretty demonstration y^t every thinge comes to fames house : he proues it by ye like, by a circle in ye water, for if you cast in a stone it will make a circle, and y^t another, and so forwarde untill it come to ye banke side : so since euery worde is but aire fractus (as flam*m*a is fumus accensus) one ayre breaketh and stirreth another, vntil it comes to fames house : and this reason is so plaine, y^t as he saith, a man may shake it by ye bill.

.   .   .   .

1608. Unknown. *The Penniles Parliament of Threed-bare Poets* ; Or, *All Mirth and wittie Conceites.* Printed at London, for William Barley, 1608. (The Harleian Miscellany, 1808, Oldys and Park, vol. i, p. 185.)

[The Chaucer reference is practically the same as that in **Fearful and lamentable effects of two dangerous Comets** by Simon Smel-Knaue [1591 ?] (*q. v.*, above, p. 134), of which book this tract is an adaptation.]

[1609 ?] **Fletcher,** John. *The Faithfull Shepheardesse.* Printed at London for R. Bonian and H. Walley, sign. I 3 *b*, act v. (Works of Beaumont and Fletcher, ed A. Dyce, 1843-6, vol. ii, p. 105 (see note), act v, sc. 3.)

Thenot . . . . . .

Her beauty euer liuing like the Rime
Our blessed *Tyterus* did singe of yore.

1609. H[eale], W[illiam]. *An Apologie for Women, or an Opposition to Mr. Dr. [Wm] G[ager] his assertion . . . That it was lawfull for husbands to beate their wiues . . .* At Oxford, Printed by Joseph Barnes . . . 1609, p. 39.

All women (you saie) are altogether evil : of men you are sure there are some good. And are they evil all ? Why then (ô graue *Plutarch*) how came it to passe thy wisdome so failed

d Chaucer.
lib. fæmi-
narum en-
comion. I.
& alterum,
de laudib.
bonarum
fæminar.

thee? ancient *Hesiode*, who corrupted thy mature iudgement? . . . *d Chaucer*, how miscaried thy golden pen? Learned and most holy Saints, *S. Hierom, S. Gregory* . . . who deceived you al? for deceived you al are (if this position be received) who have severally written several tracts in honor of honorable women.

[1609.] Jonson, Benjamin. *The Masque of Queenes Celebrated From the House of Fame:* . . . . 1609, Title, and sign. E 4. (Works, ed. W. Gifford and F. Cunningham, vol. vii, 1875, p. 140).

There rests, only, that we giue the description (we promis'd) of the *Scene*, which was the House of *Fame*. The Structure, and Ornament of which . . . . was entirely Mr. *Iones* his inuention, and designe . . . . In which, he profest to follow that noble description, made by *Chaucer*.

1609. Unknown. *Pimlyco, or, Runne Red-Cap. Tis a mad world at Hogsdon,* sign. B 2.

Skelton   By chance I found a Booke in *Ryme*,
Writ in an age when few wryt well,
(*Pans* Pipe (where none is) does excell.)
O learned *Gower !* It was not thine,
Nor *Chaucer*, (thou art more *Diuine*.)
To *Lydgates* graue I should do wrong,
To call him vp by such a *Song*.

[The book he found was Skelton's poem, the Tunning of Eleanour Rummin, which is quoted at length later in this tract. Our transcript is taken from the facsimile reprint published by the Oxford Univ. Press, ed. A. H. Bullen, 1891. The only known copy of the original is in the Bodleian.]

1609. Wyb[arne], Jos[eph]. *The New Age of old Names* by Jos. Wib. Master of Artes of Trinitie Colledge in Cambridge. To the Reader, sign. a 4 *b*. (Prefaces, etc., selected from early English books, by W. C. Hazlitt, 1874, p. 225.)

. . . . . if I have omitted something in a matter so variable remember that I talke of *Errors Denne*, celebrated by the penne of our second *Chaucer* [i. e. Spenser].

[1610.] Beaumont, Francis,}
Fletcher, John.   } *The Coxcombe*, act I. sc. i. [in] Comedies and Tragedies, written by Francis Beavmont and John Fletcher, Gentlemen . . . . 1647, p. 103. (Works of Beaumont and Fletcher, ed. A. Dyce, vol. iii, 1843, p. 151.)

[Viola is seen by the Tinker] What's this? a prayer, or a homilie, or a Ballad of good councell.

[This play, written in 1610, was acted in 1612-13, but it was not printed till it appeared in the folio edn. of 1647.]

[1610-11.] **Shakespeare,** William. *The Winter's Tale,* II, iii, 74-5.

> *Leon.*   Thou dotard ! thou art woman-tired, unroosted
> By thy dame Partlet here.

[See note to [1596-7] Shakespeare, and for the whole question of Chaucer references in Shakespeare, see below, App. A, 1589, Shakespeare.]

1611. 'Αποδημουντόφιλος [pseud]. *Commendatory verses* [to the author in] Coryat's Crudities, 1611, sign. c 3 *b* and c 4 (reprinted Glasgow University press, 1905, vol. i, pp. 23, 24).

> Incipit Αποδημουντόφιλος.
> Not *Mahound,* no nor *Tarmagaunt*
> Could euer make halfe their auaunt
> Of deedes so sterne and fell,
> As can this child Sir *Thopas* Squire
> Inspired with a sparke of fire
> Stolne out of wisdomes cell.
>
> .   .   .   .
>
> Yet would he not play *Cupids* Ape
> In *Chaucers* jest lest he should shape
> A Pigsnye like himselfe.

1611. Sydenham, George. *Note* to Poem [in] Coryat's Crudities. See below, App. A.

1611. Sylvester, Joshua. *See* below App. A, 1611.

1611. Unknown. *Melismata. Musical Phansies. Fitting the Court, Citie, and Countrey Humours* . . . London, Printed by William Stansby for Thomas Adams, 1611, sign. D i *b.* [A book of songs collected by Thomas Ravenscroft, who signs the Dedication ' T.R.'] (Reprinted in Selections from the works of Thomas Ravenscroft, Roxb. club, 1822, p. 11.)

> Citie Rounds. [no.] 9.
> My Mistris will not be content
> To take a Iest, a Iest, a Iest, as Chaucer meant,
> But following stil the womans fashion,
> Allowes it, allowes it, for the new translation,
> For with the word she would not dispence,
> And yet, and yet, and yet, and yet I know the [*sic*] loues
>   the sence.

1612. F., William. *Cornucopiæ* . *Pasquils Night-cap,* sign. D 1 *b,* O 1 *b*-O 2. Bodl. and Dyce library, S. Kensington (ed. A. B. Grosart, occasional issues of unique . . . books, vol. v, 1877, pp. 22, 102-3. *Cf. also* N. Breton's Works, ed. A. B. Grosart, 1879, vol. i, p. xxx).

[References to 'Patient Gresil' and the 'Parliament of Birds.']

[**1612.**] **Selden,** John. *From the Author of the Illustrations.—To the Reader.—Illustrations.* [Prefatory address and notes by J. Selden to] Poly-Olbion by Michaell Drayton [1612], sign. a 3, a 3 *b*, and p. 68. (Works of Drayton, ed. R. Hooper, library of old authors, 1876, vol. i, pp. xlii-iii, 114.)

He [Robert of Gloster] was, in Time, an Age before, but in Learning and Wit, as most others, much behind our Worthy *Chaucer* : . . . [here follows a long digression on the meaning of *Dulcarnon, Tr. and Cr.*, bk. iii, l. 931, which he says] is *Two-horned*, [it] well fits the passage, either, as if hee had personated Creseide at the entrance of two wayes, not knowing which to take ; . . . or else, which is the truth of his conceit, that shee was at a *Nonplus*, as the interpretation in his next Staffe makes plaine.   How many of Noble *Chaucers* Readers neuer so much as suspect this his short essay of knowledge, transcending the common Rode? and by his Treatise of the *Astrolabe* (which I dare sweare was chiefly learned out of *Messahalah*) it is plaine hee was much acquainted with the Mathematics, and amongst their Authors had it.

  .   .   .   .

[p. 68]   . . . . Some account him [St. George] an allegory of our Sauiour Christ ; and our admired *Spencer* hath made him an embleme of Religion.   So *Chaucer* to the Knights of that order

———but for Gods pleasance
And his mother, and in signifiance
That ye ben of S. Georges liuerie
Doeth him seruice and Knightly obeisance
For Christs cause is his, well knowen yee.

[*a.* **1613.**] **Commaundre,** Robert.   *Epitaph on Chaucer* [in] The Booke of Heraldrye and other thinges . . . . [Commonplace book of R. Commaundre] Egerton MS. 2,642, fol. 213 (old no. 196).

Carmina Epitaphica m*agist*ri Hickeman Auditoris composita Anno d*omi*ni 1556 in Laudem Galfridi Chawser, que denno super ipsius Tumulum renovari fuit et Inscribi in Monasterio westm*onasteriensi*, et ipsum Tumulum suis Expensis decorari et repingi procuravit.

Qui fuit Anglorum Vates ter maximus olim
Galfridus Chaucer conditur hoc Tumulo
Annum si queras Domini, Si tempora mortis,
Ecce Nota subsunt, que tibi cuncta notent.
25. Octobris Anno 1400.
Galfridus Chaucer, Vates et Fama Poesis
Maternæ, hac sacra sum tumulatus Humo.

[The Rev. Robert Commaundre, [d. 1613] from whose Commonplace book the above is taken, was Rector of Tarporley, Cheshire, and chaplain to Sir Henry Sydney ; the book was compiled in the latter part of the reign of Queen Elizabeth, and a few additions were made in the reign of James I. *See* Catalogue of Addit. MSS. B. M., 1882-7, 1889, p. 359.   As Nicholas Brigham's name is carved on the tomb of Chaucer in the Abbey as its restorer, we can only suppose that Commaundre mistook the name. *See* above, p. 94, 1556, Brigham ; the last two lines are Surigo's, *see* above, 1479, p. 59, and note.]

[1613?] **Fletcher**, John. *Prologue to The Two Noble Kinsmen* ....
Written by the memorable Worthies of their time ;

Mr *John Fletcher* and ⎱ Gent.
Mr *William Shakspeare* ⎰

Printed at London by Tho. Cotes for Iohn Waterson .... 1634, verse
of title page. (Works of Beaumont and Fletcher, ed. A. Dyce,
1843–6, vol. xi, p. 329.)

[The Prologue says of the Play it introduces :]

It has a noble Breeder, and a pure,
A learned, and a Poet never went
More famous yet twixt Po and silver Trent.
Chaucer, (of all admir'd) the Story gives ;
There constant to Eternity it lives ;
If we let fall the Noblenesse of this,
And the first sound this child heare, be a hisse,
How will it shake the bones of that good man,
And make him cry from under ground, O fan
From me the witles chaffe of such a wrighter
That blastes my Bayes, and my fam'd works makes lighter
Then Robin Hood ? This is the feare we bring ;
For to say Truth, it were an endlesse thing ;
And too ambitious to aspire to him ;
Weake as we are, and almost breathlesse swim
In this deepe water. Do but you hold out
Your helping hands, and we shall take about
And something doe to save us ; you shall heare
Sceanes though below his Art, may yet appeare
Worth two houres travell. To his bones sweet sleepe.
Content to you ! . . .

[For the general likeness of the Two Noble Kinsmen to Chaucer's Knights' Tale,
and the citation of a number of parallel passages, *see* Chaucer's Einfluss auf das
englische Drama, by O. Ballmann, in Anglia, vol. xxv, 1902, pp. 36–44.]

[1613?] **Middleton**, Thomas, *No* ⎰ *Wit* ⎱ *like a Womans,* A Comedy
⎰ *help* ⎰
.... 1657, act 2, sc. 1, p. 36. (Middleton's Works, ed. A. H.
Bullen, 1885, vol. iv, p. 322.)

. . . how many honest words have suffered corruption
since *Chaucer's* days?

1614. B[rowne], W[illiam]. *The Shepheards Pipe.* London. Printed
by N. O. for George Norton, and are to be sold at his shop without
Temple Barre, 1614, the 1st Eclogue, sign. C vi *b* and C vii.

(Browne's Works, ed. W. C. Hazlitt, Roxb. library 1868, vol. ii, pp. 197–8; Poems, ed. G. Goodwin, Muses' library 1894, vol. ii, pp. 118–9.)

[Speaking of Occleve]

There are few such swaines as he
Nowadayes for harmony.

Willie. What was he thou praisest thus?

Roget. Scholler vnto *Tityrus*:

Tityrus the brauest swaine
Euer liued on the plaine,
Taught him how to feed his Lambes,
How to cure them and their Dams:
How to pitch the fold, and then
How he should remoue agen:
Taught him when the Corne was ripe,
How to make an Oaten Pipe,
How to ioyne them, how to cut them,
When to open, when to shut them,
And with all the skill he had
Did instruct this willing lad.

.   .   .   .   .

[*Note* at end of Eclogue 1, by Browne] THOMAS OCCLEEVE, one of the privy Seale, composed first this tale, and was neuer till now imprinted . . . . Hee wrote in CHAVCER'S time.

1614. Freeman, Thomas. *Runne and a great Cast, the Second Bowle* [being the 2nd part of] *Rubbe and a great Cast.* Epigrams by Thomas Freeman . . . . Imprinted at London, and are to bee sold at the Tigers Head, 1614, epigram 14, sign. G 2.

———*Mediocribus esse Poetis*
Non homines, non dij, non concessere columne
Horat. arte.

Pitty ô pitty, death had power
Ouer *Chaucer, Lidgate, Gower*:
They that equal'd all the Sages
Of these, their owne, of former Ages,
And did their learned Lights aduance
In times of darkest ignorance,
When palpable impurity
Kept knowledge in obscurity,
And all went Hood-winkt in this Ile,
They could see and shine the while;
Nor Greece, nor Rome, could reckon vs,

As then, among the Barbarous :
Since these three knew to turne perdy
The Scru-pin of Phylosophy
As well as they ; and left behind
As rich memorials of the mind :
By which they liue, though they are dead,
As all may see that will but read ;
And on good workes will spend good howres
In *Chaucers, Lidgates,* and in *Gowers.*

1614. [**Heywood,** Thomas.] *The life and death of Hector* . . . . *written by Iohn Lidgate* . . . . At London, Printed by Thomas Purfoot. [A modernized version by Thomas Heywood of Lydgate's siege and destruction of Troy, Lydgate's Chaucer references are on pp. 102–3, 144, 183, 185 (wrongly paged 183), 317, *see* above, 1412–20, pp. 23–5.]

1614. Jonson, Benjamin. *Bartholomew Fayre, A comedie Acted in the Yeare* 1614. Printed by I. B. for Robert Allot . . . . 1631, act IV, sc. iv, sign. I 3, p. 61 [in] Workes of Beniamin Jonson, 2 vols, 1616–40, vol. ii. (Works, ed. W. Gifford and F. Cunningham, 1875, vol. iv, p. 459, act IV, sc. iii.)

Was[pe] . . . . why Mistresse, I knew *Adam* the Clerke, your husband, when he was *Adam* Scriuener, and writ for two pence a sheet, as high as he beares his head now, or you your hood, Dame.

1614. Lane, John. *Spensers Squiers tale which hath been loste* . . . *now brought to light. by J. L.* 1616. Douce MS. 170, fly-leaf. [Revised Version] *Chaucers Piller beinge his Master-peece, called the Squiers Tale, w*ch *hath binn given* [*up as*] *lost, for all most thease three hundred yeares: but now found out, and brought to light by John Lane* 1630. Ashmole MS. 53 (ed. F. J. Furnivall, Chaucer soc. 1888–90, references as below) :

[pp. 3–6]   Dedications.

[p. 8]   George Hancocke (*q. v.* below, p. 190) commendatory verses.

[pp. 8–10]   The Poet Spencer concerning this invention of Chaucers lib. 4, canto 2, stafe 31.

[pp. 10–13] The discription of the Squier as it was written by Chaucer, etc.

[p. 13]   Thus farr Chaucer ; Now followeth a supplie to what heereof is missinge ; finished by John Lane anno Domini 1615.

[pp. 234–5] Epilogue.

[p. 236]   Extra lines in Ashmole MS.

[A note in the Douce MS., fol. 35, states : This supplemente to Chaucers Squiers tale, containinge 17 sheetes, hath licence to be printed. March 2 1614. John Tauerner.]

1615. Gordon, Patrick. *See* below, App. A, 1615.

1615. Hancocke, George. *George Hancocke, Somersettensis, to his frende J. L.* Commendatory lines prefixed to Chaucer's Squire's tale, by John Lane [*q.v.* above, p. 189]. Douce MS., fol. 1 *b.* (Ed. F. J. Furnivall, Chaucer soc. 1888–90, p. 8.)

> So ringe the peale of love, truith, iustice out,
> as it, into theire choire, all heerers chime ;
>
> .   .   .   .   .   .
>
> as Chaucer, Lidgate, Sidney, Spencer dead,
> yett livinge swanns, singe out what thow haste sedd ?

1615. Jonson, Benjamin. *Masques at Court. The Golden Age Restored in a Maske at Court,* 1615 ; [printed] 1616 [in] The Workes of Beniamin Jonson, 2 vols., 1616–40, vol. i, pp. 1012–13. (Works of B. Jonson, ed. W. Gifford and F. Cunningham, 1875, vol. vii, pp. 251–2.)

> Pal[las]. Yow farre-fam'd spirits of this happie Ile,
> That, for your sacred songs haue gain'd the stile
> Of Phœbvs sons : whose notes they aire aspire
> Of th' old *Ægyptian,* or the *Thracian* lyre,
> That *Chaucer, Gower, Lidgate, Spencer* hight
> Put on your better flames, and larger light,
> To waite vpon the age that shall your names **new nourish**
> Since vertue prest shall grow, and buried arts shall flourish.
>
> *Poets descend.*

1615. Niccholes, Alex[ander]. *A discourse of marriage and wiuing . . . . by Alex. Niccholes, Batchelour in the Art he neuer yet put in practise,* London, 1620, p. 16. (Reprinted from an edn. dated 1615 in Harl. Miscell. Oldys and Park, vol. ii, 1809, p. 165.)

> [Reference to January and May.]

1615. Peacham, Henry. *Prince Henrie Revived.* Or a Poeme vpon the Birth . . . . of the . . . . yong Prince Henrie Frederick . . . . sign. B i *b.*

> I may not rash aread ; but this I wot
> How *Ianivere,* his bitter rage forgot,
> For lustie greene y'chang'd his frostie gray,
> (As if he woed the sweet and daintie May).

1615. V[allans], W[illiam]. *The Honourable Prentice :* or This Taylor is a man . . . . Where-unto is annexed the most lamentable murther of Robert Hall at the High Altar in Westminster Abbey. London. 1615. Bodl. library. (Dedication to his friend master Robert Valens, signed "W. V.")

> [p. 33, running title] The lamentable murder of Robert Hall.
>
> .   .   .   .
>
> Hall lyeth buried in the Abbey at *Westminster,* not far from

Chaucers Tombe, vnder a faire monument of a flat Marble
stone, with his image of brasse in his armour : and about the
same certaine verses in Lattin, which (though much defaced
with treading, and neere worne out,) may be found in a booke
called the *Remaines of a greater Worke*, set foorth by M[r]
Camden, al. Clarēceaulx King at Arnes.

[The account of the 'Murther of Hall' is wanting in the 1616 edition, though it is
given on the title-page. *See also* Wm. Lambarde in *Dictionarium Angliæ*, etc., *c*. 1585,
p. 390 ; p. 126, above.]

[*c.* 1615.] Beaumont, Francis, and Fletcher, John. *The Woman's
Prize: or The Tamer Tamed*, act IV, sc. i, [in] Comedies and
Tragedies, written by Francis Beaumont and Iohn Fletcher
Gentlemen . . . . 1647, p. 113. (Works of Beaumont & Fletcher,
ed. A. Dyce, vol. vii, 1844, p. 172.)

Petron[ius to Moroso who wishes to marry] Thou fond man
   Hast thou forgot the Ballard [sic], crabbed age,
   Can May and Ianuary match together,
   And nev'r a storm between 'em ?

[*a.* 1616.] Pits, or Pitseus, John. *Relationum Historicarum de Rebus
Anglicis tomus primus*, Parisiis, 1619, De illustribus Angliæ
Scriptoribus, pp. 572–5 [life of Chaucer], 576 [Gower] 632
[Lydgate] 953 [Index]. [Published after Pits's death by Dr. W.
Bishop. For extract, *see* Appendix A, 1613, Pits.]

               De Illustribus Angliæ Scriptoribus.
[pp. 572–75]   No. 730. De Galfredo Chaucero.   1400.
[p. 576]   No. 731. De Joanne Gowero.   1402.
[p. 632]   No. 820. De Joanne Lidgato.   1440.
[p. 953]   Index illustrium Angliæ Scriptorum qui fuerunt Oxoni-
               ensis Academiæ.

1616. Camden, William. *MS. lines*, in Camden's hand from Chaucer's
Nonne Preestes Tale written on the back of Grant of Arms by W.
Camden, Clarenceux, to Robert Wakeman, D.D., of Beerferris, co.
Devon. Addit. Charters 26,607 (Catalogue Addit. MSS., 1876–81,
p. 264).

      Pro Crista autem supra Cassidem et tortile ex suis coloribus,
A Cock in his proper and natiue colours, with a scrole in his
bek inscribed EVIGILA QUI DORMIS vt clarius in margine depicta
conspiciuntur ; [on the back in Camden's hand,] The Cock
giuen for the Crest in the Armes within described is like that
in Geffrey Chaucer in the Nonnes Priest his Tale and is called
Chaunteclere.

      His comb was redder then the fine corall

      .   .   .   .

      And like the burned gold was his colour.
                                        [ll. 4049–54.]

[1616.] Earle, John. *An Elegie upon Master Francis Beaumont,* [in] Poems, by Francis Beaumont, 1640, sign. K 2.

> . . . thine [fame] is lowest now,
> But thou shalt live, and when thy name is grown,
> Six ages elder, shalt be better knowne :
> When th' art of *Chaucers* standing in thy tombe,
> Thou shalt not shame [*sic, for* share], but take up all his roome.
>
> I. Earle.

[Reprinted in the First Folio of Beaumont and Fletcher's *Comedies and Tragedies* 1647, sign. C 4 *b*, where it is preceded by the remark : "Written thirty yeares since, presently after his [Beaumont's] death." Cf. Basse's epitaph on Shakespeare, below, p. 196 and note.]

1617. [Brathwait, Richard.] *Chaucer's incensed Ghost,* a poem appended to The Smoaking Age, or, the man in the mist, with the life and death of Tobacco . . . . cɔiɔ cxvii.

[A copy of this first edn. was in the Huth library, and is fully described in Collectanea Anglo-Poetica by T. Corser (Chetham soc.), part ii, 1861, pp. 355–61. It was reprinted in The Smoaking Age . . . . To which is added CHAWCER's Incensed Ghost, 1703, pp. 38–41; *see also* a reprint in R. Braithwait's Comments, etc., ed. C. Spurgeon, Chaucer soc., 1901, pp. viii–xi.]

1617. Lane, John. *The corrected historie of Sir Guy Earle of Warwick . . . . begun by Don Lidgatt, monk of St. Edmunds Berye ; but now diligentlie acquired from all antiquitie by John Lane,* 1621. Harl. MSS. 5243, ff. 4, 5 *b.*, 7, col. 1, 131, col. 2. *Coloph:* written by me John Lane, have licence to be printed July 13, 1617. (The references on ff. 4 and 5 *b* are printed in Bp. Percy's Folio MS. Ballads and Romances, ed. J. W. Hales and F. J. Furnivall, 1867–8, vol. ii, 1868, part ii, pp. 522, 524.)

[Mere passing references to Chaucer.]

[1618 ?] Bolton, Edmund. *Hypercritica ; or A Rule of Judgment for writing or reading our History's. . .* by Edmund Bolton . . now first published by Ant. Hall, Oxford, 1722 [at the end of Hall's Nicolai Triveti Annalium Continuatio, etc.], section iii, pp. 199, 235 ; Rawlinson MSS. (Reprinted in Ancient Critical Essays, etc., ed. J. Haslewood, vol. ii, 1815, p. 249.)

[p. 199]   Addresse the Fourth. Prime Gardens for gathering English : according to the true Gage or Standard of the Tongue,[1] about

[p. 235] 15 or 16 years ago.   Sect. iii. In verse there are *Ed. Spencer's* Hymns. I cannot advise the allowance of other his Poems, as for Practick *English,* no more than I can do *Jeff. Chaucer, Lydgate, Peirce Ploughman,* or *Laureat Skelton* . . . for an Historian in our Tongue to affect the like [use of " outworn Words "] out of those our Poets, would be accounted a foul Oversight.

[1] Anthony à Wood thought these addresses were written about 1610. [But see article on Bolton in D.N.B.]

1618. Savile, Sir Henry. *Thomæ Bradwardini Archiepiscopi olim Cantuariensis De Causa Dei . . . . Opera et Studio Domini Henrici Sauilii,* Lectori sign. A 3.

Nam de Galfrido Chaucero illorum ferè temporum æquali, poetarum nostrorum principe, acris iudicij, non lepidi tantum ingenij, viro, qui de Thoma hoc nostrate non tacuit, nobis nefas sit hic tacere.

1619. Gil, Alexander. *Logonomia Anglica.* Qua gentis sermo facilius addiscitur. Conscripta ab. Alexandro Gil Paulinæ Scolæ Magistro Primario. Londini. Excudit Johannes Beale, 1619, sign. B 2 *b.* (ed. from the edn. of 1621 [same title], by Otto L. Jiriczek 1903 [in] Quellen und Forschungen . . . . der germanischen Völker, ed. Alois Brandl, Heft 90.)

Præfatio ad Lectorem.

. . . .

Huc vsque peregrinæ voces in linguâ Anglicâ inauditæ. Tandem circa annum 1400, *Galfridus Chaucerus,* infausto omine, vocabulis Gallicis, & Latinis poesin suam famosam reddidit. Hic enim vulgi indocti stupor est, vt illa maximè quæ non intelligit admiretur. Hinc noua profluxit scribendi, & loquendi scabies. Nam vt quisque sciolus videri vult, & linguæ Latinæ, Gallicæ, aliusue suam peritiam venditare : ita quotidie fera vocum monstra cicuriat; horridasque, & malè sonantes, nidique infausti picas, & cicumas nostra verba conari docet.

1620. James, Thomas. *Catalogus Vniversalis librorum in Bibliotheca Bodleiana . . . auctore Thoma Iames . . .* Oxoniæ 1620, p. 123.

Galfr. *Chaucerus.* Opera Anglice, *Lond,* 1561, C. 4. 4 & MS. c. 7.11.
Of the Warre of Thebes (vt. vid.) *MS.* 40, 28.

[The war of Thebes is not entered either under War or Thebes. For the first catalogue (also by James), *see* above, 1605, p. 175 and for the third *see* below, 1674, p. 249, T. Hyde.]

[1620-35 ?]. Jonson, Benjamin. *Timber or Discoveries, Made vpon Men and Matter* . . . . 1641, The Workes of Beniamin Jonson, 1616–41, vol. ii, pp. 116, 118, 119 [pagination not continuous]. (Works, ed. W. Gifford and F. Cunningham, 1875, vol. ix, pp. 193–4, 198.)

Precipiendi modi. . . . And as it is fit to reade the best Authors to youth first, so let them be of the openest and clearest: As *Livy* *Livy* before *Salust, Sydney* before *Donne* : and beware of *Salust* *Sydney* letting them taste *Gower,* or *Chaucer* at first, lest falling too *Donne* *Gower* much in love with Antiquity, and not apprehending the weight, *Chaucer* *Spencer* they grow rough and barren in language onely. When their judgements are firme and out of danger, let them reade both, the old and the new : but no lesse take heed, that their new flowers, and sweetnesse doe not as much corrupt, as the others

CHAUCER CRITICISM.

drinesse, and squallor, if they choose not carefully. *Spencer*, in affecting the Ancients writ no Language : Yet I would have him read for his matter ; but as *Virgil* read *Ennius*.

. . . .

Consue- *Custome* is the most certaine Mistresse of Language, as the
tudo
[p. 118] publicke stampe makes the current money. But wee must
[p. 119] not . . . . fetch words from the extreme and utmost ages ; since the chiefe vertue of a style is perspicuitie, and nothing so vitious in it, as to need an Interpreter . . . . *Virgill* was
Virgil most loving of Antiquity ; yet how rarely doth hee insert
Lucre-
tius *aquai* and *pictai !* *Lucretius* is scabrous and rough in these ;
Chaucer- hee seekes 'hem : As some do *Chaucerismes* with us, which
isme.
were better expung'd and banish'd.

1620. **R[owlands]**, S[amuel]. *The Night Rauen.* By S. R. Sign. D iv *b.* (Rowland's Works, introduction by E. Gosse, notes by S. Herrtage, Hunterian club, 1880, vol. ii, p. 32.)

[A summary, in 20 lines, of part of the *Miller's Tale.*]

1620. **Taylor**, John (the Water Poet). *The Praise of Hemp-seed.* 1620, pp. 26–7. (Works of Taylor, Folio edn. of 1630, reprinted for Spenser soc., 1869, part iii, p. 72.)

> In paper, many a Poet now suruiues
> Or else their lines had perish'd with their liues.
> Old *Chaucer, Gower,* and Sir *Thomas More,*
> Sir *Philip Sidney,* who the Lawrell wore,
> *Spencer,* and *Shakespeare* did in Art excell,
> Sir *Edward Dyer, Greene, Nash, Daniell,*
> *Siluester, Beumont,* Sir *Iohn Harrington,*
> Forgetfulnesse their workes would ouerrun,
> But that in paper they immortally
> Doe liue in spight of death, and cannot die.

1621. **Heylyn**, Peter. ΜΙΚΡΟΚΟΣΜΟΣ. *A little Description of the Great World.* Augmented and reuised. Oxford. Printed by John Lichfield and William Tvrner, 1625.—*The Brittish Isles*, pp. 474–5, sign. Ff 8 *b.* and Gg 1.

The chiefe in matter of Poesie haue bin 1 *Gower*, 2 *Chaucer,* of whom *Sir Philip Sidney* vsed to say, that he maruailed how that man in those mistie times could see so clearely, and how we in these cleare times goe so stumblingly after him, 3 *Edmund Spencer,* 4 *Drayton* . . .

[The title of the first edn., printed 1621, is Microcosmus, or A little Description of the Great World . . . By P. H. At Oxford. Printed by Iohn Lichfield and Iames Short . . . 1621. This first edn. is not in the B. M. Heylyn enlarged this work and reprinted it in 1652, under the title of *Cosmographie*, where this reference, slightly altered, occurs on p. 268.]

1621. Lane, John. *Tritons Trumpet to the sweete Monethes husbanded and moralized by John Lane.* MS., Reg. 17 B xv, ff. 3, 23, 176, 181.

[fol. 176]   But Chaucer shee [Queen Mary] bidds com down off his
     spheare !

     And 'mongst the Laureat poets waite on her !

[This reference is given in An Introduction to Shakespeare's Midsummer Night's Dream by J. O. Halliwell, 1841, p. 66.]

1621. Taylor, John (the Water Poet). *Taylor's Motto Et habeo, Et careo, Et curo,* sign. E 2. (Works of John Taylor, folio edn. of 1630, reprinted for Spenser soc. 1869, part ii, p. 57.)

[In speaking of the] " Bookes that I haue read of Poesie" [Taylor says :]

> Old *Chaucer, Sidney, Spencer, Daniel, Nash,*
> I dipt my finger where they vs'd to wash.
> As I haue read these Poets, I haue noted
> Much good, which in my memory is quoted.

1621. Wither, George. *Wither's Motto Nec habeo, nec Careo, nec Curo.* London, printed for John Marriott 1621, sign. A 3 *b*, A 4. (Juvenilia, Poems by George Wither, reprinted by the Spenser soc. 1871, pt. iii, pp. 626-7.)

To any body.

The foolish *Canterbury* Tale in my *scourge* of *Vanity* (which I am now almost ashamed to read ouer), euen that, hath bin by some praysed for a witty passage.

1621-51-2. [**Burton,** Robert.] *The Anatomy of Melancholy . . . by Democritus Junior.* [1st edn. 1621, continually revised by the author till 1651, 6th edn. posthumously printed. The references are to the edn. of A. R. Shilleto, introduction A. H. Bullen, 3 vols. 1893. The subdivisions are given so that the references may be the more easily traced through the various edns.; they are all in vol. iii of the 1893 edn.]

p.	57.	Part iii,	sect. ii,	mem.	i,	subs.	ii.
	60.	„	„	„		„	
	65.	„	„	„	ii,	„	i.
	70	„	„	„		„	
	89.	„	„	„	iii,	„	ii.
	124.	„	„	„	ii,	„	iv.
	129.	„	„	„	ii,	„	iv.
	143.	„	„	„		„	
	148.	„	„	„		„	v.
	154.	„	„	„	iii,	„	i.
	161.	„	„	„		„	

p. 181.	Part iii,	sect. ii,	mem. iii,		subs.	i.
186.	,,	,,	,,		,,	
190, 197.	,,	,,	,,		,,	
233.	,,	,,	,,	v,	,,	ii.
248.	,,	,,	,,		,,	iii.
254.	,,	,,	,,		,,	
282.	,,	,,	,,		,,	v.
292 [2 refs.], 295.	,,	,,	,,		,,	
301, 302.	,,	,, iii	,,	i,	,,	i.
306, 307, 320.	,,	,,	,,		,,	ii.
339.	,,	,,	,,	iv,	,,	i.
351.	,,	,,	,,		,,	ii.

[These references are practically all quotations from Chaucer, most frequently from the Wife of Bath's Prologue (7 references), and next to that from the Knight's Tale and Troilus and Creseid (6 each). It is worth notice that Burton only quotes Chaucer in connection with ' Love.' On p. 181 he refers to Chaucer as ' our English Homer,' and in a note on p. 339 he says ' Read Petrarch's Tale of Patient Grizel in Chaucer.' These are the only references other than quotation from or allusion to some one of Chaucer's poems.]

[*c.* or *a.* **1622** ?] **Basse,** William. *Epitaph on William Shakespeare.* MS. Lansdowne 777, fol. 67 *b.* (The Shakspere Allusion Book, by C. M. Ingleby, ed. J. J. Munro, 1909, vol. i, pp. 286–9.)

On M^r· Wm Shakespeare.   he dyed in Aprill 1616.

Renowned Spencer lye a thought more nye
To learned Chaucer, and rare Beaumont lye
A little neerer Spenser, to make roome
For Shakespeare in your threefold, fowerfold Tombe.
To lodge all fowre in one bed make a shift
Vntill Doomesdaye, for hardly will a fift
Betwixt *this* day and *that* by Fate be slayne,
For whom your Curtaines may be drawn againe.
If your precedency in death doth barre
A fourth place in your sacred sepulcher,
Vnder this carued marble of thine owne,
Sleepe, rare Tragædian, Shakespeare, sleep alone ;
Thy vnmolested peace, vnshared Caue,
Possesse as Lord, not Tenant, of thy Graue,
That vnto us & others it may be
Honor hereafter to be layde by thee.

                Wm. Basse.

[There are many versions of this poem, not only in the numerous MSS. in which it exists, but in the various edns. in which it appeared ; a very complete list of these is given in the *Allusion Book.* The earliest printed version of it is in Poems, with Elegies on the Author's Death, John Donne, 1633, p. 165. A distinct reference to it is made in Jonson's own epitaph on Shakespeare, 1623, *q.v.* below, p. 198. The apparent reference to it by Earle, 1616, *q.v.* above, points to that year for its composition.]

[*a.* **1622.**] **Middleton**, Tho[mas]. *Two New Playes, viz. More Dissemblers besides Women, Women beware women,* 1657. More Dissemblers, etc., act i, sc. 4, p. 17. (Works, ed. A. H. Bullen, 1885-6, 8 vols., vol. vi, 1885, p. 397 ; *see* note as to date, *ibid.,* p. 375.)

. . . . 'Tis not good to jest, as old *Chaucer* was wont to say, that broad famous English Poet.

[For Chaucer's influence on Middleton *see* O. Ballmann ; Chaucers Einfluss auf das englische Drama, Anglia, vol. xxv, pp. 74-6.]

1622. Peacham, Henry. *The Compleat Gentleman Fashioning him absolute in the most necessary and Commendable Qualities Concerning Minde or Bodie that may be required in a Noble Gentleman.* By Henry Peacham . . . . 1622, Of Poetry, ch. 10, pp. 81-2, 94-5.

[p. 81]   Hence hath Poetry neuer wanted her Patrones, and euen the greatest Monarches and Princes . . . haue exercised their Inuention herein : . . . Euery child knoweth how deare the workes of *Homer* were vnto *Alexander* . . . in our owne Countrey, *a Chaucer* to *Richard* the second, *Gower* to *Henrie* the fourth with others I might alledge.

a Who gaue him, as it is thought, his Manuor of *Bwhelme* in Oxfordshire.

[p. 94] Sir *Geoffrey Chaucer.* Of English Poets of our owne Nation, esteeme Sir *Geoffrey Chaucer* the father; although the stile for the antiquitie, may distast you, yet as vnder a bitter and rough rinde, there lyeth a delicate kernell of conceit and sweete inuention. What Examples, Similitudes, Times, Places, and aboue all, Persons, with their speeches, and attributes, doe as in *Canterburie*-tales (like these threds of gold, the rich *Arras*) beautifie his Worke quite thorough ? And albeit diuers of his workes, are but meerely translations out of *Latine* and *French*, yet he hath handled them so artificially, that thereby he hath made them his owne, as his *Troilus* and *Cresseid*. The Romant of the Rose, was the inuention of *Iehan de Mehunes*, a French Poet, whereof he translated but onely the one halfe : his *Canterburie*-tales without question were his owne inuention, all circumstances being wholly English. Hee was a good Diuine, and saw in those times without his spectacles, as may appeare by the Plough-man and the Parsons tale : withall an excellent Mathematician, as plainly appeareth by his discourse of the Astrolabe to his little sonne *Lewes*. In briefe, account him among the best of your English bookes in your librarie.

p. 95]   *Gower* . . . was a knight, as also was *Chaucer*.

1622. Unknown. *The History of Allchester near Bircester in Oxfordshire . . . . in the year* 1622. [Appendix, pp. 683-703, in] Parochial Antiquities Attempted in the History of Ambrosden, Burcester . . . . by White Kennett [Bp. of Peterborough] MDCXCV, p. 694 (new edn., 2 vols, Oxford, 1818, vol. ii, p. 431.)

[p. 694]   . . . . The Town of *Woodstock* is a good Market and a Corporation, and more graced with the birth of ancient Learned *Chaucer* and Doctor *Case* then with any Monument of Antiquity within it.

[In the preface to the edn. of 1818, vol. i, p. xv, Dr. White Kennett gives the following account of the MS. : "There was one Manuscript communicated to me by my very worthy Friend Mr. Blackwell, B.D., which (tho' of modern age and no great authority) immediately relating to these parts, I thought good with consent of the owner to join as an Appendix to this work, under the title of the *History of Allchester near Bircester in Oxfordshire, etc. wrote in the year* 1622.]

[1623.] Dekker, Thomas. *The Wonder of a kingdome.* . . . . 1636, sign. D 1. (Dramatic works of Thomas Dekker, ed. John Pearson, vol. iv, 1873, p. 245.)

[Reference to January and May.]

1623. Jonson, Benjamin. [*Epitaph*] *To the memory of my beloued, the* AVTHOR, *M*r *William Shakespeare, and what he hath left vs* ; [prefixed to the First Folio edn. of] Shakespeare's Works, printed by Isaac Iaggard and Ed. Blount, 1623, sign. A 6.

I, therefore, will begin.   Soule of the Age !
The applause ! delight ! the wonder of our Stage !
My *Shakespeare*, rise ; I will not lodge thee by[1]
Chaucer, or *Spenser*, or bid *Beaumont* lye
A little further, to make thee a roome :
Thou art a Moniment, without a tombe,
And art aliue still, while thy Booke doth liue,
And we haue wits to read, and praise to giue.

[1 This is a reference to Basse's lines on Shakespeare, *q. v.* above, 1622, p. 196.]

1623. Painter, William. *Chaucer new painted.* Licensed to Henry Seile 25 May, 1623. [The dedication to Sir Paul Pinder signed William Painter, not the author of the Palace of Pleasure. *See* Poetical Decameron, by J. P. Collier, 1820, vol. ii, pp. 165-6 ; also W. C. Hazlitt's bibliographical collections, 2nd ser. 1882, p. 442, where it is called "a book." No copy is now known to exist.]

1624. Webster, John. *Monuments of Honor.* . . . . celebrated in the Honorable City of London . . . . Invented and Written by John Webster . . . . Printed at London by Nicholas Okes, 1624 [unique copy at Chatsworth, Duke of Devonshire's library]. (The dramatic works of John Webster, ed. W. Hazlitt, vol. iii, 1857, pp. 236-7.)

After my Lord Mayor's landing, . . . there first attends for his honor in Paul's churchyard, a beautiful spectacle, called the Temple of Honor . . . . In the highest seat a person repre-

senting Troynovant or the City . . . . beneath her . . . . sit
five eminent cities, as Antwerp, Paris, Rome, Venice and Con-
stantinople : under these sit five famous scholars and poets of
this our kingdom, as Sir Jeffrey Chaucer, the learned Gower,
the excellent John Lidgate, the sharp-witted sir Thomas More,
and last, as worthy both soldier and scholar, sir Philip Sidney,
—these being celebrators of honor, and the preservers both of
the names of men and memories of cities above to posterity
. . . . My Lord is . . . . saluted with two speeches; first by
Troynovant in these lines following.

.   .   .   .

Beneath these, [the five cities] five learn'd poets, worthy men
Who do eternise brave acts by their pen,
Chaucer, Gower, Lidgate, More, and for our time
Sir Philip Sidney, glory of our clime :
These beyond death a fame to monarchs give
And these make cities and societies live.

[This pageant was written for the Lord Mayor's (John Gore's) Show of 1624.]

1625. D[ekker], Tho[mas]. *A Rod for Run-awayes.* . . . . Written by
Tho. D., 1625. (Non-dramatic works of Thomas Dekker, ed. A. B.
Grosart, Huth. library, vol. iv, 1885, p. 302.)

[A tale of a young " Maide " of Kent, who is not allowed to
go to her sister in the town, as the citizens fear she has come
from London, and may bring the plague with her. She goes
into the fields and dies. As a side note are these words :—]

A Kentish tale, but truer than those of Chaucers.

[Grosart used an edition in the Bodleian, there is none in the B.M.]

[1625 ?] Jonson, Ben[jamin]. *The Staple of Newes, a comedie acted in
the yeare* 1625 . . . . Printed . . . . for Robert Allot 1631,
act iii, sc. ii, fol. 41. [Bound in vol. ii, of the first folio edn. of
Jonson's Works, 1640.] (ed. De Winter, 1905, Yale Studies in
English, ed. A. S. Cook, No. xxviii, p. 63.)

[speaking of the News Staple to its Register.]
P[eni-Boy] Iu [i. e. Junior] . . . . good *Register,*
We'll stand it out here, and obserue your *Office*;
What *Newes* it issues. *Reg*[ister]. 'Tis the house of *fame,* Sir,

The Office Where . . . . all doe meet,
call'd the
house of To taste the *Cornucopiæ* of her rumors,
fame.
Which she, the mother of sport, pleaseth to scatter
Among the vulgar.

[For resemblance of the 'news staple' to Chaucer's House of Fame, *see* De Winter,
in his edn. of The Staple of News . . . 1905, introduction, pp. xxii–iii, and also
Emil Koeppel in Quellen-Studien zu den dramen Ben Jonson's, etc. [in] Münchener
Beiträge zur roman. u. engl. Philologie, Heft xi, 1895, pp. 16–18.]

[*c.* 1625.] **B[arry]**, J[ames].   *A funerall Elegy on King James,* Trinity
Coll. MS. (Ireland), F. 4. 20. (652).

> Shall it be his as't was greate Henery's fate
> That none but poet Skelton should relate
> His worth, whose worke may well deserve that doome,
> Th' epitaph is more berayer than the tomb :
> Rather awake, dead Muse, thy master's prayse
> May grace thy accents and enriche thy layes
> A thought of him had made that Skelton write
> More wittily than Chaucer. . . .

[*c.* 1625.] **Unknown.**   *Gaulfridus Chaucer',* written, in an early 17th
cent. hand, in the margin of fol. 1 of the Haistwell MS. of Chaucer's
Canterbury Tales, now Egerton 2726.

[*See* above, *c.* 1450, p. 50.]

[1626-43.] **Browne**, William.   *Britannia's Pastorals,* book iii, song 2.
MS. Salisbury Cathedral library.   First printed for the Percy soc.
1852, by T. Crofton Croker. (Browne's Works, ed. W. C. Hazlitt,
Roxb. library, 1868-9, vol. ii, p. 156 ; Poems, ed. G. Goodwin,
Muses library, 1894, vol. ii, p. 66.)

> It was a shepheard that was borne by-west,
> And well of *Tityrus* had learnt to sing.

[*Cf.* above, 1579, p. 118, Edmund Spenser, who also refers to Chaucer as Tityrus.]

1627. Camden, William.   *Annales Rerum Anglicarum et Hibernicarum
Regnante Elizabetha.* . . . 1615, Tomus alter, 1627, pp. 171-2.   (The
history or Annals of England, written by William Cambden, [in]
A complete history of England, vol. ii, 1706, p. 612.)

> [Under year 1598] Edm. Spenserus, patriâ Londinensis . . . .
> Musis adeo arridentibus natus, vt omnes Anglicos superioris
> æui Poëtas, ne Chaucero quidem conciue excepto, superaret
> [p. 172] . . . . expiravit, & Westmonasterij prope Chaucerum im-
> pensis Comitis Essexiæ inhumatus, Poëtis sunus ducentibus,
> flebilibus carminibus & calamis in tumulum conjectis.

1627. Drayton, Michael.   *To my most dearely-loued friend Henery
Reynolds Esquire, of Poets and Poesie,* [in] The Battaile of Agin-
court . . . . Printed for William Lee, 1627, sign. Dd 1. (The
Barons Wars, etc., by M. Drayton, ed. Henry Morley, 1887, p. 260.)

> That noble *Chaucer,* in those former times,
> The first inrich'd our *English* with his rimes,
> And was the first of ours, that euer brake,
> Into the *Muses* treasure, and first spake
> In weighty numbers, deluing in the Mine
> Of perfect knowledge, which he could refine,

> And coyne for currant, and asmuch as then
> The *English* language could expresse to men,
> He made it doe ; and by his wondrous skill
> Gaue vs much light from his abundant quill.
> And honest *Gower*, who in respect of him,
> Had only sipt at *Aganippas* brimme,
> And though in yeares this last was him before,
> Yet fell he far short of the others store.

1627. Drayton, Michael. *Nimphidia, The Covrt of Fayrie,* [in] The Battaile of Agincourt . . . . . . Printed for William Lee, 1627, sign. Q 1 (The Barons Wars, Nymphidia, etc., by M. Drayton, ed. Henry Morley, 1887, p. 193.)

> [Verse 1] Olde CHAVCER doth of *Topas* tell,
> Mad RABLAIS of *Pantagruell*,
> A latter third of *Dowsabell*,
> With such poore trifles playing :
> .   .   .   .   .   .

[*Cf.* Drayton, 1593, above, pp. 138–9, in *Idea*, Eclogue 8, *see* p. 114 of Collier's edn. quoted under this latter reference.]

1628. Earle, John. *Micro-cosmographie* or *A Peece of the World Discovered In Essayes and Characters*, London, Printed by William Stansby for Edward Blount, 1628, sign. I 7. (English Reprints, ed. E. Arber, 1869, p. 70. In this edition "A Vulgar-Spirited Man" is numbered 49 amongst the characters.)

50. A vulgar-spirited Man [is one] . . . That cries *Chaucer* for his Money aboue all our English Poets, because the voice ha's gone so, and hee ha's read none.

1628. H[ayman], R[obert]. *Quodlibets, lately come over from New Britanolia, Old Newfoundland, . . . by R. H. sometimes Gouernour of the Plantation there*, London, Printed by Elizabeth All-de for Roger Michell, sign. D i b, p. 18. (*See* Anthony à Wood's Athenæ Oxonienses, 3rd edn., 1813, vol. ii (1815), p. 608, par. 607.)

111. To the Reuerend, learned, acute, and witty, Master *Charles Fitz-Geoffrey*, Bachelor in Diuinity, my especiall kind friend, most excellent Poet.

> Blind *Poet Homer* you doe equalize,
> Though he saw more with none, then most with eyes.
> Our *Geoffery Chaucer*, who wrote quaintly, neat,
> In verse you match equall him in conceit,
> Featur'd you are like *Homer* in one eye,
> Rightly surnam'd the Sonne of *Geoffery*.

1629. Jonson, Benjamin. *The New Inne . . . as it was . . . negligently play'd . . . by . . . the Kings Seruants, and beheld . . . 1629 . . . Now . . . to be judged . . .* 1631, act i, sc. 3 ; act ii, sc. 4 ; act iii, sc. 2, sign. B 4, C 5 *b*, C 6, E 5 and *b*. (Works, ed. W. Gifford and F. Cunningham, 1875, vol. v, pp. 313–14, act I, sc. i; p. 335, act II, sc. ii ; pp. 370–71, act. III, sc. ii.)

[For a detailed account of Chaucer's influence on Jonson's plays, *see* Chaucers Einfluss auf das englische Drama, by O. Ballman, Anglia, xxv, pp. 14–28.]

[Act i, sc. 1] [Lovel, praising men nurtured at court,]
> . . . . doe they not still
> Learne there the Centaures skill, the art of Thrace,
> To ride? or *Pollux* mystery, to fence?
>
> .   .   .   .
>
> To make their English sweet vpon their tongue !
> As reu'rend *Chaucer* says? [Prologue, l. 265]. *Host.* Sir you mistake
> To play Sir *Pandarus* my copy hath it,
> And carry messages to Madame *Cresside*.
>
> .   .   .   .

[Act ii, sc. 2] *Host.* And speakes a little taynted, fly-blowne *Latin*,
> After the Schoole *Bea*[ufort] : of Stratford o' the Bow.
> For *Lillies Latine*, is to him vnknow.
>
> .   .   .   .

[Act iii sc. 2] *Lad*[y] What pennance shall *I* doe, to be receiu'd
> And reconcil'd, to the Church of Loue?
> Goe on profession, bare-foot, to his Image,
> An say some hundred penitentiall verses,
> There, out of *Chaucers Troilus*, and *Cresside*?
> Or to his Mother's shrine vow a Waxe candle
> As large as the Towne May-pole is, and pay it !
> Enioyne me any thing the Court thinks fit,
> For I have trespass'd, and blasphemed Loue.

1630. Brathwait, Richard. *The English Gentleman, containing Sundry excellent Rules or exquisite Observations tending to Direction of Every Gentleman of selecter rank and qualitie.* Recreation, p. 190.

[Speaking of the royal patronage of letters in the past :—]
. . . to descend to our later times ; how much were *Jehan de Mehune*, and *Guillamne* [*sic*] *de Loris* made of by the French Kings? and *Jeffery Chaucer*, Father of our English Poets, by *Richard* the second; who it was supposed, gave him the Mannor of *Newholme* in *Oxfordshire*?

[*c.* **1630.**] **S[idnam]**, J[onathan]. *A Paraphrase vpon the three first Bookes of Chaucers Troilus and Cressida Translated into our Moderne English For the satisfaction of those Who either cannot, or will not take y*e* paines to vnderstand The Excellent Authors Farr more Exquisite, and significant Expressions Though now growen obsolete, and out of vse.* By J. S[idnam]. MS. Addit. B. M. 29,494, Folio, 70 leaves, in 7-line stanzas.

[Verse 1]   The double cares of Troilus to tell
    Who was y*e* Sonne of Priam King of Troy,
In his first love, how his adventures fell,
    From Woe to blisse, and after to annoy.
    Is now the task that must my Muse employ
Teach me Tysiphone how to endite
This mournefull verse, which weepes as I doe write.

[An unpublished MS. sold at Puttick and Simpson's in June 1873. There is no introductory matter. Extract from W. C. Hazlitt's Collections and Notes, 1876, p. 83.]

1630. Unknown. *The Tincker of Turvey.* London. Printed for Nath: Butter, dwelling at St. Austins Gate, 1630 [the running title is Canterburie Tales], sign. A 3, B 1, B 2. (ed. J. O. Halliwell, 1859. . . . The Epistle, p. v, and pp. 9, 11.)

[sign. A 3] *The Epistle* . . . But now to the Tinkers Tales, which were told in the Barge betweene *Billinsgate* and *Grauesend* : Herein following the steppes of old *Chaucer*, (the first Father of *Canterbury*-Tales :) These comming as farre short of his, as Bragget goes beyond the Pigs wash or small Beere.

[sign. B 1.
Head-title]   *The Tinker of Turvey,* Or *Canterburie Tales.*

    .   .   .   .

[sign. B 2] . . . lets pass away the time in telling of tales, and because I thinke most of us are for *Canterbury* we will call them *Canterbury Tales.*

[*Cf.* The Cobler of Canterburie, 1590, above, p. 132, to which there is a reference in Greene's Vision, 1592, above, pp. 137–8.]

[*c.* **1630** ?] **Unknown.** *Heading* to ll. 1428–81, of Chanon Yemannes Tale in Sloane MS. 320, fol. 35 *b*–36.

    J. Chawser   The tale of the Channons Yeoman.
    Lo thus saythe Arnolde of y*e* newe town)

    .   .   .   .   .   .

    God sende everie good man) boote of his bale &c'.
        .·. finis //

1631. [**Brathwait**, Richard.] *Whimzies: Or, A New Cast of Characters, Nova, non nota delectant*, London, printed by F. K. . . 1631, p. 119 (reprinted J. O. Halliwell, 1859, p. 75, and quoted in Restituta, by Sir S. E. Brydges 1816, vol. iv, p. 283).

A Post-Master.

Hee rides altogether upon *spurre*, and no lesse is requisite for his *dull supporter*; who is as familiarly acquainted with a *Canterbury*, as hee who makes *Chaucer* his *Author*, is with his *Tale*.

[The "Epistle Dedicatorie" is signed Clitus Alexandrinus, and under this name the book is entered in the B. M. Catalogue.]

[1631.] **H**[**enderson**], Richard. *The Arraignement of the Whole Creatvre, at the Barre of Religion, Reason, and Experience* . . . pp. 199, 256.

[p. 199]   [A discussion of the fickleness of men and women in their desires] . . . one nayle driving out another; forgetting one, as they get another : (as *Eurialus* forgets his *Lucretia*, by a new *Mistresse; Cressida*, her
* Read *Chaucer,* his *Troylus* & *Cressida.*   Trojan * *Troylus*, for the Greeke *Diomedes, Demophon* his *Phillis* for a fairer . . .

. . . .

[p. 256]   [reference to] ' *Chaucer* in his Knights Tale.'

1631. Weever, John. *Ancient Funerall Monuments*, pp. 489–91, [Chaucer's tomb and references from Hoccleve, Lydgate, etc.], pp. 727–8, [John Lydgate.]
[*See* below, p. 296, 1708, Hatton.]

[1632.] **Jonson**, Benjamin. *The Magnetic Lady* or *Humors Reconciled*, act iii, sc. 4. [Acted in 1632.]   The Workes of Beniamin Jonson, 2 vols., 1616, 40, vol. ii, 1640, sign. E 2 *b*, p. 36.   (Works, ed. W. Gifford and F. Cunningham, 1875, vol. vi, p. 60.)

Pol[*ish*]. Where there are meanes, and Doctors, learned men,
And their Apothecaries, who are not now,
(As *Chaucer* sayes) their friendship to begin,
Well, could they teach each other how to win
I' their swath bands—   [Prol. Cant. Tales, ll. 425–8.]
Rut. Leave your Poetry, good gossip,
Your *Chawcers* clouts, and wash your dishes with 'hem.

[1632 ?] **Milton**, John. *Il Penseroso* [in] Poems of Mr John Milton, Both English and Latin compos'd at several times . . . London . . . 1645, p. 41, sign. C 5.   (Milton's Poetical Works, ed. D. Masson, 1890, vol. i, p. 376, ll. 109–15.)

Or call up him that left half told
The story of *Cambuscan* bold,

> Of *Camball* and of *Algarsife*,
> And who had *Canace* to wife,
> That own'd the vertuous Ring and Glass
> And of the wondrous Hors of Brass
> On which the *Tartar* king did ride.

[*Il Penseroso* was probably written at the end of 1632, although not printed until 1645.]

[1632 ?] **R[eynolds]**, H[enry]. *Mythomystes . . . a survey . . . of true poesy* . . . London, printed for Henry Seyle, p. 8. [n. d. Preface signed H. R. In Transcript of the Register of the Stationers' Company, ed. E. Arber, vol. iv, 1877, p. 282, this book is entered by Henry Reynolds on 10 Aug. 1632.]

[p. 5]   . . . from the multitude . . . of the common rimers in these our moderne times, and moderne tongues I will exempt some few, as of a better ranke and condition than the rest . . . .

.   .   .   .

[p. 8]   I will returne home to my Countrey-men, and mother tongue : And heere, exempt from the rest, a *Chaucer*, for some of his poëms; chiefely his *Troylus* and *Cresside :* . . . [Then follow mentions of Sidney and Spenser.]

1633. Nash, Thomas (Philipolites). *Quaternio, or a fourefold way to a happie life,* p. 35. (Quoted by Sir S. E. Brydges in his Censura Literaria, vol. ix, 1809, p. 264.)

As for hawking, I commend it in some, condemne it in others ; . . . . Yet I must acknowledge, I haue in my youthfull dayes with Machabæus beene guiltie of this vanitie, & haue beene as glad as euer I was to come from Schoole, to see a little Martin in the dead time of the yeare when the Winter had put on her whitest coat, and the frosts had sealed vp the Brookes and Rivers, to make her way through the midst of a multitude of fowle-mouth'd ravenous Crows and Kites, which pursued her with more hydeous cryes and clamors, [*] <small>* Chawcer in his Nunnes Priests tale.</small> than did * Coll the dog, and Malkin the Maide, the Fox in the Apologue,

> When the geese for feare flew over the trees,
> And out of their hiues came the swarme of Bees. [ll. 4581-2.]

and maugre all their oppositions pulled down her prey, bigger than her selfe, being mounted aloft steeple-high, downe to the ground.

1633. Prynne, William.   *Histrio-Mastix; The Players Scourge or Actors Tragœdie,* . . . part ii, pp. 833–4.

Wherefore I shall here approve & not condemn, the ancient Tragedy stiled *Christus passus* . . wherein Christs passion is elegantly decyphered together with *Bernadinus Ochin* his *Tragedy of Freewil* . . &c. which like *Geffry Chaucers & Pierce* the *Plowmans tales* and Dialogues, were penned only to be read, not acted, their subjects being al serious, sacred, divine, not scurrilous wanton or prophan, as al modern Play poëms are.

1633. Ware, Sir James.   *Preface* to his edition of Spenser's *View of the state of Ireland,* Dublin, 1633, sign. ¶ 3 *b*.

[Spenser buried near Chaucer, his epitaph quoted. *See* below, App. A, 1633.]

[*c*. 1634.] Cartwright, William.   *The Ordinary, A Comedy,* . . . [in] Comedies Tragi-Comedies with other Poems, by Mr William Cartwright . . . . 1651, act III, sc. i, pp. 36, 38 ; act V, sc. iv, p. 82. (Reprinted in R. Dodsley's collection of Old English plays, ed. W. C. Hazlitt, vol. xii, 1875, pp. 253, 255, 308.)

[p 36]   Moth. . . . . I am thine Leeke, thou *Chaucer* eloquent.

[p. 37]   . . . I'll be as faithfull to thee,

[p. 38]   As Chaunticleere to Madam Partelot.

[p. 82]   [Moth on his marriage changes his name to ' Giffery.']

[*Cf. also* note in Hazlitt, p. 240, where the editor points out that Moth's words are generally borrowed from Chaucer, and gives their meaning from Tyrwhitt's Glossary. For an account of Chaucer influence on this play, *see* Chaucers Einfluss auf das englische Drama, by O. Ballman, Anglia, xxv, pp. 63–6.]

[1634.] Fletcher, John, [and Massinger, Philip.]   *The Lovers Progres,* act. v, sc. 1 [in] Comedies and Tragedies, written by Francis Beaumont and Iohn Fletcher, Gentlemen . . . . 1647, p. 92. (Works of Beaumont and Fletcher, ed. Alexander Dyce, vol. xi, 1846, p. 105.)

[Speaking of Calista, Lysander says to lay down his life] . . . . will cleare her, and write her name a-new in the faire legend of the best women.

[*a*. 1635.] Corbet, Richard, Bishop of Norwich.   *Certain Elegant Poems, written by Dr. Corbet, Bishop of Norwich. London,* Printed by R. Cotes for Andrew Crooke at the Green Dragon in Pauls Churchyard, 1647.   Iter Boreale . . p. 11.   (Poems, ed. 1807, p. 193.)

The shot was easie, and what concernes us more,

The way was so, mine host did ride before,

Mine host was full of Ale, and History,

And on the morrow when he brought us nigh

Where the two Roses joyned [Bosworth Field], you would suppose,

Chaucer nere writ the *Romant* of the Rose.

1635. Kynaston, Sir Francis. *Amorum Troili et Creseidæ libri duo priores Anglico-Latini.* Oxoniæ. Two prefatory addresses, one to Patrick Junius, the other to the Reader, dated 1634, signs. A 2–†2 *b*, contain many references to Chaucer; for extracts from them, and for a specimen of the translation, *see* below, Appendix A, 1635, Kynaston.

[This is a translation of the two first books of Chaucer's *Troilus and Criseyde* into Latin rhymed verse, the English and Latin being on opposite sides of the page. Kynaston completed this work, and wrote an erudite Latin commentary on it, but only the first two books were printed. In 1793 Kynaston's MS. was bought by F. G. Waldron (*see* below, p 49, 1796, Waldron), who, in 1796, published a small book entitled: 'The loves of Troilus and Creseid, written by Chaucer; with a commentary by Sir Francis Kinaston : never before published.' This consists of an Advertisement by Waldron (*see* 1796, *infra*), followed by introductory extracts from various authors, relating to Kynaston, his MS., and its purchase by Waldron ; then a few passages are quoted from Kynaston's commentary. Waldron prints (pp. vii, xii–xiii) from the MS., the note on *Morter*, which was incorrectly printed in the Glossary to Urry's Chaucer, 1721, and there signed 'Kyn'. Also Kynaston's note on the *Tale of Wade* is printed (pp. xvi–xvii), and his long note on Henderson's authorship of the *Testament of Creseid* (pp. xxix–xxxi), a portion of which had been misquoted, without acknowledgment, by Urry at the head of the Testament of Creseid. Then follow the twelve first stanzas of Troilus (from Chaucer), and after that 12 pp. of Kynaston's commentary on it (in English), expanded by Waldron's own notes. Nothing further was published, although Waldron intended to print the whole poem and the commentary. *See* extracts in Hearne's diary, 1711, p. 315 below ; T. Corser, Collectanea, iv, Chetham soc., pp. 334–39, *also* a long review in the Retrospective Review, vol. xii, 1825, pp. 106–23 ; *and* Chaucer, a bibliographical manual, by E. P. Hammond, N. York, 1908, pp. 396–98. Kynaston's MS. was sold in the Crossley Sale, 1884, no. 2951.]

1635. Barker, William. *In Translationem Authoris,* [prefatory verses in] Kynaston's Amorum Troili et Creseidæ libri duo, sign. *3 *b*–*4.

OLIM *Chaucerus* Anglicus, Romano
    Nunc ore loquitur, & ita Plano,
Vt ipse se, si reuiuisceret,
Hinc intelligere fortassè disceret,
Tam bellè ardores suos vrget *Troilus,*
Vt nullus damnet, nullus Carpat *Zoilus*;
Tam lepidè *Creseida* petulantiam
Parem Amorem, parem inconstantiam ;
Vt ego, si iam viueret, amarem,
Fortassis etiam plusquam Basiarem.

I'ME glad the stomacke of the time's so good,
    That it can relish, can digest strong food :
That Learning's not absurd ; and men dare know,
How Poets spake three hundred yeares agoe.
Like travellors, we had bin out so long,
Our Natiue was become an vnknowne tongue,
And homebred *Chaucer* vnto vs was such,
As if he had bin written in High Dutch :
Till thou the Height didst Leuell, and didst Pierce
The depth of his vnimitable verse

Let others praise thy how ; I admire thy what.
Twas Noble, the adventure ; to Translate
A booke, not tractable to every hand,
And such as few presum'd to vnderstand :
Those vpstart verse-wrights, that first steale his wit,
And then pronounce him Dull : or those that sit
In judgement of the Language they nere view'd,
And because they are lazie, *Chaucer's* Rude ;
Blush they at these faire dealings, which haue shown
Thy worth, and yet reseru'd to him his owne.
  Wake, wake renowned ghost from that cold clay,
Where Thou and Poetry both buried lay.
And in White Hall appeare, among those men
For whom thou'lt ioy thou art aliue agen.
Where Mighty *Charles* his Rayes dar't [*sic*] Influence
Into a Thousand Poets, which from hence,
To after ages shall trans-mit his deeds
The subject of a Second *Æneids.*
If there among those Swans thou Him shal see,
That to our knowledge thus hath rescued thee.
Then call thine Eagle downe to raise his Name
From *Troilus* vp to the *Howse of Fame.*

Guil. Barker, *Art. Mag. Nov.*
Coll. Socius.

1635. Cartwright, William. *To the worthy Author on this his Approved Translation,* [prefatory verses in] Kynaston's Amorum Troili et Creseidæ libri duo, sign. **1. (Reprinted in Comedies, Tragi-Comedies . . . by Mr. William Cartwright, 1651, p. 250.)

.   .   .   .   .

'TIS to your Happy cares wee owe, that wee
   Read *Chaucer* now without a Dictionary ;
Whose faithfull Quill such constant light affords,
That we now read his thoughts, who read his words,
And though we know't done in our age by you,
May doubt which is the Coppy of the two.

.   .   .   .

                    Hee, that hitherto
Was dumbe to strangers, and 's owne Country too,
Speakes plainly now to all ; being more our owne
Eu'n hence, in that thus made to Aliens knowne.

Guil. Cartwright.

1635. Corbet, sir John. *In Chaucerianam Francisci Kinaston Equitis Aurati translationem,* [prefatory verses in] Kynaston's Amorum Troili et Creseidæ libri duo, sign. *2 b–*3.

TVrpes susurri, proba nefaria,
   Ronchi maligni iam sileant, Enim
Musas potentes Nobilitas amat :
    Et Literæ ducunt genus,
    Stirpem & suam à multis avis :
    Clarus libris qui sanguine.
Doctrina tecto haud paupere clauditur,
Nec veste semper carmina rusticâ
Contenta : Sordes abstulit has tua
    (Romane *Chaucer*) Gloria :
    Et Nobilem gentem Tui
    Noctes laboris vindicant.
Omnes Poetæ Numen habent, Poli
Fervore, flammâ & Sidereâ calent.
Et nocte damnant, & Tenebris malis,
    Quos Ense tangunt carminis :
    Famâ & vetant dignos mori.
    Quantus (Precor) sancto frui
Ipsos Poetas qui facit Æthere ?
Cæli Magistros, Lucis & arbitros
Qui donat Astris, Quantus habebitur ?
    Curis (*Eques*) vivit Tuis
    Chaucer, Britannis cognitus
    Olim, manet Mundi incòla.

          Ioh. Corbet Baronetti filius natu
          maximus ex Aulâ Alb.

1635. Crouther, John. *In Translationem Authoris,* [prefatory verses in] Kynaston's Amorum Troili et Creseidæ libri duo, sign. †4 b–*1.

ADèone nil est fas habere privatum,
   Britannidumque arcana sacra Musarum
Vulganda ? Nosterque (& nec omnium noster)
Chaucerus orbi perlegendus est toti ?
Itane insolentis semper in sinum Tybris
Exonerat Helicon alueos suos omnis ?
Nos quoque tributum liberè damus Linguæ ?
En quàm superbit invidenda linguarum

CHAUCER CRITICISM.

Regina, quàm se divitem hoc libro gestit.
Sic continenti quando reddit *Ægyptum*
In mare relabens ore Nilus averso.
Stupere Mediterraneus novas vndas,
Et intumescere haud suæ capax molis.

. . . . . .

Ios. Crouther, Art. Mag.,
Col. D. Ioh. Socius.

1635. Digges, Dudley. *In pulcherimos conatus Domini,* Fran. Kinaston, Equit. Aur. Amores *Troili & Creseidæ* CHAVCERO Anglicè decantatos latino idiomate donare parantis, [prefatory verses in] Kynaston's Amorum Troili et Creseidæ libri duo, sign. *1–*1 *b*.

SIC sic decebat Vatis Angli manibus
Cumulare vitam post humam. Britannia
Arctum sepulchrum est.   Fama tanti nominis
Iacere mundo debuit, non Insulâ.
Dudum sepultus cur at hoc vnum cinis
Spirare laxiùs : vmbra iam felix satis
Tumulo soluta iactat hoc solatium ;
Orbis*que* lucis conscius novæ stupet.
Generose Vates feceris Nostrum magis,
Quòd eruditum iuris exteri facis.
Neglecta penè Musa *Chauceri* iacet,
Tineæ triumphus, blattulis spolium frequens :
Dediscit Anglus nuper indigenos sales,
Sui*que* prorsus exul haud intelligit
Dulces lepores Musa quos vetustior
Effudit : aliâ debuit linguâ loqui
Chaucerus, aliter lateat ignotus domi.
Fruéntur Angli vate clariùs suo,
Quòd orbis vnà gloriæ, iubar colet.

. . . . . .

Dudleius Digges, Equit. Aur. filius,
Col. Omn. An. Socius.

1635. Evans, Samuel. *Vpon the Translation of Chaucers Troilus and Creseide, by Sir Francis Kinaston,* [prefatory verses in] Kynaston's Amorum Troili et Creseidæ libri duo, sign. **1–**1 *b*.

THANKS Noble *Kinaston,* to whose Learn'd Arte
We owe a limbe of *Chaucer,* th' other part
Expects thy happy hand, Me thinks I see
It pant, and heaue for a recovery :

First let the *Troian* Boy arise, and then
True *Troians* all, they are his Countrymen.
The *Sumner, Franklin*, oh that I might heare
The *Manciple*, and early *Chaunticleare*
Crowe latin, next might see the *Reue*, and *Logge*,
The *Miller* and learne Latine for a Cogge,
The *Merchant*, and Sir *Topas* height, the *wife*
Of *Bathe*, in vulgar Latine scold for life.
But aboue all the *famous Legacie*
Amongst the Couent dealt, so Legally,
Where twelue divide the As, and everyone
Hath part 𝔴𝔦𝔱𝔥𝔬𝔲𝔱𝔢𝔫 𝔇𝔢𝔣𝔞𝔩𝔠𝔞𝔱𝔦𝔬𝔫
And all in Latine, surely when the Pope
Shall heare of this and all the sacred Troupe
Of Cardinalls pervse the Worke, theyle all
In generall Councell mak't Canonicall.

Sam. Evans, LL. Bac. Nov.
Coll. Socius.

1635. Foulis, Ed. *Vpon that worthy Poet Sir Geofrey Chaucer & Sir Francis Kinastons Translation,* [prefatory verses in] Kynaston's Amorum Troili et Creseidæ libri duo, sign. *4 b.

TRUE Poet! Who could words endue
    With life, that makes the fiction true;
    All passages are seene as cleare
As if not pend, but acted here:
Each thing so well demonstrated
It comes to passe, when tis but read.
    Here is no fault, but ours: through v૩
True Poetry growes barbarous:
While aged Language must be thought
(Because 'twas good long since) now naught.
    Thus time can silence *Chaucer's* tongue,
But not his witte, which now among
The Latines hath a lowder sound;
And what we lost, the World hath found.
    Thus the Translation will become
Th' Originall, while that growes dumbe:
And this will crowne these labours: None
Sees *Chaucer* but in *Kinaston*.

Ed. Foulis, *Equitis & Baronetti filius*
Coll. Om. An. Socius.

1635. Gowen, T.   *Authori in Chaucerum Virbium,* [prefatory verses in]
Kynaston's Amorum Troili et Creseidæ libri duo, sign. *2.

ESTO ; dixeris omnibus renasci
  Fatum Vatibus esse, sed renasci
Fato dixeris Auspicatiori.
Sic in *Virgilio* legas *Homerum,*
Sed præ *Virgilium* eligas *Homero* :
Est in Carmine *Nævius Terenti,*
Sed carmen melius *Terentianum* :
Sic tandem Numeris Tuis recoctum,
Iucundum, lepidum, aureum Poetam,
Quantumcunq*ue* fremant Tenebriones
Scabrarum Tineæq*ue* Capsularum,
Iucundum, lepidum, aureum Poetam,
Chaucerum Ingenij redintegrati
Vitâ crescere duplici videmus ;
Atque addi poterat Venustiori,
Sed Nostros pudor hîc Tuus refrænat
Proclives Calamos : tamen, Calore
Cum sitis similes ; pares Camænis ;
Aptè cum Stichus in Stichum recurrat ;
Rythmum Rhymus agat sequens priorem
Primam Schedula Schedulam reflexa,
Cum sic assimilentur, hinc & inde
Versus versibus Anglicis Latini ;
Astabis lateri Comes, locumq*ue*
Phœbi iudicio parem obtinebis ;
Et Musæ Tibi Gratias rependent,
Quòd iam, Deliciis reduplicatis
Chaucero liceat frui *Gemello.*

     T. Gowen, Nov. Col. Socius.

1635. James, Francis.   *Vpon Noble Sir Francis Kinastons Translation
of the excellent Poem of Troilus and Creseide,* [prefatory verses in]
Kynaston's Amorum Troili et Creseidæ libro duo, sign. **3-3 *b.*
[Printed in blackletter.]

CERTES, yt is a thinge right hard to done
  Thee myckel Prayse, o doughtie KYNASTONE,
I peyne me sore to done Thee grace, for here
I thee alowth there no wight nys thy peere,
And who that saith it nat he is right nice,
I dare well wage, tho mote mine herte agrise

In bytter stound, all were my life etern,
Bote if I should thee prayse both late and yern.
There nas none wight couth wryte more thriftely
Ne eke more bet, ne eke more Clerkly,
There nyst none speken bet of *Troilus,*
Ne of dame *Creseid* ne of *Pandarus.*

For that thy boke beareth alder prize,
That I nat how vnneth thou couth devise,
To maken *Chaucer* so right wise and sage.
Who couth all craft in werkes, take pilgrimage
To *Rome,* and sothly there lerne Latine verse
In little throwe, so seemlyche to reherse.

. . . .

Withouten maugre, thou hast mowen the flower
Fulfilled of all Courtship and all honour,
Farced with pleasaunce and all goodlyhede
That deyntie is to see : Thee thus I reade,
Faire mought thee fall, who art the second Poet,
Fro Brittons *Homer* nephew to *Payne Roet.*

Sic officiose αρχαιζειν conatus est *Franc James*
Art. Bac. Nov. Coll. Socius.

[*Cf.* verses by James, below, pp. 218-19.]

1635. Johnston, Arthur. *In translationem Authoris,* [prefatory verses
in] Kynaston's Amorum Troili et Creseidæ libri duo, sign. †3.

INSULA quos genuit Phœnices adspice, quorum
Alter ab alterius lumine lumen habet.
Chaucerus patriam, sibi Kinastonus at orbem
Devinxit, Latio sub Iove quantus erat.
Hic comes ingenio est tersæ facundia linguæ,
Et nitor, immensus vincit vtram*que* labor.
Si quà fides vero, nil maius civibus istis
Insula quos genuit, maximus orbis habet.

Art. Ionstonus
Med. Reg.

1635. Kynaston, Samuel. *In Translationem Authoris,* [prefatory verses
in] Kynaston's Amorum Troili et Creseidæ libri duo, sign. *2 b.

*C*Hauceri ingenium densam quæ condidit vmbra*m,*
Vicit Sol Doctus radiis felicibus. Arcto
Carcere qui clausus regni, cantabitur orbe
Toto ; Contendent ventura*que* secula, Vates
Vtrum Romano, an nostro sermone locutus ?
Vrbes quot celebrant *Chauceri* carmina Græci,

Angliacum poscent tot Regna ingentia Homerum.
Quam dedit ergo Interpres vitâ & laude fruatur :
Non aliud funus Calamus quam mundus habebit.

Sam. Kinaston, Art. M. Col.
Om. An. Socius.

1635. Lloyd, Thomas. *Invidus in Chauceri interpretem*, [prefatory verses in] Kynaston's Amorum Troili et Creseidæ libri duo, sign. †3 *b*–†4 *b*.

*C*HAUCERUS redivivus audit ; *Æson*,
    Pelops Hipplitusue vis potitus
Vitæ stamine non ministret omen ;
Frustrato *Peliæ* exitu fruatur.

. . . . . .

Sermo Britanicus in invidum.

Quin siste, livor, numen in partes tuas
Vocare nostrum. Conditum tandem caput,
Chaucere, tolle. Fata subijsti miser
Poetatantùm ; surge sed felix simul
Pater Poetæ : Dubiæ & ignotæ Sonant
Voces amæni Vatis. En veris modis
Resurgit Echo purior. Mirum cano,
Parente salvo nascitur Phænix novus.
Conduplicatos nec decet quæstus sonos ;
Meum *Maronem* qui dicat flammis, magis
Est sævus ipsis. Perge ; meruisti benè,
Interpres alme. Flamma sic crescat tibi
Cælestis ignis æmula : auspiciis tuis
Spencerus olim sentiat sortes pares.
Extende Linguam patriam ; discent Phrasin
Angli Latinam sedulò : Latii scient
Voces Britannas ; sentient omnes, eos
V*t*rin*que* victos, præmio & dignos simul.
Obscurasne velis *Chauceri* exponere voces ?
Siste : sat exposuit, qui transtulit Angla Latinis.

Tho. Lloyd, LL. Bac.
è Col. Divi Iohan. Bapt.

1635. Read, or **Reade,** Thomas. *Vpon the Authors Translation,* [prefatory verses in] Kynaston's Amorum Troili et Creseidæ libri duo, sign. **2 *b*–**3.

*C*HAVCER, thou wert not dead ; nor can we feare
    Thy death, that hast out liu'd three hundred yeare.
Thou wert but out of fashion ; then admit
This courtly habit, which may best befit

Thee and the times.   Thou hast a *friend*, that while
He studies to translate, his Latine stile
Hath Englisht thee, and cunningly in one
Fram'd both a comment and Translation.
   Once more thou'rt ours, by him whose happy veine
Hath not reviu'd, but made thee young againe.
Nor wert thou old, but in thy outward hew
Thy judgement and invention yet are new.
Thy seeming rudenesse might some ballad-poet,
That skill'd thee not, amaze, whereas we know it
The best adore thee ; from which learned sect
Thou differ'st not in worth, but Dialect.
That was the vaile obscur'd thee ; that the cloud
Ecclipst thy lustre, and is now remou'd
By our Sir *Francis* pen ; to whose each line
Thou honour giu'st, whilst he addes light to thine.

Tho. Reade LL. Bac. *Nov.*
Col. Socius.

1635. Strode, William. *In Galfridi Chauceri Troilum, à Domino Fran-
cisco Kinaston, Equite Aurato, Latinè redditum,*[prefatory verses in]
Kynaston's Amorum Troili et Cresidæ libri duo, sign. †3—†3 *b*.

Q Vibus obsoleta Verba, carmen hirsutum,
         Et Musa visa est rusticana *Chauceri*,
Quibus is profundè Lepidus, Acer, Antiquus,
Et visus obstupendus arte celatâ,
Vtriusq*ue* partes factionis accedant,
Et consulant interpretem *Kinastonum ;*
Galfridiorem perlegantq*ue* *Chaucero ;*
Equiti Equitem, Aulico Aulicum coaptatum,
Verum Iudicem Poematis, Poetæq*ue*.
Troiam Britannam transferens Hic in Roman
Lapis esto Lydius Ingeniq*ue*, Versusq*ue*,
Si dicat Illum lector Ingeni plenum,
Deprædicare non dubito fidelemistum.
At non in eius laude stat *Kinastoni*
Laus summa : turpem turpiterne depinxit
Thersitem Homerus, Chœrilusve Alexandri
Decus decorè ?   Tabula par suo exemplo,
Seu pulchra Veneris Ora, siuè rugosæ
Referat Sybillæ membra, pariter oblectat.

Guil. Strode, Publicus Acad.
Oxon. Orator.

1635. Habington, William. *Castara.* The second Edition Corrected and Augmented, first part, p. 59 [not in the first edn. of 1634.] (ed. E. Arber, English reprints, 1870, p. 50.)

> *To my most honoured Friend and Kinsman R. St. Esq.*
> Since *Spencer* hath a Stone; and *Draytons* browes
> Stand petrefied ith' wall, with Laurell bowes
> Yet girt about; and nigh wise *Henries* herse,
> Old *Chaucer* got a Marble for his verse:
> So courteous is Death; Death Poëts brings
> So high a pompe, to lodge them with their Kings:
> Yet still they mutiny.

1635. Marten, Sir Henry. *Letter to King Charles I.,* Feb. 9, 1639. (Calendar of State Papers, Dom., 1634–5, 1864, vol. cclxxxiii, no. 27, ii, p. 506.)

[Arthur Champernoon of Dartington petitions the King. He has had goods to the value of £570 seized in France, to pay compensation due on a French ship captured, 35 years previously, by an Englishman, Captain Andrew French. The case was heard at the time in the Admiralty Court, French was condemned, and a certain Arthur Champernoon of Childhay was surety for him. The Petitioner proved, but with no result, that he was not this Arthur Champernoon. Sir H. Marten (judge of the Court of Admiralty) says it seems strange that one man should be condemned for another without proof of identity, but it is evident that the judges (in Paris) did not much regard that point, because it is expressly stated in the sentence against French that the debt was to be supplied by the goods of any Englishman in France], so as if the petitioner's name had been Jeffrey Chaucer, he would have suffered the like judgment and condemnation.

1636. Haxby, Stephen. *Clarissimo viro Domino Carolo Fitz-geofrido, Steph. Haxby Cantabrigiensis. S. P. D.,* [in] The Blessed Birthday, by Charles Fitz-Geffry, 1636. 2nd edn. [not in 1st], sign. *4. (The Poems of the Rev. Charles Fitzgeoffrey, ed. A. B. Grossart, 1881, p. 117.)

> Who wisely reades thy lines may well be bolde,
> Pythagoras his Paradoxe to holde
> That dead mens soules (for which men fondly mourne)
> Are not extinct, but after death returne
> To other bodies, and may plainely see
> Old *Geffry Chaucers* soule reviu'd in thee.

Such heavenly Raptures, sentences divine
No soule could vtter, but or his or thine;
If not his soule (which now to heaven is gone)
Yet is his verse reviu'd in thee (his Sonne).
So long as the worlds eye his light shall giue,
So long shall both you (Divine Poets) liue.

[*Cf.* 1646, G., E., below, pp. 224–5.]

1636. Taylor, John (the Water Poet). *The Honourable and Memorable Foundations . . . . of divers Cities . . . . Also a Relation of the Wine Tavernes . . . .* sign. D 7. (Works of John Taylor, not included in the Folio vol. of 1630, repr. for the Spenser soc. 1870–78, 4th collection 1877, p. 59.)

A catalogue of Tavernes.

Oxfordshire. Woodstocke . . . . The town is a pretty Market towne, and chiefly famous for the breeding of the worthy *Ieffrey Chaucer,* the most ancient Arch-Poet of *England.*

[*a.* **1637.**] **Jonson,** Benjamin. *The English Grammar, Made by Ben Iohnson* . . . 1640. The Second Booke, Of Syntaxe . . . . ch. i, p. 70 (1 ref.), ch. ii, p. 72 (3 refs.), ch. iii, p. 74 (2 refs.), p. 75 (3 refs.), p. 76 (2 refs.), ch. iv, p. 76 (2 refs.), ch. v, p. 77 (2 refs.), p. 78 (2 refs.), ch. vii, p. 80 (2 refs.), ch. viii, p. 82 (3 refs.), ch. ix, p. 83 (1 ref.), p. 84 (2 refs.). (Works, ed. W. Gifford and F. Cunningham, 1875, vol. ix, pp. 291–319.)

[p. 70]   *Apostrophus* . . . .

Vowells also suffer this *Apostrophus* before the Consonant *h Chaucer* in the 3. Booke of *Troilus.*

> *For of Fortunes sharpe adversitie,*
> *The worst kind of infortune is this:*
> *A man to have beene in prosperitie,*
> *And it to remember when it passed is.*

. . . .   [ll. 1625–28.

[p. 76] *Him* and *Them,* be used reciprocally for the Compounds, himselfe, themselves: . . . .

Chaucer *in the Squires tale:*

> *So deepe in graine he dyed his colours*
> *Right, as a Serpent hideth* him *under flowers.* [ll. 511–12.]

His, their and *theirs* have also a strange use; that is to say, being *Possessives,* they serve instead of Primitives:

Chaucer: *And shortly so farre forth this thing went,*
That my will was his *wills instrument.*

. . . . . .

Certaine Pronounes, governed of the Verbe doe, here abound
. . . .

[p. 78] Chaucer, 3 *booke of Fame* :

> *And as* I wondred *me*, ywis
> *Upon this house.*   [ll. 1988–9.]

&c., &c.

[Altogether Jonson in his Syntax gives 25 references to Chaucer, as illustrating points of construction. They are taken from the Hous of Fame, (the most frequently quoted) Troilus, Prol. to Man of Law's Tale, Nonne Preestes Tale, Reeves Tale, Squires Tale, etc.]

1637. Terrent, T. *Elegy* [in] *Jonsonus Virbius, or the Memorie of Ben : Johnson, Revived by the Friends of the Muses.* Printed by E. P. for Henry Seile, 1638, p. 64 [colophon dated Jan. 23, 1637].

In obitum Ben: IONSONI Poetarum facile Principis.

. . . .

> Haud aliter nostri præmissa in principis ortum
> Ludicra *Chauceri*, classis*que* incompta sequentum ;
> Nascenti apt a parum divina hæc machina regno,
> In nostrum servanda fuit, tantæ*que* decebat
> Prælusisse Deos ævi certamina famæ ;
> Nec geminos vates, nec Te *Shakspeare* silebo,
> Aut quicquid sacri nostros conjecit in annos
> Consilium Fati : . . . .

. . . .

T. Terrent.

1638. James, F[rancis]. *To his Friend, A. H. on his translation of Achilles Tatius, on the loves of Leucippe and Clitophon,* [in] **The** loves of Clitophon and Leucippe . . . . written in Greek by Achilles Tatius : and now Englished, Oxford, 1638, sign. A 6 *b*–A 7. [The notes are by James.]

> As whilom for the lore of Engelond
> *Gaufrid* an orpyd Knight toke upon hond
> To wryten thilk throwe ; for all ages after
> Of *Troyl* hight *Pryam*s son and [1] *Calchas daughter* ;
> " [2] The double sorrows of those wights to tellen
> " Froe woe to wele how their aventures fellen.
> Clepend on Muse, to help for to endite
> His balefull verse that weepen as he write [2]
> Forthy a [3] *Muses sonne* in gret nobles,
> That can of *Knighthode* chivalrie and prowes

---

[1] *Cressida.*   [2–2] paraphrase of ll. 1–7 *Troil. and Cres.*
[3] *Sir Francis Kynaston.*

The lore; whos goodship algates did deserve
The *studdie* of thilk Goddess [1]hight Minerve,
[2]*Payne Roëts Nephew* so did understond,
As shope him to the lenguage of Rome's lond.

 [1] *Minervæ Musæum.*   [2] *Chaucer.*

 [*Cf.* dedicatory verses by the same author to Kynaston's translation of Troilus and Cressida, 1634, pp. 212–13 above.]

[**1638–39.**] **Milton,** John. *Mansus.* 34. Poems of Mr John Milton . . . .
1645, pp. 73–4. (Poetical works of J. Milton, ed. D. Masson, 1890,
vol. i, pp. 522, 313 (English translation).)

> Nos etiam in nostro modulantes flumine cygnos
> Credimus obscuras noctis sensisse per umbras,
> Quà Thamesis latè puris argenteus urnis
> Oceani glaucos perfundit gurgite crines ;
> Quin & in has quondam pervenit Tityrus oras.

    English Translation [by Masson].
 [*We* also think that *we* have heard the swans in our river
 Making music at night through all the shadowy darkness,
 Where our silver Thames, at breadth of her pure-gushing current,
 Bathes with tidal whirl the yellow locks of the Ocean :
 Nay, and our Chaucer once came here [Italy] as a stranger before me.]

1638. Pick, Samuel. *Festum Voluptatis, or the Banquet of Pleasure,*
p. 32.

> Friscus in secret jesting with a Lady,
> (Which jesting *Chaucer* far more broadly stiles).

[*c.* **1640 ?** **Browne,** William ?] *A catalogue* of the poems in MS.
Addit. 34,360 (formerly Phillipps 9053), on fol. 3, probably by
Browne, who was a former owner of this MS. Entries 2, 3, 8, 9
refer to Chaucer's Poems in this collection. For Stowe's notes in
this vol. *see* above, *c.* 1600, p. 164. [A late 18th or early 19th cent.
hand has written "Poems by Chaucer, Lydgate, etc." on fol. 1 of
this MS.]

1641. B[rome], A[lexander]. *A Canterbury Tale, Translated out of
Chaucers old English Into our now vsuall Langvage. Whereunto is
added the Scots Pedler. Newly enlarged by A. B.* [These are
satirical verses against Laud, archbp. of Canterbury, and other prelates. The Scots Pedler is an imitation of Chaucer's Pardoner (see
Prol. ll. 671–716, also Prol. to Pard. Tale, ll. 329–462). For a full
account of the pamphlet, *see* Chaucer's Influence on English Literature, by Alfred Tobler, Berne, 1905.]

1641. Unknown. *Witt's Recreation, Augmented with Ingenious Con-
ceites* . . . . Epitaph 140. On our prime English Poet, *Geffery
Chaucer* an ancient Epitaph, sign. R 7. (Facetiæ Musarum Deliciæ
. . . . Wits Recreations [ed. T. Park], 2 vols., 1817, vol. ii, pp. 260–1.)

 [This is a stanza from John Lydgate's *Fall of Princes, c.* 1430, Harl. 1766, fol. 8,
quoted on p. 87 above. It is not in the first edn. of *Wit's Recreation,* 1640, but it is
reprinted in the augmented edns. of 1645 and 1650, Epitaph 152 and 168 respectively.]

1641. Jonson, Benjamin.   *The Sad Shepherd* . . . . act II, sc. vi, sign.
T 4, p. 147, printed London, 1641.   The Workes of Beniamin
Jonson, 2 vols., 1616, 1640, vol. ii, 1640.   (Works, ed. W. Gifford
and F. Cunningham, 1875, vol. vi, p. 271, act II, sc. ii.)

> Mau[dlin] The Swilland Dropsie enter in
> The Lazie *Cuke*, and swell his skin ;
> And the old Mort-malon his shin
> Now prick, and itch, withouten blin.
> [*Prol. Cant. Tales*, l. 386.]

1641. Marmion, Shakerley.   *The Antiquary, a Comedy* . . . . *written
by Shackerly Mermion, Gent,* act I, sign. C 2.   (R. Dodsley's Old
English Plays, ed. W. C. Hazlitt, vol. xiii, 1875, p. 432.)

The Actors names.

Moccinigo, *an old Gentleman that would appear yong.*

. . . .

> *Moc.* Yet this I resolve on,
> To have a Maid tender of age, and fair :
> Old fish, and yong flesh, that's still my dyet.

[This is a reference to Merchant's Tale, ll. 1415–18 :—
But one thing warn I you, my friendis dere,
I wol no old wife have in no manere.
She shall not passin sixtene yere certeine
Old fish, and young flesh woll I haue full faine.
For the influence of Chaucer's Merchant's T. on this play, *see* Chaucers Einfluss auf
das englische Drama, by O. Ballman, Anglia, xxv, pp. 56–63.]

1641. [Milton, John.]   *Of Reformation touching Church-Discipline in
England,* pp. 31, 41, 50–1.   (English prose writings of Milton, ed.
Henry Morley, Carisbrook library, vol. v, 1889, pp. 71, 77, 83.)

[p. 31] [Constantine did much harm to the Church.]   And this was
a truth well knowne in *England* before this *Poet* [Ariosto]
was borne, as our *Chaucers* Plowman shall tell you by and by
upon another occasion.

. . . .

[p. 41] 'Tis only the merry Frier in *Chaucer* can disple [*sic*, i.e.
discipline] them.

> Full sweetly heard he confession
> And pleasant was his absolution
> He was an easie man to give pennance.
> [*Prol. Cant. Tales*, ll. 221–3.]

. . . .

[pp. 50–1] This [the encroachements of Rome] our *Chaucer* also hath
observ'd and gives from hence a caution to England to beware
of her Bishops in time . . . . [Quotes 2 stanzas from spurious
Plowmans Tale, ll. 693–708].   Thus he brings in the Plow-

man speaking. . . . . Whether the Bishops of *England* have
deserv'd thus to be fear'd by men so wise as our *Chaucer* is
èsteem'd . . . . he that is but meanly read in our Chronicles
needs not be instructed.

1641. [Milton, John.] *Animadversions upon the Remonstrants Defence,
against Smectymnuus*, p. 6. (Milton's Prose Works, Bohn's edn.,
1848, vol. iii, p. 46.)

Remember how they mangle our British names abroad ; what
trespasse were it, if wee in requitall should as much neglect
theirs ? and our learned *Chaucer* did not stick to doe so,
writing *Semyramus* for *Semiramis, Amphiorax* for *Amphioraus,*
K. *Sejes* for K. *Ceyx* the husband of *Alcyone*, with many other
names strangely metamorphis'd [*sic*] from true *Orthography*,
if he had made any account of that in these kind of words.

1641. Parker, Martin.   *The Poet's Blind mans bough,* or *Have among
you my blind Harpers*, etc.   Printed at London by F. Leach for
Henry Marsh, 1641, sign. A 4.   (British Bibliographer, ed. Sir
S. E. Brydges, 1810–14, vol. ii, 1812, p. 433. Reprinted in Miscellanea
Antiqua Anglicana, the old book collector's miscellany, ed. C.
Hindley, vol. ii, 1873, p. 4.)

> All Poets (as adition to their fames)
> Have by their Works eternized their names,
> As Chaucer, Spencer, and that noble earle,
> Of Surrie, thought it the most precious pearle,
> That dick'd his honour, to subscribe to what
> His high engenue ever amed at . . . .

[a. 1642. Barkham, John ?]   *MS. note* at beginning of MS. Laud misc.
600 Bodl. library [formerly MS. Laud. K. 50].

[The first page contains two lists, side by side, of the Tales,
viz., "The Order of this book MS." and "The order of the
Printed."   The latter list ends :—]

13. The Franklin.

14 &c. All the rest are in the same order in both Bookes.

> Onely the *Plowmans Tale*, is not MS. & if it were
> Chaucers, it was left out of his Canterbury Tales
> for the tartnes against the Popish Clergie.

> It is very probable y[t] it was severally *written* by
> Chaucer, & not as one of the Tales ; w[ch] were
> supposed to be *spoken*, & not *written :* for so the
> Plowman concludeth : f. 92 of the printed :

> To holy Church I will me bow ;
> Each man to' amend him Christ send space,
> And for my *writeing* me allow,
> He, that is Almighty, for his Grace.

The same word of *writeing* is there vsed diuers times : as, *For my writeing if I haue blame,—&, Of my writeing haue me excused* [Er?]*go*, it was not deliuered as a Tale told by mouth and all the rest were.

[Thomas Hearne says this note was written by John Barcham, [or Barkham] to whom the MS. belonged ; see Hearne's Diary, May 9, 1709, vol. ii, p. 196, also the end of his long letter to Bagford [undated] 1709. *See* below, p. 309. In the last paragraph : *Of my writeing haue me excused go*, 'excused' comes at the end of the line in the MS., and possibly it may have been followed by an 'Er,' but if so the 'Er' has got rubbed away, which is quite likely.]

1642. [**Hall**, Joseph, Bp. of Norwich?] *A Modest Confutation of a Slanderous and Scurrilous Libell Entituled Animadversions vpon the Remonstrants Defense against Smectymnuus*, pp. 11–13.

[p. 11 quotes Pardoners tale, ll. 413–22.
p. 12 „ Parliament of Foules, ll. 288–9.
„   „ Book of the Duchesse, ll. 62–5.
p. 13 „ Lydgate's (as Chaucer's) Complaint of the Black Knight, ll. 92–3.]

1642. Kynaston, Sir Francis. *Leoline and Sydanis*, p. 89. [The author must surely, owing to his recent translation of Troilus, have had Chaucer's story in his mind when he wrote]

'Mongst other stories he did call to minde
That of the fairy *Creseid*, who insteed
Of faithfull *Troilus* lov'd false *Diomed*.

1643. Baker, Sir R[ichard]. *A Chronicle of the Kings of England*, pp. 181, 29, 45, sign. Z, Dd 3, Ff. 3.

[p. 181] The Life and Raigne of King EDWARD the Third.
Of men of note in his time.
. . . . *Sir Geoffrey Chaucer*, the *Homer* of our Nation ; and who found as sweete a Muse in the Groves of *Woodstocke*, as the Antients did upon the banks of *Helicon*.

[p 29] The Reigne of King RICHARD the Second. Men of note in this Kings time . . . . *John Moone*, an English man, but a student in *Paris*, who compiled in the French tongue, the *Romant of the Rose* ; translated into English by *Geoffrey Chaucer* and divers others.

[p. 45] The Reigne of King HENRY the Fourth.

Of men of note in his time.

The next place after these [William Wickham and Roger Walden] is justly due to *Geoffry Chaucer* and *John Gower*, two famous Poets in this time, and the Fathers of English Poets in all the time after : *Chaucer* died in the fourth yeare of this king, and lyeth buried at *Westminster* : *Gower*, in this king's ninth yeare, and was buried in St. *Mary Overys* Church in *Southwarke.*

[The pagination is not continuous.]

1643. Unknown. *Powers to be Resisted*, pp. 39, 40. *See* App. A.

[1643.] Unknown. *The Cities Warning-Peece . . . . or the Round-head turn'd Poet*, pp. 5, 6.

Written long since, but Printed in the Yeere
That every knave and foole turn'd Cavaleere.

[Date of publication, February 27, 1642[-3], added in MS. by Thomason, from whose collection in B. M. this copy comes (E 246/28). Catalogued under London.[1]

The Spanish Fleete in the Downs.

Twixt our Religions, *Rome* and *Spaine*, and we
Put all together, make but one of three :
And shall you feare us, or shall we feare you ?
Tush, *Spain* is *England, England* is *Spain* now.

    .   .   .   .

Pauls for your sakes is almost newly built,
And 'tis not long since *Cheapside-crosse* was gilt,
Old *Charing* shall be now re-edified
That lost his glory when old *Chaucer* died.

1645. Cavendish, William (Marquis, afterwards 1st Duke, of New-castle). *The Phanseys of the Marquesse of Newcastle, sett by him in verse at Paris* [date in pencil under the last words 1645]. Old numbering pp. 77, 78 ; new numbering ff. 69 and 69 *b*. [MS. copy in B. M., Addit. 32,497.]

Loues Pretty Answer.

. . . . Oh what is woman att the best they fall
Under the title of Dissembling all
If wicked, weare the Otian all turnd Inkĕ
Each floatingĕ Riuer Siluer Brooke & Sinkĕ
And Eury stick a Pen for to Enditĕ
And all the Earth smooth Parchment on to writĕ
It were too litlĕ for their wickednessĕ
Old Jeffry Chauser thought them sure no lessĕ
For those four lines arĕ his Expression, knew
Women so well he sworĕ that it was truĕ.

[Refers to Lydgate's "Balade : warning men to beware of deceitful women," formerly attributed to Chaucer. *See* Chaucerian and other pieces, ed. W. W. Skeat, Chaucer soc. 1897, p. 296, ll. 43-9. *Cf.* 1601, Winwood, Ralph, above, p. 167.]

[1645-6.] **Unknown.** A Parliament-Officer at Grantham, [name unknown.] *A Letter* [undated] *sent from a Parliament-Officer at Grantham* to John Cleveland (the royalist poet) in Newark, [printed in] The works of Mr John Cleveland, containing his Poems, Orations, Epistles, Collected into one volume . . . London . . . 1687, pp. 95–6.

[The Officer writes satirically, saying Cleveland is such a good preacher, he is a great loss to the Church.] Such an Holy Father might have begot as many Babes for the Mother-Church of *Newark*, as our Party of late hath done Garrisons, and converted as many Souls as *Chaucer's* Friar with the Shoulder-bone of the lost Sheep.

[John Cleveland was appointed Judge-Advocate to Charles I.'s garrison at Newark in 1645, and remained there until the surrender of the city in May 1646. The reference is of course to Chaucer's Pardoner, not to the Friar. Prol. to Pardoner's Tale, ll. 22–29.]

1646. Daniel, George. *Poems written upon Severall Occasions* . . . . MSS. Addit. 19,255. To Time and Honour, p. 33. An Essay; Endeavouring to ennoble our English Poesie, p. 80. (Poems of G. Daniel of Beswick, MSS. in B. M. hitherto unprinted, ed. A. B. Grosart, 4 vols., vol. i, 1878, pp. 33, 80.)

But thinke thee [Albion] fairest, Sweetest, richest, Best;
fforgetting Chaucer, and Dan Lidgate's Rhime;
Loe here, the Glorie of our modern time,
A learnèd Age; Since great Eliza^e's reigne
And peace came in; the proud Italian
[p. 34] And iustly proud in Poesie, will allow
The English (though not Equall) next him now
      [goes on to mention Sidney, Spencer, Jonson, etc.]
            .   .   .   .   .   .
[p. 80]   Shall we derive
Our English fflame our Glories Primitive
From antique Chaucer? Blesse me witt, if right
Were onlie right, I feare a present night
Would cover all his credit. This I wage
Onlye for Truth; in reverence to the Age
Wherein he writ.

1646. G., E. *Commendatory Verses to the author* [in] *Men Miracles with other Poems* by M[artin] Ll[uelyn], St[udent] of Ch[rist] Ch[urch] *in* Oxon, Printed in the yeare 1646, sign. A 5. (These verses are reprinted in T. Corser's Collectanea, Chetham soc., part 8, 1878, p. 366.)

To the Author.

If ever I believ'd *Pythagoras*,
(My dearest friend) even now it was

While the grosse Bodies of the *Poets* die
Their Souls doe onely shift.   And *Poesie*
Transmigrates, not by chance or lucke
So *Chaucers* learned soule in *Spencer* sung,
(*Edmund* the quaintest of the Fairy throng)
And when that doubled Spirit quitted place
It fill'd up *Ben* . . . .

                                        E. G.

[*Cf.* 1636, above, pp. 216–17, Haxby, Stephen.]

1646. Selden, John. *Uxor Ebraica*, lib. ii, cap. 27, p. 285. [In the edn. of 1695 the reference is lib. ii, cap. 27, p. 203.]

. . . . unde Galfredus Chaucerus qui sub Edwardo tertio floruit, de uxore sua Bathoniensi

Shee was a worthy woman all hir live
Husbands at the Church dore had she five. [*Prol. Cant. Tales,* ll. 459–60.]

Id est; fœmina erat quamdiu vixit celebris, & ad ostium Ecclesiæ quinque maritos acceperat.

1647. T[ooke], G[eorge]. *The Belides, or Eulogie of that Noble Martialist Major William Fairefax . . . To the Reader, Epistle Dedicatorie,* p. 22. [This 1st edn. of 1647 is bound with "the Belides, or Eulogie of John, Lord Harrington," by G. T., London. Printed, 1647. The pagination is continuous; the copy in B. M. is supposed to be unique. A separate edn. was printed in 1660; reference on sign. A 2 *b*.]

A Poet also has the prerogative freely to follow the propensitude of his *Genius*; and our language as supplyed from abroad, is of richer variety for the cadence of either Prose or Verse. *Verstegan* will indeed upbraid *Chauc*[er] with it as prejudiciall; and another Netherlander has objected our English to me, for made up of severall shreds like a Beggars Cloake

[*See* above, p. 176, 1605, Verstegan.]

1648. Unknown. *A Fraction in the Assembly* [of the Divines at Westminster] *or the Synod in Armes,* pp. 7, 10.

[p. 7]   . . . till her Tongue travel'd tantivie, and more then a *Canterbury* pace.

[p. 10]   . . . . is not this in the Devills name, a trick of the beast, to tell the people of a *Cock* and a *Bull*, and bind them to beleeve all the stories in *Chawcer* for Articles of Faith . . . .

CHAUCER CRITICISM.

1649. Daniel, George. *Trinarchodia. The Raigne of Henrie the Fifth,* stanzas 36-7, 290, Addit. MSS. 19,255. (Poems of G. Daniel . . . . ed. A. B. Grosart, 4 vols., vol. iv, 1878, pp. 110, 173.   A Chaucer reference is given in Restituta, ed. Sir S. E. Brydges, vol. iv, 1816, p. 168.)

(36)

ɔ)   .   .   .   .

Or was it Number'd verse ? let Orpheus play ;
Our Harrye has a deeper Sweeter Note
    And from soft Groves, could his owne Act reherse
    As high as Pindare, or Tyrtæus' verse.

(37)

That infancy of Time, (when vnfledg'd Witt
Imp't from the ragged Sarcill Chaucer drop't)
Was Smooth'd by him a-new ; & fancy knitt
Harmonious Sence ; it is but to be hop'd
    A King & Poet ; if it shall be Seene
    Nature full-handed, made that Age to Him.

.   .   .   .

(290)

Like Rites perform'd to (him who like him fell)
Suffolke ; old Chaucer's late inheritance
Proud to entombe him ; as the first Summd Quill
Of England, not enough were to advance
    Eweline [*i. e.* Ewelme] ; an Athens, if his Pen that Fame
    May merit ; Sure this Sword, asserts that Claime.

[*c.* **1649–64.**] **Plume,** Thomas. *Anecdotes of English writers* in Dr. Plume's pocket book, MS. no. 25, Maldon library.   (A transcript has been made for the Bodl. library ; the references here are, however, taken from Dr. Plume's pocket book, by Andrew Clark [in] Essex Review, vol. xiv, no. 53, 1905, pp. 13–14.)

Tis now the sign of *the Talbott* in Southwark but anciently it was of *the Tabbert,* i. e.—Herald's coat—old Chaucer's inne, from whence the Canterbury Tales come.

The time's coming when Doctors and Knites
Will be as common as woodcocks and snites

says old Chaucer's prophecy.   You cannot quoit a stone up, but 'twill fall down upon a Doctor.

[The latter reference was "made in connection with the deluge of honorary degrees exacted by Court pressure from the universities/at the time of the Restoration." The editor also adds, "the Chaucerian attribution of the lines will hardly earn their inclusion in Professor Skeat's monumental edition."]

[*c.* **1650**. **Sheppard,** Samuel.] *The Faerie King Fashioning Love and Honour In an Heroicall Heliconian Dresse,* lib. 5. canto 6. verse 41. MS. Rawlinson, Poetry 28, fol. 65 *b.*

> neare these were foure and twentie pillars more
> equall for height, and bulke, with any there
> the first supported by a Swaine of yore
> the bonniest and the blythest one yfere,
> CHAWCER a Knight readen in vertues lore
> who knew full wellen how to Jape and Jeere
> by MERCURY, compare these barbarous Times
> with his conceits, and you'll applaud his Rimes.

1650. **Simpson,** John. *Catalogus universalis librorum omnium in Bibliotheca Collegii Sionii apud Londinenses . . . Omnia per J. S. Bibliothecarium . . . collecta,* p. 37.

> Galfrid. *Chaucer.*   Opera Anglicè *Lond.* 1602.   C. 6. 8.

[The copy in B. M. (pr. mk. C. 28 e. 13) has copious MS. notes by the author and Richard Smyth.]

1650. **Toll,** Tho[mas]. *To the Author* [in] Fragmenta Poetica . . . by Nich. Murford, sign. A 5. *See* App. A.

[*c.* **1650** ?] **Unknown.** *MS. note* on the date of the death of Chaucer and Gower, and their places of burial. Trentham MS. (Duke of Sutherland's), fol. 39 *b.* (Gower's Works, ed. G. C. Macaulay, vol. i, French works, 1899, p. lxxxi.)

1652. **Ashmole,** Elias. *Theatrum Chemicum Britannicum;* Prolegomena, signs. A 3 and A 3 *b,* pp. 227–56. The tale of the Chanons Yeoman, Written by our Ancient and famous English Poet, Geoffry Chaucer ; p. 226 a print of Chaucer's tomb erected by Nicholas Brigham. Annotations . . . . upon some part of the preceding Worke, pp. 440, 447, 456, 465, 467–72 [470–72, life of Chaucer], 484–5.

[These references are chiefly quotations from Chaucer.]

[p. 470]   Now as Concerning *Chaucer* (the *Author* of this *Tale*) [*i. e.* Chanon Yeoman's] he is ranked amongst the *Hermetick Philosophers,* and his *Master* in this *Science* was Sir *John Gower . . .* He is cited by *Norton* for an *Authentique Author,* in these words ;

> And Chaucer rehearseth how Tytans is the same.

Besides he that Reads the latter part of the *Chanon's Yeoman's Tale,* wil easily perceive him to be a *Iudicious Philosopher,* and one that fully knew the *Mistery.* [Ashmole then quotes Speght, Bale, Pits and Stow.]

[*Cf.* above, *c.* 1477, Norton, p. 57.   For Alchemy in general, and Chaucer's relation to it, *see* The Alchemist, by Ben Jonson, ed. C. M. Hathaway, N. York. 1903, Introduction.]

1652. Wharton, G [Sir George ?]. *To my very Honoured Friend Mr Robert Loveday upon this His Matchlesse Version, Entituled Love's Master-piece.* Prefatory verses to Hymen's Præludia : or Love's Master-piece. Being the first Part of that so much admir'd Romance, intituled Cleopatra. Written originally in the French, [by Gauthier de Costes, Seigneur de la Calprenède] and now rendred into English by R. Loveday . . . 1652, sign. A 6 *b*.

> *Chawcer* and *Gow'r* our *Language* but *Refin'd,*
> You (SIR) true *Chemist*-like, have it *Calcin'd,*
> *Hew'd* out the *Barbarous Knots,* and made it *Run*
> As *Smooth,* as doth the *Chariot* of the *Sun.*

[This poem does not appear in the later edns. of 1654 and 1655.]

[1653 ?] Bowyr, Ann. *Ann Bowyr's writing-book,* containing : Exercises or Extracts from various English poets ; Chaucer, the Earl of Surrey, the Mirror for Magistrates, etc. MS. Ashmole 51, f 1 *b,* 7 *b,* 20 leaves of paper (Catalogue of Ashmole MSS., by W. H. Black, 1845, col. 91.)

[fol. 2]

Chascer vpon The mancipels Talle.

harde it is to be restraned that
Which nature hath ingraft in ani creture.

[ll.161-2]

Chascer the Romont on the rose.

What is the cas that men complan in comon
of godes hie prouidenc & folish fortune
God giueth vnto vs in sundri wis
far beter then our wits can deuis.

[fol. 3 *b*]

Chauser The Romont on the rose.

Alle knoledg is not toute in scouls
manitimes on may learne wit of foules
out of oulde feldes as men may say
haue wee our new come [corn ?] from day to day
but out of oulde boukes in good fay
comes our new learning day by day.

[Not in *R. of Rose,* but the last 4 lines are taken from the *Parlement of Foules,* ll. 22-25.]

Chascer vpon yᵉ wife of bathes prologue.

[fol. 4 *b*]

Who so buildeth his hous all of salowes
& pricketh his blind hors oure yᵉ falowes
& suffreth his wife for to seche hallowes
he is worthy to be honged on yᵉ gallowes.

[ll. 655-8]

Chascer on yᵉ man of Lawes tale.

in hir is hie beautie without pride
youth without grenhed or folie
to all her workes vertue is her guide

humblenes hath slain in her all tyrannie
she is a mirrour of all curtesie
her hert is very chamber of holinens [*sic*]
her hand minister of fredome & almes.

[ll. 162–8]

[There may be other extracts from Chaucer in this MS., but the above are the only ones that are noted as his. There is no date in the MS., but it is probably *c.* 1653.]

1653. Langbaine, Gerard. *Letter to Mr. Selden* [dated] Queen's Coll. Oxon, 11 Oct. 1653 [printed in] Joannis Lelandi . . De rebus Britannicis collectanea . cum Thomæ Hearnici, Prefatione Notis et Indice ad Editionem primam . . . Londini, 1770, vol. v. [Appendi Ludovici Savoti . . . e collectaneis Smithianis . . .], p. 270.

Sir,
  I give you many thanks for imparting so much (as I earnestly desired to know) of that Scotch Copy of Chaucer. . .

[This no doubt refers to the Selden MS. of the Canterbury Tales now in the Bodleian library.]

1653. Wallis, John. *Grammatica Linguæ Anglicanæ. Oxoniæ*, 1653, p. 34.

[Brief reference to certain spelling and word forms in Chaucer.]

1654. Evelyn, John. *Diary*, June 9th, 1654. (Diary and Correspondence of John Evelyn, ed. William Bray, new edn. by H. B. Wheatley, 1906, vol. ii, p. 52.)

Din'd at Marlborough . . . . thence, to Newberry, a considerable towne, and Donnington, famous for its battle, siege, and castle ; this last had ben in the possession of old Geofrie Chaucer.

1654. Gayton, Edmund. *Pleasant Notes upon Don Quixot.* By Edmund Gayton, 1654, book 3, chap. xi, p. 150.

Our Nation also had its Poets, and they their wives : To passe the Bards : Sir *Jeffery Chaucer* liv'd very honestly at Woodstock, with his Lady, (the house yet remaining), and wrote against the vice most wittily, which Wedlocke restraines. My father *Ben* begate sonnes and daughters ; so did *Spencer, Drayton, Shakespeare* and more might be reckoned, who doe not only word it, and end in aiery *Sylvia's, Galatea's, Anglaura's,*
                    Sed de virtute locuti,
      Clunem agitant . . . .

1655. Fuller, Thomas. *The Church-History of Britain*, book iv, pp. 151–2, book vi, p. 268. (The Church History of Britain, by Thomas Fuller, ed. J. S. Brewer, 1845, vol. ii, pp. 382–4.)

[p. 151]
[Trevisa]
escaped
persecution,
. . . . .
As did his
contempor-
ary *Geoffery
Chaucer.*

46. We may couple with him [*John de Trevisa*], his contemporary, *Geffery Chaucer*, born (some say) in *Berke-shire*, others in *Oxford-shire*, most and truest in *London*. If the Grecian *Homer* had seven, let our English have three places contest for his Nativity. Our *Homer* (I say) onely herein he differed.

> *Mœonides nullas ipse reliquit opes*
> *Homer* himself did leave no pelf,

Whereas our *Chaucer* left behinde him a rich and worshipful estate.

[p. 152]
His parent-
age and
armes.

47. His Father was a Vintner in *London ;* and I have heard his Armes quarell'd at, being *Argent* and *Gules* strangely contrived, and hard to be blazon'd. Some more wits have made it the dashing of white and red wine (the parents of our ordinary Claret) as nicking his father's profession. But, were *Chaucer* alive, he would justifie his own Armes in the face of all his opposers, being not so devoted to the Muses, but he was also a son of *Mars.* He was the Prince of English Poets ; married the daughter of *Pain Roët*, King of Armes in *France*, and sister to the Wife of *John* of *Gaunt*, King of *Castile*.

He refined
our English
tongue.

48. He was a great *Refiner*, and *Illuminer* of our English tongue (and, if he left it so bad, how much worse did he finde it ?) witness *Leland* thus praising him, [quotes and translates Leland's lines beginning 'Prædicat Algerum,' *see* below, App. A., Leland, c. 1545.] . . .

ᵃ In his
restitution
of decaied
intelligence,
p. 203.
[*See* above,
p. 176 *b.*]

Indeed *Verstegan*, a learned ᵃ Antiquary, condemns him, for spoiling the purity of the English tongue, by the mixture of so many French and Latin words. But, he who mingles wine with water, though he destroies the nature of water, improves the quality thereof.

A great
enemy to
Friers.

49. I finde this *Chaucer* fined in the Temple two shillings, for striking a Franciscan Frier in *Fleet-street*, and it seems his hands ever after itched to be revenged, and have his penniworths out of them, so *tickling* Religious Orders with his *tales*, and yet so *pinching* them with his *truths*, that Friers in reading his books, know not how to dispose their faces betwixt *crying* and *laughing*. He lies

buried in the South-Isle of *St. Peters, Westminster,* and since hath got the company of *Spencer* and *Drayton* (a pair-royal of Poets), enough (almost) to make passengers feet to move metrically, who go over the place, where so much *Poetical dust* is interred.

. . . .

[bk. vi, p. 268]   These Augustinians were also called *Canons Reguar,* where, by the way, I meet with such a nice distinction, which disheartens me from pretending to exactnesse in reckoning up these Orders.   For, this I finde in our *English* Ennius :

Chaucer in the Plowmans Tale.

> And all such other Counter faitours
> Chanons, Canons and such disguised
> Been Goddes enemies and Traytours
> His true religion hau[e] foule despised
> [Chaucerian and other pieces, ll. 1061-4]

It seems that the H here amounteth to a letter so effectuall as to discriminate chanons from canons (though both Canonici in Latine) but what should be the difference betwixt them, I dare not interpose my conjecture.

1655. **M**[ennis], Sir J[ohn], and **S**[mith], Ja[mes].   *Musarum Deliciæ or The Muses Recreation,* by Sʳ J. M. and Ja. S. London. Printed for Henry Herringman, 1655, pp. 71–3 : *Partus Chauceri Post-humus Gulielmi Nelson,* p. 73 : *Vpon the same,* pp. 74–5 : *Imitatio Chauceri altera, In eundem.* (Facetiæ. Musarum Deliciæ. etc. [ed. T. Park], 2 vols, 1817, vol. i, pp. 85–9.)

[In the 2nd edition of 1656 the above references are on pp. 85–9.]

1656. **B**[lount], T[homas].   *Glossographia, or a Dictionary, interpreting all . . . . hard . Words,* by T. B. of the Inner-Temple, sign. A. 4 and O 1 *b*.   Fifth edn. 1681, sign. A. iv *b*, and p. 213.

To the Reader.

. . . . words in Common Tongues like leaves, must of necessity have their buddings, their blossomings, their ripen-ings & their fallings : Which old *Chaucer* also thus remarks :—

> I know that in form of speech is change
> Within a hundred years, & words tho
> That hadden price, now wonder nice & strange
> Think we them, yet they spake them so
> And sped as well in love as men now do.
> [*Tr. & Cres.* ii, ll. 22–6.]

[The reference on sign. O 1 *b* is a note under Dulcarnon.]

1656. Cowley, Abraham.   *Poems* .... *iii. Pindarique Odes* [separate
title-page and pagination]—*To Dr. Scarborough,* note on verse 2,
p. 37.   (Works of A. Cowley, ed. A. B. Grosart, Chertsey worthies
library, 1881, vol. ii, p. 23.)

> *Find, Refind*—These kind of *Rhymes* the *French* delight in,
> and call *Rich Rhymes*; but I do not allow of them in *English*
> .... They are very frequent in *Chaucer,* and our old Poets,
> but that is not good Authority for us now.   There can be no
> *Musick* with only *one Note.*
>
> [*See* also below, App. A., *a.* 1664.]

1656. [Holland, Samuel].   [secondary title] *Don Zara del Fogo.*   A
Mock Romance.   [title-page] *Wit and Fancy in a Maze,* or the
incomparable Champion of Love and Beautie ....   Written originally in the British Tongue, and made English by a person of much
Honour, London, Printed by *T. W.* for *Tho. Vere,* 1656, bk. 2,
ch. 4, pp. 101–2.

> . . . the Brittish Bards (forsooth) were also ingaged in
> quarrel for Superiority; and who think you, threw the Apple
> of Discord among them, but *Ben Johnson,* who had openly
> vaunted himself the first and best of English Poets; this
> Brave was resented by all with the highest indignation, for
> *Chawcer* (by most there) was esteemed the Father of English
> Poesie, whose onely unhappines it was, that he was made for
> the time he lived in, but the time not for him . . . [the various
> poets take sides] *Skelton Gower* and the Monk of *Bury* were at
> Daggers-drawing for *Chawcer*; . . . .

> [In another issue of the above, with same printers' names and date, the title runs
> differently, *Don Zara del Fogo,* A Mock Romance, Written originally in the *Brittish*
> Tongue, and made *English* by a person of much Honor, Basilivs Mvsophilvs. This
> book was reprinted in 1660, with the author's name, under the title of *Romancio-
> mastrix*; and later in 1719 under the title of *The Spaniard,* or *Don Zara del Fogo.*
> Translated from the *Original Spanish* by Basilius Musophilus. London. Printed
> for *W. Chetwood* . . . and *R. Franklin,* MDCCXIX; in which edn. the above reference
> is on p. 71.]

1656. Leigh, Edward.   *A Treatise of Religion and Learning, and of
Religious and Learned Men,* sign. A 6, pp. 91, 160, 211.

[sign. A, 6]   The Epistle To The Reader.

> I shall endeavour to marshall up some of our English
> Schollers . . . .

> For Poets of old, *Chaucer, Spenser, Ockland.*

[p. 91]   *England* hath been famous for Learned men, and for her
Seminaries of Learning, as well as other things.

> For Poetry.   *Gower, Chaucer, Spencer, Sir Philip Sidnie,
> Daniel and Draiton, Beaumont and Fletcher, Ben: Johnson.*

[p. 160]   *Galfridus Chaucerus, Jeffery Chaucer,* he was born in *Oxford-shire.* He first of all so illustrated the English Poetry, that he may be esteemed our English *Homer.* He is our best English Poet and *Spencer* the next.   [quotes Latin verse from Leland beginning, ' Prædicat Algerum ' ; *see* below, App. A, *c.* 1545, Leland.] He seems in his Works to be a right *Wiclevian,* as that of the Pellican and Griffin shews.

He was an acute Logician, a sweet Rhetorician, a facetious Poet, a grave Philosopher, and a Holy Divine.

His Monument is in *Westminster-*Abbey.

Chaucerus *linguam patriam magna ingenii solertia ac cultura plurimùm ornavit, itemque alia, cum* Joannis Mone *poema de arte amandi Gallicè tantùm legeretur, Anglico illud metro feliciter reddidit.* Voss. *De Histor. Lat.* l. 3–c. 2 [*see* App. A, below]. [note partly in margin and text].   Vixit Anno Domini 1402. Propter docendi gratiam & libertatem quasi alter Dantes aut Petrarcha quos ille etiam in linguam nostram transtulit, in quibus Romana Ecclesia tanquam sedes Antichristi describitur, & ad vivum exprimitur. *Humphr* : Præfatio ad lib. de Jesuitismo. [See above, p. 122, 1582, Humphrey.]   Fuere & in Britannorum idiomate & eorum vernaculo sermone aliqui poetæ ab eis summo pretio habiti inter quos *Galfredus Chaucerus* vetustior qui multa scripsit, & *Thomas Viatus,* ambo insignes equites. *Lil. Gyrald* De Poet : nost Temp. ii Dial 2 [*see* Giraldus, 1551, App. A, below].

. . . .

[p. 211]   *Joannes Goverus,* sive *Gouerus,* a learned English Knight, and Poet *Laureate.*

Hic nomen suum extulit partim iis quæ & Gallicè & eleganter Anglicè elaboravit.   Sane is & Gualterus Chaucerus primi Anglicam linguam expolire cœperunt. Vossius *de Histor: Lat: l. 3. c. 3.*

[For the question of Chaucer and Dante, *see* note above, p. 38.]

1656. S[mith], J[ames]. *The Preface to that most elaborate piece of Poetry entituled Penelope and Ulysses* [in] Wit and Drollery. Jovial Poems by Sir J[ohn] M[ennis], Ja[mes] S[mith], Sir W[illiam] D[avenant], J. D. and other admirable Wits, London, Printed for Nath. Brook, 1656, p. 2 ; [also in] Wit Restor'd . . . 1658, p. 149 (reprinted Facetiæ, Musarum Deliciæ, Wit Restor'd [ed. T. Park], 2 vols., 1817, vol. i, p. 254.]

Why didst thou [the author's muse] play the wag? I'm very sure
I have commended thee above old *Chaucer*

And in a Tavern once I had a Sawcer
Of white-wine Vinegar dasht in my face
For saying thou deservedst a better grace.

1656. Unknown. *Verses written over the Chair of Ben Johnson* [in] Wit and Drollery. Jovial Poems, by Sir J[ohn] M[ennis], etc. [*see* last entry, under James Smith], p. 79.

And though our nation could afford no room
Near *Chaucer*, Spencer, *Drayton*, for thy tomb . . .

1656. Unknown. *Choyce Drollery:* Songs and Sonnets, Being a collection of divers excellent pieces of Poetry, of severall eminent Authors. Never before printed. London, Printed by J. G. for Robert Pollard, at the Ben Johnson's head . . . 1656. (No copy of original in B.M., but there is one in the Bodleian and there was one in the Huth collection. Reprinted by J. W. Ebsworth, 1876, p. 7.)

On the Time Poets.

. . . Of these sad Poets this way ran the stream,
And *Decker* followed after in a dream ;
Rounce, Robble, Hobble, he that writ so high big[;]
Basse for a Ballad, *John Shank* for a Jig ;   [*Wm. Basse*]
Sent by *Ben Jonson,* as some Authors say,
Broom went before and kindly swept the way :
Old *Chaucer* welcomes them into the Green,
And *Spencer* brings them to the fairy Queen.

1657. Poole, Josua. *The English Parnassus : or, A Helpe to English Poesie. Containing a short Institution of that Art ; a Collection of all Rhyming Monosyllables, the choicest Epithets and Phrases,* p. 41.

[The book practically consists of lists of adjectives suitable to be applied to certain nouns. The reference to Chaucer consists of his name among the list of ' Books principally made use of in the compiling of this work.']

1658. Atkins, James. *To his Worthy Friend, Mr. J. S. Upon his happy Innovation of Penelope and ulysses* [signed] James Atkins. [in] Wit Restor'd. In severall Select Poems not formerly publisht. London, Printed for R. Pollard, N. Brooks [etc.], 1658, sign. K 8. [There is a separate title-page for this poem] The Innovation of Penelope and Ulysses. A mock Poem by J[ames] S[mith], 1658. (Facetiæ. Musarum Deliciæ. Wit Restor'd [ed. T. Park], 2 vols., 1817, vol. i., p. 243.)

She [Thalia] lowr'd her flight, and soone assembled all
That since old *Chaucer,* had tane leave to call
Upon her name in print . . . . .

[*See* above, 1656, Smith, James, p. 233.]

1658. Austin, Samuel (the Younger). *To his ingenuous Friend, the Author, on his incomparable Poem.* Naps upon Parnassus . . . 1658, sign. B 4 *b* and B 5. (Printed in Fresh allusions to Shakspere, ed. F. J. Furnivall, New Shakspere soc., 1886, pp. 181–2.)

Carmen Jocoserium.

If I may guess at Poets in our Land,
Thou beat'st them all *above,* and *underhand;*

.   .   .   .

To thee compar'd, our English Poets all stop,
An vail their Bonnets, even *Shakespear's Falstop.*[1]
Chaucer the first of all wasn't worth a farthing,
Lidgate, and *Huntingdon,* with Gaffer *Harding.*

.   .   .   .

S. W., W. C. C. Oxon.

[1] It should have been Falstaff, if the rhyme had permitted it.

[The poet here addresses himself in a commendatory " Carmen Jocoserium " under the initials S.W., W. C. C. Oxon. The Advertisement to the Reader is signed Adoniram Banstittle, alias Tinderbox. This book may be found in the B.M. Catalogue under Q. K., with references from Banstittle and Austin.]

[a. 1658.] Cleveland, John. *The Rustick Rampant or Rural Anarchy, affronting Monarchy : in the Insurrection of Wat Tyler,* by J. C. London. Printed by *R. Holt,* for *Obadiah Blagrave,* 1687, p. 424 (Works of Mr. John Cleveland, 1687, p. 424).

Our most famous *Chaucer* flourishing then, in his Description of the terrible Fright and Noise, at the carrying away of *Chanticlere* the Cock by *Reinold* the Fox, reflects upon these Crys, but in an Hyperbole of his Poetical feigned ones, and much undervaluing the Honor of the *Kentish* Throats, as he will have it.

They yellen as Fiends do in Hell, etc.
So hideous was the Noise, Ah benedicite !

Certes Jack-Straw ne his meney
Ne made Shouts half so shrill,
When they would any Flemming kill.

[Nonne Preestes Tale, ll. 4579 and 4583–6.]

1658. Cokayne, Sir Aston. *Small Poems of Divers Sorts.* London. Printed by Wil. Godbid, 1658, pp. 8, 105, 155. (Poems, ed. A. E. Cokayne, Congleton, 1877, privately printed, pp. 10–11, 118.)

A Remedy for Love.

[p. 8]

Theré [London] thou upon the Sepulchre maist look
Of *Chaucer,* our true *Ennius,* whose old book
Hath taught our Nation so to Poetize,
That English rythmes now any equalize ;

That we no more need envy at the straine
Of *Tiber*, *Tagus*, or our neighbour *Seine*.

.   .   .   .

[p. 105]   *To Mr. Humphry C. on his Poem entitled Loves Hawking-Bag.*

Chaucer, we now commit thee to repose,
And care not for thy Romance of the *Rose*.
In thy grave at *Saint Edmunds Bury*, thy
Hector henceforth (*Lydgate*) may with thee ly;
Old *Gower* (in like manner) we despise,
Condemning him to silence for his Cryes
And *Spencer* all thy Knights may (from this time)
Go seek Adventures in another Clime
These Poets were but Footposts that did come
Halting unto 's, whom thou hast all outrun:

.   .   .   .

[p. 155]   *Epigrams.*   The first Book, 36 *Of Chaucer* [not in modern edition].

Our good old *Chaucer* some despise: and why?
Because say they he writeth barbarously.
Blame him not (Ignorants) but your selves, that do
Not at these years your native language know.

1658. P[hillips], E[dward].   *The Mysteries of Love and Eloquence, or the Arts of Wooing and Complementing* . . . . 1658, p. 180.

Miscellania.   Fancy Awakened: Natural . . . . Jovial Questions with their several Answers . . . .

Q. What was old Chaucers *Saw?*

A. Lord be merciful unto us,
Fools or Knaves will else undo us.

1658. P[hillips], E[dward].   *The New World of Words, or a generall dictionary*, by E. P., preface, sign. b 4 *b*.   [On the title-page are pictures of Spenser, Chaucer, Lambard, Camden, Selden, and Spelman.]

. . . . it is evident, that the Saxon, or German tongue is the ground-work upon which our language is founded, the mighty stream of forraigne words that hath since *Chaucers* time broke in upon it, having not yet wash't away the root.

1658. Topsell, Edward.   *The History of Four-footed Beasts and Serpents*, pp. 780, 781.

[Quotes Chaucer's description of the Franklin.]

1659. J[ones], B[assett]. *Hermælogium; or an Essay at the rationality of the Art of Speaking. As a Supplement to Lillie's Grammar.* Offered by B. J., pp. 42, 43, 69.

[p. 42]   In that the first and second persons of the Verb be aswell digitally as vocally notified; but this third person never digitally, saving in order to contempt. So that it was not without reason that the old *English* usurped it for the heightning of perswasion. As Sir *Geoffery Chaucer* when representing the cheating Alchymist,

The Chanons Yeoman's Tale [ll. 1326– 29]

Thus said he in his game.
. . . .
Put in your hond and looketh what is there.

[p. 43]   The Verb Impersonal of the Passive Voice, I observe to vary from the sense of its personality only while it fixeth our observance to it self; just as the fore-quoted noble *Chaucer* doth by a personal Active, where* he thus singeth

*In *Assembly of fowls* [ll. 22–25]

As from awd ground Men Saith commeth Corn fro yeer to year [*sic*]
So from awd books, by my faith, commen all new Science that men lere.
. . . .

[p. 69]   Whether there be any Books writ on this subject [*i. e.* of interjections conveyed by actions] I am not certain. But observe that before the use of Bandstrings, this gravity hath been emulated by the English. The noble *Chaucer*, as he encomiats the deportment of the Arabian Envoy in the Tartarian presence thus singing,

The Squier' Tale [ll. 103–4]

Accordant to his woordes was his chere
As teacheth art of speech hem that it lere.

1659. With, Elizabeth, of Woodbridge. *Elizabeth Fools Warning . . . Being a caveat for all young women to marry with old men . . . By Elizabeth With of Woodbridge,* pp. 4, 5.

[p. 4]   Instead of smiles he gave me a frown
In his locking up my best silk gown,
Which with my pettycoats so neatly wrought
Into his Sisters Chest after he brought
. . . .
Now patient Grisill what dost thou now say
Art thou contented with thy gown of gray.
. . . .

[p. 5]   At length I left this crying strain :
And when old Naboth plaid his part,
I did get patient Grisills heart.

1660. P[arker], M[artin]. *The Famous History of That Most Renowned Christian Worthy Arthur King of the Britaines*, p. 13. [The preface is signed M. P., Parker's initials, under which he often wrote.]

King Arthur . . . . instituted at the City of Winchester where he was then residing the Order of the Round Table . . . . into this order were received 150 men . . . . which were called Knights of the Round Table, and because I find many of their names to be at this day great sirnames in the Monarchy of great Britain, I think it convenient . . . . to set down the names of the first Knights of the Round Table in Alphabeticall order, as I found them long since in an old Chaucerian manuscript.

1660. Tatham, John. *The Character of the Rump*, p. 1. [In Thomason Tracts, B.M. pr. m. E. 1017.] (Tatham's Dramatic Works, ed. J. Maidment and W. H. Logan, Edinburgh, 1879, p. 287.)

. . . the devil's tail in Chaucer, being stuck in this, would look but like a maggot in a Tub of Tallow, and yet he saith—

That certainly Sathanas hath such a tail
Broader than of a Pinnace is the Sail.

1660. Winstanley, William. *Englands Worthies*, sign. A 7 b, A 8 b, pp. 79, 91–8. [Life of Chaucer based on Speght, *cf.* Winstanley's Lives of the Most Famous English Poets, 1687, below, p. 261.]

[p. 79]   His body [Edward III] was solemnly interred at *Westminster* Church, where he hath his monument, with this Epitaph engraven thereon, made by *Geffery Chaucer* the Poet.

Hic decus Anglorum, flos regum præteritorum,
Forma futurorum, Rex clemens, pax populorum,
Tertius Edwardus, regni complens Jubilæum,
Invictus Pardus, pollens bellis Machabæum.

[c. 1660.] Widdrington, Sir Thomas. *Analecta Eboracensia*. *See* below, App. A.

1661-6. Wood, Anthony à. *Survey of the Antiquities of the City of Oxford*. MS. Wood F. 29a, Bodl. ff. 7 b, 38 b, 220, 275 b. (Survey, etc., ed. Andrew Clark, 1889–99, vol. i, pp. 55, 173, 402 ; vol. ii (1890), pp. 225, 287. Merely passing references to Chaucer.)

vol. i, ch. iv, p. 55, fol. 7 b. [Reference to Astrolab.
    „   viii, p. 130, „   24 b. Tabard Inn in Oxford.
                        Reference in Clark's note.

vol. i, ch. viii, p. 173, fol. 38 *b*. Soller Hall and Reeves Tale.

„ „ xxi, p. 402, „ 6 *a*. Reference in Wood, marginal note to Chaucer.

„ ii „ xxxi, p. 225, „ 220 *a*. Reference in text and marginal note—Wood.

„ „ „ p. 287, „ 275 *b*. Chaucer and Wijclyve.

„ „ „ p. 290, „ 276 *a*. Reference in margin by Clarke to Twyne, xxiii, 729.]

1662. E[velyn], J[ohn]. *Sylva, or a Discourse of Forest-Trees* . . . . by J. E., Esq. . . . as it was Deliver'd in the Royal Society . . . . 1662 . . . Printed 1664 ; ch. xxix, p. 83. (Sylva, ed. John Nisbet, 1908, vol. ii, p. 43.)

Nor are we to over-pass those memorable Trees which so lately flourished in *Dennington* [*sic*] *Park* neer *Newberry* ; amongst which three were most remarkable from the ingenious *Planter,* and *dedication* (if *Tradition* hold) the famous English *Bard Jeofry Chaucer* ; of which one was call'd the *Kings,* another the *Queens,* and a third *Chaucers Oak.* . . . *Chaucers Oak,* though it were not of these dimensions, yet was it a very goodly Tree.

1662. Fuller, Thomas. *The History of the Worthies of England.* Endeavoured by Thomas Fuller, p. 106, sign. P 1 *b*, Barkshire, [Thomas Chaucer] ; p. 97, sign. Oo 1, Kent ; pp. 219–20, sign. Eee 4 and 4 *b*, London ; pp. 337–8, sign. Vvv 4 and *b*, Oxford-shire ; pp. 68–9, sign. Iii 2 *b* and 3, Suffolk ; p. 207, sign. Cccc 4, Yorkshire [Gower]. (ed. John Nichols, 1811, vol. i, pp. 107, 527 ; vol. ii, pp. 80–1, 230–1, 341–2, 514.)

Proverbs

[p. 97 sign. Oo 1] *Canterbury Tales*]

So *Chaucer* calleth his Book, being a collection of several *Tales,* pretended to be told by Pilgrims in their passage to the Shrine of Saint *Thomas* in *Canterbury.* But since that time *Canterbury Tales* are parallel to *Fabulæ Milesiæ,* which are charactered, *Nec veræ, nec verisimiles,* meerly made to marre precious time, and please fanciful people.

. . . .

[p. 219 sign. Eee 4] EDMOND SPENCER . . . especially most happy in English Poetry, as his works do declare. In which the many *Chaucerisms* used (for I will not say affected by him) are thought by the ignorant to be *blemishes*, known by the learned to be *beauties* to his book ; which notwithstanding had been more alable, if more conformed to our modern language. . . .

[p. 337 sign. Vvv 4] JEFFREY CHAUCER was by most probability born at *Woodstock* in this County [Oxfordshire], though other places lay stiff claim to his Nativity [i. e. Berkshire and London, the claims of all three places are then stated in parallel columns.]

. . . .

[p. 338] He was a terse and elegant Poet, (the *Homer* of his Age), and so refined our *English* Tongue, *Ut inter expolitas gentium linguas potuit recte quidem connumerari*,[1] His skill in *Mathematics* was great (being instructed therein by Joannes Sombus and Nicholas of Linn) ; which he evidenceth in his book "De Sphaerâ." He, being contemporary with Gower, was living anno Domini 1402. . . .

[p. 68 sign. Iii 2 b] JOHN LYDGATE . . . If *Chaucers coin* were of a *greater weight* for *deeper learning*, *Lydgates* were of a more *refined standard* for *purer language*, so that one might mistake him for a modern Writer.

[[1] Bale, de Scriptoribus Britannicis, cent. vii, num. 14.]

1662. Wilson, John. *The Cheats: a Comedy*. Written in the year 1662 . . . . Printed . . . . 1664. Second edition, 1671. The Author to the Reader, sign. A 3. (Dramatic works of J. Wilson, ed. J. Maidment and W. H. Logan [1873], p. 13.)

There is hardly any thing left to write upon, but what either the Ancients or Moderns have some way or other touch'd on :—Did not *Apulejus* take the Rise of his *Golden Asse*, from *Lucian's Lucius* ? and *Erasmus*, his *Alcumnistica*, from *Chaucer's Canons Yeomans Tale* ? and *Ben Johnson* his more happy *Alchymist* from both ? The Argument were everlasting.

1663. Gayton, Edmund (Batchelor of Physick). *The Religion of a Physician. Or, Divine Meditations upon the Grand and Lesser Festivals.* Epistle to the Favourable *Reader*, sign. A 4 b and B 1. (This reference is given in T. Corser's Collectanea, Chetham soc., part vi, 1877, p. 463.)

'Tis true, that Sir *Jeffrey Chaucer* had but an ill opinion of my Faculty, when he saith of a Doctor of Physick,

> *His meat was good and digestible,*
> *But not a word he had o' th' Bible.* [*Prol. Cant. Tales,* ll. 437–8]

To wipe off that stain and aspersion from our *Botanick Tribe*,

I wrote these *Meditations,* to show the world, that it is possible
for a Physician of the Lower Form to be *Theologue,* at least-
wise to seem to be one . . . .

1663–4. Pepys, Samuel. *Diary for June 14ᵗʰ and Dec. 10ᵗʰ 1663,
July 8, 9, Aug. 10,* 1664. (The Diary of Samuel Pepys, ed. H. B.
Wheatley, 1893–99, vol. iii, pp. 168, 370–1 ; vol. iv, pp. 178, 213.)

[vol. iii, p. 168]   June 14ᵗʰ 1663 . . . . So to Sir W. Pen's to visit him . . . .
By and by in comes Sir J. Minnes, and Sir W. Batten, and so
we sat talking.   Among other things Sir J. Minnes brought
many fine expressions of Chaucer, which he doats on mightily,
and without doubt he is a very fine poet.

[p. 370]   Dec. 10, 1663.   To St. Paul's Church Yard to my booksellers . . . . I could not tell whether to lay out my money
for books of pleasure, as plays, which my nature was most
earnest in ; but at last, after seeing Chaucer, Dugdale's History
of St. Paul's, Stow's London, Gesner, History of Trent, besides
Shakespeare, Jonson, and Beaumont's plays, I at last chose
Dr. Fuller's Worthys, the Cabbala or Collections of Letters of
State, and a little book, Delices de Hollande, with another
little book or two, all of good use or serious pleasure ; and
[p. 371] Hudibras both parts, the book now in greatest fashion for
drollery, though I cannot, I confess, see enough where the
wit lies.

[vol. iv, p. 178]   1664. July 8ᵗʰ . . . . So to Paul's Churchyarde about my
books, and to the binder's and directed the doing of my
Chaucer, though they were not full neate enough for me, but
pretty well it is ; and thence to the clasp-maker's to have it
clasped and bossed.   [This was Speght's edn. of 1602, still in
the Pepysian library, bound in calf, with brass clasps and
bosses.]

July 9ᵗʰ . . . . So home, by the way calling for my Chaucer
and other books, and that is well done to my mind, which
pleased me well.

[p. 212]   Aug. 10ᵗʰ Up, and . . abroad to do several small busi-
nesses, among others to find out one to engrave my tables
upon my new sliding rule with silver plates. . . . So I find
out Cocker, the famous writing master, and get him to do
CHAUCER CRITICISM.

[p. 213] it . . . he says that the best light for his life to do a very small thing by (contrary to Chaucer's words to the Sun, "that he should lend his light to them that small seals grave "), it should be by an artificial light to a candle, set to advantage, as he could do it.

[Pepys here refers to the passage in *Troilus & Criseyde*, book iii, st. 209, ll. 1457–63.]

[*a.* 1665.] **Fairfax**, Henry. *The Catalogue of the library of Henry Fairfax* (4th son of Thomas, first Lord Fairfax, who died in 1665). Sloane MS. 1872, f. 81. (*See* Edw. J. L. Scott in Athenæum, Mar. 3, 1898, p. 320, col. 2.)

> [Under the heading of] Poesis—Anglici. Chaucer's workes. fol.
> Spenser's fairy Queen. fol.
> Johnsons .2. vol.
> Beaumont & ff. Fletcher.
> Shakespeare.

1665. Brathwait, Richard. *A comment upon the Two Tales of our Ancient . . . . Poet . Sr Jeffray Chaucer . . . . The Miller's Tale* [and the] *Wife of Bath* (ed. C. Spurgeon, Chaucer soc. 1901). [The whole is a running commentary on these Tales, we quote only *Appendix*, p. 98.]

A Critick . . . . said " that he could allow well of Chaucer, if his Language were Better."—Whereto the Author of these Commentaries return'd him this Answer: " Sir, it appears, you prefer Speech before the Head piece; Language before Invention; whereas Weight of Judgment has ever given Invention Priority before Language. And not to leave you dissatisfied, As the Time wherein these Tales were writ, rendered him incapable of the one; so his Pregnancy of Fancy approv'd him incomparable for the other."

Which Answer still'd this Censor, and justified the Author; leaving New-holme to attest his Deserts; his Works to perpetuate his Honour.

1666. Dugdale, Sir William. *Origines Juridiciales*, pp. 136 *b*, 137 *a*.

[Concerning the robes of serjeants at law], I am of opinion, that the form of the Robe, and colour thereof, which they use at their Creation, is very antient: for in *Chaucer's* time (which is 3 hundred years since) it is evident, that parti-coloured Garments were much in fashion; and that the people of that age were grown to a great exorbitancy therein; so that in his

Parson's Tale he sharply inveighs against the vanity thereof : and amongst other particulars which he there instanceth, takes notice, that the one half of their Hose was *white*, and the other *Red.*]

[c. **1667.**] **Butler**, Samuel. *Remains.* MSS. Add. 32625, fol. 186 *b* ; Transcript Add. 32626, ff. 83, 92.

[fol. 186 *b*] When King Henry 8th had dissolu'd all Monasteries and turnd the Friers out to grass, they overspred the whole Nation as Chaucer's Friers did Hell.   [Somnour's Prologue.]

Character of a Banker . . . .

[fol. 83] He borrows the king's money of his officers to break his laws with, as Chaucer's fryar borrow'd money of a merchant to corrupt his wife with, and makes him pay for his own injury.   [Shipmannes Tale.]

[fol. 92] These are all that is left of the Devils oracles, that give answers to those that come to consult him, not as their forefathers did by being inspired & possest, but as if they possessed the Devil himself, & had him perfectly at command : for if they were not intrenched in their circles, he would serve them as they did Chaucer's Sumner for daring to cite him to appeare . . . .   [Freres Tale, ll. 1610—40.]

[*a.* **1667.**] **Cowley**, Abraham. *See* below, App. A.

1667. Evelyn, John. *Diary*, Aug. 3rd 1667. (Diary and Correspondence of John Evelyn . . . . ed. William Bray, new edn. 1850-2. vol. ii, 1850, p. 27.)

Went to Mr Cowley's funerall ; whose corpse lay at Wallingford House, and was thence convey'd to Westminster Abby in a hearse with six horses and all funeral decency . . . . He was interred next *Geoffry Chaucer* and near *Spenser.*

[*a.* **1667.**] **Skinner**, Stephen. *Etymologicon Linguæ Anglicanæ*, 1671. *Præfatio*, sign. B 3. [Licence to be printed Sept. 7, 1668 ; Skinner died 1667. Throughout the whole work there are continual references to Chaucer, see specially the 3rd appendix to the Glossary.]

Ex hoc malesano novitatis pruritu, *Belgæ* Gallicas voces passim civitate sua donando, patrii sermonis puritatem nuper non leviter inquinarunt, & *Chaucerus* poeta, pessimo exemplo, integris vocum plaustris ex eadem Gallia in nostram Linguam invectis, eam, nimis antea à Normannorum victoria adulteratam, omni fere nativa gratia & nitore spoliavit, pro genuinis coloribus fucum illinens, pro vera facie larvam induens.

1667. Sprat, Dr. Thomas (Bishop of Rochester). *History of the Royal Society of London,* 1667, pp. 41–2.

The Truth is, it [the English language] has been hitherto a little too carelessly handled ; and I think has had less labor spent about it's polishing, then it deserves.   Till the time of *King Henry* the *Eighth,* there was scarce any man regarded it, but *Chaucer* ; and nothing was written in it, which one would be willing to read twice, but some of his *Poetry.*   But then it began to raise it self a little, and to sound tolerably well.

1668. Denham, Sir John.   *Poems and Translations, with The Sophy,* 1668, p. 89.   (Works of English Poets, ed. Samuel Johnson, additional lives by A. Chalmers, vol. vii, 1810, p. 247.)

On Mr Abraham Cowley, his Death and Burial amongst the Ancient Poets.

Old *Chaucer,* like the Morning Star,
To us discovers day from far,
His light those Mists and Clouds dissolv'd,
Which our dark Nation long involv'd ;
But he, descending to the shades,
Darkness again the Age invades.
Next (like *Aurora*) *Spencer* rose,
Whose purple blush the day foreshows.

1668. Waller, Edmund.   *Poems . . . . upon several Occasions. . . . The third Edition with several Additions . . . .* pp. 234–5.   **Of** English Verse [not in earlier edns.].   (Poems of Edmund Waller, ed. G. Thorn Drury, Muses Library, 1904, vol. ii. p. 70.)

Poets that lasting Marble seek
Must carve in *Latine* or in *Greek,*
We write in Sand, our Language grows,
And like the Tide our work o're flows.

Chaucer his Sense can only boast,
The glory of his numbers lost,
Years have defac'd his matchless strain,
And yet he did not sing in vain,

The Beauties which adorn'd that age
The shining Subjects of his rage,
Hoping they should immortal prove
Rewarded with success his love.

1669-96. Aubrey, John. *Brief Lives,* chiefly of Contemporaries, set down by John Aubrey, between the years 1669 & 1696. Edited from the Author's MSS. by Andrew Clark, . . . 1898. [MSS Aubrey 6, 7, 8, 9, Ashmole ; for descriptions of MSS. see introduction, pp. 8-23.] Vol. i, pp. 96 (MS. Aubrey 6, fol. 116 *b*), 170-1 (8, fol. 27), 189 (6, fol. 113 *b*), 193 (8, fol. 25), 219 (6, fol. 105 *b*), vol. ii, pp. 318 (6, fol. 11 *b*), 319 (8, fol. 10 *b*).

[p. 96] [Francis Beaumont's prefatory letter in Speght's edn. of Chaucer.]

.   .   .   .

[p. 170]   Sir Geffrey Chaucer: memorandum—Sir Hamond L'Estrange, of . . . [Hunstanton ?] in [Norfolk ?] had his Workes in MS., a most curious piece, most rarely writt and illumined, which he valued at 100 *li.* His grandson and heire still haz it.—From Mr. Roger L'Estrange.

He taught his sonne the use of [the] astrolabe at 10 ; prout per his treatise of the Astrolabe.

Dunnington Castle, neer Newbury was his, ...

Memorandum :—near this castle was an oake under which Sir Jeofrey was wont to sitt, called *Chaucer's-oake,* which was cutt downe by . . . . tempore Caroli I^mi ; and so it was that . . . . was called into the starre chamber, and was fined for it . . . . Judge Richardson[1] harangued against him long, and like an orator, had topiques from the Druides, etc. This information I had from . . . . an able attorney that was at the hearing.

His picture is at his old howse at Woodstock (neer the parke-gate), a foot high, halfe way : has passed from proprietor to proprietor.

One Mr. Goresuch of Woodstock dined with us at Rumney marsh, who told me that at the old Gothique-built howse neere the parke-gate at Woodstock, which was the howse of Sir Jeffrey Chaucer; that there is his picture, which goes with the howse from one to another—which see.

.   .   .   .

[p. 189]   [Cowley buried next to Chaucer].

.   .   .   .

[p. 193]   [Elizabeth Danvers, dau. of John Nevill, last lord Latimer.] His [*i.e.* Henry, earl of Danby's] mother, an Italian, prodigious parts for a woman. I have heard my father's mother say that she had Chaucer at her fingers' ends.

.   .   .   .

[1 Sir Thomas Richardson, Chief Justice of the King's Bench, 1631 ; we have been unable to trace this case.]

[p. 219] [Sir John Denham buried near Chaucer].

. . . .

[vol. ii, p. 818] [reference to Chaucer's 'Prologue of the Doctor of Physick '].

. . . . . .

[p. 319] [reference to *clocks* in Chaucer's Nonnes Priest's Tale].

1669. Ramesey, William.] *The Gentlemans Companion or a Character of true Nobility* . . . . by a Person of Quality . . . . 1672, p. 129. [The epistle dedicatory is dated 1669.]

[The author gives a list of books to be read, amongst others] and among our selves, old *Sir* Jeffery Chaucer, Ben. Johnson, Shakespear, Spencer, Beaumont and Fletcher, Dryden, and what other Playes from time to time you find best Penn'd.

[c **1669.**] **Unknown.** *Verses, set to music.* Harl. MS. 6947, fol. 401. (*See* Athenæum, Aug. 9, 1902, p. 191, col. 3, where these verses are given by Dr. E. J. L. Scott, who dates them as above.)

To heauen once ther caime a poett / a frend of mine swore hee did know itt
No sooner ther butt hee did cale / the aengills littell Cupitts all
Ther haleluiaes sunge in time butt angry cause itt was not rime
And when ther prayers they did reherse hee wondred thát is [*sic*] was not verse
Seeing sutch gloris hee did aske whether twere not a twelph night mask.

Then hee satt downe vppon a bench askt for a tauerne and a wench
What sports they had ther in ther dayes and who eatch terme did wright new playes
What joyes to sencis great delights and how they past long winters nights
In sweet discorce tongs best depaints the ould wiues tales of liues of saints
Butt had no aunser mayd him there wondred wher all his ould frends weare.

No store of companey ther hee then did jeere the shepperds fishermen
And asked wher the good fellowes bee and could not one jentillman see
Swore that the place was dull so fell from thence to Lusefer in hell

Ould Chauser mett him in great state Spenser and Johnson at the gate

Beamon and Flettchers witt mayd one butt Shakspeers witt did goe aloane.

Butt ther the poetts nothing lack they had burnt Claritt and muld sack

And for a rasher of the coales the had good tuff vserers sooles

And neuer ther did want a fire to light ther pipes to ther desire

Will Dauenants health they drunke amaine to all the poets of the trayne

By no meanes they would goe from thence drunke a full quart to his exselence.

1670. Baker, Sir Richard. *Theatrum Triumphans*, p. 34.

. . . for let him try it when he will, and come himself upon the *stage*, with all the scurrility of the Wife of *Bath* . . .

1670. *John Dryden's Patent* [as Poet Laureate] Pat. 22. Car. II, p. 6, n. 6. Printed by Edmond Malone in The . . . Prose Works of John Dryden, 1800, vol. i, part i, Appendix, p. 557.

Know yee, that wee . . . . do . . appoint . . John Dryden, our POET LAUREAT and HISTORIOGRAPHER ROYAL; giving and granting unto him the said John Dryden all & singular the rights, privileges, benefits, and advantages, thereunto belonging, as fully & amply as Sir Geoffery Chaucer, Knight, Sir John Gower, Knight, John Leland, Esquire, William Camden, Esquire, Benjamin Johnson, Esquire, James Howell, Esquire, Sir William D'Avenant, Knight . . . . .

1671. [Culpeper, Sir Thomas.] *Essayes or Moral Discourses on several Subjects Written by a Person of Honour*, 1671, pp. 110, 118.

[p. 110]   I would willingly be resolved if *caress, trepan, harange,* and the like, had been written by *Chaucer*, whether they had not appeared as harsh and barbarous to us now, as any of the most obsolet used by him; . . .

[p. 118] Some have thought to honour Antiquity by using such [words] as were obsolete, as hath been done by our famous *Spencer* and others, though the times past are no more respected by an unnecessary continuing of their words then if wee wore constantly the same trimming to our Cloaths as they did, for it is not Speech, but things which render antiquity venerable, besides the danger of expressing no

Language, if as *Spencer* made use of *Chaucers*, we should likewise introduce his ; . . .

1672. Unknown. *Chaucer's Ghoast; Or a Piece of Antiquity.* Containing twelve pleasant Fables of Ovid penn'd after the ancient manner of writing in England, Which makes them prove Mock-Poems to the present Poetry . . . By a Lover of Antiquity.

> [No mention of Chaucer save in the title and in a short poem at end of the book, entitled *The Authours Friend to the Readers. See* next entry. It is not the ghost of Chaucer, but of Gower, which is here revived. *See* Studies in Chaucer, by T. R. Lounsbury, vol. iii, pp. 118–19.]

1672. Unknown. *The Authours Friend to the Readers upon his perusal of the Work.*

> . . . . . . *my loving friend*
> *His Conjuring-glass unto the World doth lend ;*
> *Where both his worth appearing we may finde,*
> *And* Chaucer's *Ghoast, or else we all are blinde.*

1672. V[eal], R[obert]. *See* below, App. A.

1673. Phillips, John. *Maronides or Virgil Travesty, . . a . . . paraphrase upon the Sixth Book of Virgil's Æneids,* p. 108.

> [p. 103] They came to the capacious High-lands,
>   That always look like *Summer-islands ;*
>
> .   .   .   .
>
> [p. 108] There sits *Ben Johnson* like a Tetrarch
>   With *Chaucer, Carew, Shakespear, Petrarch,*
>   *Fletcher* and *Beaumont,* and *Menander,*
>   *Plautus* and *Terence* .   .   .   .   .

[a. 1674.] Hyde, Edward, Earl of Clarendon. *The History of the Rebellion and Civil Wars in England, begun in* . . . 1641, by Edward, Earl of Clarendon. (1st edn. 1702 ; re-ed. from MSS. by W. Dunn Macray, 1888, vol. iii, bk. vii, § 212, p. 176.)

> 1641 . . . his majesty . . . leaving a garrison . . . in Donnington castle (a house of John Packer's, but more famous for having been the seat of Geoffrey Chaucer).

[a. 1674 ?] Milton, John. *Common Place Book,* MSS. in possession of Sir F. V. Graham. Matrimonium Vide de Divortio, fol. 109, De liberis educandis. Vide de scientia literarum, fol. 111, Paupertas, fol. 150, Nobilitas, fol. 191. (Ed. A. J. Horwood, Camden soc., revised edn. 1877, pp. 14, 16, 19, 38 ; *see* also A Common Place Book of John Milton reproduced . . . . from the original MS. . . . introduction by A. J. Horwood, under the direction of the Roy. Soc. of Literature, 1876.)

[fol. 109] *Matrimonium. Vide de Divortio.* The discommoditie of marriage. See *Chaucer,* marchants tale, and wife of Baths prologue.

.   .   .   .

[fol. 111] *De liberis educandis. Vide de scientia literarum.* Not to labour, as most men doe, to make them bold and pert while they are young, which ripens them too soon; and true boldnes and spirit is not bred but of vertuous causes, which are wrought in them by sober discipline : to this purpose *Chaucer* speaking of feasts revells and daunces, "such things maken children for to be too soon ripe and bold, as men may see, which is full perillous," &c., Doctor of Phis. tale, fol. 58.

[Physiciens Tale, ll. 67–9.]

.   .   .   .

[fol. 150] *Paupertas.* See *Chaucer.* No poverty but sin. Wife of Bath's Tale, p. 36.   [ll. 1177–1206 ?]

.   .   .   .

[fol. 191] *Nobilitas.* See *Chaucer,* Wife of Bath's Tale, fol. 36, and Romant of the Rose, fol. 118.

[ll. 1109–76; R. of the R., ll. 2187–2205.]

1674. Hyde, Thomas. *Catalogus impressorum librorum bibliothecæ Bodlejanæ in Academia Oxoniensi Curâ et operâ Thomæ Hyde,* p. 157.

Geffrey CHAUCER. His Works, *Lond.* 1561, C. 4.4. *Art.* Et *Lond.* 1602. C. 1, 9. Art. Seld.

The Plough-man's Tale, shewing that the Pope is Antichrist with an Exposition on the same. Lond..1606, 4°. C. 22, Art.

[For the two first Bodleian catalogues *see* above, 1605, p. 175, and 1620, p. 193.]

1674. Ray, John, F.R.S. *A Collection of English Words not generally used, with their significations and Original . . .* , pp. 38, 45, 53, 55, 60.

[Chaucer's use of ' recketh,' ' stot,' ' to wite,' ' yed,' ' bucksome.']

1674. [Rymer, Thomas.] *The Preface of the Translator* [to] Reflections on Aristotle's Treatise of Poesie . . . by R. Rapin, sign. A 6 *b*.

[Rymer is about to discuss the " Heroick Poets " of England.] I shall leave the Author of the *Romance of the Rose* (whom Sir *Richard Baker* makes an *Englishman*) for the *French* to boast of, because he writ in their Language. Nor shall I speak of *Chaucer*, in whose time our Language, I presume, was not capable of any Heroick character. Nor indeed was the most polite Wit of *Europe* in that Age sufficient to a great design . . . . . *Spencer* I think may be reckon'd the first of our *Heroick Poets.*

1674. Speed, Samuel (Stationer and Bookseller). *The Legend of the Thrice-Honourable, Ancient, and Renowned Prince, His Grace Humphrey, Duke of St. Paul's Cathedral Walk* . . . . [in] *Fragmenta Carceris or The Kings-Bench Scuffle.* London. Printed by J. C. for S. S. 1674, sign. G. 1.

> Old *Chaucer*, who though sickly, full of ails,
> From hence collects a Book as full of Tales.
> His Neighbour *Drayton*, who was his *Amoris*,
> Studying to write *Encomiums* on *Authoris*.

1675. Phillips, Edward. *Theatrum Poetarum, or a Compleat Collection of the Poets, especially the most Eminent, of all Ages.* By Edward Phillips, sign. **2 and *b*, The Modern Poets, pp. 50–1, 109, 112, 223.

[Preface sign. **2] . . . True it is that the style of Poetry till Henry the 8th's time, and partly also within his Reign, may very well appear uncouth, strange and unpleasant to those that are affected only with what is familiar and accustom'd to them, not but there were even before those times some that had their Poetical excellencies if well examin'd, and chiefly among the rest CHAUCER, who through all the neglect of former ag'd Poets still keeps a name, being by some few admir'd for his real worth, to others not unpleasing for his facetious way, which joyn'd with his old *English* intertains them with a kind of Drollery.

. . . .

[pp. 50–51] *Sir Geoffry Chaucer*, the *Prince* and *Coryphæus*, generally so reputed, till this Age, of our *English* Poets, and as much as we triumph over his old fashion'd phrase, and obsolete words, one of the first refiners of the *English* Language, of how great Esteem he was in the Age wherein he flourish'd, namely the Reigns of *Henry* the 4th, *Henry* the 5th, and part of *Henry* the 6th, appears, besides his being Knight and Poet Laureat, by the Honour he had to be allyed by marriage to the great Earl of *Lancaster, John* of *Gaunt :* How great a part we have lost of his Works above what Extant of him is manifest from an Author of good Credit, who reckons up many Considerable Poems, which are not in his publisht works ; besides the Squires Tale, which is said to be compleat in *Arundel-House* Library.

. . . .

[p. 109]   *Sr John Gowr*, a very famous English Poet in his time, and counted little inferiour, if not equal to Chaucer himself; who was his Contemporary, and some say his Scholar and Successor in the Laurel. For Gower was also both Poet Laureat and Knight.

    .   .   .   .

[p. 112]   *John Lane* . . . but they [his poems] are all to be produc't in Manuscript, namely . . . . . his Supplement to *Chaucers* Squires Tale.

    .   .   .   .

[p. 223]   The Supplement. *Gaulfrid*, one of the oldest of our Modern Poets, for he was contemporary with *Joseph of Exeter*: he is mentioned by Chaucer in his Description of *Chaunticleer*, the Cock's being carried away by *Reynard* the Fox, with great veneration . . . .

    .   .   .   .

[p. 233]   *Thomas Ocleave*, a very famous English poet in his time, which was the reign of King *Henry* the Fourth and *Henry* the Fifth; to which last he dedicated his *Government of a Prince*, the chiefly remember'd of what he writ in Poetry, and so much the more famous he is by being remember'd to have been the Disciple of the most fam'd *Chaucer*.

[*a.* 1675.] **Whitelock**, Bulstrode. *Memorials of the English Affairs.* London. Printed for Nathaniel Ponder. MDCLXXXII, p. 348 col. *b.* (Memorials of the English Affairs by Bulstrode Whitelock. A new edition . . . Oxford, at the University Press, 1853, vol. ii, p. 452.)

[p. 347 col. *a*]   *Anno* 1648. The new Serjeants appeared at the Chancery Bar, and *Whitelock* made the speech to them to this Effect:

    .   .   .   .

  Our old English Poet *Chaucer* (whom I think not unproper to cite, being one of the greatest Clerks and Wits of his time) had a better Opinion of the state of a Sergeant, as he expresseth in his Prologue of the Sergeant.

> *A Sergeant at Law wary and wise,*
> *That oft had been at the pervise,*
> *There was also, full of rich Excellence,*
> *Discreet he was, and of great Reverence.*

[Cant. T., prol. ll. 309–12.]

And in his description of the *Franklyn* he saith of him,

> *At Sessions there was he Lord, and Sire,*
> *Full oft had he bin Knight of Shire;*
> *A Sheriff had he bin, and Countor,*
> *Was no where such a worthy* Vavasor.
>
> [Cant. T., prol. ll. 355–6, 359–60.

A *Countor* was a Sergeant, and a *Vavasour* was the next in degree to a *Baron.*

[1676 ? **Adam,** Ben.] *Lennæ Redeuiua, or a Description of Kyngs Lynn in Norfolk . . . . in English by Ben Adam.* [Poem in MS. formerly lost, and now in the Castle Museum, Norwich; the MS. is a transcript on paper dated 1814 : see N. & Q., 3rd series, vol. iv, p. 326, 1863; vol. vii, pp. 399 and 445, 1865. Mr. H. J. Hillen published the whole MS. in the "Lynn News," and reprinted it as a pamphlet in 1909. The date 1676 occurs on the margin of the MS.; but the style suggests a date of perhaps a generation earlier. Mr. Hillen's attribution of it to *temp.* Edward IV (History of the Borough of King's Lynn [1907], pp. 249, etc.) is impossible; the chronicle stops at that period. (Information kindly given by the Curator.)

[fol. 5]   Lynn had the honour to present the world
             With Geoffrey Chaucer, Capgrave, and the curled
             Pate Allanus de Lenna . . . .

             .   .   .   .

             All famous in theyr time, Lynn, nursed by thee.

1676. Coles, E[lisha]. *An English Dictionary,* explaining . . . . difficult Terms . . . . by E. Coles, School-Master and Teacher of the Tongue to Foreigners. To the Reader, sign. A 3 *b* and L 3.

Those that I call Old Words, are generally such as occur in *Chaucer, Gower, Pierce Ploughman,* and *Julian Barns.*

.   .   .   .

At Dulcarnon, in a maze, at my wits end.   *Chaucer,* l. 3,
fol. 161.   [Tro. & Cres. iii. 933.]

1676. Plot, Robert. *The Natural History of Oxford-shire,* pp. 7–8, § 15.

§ 15. As for *Polysyllabical articulate Echo's,* the strongest and best I have met with here, is in the Park at *Woodstock* . . . . The object of which *Echo,* or the *Centrum phonocampticum,* I take to be the hill with the trees on the summit of it, about half a mile distant from Woodstock town . . . . And the true place of the speaker or *Centrum phonicum* the opposite Hill just without the gate at the Townsend, about thirty paces directly below the corner of a wall inclosing some hay-ricks, near *Chaucer's* house . . . .

[*a.* **1677.**] **Junius,** Francis. (1) *An annotated copy of Speght's edition* (1598) *of Chaucer's works.* (2) *A large quarto filled with slips in Junius's handwriting,* entitled 'Dictionarium Veteris Linguæ Anglicanæ.' Junius MSS. 9, Bodl. library. (*See* Athenæ Oxoniensis, by A. à Wood, 2nd edn. 1721, vol. ii, col. 604.)

[(1) The annotations, which are very numerous, are almost all such as the following: "Vide Annotat.," "404 m," "5971," "64 i." There are one or two references to other works, *e. g.* "Vide Aulum Gellium," "vide etymol. Anglicum." There are some Latin notes on the text, but not many. At the end is a "Syllabus operum Chauceri hoc libro contentorum," in Junius's handwriting, preceded by a few notes, such as the following: "Spelmanni glossarium, in *Colobium.* Huc pertinet illud Chauceri de Colono peregrinante, *Hee tooke his taburd, and his staffe eke.*" (2) The references in this dictionary correspond with the notation used by Junius in the copy of Speght's Chaucer, so that no doubt the two volumes belong together. *See* Wanley's Catalogus, 1705, p. 292; and Hearne, 1711, p. 317 below. For a further account of all these notes, and evidence that Junius really planned a new edition of Chaucer's works, with notes, *see* Mark Liddell in Athenæum, June 12, 1897, p. 779.]

1677. *A Catalogue of all the Bookes in his Highnesse Prince Ruperts Library,* November 1677. Sloane MSS. 555, fol. 5.

Titles.	Folio.	Authores.	Printed
136. The Workes of Chaucer		Jeffery Chaucer	Lond. 1602.

1678. **Perrot,** Charles. *Inscription in a printed copy of Chaucer's Works,* chained in his house at Woodstock, transcribed [by Timothy Thomas] and given as a note to the Life of Chaucer [by Dart] in Urry's edn. of Chaucer, 1721. Sign. *b* 2, note K.

Ædium harum

Quas olim vivus incoluit,

Ut per hac ingenii monumenta,

In quibus æternum vivet

Unà cum antiquæ prosapiæ, fidei, fortitudinis Viro

Nicolao Bayntun

rursus incoleret,

Galfrido Chaucer,

Poetarum sui temporis facile Principi,

Principum Poetæ, amico, adfini,

A priori hospite vi dejecto

Læto lubenti, lætus lubens.

Possessionem restituit

Carolus, Perrot L.L.D.

MDCLXXVIII

[In W. Thomas's handwriting, in his interleaved copy of Urry's Chaucer (B. M. pr. m. 643. m. 4) there is the following unfinished note: 'Since this Inscription was transcribed by T. T. it has been taken out of the Book; and I saw the original since in the hands of——.']

1679. Dryden, John. *Troilus and Cressida, or Truth Found too Late.* Epistle Dedicatory to the Right Honourable Robert Earl of Sunderland, sign. A 3 *b*, preface to the Play, sign. A 4 *b*. (Dryden's works, ed. Sir W. Scott; revised G. Saintsbury, 1882–93, vol. vi, 1883, pp. 252, 255.)

[p. 252]   It would mortify an Englishman to consider that from the time of Boccace and Petrarch the Italian has varied very little ; and that the English of Chaucer their contemporary, is not to be understood without the help of an old dictionary.

.   .   .   .

[p. 255]   The original story was written by one Lollius, a Lombard, in Latin verse, and translated by Chaucer into English.

[1679 ?] Howell, Dr. William. *Medulla Historiæ Anglicanæ, The Ancient and Present State of England.* . . . Written by Dr. Howel ; and Continued by an Impartial Hand . . . 1712, p. 123.

[Richard II, end].   Now flourished Sir *John Hawkwood*, whose chivalry had made him Renowned thro' the Christian World.   Sir *Geoffry Chaucer*, Poet-Laureat, now also lived.

[The earliest edn. of this work mentioned by Wood is 1679; the above extract is taken from the 6th edn., the earliest in the B. M.]

1679. Phillips, Edward. *Tractatulus de Carmine Dramatico Poetarum Veterum* . . . . Cui Subjungitur Compendiosa Enumeratio Poetarum . . . . Ab. Edv. Philippo, 1679. [Printed in] Sacrarum prosanarumque phrasium poeticarum thesaurus . . . . opera M^{ri} Joannis Buchleri, editio decima octava . . . 1679, p. 395.

[Under the heading Poëtae recentiores Angli & Scoti, a very brief notice of Chaucer, Gower, Lydgate, etc.]

1680-3. [Dryden, John ?] *The Art of Poetry,* Written in French by the Sieur de Boileau, Made English, 1683, p. 25, ll. 165–8. (Dryden's works, ed. Sir W. Scott, revised G. Saintsbury, 1882–93, vol. xv, 1892, p. 235.)

> *Chaucer* alone fix'd on this solid Base ;
> In his old Stile, conserves a modern grace :
> Too happy, if the freedom of his Rhymes
> Offended not the method of our Times.

> [*Corresponding French lines.*
> De ces maîtres savans disciple ingénieux,
> Régnier, seul parmi nous formés sur leurs modèles
> Dans son vieux style encore a des graces nouvelles ;
> Heureux, si ses discours, craints du chaste lecteur,
> Ne se sentoient des lieux où fréquentoit l'auteur

> Et si, du son hardi de ses rimes cyniques
> Il n'alarmoit souvent les oreilles pudiques.]

[This is Sir William Soames's translation made in 1680 ; the reference is placed under Dryden's name on account of the following remark of Tonson's (reprinted in Dryden's works, ed. Sir W. Scott, revised G. Saintsbury, 1882–93, vol. **xv**, 1892, p. 223): "I saw the MS. lie in Mr. Dryden's hands for above six months, who made very considerable alterations in it . . . . and it being his opinion, that it would be better to apply the poem to English writers, than keep to the French names as it was first translated, Sir William desired he would take the pains to make that alteration, and accordingly that was entirely done by Mr. Dryden."]

[*c.* **1680–90.**] **Unknown.** *Note* at foot of Egerton MS. 2622, fol. 50. *A Treatise of yᵉ Fabrique and use of yᵉ Astrolabe,* written by yᵉ famous Clerke Sʳ Geffery Chaucer Kᵗ. (In contents, fol. 1.)

Chaucer of the Astrolabe.

[*c.* **1680**?] **Unknown.** *MS. note,* referring to Brigham's tomb of Chaucer, in a copy of Petit's edn. of Chaucer's works, in the Library of the Royal College of Physicians, at foot of last leaf, fol. 355 *b.*

Galfridus Chaucer poeta celeberrimus qui primus Anglicam poësin ita illustravit ut Anglicus Homerus habeatur, obiit 1400. anno verò 1555 Nicholaus Brigham Musarum nomine hujus ossa transtulit et illi novum tumulum ex marmore in Australi plaga ecclesiæ Beati Petri Westmonasterii his versibus inscriptum posuit

> Qui fuit Anglorum vates ter maximus olim
> Galfridus Chaucer conditur hoc tumulo
> Annum si quæras domini, si tempora mortis,
> Ecce nota [*sic, for* notæ] subsunt, quæ tibi cuncta notant.

25 Oct : 1400

Ærumnarum requies mors .

> N : Brigham hoc fecit Musarum nomine sumptus
> Si rogitas quis eram, forsan te fama docebit
> Quod si fama neget, mundi quia gloria transit.

[One word, possibly signature, cut off.]

[*Cf.* above, 1479, pp. 58–9.]

1681. K[eepe], H[enry]. *Monumenta Westmonasteriensia, by H. K. of the Inner Temple, Gent,* 1681. London . . 1682, p. 47.

And now come we to the first and last best Poets of the English Nation *Geffrey Chaucer* and *Abraham Cowley,* the one being the Sun just rising, and shewing itself on the *English Horizon* and so by degrees increasing and growing in strength till it came to its full *Glory* and *Meridian* in the incomparable

Cowley, whose admirable *Genius* hard to be imitated but never equalled, hath set the bounds to succeeding times. *Chaucer* lies in an antient Tomb, Canopied of grey Marble, with his Picture painted thereon *in plano*, with some Verses by; he died in the Year 1400.

1681. Oldham, John. *Horace His Art of Poetry. Imitated in English.* [In] Poems and Translations by John Oldham, 1684, sign. A 4, p. 5, [bound up in] The Works of Mr. John Oldham Together with his Remains 1686. [A separate pagination begins with Poems and Translations; the last page before the fresh title is 148.] (Poetical works of J. Oldham, ed. R. Bell, 1854, p. 147.)

> 'Tis next to be observ'd that care is due,
> And sparingness in framing words anew.
>
> •   .   .   .   .   .   .
>   .   .   .   .   . if there be need
> For some uncommon matter to be said
> Pow'r of inventing terms may be allow'd,
> Which *Chaucer* and his Age n'eer understood.

[1682. Chiswel, Richard.] *Bibliotheca Smithiana, sive catalogus librorum* [the sale catalogue of Richard Smith's library], p. 274.

English books in Folio 77. *Chaucer's* (*Geoffery*) Works of Antient Poetry; best Edition (with a MS. of a Tale of Gamelyn taken out of a MS. of *Chaucer's* Works in the University Library of *Oxford*, 1602).

[This catalogue was compiled by Richard Chiswel at the Rose and Crown in St. Paul's Churchyard.]

1683–4. Aubrey, John. *An Idea of Education of young Gentlemen.* By Mr. John Aubrey, Fellow of the Royal Societie [a private Essay only]. 168¾. MS. Aubrey 10, Bodl. library, Ch. **xx.** Mundane Prudence, ff. 95, 84, 83.

Chapter XX. Mundane Prudence.

[fol. 95] Mr. J. Dreyden, in his preface to the Spanish Fryar, saies that Description is the most principal part of Poetrie, and deserves the greatest Prayse : in order to this, and to please their ingeniose minds, let 'em read Mr. J. Milton's Paradise lost; and Paradise regain'd : as also The Tales of Sr Geofry Chaucer, "who may be rightly called the pith, and Sinews of Eloquence, and very life it selfe of all mirth and pleasant writing. Besides one gift he hath above other Authors, and that is, By excellency of his Descriptions, to possesse his Readers with a more forcible imagination of seeing that (as it were)

done before their eies, which they read, than any other that
ever hath written in any tongue." [1]

These exercises of Descriptions, I would have in Blank
verse: in English or in prose (Latin, and English for variety).

Chapter XX. Mundane Prudence.

[fol. 84]   *Courtesie* [or common Civility] is the cheapest thing in the
World, and the most usefull. Great men doe understand
well, the Respect that is due unto them . . . .

S[r] Geofrey Chaucer's Character of a Young Knight.
        That from the time he first began
        To riden out, he loved Chevalrie,
        Trouth, honour, freedome, and Courtesie.
                                [Prol. Cant. Tales, ll. 44–6.]

Chapter XX. Mundane Prudence.

[fol. 88]   [The following is among a list of quotations from various
writers, which Aubrey introduces in speaking of the advantages
of boys brought up in towns :]

Chaucer, p. 71 *b*. With Scorners ne make no company,
        but fly her words of venome.
                                [Tale of Melibeus, l. 2519.]

    [1] M[r] Francis Beaumont's letter to M[r] Th. Speght before S[r] Geofry Chaucers
workes printed London 1602. [*See* above, 1597, pp. 145–6.]

1684. Chetwood, Knightly. *To the Earl of Roscomon on his Excellent
    Poem*, sign. A 3 *b*. [Commendatory Verses prefixed to] An Essay
    on Translated Verse, by the Earl of Roscommon, 1684. [In B. M.
    Catalogue, *see* under Dillon, Wentworth.]

        Such was the case when *Chaucer's early* toyl
        Founded the *Muses* Empire in *our* Soyl.
        Spencer improv'd it with his painful hand
        But *lost* a *Noble* Muse in *Fairy-land.*
        Shakspear say'd all that *Nature* cou'd impart,
        And *Johnson* added *Industry* and *Art.*
        Cowley, and *Denham* gained immortal praise ;
        And some who *merit* as they *wear*, the Bays, [etc.].

1684. S., G. *Anglorum Speculum, or the Worthies of England in Church
    and State.* Alphabetically digested into the several Shires and
    Counties therein contained. London . . 1684, pp. 497–8. [The Pre-
    face is signed G. S. He was once Chaplain to the Princess Henrietta.]

    Edm. Spencer, bred in *Camb.* A great Poet who imitated
Chaucer . . . Returning into England, he was robb'd by the
Rebels of that little he had, and dying for Grief in great Want
1598, was honourably buried nigh *Chaucer* in *Westminster.*
CHAUCER CRITICISM.

1685. Evelyn, [John]. *The Immortality of Poesie. To Envy* [in]
Poems by Several Hands, and on Several Occasions. Collected by
N. Tate, p. 91.

> Old *Chaucer* shall, for his facetious style,
> Be read, and prais'd by warlike *Britains*, while
> The Sea enriches, and defends their Isle.

[1685. Wesley, Samuel.] *Maggots: or, Poems on several subjects* . . .
by a Schollar, p. 97, *note.*

[p. 95] Scarce peeps out the Sun with a blushing young Ray,
> ᵉEre my brisk feather'd Bell-man will tell me 'tis Day;

[Note ᵉ, p. 97] : *Meaning* Chaunticleer,—*as Gransire* Chaucer
has it ; or in new English, *no better nor worse than a* Cock,—

1685. Unknown. *Miscellany Poems and Translations By Oxford
Hands* . . London, Printed for Anthony Stephens, Bookseller near
the Theatre in Oxford, 1685. Elegy the Fifteenth, p. 155.

> The Fame, I seek, shall know Eternity :
> My Wit a lasting Monument shall raise,
> And all the world shall loudly sing my Praise.
> *Chaucer* shall live, whilst this our *Brittish* Land,
> Or the vast *Cornwall-Mount* in it shall stand :
>
> .   .   .   .
>
> *Sidneys* great Name shall last, whilst there are Swains,
> That feed their Flocks on the *Arcadian* Plains;
>
> .   .   .   .
>
> The Majesty of mighty *Cowley's* name,

[p. 156] Shall travel thro' the farthest coasts of Fame ;

> .   .   .   .
>
> *Dryden,* great King of Verse, shall ever live,
>
> .   .   .   .
>
> The Lawrel shall the matchless *Johnson* Crown.
> *Shake'spear* [*sic*], tho rude, yet his immortal Wit
> Shall never to the stroke of time submit,
> And the loud thund'ring flights of lofty *Lee ;*
> Shall strike the Ears of all Posterity.
> *Creeches* Sublimest Verse in God-like State,
> Shall soar above the reach of humble Fate ;
>
> .   .   .   .
>
> *Spencer*'s Heroick Lines no death shall fear—

[*Stephen* and *Suckling* are the two last poets praised.]

1687. The Works of our Ancient, Learned & Excellent English Poet, Jeffrey Chaucer : As they have lately been Compar'd with the best Manuscripts ; and several things added, never before in Print.   To which is adjoyn'd, The Story of the Siege of Thebes, By John Lidgate, Monk of Bury. Together with The Life of Chaucer, Shewing His Countrey, Parentage, Education, Marriage, Children, Revenues, Service, Reward, Friends, Books, Death.   Also a Table, wherein the old and Obscure Words in Chaucer are explained, and such Words (which are many) that either are, by Nature or Derivation, Arabick, Greek, Latine, Italian, French, Dutch, or Saxon, mark'd with particular Notes for the better understanding their Original.   London, Printed in the Year MDCLXXXVII.

[This edition is really a reprint of Speght's 2nd edition of 1602 (*see* above, p. 168), with a different title page, otherwise the only differences are the following small additions under ' J. H.' below, and the omission of ff. 376–7 of Speght's edn., which contain a catalogue of Lidgate's works, and a list of Errata. The text is in black letter.]

1687. H., J. *Advertisement to the Reader* and *Advertisement* [on last page] in The Works of our Ancient . . Poet, Jeffrey Chaucer . . . 1687, ff. b 4, Ssss 1 *b.*

Advertisement to the Reader.

Having, for some Years last past, been greatly sollicited by many Learned and Worthy Gentlemen, to Re-print the Works of this Ancient Poet ; I have now, not only to answer their Desire, but I hope to their full satisfaction, perform'd the Obligation long since laid upon me, and sent *Chaucer* abroad into the World again, in his old dress, and under the Protection of his own Merits, without any new Preface or Letters Commendatory, it being the Opinion of those Learned Persons, that his own Works are his best Encomium.

Whereas in the *Life of Chaucer*, mention is made of a Tale call'd the *Pilgrims Tale*, which is there said to have been seen in the Library of Mr. *Stow*, and promis'd to be printed so soon as opportunity should offer ; I have, for the procuring of it, used all Diligence imaginable, not only in searching the publick Libraries of both Universities, but also all private Libraries that I could have Access unto ; but having no Success therein I beg you will please to accept my earnest Endeavour to have serv'd you, and take what is here printed, it being all that at present can be found that was *Chaucer's*.

J. H.

· · · · · · · · · · ·

Advertisement.

Whilst this Work was just finishing, we hapned to meet
with a Manuscript, wherein we found the Conclusion of the
Cook's Tale, and also of the *Squires Tale*, (which in the
Printed Books are said to be lost, or never finish'd by the
Author,) but coming so late to our hands, they could not be
inserted in their proper places, therefore the Reader is desir'd
to add them, as here directed.

Immediately after what you find of the Cooks Tale, add this:

What thorow himself & his felaw y^t fought,
Unto a mischief both they were brought,
The tone ydamned to prison perpetually.
The tother to deth, for he couth not of clergy,
And therefore yong men learne while ye may,
That with many divers thoughts beth pricked all the day,
Remembre you what mischief cometh of misgovernaunce,
Thus mowe ye learn worschip and come to substaunce:
Think how grace and governaunce hath brought aboune
Many a poore man'ys Son chefe state of the Town
Euer rule thee after the best man of name,
And God may grace thee to come to ye same.

Immediately after these words, at the end of the Squires Tale,

Apollo whirleth up his chare so hie,
Untill the God Mercurius house he flie.

Let this be added,

But I here now maken a knotte,
To the time it come next to my lotte,
For here ben felawes behind, an hepe truly,
That wolden talk full besily,
And have here sport as well as I,
And the day passeth certainly,
So on this mattere I may no lenger dwell,
But stint my clack, and let the other tell,
Therefore oft taketh now good hede
Who shall next tell, and late him spede.

[Possibly 'J. H.' stands for Joseph Hindmarsh the printer. All the above lines
are spurious additions. The twelve lines in conclusion to the Cook's Tale are in MS.
Bodley 686; and those at end of the Squire's Tale in MS. Selden B 14. See Tyrwhitt's
edn. of the C. Tales, 1775–8, Appendix to the preface note m. *See also c.* 1450,
Spurious links, above, p. 51.]

[*c.* **1687. Wharton,** Henry.] *Historiola de Chaucero nostro, scripta etiam à Reverendiss. Tho. Tenison, Archiepiscopo Cant. ad calcem Historiæ Cl. Cavei Literariæ,* [printed · in] Notæ MSS. & Accessiones Anonymi ad Cavei Historiam Literariam, Codicis Margini adscriptae, in Bibliotheca Lambethana [separate pagination]. [in vol. ii of] Scriptorum Ecclesiasticorum Historia Literaria, by William Cave, 1740-3, pp. 13-15.

[For extract, *see* below, Appendix A, under *c.* 1687, Wharton.]

[Note from Illustrations of Gower and Chaucer by H. J. Todd, 1810. Introduction, p. xxxvi—". . . the celebrated Henry Wharton has left in manuscript a sketch of Chaucer [as a theological writer], which is preserved in the Manuscript Library at Lambeth, and was intended by him as an addition to Cave's *Scriptores Ecclesiastici ;* although in the republication of Cave's work in 1740, this *Historiola* of Chaucer . . . is given, but not correctly, to Archbishop Tenison. *See* MSS. Lamb 956." Todd gives an extract from Wharton.]

1687. Winstanley, William.   *The Lives of the most Famous English Poets,* pp. 18, 19, 20, [Gower] 23–32 [life of Chaucer, slightly enlarged, *cf.* Winstanley's England's Worthies, 1660, above, p. 238], 33–35, 37, [Lydgate] 89, 92, [Spenser] 100, 107, 133 [Basse's epitaph, *see* above, p. 196].

1689. Evelyn, John.   *Letter To Mr. Pepys* [dated] *Says-Court,* 12 Aug. 1689 (Diary and Correspondence of John Evelyn, ed. William Bray, new edn. by H. B. Wheatley, 1906, vol. iii, pp. 436, 444).

. . . The late Lord Chancellor Hyde . . . to adorne his stately palace (since demolished) he collected the pictures of as many of our famous countrymen as he could purchase or procure . . .

[p. 444]   . . . There were the pictures of Fisher, Fox, Sʳ Tho. More, Tho. Lord Cromwell, Dʳ Nowel, &c. And what was most agreeable to his Lᵖˢ general humor, old Chaucer, Shakspere, Beaumont & Fletcher, who were both in one piece, Spencer, Mr. Waller, Cowley, Hudibras, which last he plac'd in the roome where he vs'd to eate & dine in publiq, most of which, if not all, are at the present at Cornebery in Oxfordshire.

1689. [Howard, Edward.]   *Caroloiades, or, the Rebellion of Forty One . . . A Heroick Poem.* London . . . 1689, p. 137. [Re-issued 1695 with a fresh title-page—Caroloiades Redivivus ; or the War and Revolutions in the Time of King Charles the First. An Heroick Poem. By a Person of Honour.—Preface signed by Edward Howard. *See* N. & Q., 7th ser. vii, 1889, p. 285, for Chaucer reference.]

[A description of Polyaster's study " a Character of Science . . Whose then aboad near *Oxfords* confines stood," which is adorned by busts of the poets.]

[p. 137]   . . . around their brows were Lawrells plac'd,
Large next to those *Apollo*'s Temples Grac'd :
Of which, he *Chaucer, Spencer,* much beheld,
And where their Learned Poems most excell'd.
Tho' words now obsolete express their Flame,
Like Gemms that out of Fashion value Claim.
Near these in Statue witty *Shakspere* stood,
Whose early Plays were soonest next to Good.

1689. Unknown. [*Entry* in] *The Term Catalogues,* Easter 1689, [printed
in] The Term Catalogues, ed. E. Arber, 1905, vol. ii, p. 261 [May]
1689.

The works of . . Jeffry [*sic*] Chaucer, as they have lately been
compared with the best Manuscripts. . . . Sold by S. Crouch
in *Cornhill ;* Math. Gilliflower, and W. Hensman in *Westminster* Hall ; and A. Roper, and G. Grafton, in *Fleet Street.*

[For full title, *see* above, 1687, p. 259 ; this is an entry of the 1689 reprint.]

1690. Blount, Sir Thomas Pope. *Censura Celebriorum Authorum,* pp.
312, 313. *Galfredus Chaucerus* [a collection of references to Chaucer
by Pits, Lilius Giraldus, Vossius, Camden, Sir H. Savil, Leland,
Sprat, Sir R. Baker, Verstegan, Speght's Preface to Chaucer's
works, Skinner].

1691. G[ibson, Edmund]. *Notes* [to] *Polemo-Middinia, see* below,
Appendix A, 1691.

1691. Langbaine, Gerard. *An Account of the English Dramatick
Poets.* [Copy in B. M., C. 45. d. 14, with MS. notes of Bishop Percy
and Oldys, etc. *See* J. Haslewood's note on first page], pp. 86, 127,
173, 215 [for last page *see* under Oldys, 1725].

[p. 86]   [Abraham Cowley] He was Buried at *Westminster* Abby,
near Two of our most eminent English Bards, *Chaucer* and
Spencer . . .

[p. 127]   [Sir John Denham] . . . was Buried the Twenty-third
Instant [March 1668] at *Westminster,* amongst those Noble
Poets, *Chaucer, Spencer,* and *Cowley.*

. . . .

[p. 173]   [Dryden's] *Troilus and Cressida,* or *Truth found out too
late ;* a Tragedy acted at the Duke's Theatre, to which is
prefixt a Preface containing the Grounds of Criticisme in
Tragedy, printed in quarto *Lond.* 1679 . . . . . This Play
was likewise first written by *Shakespear* and revis'd by Mr.
Dryden, to which he added several new Scenes, and even
cultivated and improv'd what he borrow'd from the Original.
The last scene in the third Act is a Masterpiece, and whether
it be copied from *Shakespear, Fletcher,* or *Euripides,* or all of

them, I think it justly deserves Commendation. The Plot of
this Play was taken by Mr. *Shakespear* from *Chaucer's Troilus
and Cressida ;* which was translated (according to Mr. *Dryden*)
from the Original Story, written in Latine Verse, by one
Lollius, a *Lombard.*

[For a later edition *see* below, 1699, Gildon, p. 270.]

1691. Unknown. *The Athenian Mercury,* vol. ii, no. 14, Saturday,
July 11, 1691. [The Athenian Mercury began March 17, 1691,
under the title *The Athenian Gazette or Casuistical Mercury,
Resolving all the most Nice and Curious Questions proposed by the
Ingenious . . . . Printed for John Dunton at the Raven in the
Poultry.* The second and following numbers are called *The
Athenian Mercury,* but the original title is preserved at the head
of each vol. *See* extract from a later vol., below, p. 265.]

[In answer to] Question 3. *Which is the best* Poem *that
ever was made, and who in your Opinion, deserves the* Title *of
the best* Poet *that ever was ?* [the following occurs]: *Plautus*
wrote *wittily, Terence* neatly—and *Seneca* has very fine
thoughts.—But since we can't go through all the world, let's
look home a little. *Grandsire Chaucer,* in spite of the Age,
was a Man of as much wit, sence and honesty as any that have
writ after him. Father *Ben* was excellent at *Humour,
Shakespeare* deserves the Name of *sweetest* which *Milton* gave
him.—*Spencer* was a noble poet, his *Fairy-Queen* an excellent
piece of Morality, Policy, History. *Davenant* had a great
genius.—Too much can't be said of Mr. *Coley* [*sic*]. *Milton's
Paradise lost* and some other Poems of his will never be
equal'd. Waller is the most *correct* Poet we have.

1691. Harington, James. *The Introduction* [to vol. ii of] Anthony à
Wood's *Athenæ Oxonienses,* 1691, sign. a i *b.*

As to the Poetry of the Age, the beauty of Speech, and
the Graces of measure and numbers, which are the inseparable
ornaments of a good Poem, are not to be expected in a rude
and unsettled Language; And tho *Chaucer,* the Father of
our Poets, had not taken equal care of the force of expression,
as of the greatness of thought; yet the refining of a Tongue
is such a Work, as never was begun, and finished by the same
hand. We had before only words of common use, coin'd by
our need, or invented by our passions : Nature had generally
furnish'd this Island with the supports of Necessity, not the
instruments of Luxury; the elegance of our speech, as well as
the finess [*sic*] of our garb, is owing to foreign Correspondence.
And as in Clothes, so in Words, at first usually they broke in

unalter'd upon us from abroad; and consequently, as in *Chaucer's* time, come not over like Captives, but Invaders. But then only they are made our own, when, after a short Naturalization, they fit themselves to our Dress, become incorporated with our Language, and take the air, turn, and fashion of the Country that adopted them.

1691-2. [Wood, Anthony à.] *Athenæ Oxonienses.* [1st edn.] 1691-2; [2nd edn.] . . . . enlarged, 1721; [3rd edn.] ed. P. Bliss, 1813, vol. i, pp. 10, 48, 136-7, 309-10, and clxxv; vol. ii, 1815, p. 109; vol. iii, 1817, pp. 38, 1142.

vol.	page	[1st edn]	vol.	page	[2nd edn]
i	6.	Stephen Hawes.	i	6.	Stephen Hawes.
„	52-3.	William Thynne.	„	22.	Thomas Richard [not in 1st edn.].
„	99.	Nicholas Brigham.			
„	319-20.	Francis Thynne.	„	61.	William Thynne.
			„	130.	Nicholas Brigham.
			„	376.	Francis Thynne.
ii		Introduction by J. Harington, sign. a 1 and a 1 *b* [*q. v.*, p. 263].	ii		Introduction by James Harington, sign. a 2.
			„	21.	Francis Kynaston.
„	11.	Francis Kynaston.	„	604.	Franciscus Junius [not in 1st edn.].

[*a*. **1692.**] **Ashmole**, Elias. *Marginal notes* in shorthand at the end of Chaucer's Coke's Tale, with the prologue and spurious tale of Gamelyn, written by Ashmole in MS. Ashmole no. 45, 18 leaves of paper. Another transcript of Gamelyn by Ashmole is on 20 leaves inserted between ff. xx–xxi of Godfray's [*i.e.* Thynne's] edn. of Chaucer's works (1532 fol.), MS. Ashmole 1095. (Catalogue of Ashmole MSS., ed. W. H. Black, 1845, cols. 70, 720.)

[*a*. **1692**]. **Ashmole**, Elias. *Marginal note* (in MS. Ashmole 59 (Shirley's), no. 9, fol. 27) to Scogan's Moral Ballad. (Catalogue of Ashmole MSS., ed. W. H. Black, 1845, col. 97.)

[Ashmole notes that Scogan's Moral Ballad was printed in Godfray's [*i. e.* Thynne's] edn. of Chaucer's works, 1532, *see* above, p. 79, and against the 14th stanza he notes,] These 3 following verses were made by Geffrey Chaucer.

1692. Dryden, John. *The Satires of Decimus Junius Juvenalis Translated into English Verse, by Mr Dryden . . . 1693. Dedication to the Right Honourable Charles Earl of Dorset and Middlessex*, pp. viii, l., [dated] Aug. 18, 1692. (Dryden's works, ed. Sir W. Scott; revised G. Saintsbury, 1882-93, vol. xiii, 1887, pp. 19, 117; *also* Dryden's Essays, ed. W P. Ker, 1900, vol. ii, pp. 29, 109.)

[p. viii] His [Milton's] Antiquated words were his Choice, not his Necessity; for therein he imitated *Spencer*, as *Spencer* did

Chawcer. And tho', perhaps, the love of their Masters, may have transported both too far . . . .

. . . .

[p. 1] I found in him a true sublimity, lofty thoughts, which were cloath'd with admirable *Grecisms*, and ancient words, which he had been digging from the Mines of *Chaucer*, and of *Spencer*, and which, with all their rusticity, had somewhat of Venerable in them.

1692. Rymer, [Thomas]. *A Short View of Tragedy*, 1693. [published late in 1692], sign. A 7. (Contents of ch. vi, repeated on p. 73), pp. 78, 79. [Bound with the 2nd edn. of The Tragedies of the Last Age, 1692 ; this is, however, really the 1st edn. of A Short View of Tragedy. The pagination for the two parts is distinct.]

[sign. A 7] Chap. 6. . . . *Chaucer* refin'd our English. Which in perfection by *Waller*.

. . . .

[p. 78] But they who attempted verse in English, down till *Chaucers* time, made an heavy pudder, and are always miserably put to't for a word to clink : . . . *Chaucer* found an Herculean labour on his Hands ; And did perform to Admiration. He seizes all Provencal, French or Latin that came in his way, gives them a new garb and livery, and mingles them amongst our English : turns out English, gowty, or superannuated, to place in their room the foreigners, fit for service, train'd and accustomed to Poetical Discipline.

But tho' the Italian reformation was begun and finished well nigh at the same time by *Boccace, Dante*, and *Petrarch.* Our language retain'd something of the churl ; something of the Stiff and Gothish did stick upon it, till long after *Chaucer.*

Chaucer threw in Latin, French, Provencial [*sic*], and other
[p. 79] Languages, like new Stum to raise a Fermentation ; In Queen *Elizabeth's* time it grew fine, but came not to an Head and Spirit, did not shine and sparkle till Mr. *Waller* set it a running.

1693. Unknown. [*Answers to*] *Questions from the Poetical Lady* [in] The Athenian Mercury, vol. xii, no. 1, Oct. 24, 1693 [no pagination or signature. For full title and extract *see* earlier vol., above, p. 263].

Quest. 4. *What Books of Poetry wou'd you Advise one that's Young, and extreamly delights in it, to read, both Divine and other ?*

Answ. For Divine, *David's* Psalms, *Sandys's* and *Woodford's* Versions, *Lloyd's* Canticles, *Cowley's* Davideis, *Sir J.*

Davis's Nosce Teipsum, *Herbert*'s and *Crashaw*'s Poems, *Milton's*
Paradices, and (if you have Patience) *Wesley*'s Life of Christ.
For others, Old Merry *Chaucer, Gawen Douglas*'s Æneads
(if you can get it) the best Version that ever was, or We
believe, ever will be, of that incomparable Poem ; *Spencer's*
Fairy Queen, *&c., Tasso*'s Godfrey of Bulloign, *Shakespear,
Beaumont* and *Fletcher, Ben. Johnson, Randal, Cleaveland,*
Dr. *Donne, Gondibert,* WALLER, all DRYDEN, *Tate,
Oldham, Flatman, The Plain Dealer*—and when you have
done of these, We'll promise to provide you more.

1693. Yalden, Thomas. *To Mr. Congreve . . An Epistolary Ode,* 1693,
[in] Works of the English Poets, ed. Samuel Johnson, vol. x,
1779, p. 373. (*Ibid.,* ed. A. Chalmers, vol. xi, 1810, p. 68.)

[Speaking of the neglect shown to poets :—]

> Thus did the world thy great fore-fathers use ;
> > Thus all th' inspir'd bards before
> > Did their hereditary ills deplore ;
> From tuneful Chaucer's down to thy own Dryden's Muse.

1694. Addison, Joseph. *An Account of the Greatest English Poets.*
To Mr H[enry] S[acheverell]. Ap. 3d, 1694. [in] The Annual
Miscellany for the year 1694, Being the Fourth Part of Miscellany
Poems . . . . published by Mr Dryden, [2nd edn. 1692, 85–1709, 6
parts]. Printed by R. E. for Jacob Tonson, 1694, pp. 317–18.
(Addison's works, ed. Richard Hurd, Bohn series, 1854–6, 6 vols.,
vol. i, p. 23.)

> *Since, Dearest* Harry, you *will needs request*
> *A short Account of all the Muse possest ;*
> *That, down* from Chaucer's *days to* Dryden's *Times,*
> *Have spent their Noble Rage in* Brittish Rhimes ;
>
> .　.　.　.　.　.　.　.　.
>
> *I'll try to make they're sev'ral Beauties known*
> *And show their Verses worth, tho' not my Own.*
>
> Long had our dull Fore-Fathers slept Supine,
> Nor felt the Raptures of the Tuneful Nine ;
> Till *Chaucer* first, a merry *Bard,* arose ;
> And many a Story told in Rhime and Prose.
> But Age has Rusted what the *Poet* writ,
> Worn out his Language, and obscur'd his Wit :
> In vain he jests in his unpolish'd strain
> And tries to make his Readers laugh in vain.

1694. Blount, Sir Thomas Pope. *De Re Poetica : or Remarks upon Poetry, with Characters and Censures of the most considerable Poets.* [Part 2] *Characters and Censures,* pp. 41–44. *Geoffry Chaucer* [followed by references to Leland, Bale, Pits, Winstanley, Ascham, Sir P. Sidney, Sir J. Denham, Sir H. Savil, Sir R. Baker, Camden, Dr. Spratt, Verstegan, and Brigham], pp. 55. 137 [Dryden, Trans. Juvenal, p. 50], 216, 247 [quotation from Rimer, Short View of Tragedy, p. 78, *see* above, p. 265].

[p. 41]   *Geoffry Chaucer.*

Three several Places contend for the Birth of this Famous *Poet. First, Berkshire,* from the words of *Leland,* that he was born in *Barocensi Provinciâ* ; and Mr. *Cambden* affirms,
[p. 42] that *Dunington Castle,* nigh unto *Newbury,* was Anciently his Inheritance. *Secondly, Oxfordshire,* where, *John Pits* is positive, that his Father (who was a Knight) liv'd, and that he was born at *Woodstock. Thirdly,* the Author of his Life, Printed 1602. Supposes him to be born at *London* [*see* note, p. 148 above]. But though the place of his Birth is not certainly known, yet this is agreed upon by all hands, that he was counted the chief of the *English Poets,* not only of his time, but continued to be so esteem'd till this Age ; and as much as we despise his old fashion'd Phrase, and Obsolete Words, *He* was one of the first Refiners of the *English* Language.

Of how great esteem he was in the Age wherein he flourish'd, *viz.* the Reigns of *Henry* the IV. *Henry* the V. and part of *Henry* the VI. appears, besides his being Knighted, and made *Poet Lauriate* [*sic*] by the Honour he had to be ally'd by Marriage to the great Earl of *Lancaster, John* of *Gaunt.*

We have several of his Works yet extant, but his *Squires Tale,* and some other of his Pieces are not to be found.

[1695 ?] B., T. *Commendatory verses* on the Author, in *England's Heroical Epistles . . . .* by Michael Drayton. Newly Corrected and Amended. Printed for S. Smethwick. *A Dedication of These and the foregoing Verses to Mr* Drayton's *Heroick Epistles,* sign. **A** 3 *b.* [These first appear in the edn. of 1695.]

> Time has devour'd the Younger Sons of Wit,
> Who liv'd when *Chaucer, Spencer, Johnson* writ :
> Those lofty Trees are of their Leaves bereft,
> And to a reverend Nakedness are left. . .
>   T. B.

1696. Aubrey, John. *Miscellanies,* pp. 28, 29.

[Reference to Thinne's explanation of 'Gawyn' in his edn. of Chaucer, with a quotation from Chaucer's Squire's Tale.]

1696. Smith, Thomas, Fellow of Magdalen College, Oxford. *Catalogus librorum manuscriptorum bibliothecæ Cottonianæ* . . . . pp. 65, 69. (*Cf.* Parallel text of Chaucer's minor poems, ed. F. J. Furnivall, Chaucer soc. 1871, etc., p. 407.)

[p. 65. Cotton, Galba E ix] Chaucer . Exemplar emendate scriptum.

. . . .

[p. 69. Cotton, Otho A xviii, 24] A Ballade made by Geffrey Chaucer upon his death-bed, lying in his anguish [this is a copy of " Truth," since burnt]. [25] Ballade ryall, made by Chaucer. [26] Chaucer's ballade to his purse. [27] Cantus Troili. [28] Pictura Galfridi Chauceri.

1696. Unknown (?). *Parnassus. The Session of the Poets, Holden at the Foot of Parnassus Hill, July 9th, 1696.* Printed for E. Whitlock, near Stationers-Hall, 1696, sign. C 4, p. 37.

Indeed his [A. O.] chiefest Talent lies in composing such sort of Ballads, as *Patient Grissel,* or old *Chaucers* goodly Ballad of our Lady, whose Title is usually a most lamentable Example of the doleful Desperation of a miserable Worldling, who alas ! most wickedly forsook the Truth of Gods Gospel, for fear of the loss of Life, and worldly goods.

[This poem is evidently a satire on the smaller writers of the day ; a kind of mock Court is held, each poet (designated by initials only) appearing before the bar in turn, and ' A. O.' is one of these.]

1696. Unknown. *A Pastoral on the Death of the Earl of Rochester,* [in] Poems on several Occasions : with Valentinian . . by . . John, late Earl of Rochester, p. x.

Old *Chaucer,* who first taught the use of Verse,
No longer has the Tribute of our Tears.

[*a.* **1697.**] **Aubrey,** John. [*Anecdotes and traditions.*] Lansdowne MS. 231, ff 110, 129, 178, [printed in] Anecdotes and Traditions . . ed. W. J. Thoms . . Camden soc., 1839, pp. 86, 98, 110.

[p. 86] In time of thunder they invoke St. Barbara. So Sir Geof. Chaucer, speaking of the great hostesse, her guests would cry St. Barbara when she let off her gun [ginne].

. . . .

[p. 98] Chaucer's Tregetours.

For I am siker that ther be sciences,
By which men maken divers apparences,
Swiche as thise subtil Tregetoures play.
For oft at festes have I wel herd say
That Tregetoures, within an hall large,
Hath made come in a water and a barge,
And in the halle rowen up and down.
Sometime hath seemed come a grim leoun

> And sometimes floures spring as in a mede,
> Sometime a vine and grapes white and red,
> Sometime a castel al of lime and ston,
> And when hem liketh voideth it anon.
> *Chaucer's Franklein's Tale,* [ll. 1139–1150].

I have heard my grandfather Lyte say, that old father Davis told him, he saw such a thinge doune [*sic*] in a gentleman's hall at Christmas, at or near Durseley in Gloucestershire, about the middle of King Henry the Eighth's reigne. Edmund Wylde, Esq. saies that it is credibly reported that one shewed the now King of France, in anno 1689 or 1690, this trick, sc. to make the apparition of an oake, &c. in a hall, as described by Chaucer : and no conjuration. The King of France gave him (the person) five hundred Louis d'or for it.

M^m. a Hamborough merchant, now (or lately) in London, did see this trick donne at a wedding in Hamborough about 1687, by the same person that shewed it to the King of France.

. . . .

[p. 110]	The Friars Mendicant heretofore would take their opportunity to come into houses when the good women did bake, and would *read a Ghospel over the batch,* and the good women would give them a cake, &c. It should seem by Chaucer's tale that they had a fashion to beg in rhyme.

> Of your white bread I would desire a shiver,
> And of your hen the liver.
> *From old Mr. Frederick Vaughan.*

1697. De la Pryme, Abraham. *See* below, Appendix A, 1697.

1697. Dryden, John. *The Works of Virgil . . . . Translated into English Verse by Mr Dryden.* Dedication to . . . . Lord Clifford, sign. A 2, postscript to the reader, p. 621. (Dryden's works, ed. Sir W. Scott, revised G. Saintsbury, 1882–93, vol. xiii, 1887, p. 325, vol. xv, 1892, p. 188 ; *also* Dryden's Essays, ed. W. P. Ker, 1900, vol. ii, p. 241, postscript only.)

[sign. A 2] *Spencer* being Master of our Northern Dialect, and skill'd in *Chaucer's* English. . . . .

[p. 621]	One [speaking of Poets] is for raking in *Chaucer* (our *English Ennius*) for antiquated Words, which are never to be reviv'd, but when Sound or Significancy is wanting in the present Language. But many of his deserve not this Redemption.

1698. Dennis, [John]. *The Usefulness of the Stage*, pp. 39, 40.

And tho I will not presume to affirm, that before the Reign
of King *Henry* the Eighth we had no good Writers, yet I will
confidently assert, that, excepting *Chaucer*, no not in any sort
of Writing whatever, we had not a first rate Writer.

1698[–9]. Dryden, John.   *Letter to Mrs. Steward*, [dated] *Candlemas-
Day*, 1698, in Dryden's works, ed. Sir W. Scott, revised G. Saintsbury, 1882–93, vol. xviii, pp. 147–8.   [The original letter was in the
possession of Mr. Huth, *see* ibid. vol. xviii, p. 87.]

I pass my time sometimes with Ovid, and sometimes with
our old English poet Chaucer ; translating such stories as best
please my fancy ; and intend, besides them, to add somewhat
of my own.

1699. Dryden, John.   *Letter to Samuel Pepys, Esq., no. XXXV* (Dryden's
works, ed. Sir W. Scott, revised G. Saintsbury, 1882–93, vol. xviii,
p. 154).   [*See* below under Pepys, p. 271, for his reply.]

July the 14th, 1699.

PADRON MIO,

I REMEMBER last year, when I had the honour of dineing
with you, you were pleased to recommend to me the character
of Chaucer's " Good Parson."   Any desire of yours is a command to me ; and accordingly, I have put it into my English,
with such additions and alterations as I thought fit.   Having
translated as many Fables from Ovid, and as many Novills
from Boccace and Tales from Chaucer, as will make an indifferent large volume in folio, I intend them for the Press in
Michaelmas term next.   In the mean time my Parson desires
the favour of being known to you, and promises, if you find
any fault in his character, he will reform it.   Whenever you
please, he shall wait on you, and for the safer conveyance, I
will carry him in my pocket; who am

My *Padrons* most obedient servant,

JOHN DRYDEN.

For Samuel Pepys, Esq.
Att his house in York-street, These.

[1699. Gildon, Charles.]   *The Lives and Characters of the English
Dramatic Poets . . . First begun by Mr Langbain, improv'd and
continued down to this Time by a Careful Hand* [i. e. Gildon], pp. 27,
47, 129.

[p 129]   *Troilus and Cressida*, a Tragedy, *fol.*   This was reviv'd with
Alterations, by Mr *Dryden* ; who added divers new Scenes.
Plot from *Chaucer's Troilus and Cressida.*   [The reference on
p. 47 is of the same kind, that on p. 27 to the burial of Cowley
next Chaucer. *See* above, 1691, Langbaine, p. 262.]

1699. Pepys, Samuel. *Letter to John Dryden dated July* 14, 1699. [in] (The Works of John Dryden, ed. Sir W. Scott, revised G. Saintsbury, 1882–93, vol. xviii, p. 155). [*See* above, under Dryden, for the letter to which this is the answer.]

Sir,

You truly have obliged mee; and possibly in saying so, I am more in earnest then you can readily think; as verily hopeing, from this your copy of one "Good Parson" to fancy some amends made mee for the hourly offence I beare with from the sight of so many lewd originalls.

[*a.* **1700. Cobb,** Samuel.] *Poetæ Britannici. A Poem,* p. 10. [A pamphlet, folio, no title page; from internal evidence (Dryden, old, but alive, &c.) it must have been written just before 1700. It is reprinted in *Poems on Several Occasions,* by Samuel Cobb, 3rd edition, London, 1710, pp. 188–9, under the title *Of Poetry.* 1. Its Antiquity.   2. Its Progress.   3. Its Improvement.]

Sunk in a Sea of Ignorance we lay,
Till *Chaucer* rose, and pointed out the Day,
A joking Bard, whose Antiquated Muse
In mouldy Words could solid Sense produce.
Our *English Ennius* He, who claim'd his part
In wealthy Nature, tho' unskilld in Art.
The sparkling Diamond on his Dung-hill shines,
And Golden Fragments glitter in his Lines.
Which *Spencer* gather'd for his Learning known,
And by successful Gleanings made his own.
So careful Bees, on a fair Summer's Day,
Hum o'er the Flowers, and suck the sweets away.
Of *Gloriana,* and her Knights he sung,
Of Beasts, which from his pregnant Fancy sprung.
O had thy Poet, *Britany,* rely'd
On native Strength, and Foreign Aid deny'd!
Had not wild Fairies blasted his design,
Mæonides and *Virgil* had been Thine!
Their finish'd Poems he exactly view'd,
But *Chaucer's* steps Religiously pursu'd.
He cull'd and pick'd, and thought it greater praise
T'adore his Master, than improve his Phrase.
Twas counted Sin to deviate from his Page;
So sacred was th' Authority of Age!
The Coyn must sure for currant Sterling pass
Stamp'd with old *Chaucer's* Venerable Face.

But *Johnson* found it of a gross Alloy,
Melted it down and flung the Scum away.
He dug pure Silver from a *Roman* Mine
And prest his Sacred Image on the Coyn.

[The 1710 edn. omits 'Of *Gloriana*, and her knights he sung **and the following**
line, and reads 'Dross' for 'Scum' in the 3rd line from the bottom. In the Bodleian
Catalogue there is an edn. of Cobb's 'Poems on Several Occasions' printed in 1709.
Allibone and Watts mention a Collection of Poems 1707.]

1700. Dryden, [John]. *Fables Ancient and Modern, Translated into
Verse from Homer, Ovid, Boccace & Chaucer: With Original Poems.
Preface*, sign. *A 1 to *D 2 *b.* (Dryden's works, ed. Sir W.
Scott, revised G. Saintsbury, 1882-93, vol. xi. 1885, Preface,
pp. 208-44 ; *also* Dryden's Essays, ed. W. P. Ker, 1900, vol. ii,
pp. 246-73.)

[sign.*A 1] . . . *Spencer* and *Fairfax* both flourish'd in the Reign of
Queen *Elizabeth* : Great Masters in our Language . . . *Milton*
was the Poetical Son of *Spencer*, and Mr. *Waller* of *Fairfax* ;
for we have our Lineal Descents and Clans, as well as other
Families : *Spencer* more than once insinuates, that the Soul of
Chaucer was transfus'd into his Body ; and that he was begotten by him Two Hundred years after his Decease. *Milton*
has acknowledg'd to me that *Spencer* was his Original ; . . .

But to return : Having done with *Ovid* for this time, it came
into my mind, that our old *English* poet, *Chaucer*, in many
[sign. *A 1 *b*] Things resembled him, and that with no disadvantage on the
Side of the Modern Author, as I shall endeavour to prove when
I compare them : And as I am, and always have been studious
to promote the Honour of my Native Country, so I soon resolv'd
to put their Merits to the Trial, by turning some of the *Canterbury* Tales into our Language, as it is now refin'd : For by this
Means, both the Poets being set in the same Light, and dress'd
in the same *English* habit, Story to be compared with Story, a
certain Judgment may be made betwixt them, by the Reader,
without obtruding my Opinion on him : Or if I seem partial to
my Country-man, and Predecessor in the Laurel, the Friends of
Antiquity are not few : And, besides many of the Learn'd, *Ovid*
has almost all the *Beaux*, and the whole Fair Sex his declar'd
Patrons. Perhaps I have assum'd somewhat more to my self
than they allow me ; because I have adventur'd to sum up the
Evidence ; but the Readers are the Jury ; and their Privilege
remains entire to decide according to the Merits of the Cause :
Or, if they please, to bring it to another Hearing, before some

other Court. In the mean time, to follow the Thrid of my
Discourse (as Thoughts, according to Mr. *Hobbs*, have always
some Connexion,) so from *Chaucer* I was led to think on
Boccace, who was not only his Contemporary, but also pursu'd
the same Studies ; wrote Novels in Prose, and many Works in
Verse ; particularly is said to have invented the Octave Rhyme,
or *Stanza* of Eight Lines, which ever since has been maintain'd
by the Practice of all *Italian* Writers, who are, or at least
assume the title of *Heroick Poets :* He and *Chaucer*, among
other Things, had this in common, that they refin'd their
Mother-Tongues ; but with this difference, that *Dante* had
begun to file their Language, at least in Verse, before the time
of *Boccace*, who likewise receiv'd no little Help from his Master
Petrarch : But the Reformation of their Prose was wholly
owing to *Boccace* himself ; who is yet the Standard of Purity
in the *Italian* Tongue, though many of his Phrases are become
obsolete, as in process of Time it must needs happen. *Chaucer*
(as you have formerly been told by our learn'd Mr. *Rhymer*)
first adorn'd and amplified our barren Tongue from the
Provençall, which was then the most polish'd of all the
Modern Languages : But this Subject has been copiously treated
by that great Critick, who deserves no little Commendation
from us his Countrymen. For these Reasons of Time, and
Resemblance of Genius, in *Chaucer* and *Boccace*, I resolv'd to
join them in my present ·Work ; to which I have added some
Original Papers of my own ; which whether they are equal or
inferiour to my other Poems, an Author is the most improper
Judge ; and therefore I leave them wholly to the Mercy of the
Reader : I will hope the best, that they will not be condemn'd ; but if they should, I have the Excuse of an old
Gentleman, who, mounting on Horseback before some Ladies,
when I was present, got up somewhat heavily, but desir'd of
the Fair Spectators, that they would count Fourscore and
eight before they judg'd him. . . .

[sign. *B1] I proceed to *Ovid*, and *Chaucer* ; considering the former
only in relation to the latter. With *Ovid* ended the Golden
Age of the *Roman* Tongue : From *Chaucer* the Purity of the
English Tongue began. The Manners of the Poets were not
unlike : Both of them were well-bred, well-natur'd, amorous,
and Libertine, at least in their Writings, it may be, also in their
Lives. Their Studies were the same, Philosophy, and Philology.
Both of them were knowing in Astronomy ; of which *Ovid's*

CHAUCER CRITICISM.

Books of the *Roman* Feasts, and *Chaucer*'s Treatise of the *Astrolabe*, are sufficient Witnesses. But *Chaucer* was likewise an Astrologer, as were *Virgil, Horace, Persius,* and *Manilius.* Both writ with wonderful Facility and Clearness ; neither were great Inventors : For *Ovid* only copied the *Grecian* Fables ; and most of *Chaucer*'s Stories were taken from his *Italian* Contemporaries, or their Predecessors : *Boccace* his *Decameron* was first publish'd, and from thence our *Englishman* has borrow'd many of his *Canterbury* Tales : Yet that of *Palamon* and *Arcite* was written in all probability by some *Italian* Wit, in a former Age ; as I shall prove hereafter : The tale of *Grizild* was the Invention of *Petrarch* ; by him sent to *Boccace* ; from whom it came to *Chaucer* : *Troilus* and *Cressida* was also written by a *Lombard* Author ; but much amplified by our [sign. *B 1 b*] *English* Translatour, as well as beautified ; the Genius of our Countrymen, in general, being rather to improve an Invention than to invent themselves ; as is evident not only in our Poetry, but in many of our Manufactures. I find I have anticipated already, and taken up from *Boccace* before I come to him : But there is so much less behind ; and I am of the Temper of most Kings, *who love to be in Debt,* are all for present Money, no matter how they pay it afterwards : Besides, the Nature of a Preface is rambling ; never wholly out of the Way, nor in it. This I have learn'd from the Practice of honest *Montaign,* and return at pleasure to *Ovid* and *Chaucer,* of whom I have little more to say. Both of them built on the Inventions of other Men ; yet since *Chaucer* had something of his own, as *The Wife of Baths Tale, The Cock and the Fox,* which I have translated, and some others, I may justly give our Countryman the Precedence in that Part ; since I can remember nothing of *Ovid* which was wholly his. Both of them understood the Manners ; under which Name I comprehend the Passions, and, in a larger Sense, the Descriptions of Persons, and their very Habits : For an Example, I see *Baucis* and *Philemon* as perfectly before me, as if some ancient Painter had drawn them ; and all the Pilgrims in the *Canterbury* Tales, their Humours, their Features, and the very Dress, as distinctly as if I had supp'd with them at the *Tabard* in *Southwark* : Yet even there, too, the Figures of *Chaucer* are much more lively, and set in a better Light : Which though I have not time to prove ; yet I appeal to the Reader, and am sure he will clear me from Partiality. The Thoughts and Words remain to be consider'd, in the Comparison of the two Poets ; and I have sav'd my self one half of that Labour, by owning that *Ovid* liv'd when the *Roman* Tongue was in its Meridian ; *Chaucer*, in the Dawning of our Language : Therefore that Part of the Comparison stands not on an equal Foot, any more than the Diction of *Ennius* and *Ovid* ; or of *Chaucer* and our present *English.* The Words are given up as a Post not to be defended in our Poet, because he wanted the Modern Art of Fortifying. The Thoughts remain to be consider'd : And they are to be measur'd only by their Propriety ; that is, as they flow more or less naturally from the Persons describ'd, on such and such Occasions. The Vulgar Judges, which are Nine Parts in Ten of all Nations, who call Conceits and Jingles Wit, who see *Ovid* full of them, and *Chaucer* altogether without them, will think me little less than mad for preferring the *Englishman* to the *Roman* : Yet, with their leave, I must presume to say, that the Things they admire are only glittering Trifles, and so far from being Witty, that in a serious Poem they are nauseous, because they are unnatural. Wou'd any Man, who is ready to die for Love, describe his Passion like *Narcissus* ? Wou'd he think of *inopem me copia fecit*, and a Dozen more of such Expressions, pour'd on the Neck of one another, and signifying all the same Thing ? If this were Wit, was this a Time to be witty, when the poor Wretch was in the Agony of Death ? This is just *John Little-wit*, in *Bartholomew Fair*, who had a Conceit (as he tells you) left him in his Misery ; a miserable Conceit. On these Occasions the Poet shou'd endeavour to raise Pity : But, instead of this, *Ovid* is tickling you to laugh. *Virgil* never made use of such Machines when he was moving you to commiserate the Death of *Dido* : He would not destroy what he was building. *Chaucer* makes *Arcite* violent in his Love, and unjust in the Pursuit of it : Yet, when he came to die, he made him think more reasonably : He repents not of his Love, for that had alter'd his Character ; but acknowledges the Injustice of his Proceedings, and resigns *Emilia* to *Palamon.* What would *Ovid* have done on this Occasion ? He would certainly have made *Arcite* witty on his Death-bed. He had complain'd he was further off from Possession, by being so near, and a thousand such Boyisms, which *Chaucer* rejected as below the Dignity of the Subject. They who think otherwise, would by the same Reason, prefer *Lucan* and *Ovid* to *Homer* and *Virgil*, and *Martial* to all Four of them. As for the Turn of Words, in

[sign.
•B 2]

which *Ovid* particularly excels all Poets; they are sometimes a Fault, and sometimes a Beauty, as they are us'd properly or improperly; but in strong Passions always to be shunn'd, because Passions are serious, and will admit no Playing. The *French* have a high Value for them; and, I confess, they are often what they call Delicate, when they are introduc'd with Judgment; but *Chaucer* writ with more Simplicity, and follow'd Nature more closely, than to use them. I have thus far, to the best of my Knowledge, been an upright Judge betwixt the Parties in Competition, not medling with the Design nor the Disposition of it; because the Design was not their own; and in the disposing of it they were equal. It remains that I say somewhat of *Chaucer* in particular.

In the first place, as he is the Father of *English* Poetry, so I hold him in the same Degree of Veneration as the *Grecians* held *Homer*, or the *Romans Virgil*: He is a perpetual Fountain of good Sense; learn'd in all Sciences; and, therefore speaks properly on all Subjects: As he knew what to say, so he knows also when to leave off; a Continence which is practis'd by few Writers, and scarcely by any of the Ancients, excepting *Virgil* and *Horace*. One of our late great Poets is sunk in his Reputation, because he cou'd never forgive any Conceit which came in his way; but swept like a Drag-net, great and small. There was plenty enough, but the Dishes were ill sorted; whole Pyramids of Sweet-meats for Boys and Women; but little of solid Meat for Men: All this proceeded not from any want of Knowledge, but of Judgment; neither did he want that in discerning the Beauties and Faults of other Poets; but only indulg'd himself in the Luxury of Writing; and perhaps knew it was a Fault, but hoped the Reader would not find it. For this Reason, though he must always be thought a great Poet, he is no longer esteemed a good Writer: And for Ten Impressions, which his Works have had in so many successive Years, yet at present a hundred Books are scarcely purchased once a Twelvemonth: For, as my last Lord *Rochester* said, though somewhat profanely, *Not being of God, he could not stand.*

Chaucer follow'd Nature every where, but was never so bold to go beyond her: And there is a great Difference of being *Poeta* and *nimis Poeta*, if we may believe *Catullus*, as much as betwixt a modest Behaviour and Affectation. The Verse of
Chaucer, I confess, is not Harmonious to us; but 'tis like the

Eloquence of one whom *Tacitus* commends, it was *auribus istius temporis accommodata* : They who liv'd with him, and some time after him, thought it Musical ; and it continues so even in our Judgment, if compar'd with the Numbers of *Lidgate* and *Gower*, his Contemporaries : There is the rude Sweetness of a *Scotch* Tune in it, which is natural and pleasing, though not perfect. 'Tis true, I cannot go so far as he who publish'd the last Edition of him ; for he would make us believe the Fault is in our Ears, and that there were really Ten Syllables in a Verse where we find but Nine : But this Opinion is not worth confuting ; 'tis so gross and obvious an Errour, that common Sense (which is a Rule in everything but Matters of Faith and Revelation) must convince the Reader, that Equality of Numbers, in every Verse which we call *Heroick*, was either not known, or not always practis'd, in *Chaucer*'s Age. It were an easie Matter to produce some thousands of his Verses, which are lame for want of half a Foot, and sometimes a whole one, and which no Pronunciation can make otherwise. We can only say, that he liv'd in the Infancy of our Poetry, and that nothing is brought to Perfection at the first. We must be Children before we grow Men. There was an *Ennius*, and in process of Time a *Lucilius*, and a *Lucretius*, before *Virgil* and *Horace* ; even after *Chaucer* there was a *Spencer*, a *Harrington*, a *Fairfax*, before *Waller* and *Denham* were in being : And our Numbers were in their Nonage till these last appear'd. I need say little of his Parentage, Life, and Fortunes : They are to be found at large in all the Editions of his Works. He was employ'd abroad, and favour'd by *Edward* the Third, *Richard* the Second, and *Henry* the Fourth, and was Poet, as I suppose, to all Three of them. In *Richard's* Time, I doubt, he was a little dipt in the Rebellion of the Commons ; and being Brother-in-Law to *John of Ghant*, it was no wonder if he follow'd the Fortunes of that Family ; and was well with *Henry* the Fourth when he depos'd his Predecessor. Neither is it to be admir'd, that *Henry*, who was a wise as well as a valiant Prince, who claim'd by Succession, and was sensible that his Title was not sound, but was rightfully in *Mortimer*, who had married the Heir of *York*; it was not to be admir'd, I say, if that great Politician should be pleas'd to have the greatest Wit of those Times in his Interests, and to be the Trumpet of his Praises. *Augustus* had given him the Example, by the Advice of

Mecænas, who recommended *Virgil* and *Horace* to him ; whose Praises helped to make him Popular while he was alive, and after his Death have made him Precious to Posterity. As for the Religion of our Poet, he seems to have some little Byas towards the Opinions of *Wicliff*, after *John of Ghant* his Patron ; somewhat of which appears in the Tale of *Piers Plowman* : Yet I cannot blame him for inveighing so sharply against the Vices of the Clergy in his Age : Their Pride, .their Ambition, their Pomp, their Avarice, their Worldly Interest, deserv'd the Lashes which he gave them, both in that, and in most of his *Canterbury Tales* : Neither has his Contemporary *Boccace*, spar'd them. Yet both those Poets liv'd in much esteem, with good and holy Men in Orders : For the Scandal which is given by particular Priests reflects
[sign. *C 1] not on the Sacred Function. *Chaucer's Monk*, his *Chanon*, and his *Fryar*, took not from the Character of his *Good Parson*. A Satyrical Poet is the Check of the Laymen on bad Priests. . . . . .

I have followed *Chaucer*, in his Character of a Holy Man, and have enlarg'd on that Subject with some Pleasure, reserving to myself the Right, if I shall think fit hereafter, to describe another sort of Priests, such as are more easily to be found than the Good Parson ; such as have given the last Blow to Christianity in this Age, by a Practice so contrary to their Doctrine. But this will keep cold till another time. In the mean while, I take up *Chaucer* where I left him. He must have been a Man of a most wonderful comprehensive Nature, because, as it has been truly observ'd of him, he has taken into the Compass of his *Canterbury Tales* the various Manners and Humours (as we now call them) of the whole *English* Nation, in his Age. Not a single Character has escap'd him. All his Pilgrims are severally distinguish'd from each other ; and not only in their Inclinations, but in their
[sign. *C 1 b] very Phisiognomies and Persons. *Baptista Porta* could not have describ'd their Natures better, than by the Marks which the Poet gives them. The Matter and Manner of their Tales, and of their Telling, are so suited to their different Educations, Humours, and Callings, that each of them would be improper in any other Mouth. Even the grave and serious Characters are distinguish'd by their several sorts of Gravity : Their Discourses are such as belong to their Age, their Calling, and their Breeding ; such as are becoming of them, and of them

only. Some of his Persons are Vicious, and some Virtuous;
some are unlearn'd, or (as *Chaucer* calls them) Lewd, and
some are Learn'd. Even the Ribaldry of the Low Characters
is different: the *Reeve*, the *Miller*, and the *Cook*, are several
Men, and are distinguish'd from each other, as much as the
mincing Lady-Prioress, and the broad-speaking, gap-toothed
Wife of *Bathe*. But enough of this: There is such a Variety
of Game springing up before me, that I am distracted in my
Choice, and know not which to follow.   'Tis sufficient to say
according to the Proverb, that here is God's Plenty. We have
our Fore-fathers and Great Grand-dames all before us, as they
were in *Chaucer*'s Days; their general Characters are still
remaining in Mankind, and even in *England*, though they are
call'd by other Names than those of *Moncks*, and *Fryars*, and
Chanons, and *Lady Abbesses*, and *Nuns*: For Mankind is ever
the same, and nothing lost out of Nature, though everything
is alter'd.   May I have leave to do myself the Justice, (since
my Enemies will do me none, and are so far from granting me
to be a good Poet, that they will not allow me so much as to
be a Christian, or a Moral Man), may I have leave, I say, to
inform my Reader, that I have confined my Choice to such
Tales of *Chaucer* as savour nothing of Immodesty. If I desir'd
more to please than to instruct, the *Reve*, the *Miller*, the
Shipman, the *Merchant*, the *Sumner*, and above all, the *Wife
of Bathe*, in the Prologue to her Tale, would have procur'd me
as many Friends and Readers, as there are *Beaux* and Ladies
of Pleasure in the Town. But I will no more offend against
Good Manners: I am sensible as I ought to be of the Scandal
I have given by my loose Writings; and make what Reparation
I am able, by this Public Acknowledgment. If anything of
this Nature, or of Profaneness, be crept into these Poems, I
am so far from defending it, that I disown it. *Totum hoc
indictum volo. Chaucer* makes another manner of Apologie for
his broad speaking, and *Boccace* makes the like; but I will
follow neither of them. Our Country-man, in the end of his
Characters, before the *Canterbury Tales*, thus excuses the
Ribaldry, which is very gross in many of his Novels.

> *But firste, I pray you of your courtesy,*
> *That ye ne arrete it nought my villany,*
> *Though that I plainly speak in this mattere,* [etc.].

[quotes ll. 725-42 of Prologue.]

[sign. *C 2] Yet if a Man should have enquir'd of *Boccace* or of *Chaucer*,

what need they had of introducing such Characters, when
obscene Words were proper in their Mouths, but very undecent
to be heard; I know not what Answer they could have made :
For that Reason, such Tales shall be left untold by me.   You
have here a *Specimen* of *Chaucer's* Language, which is so
obsolete, that his Sense is scarce to be understood ; and you
have likewise more than one Example of his unequal Numbers,
which were mention'd before.   Yet many of his Verses consist
of Ten Syllables, and the Words not much behind our present
English : as for Example, these two Lines, in the Description of
the Carpenter's Young Wife :

> *Wincing she was, as is a jolly Colt,*
> *Long as a Mast, and upright as a Bolt.*

I have almost done with *Chaucer*, when I have answer'd some
Objections relating to my present Work.   I find some People
are offended that I have turn'd these Tales into modern
English ; because they think them unworthy of my Pains,
and look on *Chaucer* as a dry, old-fashion'd Wit, not worth
receiving [edn. of 1723 ' reviving ']. I have often heard the
late Earl of *Leicester* say, that Mr. *Cowley* himself was of that
opinion ; who, having read him over at my Lord's Request,
declared he had no Taste of him.   I dare not advance my
Opinion against the Judgment of so great an Author : But I
think it fair, however, to leave the Decision to the Publick.
Mr. *Cowley*, was too modest to set up for a Dictatour ; and,
being shock'd perhaps with his old Style, never examin'd
into the depth of his good Sense.   *Chaucer*, I confess, is
a rough Diamond, and must first be polish'd, e'er he shines.
I deny not likewise, that, living in our early Days of Poetry,
he writes not always of a piece ; but sometimes mingles
trivial Things with those of greater Moment.   Sometimes also,
though not often, he runs riot, like *Ovid*, and knows not
when he has said enough.   But there are more great Wits
besides *Chaucer*, whose Fault is their Excess of Conceits, and
those ill sorted.   An Author is not to write all he can, but
only all he ought.   Having observ'd this Redundancy in
Chaucer, (as it is an easie Matter for a Man of ordinary
Parts to find a Fault in one of greater,) I have not ty'd
my self to a Literal Translation ; but have often omitted what
I judg'd unnecessary, or not of Dignity enough to appear in
the Company of better Thoughts.   I have presum'd farther
in some Places, and added somewhat of my own where I

thought my Author was deficient, and had not given his [sign. •C 2 b] Thoughts their true Lustre, for want of Words in the Beginning of our Language. And to this I was the more embolden'd, because, (if I may be permitted to say it of my self) I found I had a Soul congenial to his, and that I had been conversant in the same Studies. Another Poet, in another Age, may take the same Liberty with my Writings; if at least they live long enough to deserve Correction. It was also necessary sometimes to restore the Sense of *Chaucer*, which was lost or mangled in the Errors of the Press : Let this Example suffice at present in the Story of *Palamon* and *Arcite*, where the temple of *Diana* is describ'd, you find these Verses in all the Editions of our Author :

> *There saw I* Danè *turned unto a Tree,*
> *I mean not the goddess* Diane,
> *But* Venus *Daughter, which that hight* Danè.

Which, after a little Consideration, I knew was to be reform'd into this Sense, that *Daphne*, the daughter of *Peneus*, was turn'd into a Tree. I durst not make thus free with *Ovid*, lest some future *Milbourn* should arise, and say, I varied from my Author, because I understood him not.

But there are other Judges, who think I ought not to have translated *Chaucer* into *English*, out of a quite contrary Notion : They suppose there is a certain Veneration due to his old Language; and that it is little less than Profanation and Sacrilege to alter it. They are farther of opinion, that somewhat of his good Sense will suffer in this Transfusion, and much of the Beauty of his Thoughts will infallibly be lost, which appear with more Grace in their old Habit. Of this Opinion was that excellent Person, whom I mention'd, the late Earl of *Leicester*, who valued *Chaucer* as much as Mr. *Cowley* despis'd him. My Lord dissuaded me from this Attempt, (for I was thinking of it some Years before his Death,) and his Authority prevail'd so far with me, as to defer my Undertaking while he liv'd, in deference to him : Yet my Reason was not convinc'd with what he urg'd against it. If the first End of a Writer be to be understood, then, as his Language grows obsolete, his Thoughts must grow obscure, *multa renascuntur, quæ nunc cecidere; cadentque quæ nunc sunt in honore vocabula, si volet usus, quem penes arbitrium est et jus et norma loquendi.* When an ancient Word for

its Sound and Significancy, deserves to be reviv'd, I have
that reasonable Veneration for Antiquity, to restore it. All
beyond this is Superstition. Words are not like Land-marks,
so sacred as never to be remov'd: Customs are chang'd, and
even Statutes are silently repeal'd, when the Reason ceases
for which they were enacted. As for the other Part of the
Argument, that his Thoughts will lose of their original Beauty
by the innovation of Words; in the first place, not only their
Beauty, but their Being is lost, when they are no longer
understood, which is the present Case. I grant that something
must be lost in all Transfusion, that is, in all Translations; but
the Sense will remain, which would otherwise be lost, or at
least be maim'd, where it is scarce intelligible; and that but to
a few. How few are they who can read *Chaucer*, so as to
understand him perfectly? And if imperfectly, then with
less Profit, and no Pleasure. 'Tis not for the Use of some old
Saxon Friends, that I have taken these Pains with him: Let
them neglect my Version, because they have no need of it. I
made it for their sakes, who understand Sense and Poetry, as
well as they; when that Poetry and Sense is put into Words
which they understand. I will go farther, and dare to add,
that what Beauties I lose in some Places, I give to others
which had them not originally : But in this I may be partial to
my self; let the Reader judge, and I submit to his Decision.
Yet I think I have just Occasion to complain of them, who because they understand *Chaucer*, would deprive the greater part
of their Countrymen of the same Advantage, and hoord him up,
as Misers do their Grandam Gold, only to look on it themselves,
and hinder others from making use of it. In sum, I seriously
protest, that no Man ever had, or can have, a greater Veneration for *Chaucer* than my self. I have translated some part
of his Works, only that I might perpetuate his Memory, or at
least refresh it, amongst my Countrymen. If I have alter'd
him anywhere for the better, I must at the same time acknowledge, that I could have done nothing without him : *Facile est
inventis addere*, is no great Commendation ; but I am not so
vain to think I have deserv'd a greater. I will conclude
what I have to say of him singly, with this one Remark :
A Lady of my acquaintance, who keeps a kind of Correspondence with some Authors of the Fair Sex in *France*, has been
inform'd by them, that *Mademoiselle de Scudery*, who is as old
as *Sibyl*, and inspir'd like her by the same God of Poetry, is at

[sign.
*D 1]

this time translating *Chaucer* into modern *French*. From which
I gather, that he has been formerly translated into the old
Provençall; (for, how she should come to understand Old *English*, I know not). But the Matter of Fact being true, it makes
me think that there is something in it like Fatality; that, after
certain Periods of Time, the Fame and Memory of Great Wits
should be renew'd, as *Chaucer* is both in *France* and *England*.
If this be wholly Chance, 'tis extraordinary; and I dare not
call it more, for fear of being tax'd with Superstition.

Boccace comes last to be consider'd, who, living in the
same Age with *Chaucer*, had the same Genius, and followed
the same Studies : Both writ Novels, and each of them cultivated his Mother-Tongue : But the greatest Resemblance of
our two Modern Authors being in their familiar Style, and
pleasing way of relating Comical Adventures, I may pass it
over, because I have translated nothing from *Boccace* of that
Nature. In the serious part of Poetry, the Advantage is wholly
on *Chaucer*'s Side; for though the *Englishman* has borrow'd
many Tales from the *Italian*, yet it Appears, that those of *Boccace*
were not generally of his own making, but taken from Authors
of former ages, and by him only modell'd : So that what there
was of Invention, in either of them, may be judg'd equal.
But *Chaucer* has refin'd on *Boccace*, and has mended the
Stories, which he has borrow'd, in his way of telling; though
Prose allows more Liberty of Thought, and the Expression is
more easie, when unconfin'd by Numbers. Our Countryman
carries Weight, and yet wins the Race at disadvantage. I
desire not the Reader should take my Word; and, therefore, I
[sign. ⁕D 1 *b*] will set two of their Discourses, on the same Subject, in the
same Light, for every Man to judge betwixt them. I trans-
lated *Chaucer* first, and amongst the rest, pitch'd on The Wife
of *Bath*'s Tale; not daring, as I have said, to advance on her
Prologue, because 'tis too licentious: There *Chaucer* introduces an old Woman of mean Parentage, whom a youthful
Knight of Noble Blood, was forc'd to marry, and consequently
loath'd her: The Crone being in bed with him on the
wedding Night, and finding his Aversion, endeavours to win
his Affection by Reason, and speaks a good Word for herself,
(as who could blame her?) in hope to mollifie the sullen Bride-
groom. She takes her Topiques from the Benefits of Poverty,
the Advantages of old Age and Ugliness, the Vanity of Youth,
and the silly Pride of Ancestry and Titles, without inherent

Vertue, which is the true Nobility.   When I had clos'd
Chaucer, I return'd to *Ovid*, and translated some more of his
Fables ; and, by this time, had so far forgotten The Wife of
Bath's Tale, that when I took up *Boccace*, unawares I fell
on the same Argument of preferring Virtue to Nobility of
Blood, and Titles, in the Story of *Sigismonda*; which I had
certainly avoided for the Resemblance of the two Discourses,
if my Memory had not fail'd me.   Let the Reader weigh both ;
and if he thinks me partial to *Chaucer*, 'tis in him to right
Boccace.

   I prefer in our Countryman, far above all his other Stories,
the Noble Poem of *Palamon* and *Arcite*, which is of the
Epique kind, and perhaps not much inferior to the *Ilias* or
the *Æneis*: the Story is more pleasing than either of them, the
Manners as perfect, the Diction as poetical, the Learning as
deep and various ; and the Disposition full as artful : only it
includes a greater length of time ; as taking up seven years at
least ; but *Aristotle* has left undecided the Duration of the
Action ; which yet is easily reduc'd into the Compass of a
year, by a Narration of what preceded the Return of *Palamon*
to *Athens*.   I had thought for the Honour of our Nation,
and more particularly for his, whose Laurel, tho' unworthy,
I have worn after him, that this Story was of *English* Growth,
and *Chaucer*'s own : But I was undeceiv'd by *Boccace*; for
casually looking on the End of his seventh *Giornata*, I found
Dioneo, (under which name he shadows himself,) and *Fiametta*,
(who represents his Mistress, the natural Daughter of *Robert*,
King of *Naples*) of whom these Words are spoken.   *Dioneo e
Fiametta gran pezza cantarono insieme d'Arcita, e di Palemone:*
by which it appears, that this Story was written before the
time of *Boccace*; but the Name of its Author being wholly
lost, *Chaucer* is now become an Original; and I question not
but the Poem has receiv'd many Beauties, by passing through
his Noble Hands.   Besides this Tale, there is another of his
own Invention, after the manner of the *Provençalls*, call'd *The
Flower and the Leaf*; with which I was so particularly pleas'd,
both for the Invention and the Moral, that I cannot hinder
myself from recommending it to the Reader.

[sign. A 1]   [Poem] To Her Grace The Dutchess of Ormond.
   Madam,
         The Bard who first adorn'd our Native Tongue
         Tun'd to his *British* Lyre this ancient Song :

Which *Homer* might without a Blush reherse,
And leaves a doubtful Psalm in *Virgil's* Verse :
He match'd their Beauties, where they most excell ;
Of Love sung better, and of Arms as well.

[sign. A 1 *b*]   Vouchsafe, Illustrious *Ormond*, to behold
What Pow'r the Charms of Beauty had of old ;
Nor wonder if such Deeds of Arms were done,
Inspir'd by two fair Eyes, that sparkled like your own.

If *Chaucer* by the best Idea wrought,
And Poets can divine each others Thought,
The fairest Nymph before his Eyes he set ;
And then the fairest was *Plantagenet* ;
Who three contending Princes made her Prize,
And rul'd the Rival-Nations with her Eyes :

.   .   .   .

Thus, after length of Ages, she returns,
Restor'd in you, and the same Place adorns ;
[sign. A 2]   Or you perform her Office in the Sphere,
Born of her Blood, and make a new Platonick Year.

O true *Plantagenet*, O Race Divine,
(For Beauty still is fatal to the Line,)
Had *Chaucer* liv'd that Angel-Face to view,
Sure he had drawn his *Emily* from You :
Or had You liv'd to judge the doughtful Right ;
Your noble *Palamon* had been the Knight :
And Conqu'ring *Theseus* from his Side had sent
Your Gen'rous Lord, to guide the *Theban* Government.
Time shall accomplish that ; and I shall see
A *Palamon* in Him, in You an *Emily*.

.   .   .   .

Palamon and Arcite, or the Knight's Tale from Chaucer.
                                                    [pp. 1–90.]
The Cock and the Fox ; or The Tale of the Nun's Priest from
    Chaucer.   [pp. 223–53.]
The Flower and the Leaf ; or The Lady in the Arbour.   A
    Vision.   [pp. 383–405.]
The Wife of Bath Her Tale.   [pp. 477–99.]
The Character of a Good Parson. Imitated from Chaucer and
    Inlarg'd.   [pp. 531–36.]

[Chaucer's original versions of the above Tales are given later,
on pp. 567 to 646.]

1700. Tanner, Rev. Thomas. *Letter to Dr. Arthur Charlett,* [dated] May 6, 1700.   [printed in] The Prose Works of John Dryden . . . [ed.] Edmond Malone . . . 1800, vol. i, part 1, p. 368, note 2.

[Dryden to be buried] with Chaucer, Cowley, &c., at Westminster-Abbey on Munday next.

1700. Playford, Henry. *Advertisement* [in] The Postboy, Tuesday, May 7, 1700. [printed in] The Prose Works of John Dryden, [ed.] Edmund Malone, 1800, vol. i, p. 382, note 9.

The death of the famous John Dryden Esq., . . . being a subject capable of employing the best pens; and *several persons of quality, and others, having put a stop to his interment,* which is designed to be in Chaucer's grave, in Westminster-Abbey; this is to desire the gentlemen of the two famous Universities, and others, who have a respect for the memory of the deceased, and are inclinable to such performances, to send what copies they please, as Epigrams, &c., to Henry Playford . . . and they shall be inserted in a Collection. . . .

[This collection was published on June 19, 1700, under the title of Luctus Britannici, see below.]

1700. Unknown. *Notice of Dryden's funeral* [in] *The Postboy,* May 7, 1700. *Account of Dryden's funeral* [in] *The Postman,* May 14, 1700. *Ditto* [in] *The Flying Post,* May 14, 1700. [all printed in] The Prose Works of John Dryden, [ed.] Edmond Malone, 1800, vol. i, part 1, pp. 367, note 1, 378–9, note 8.

[Dryden buried near Chaucer.]

1700. Ward, Edward. *Account of John Dryden's funeral* [in] *London Spy,* p. 422. [pr. in] The Prose Works of John Dryden, [ed.] Edmond Malone, 1800, vol. i, part 1, p. 379.

1700. Hall, Henry. [*Verses*] *To the Memory of John Dryden,* Esq., [in] Luctus Britannici : or the Tears of the British Muses for the Death of John Dryden, Esq. . . . written by the most Eminent Hands in the two Famous Universities, and by several Others. London . . . 1700, pp. 18, 19.

Nor is thy latest Work, unworthy Thee.
New Cloath'd by You, how *Chaucer* we esteem;
When You've new Polish'd it, how bright the Jem !
And lo, the Sacred Shade for thee make's room,
Tho' Souls so like, should take but up one tomb.

· · · · · · · · · ·

Let us look back, and Noble Numbers trace
Directly up from Ours, to *Chaucer's* days ;
Chaucer, the first of Bards in Tune that Sung,
And to a better bent reduc'd the stubborn Tongue.

1700. Unknown. [*Verses*] *To Dr. Samuel Garth, occasioned by the much Lamented Death of John Dryden, Esq.*, [in] Luctus Britannici, pp. 54–5.

But if the *Greek*, and if the *Latin* share
The Bounties of his Favours, and his Care,
If *Foreign* Tongues have His assistance known,
What Thanks are owing to Him from his own ?

. . . .

Rugged, and rough, the Bard her Language found,
Without a *Meaning*, or a proper *sound*,
As *Saxon Syllabs* Choak'd the *Roads* of Sence,
And *Foreign Words* were all Her Tongues *Defence*.
But *Dryden's* Diligence, and *Dryden's* Thought,
Chas'd back the Troops, which false *Invaders* brought,
New stamp'd the Language with another *Face*,
And gave it *Majesty* as well as *Grace*,

. . . .

Yet though his Works are all sublimely Great ;

. . . .

Though, All H' [Dryden] has done dares Envy's Nicest Test,
And His *worst* Poem's better than our *Best*.
His latest Work, though in His last decays,
As far exceeds His former as Our Praise.
And *Chaucer* shall again with Joy be Read,
Whose Language with its Master lay for Dead,
Till *Dryden*, striving His Remains to save,
Sunk in His *Tomb*, who *brought* him from his *Grave*.

1700. Unknown. [*Verses*] *To the Memory of John Dryden, Esq.*; [in] Luctus Britannici, p. 36.

Methinks I see the Reverend Shades prepare
With Songs of Joy, to waft thee through the Air

. . . .

Where *Chaucer, Johnson, Shakespear*, and the rest,
Kindly embrace their venerable Guest.

. . . .

Whilst we in pensive Sables clad below
Bear hence in solemn Grief, & pompous Woe,
Thy sacred Dust to *Chaucer's* peaceful Urn.

1700. Unknown. *A Description of Mr. D[ryde]n's Funeral.* A Poem
. . . p. 8, [a separate tract bound up with the B. M. copy of Luctus
Britannici].

> A Crowd of Fools attend him to the Grave,
> A Crowd so nauseous, so profusely lewd,
> With all the Vices of the Times endu'd,
> That *Cowley*'s Marble wept to see the Throng,
> Old *Chaucer* laugh'd at their unpolish'd Song,
> And *Spencer* thought he once again had seen
> The Imps attending of his *Fairy Queen*.

1700. Unknown. *Gallus* [*Latin Verses in Memory of John Dryden*,
bound as a supplement with the B.M. copy of Luctus Britannici]
signed Ex Aul. C. [probably Catherine Hall, Cambridge], p. 5.

1700. H., N. [*Latin verses*] *In obitum celeberrimi Joannis Dryden* . . . in
Gallus [bound up with] Luctus Britannici, p. 15.

1700. Higgons, Bevill. [*Latin verses*] *In celeberrimum Joannem
Dryden Chauceri Sepulchro Intectum,* [in] *Gallus* [bound up with]
Luctus Britannici, p. 8.

1700. Vernon, Henry. [*Latin verses*] *In Memoriam Johannis Dryden*
. . . in *Gallus* [bound up with] Luctus Britannici, p. 18.

1700. W., P., Trin. Coll. Cant. [*Latin verses in memory of John
Dryden*] in *Gallus* [bound up with] Luctus Britannici, p. 19.

1700. Unknown. *The New Wife of Beath* [sic], *much better Reformed,
Enlarged, and Corrected, than it was formerly in the old uncorrect
Copy. With the Addition of many other Things.* Glasgow.

> In Beath, once dwelt a worthy Wife,
> Of whom brave Chaucer mention makes. . . .

[An enlargement, ultimately, of the ballad "The Wanton
Wife of Bath" (*q.v.* below, Appendix A, c. 1670), but the first
words of the address "To the Reader," "Courteous Reader,
What was Papal or Heretical in the former copy is left out here
in this second edition," must refer to an intermediate version.
The address to the reader was omitted in later editions. That
of [1785?] has the misprint "Sanquer" for "Chaucer." It
was reprinted in Fugitive Poetical Tracts. ed. W. C. Hazlitt,
1875, Ser. ii, No. xxviii.]

1700. Wesley, Samuel. *An Epistle to a Friend Concerning Poetry.*
London. Printed for Charles Harper at the Flower de Luce in
Fleetstreet, MDCC, p. 12.

> Of CHAUCER's Verse we scarce the *Measures* know,
>
> So *rough* the *Lines*, and so *unequal* flow ;
>
> Whether by Injury of *Time* defac'd,
>
> Or *careless* at the *first*, and writ in *haste ;*
>
> Or *coursly*, like old *Ennius*, he design'd
>
> What After-days have *polish'd* and *refin'd.*

1701. Collier, Jeremy. *The Great Historical, Geographical, Genea-
logical, and Poetical Dictionary.* . . . [chiefly] collected from
. . . Lewis Morery his Eighth Edition. The Second Edition,
Revis'd, Corrected and enlarged to the Year 1688, vol. i, sign
B.b.b.2. [Life of] Jeffrey Chaucer.

> CHAUCER (*Jeffrey*), born at *Woodstock* in *Oxfordshire*, in
> the Fourteenth Century. He was called *The English Homer*,
> and was not only a Poet but a Mathematician, and under-
> stood, according to the Talent of his Time, the Polite Part of
> Learning. He died in 1440, and has a Tomb in *Westminster-
> Abby*. His Works are Printed in Folio, at *London* in 1561.
> Besides these, he left a Manuscript, in which he Laments the
> Liberties he had taken in some Part of his Poems, incon-
> sistent with Modesty and Religion. This Manuscript is now
> in the Hands of the *Reviser*.
>
> [Authorities] *Leland, Bale, Cambden.*

1701. Le Neve, Peter. *Letter* to Sir John Perceval, [printed in]
Report on the Manuscripts of the Earl of Egmont, vol. ii (Hist.
MSS. Comm.), 1909, p. 198.

> This I am sure of, that at Henham Hall and Park by the
> road side, the lovers of antiquity will find occasion of con-
> templation, when they recollect that the famous Charles
> Brandon, Duke of Suffolk, in Henry VIII's time lived here ;
> and before him the family of Kederston, whose estate devolved
> by heirs female to Thomas Chaucer, Esq., a descendant of the
> famous poet of that name . . .

1701. Unknown. *Chaucer's Whims: Being some select Fables and
Tales in Verse, very applicable to the Present Times.* [See specially
the] Preface.

> If I have not done Justice to *Chaucer* by putting his
> Name to Fables and Stories which are Collected by another
> Hand; I have several Precedents to excuse me. . . .

CHAUCER CRITICISM.

1701. **Wanley,** [Humphrey]. *Letter to Dr.* [*Arthur*] *Charlett, May* 21, 1701, [printed in] Letters written by eminent persons, 1813, vol. i, p. 127.

[The letter is on the meaning of the title "Dan" in connection with the song of "Dan Hew."] And this Monk is all along called by his Christian name in the rude song about him, as *Absolom*, *Nicholas*, and others in Chaucer; Sirnames being not yet universally received.

1701. **White,** John. *The Country-Man's Conductor in Reading and Writing True English* . . . by John White. Sometime Master of *Mr. Chilcot's* English-Free-School in *Tiverton*, and now Master of a Boarding School in *Butterly*, near *Tiverton* aforesaid. . . . Exeter, 1701, p. 125.

From this Age [the time of *Robert* of *Gloster*] 'till *Chaucer's* time, I find but little variation in the *English*; his Works are extant, and the Readers of any thing of Antiquity will find him often quoted in Examples of his own *English*. He was a great Refiner of our *English*, as *Leland* saith,

> *Our* England *honoureth* Chaucer *Poet, as principal,*
>
> *To whom our Country Tongue doth owe her Beauties all.*

Chaucer died in October 1400, aged about 72 years: Such as have his Works may find a great alteration in his own *English*; his Lamentation of *Mary Magdalen* being much finer than his Works done in his younger days. You may read his life in *Mr. Winstanly's* Worthies. [*q.v.* above, 1660, p. 238.]

1702. **Bysshe,** Edw[ard]. *The Art of English Poetry, containing, I, Rules for making Verses. II, A Dictionary of Rhymes. III, A Collection of the most Natural, Agreable, and Noble Thoughts, viz: Allusions; Similes, Descriptions, and Characters, of Persons and Things; that are to be found in the best English Poets.* Preface sign *2b *3 ; p. 25.

[sign *2b] [Bysshe says he has inserted quotations from all our modern poets]; I say of our Modern: For though the Ancient, as *Chaucer, Spencer,* and others, have not been excell'd, perhaps not equall'd by any that have succeeded them, either in Justness of Description, or in Propriety and Greatness of Thought, [sign *2] yet the Garb in which they are Cloath'd, tho' then Alamode, is now become so out of Fashion, that the Readers of our Age have no Ear for them: And this is the Reason that the

Good *Shakespear* himself is not so frequently Cited in the following Pages, as he would otherwise deserve to be. . . . . .

[p. 25] Thus the *Troilus* and *Cressida* of *Chaucer* is compos'd in Stanzas consisting of 7 Verses.

1703. Hickes, George. *Linguarum Vett. Septentrionalium Thesaurus Grammatico-Criticus et Archæologicus,* 1705, pp. 17 note, 27 note, 38 and note, 57–58, 65 note, 105. (For p. 65 *n. see* Urry's Chaucer, 1721, p. xxi.)

[p. 65, note] Legitur hæc Præpositio in veteribus nostris Scriptoribus, ut in carmine *Chauceri,* quod inscribitur the Testament of Creseide.

𝕬 𝖉𝖔𝖑𝖞 𝖘𝖊𝖆𝖘𝖔𝖓 𝖙𝖎𝖑 𝖆 𝖈𝖆𝖗𝖊𝖋𝖚𝖑𝖑 𝖉𝖎𝖙𝖊
𝕾𝖍𝖔𝖚𝖑𝖉 𝖈𝖔𝖗𝖗𝖊𝖘𝖕𝖔𝖓𝖉— . . .

[Throughout the book there are numerous references to Chaucer. There are separate title-pages for parts 1 and 2, each dated 1703.]

[*a.* **1704.**] **Brown,** Thomas (of Shifnal). *Letters from the Dead to the Living. The third and last letter of News from* Signior Giusippe Hanesio, *high* German *Doctor in* Brandipolis, *to his Friends at* Will's *Coffee-house.* . . . [in] The Works of Mr. Thomas Brown, ed. James Drake, 1707, vol. ii, the third part, pp. 206–7. [The title page of the 2nd vol. states that the 3rd pt. was never before printed. Brown died in 1704.]

[A dialogue in one of the coffee-houses of hell, between Dryden and Chaucer.] Sir, cries he [Chaucer], you have [p. 207] done me a wonderful Honour to Furbish up some of my old musty Tales, and bestow modern Garniture upon them, and I look upon my self much oblig'd to you for so undeserv'd a favour; however, Sir, I must take the Freedom to tell you that you overstrain'd Matters a little, when you liken'd me to *Ovid,* as to our Wit and manner of Versification. Why, Sir, says Mr. *Dryden,* I maintain it, and who then dares be so sawcy as to oppose me? But under favour, Sir, cries the other, I think I should know *Ovid* pretty well, having now conversed with him almost three hundred Years, and the Devil's in it if I don't know my own Talent, and therefore tho' you past a mighty compliment upon me in drawing this Parallel between us, yet I tell you there's no more resemblance between us as to our manner of Writing, than there is between a Jolly well complexion'd *Englishman* and a black-hair'd thin-gutted *Italian.* Lord, Sir, says *Dryden* to him, I tell you that you're mistaken, and your two Stiles are as like one another as two Exchequer Tallies. But I, who should know it better, says *Chaucer,* tell you the contrary.

1705. Hearne, Thomas. *Extracts from his Diary,* Nov. 19, Dec. 15, 1705, (in Remarks and Collections of Thomas Hearne, ed. C. E. Doble, Oxford Hist. Soc., 1885, vol. i, pp. 87, 129.)

Nov. 19 (Mon.) . . . In the story of Thebes compiled by *John Lidgate,* pag. 374, at yᵉ End of Chaucer's Works, is a Testimony of *Martianus* Capella ; wᶜʰ yᵉ Gentleman of *Cambridge* (of *Queen's* Col. viz : Mʳ *Wasse*) who is publishing *Capella* anew should remember to put down among yᵉ *Testimonia.*

Dec. 15. Quære wᵗ Armes are now in the Church of Ewe-Elme in Oxfordshire. There are several of them in the last Editions of Sr. Jeoff. Chaucer's Works. His Arms were parted per Pale, Argent and Gules, a Bend Counter-changed . . .

1705. Unknown. *The Tale of a Tub revers'd for the universal improvement of Mankind* [a rehandling of Furetière's Nouvelle allégorique des troubles arrivés au royaume d'éloquence], p. 35.

Not a part of the *Poetick* Country, but shewed their hearty Zeal upon this occasion, nay *Chaucer* himself, notwithstanding his *Age,* march'd at the head of his *Invalides* to Queen RHETORICK's Assistance ; and for the convenience of being supplied with an interpreter, had leave to take his post near Dryden.

[The only copy of this book now known is at Lambeth. Information was kindly supplied by Mr. A. Guthkelch.]

1705. Wanley, Humphrey. *Codices Anglo-Saxonici Bibliothecæ Bodleaianæ* [in] Antiquæ literaturæ Septentrionalis. Liber alter, seu Humphredi Wanleii Librorum Vett. Septentrionalium . . . Catalogus, [being the second volume of] Linguarum Vett. Septentrionalium Thesaurus . . . auctore Georgio Hickesio. Oxoniæ, 1705, vol. ii, p. 102.

Jun. 26. Superioris Dictionarii Saxonico-Anglici . . . [William Lambarde's note in the beginning of this Dictionary is then quoted, as given by Hearne 1711, *see* above, p. 104, below, p. 316.]

Libri impressi à cl. *Junio* notati & emendati.

Jun. 9. Galfridi Chauceri *opera, edit. Lond.* 1598. *ad quæ*

pariter pertinet opus Junii *manu scriptum,* & Jun. 6. *sig-
natum, in quo omnes obsoletæ apud* Chaucerum *voces collectæ
sunt, præter illas quæ incipiunt à littera* A, *quæ desiderantur.*
[Cf. *a.* 1677, Junius, above, p. 253.]

1706. Harrison, William. *Woodstock Park, a Poem,* [in] A Collection
of Poems by several hands, ed. R. Dodsley, 1758, vol. v, pp.
192-3.

Goddess, proceed ; and as to relicks found
Altars we raise, and consecrate the ground,
Pay thou thy homage to an aged seat,
Small in itself, but in its owner great ;
Where Chaucer (sacred name !) whole years employ'd
Coy Nature courted, & at length enjoy'd ;
Mov'd at his suit, the naked goddess came,
Reveal'd her charms, & recompens'd his flame.
Rome's pious king with like success retir'd,
And taught his people, what his Nymph inspir'd.
Hence flow descriptions regularly fine,
And beauties such as never can decline :
Each lively image makes the reader start,
And poetry invades the painter's art.
This Dryden saw, and with his wonted fate
(Rich in himself) endeavour'd to translate ;
Took wond'rous pains to do the author wrong,
And set to modern time his ancient song.
Cadence, and sound, which we so prize, and use,
Ill suit the majesty of Chaucer's Muse ;
His language only can his thoughts express,
Old honest Clytus scorns the Persian dress.
   Inimitable bard !
In raptures loud I would thy praises tell,
And on th' inspiring theme for ever dwell.

[A copy of Harrison's poem is in the Bodleian (Gough, Oxford, 103). The title runs :
Woodstock Park, a poem, by William Harison [*sic*], of New College. Oxon, 1706. *See*
D. N. B.]

1706. Unknown. *The British Warrior, a poem addressed to Lord
Cutts,* Oct. 30, 1706.

[The beginning of this poem is written by J. Haslewood in his interleaved copy of
Winstanley's Lives of the Poets, to face p. 23. *See* below, *c.* 1833.]

The British muse in Chaucer first began,
All nature list'ning to the wondrous Man,
Our rugged youth upon his accents hung,
And melted at the musick of his song ;

Strong was his voice, and sprightly were his lays,
Which warm'd, but wanted still the pow'r to raise,
Till the muse taught the following Bards to soar
Thro' beauteous worlds of Wit unknown before,
The tree he planted took a gen'rous root,
Shot into boughs and bent with golden fruit ;
Under whose fair auspicious shade were seen
An Eden lost and won, a Fairy Queen,
A Moor to doubts betray'd, and lofty Cataline [*sic*].

.   .   .   .   .   .

c. **1707.**] **Hughes,** Jabez. [*Verses*] *Upon Reading Mr. Dryden's Fables* [printed in] Miscellanies in Verse and Prose, by Mr. Jabez Hughes, 1737, pp. 95–97. (Appendix A, No. ix, in G. Saintsbury's revision of Sir Walter Scott's edition of the Works of John Dryden, 1893, vol xviii, p. 237.)

Upon Reading
Mr. *Dryden's* Fables.

Our great Forefathers in Poetic Song,
Were rude in Diction, tho' their Sense was strong ;
Well-measur'd Verse they knew not how to frame,
Their Words ungraceful, and the Cadence lame :
Too far they wildly rang'd to start the Prey,
And did too much of Fairy Land display ;
And in their rugged Dissonance of Lines,
True manly thought debas'd with Trifles shines.

.   .   .   .   .   .

Such was the Scene, when *Dryden* came to found
More perfect Lays, with Harmony of Sound :
What lively Colours glow on ev'ry Draught !
How bright his Images, how rais'd his Thought ! . . .

.   .   .   .   .   .

[p. 97] Revolving Time had injur'd *Chaucer's* Name,
And dimm'd the brilliant Lustre of his Fame ;
Deform'd his Language, and his Wit depress'd,
His serious Sense oft sinking to a Jest ;
Almost a Stranger ev'n to *British* Eyes,
We scarcely knew him in the rude Disguise :
But cloath'd by Thee, the burnish'd Bard appears
In all his Glory, and new Honours wears.
Thus *Ennius* was by *Virgil* chang'd of old ;
He found him Rubbish, and he left him Gold.

1707. Unknown. *Of the Old English Poets and Poetry; An Essay* [in] The Muses Mercury or Monthly Miscellany, for the Month of June, vol. i, no. 6, pp. 127–33.

.... the French stand in as much need of a Dictionary to understand the old Poem, call'd the *Romance of the Rose*, which is one of their oldest Pieces in Verse, as we do to read *Robert of Gloucester ;* not to say *Chaucer*, with whom how-

[p. 128] ever his Readers will now and then be puzzl'd, if they don't know a little *French* and a little *Dutch* too, there is so much of the *Saxon* or *German* Tongue in his Language. ... The French ... As for their *Romance of the Rose*, of which they talk as much as we do of *Chaucer's* Poems, we have more Right to it than they, for the Author was an *English-man*, his name *John Moon :* He was a Student in *Paris*, and there writ that Poem, which *Chaucer* translated into *English* ... The *English*, till *Chaucer's* time, might be look'd upon to be no more than a confus'd Mixture of *Saxon* and the *Norman* Jargon . . . .

[p. 130] About 70 Years after *Longland* [*sic*] came *Chaucer*, the Father of the English Poesy, of whom an old Historian writes, *He was a Man so exquisitely learn'd in all Sciences that his Match was not easily found anywhere in those days*, etc., etc. [*i. e.* John Pits, *see* below, p. 659, Appendix A, *a.* 1616.]

Chaucer, as much as he reform'd our Tongue, found it so rude, that he left a great deal to be done by those that came after him. His Numbers are in some places as hobling as his Contemporaries ; in others as harmonious as ours. [Then follows a comparison between Chaucer and Lydgate, greatly

[p. 131] in favour of the latter, including this remark :] Let the Wit of this Monk be what it will, his English, and his Numbers, are more polish'd than his Master's . . . .

1708. Downes, John. *Roscius Anglicanus or an Historical Review of the Stage*, p. 30.

The *M*an's the *M*aster, Wrote by Sir *William Davenant*, being the last Play he ever Wrote, he Dying presently after ; and was Bury'd in *Westminster-Abbey*, near *M*r. *Chaucer's* *M*onument, Our whole Company attending his Funeral.

1708. [Freind, Robert.
  Atterbury, Francis.
  Smalridge, George.] *Monument to John Philips in Westminster Abbey erected by Simon Harcourt Knight.* Westmonasterium by John Dart, 1742, vol. i, pp. 82–4.]

[The long latin inscription contains the following lines :]

O Poesis Anglicanæ Pater atq*ue* Conditur [*sic*] CHAUCERE
Alterum Tibi latus claudere
Vatum certe Cineres Tuos undiq*ue* stipantium
Non dedecebit Chorum.

[Philips died in Feb. 1708. The article under his name in D. N. B. states that this inscription has been attributed to all three of the above.]

1708. [**Hatton,** Edward.] *A New View of London or an ample account of that City,* vol. ii, pp. 527–8.

St. Peter's Westminster, . . . *Geoffrey Chaucer,* a learned and admirable Poet, his Monument is on the E. side of the S. Cross. . . .

[Then follow a description of the Monument, a copy of the inscription and references to John Weever's account of the tomb. *See* above, 1631, p. 204.]

1708. Hearne, Thomas. *Extract from his Diary,* Sept. 29, 1708. [in] Remarks and Collections of Thomas Hearne, ed. C. E. Doble, Oxford Hist. Soc., vol. iii, 1886, p. 136.

Look upon Chaucer's Translation of Boëthius de Consolatione, in 8vo, p[r]inted at y° Exempt Monastery of Tavistoke in Denshire . . .

At yᵉ end of yᵉ Translation of Boethius by Chaucer (quære) 4°. L. 21, Art. in Bibl. Bodl. [Here Hearne gives the colophon.]

1708. Hearne, Thomas. *Letter to Mr. Bagford,* [dated] Oxon, Dec. 20, 1708, [in] Robert of Gloucester's Chronicle, ed. T. Hearne, 1724, vol. ii, Glossary, p. 708.

[The letter describes an edition of John Walton of Osney's translation of Boethius, 1525.] When I first saw this Book, I guess'd, that it might have been *Chaucer's*; but I presently recollected, that his is in Prose.
[*See* above, 1410, pp. 20–1.]

1708. Prior, Matthew. *The Turtle and Sparrow. An Elegiac Tale Occasioned by the Death of Prince George,* 1708. (Prior's Poetical Works, ed. R. Brimley Johnson (Aldine edn.), 1892, vol. ii, p. 209.)

Those fowl who seem alive to sit,
Assembled by Dan Chaucer's wit,
In prose have slept three hundred years :
Exempt from worldly hopes and fears,

And, laid in state upon their hearse,
Are truly but embalm'd in verse.

[This poem was printed separately in 1723 as "The turtle and the sparrow, a poem by the late Matthew Prior." It did not appear in the 1718 edn. of his poems, but the title given is in the edn. of 1892.]

1708. Rymer, Thomas. *Foedera,* etc., 1704–32, vol. vi (1708), pp. 567, 756.

[p. 567. Grant to Chaucer of 20 marks yearly, 20 June, 1367; *see* above, p. 1. *Ib.*, p. 756: Commission, appointing Chaucer and others as envoys to treat with the Duke, citizens and merchants of Genoa, 12 Nov., 1372; *see* above, p. 2.]

1709. Bagford, John. *Letters to Thomas Hearne,* dated April 14 and May 3, 1709. MS. Rawl. Lett: 21, ff. 8 and 9. [abstracts in] Remarks and Collections of T. Hearne, Oxford Hist. Soc., vol. ii, ed. C. R. Doble, 1886, pp. 186, 192.

[To T. Hearne] Apr. 14. . . . as for yᵉ Chausier I neuer intended the returne of it nor any thin else I euer send if ther [*sic*] are worth you exceptance and paying yᵉ Carridge in a lettle time I shall send you a shet of paper by me Collected Relating to yᵉ seuirall Imprison of Chausier which will geue you less troble. . . .

May 3. I geue you my hartey thanks for your last kind Letter and next thursday you will receue a parsell by yᵉ Cayrier with my obseruations and yᵉ seuirall Impresiones of Chausers Workes which I am apt to thinke none hetherto as I haue herd of hath taken yᵉ like paynes and all of them from yᵉ Bookes themselues which haue run throw my handes.

I would not haue you Rune ouer yᵉ MSS. of Chausier [*sic*] Workes but onley to know what [MS. torn] n[um]ber: you haue & whare lodged for that would be an enless [*sic*] worke.

My desier is onley to haue yᵉ printed Copeyes loked ouer with yᵉ dates & printers Names.

1709. Hearne, Thomas. *Extracts from his Diary,* April 18, 24, May 9, 12, 18, 24, 1709 [in] Remarks and Collections of Thomas Hearne, ed. C. E. Doble, Oxford Hist. Soc. vol. ii, 1886, pp. 188, 190, 194–202.

[p. 188]   April 18 (Mon.) . . . Chaucers in yᵉ Bodlej. Library, MS.— Laud G. 69. His Canterbury Tales.—K. 50. His Canterbury Tales, except yᵉ Plow-man's Tale.—Of yᵉ Astrolabe Digby,

72.—N.E. D. 1. 16. Of yᵉ Astrolabe.—Super Art. A. **32.**
His Tales.—Archiv. Seld. B. 24. His Troylus, with other
Poëms of his.—Arch. Seld. B. 30. His Tales.—Seld. Supra
56. His Troilus and Cressida.—Seld. Supra 60. His Workes
printed by Richard Pynson.—Mus. 64. Of yᵉ Astrolabe.—
Fairfax 16. Some Poëms by Chaucer, & others.—Charles
Hatton. Numb. 1. Chaucer's Works.—Junius 9. His Works,
with some Marginal notes MS. by Junius.—About Sʳ. G.
Chaucer in Leland's Itin. vol. II, fol. 6.—Pedigree of Geff.
Chaucer. See at yᵉ Beginning of his Works. Edit. opt. . . .
—Chaucer in his Man of Lawes Tale, Part 2ᵈ. calleth yᵉ
Baptisterium the *Font-Stone.*—Mauricius at Fontstone they
hym calle.

[p. 190] April 24 (Sun.). [Notes from Chaucer in the *Clerke of
Oxenfordes Prologue*] . . .

[p 194] May 9 (Mon.). Arch. Seld. B. 30. Chaucer's Canterbury
Tales. A very good MS. written in Velam, I believe not long
after yᵉ time that Chaucer liv'd. [Here follows the order of
[p 195] the Tales, and the conclusion of the MS. "Here enden the
Talis of Caunturbury, and next thautour taketh leve" . . .
"the booke of Seint Valenty."] The Conclusion conteyning
Chaucer's acknowledgment of his Faults &c. not in the Print.
The Booke of Seint Valenty, & the Booke of xxv Ladies
(unless it be the same with the Assembly of Ladies) not in
his Printed Works. List of yᵉ Canterbury Tales, alphabetical,
from the last Edition.[1]

The Wife of Bathe's Tale. 1. 2. 3. 4. 5.
The Chanon's Yeoman's T. 1. 2. 4. 5. deest 3.
Chaucer's T. 1. 2. 4. 5. deest 3.
The Cookes T. 1. 2. 3. 4. 5.
The Frankeleine's T. 1. 2. 3. 4. 5.
The Freres T. 1. 2. 3. 4. 5.
The Knight's T. 1. 2. 3. 4. 5.
The Man of Laws T. 1. 2. 3. 4. 5.
The Manciple's T. 1. 2. 4. 5. deest 3.
The Marchant's T. 1. 2. 3. 4. 5.
The Miller's T. 1. 2. 3. 4. 5.
The Monke's T. 1. 2. 4. 5. deest 3.

[1] The Mark 1. denotes MS. Arch. Seld. B. 30. When only 1. or 2.
&c., is put it shows that tale is in the MS.: but deest added it shews that
the same Tale is wanting.—The Mark 2. Laud K. 50.—3. Cod. super.
Art. A. 32.—4. Pynson's Edition of yᵉ Tales. 5. MS. Caroli Hatton
num. 1. [Hearne's note.]

The Second Nonne's T. 1. 2. 3. 4. 5.
The Nonne's Priest's T. 1. 2. 4. 5. deest 3.
The Clerk of Oxenford's T. 1. 2. 3. 4. 5.
The Pardoner's T. 1. 2. 3. 4. 5.
The Parson's . 1. 2. 4. 5. deest 3.
The Doctor of Phisick's T. 1. 2. 3. 4. 5.
The Plowman's T. deest 1. 2. 3. 4.
The Prioresse's T. 1. 2. 3. 4. 5.
The Prologues to ye whole. 1. 2. 3. 4. 5.
The Reve's T. 1. 2. 3. 4. This is call'd the **Carpenter's**
    Tale in Cod. 5.
The Shipman's T. 1. 2. 3. 4. 5.
The Sompnour's T. 1. 2. 3. 4. 5.
The Squire's T. 1. 2. 3. 4. 5.
The Rime of S^r. Topas. 1. 2. 3. 4. 5.

The Plowman's Tale is not in the MSS. If it were Chaucer's, it was left perhaps out of his Canterbury Tales, for ye Tartness against the Popish Clergy. It is very probable that it was severally *written* by Chaucer, and not as one of the Tales; which were supposed to be *spoken*, & not *written*. [Here follow some remarks, with quotation from Plowman's Tale, as at end of Hearne's Letter to Bagford *q.v.* below, p. 309] . . .

  .   .   .   .

At the Beginning of the Astrolabe of the last Ed.—
This Booke (written to his Sonne in the year of our Lord 1391, and in the 14 of K. Richard 2) standeth so good at this day, especially for the Horizon of Oxford, as in the opinion of the learned, it cannot be amended.

It was therefore written 9 years before his Death, viz. in the 63 year of his age, he being 72 Years old when he died. See his Life, written it was to his son Lewis, whom he calleth his little sonne Lewys, at ye beginning.

Arch. Seld. B. 24. Troilus & Cressida, and several other Pieces of Chaucer. At the End of Troilus is this Note, written in ye same Hand with ye Book, viz. Nativitas principis nostri Jacobi quarti anno Domini miiij^c. lxxij^o. & vij die mensis Marcij, viz. in festo Sancti Patricij Confessoris In Monasterio sanctæ Crucis prope Edinburgh. That wch is in ye Print call'd *The Complaint of the blacke Knight* is here call'd *the Maying and Disporte of Chaucere*.

The Parson's Tale in Chaucer's Cant. Tales in MS. Hatton (Caroli) num. 1, wch MS. seems to have been written either

in the author's Life Time, or very soon after, concludes thus:
[quotes the full ending, 'This blisfull regne' . . . 'Qui cum
patre, &c.'].

[p. 197] Chaucer not of Oxfordsh.—or Barksh. as Leland supposed,
but of London, as appears from his Testament of Love. His
Father suppos'd to be Rich. Chaucer vintner of Lond. in
the 23 of Ed. 3. Eliz. Chaucer, in Rich. II^{ds}. time, a
Nunne, who was perhaps his sister, or at least one of his
Relations. The nobili loco of Leland & Bale to be understood of the Place of his Nativity, he being not of great Birth,
as appears from his arms, wch were parted per Pale arg. & g.
a Bend counterchang'd. Yet this argument rejected by the
writer of his Life. Chaucer came in withe ye Conqueror, as
appears from the Roll of Battle-Abbey. Some think his
Father was a Merchant, but y^t is uncertain. 'Tis however
certain that his Parents were wealthy, otherwise they could
not have given their son such Education as to render him fit
for the Court, & to qualify for Business of State abroad. He
was educated both at Oxford and Cambridge.

May 12 (Th.). . . . .

[p. 198] Troilus and Creseida of Chaucer MS. in Bibl. Bodl. Seld.
supra 56. written anno Dni. 1441, anno Regni H. VI. 19.—
MS. Fairfax 16. contains several Poetical Pieces. Some
bear Chaucer's Name, others have no Name, but I conjecture
that they were however written by him, tho' not amongst his
printed Pieces.

[p. 199] May 18 (Wed.). Leland saith that Chaucer was nobili loco
natus, & summæ spei juvenis.—William Botevil alias Thinne
Esqr. publish'd Chaucer & dedicated it to K. Hen. VIII.
anno 1540. After y^t in 1560 John Stow corrected the same
with divers MSS., and added several Pieces not printed
before. Afterwards in 1597 he added to it several Pieces of
Lidgate, and drew up an Account of Chaucer's Life, Preferment, Issue & Death, collected out of Records in ye Tower
& other Places, wch he communicated to Thomas Spight
[*sic*] to be publish'd, wch was accordingly performed. Stow's
Annals Edit. fol. p. 326.—Thinne found the Editions before
his time of Chaucer very faulty, wch he therefore corrected
according to MSS. See his Ded. to K. Hen. 8. His Edition was
printed at Lond. in 1540. by Thomas Bertholet [*sic*] as appears
from Leland.—Mr. Ashmole p. 227. of his Theatrum Chem.
Lond. 1652, 4°. has printed Geoff. Chaucer's Tale of y^e

Chanon's Yeoman, and before it he has added Chaucer's
Picture and Epitaph from Westminster Abbey. Pitts says
Chaucer was born of Noble Parents, and that Patrem habuit
equestris ordinis virum, his Father was a Knight.—

The Plough-Man's Tale.   Shewing by y⁰ Doctrine and lives
of the Romish Clergie that the Pope is anti-christ and they
his ministers, written by sir Geffrey Chaucer, Knight, amongst
his Canterburie Tales : and now set apart from the rest, with
short exposition of the words & matters, for y⁰ capacitie and
understanding of y⁰ simpler sort of Readers.   Lond. 1606,
printed by G. E. for Samuell Macham & Matthew Cooke. 4⁰.
S. 77, Art. Seld.   There is no Preface, nor any Account of
y⁰ Publisher in this Copy.   At y⁰ Beginning the Author of y⁰
Notes (wᶜʰ are very good) says, . . . [quotes from these : "In
the former Editions . . . written near to Chawcer's time."
See above, p. 177, Ploughman's Tale, 1606].   The Title Page of
our Pynson's Edition of Chaucer's Tales, amongst Mr. Selden's
MSS. is wanting, as is also the date.   But there is the
Preface of Mʳ. Pynson.   From yᵗ Preface it appears that he
printed these Tales according to a Copy prepared in due
Method by Mʳ. Wᵐ. Caxton, but I much doubt whether
Caxton ever printed all y⁰ Tales, & am of opinion that he
printed only some Pieces of his works, notwithstanding what
Stow and others say.

In the Bodl. Library is a Collection of old Romantick Pieces,
the first of wᶜʰ is The story of y⁰ Noble Kynge Richard Cure de
lyon, pr. at Lond. by Wynkyn de Worde an. 1528, without
[p. 200] y⁰ Author's Name, but somebody has written at y⁰ Beginning
these words, *By Jeffree Chawsher Pooet Laret.*   It is adorned
with wooden Cutts.   .   .   .   .   .   .
John Shirley Esqr. lyes buried in St. Bartholomew's Church,
Lond.   He was a great Traveller in divers Countries, &
amongst other his Labours, painfully collected the works of
Geffrey Chawcer, John Lidgate, and other learned writers ; wᶜʰ
workes he wrote in sundry volumes, to remain for posterity :
Mʳ. Stow says he had seen them, and that he had some of
them in his Possession.   See Survey of London, p. 416.   He
died anno 1456.   .   .   .   .   .   .

I believe the Revocation annex'd to the Parson's Tale in
some Copies of Chaucer not to be genuine, but made by the
Monks, who were strangely exasperated for the Freedom he
took, especially in the Plow-man's Tale of exposing their

Pride, Loosness and Debauchery. . . . Pitts
mentions among Chaucer's Works *Oratoris* (read *aratoris*)
narratio, wch he takes to be the same with Pierce Plow-man,
and tells us 'tis exstant in MS.^t at Oxon. and Cambridge.
He also mentions Chaucer's Canterbury Tales, with his
Retractation, as being in MS. in the Lord Lumley's Library.

[p. 201]   May 24 (Tu.). It appeareth from ye Testament of Love
that G. Chaucer was in some Trouble in the days of Rich.
2^d. where he complains very much of his own Rashness in
[p. 202] following the multitude, & of their hatred against him for
bewraying their Purpose. And in that complaint wch he makes
to his empty purse M^r. Speght found ten times more adjoyned
in a MS.^t of it in Mr. Stowes hands than is in the Print,
making therein great Lamentation for his wrongfull Imprisonment, wishing Death to end his Dayes. And 'tis plain from
a Record in ye Tower that the King took Geff. Chaucer & his
Lands into his Protection in ye 2^d. year of his Reign, because
there was much Danger from him by reason of his favouring
some rash attempt of the common People.—Some of his
Canterbury Tales were translated and penned in the Days of
Rich. 2^d., after the insurrection of Jack Straw, wch was in
the 4th year of y^t King's Reign, & whereof Chaucer maketh
Mention in the Tale of the Nunne's Prest.

[1709.] Hearne, Thomas. *A Letter to Mr.* Bagford, *containing some
Remarks upon* Geffry Chaucer *and his Writings* [in] Robert of
Gloucester's Chronicle, ed. Thomas Hearne, 1724, vol. ii, Appendix
iv, pp. 596–606.

Sir,

§ 1. A laudable   I cannot but highly commend your In-
Undertaking, to   dustry, in being so inquisitive into the Life
endeavour to give
an Account of the and Writings of *Geffry Chaucer*, the Prince
Life and Writings of our *English* Poëts; and I am extremely
of *Geffry Chaucer*. oblig'd to you, for the Account you sent me
of the Editions of him, that you have hitherto met with.
Would others but imitate your Diligence, we should understand this excellent Poët much better than we do, and be
able to give a far more correct Edition of him than has hitherto appear'd. Such an Undertaking will derive great Honour
upon those, that shall ingage in it, and will be gratefully
receiv'd by all true Scholars and Antiquaries. For *Chaucer*
was not only an excellent Poët, but was admirably well

vers'd in most Parts of Learning. And besides his profound
Learning, he was a compleat Gentleman, & skill'd in all the
Arts of Address. These Qualifications made him belov'd and
honour'd, and his Conversation & Acquaintance were courted
by the Greatest Personages, insomuch that he was sent
Ambassadour into Forreign Parts, where he came of [*sic*] with
as much Applause, as he did in any of his Performances in his
own Native Country. This does not seem to be at all owing
to his Birth, his Father, notwithstanding wealthy, being, in
all probability, only a Merchant; tho' I know, that *Leland*,
in which he is follow'd by *Bale*, tells us, that he was *nobili
loco natus*, which seems to be a mistake, there being no
Evidence now remaining, that we know of, to confirm such an
[p. 597] Assertion, unless it be that from the Roll of *Battle-Abbey* we
learn, that the *Chaucers* came with the Conqueror into
England, and that *Pitts* tells us, that his Father was a Knight.
Nor are we uncertain only as to his Ancestors, and his Quality,
but there are a great many other Particulars relating to him,
which, at present, we know nothing of, which I am perswaded
we might be satisfied in by a diligent Inspection into antient
Records. I have not time myself to assist in any such
Attempt : and therefore I leave it to your self and others, who
have both leisure and opportunity of going through so desirable
a Work.

§ 2. In which
we have *William
Caxton*, and
several other
eminent Persons
for Precedents.
We have several eminent Persons for
Precedents in this usefull Inquiry, which
cannot but add Life and Vigour to those
who concern themselves in it. For soon
after Printing was established in this Island,
William Caxton, besides divers other good Books, set himself carefully about searching out and publishing the several
Pieces of *Geffry Chaucer ;* but I much question whether he
printed divers of them together. For tho' *Stow* and some
others inform us, that he was the first that publish'd his
Works, yet I believe they are to be understood of some Pieces
printed by him in distinct and small Volumes, and not after
the Method that was follow'd by his Successors. For *Richard
Pynson*, in his Preface to his Edition of the *Canterbury Tales*
(which we have amongst Mr. *Selden*'s MSS., and contains
nothing else) acquaints us, that he printed them from a Copy,
that was prepar'd for the Press by his Master *William Caxton*,
but gives not the least Hint that they had been before

printed. *Caxton* and *Pynson* having spent their time so
successfully upon *Chaucer*, and so much to the Content and
Approbation of learned Men, others were soon animated to
[p. 598] advance and promote what they had begun ; and accordingly
several Editions follow'd with Improvements, as you have
particularly specify'd in your Paper : but *Caxton* and *Pynson*
were exceeded in their Labours by *William Botevil*, alias
Thinne, Esq., who having collected all the old Copies of
Chaucer that he could any ways procure, and having with great
Exactness corrected a vast number of Places, and made considerable Additions, amongst which must not be passed by his
Notes and Explications, publish'd the Work in one Volume in
Folio in the Year [1] MDXL. (not in MDXLII. as Mr. *Wood* insinuates [2]) which was printed at *London* by *Thomas Bertholet* [*sic*],
as is noted by Mr. *Leland*,[3] and dedicated to K. *H.* VIII.
Twenty Years after this *John Stow* [4] the Antiquary collated
this Edition with several MSS. (some of which, I suppose,
are part of those that had been collected a great many Years
before by *John Shirley* Esq., who died in the Year MCCCLVI [5]
and not in MCCCLXV. as you mistake) added some Pieces not
printed before, and in the Year MDXCVII. joyn'd to him divers
Poëms of *Lidgate ;* which being done, he drew up an Account
of *Chaucer's* Life, of his Preferment, Issue and Death, collected
out of Records in the Tower and other Places, which he at
length communicated to *Thomas Speght*, who publish'd him
the same Year, with the said Improvements of *Stow* and his
own, and methodiz'd his Life according to his own Judgment.
After this *Francis Thinne*, *Lancaster*-Herald at Arms, a
Person very well vers'd in Antiquities, and descended, as it
seems,[6] from the before mentioned *William Thinne*, but not
[p. 599] his Son as is affirm'd by *Speght* in his Life of *Chaucer*, corrected
this Edition in abundance of Places, drew up several Notes to
it, and put them into the Hands of the said Mr. *Speght*, who
remitted them into another Edition of *Chaucer* printed in
Folio in MDCII. which is the most compleat Edition we have
yet, and, besides the Explication of old and obscure Words,
contains great Variety of Improvements, that were not in
former Impressions. But I shall not trouble you with a
Catalogue of the Editions of *Chaucer*, which you are acquainted

[1] See *Stow's* Annals Edit. fol. p. 326, and Mr. *Leland* de Scriptorib.
in vita *Chauceri.*
[2] *Athenæ Oxon.*, vol. i, col. 53.   [3] Loco citato.
[4] See his Annals loc. cit.   [5] See *Stow's Survey of London*, p. 416.
[6] See *Wood's Athenæ Oxon.*, vol. i, col. 320.

with far better than I can pretend to. I shall, however, if I
meet with any Edition, that you have not specify'd, let you
know of it; and in the mean time I must take notice, that I
have seen some Pieces of him printed separately that you
have not mention'd, and 'tis likely I may meet with others
hereafter in my Searches. Amongst Mr. *Selden's* printed
Books in the *Bodleian* Library is a *Quarto* Collection of old
Romantick Pieces, the first of which is, *The story of the noble
Kynge Richard Cure de Lyon*, pr. at *London* by *Wynkyn de
Worde an.* MDXXVIII. The Author's name is not added, and
therefore 'tis put down in Dr. *Hyde's* Catalogue as an
anonymous Tract; but, upon consulting the Book, I find, that
some body, perhaps one that was formerly Owner of it, has
writ the following Words at the Beginning, *By Jeffree Charsher
Pooet Laret*. What Authority he had for this, I will not
pretend to guess; but I thought fit to give you an account of
it, that you may, at your leisure, examine into it. In the
same Library we have another Collection of old *English* Pieces,
which was also Mr. *Selden's*, in which is the *Ploughman's
Tale*, with a short Exposition of the Words and Matters, pr.
at *Lond*, MDCVI. *Quarto*. This Exposition is very usefull, and
the Author, who, it may be, was the said *Francis Thinne*,
[p. 600] shews himself to be a Man of Skill, and to have been a Master
of *Chaucer*. Besides these two Pieces, I must hint to you,
that the famous Mr. *Elias Ashmole* has printed, *The Tale of
the Chanon's Yeoman*, in his *Theatrum Chem.*[1] [*see above*, 1652,
p. 227] (before which he has put *Chaucer's* Picture and
Epitaph from *Westminster-Abbey*) and that in his *Museum*
at *Oxford* is *The Miller's Tale*, and *The Tale of the Wife of
Bath*, with Comments, pr. at *London* in MDCLXV. [*see ante*, 1665,
p. 242] which last I have not yet seen; but I shall take the
first opportunity to do it, and I will not fail to let you
know the Issue of my Inquiry.

§ 3. Who nevertheless have not been so exact in their Editions, but that they might be still corrected and supply'd from MSS. and some Tracts added that were never yet publish'd.

But notwithstanding these excellent
Persons Labours were so successfull, as that
they may seem, perhaps, to some to have
superseded all future Attempts, yet I may
with Modesty assert, that a much more
correct and compleat Edition of *Chaucer*
might be given than any that has hitherto
appear'd. I have consulted some of our
Oxford MSS. and find that the Print is in a

[1] Pag. 227.

CHAUCER CRITICISM.

great many Places corrupted, that in other Places whole Verses
are wanting, which might by these Helps be supply'd, that
sometimes the Titles of the Tales are chang'd, and that, lastly,
intire Tracts might be added, that were never yet made publick.
I took more particular notice of one MS. there,[1] which is a
Collection of Poëms, some whereof bear *Chaucer*'s name, and
others have no name at all, which, nevertheless, I take to
have been written by him, as being in the same Style, and all
in the same Hand, which I guess to have been of the very
Age of *Chaucer*. From this Collection, from those that were
in Mr. *Stow*'s Library, from that mention'd by Mr. *Edw.*
Philips in his *Theatrum Poëtarum* [*see* above, 1675, p. 250],
[p. 601] and from a multitude of others, we might, in all likelyhood,
make another intire Volume of *Chaucer* in *Folio*.

§ 4. A Frag-
ment of *The*
Squire's Tale,
with a Passage at
the End of *The*
Parson's Tale, by
which *Chaucer*
revokes some of
his Works.

I shall not give myself the Trouble of
multiplying Instances, to confirm what is
before asserted, since those cannot but be
obvious to every one, that shall have the
Curiosity to inspect and examine a little the
MSS. Yet I think it proper at present to
inform you, that as the Prologue of *the*
Squire's Tale, in an excellent MS. of Mr. *Selden*'s,[2] is quite
different from that in the Print, so there are eight Verses in
the Tale itself, which are not in the Common Editions. For
whereas we have receiv'd as yet but two Verses of the third
Part, with a Note signifying, that none of the rest, notwithstanding diligently sought after, could be recover'd, we have
here the following ones, which immediately precede the two
already printed, *viz.*

> But I here now wol maken a knotte,
> To the tyme it come nexte to my lotte.
> For here ben felawes behynde an hepe truly,
> That wolden talke ful besily,
> And habe here sporte, as wel as I,
> And the day passith certeynly.
> Therfore Oste taketh now good hede,
> Who shal nexte telle, and late him spede.

And whereas you mention a Passage, intit'led *Penitentia ut*
dicitur pro fabula Rectoris, by which *Chaucer* revok'd several

---

[1] Inter Codd. *Fairfaxii*, num. **16.**
[2] Arch. B. 30, in Bibl. *Bodl.*

of his Books, that you found printed in an Edition of his
Poëms with Mr. *Tanner*, which you have not seen in any
other, I must, withall, acquaint you, that I have found the
[p. 602] same Revocation in a[1] MS. in the *Bodleian* Library, which
because it is fuller than that you mention, and somewhat
different, I shall transcribe at large. *Now prey I to hem
all, that herken this litul tretise or reden, that if ther be
any thing in it, that liketh hem, that thereof thei thanken
our Lorde Ihesu Crist, of whom procedeth alle witte and
all goodenesse. And if there be anything, that displese
hem, I prey hem also, that thei arrecte it to the defaute of
myn unkonnyng, and not to my will, that wold fayne habe
seid better, if I hadde konnyng: for our boke seith, that
al that is written for oure doctrine, & that is myn entent.*
. . . [Here the whole passage is given which is printed at the
end of the *Persones Tale*, ll. 1082–92.]

This Passage immediately follows these words, *And the
rest by trabaile and the life by deth and mortification of*
[p. 603] *Syn*, and is so continued with the Tale, as if it were part of
it; but tho' this Revocation be also extant in the above mention'd MS. of Mr. *Selden*, yet it is written as distinct from the
Tales, which conclude with that of *the Parson*. For thus
it is brought in, *Here enden the Talis of Caunturbury, and
next thantour taketh leue.—Now preye I to hem alle &c.*
So that it begins just as that which I have transcrib'd
above; but however is much shorter, ending with *the Booke
of Seint Valenty*.

Besides the Tracts said in this Revocation to have been
written by *Chaucer*, and the Difference of
§ 5. This Revo-
cation seems not
genuine, but to
have been added
by the Monks.
the three Copies, *viz.* our two, and that in
Mr. *Tanner*'s Book, we may observe, that
the Scribe has intit'led himself to a share in
the Petition: whence I begin to think,
that the Revocation is not genuine, but that it was made
by the Monks. For not only the Regular, but Secular,
Clergy were exasperated against *Chaucer*, for the Freedom he
had taken to expose their Lewdness and Debauchery; but
nothing gave them so much offense, as the *Plowman's Tale*,
in which he has, in lively Colours, describ'd their Pride,
Covetousness, and abominable Lusts, and shew'd that the

---

[1] Inter Codd. *Caroli Hattoni*, num. 1.

Pope is *Anti-Christ,* and they his Ministers. Such a Satyr, made by a Person of his Note and Distinction, and so much celebrated for his wonderfull fine Parts and exquisite Learning and Judgment, could not but work mightily upon them, especially when many of them had arriv'd at so high a Pitch of Wickedness, and were, as it were, drown'd in Sloath and Luxury, being much worse now than their Predecessors above three hundred Years before, when most of even the Bishops themselves were illiterate, tho' ador'd and flatter'd upon account of their Dignity and unbounded Wealth, and attended [p. 604] upon by an amazing Number of Servants and Sycophants.

§ 6. If it be sup-
pos'd to be authen-
tick, 'tis likely
'twas written by
Chaucer towards
the latter end of
Richard the
second's Reign, he
being then old
and in disgrace,
for striking in
with the Multi-
tude in some dan-
[p. 605] gerous Enterprize.

But if, notwithstanding, what has been alleg'd, it be suppos'd, that this Revocation is authentick, and that 'twas penn'd by *Chaucer* himself, we may then conjecture, that 'twas done by him towards the latter end of the Reign of *Richard* II. when having lost the favour of his Prince, and most of his noble Friends here, and being, withall, grown old, he retired himself from the Pleasures of the World, and reflected seriously upon the Changes and Infirmities to which humane Nature is subject. This Consideration, with the thoughts of a future State, could not but make him renounce the Vanities of this Life, and retract those Passages, which he perceiv'd, either had [done] or might do Mischief to Religion and Morality. After which he became quite weary of this Life, and seem'd to have no relish for any thing in it; tho' that may be attributed chiefly, perhaps, to the Mis-fortunes which happen'd to him, he and his Lands being taken into the King's Protection in the second Year of his Reign, because of some danger that seem'd to threaten from his favouring and striking in with the rash Attempts of the common-people. Whatever this Attempt was, whether Rebellion, or something bordering upon it, 'tis certain he forfeited the Love of his Prince and most of his Friends, and he was forced to lead afterwards a melancholy Life, which often extorted from him grievous Complaints, parti-cularly of his own Rashness in following the Multitude, and sometimes would wish to exchange Life for Death,[1] which

---

[1] This may be seen in the Complaint he made to his empty Purse, which *Mr. Speght* found ten times larger in *Mr. Stow's* MS. than in the Print.

Misery, however, was fortunate in this, that it prepar'd him
the better for Eternity, and influenced him to retract all the
loose Things in his Writings.

§ 7. The reason
why the *Plough-*
man's Tale is
found but in few
MSS. Some think
'twas not *Chau-*
cer's, but if his,
it is improperly
call'd a Tale.

Now the *Plough-man's Tale* having given
more offence than all the rest of *Chaucer's*
Works, perhaps that is the reason why it
appears in so few MSS. I have not
found it in one of those I have consulted at
Oxford, which has made some think, that
'tis not *Chaucer's*, and this they believe
confirm'd from the Style, which is different
from his other Poëms. *Mr. Pitts* confounds it with the
Satyr, that is call'd *Piers Plowman*; but the Publishers have
skillfully ascrib'd it to him, being warranted from a MS. in
Mr. Stow's Library; tho' it must be confessed, that 'tis not
properly term'd a Tale, and it does not seem to have been put
as one of the Tales by the Author himself: for they were
suppos'd[1] to have been *spoken* and not *written*, as this is
plainly said to be, the Plowman concluding thus:

> To holy Church I will me bow,
>   Ech man to amend him Christ send space:
> And for my writing me allow
>   He, that is almighty, for his Grace.

The same word of *writing* is there made use of several
times: as, *For my writing if I habe blame* —— and,
Of my writing habe me excused: which seems to me an
undeniable Argument, that it was not delivered as all the
rest were.

I might from this occasion insist upon divers other Particulars, but I have already exceeded the Bounds of a Letter,
and I am afraid I have quite tired your Patience. I hope,
however, you will take what I have said as an instance of my
Readiness to serve you, being, with all sincerity,

   Sir,

     Your very humble Servant,

       Tho. Hearne.

[A MS. note by W. Thomas in Urry's edn. of Chaucer's Works, 1721, B.M. pr. m.
648. m. 4, on blank leaf to f. p. 32, states that this letter was written in 1709.]

[1] See a Note at the Beginning of the Tales in MS. (in Bibl. *Bodl.* inter Codd.
Laud. K. 50) by *John Barcham.* [*See above*, 1642, pp. 221-2.]

1709. Hearne, Thomas. *Letter to Robert Harley, after Earl of Oxford,* May 28, 1709. MSS. Marquis of Bath, Longleat [in Report iii of Roy. Comm. Hist. MSS., p. 198, col. i, 1872].

[This letter (which is not printed in the Hist. MSS.) concerns the various edns. and copies of Chaucer's poems. MSS. Cod. Fairfax, 16 ; Cod. Hatton, 1, and Selden MS. B. 30 are cited.]

[1709.] King, William. *The Art of Love: in Imitation of Ovid De Arte Amandi.* London . . [1709], pp. 59, 60.

> *Achilles,* a Gigantick Boy,
> Was wanted at the Siege of *Troy :*
>
> .   .   .   .
>
> *Venus,* although not over virtuous,
> Yet still designing to be courteous,
> Resolv'd for to procure the Varlet
> A flaming and triumphant Harlot ;
> First stol'n by one she would not stay with,
> Then married to be run away with.
> Her *Paris* carried to his Mother,
> And thence in *Greece* arose that Pother,
> Of which old *Homer, Virgil, Dante,*
> And *Chaucer* make us such a Cant.

1709. [Maynwaring or Mainwaring, Arthur.] *The Court of Love. A Tale from Chaucer* [in] Ovid's Art of Love . . . . translated into English Verse by Several Eminent Hands . . . To which are added The Court of Love . . . Printed for Jacob Tonson . . . 1709, pp. 351–68.

[The central idea of the poem and a few images are all that Maynwaring has given here. *See* below, 1715, p. 341, Oldmixon, John.]

1709. Pope, Alexander. *January and May, or the Merchant's Tale from Chaucer.* [in] Poetical Miscellanies, The Sixth Part, London, Printed for Jacob Tonson, 1709, pp. 177–224. (Works of Alexander Pope, ed. Rev. Whitwell Elwin and W. J. Courthope, 1871, vol. i, pp. 115–53.)

[The modern references to Pope are all to this latter edition, and are referred to in the entries below as " Works, 1871."]

[1709.] [Pope, Alexander.] *An Essay on Criticism,* Printed for W. Lewis, 1711, p. 28. (Works, 1871, vol. ii, p. 63.)

> Short is the date, alas ! of modern rhymes,
> And 'tis but just to let them live betimes.
> No longer now that golden age appears,
> When patriarch wits survived a thousand years

Now length of fame (our second life) is lost,
And bare threescore is all ev'n that can boast;
Our sons their fathers' failing language see,
And such as Chaucer is shall Dryden be,

[In "The Works of Mr. Alexander Pope," printed 1717, it states under the title that the Essay on Criticism was written in 1709. *See* below, p. 314-15, 367, 369, 379, 383.]

1709. Rymer, Thomas. *Foedera,* etc., 1704-1732, vol. vii (1709), p. 35 ; vol. viii (1709), pp. 39, 51, 94.

[Vol. vii (1709), p. 35. Grant to Chaucer of a pitcher of wine, 23 April, 1374 ; *see* above, p. 3.—Vol. viii (1709), p. 39. Royal protection for Chaucer for two years, 4 May 1398 ; *see* above, p. 13.—*Ib.* p. 51. Grant to Chaucer of a butt of wine yearly, 13 Oct. 1398 ; *see* above, p. 13.—*Ib.* p. 94. Confirmation by **Henry IV** to Chaucer of Richard II's two patents of 20 marks and a butt of wine yearly (Feb. 28 and 13 Oct. 1398), 18 Oct. 1399 ; *see* above, p. 13.]

[1709 ?] Smith, Edmund. *A Poem on the Death of Mr. John Philips, Author of the Splendid Shilling* . . . p. 7. Reprinted in Miscellaneous Poems and Translations by several Hands, B. Lintot, 1712, p. 156. (Works of the English Poets, by Dr. S. Johnson, additional lives by Alexander Chalmers, vol. ix, 1810, p. 205.)

Rail on, ye Triflers, who to *Will's* repair
For new Lampoons, fresh Cant, or modish Air ;
Rail on at *Milton's* Son, who wisely bold
Rejects new Phrases, and resumes the old :
Thus *Chaucer* lives in younger *Spencer's* Strains,
In *Maro's* Page reviving *Ennius* reigns ;
The ancient Words the Majesty compleat,
And make the Poem venerably great.

1709. Steele, Richard. *The Tatler,* No. 110, col. 2, Dec. 22, 1709. (The Tatler, ed. George A. Aitken, vol. ii, 1898, p. 402.)

I did not care for hearing a Canterbury tale.

17⅒. Steele, Richard. *The Tatler,* No. 132, Feb. 11, 1709. (The Tatler, ed. George A. Aitken, vol. iii, 1899, p. 102.)

I must own, it makes me very melancholy in Company when I hear a young Man begin a Story ; and have often observed that one of a Quarter of an Hour long in a Man of Five and Twenty, gathers Circumstances every Time he tells it, till it grows into a long *Canterbury* Tale of Two Hours by that Time he is Threescore.

[*a.* **1710.**] **Betterton,** Thomas. *Chaucer's Characters or the Introduction to the Canterbury Tales—The Miller of Trompington or the Reve's Tale from Chaucer.* [Printed in] Miscellaneous Poems and Translations by Several Hands, Printed for Bernard Lintot, 1712, pp. 245–82, and 301–20. Reprinted 1720, 1722. [A very free rendering of Chaucer's Prologue and Reeve's tale.]

[Betterton died in 1710. Warton relates that Harte told him that Fenton believed this version of the Prologue to be by Pope. *See* below, p. 500, 1797, Warton, and also Johnson's Lives of the Poets, below, p. 459, 1779–81.]

1710. [**Gildon,** Charles.] *Remarks on the Plays of Shakespear* [in] The works of . . . Shakespear, vol. vii, 1710, p. 358.

Shakespear is to be Excus'd in his falsifying the Character of *Achilles,* making him and *Ajax* perfect Idiots, . . . I say Shakespear is excusable in this because he follow'd *Lollius,* or rather *Chaucers* Translation of him. But Mr. *Dryden* who had *Homer* to guide him right in this particular, is unpardonable.

1710. Hearne, Thomas. *Extracts from his Diary,* Feb. 19, Aug. 2, Aug. 11, 1710, [in] Remarks and Collections of Thomas Hearne, ed. C. E. Doble, Oxford Hist. Soc., vol. ii, p. 347, vol. iii, pp. 32, 39.

Feb. 19 (Sun.). The Picture of Geofrey Chaucer in a MS^t. of his Tales in Bibl. Bodl. super. Art. A. 32.—

Aug. 2 (Wed.). . . . F. 1. 18. Th.—G. 2. 16. Th. We have in this Volume Geffry Chaucer's Translation of Boecius, printed by Caxton in the year I think 1515, & I believe 'tis not express'd in our Catalogue. Quære. At the End is a large Memorandum, about Chaucer by Caxton, & his Epitaph. . . .

Aug. 11 (Fri.). . . . 4to H. 24. Art. Chaucer's Troilus and Cresseida, in Latin & English. The Latin is a Translation by Sir Francis Kinaston, & the second Part is dedicated to M^r. John Rouse, Keeper of the Bodlejan Library, the first Part being dedicated to Patrick Young the King's Librarian.

[*See* above, p. 207, 1635, Kynaston.]

1710. [**Ruddiman,** Thomas.] *Virgil's Æneis translated into Scottish Verse by the famous Gawin Douglas Bishop of Dunkeld. A new edition . . . to which is added a large Glossary. Edinburgh,* 1710. Preface [pp. 2, 4], Glossary sign. C 2, F 2–G 1, H 1 *b.,* etc.; Y 1.

[Preface] . . . By the help of the *Glossary* one may not only understand this *Translation of Virgil,* but be also very much assisted to Read with profit any other book written in the same Language. Yea *Chaucer* and the other *English* Writers about that time are rendred more plain and easy by it . . .

[Pref.
p. 4] Some have blam'd Him for the *Inequality* of the *Measures* . . . but this has been no less objected against the *English Ennius Chaucer* himself . . .

1710. Bubb, Geo[rge]. *The Laurel and the Olive,* Inscrib'd to George Bubb, Esq. by Geo. Stubbes . . . p. iv. (Quoted by Dr. F. J. Furnivall in his edn. of Phil. Stubbes's Anatomie of Abuses, New Shaks. soc., pt. ii, 882, pp. xxxi[x]–xxxii[x].)

To the Author

. . . .

So when revolving Years have run their Race,
Bright the same Fires in different Bosoms blaze :
Known by his glorious Scars, and deathless Lines,
Again the *Hero,* and the *Poet* shines.
In gentler *Harison* soft *Waller* sighs,
And *Mira* wounds with *Sacharissa's* Eyes.
Achilles lives, and *Homer* still delights,
Whilst *Addison* records, and *Churchill* fights.
This happy Age each Worthy shall renew,
And all dissolv'd in pleasing Wonder, view
In Ann *Philippa, Chaucer* shine in You.

Geo. Bubb.

[1710.] Welsted, Leonard. *A Poem to the Memory of the incomparable Mr. J. Philips* [in] The Works in Verse and Prose of Leonard Welsted . . . collected . . . by John Nichols, 1787, pp. 23–4.

[p. 23] . . . Rearing with majestick pomp thy tomb,
Swells the big honours of that hallow'd dome,
Where their dark gloomy vaults the Muses keep.
And, lov'd by Monarchs, near those Monarchs sleep ;

. . . .

[p. 24] Justly in death with those one mansion have,
Whose works redeem their glories from the grave ;
Where venerable Chaucer's antient head,
And Spenser's much-ador'd remains are laid ;
Where Cowley's precious stone, and the proud mould
That glories Dryden's mortal parts to hold,
Command high reverence and devotion just
To their great relicks and distinguish'd dust.

17$\frac{1}{1}\frac{9}{7}$. Fenton, El[ijah]. *An Epistle to Mr. Southerne from Mr. El. Fenton,* From Kent, Jan. 28, 17$\frac{1}{1}\frac{9}{7}$, p. 14. (Works of the English Poets, ed. Dr. S. Johnson, additional lives by A. Chalmers, vol. x, 1810, p. 401.)

Chaucer had all that Beauty cou'd inspire,
And *Surry's* Numbers glow'd with warm Desire :

Both now are priz'd by few, unknown to most,
Because the Thoughts are in the Language lost;
Ev'n *Spencer's* Pearls in muddy Waters lye,
Rarely discover'd by the Diver's Eye :
Rich was their Imag'ry, till Time defac'd
The curious Works ; but *Waller* came at last.
Waller the Muse with Heavenly Verse supplies . . .

[Quoted by Samuel Pegge (the Elder) in Anonymiana, 1778, pr. 1809, pp. 344-5,
see below, 1778, p. 451 ; and by Dr. George Sewell, in his Memoirs prefixed to the
Poems of Henry Howard, Earl of Surrey, 1717, pp. xv-xvi, *see* below, 1717, p. 346.
In Chalmers the line " Rarely discover'd . . ." reads " Yet soon their beams attract
the diver's eye."]

1711.   Addison, Joseph.   *The Spectator* for May 24, 1711, No. 73,
fol. 1 *b*. (The Spectator, ed. G. Gregory Smith, 1897-8, vol. i,
p. 278.)

This Humour of an *Idol* is prettily described in a Tale of
Chaucer : He represents one of them sitting at a Table with
three of her Votaries about her, who are all of them courting
her Favour, and paying their Adorations : She smiled upon
one, drank to another, and trod upon the other's Foot which
was under the Table.   Now which of these three, says the
old Bard, do you think was the Favourite.   In troth, says he,
not one of all the three.

¶ The Behaviour of this old *Idol* in *Chaucer* puts me in
mind of the Beautiful *Clarinda*, one of the greatest *Idols*
among the Moderns.

[The reference is to the ' Remedy of Love,' not by Chaucer, but first printed by
Thynne in the 1532 edn. of Chaucer's collected Works.]

[1711.] Dennis, John.   *Reflections, Critical and Satyrical, upon a late
Rhapsody call'd an Essay on Criticism*, pp. 18-20.

In the 28th Page there are no less than two or three
Absurdities in the compass of four Lines :

Now length of Fame our second Life is lost,
And bare Threescore is all ev'n that can boast.
[p. 19]   Our Sons their Fathers failing Language see
And such as *Chaucer* is shall *Dryden* be.

.   .   .   .

That is shall grow obsolete and neglected, and be either forgot
[p. 20] or be read by but a few. . . . Mr. *Dryden* had one Quality
in his Language, which *Chaucer* had not, and which must
always remain.   For having acquir'd some Justness of
Numbers and some Truth of Harmony and of Versification, to
which *Chaucer* thro' the Rudeness of the Language or want
of Ear, or want of Experience, or rather perhaps a mixture of

all, could not possibly attain, that Justness of Numbers, and
Truth of Harmony and of Versification can never be destroy'd
by any alteration of Language; and therefore Mr. *Dryden,*
whatever alteration happens to the Language, can never be
like *Chaucer.*

[This extract is not complete. *See* above, pp. 310–11, 1709, A. Pope, and below,
pp. 367, 369, 379, 383.]

1711. Hearne, Thomas. *Extracts from his Diary,* April 28, Aug. 27,
Sept. 20, Nov. 16, Dec. 5, 1711, [in] Remarks and Collections of
Thomas Hearne, ed. C. E. Doble, Oxford Hist. Soc., vol. iii,
pp. 155–6, 217, 234, 264, 274.

[p. 155]   April 28 (Sat.). . . . Note out of Sr Fra. Kinaston of
Oatly in Salop his Comments on Chaucer's Troilus & Cresida
[*see* above, 1635, p. 207]. (The said S^r. Fr. turn'd that piece
into Latin Rhyme, & writ also Latin Notes upon it.)

For Chaucer's Personage it appears by an excellent piece
of him, limm'd by the Life by Thomas Occleve his Schollar
and now remaining as a high priz'd Jewell in the Hands of
my honoured Friend S^r. Thomas Cotton K^t. and Bart. that
Chaucer was a Man of an even Stature, neither too high
nor too low, his Complection sanguine, His Face fleshie, but
pale, his Forehead broad, but comly smooth and even.
His Eyes rather little than great cast most part downward,
with a grave Aspect, His Lipps plump and ruddy & both
of an equal thickness, the hair on the upper being thin and
short of a wheat Colour, on his Chin 2 thin forked Tuffs.
His Cheeks of like coller with the rest of his Face being
either shaved or wanting Hair. All which considered
together with his Witt and Education in ye Cort, and his
Favour among Great Ladys one of whose Women he married:
it was his Modesty made him speake of his Unlikeliness to
be a Lover.

This Note I took out of a Book of Mr. Urry of X^t. Church,
who transcrib'd several things of the English Comment from
the MS. in the Dean of X^t. Church (Dr. Aldrich's) Study.

.   .   .   .

[p. 156]   Ibid. [i.e. Kinaston's Comments] 157. *passed prime.*
Our Ancestours in Chaucer's time and before divided their
Morning Devotions into two Space 1$^{o.}$ fr. 6 of the Morning
'till nine & it was called *Spacium orationum primarum.* The
other from 9 a clock 'till twelve, wch was call'd *Spacium
Orationum nonarum* & hence we have our word NOON. . . .

.   .   .   .

Ibid.] 159. *Game in mine hood.*]

In Chaucer's time they had but found out the Invention of
Felt & Beaver Hatts.   Before that time they either wore
Knitt Capps or Silk, or Cloath Hoods, as you may see in the
prologues.   The Invention of Hatts there you may see (in the
Description of the Merchant, who wore a Flanders Bever
Hatt [l. 272]).   His Meaning is that Cresid should find in or
under his Hood some Waggery or Merry Conceits.

. . . .

[p. 216]   Aug. 27 (Mon.). . . . Mr. W^m. Lambard writ a Saxon
Dictionarie [*see* above, p. 104], wch we have in MS. in Bodley,
inter Codd. Seld. supra n. 63, at ye Beginning of wch he hath
this Note :

> *For the Degrees of the Declination of the old Inglishe, or*
> *Saxon tongue, reade*   1. *The Lawes before the Conquest.*
> 2. *The Saxon Chron. of Peterborough, after the Conquest.*
> 3. *The Saxon Writte of H.* 3. *to Oxfordshyre : in the litle*
> *Booke of olde Lawes, fo.*   4. *The Pater nostre, & Crede, of*
> *Rob. Grosted : in the Booke of Patrices Purgatiorie &c.*
[p. 217]
> 5. *The Rythme of Jacob : in the Booke called flos florum.*
> 6. *The Chronicles called Brute : Gower, Chaucier, &c.*
> *By the w^ch, and such like it may appeare, how, and by what*
> *Steps, our Language is fallen from the old Inglishe, and*
> *drawen nearer to the Frenche.   This may well be lightened*
> *by shorte Examples, taken from theise Bookes, and is meete to*
> *be discover'd when this Dictionarie shal be emprinted.*
>
> W. Lambarde 1570.

Seld supra 57. Romanz de la Rose in French.   W^ch hath
been translated by Chaucer & is to be found in his Works.
In this MS^t. are abundance of Pictures, from one of wch it
appears y^t women rid astride when 'twas written.

. . . .

[p. 234]   Sept. 20 (Th.).   Mr. Urry tells me that he saw a MS.
Chaucer in the Study of the L^d. Treasurer Harley, written,
he believes, in, or very near, the time in which Chaucer liv'd,
and that several things of the Cooks Tale are in this MS^t.
that are not in the common Editions.

. . . .

[p. 264]   Nov. 16 (Fri.). . . . De re literaria promovenda valde est
sollicitus, & ut Ædis X^ti. alumni bonæ notæ scriptores
recenseant, notisque brevibus, sed necessarijs, illustrent sæpe

monet atque incitat. Quin & D. Joannem Urrium, amicum
nostrum probum integrumque ut novam Galfridi Chauceri
operum Editionem aggrediatur hortatus est. Ut Urrius opus
istud in se suscipiat ideo optandum esse puto, quod linguæ
Anglo-Saxonicæ, & vocum obsoletarum nostrarum apprime sit
peritus, & in hisce studijs non mediocriter versatus. Unus
porro ex intimis Hickesij est familiaribus, qui proculdubio
consilijs commodis Urrium sublevabit, & locos paullo
difficiliores pro virili elucidabit.—

. . . .

[p. 273] Dec. 5 (Wed.). Yesterday M^r. Urry came to the Bodlejan
Library on purpose to look over Junius's MSS. he having had
a Letter from D^r. Hickes (whose Advice he ask'd about the
[p. 274] Matter) that an Edition of Chaucer was there in great measure
done to his Hands. Num. 9th of those MSS. is a printed
Chaucer in Folio, with divers MSS. Notes throughout by
Junius's own Hand, & divers of his other Books will be of
signal Service in the Work, especially the Etymologicon of the
English Tongue, & the Original of old English Words, w^ch
are distinctly handled in three Volumes, wch Mr. Urry designs
carefully to read over. . . . [*see* above, 1677, p. 253].

[*See* above, p. 292, 1705, Wanley, Humphrey.]

1711. Nicols, William. *De Literis Inventis Libri Sex*, London . . .
1711. Lib. ii, p. 49. [The B. M. copy has 1716 pasted on the
title-page over 1711, which was the original date. This passage
is referred to in Memoirs of Literature, 2nd edition, 1722, vol. iv,
article 70, p. 422.

Aut quam nunc Anglis sunt hæc quæ nobilis olim
  Vates *Chaucerus* carmina scripta dedit,
Chaucerus (quo olim tantum Woodstoca superba
  Civè fuit, quantum Mantua Virgilio),
Jam lectore caret; dum tot post secla leguntur
  Tityrus, & segetes, armaque clara ducum.

. . . .

Pauca manent nobis lingua monumenta Britanna,
  Quæ modo *Chauceri* tempore scripta forent,
Quamvis ter centum vatis non amplius amnis
  Temporibus duris abfuit ille meis.
Nulla diu vivent, quae vulgi condita lingua
  Quamvis nec careant arte nec ingenio:

At quae Romano sublimia carmina felix
Eloquio condas, sæcula cuncta legent.

[This Index also gives under Chaucer, " Homerus Anglicus
Cambdeno.   Ibid. N." : but this has not been found.
For a review of this work and reference to Chaucer, *see*
below, 1722, Delaroche, p. 362.]

1711. Pope, Alexander. *The Temple of Fame: A Vision.* Printed for
Bernard Lintot 1715, p. 5, sign. A 3, advertisement, p. 46 Notes.
The Works of Alexander Pope, Esq. Printed for H. Lintot, 1736.
The Temple of Fame, vol. iii, pp. 1-35. [In this edn. another
sentence is added to the Advertisement and also on each page there
are numerous passages drawn from Chaucer. In the 1717 edn. of
Pope's Works, and in several subsequent ones, the remark, " written
in 1711" is placed under the Title "The Temple of Fame."]
(Works, 1871, vol. i, pp. 185-230.)

[Works, p. 187] Advertisement. The hint of the following piece was taken
from Chaucer's House of Fame. The design is in a manner
entirely altered, the descriptions and most of the particular
thoughts my own : yet I could not suffer it to be printed
without this acknowledgment, or think a concealment of this
nature the less unfair for being common. The reader who
would compare this with Chaucer, may begin with his third
Book of Fame, there being nothing in the two first books
that. answers to their title.   [The following sentence, and the
parallel passages from Chaucer were not added until 1736.]
Whenever any hint is taken from him, the passage itself is
set down in the marginal notes.

[Note by Pope to 1st edn. Speaking of allegory :—]

[Works, p. 189.] . . . Chaucer introduced it here, whose Romaunt of the
Rose, Court of Love, Flower and the Leaf, House of Fame,
and some others of his writings, are master pieces of this sort.
In epic poetry, it is true, too nice and exact a pursuit of the
allegory is justly esteemed a fault ; and Chaucer had the
discernment to avoid it in his Knight's Tale, which was an
attempt towards an epic poem.

1711. Pope, Alexander. *Letter to Henry Cromwell, Esq.,* July 24th,
1711 [in] Miscellanea in 2 vols, Never before published. London.
Printed in the year 1727. Letter xxi, vol. i, pp. 59-60. (Works,
1871, vol. vi, p. 124.)

Your heroick Intention of Flying to the Relief of a distressed
Lady, was glorious and noble ; such as might be expected from
your Character, for as *Chaucer* says (I think)

As noblest Metals are most soft to melt
So Pity soonest runs in gentle Minds.

[The second line is a paraphrase of Chaucer, Knight's Tale, l. 903, Merchant's Tale,
l. 742, Squire's Tale, l. 471, and Legend of Good Women, B., l. 503.]

1711. Unknown (?). *Preface* to *Expostulatoria*, by Thomas Ken,
Bishop of Bath and Wells, sign. A 4 b.

Take his [Bishop Ken's] Character from the following
Lines, in which Mr. *Dryden* has very accurately and justly
drawn his Picture.

[Here follows Dryden's version of Chaucer's character of a
Good Parson.]

1712. Cobb, Samuel. *The Carpenter of Oxford* or *The Millers Tale
from Chaucer. Attempted in Modern English. To which are added
Two Imitations of Chaucer by Matthew Prior.* London. Printed
for E. Curll, R. Gosling, and I. Pemberton, 1712.
    (Also in The Canterbury Tales of Chaucer Modernis'd, by
Several Hands. Published by Mr. Ogle, 1741, vol. i, pp. 191–
228, *see* below, 1741, pp. 389–90.)

1712. [Gay, John.] *Verses* addressed to Bernard Lintot [in] Miscellaneous Poems and Translations by several Hands, [published by
Lintot], 1712, pp. 168, 171, 172. [For Thomas Betterton's Chaucerian contribution to this volume, *see* above, 1710, p. 312.] (Poetical . . . and Miscellaneous Works of John Gay, in 6. vols. . . .
printed for Edward Jeffrey . . . 1795, vol. vi, p. 80.)

On a Miscellany of Poems.   To *Bernard Lintott.*

.   .   .   .

So, *Bernard,* must a Miscellany be
Compounded of all kinds of Poetry ;

.   .   .   .

Let *Prior*'s Muse with soft'ning Accents move,
Soft as the Strains of constant *Emma*'s Love :
Or let his Fancy chuse some jovial Theme,
As when he told *Hans Carvel*'s jealous Dream ;
Prior th' admiring Reader entertains,
With *Chaucer*'s Humour, and with *Spenser*'s Strains.

1712. Hearne, Thomas. *Extracts from his Diary,* Jan. 4, 24, March 3,
April 9, May 21, 24, June 9, Aug. 7, Sept. 3, Dec. 26, [in]
Remarks and Collections of Thomas Hearne, ed. C. E. Doble,
Oxford Hist. Soc., vol. iii, 1889, pp. 288, 295, 317–18, 330, 363,
365, 373, 425, 444, vol. iv, ed. D. W. Rannie, 1898, p. 42.

[p. 288] .Jan. 4 (Fri.). An old Geffrey Chaucer in M^r. Urry's Hands
(belonging to my L^d. Harley) printed by Rich. Rele [Kele]
dwellyng in Lombard Street. [*See* above, 1542, p. 83.] In it
is a MS^t. Bill of Fare at ye Beginning wch may be of use.

it seems to have been by the Hand in tem. Reg. Eliz. or
soon after.

. . , ...

[p. 295]   Jan. 24 (Th.).   The word Stele is in Geffery Chaucer's Tale
of the Miller.   It signifies an Handle.   I find it so written
in the MSS.

[C. Tales, A, l. 3785.]

. . . .

[p. 317]   March 3 (Mon.). . . On the Prologue to Chaucer's Franke-
leyn's Tale about the Welch or British Songs upon their
Instrum^ts.

. . . .

[p. 318]   Ashmole 6928.   The Cook's Tale, written by M^r. Ashmole's
own hand . 43 . 4.—6937.   Chaucer's Piller, or the Squire's
Tale found out by John Lane, 1630. 4to. 53. [*See* above,
1614, p. 189.]

. . . .

[p. 330]   April 9 (Wed.). . . . M^r. Urry . . . hath got a Chaucer
MS. from M^r. Pepys in wch are some Fragments not printed.

. . . .

[p. 363] May 21 (Wed.).   D^r. Sloane hath lent M^r. Urry (who is preparing for the Press a new Edition of Chaucer's Works) a MS.
call'd *The Conclusions of the Astrolabye Compiled by Geffray
Chaucer newlye amendyd* [now Sloane MS. 261].   The Author
of these Emendations was Walter Stevins, as appears from his
Dedication of the Work *to the right honorable & his vearie
good Lorde Edwarde* (Courtney) *Earle of Devonshire.* M^r.
Stevins, of whose Composition I never saw nor heard of any
thing before, hath added a Comment or Paraphrase all along:
Quære what this Stevins was, & whether he was of any
University, & particularly whether of Oxford? [*See* above,
c. 1555, p. 192.]

. . . .

[p. 364]   May 24 (Sat.). . . M^r. Urry hath borrow'd of D^r. Sloane a
Q^to. MS. [now Sloane 314] which is written in Paper, and at
[p. 365] the Beginning is thus intitled, Tractatus Astrologico-Magicus,
with a Discourse written by S^r. Geoffrey Chaucer's own Hand
of the Astrolabe.   I know not what Ground there was for
saying the Discourse of the Astrolabe was written by Chaucer's
own Hand; for tho' he was the Author of it, & it be written
in an Hand of about the Age of Hen. IVth. yet 'tis certain

from the Faults and Corruptions of the MS. that it cannot
have been written with his own Hand.   Some Body or other
(perhaps some body that publish'd Chaucer's Works) hath
made Corrections and observations throughout.   'Tis possible
the Person that put that Title had no other Ground for what
he did than these Words that are added by some Body just at
the Beginning of Chaucer's Discourse, viz. 1391. S^r. Jeffery
Chawser's Worke.   There had been another Discourse in this
MS. but 'tis intirely cut out all but the first Page which is
the 2^d. Page of the last Leaf of Chaucer, & is thus intitled,
Experimentum bonum Magistri Johannis de Belton . . .

    .   .   .   .

[p. 373]   June 9 (Mon.). . . . D^r. Sloane hath an imperfect Copy of
William Caxton's Ed. of Chaucer's Canterbury Tales.   It is
now in M^r. Urry's hands.   Caxton's Name does not appear.
But, I think, there is no doubt of his being the Printer, the
Letter agreeing with the other Pieces I have seen printed by
Caxton. . . .

[p. 425]   Aug. 7 (Th.).   To M^r. Urry.

Sir,—I haue at last sent you three Copies of the 8th Vol. of
Leland's Itin. . . . I hope you continue to meet with excellent
Materials for your Edition of Chaucer.

[p. 444]   Sept. 3 (Wed.). . . . The following old Fragments given
me by Thomas Rawlinson, Esqr.—Two old Love Songs.   I
know not who the Author.   Perhaps Chaucer. . . . . Two
other Love Songs.   Perhaps also by Chaucer.

    .   .   .   .

[Vol. iv.
p. 42]   Dec. 26 (Fri.).   Hesterna die D. Urry ex Æde X^{ti} mihi
ostendit vetustam Editionem Chauceri, sed mutilam cum ad
initium tum ad finem.   Est in folio, multis adjectis quæ non
comparent in Edd. Caxtoni & Pynsoni.   Quisnam Editor fuit
mihi non constat.   Edisci tamen, ni fallor, potest è schedula
quadam mecum à Bagfordo communicata.   Typi sunt alij ab
ijs qui in ceteris, quas vidi, Edd. habentur.   In una parte libri
hæc verba *constat W. Thynne* leguntur.   An fuerit olim
Thynni illius, qui prelo Chaucerum paravit ?   De qua re consul-
endus Stoveus in Annalibus.   Hoc etiam Urry indicavi.   Sed
Annales hosce non penes se habuit.

[With regard to the two Fragments referred to above, Doble adds the following
note, iii, 444: On vellum, two leaves : pasted in.   Printed : *Reliquiae Hernianae* (1869),
i, p. 265 seq.]

CHAUCER CRITICISM.

[1712 ?] **Johnson**, Maurice. *An Introduction to the Minute Books of the Spalding Society;* being an Historical Account of the State of Learning in Spalding, Elloe, Holland, Lincolnshire . . written by Maurice Johnson, Junior, Secretary to the Society. [Printed by John Nichols in] Literary Anecdotes of the 18th century, vol. vi, 1812, pp. 45, 46.

[p. 45]   Thus this house [Priory at Spalding] flourished ; but never more than under the influence of its great and proper patron John of Gaunt . . . who . . . . made frequent visits to this Convent, with his brother Geffrey Chaucer, who married his lady's sister. No question but learning then flourished in this place when honoured by such company, the fathers of our kings, our language, and our verse ; and most probably this place was the scene of action of that severest satire of Chaucer, mentioned by Mr. Dart in his life of that poet before Mr. Urry's edition from Mr. Speght which yet hath not been published, beginning thus :

> In Lincolnshire fast by a fenne
> Standeth a religious house who doth it kenne.

[The Society was founded in 1712, when Maurice Johnson junr. was among the Members, and Mr. Lyon was elected President. This introduction to the Minute books is addressed to Mr. Lyon, so possibly the date is 1712, it is certainly before 1721, when Urry's Chaucer was published. See Literary Anecdotes, vi, pp. 29, 34, 37.]

[*a.* 1712.] **King**, William. *Adversaria ; or Occasional remarks on men, manners, & books;* [printed in] Remains of Dr. William King, 1732, pp. 45-6 ; [and in] The Original Works of William King, LL.D., 1776, vol. i, p. 235.

He [William Cartwright the poet] has a Copy of Verses on Sir *Francis Kynaston*'s Translation of *Troilus* and *Cressida . . .* [*See* above, 1635, p. 207.]

Criticisms and Remarks in Poetry, &c. as might tend to the Honour of the British Name and Literature.

To collect some of *Spencer*'s ; particularly an *Eclogue* of *Colin,* very well turned into *Latin* verse. *Kynaston*'s *Chaucer,* a peculiar Piece of Poetry ; Dean Aldrich has taken Pains to give us Notes. The first Book only published.

[1712 ? **Oldmixon**, John.] *Reflections on Dr. Swift's Letter to the Earl of Oxford about the English Tongue,* [n. d.] pp. 24-5.

[p. 24]   When a Tongue is come to any degree of Perfection, whoever writes well in it will Live ; ther'es [*sic*] a Thirst after Wit in all Ages, and those that have a Taste of it will distinguish
[p. 25]   the Thought from the Diction. *Chaucer* will, no doubt, be

admir'd as long as the *English* Tongue has a Being; and the
changes that have happen'd to our Language have not hinder'd
his Works out living their Contemporary Monuments of Brass
or Marble.

[Swift wrote his letter, entitled, A Proposal for correcting, improving and ascertaining the English tongue, in Feb. 1712, printed in May 1712. It was addressed to Robert Harley, Earl of Oxford. Various answers were published on its appearance, amongst others Oldmixon's—whose name, however, does not appear. There are no references in Swift's letter to early English writers, and but one passing mention of Spenser.]

1712. Pope, Alexander. *Letters of Mr. Pope to Mr. Gay, Dec.* 24, 1712, [in] Letters of Mr. Pope and Several Eminent Persons. London. Printed and sold by the Booksellers of London and Westminster, 1735, p. 120. (Works, 1871, vol. vii, p. 410.)

He who is forced to live wholly upon those ladies' favours, is indeed in as precarious a condition as any He who does what Chaucer says for sustenance.   [Cokes Tale]

[This edition, known as the P. T. edition, is in 2 vols. bound together. The letters to Gay are the last in the book, and begin on p. 117; the preceding page being numbered 194.]

1712. Prior, Matthew. *Two Imitations of Chaucer: viz. I. Susannah and the Two Elders; II. Earl Roberts' Mice, by Matthew Prior, Esq.* London.   Printed 1712 [with] Samuel Cobb's The Carpenter of Oxford, or The Miller's Tale from Chaucer, sign. H 1.–H 2 b. [*See* above, p. 319.]   (Prior's poetical Works, R. Brimley Johnson (Aldine edn.) 1892, vol. ii, pp. 1–4.   The text in this edn. is from Prior's Poems, published 1718, pp. 287–9, our extract is from the original of 1712.)

[sign. H i] Susannah and the Two Elders, in Immitation of Chaucer.

Earl Robert's Mice.

[sign. H 2]   Twa Mice, full Blythe and Amicable
        Batten beside Earl Robert's Table.

          .   .   .   .

            . . . Eftsoons the Lord
        Of Boling, whilome John the Saint,

          .   .   .   .   .   .

        Laugh'd Jocound, and aloud he cry'd
        To Matthew seated on the other side;
[sign. H 2 b]   To thee lean Bard it doth pertain
        To understand these Creatures Twain.
        Come frame us now some clean Device,
        Or pleasant Rhyme on yonder Mice:

They seem, God shield me, MAT. and CHARLES,
Bad as Sir *TOPAZ*,* or Squire *QUARLES*.
MATTHEW did for the nonce reply
At Emblem, or Device am I,
But could I Chant or Rhyme pardie,
Clear as Dan *CHAUCER*, or as Thee,
Ne Verse from me, so God me shrive,
On Mouse, or any Beast alive.

[Note]   * A sort of Ballad Rhymes, so call'd by CHAUCER.

[The two versions on Susannah were reprinted in Miscellaneous Poems. Translations by Several Hands. B. Lintot, 1712, p. 74.]

1712. Tickell, [Thomas]. *A Poem to His Excellency The Lord Privy Seal, on the Prospect of Peace*, pp. 10, 11, 19, [published Oct. 1712, dated 1713]. (English Poets, by Dr. S. Johnson, with additional lives by A. Chalmers, vol. xi, pp. 104, 5.)

[p. 11]   From Fields of Death to *Woodstock's* peaceful glooms
The Poets Haunt, *Britannia's* Hero [Duke of Marl-
      borough] comes :
Begin, my Muse, and Softly touch the String :
Here *Henry* lov'd ; and *Chaucer* learn'd to sing.
Hail fabled Grotto ! hail Elysian Soil !
Thou fairest Spot of fair *Britannia's* Isle !
Where Kings of old conceal'd forgot the Throne,
And Beauty was content to shine unknown,
Where Love and War by turns Pavilions rear,
And *Henry's* Bowr's near *Blenheim's* Dome appear ;
Thy weary'd Champion lull in soft Alcoves,
The noblest Boast of thy Romantick Groves.
Oft, if the Muse presage, shall He be seen
By *Rosamonda* fleeting o'er the Green,
In Dreams be hail'd by Heroes mighty Shades
And hear old *Chaucer* warble through the glades.

.   .   .   .

[p. 19]   Nor, *Prior*, hast thou hush'd the Trump in vain,
Thy Lyre shall now revive her mirthful Strain,
New Tales shall now be told ; if right I see,
The Soul of *Chaucer* is restor'd in Thee.

1712. Unknown. *Parliament of Birds*, 1712. [A satire in verse, with no reference to Chaucer, the only connection with him being similarity of title.]

1712. Urry, John. *Letter to Lord Harley,* [printed in] Report on the Manuscripts of his Grace the Duke of Portland, preserved at Welbeck Abbey, vol. v (Historical MSS. Commission), 1899, pp. 247–8.

[p. 247] 1712, November 24—Mr. Dean of Christ Church tells me from Mr. Broxholm, your honour has found out another Tale [p. 248] of Chaucer's, that never was in print. I need not tell you I shall be glad to see it, and hope you will favour me with a sight of it when I come to Christ Church, which will be very soon. . . . Last week the Honourable Mrs. Thynn of Cawston sent me a MS. Chaucer, which she has lately purchased; it belonged to Mr. Long, Prebendary of Exeter Church. 'Tis all unbound and wants several leaves, and some whole Tales, but yet there are two in it that I have not met with anywhere else. The one is what passed at the inn at Canterbury, and how the Pilgrims disposed of themselves, and the Pardoner's misadventure with the Tapster of that inn [Prologue to *Beryn*]. The other is the Merchant's tale as they return from Canterbury; 'tis long; I have not read it, but after it are these two lines in the same hand with the rest of the MS —

> Nomen autoris presentis cronica Romæ
> Et translatoris filius Ecclesiæ Thomæ.

If what you have discovered is one of these, I shall be the better enabled to put it forth from two MSS., but if it is different from these, I shall thereby enlarge my collection of Chaucer's works, and that will be some commendation to the edition I am preparing. I transcribe every line, so that I, that am not a swift penman, find I have set myself a tedious task. I am advanced a great way in the Tales, and have taken as great care of the versification as I can, being persuaded Chaucer made them exact metre, but the transcribers have much injured them. In his Troilus and Creseide he says to his book—

> And for there is so great diversitie
> In English and in writing of our tonge,
> So pray I God, that none miswrite the
> Ne the mismetre for default of tonge.

So that if I, by the help of MSS. and several printed editions can restore him to his feet again, I shall have done, though no great matter, as much as I am able to do, and that in a good measure I think I shall do.

I shall make no complaints of the difficulties I meet with in this trifling business. I shall reserve them to a paragraph in the preface, and there I'll magnify my labours and talk as big, though but a paltry editor, as if I were the very author himself. But Chaucer was a modest man, and boasting will not become me. However, you will give me leave, I hope, to mention how much I am beholden to you in procuring me that valuable MS. from my Lord Treasurer's library, and promising to get me the habits of the pilgrims, and finding out a new Tale to grace the edition, and many other favours, for all which I most humbly thank your Lordship, and with all respect kiss your hands.

[Mrs. Thynne's MS. afterwards passed to the Northumberland Collection at Alnwick. *See* below, Horwood and Martin, 1872.]

1713. Diaper, [William]. *Dryades; or the Nymphs Prophecy. A Poem,* p. 2.

How happy, when I view'd the calm Retreat,
And Groves o'er-look'd by *Winchcomb*'s ancient Seat?
Here the smooth *Kennet* * takes his doubtful Way
In wanton Rounds the lingring Waters play,
And by their circling Streams prolong the grateful Stay.
Here good old *Chaucer* whilom chear'd the Vale,
And *sootely* sung, and told the *jocund* Tale.

* *A River in* Berkshire.

1713. Gay, John. *The Wife of Bath, a comedy,* . . . by Mr. Gay . 1713.

Prologue.

If ancient Poets thought the *Prologue* fit,
To sport away superfluous Starts of Wit;
Why should we Moderns lavish ours away,
And to supply the *Prologue* starve the *Play?*
Thus *Plays* of late, like Marriages in Fashion,
Have nothing good besides the Preparation.
How shall we do to help our Author out,
Who both for *Play* and *Prologue* is in doubt?
He draws his Characters from *Chaucer*'s Days,
On which our Grandsires are profuse of Praise.

•   •   •   •   •   •   •   •   •

Dramatis Personæ.

Men.

    Chaucer.

    Doggrell.

    Franklyn, *a Rich Yeoman of* Kent.

    Doublechin, *a Monk.*

    Merit *in Love with* Florinda.

    Astrolabe, *an Astrologer.*

    Antony,   } *Servants to* Franklyn.
    William, }

    A Drawer.

Women.

    Myrtilla, *a Lady of Quality.*

    Florinda, Franklyn's *Daughter.*

    Alison, *the Wife of* Bath.

    Busie, Myrtilla's *Woman.*   Scene, *an Inn lying in the Road between* London *and* Canterbury.

[Act i, sc. 1, *Frank.* You must know, Sir, that we came thus far with
sign. B 2] the *Canterbury* Pilgrims,—certainly the most diverting
Company that ever travell'd the Road—and my House
lying in the way, I design to invite them all to the
Wedding to Morrow.

   Dog. And there is a Nun of Quality, I am told, hath just
now joyned them.

   Frank. The Wife of *Bath* is enough to make any Mortal
split his Sides.   She is as frolicksome as a young Wench
in the Month of *May*, plays at Romps with the Pilgrims
all round, throws out as many quaint Jokes as an *Oxford*
Scholar;—and, in short, exerts herself so facetiously, that
she is the Mirth of the whole Company.

   Dog. But the Support of the Society is Mr. *Chaucer*—he
is a Gentleman of such inexhaustible good Sense, Breeding, and Civility, that since I have had the Happiness to
converse with him, he hath honour'd some of my
Productions with his Approbation.

[This original 'Chaucer' form of the 'Wife of Bath' was not a success, so in 1730,
Gay altered and revised it, striking out the characters of 'Chaucer' and 'Franklyn,'
and substituting the modern characters of 'Sir Harry Gauntlet' and 'Plowdon' in
their place. In this 2nd edn. the old Prologue is kept, and there is no word of the
reason for the change. See Johnson, in his Life of Gay (Lives of the Poets, 1781),
where he says : 'In 1713 he [Gay] brought a comedy called "The Wife of Bath" upon
the stage, but it received no applause ; he printed it, however ; and seventeen years

after, having altered it, and, as he thought, adapted it more to the public taste, he
offered it again to the town; but though he was flushed with the success of the
"Beggar's Opera," had the mortification to see it again rejected.' Both versions are
reprinted in vol. iii of Gay's *Miscellaneous Works*, 1772–3.

See letter from Gay to Swift, 9 Nov. 1729; also one of 3 March, 1729–30, in which he
says, 'My old vamped play [The Wife of Bath] got me no money, for it had no
success.' Pope, Works, 1871, pp. 165, 183.]

1713. Hearne, Thomas. *Extracts from his Diary,* April 5, Nov. 28,
1713 [in] Remarks and Collections of Thomas Hearne, Oxford Hist.
Soc., vol. iv, 1898, ed. D. W. Rannie, pp. 150–1, 261.

April 5 (Sun.).   Mr. Urry tells me y^t ye Name Cornhil
appears at ye End of the Retractation of Chaucer's Parson's
Tale in a MS. he hath.   Who [was] this Cornhill?

In a MS. Chaucer lent by the present L^d. Treasurer to
M^r. Urry. 'Tis in Vellam, very near the time in wch the Author
lived: [Here follow a list of births, &c. mostly of the Fox
[p. 151] family, 1548 to 1585.]   At the End of the said Book:

Edwarde Foxe oweythe this booke ex dono patris sui.   In
red Letters this followeth: Here endeth the book of the tales
of Cauntirburye, Compyled by Geffraye Chaucers. Of whos
soule Ihesu Crist have mercye.   Amen quod Cornhyl.

At the beginning in a spare Leaf: Thys boke belongith to
me Edmond Foxe felow of Lyncolls Inne.

Equus de stanno for a Horse of Brass in one of the MS.
Chaucers y^t Mr. Urry hath, being a note of ye Scribe.

The same ignorant Scribe in the Title of the D^r. of
Physick's Tale, Fabula de le Fisician de Virginius Apius &
Claudius.

In the Tale of the Shipman he writes, fabula cujusd.
Shipman.

In the title of the Manciple's Tale ye same scribe: Mancipij
fab: de la Crowe.

In ye Margin of a Paper MS. (very much Shattered) of
Chaucer, y^t Mr. Urry borrowed of Col. Hen. Worsley at y^e
Beginning of the Sergeant of Law's Tale, where he mentions
Europe, this Note: Europa est tercia pars mundi.   It is ag^t
these words *of all Europe Queen.*   Hence, I think, it is plain
y^t this Book was written before ye Discovery of America.

[p. 261]   Nov. 28 (Sat.). . . . Mr. Bagford tells me y^t Caxton printed
Chaucer's Fragm^ts. in 4to. w^thout Date wch are not taken into
his Ed. of the Tales. This is now in the Hands of ye B^p. of
Ely, who had it of M^r. Bagford. D^r. Tanner hath seen this
Book. And 'tis certainly a Treasure.—K. Henry VIIIth. hath

an Act for reading of the Scriptures, in wch also Chaucer's Canterbury Tales and Gower de Amore are allow'd to be read by the common People, and likewise the Legenda Aurea.

[*See* above 1477-8, p. 58, for Caxton, and 1542-3, p. 84, an Acte for thadvauncement of true Religion.]

1713. [**Oldmixon**, John?] *Note to* The Salisbury Ballad : *with curious, learned and critical notes, by Dr. Walter Pope.* London. Printed in the year 1713 [in] Poems and translations by Several Hands . . . printed for J. Pemberton . . . 1714, p. 8. [The sub-title runs] The Salisbury Ballad With the Learned Commentaries of a friend to the *Author's* memory. [The dedication to the whole collection is signed by John Oldmixon, who was probably the author of these notes.]

[Text]   With a Cup of Old Sack he'll wind up his * Jack.

[Note]   *His Engine wherewith he makes Verses. So CHAUCER.

'As Winding up makes a Jack go,
So good Wine makes good Verses flow.'

[1713-14.] Montagu, Lady Mary Wortley. *Unfinished Sketches of a larger poem*, [in] The Letters and Works of Lady Mary Wortley Montagu, ed. Lord Wharncliffe, 1837, vol. iii, p. 391.

[Dulness is speaking :]

Shall mortals then escape my power ? she cried . .
Shall Addison my empire here dispute
So justly founded, lov'd, and absolute,
Explode my children, ribaldry and rhyme,
Rever'd from Chaucer's down to Dryden's time ?

1714. Fortescue-Aland, John. *The Difference between an Absolute and Limited Monarchy . . . . being A Treatise Written by Sir John Fortescue. Kt. . . . . Publish'd with some Remarks by John Fortescue-Aland*, Preface, pp. lxxviii-ix, pp. 2-4, 15, 18, 23, 56, 90.

[The above references (except those to the Preface) are to notes on the pages indicated, and are chiefly on similarities of words and expressions between Sir John Fortescue and Chaucer.]

1714. Gay, John. *The Shepherd's Week. In Six Pastorals*, by Mr. J. Gay. London . . . 1714, Notes, sign. B 2, B 4 *b*, C 5 *b*. (Poetical Works of Gay, ed. John Underhill, 1893, Muses Library, vol. i, pp. 74, 78, 89.)

[First Pastoral]

[Line 3]   *Welkin,* the same as *Welken,* an old *Saxon* word signifying a *Cloud ;* by Poetical License it is frequently taken for the *Element* or *Sky,* as may appear by this Verse in the Dream of *Chaucer, Ne in all the Welkin was no Cloud.*

.   .   .   .

[First Pastoral]

[Line 79] *Queint* has various Significations in the ancient *English* Authors. I have used it in this Place in the same Sense as *Chaucer* hath done in his *Miller's Tale. As Clerkes been full subtil and queint,* (by which he means *Arch* or *Waggish*), and not in that obscene Sense wherein he useth it in the Line immediately following.

. . . .

[Third Pastoral]

[Line 89] *To ken,* Scire *Chaucero,* to Ken; and *Kende* notus. A.S. *cunnan.* . . . This word is of general use, but not very common, though not unknown to the vulgar . . . Ray, F.R.S.
[*See* above, p. 249, 1674, Ray. The reference may be to the 2nd ed. of Ray's Collection, 1691, with which, however, it does not really correspond.]

1714. Hearne, Thomas. *Extract from his Diary,* Dec. 27, 1714 [in] Remarks and Collections of Thomas Hearne, Oxford Hist. Soc., vol. v, ed. D. W. Rannie, 1901, p. 7.

Dec. 27 (Mon.). Mr. Urry shew'd me a fine MS. of Chaucer's Works written in Vellam (in an Hand of that time, as I take it) at the Beginning of which is Chaucer's Picture in a Fragment of Ocleve. There are Pictures of some of the Pilgrims, & there have been others, but they have been taken out. This Book (which is a great Curiosity), belongs to the Publick Library of Cambridge, from whence M^r. Urry borrow'd it.

1714. Pope, Alexander. *The Wife of Bath, her prologue, from Chaucer,* [in] Poetical Miscellanies . . . publish'd by Mr. Steele, 1714, pp. 3–27. (Works, 1871, vol. i, pp. 163–183.)

1714. Urry, John. *Sketch of a Preface* [to] *Edition of Chaucer's Works,* not published until 1721 [*q. v.* below, pp. 353–6], also some remarks, quoted by Timothy Thomas in his Preface to Urry's Chaucer 1721, [*q. v.*], also a note before the Coke's Tale of Gamelyn, Urry's edn. of Chaucer's Works, 1721, p. 36. [For the licence for Urry's edition, dated 20 July, 1714, *see* below, App. A., 1714.]

[Quoted at end of the Preface as being Urry's own Words to the Reader:—] If this is the First Edition of *Chaucer* that ever thou didst read, it will be to little purpose to tell thee what pains I have been at to fit out this Edition for thee, Thou wilt, maybe, not thank me for what I have done, and complain of me for having left so much undone. All this I do believe thou mayst do justly: But if thou hast read any of the former Editions, thou wilt be my witness that I have been at some trouble in settling the Text, and giving Metre to the Poet's Verse, in collating many MSS., and not a few Printed

Books, writing out Indexes, looking over a great many Dictionaries for words I could not find, as well as for words I could. In short, if thou ever wert an Editor of such Books thou wilt have some compassion on my failings, being sensible of the toil of such sort of creatures; and if thou art not yet an Editor, I beg truce of thee till thou art one, before thou censurest my Endeavours.

[Note before Tale of Gamelyn which, in the annotated copy, has "Urry" in Thomas's handwriting at foot.]

[p. 36]   So many of the MSS. have this Tale, that I can hardly think it could be unknown to the former Editors of this Poet's Works. Nor can I think of a Reason why they neglected to publish it. Possibly they met only with those MSS. that had not this Tale in them, and contented themselves with the Number of Tales they found in those MSS. If they had any of those MSS. in which it is, I cannot give a Reason why they did not give it a Place amongst the rest, unless they doubted of its being genuine. But because I find it in so many MSS., I have no doubt of it, and therefore make it publick, and call it the Fifth Tale. In all the MSS. it is called the Cooke's Tale, and therefore I call it so in like manner: But had I found it without an Inscription, and had been left to my Fancy to have bestow'd it on which of the Pilgrims I had pleas'd, I should certainly have adjudg'd it to the Squire's Yeoman; who tho as minutely describ'd by Chaucer, and characteriz'd in the third Place, yet I find no Tale of his in any of the MSS. And because I think there is not any one that would fit him so well as this, I have ventur'd to place his Picture before this Tale, tho' I leave the Cook in Possession of the Title.

$17\frac{14}{15}$. **Hearne,** Thomas. *Letter to Richard Rawlinson,* dated Feb. 2, $17\frac{14}{15}$ (MS. Rawl. Lett. 111, f. 31), [abstract of it printed in] Remarks and Collections of Thomas Hearne, Oxford Hist. Soc., vol. v, ed. D. W. Rannie, 1901, p. 20.

. . . I find Mr. Urry's Chaucer advertised as being to go to y^e Press in a little time. I have not seen any specimen.

$17\frac{14}{15}$. **Hearne,** Thomas. *Extracts from his Diary,* Feb. 16, Mar. 19, $17\frac{14}{15}$ [in] Remarks and Collections of Thomas Hearne, Oxford Hist. Soc., vol. v, ed. D. W. Rannie, 1901, pp. 23, 33, 34, 36.

[p. 23]   Feb. 16 (Wed.). Last Night M^r. Urry shew'd me a very fine Chaucer in Vellam, the best preserved y^t I have seen which formerly belong'd to Hamon Le Strange, and afterwards

to S^r. Nich. Le Strange to whom it belongs at present. [Now
at Chatsworth.]

[p. 33] March 19 (Sat.). Yesterday about 3 Clock in the Afternoon
died of a Feaver my great and good Friend M^r. John Urry,
Student of Christ-Church. This Gentleman was Bachelor of

[p. 34] Arts, & bore Arms against Monmouth in the Rebellion called
Monmouth's Rebellion, as several other Oxford Scholars did.
He was a stout, lusty Man, & of admirable Principles. His
Integrity & Honesty & Loyalty gain'd him great Honour &
Respect. He refused the Oaths, & died a Non-Juror . . . .
He had published Proposals for a new Edition of Chaucer,
which he had almost prepared for the Press before he died, &

[p. 36] he was like to meet with very great Encouragement. . . . He
was somewhat above 50 Years of Age, & had begun an
Epitaph upon himself, which was found in his Pocket soon
after his Decease, & is as follows: [Here Hearne quotes the
epitaph, for the last verse of which see immediately below.]

[17$\frac{14}{15}$? **Urry**, John.] *Epitaphium Johannis Urry* [in MS. on a piece of
letter paper, inserted before the title page of Urry's edn. of
Chaucer, with notes by T. and W. Thomas, B. M. pr. m. 643, m. 4.
The following note is at the end of it: 'This is supposed to have
been made by Mr. Urry himself; It was found in his Pockett
after his Death (I think it was written in his own Hand). Tim^t.
Thomas, 1717.']

[The epitaph ends thus:]

> Et quamvis memorabile
> Nihil perfecit unquam,
> Jussus tamen est aggressus
> Opus ultra vires magnum
> Chaucerum, nec absolvit,
> Magno sed ausu excidit.

[For the date of above epitaph, see diary of Thomas Hearne for April 1, 1715,
in Remarks and Collections of Thomas Hearne, Oxford Hist. Soc., vol. v, ed.
D. W. Rannie, 1901, p. 39. 'Mr. Urry made his Epitaph as 'tis supposed a little
before he kept his Bed, he being up one whole Night, or at least a good part of one.'
Hearne also quotes the epitaph in full, *ibid.* p. 36.]

17$\frac{14}{15}$. **Hickes**, George. *Letter to Thomas Hearne*, dated March 22, 17$\frac{14}{15}$,
MS. Rawl. Lett. f. 15, (75). [abstract of it in] Remarks and
Collections of Thomas Hearne, Oxford Hist. Soc., vol. v, ed.
D. W. Rannie, 1901, p. 35.

I am as sensible & sorry for the great Loss of Mr. Urry,
as any Friend he hath left behind him, and desire to know to
whom he hath left his Chaucer.

17$\frac{14}{15}$. Hearne, Thomas. *Letter to George Plaxton* [dated] March 23,
17$\frac{14}{15}$, MS. Hearne's Diaries 56, pp. 72–3. [abstract printed in]
Remarks and Collections of T. Hearne, Oxford Hist. Soc., vol. v,
ed. D. W. Rannie, 1901, pp. 35–6.

Mar. 23.   On Saturday Night last I was at the ffuneral of
Mr. John Urry Student of X^t Church, who died of a ffeaver
the Day before.   He was a couragious, brave, honest, virtuous
and learned man, and is much lamented.   He was about an
Edition of Chaucer, but what will become of it now I cannot
tell. . . .

1715. *Abstract of the Articles for Printing Chaucer's* [sic], *26th Aug^t., 1715.*
A MS. sheet inserted at the beginning [before the title page] of the
interleaved copy of Urry's edition of Chaucer's Works with MS.
notes by T. and W. Thomas [B. M. 643, m. 4].

An Agreement dat. 26. Augt. 1715, Between M^r. W^m.
Brome Ex^r. to M^r. John Urry, The Dean & Chapter of C. C.
Oxon & Bern^d. Lintot Bookseller.   Reciting the Queen's
License to M^r. Urry for the sole Printing of Chaucer for 14
y^{rs} from 25 July 1714.   Assigned over by him to Lintot
17. Decr foll^g, & M^r. Urry Dying soon after left M^r. Brome
Ex^r.   And Reciting M^r. Urry's Intention to Apply part of the
Profits tow^{ds}. Building Peckwater Quadrangle.

M^r. Brome assigns his Right to Chaucer, Glossary & License
to M^r. Lintot for the Rem^r. of the Term.

The Dean & Chapter and M^r. Brome to Deliver to Lintot
a Compleat Copy of Chaucer & Glossary & to Correct y^e same
or get a person to Correct it at their Charge.

R.P. 250
S.P.1000
$\frac{}{1250}$ M^r. Lintot to print off 1250 Copys on Royal pap^r & Demy
—the No of each pap^r to be determined by y^e parties before
—the Printing begins.   M^r. L. to be at the Charge of printing
Proposals and Rec^{ts} and if the Subscription exceed 1250,
He is at his Charge to furnish Copys so they do not exceed
1500, Mr. L. being to have of the produce of the Subscription Books.

If the Subscriptions do not amount to 1250 Then such
Books are [as ?] remain to be Disposed of to Booksellers & the
Produce to be equally Divided between the Three partys.

The Neat and Clear Share of ye Dean & Chapter to be
apply'd to the Finishing of Peckwater.   Subscriptions to be
taken by all the partys & to acco[un]t to one another & M^r.
Brome for w^t. money had been received by M^r. Urry.

Subscriptions to be taken in till publication & then Books

to be Delivered to the Subscribers Compl^t in Quires on paym^t of their Subscription Money & not otherwise.

M^r. Lintot to begin Printing as soon as the Copy is Certifyed by the Dean & M^r. Brome to be Compleat & to finish it *with all convenient Speed & assoon as possible*, & he is not to print nor wittingly or willingly suffer to be printed any more than 1500 Copys as above without Consent of the rest of the Partys, nor print or suffer to be printed the s^d Work, or any part thereof in any manner then as afores^d, untill this Agreement be in all respects fulfilled & Compleated.

If any Difference arise, the parties to be Determined by M^r. Arthur Trevor & D^r. Henry Levet.

The College Seal annext.

Witnesses	G. Brookes	Signed	Will Brome
	Rob. Philips		Bern^d Lintot
	J. Holloway		

Printed in pursuance of this Agreement of the Large paper	250
—— Do. Small pap^r	1000
	1250

[*See*, in connection with this edn., a letter from Wm. Brome to Mr. Rawlins, below, June 23, 1733, p. 375.]

[1715? **Thomas,** Timothy?] *Est. of the produce of the Ed^n of Chaucer;* a small MS. sheet inserted in beginning of annotated copy of Urry's edition of Chaucer [B.M. 643. m. 4] endorsed as above.

There are printed 1000 Copys of Chaucer, wch at £1. 10. p Book (in Small Paper)	1500
250 on Large Paper at £2. 10.	625
The Gross Product	2125
Out of wch by the Articles Lintot is to have ⅓ for the Charges of Paper, printing, Graving &c.	708 · 6 · 8
To be Divided between Christ Church and Brome, they paying for Correcting & Glossary.	1416 · 13 · 4

N.B. Lintot tells me he is assured all the Copys will go off.

If you are allowed a proportional part You may insist on ⅓ of £1416 13 4 ...	472 · 4 · 5½
¼	354 · 3 · 4
⅕	283 · 6 · 8

1715. Sloane, Sir Hans. *Three Letters to Thomas Hearne,* dated respectively May 5, June 30, and Oct. 29, 1715. MS. Rawlinson, Lett. 16, ff. 71, 75, 77 [abstracts of them in] Remarks and Collections of Thomas Hearne, Oxford Hist. Soc., vol. v, ed. D. W. Rannie, 1901, pp. 54, 72, 130.

May 5, 1715. . . . I am to begg yor favour in another matter which is the getting for me some MSS. & printed copies of Chaucer I lent M^r. Urry for forwarding his edition of that author. He had one in his own handwriting or at least said to be so, another of the Astrolabe fitted for the presse in folio & some more. You may find them out by 2 marks either MSS. or a letter of the alphabet in the under part of the back and a number on the upper. The same marks are generally on the inside. I should be glad to hear one of yor qualifications would undertake the publication of so usefull a work even for the language. I begg pardon for this trouble and remain. . . .

June 30, 1715. . . . As to my MSS. of Chaucer, I shall only desire, as occasion offers, that you would (if you can easily) gett my books.

Oct. 29, 1715. . . . I have at last found the list of my books in Mr. Urry's hands, viz. :

The works of G. Chaucer London. 1518. in fol., markd P. 150.

The conclusion of the astrolabe by G. Chaucer mark'd MS. 324 in fol.

Tractatus Astrologico Magicus w^t. a discourse written by S^r. G. Chaucers own hand of the astrolabe mark'd MS. 378. in 4°.

You will do me a great favour to gett these books for me from M^r. Brome or any body may have the looking into M^r. Urry's papers. . . .

[Sir Hans Sloane had some difficulty in getting back the books he had lent to Urry, Mr. Brome on being applied to says [Brome to Hearne, c., Nov. 1, 1715, MS. Rawl. Lett. 13, f. 139] that all MSS. and printed books lent to Urry which came into his [Brome's] possession were delivered to Dr. Terry, Subdean of Ch: Ch:. Next follows Hearne's letter to Sloane, Nov. 13, 1715, q.v., and Sloane to Hearne, Nov. 15, 1715 [MS. Rawl. Lett. 9, f. 74, and Remarks, etc., ed. Rannie, v. p. 139]. The MS. was finally found with Dr. Keil [see Hearne's letter to Brome, Nov. 20, 1715], but Sir Hans Sloane did not get all his Chaucers back until Feb. 29, 17$\frac{1}{16}$, when he writes to Hearne in acknowledgment of them, q.v. Mar. 1, 17$\frac{1}{16}$. *See* Remarks and Collections of T. Hearne, vol. v, pp. 130–2, 138–40, 152, 175, 178–9. For present nos. of these MSS. see Skeat's Chaucer, vol. iii, p. lx.]

1715. Hearne, Thomas. *Three Letters to Sir Hans Sloane*, dated Nov. 1 and 13, and Dec. 12, 1715. MS. Hearne's Diaries, 58, pp. 54, 68, 106. [abstracts in] Remarks and Collections of T. Hearne, Oxford Hist. Soc., vol. v, ed. D. W. Rannie, 1901, pp. 138, 152. [The Chaucer reference in letter of Nov. 1 is only given in the MS.]

Nov. 1. [Hearne has communicated to M^r. Brome particulars in H. S.'s letter relating to Chaucer.]

Nov. 13, 1715. . . . I have been since my last, with D^r. [Moses] Terry, the Subdean of X^t Church, and look'd over the Chaucers in his Hands. I find two of these you mention, viz. that mark'd P. 150 and that mark'd MS. 378, but the 3^d mark'd MS. 324 (which is the Conclusion of the Astrolabe) we did not meet with. D^r. Terry is ready to deliver up the two foresaid Books when he hath a Note of Release from Mr. Brome, to whom he gave his Hand for them, and to whom I design to write upon this Occasion. I intend also to ask D^r. [Edmund] Halley and D^r. [John] Keil, whether either of them know any thing of the MS. that is wanting. I mention them, because, if I am not much mistaken, I formerly heard M^r. Urry say that he would let one or both of them have it for a little while, that he might by that means be able to receive some Assistance in his Design, these Gentlemen being great Mathematicians.

Dec. 12. . . . [Hearne would have answered sooner Sloane's letter of Nov. 15 last] had I not waited for Mr. [William] Brome's Order to have the two Books of yours that are in D^r. Terry's Hands restored to me. But having receiv'd as yet no such Order, I could not defer writing to you any longer, especially since the 3^d Book, mark'd MS. 324 hath been delivered to me by D^r. Keil, who gives you his humble service. I shall send this Book to-morrow by the Carrier that sets up at the Oxford Arms, and I will write again to M^r. Brome about the others. . . .

1715. Hearne, Thomas. *Letters* (1) to William Brome, dated Nov. 20, 1715 ; (2) to John Bagford [c. Nov. 28, 1715] MS. Hearne's Diaries 58, pp. 80, 94. [abstracts in] Remarks and Collections of T. Hearne, Oxford Hist. Soc. vol. v, ed. D. W. Rannie, 1791, pp. 140, 148.

[To W. Brome] Nov. 20, 1715. Sir, I have been with Dr. Terry, and found two of Dr. Sloane's Books. The third is in Dr. Keil's Hands. I have spoke with Dr. Keil, who is ready to deliver it to me. Dr. Terry is likewise ready to put the other two into my Hands, as soon as he hath an order from You. I therefore desire that you would be pleased to let him have your leave as soon as you can, and at the same time to give him leave withall to deliver to me Mr. Bagford's Chaucer of Caxton's Edition, Mr. Bagford having commission'd me to receive it by virtue of the following Note, viz.

Mr. Hearne, I would have you to demand my Chaucer's Canterbury Tales, printed by William Caxton, lent to Mr. Urry sometime since. John Bagford.

. . . As soon as I have these Books I will deliver them to the right owners, tho' I wish with all my heart the Edition were carried on.

[To J. Bagford, *c.* Nov. 28, 1715.] . . . I have writ to Mr. Brome about your Chaucer. But have rec^d no Answer as yet.

1715. Hearne, Thomas. *Extract from his Diary,* Oct. 24, [printed in] Remarks and Collections of T. Hearne, Oxford Hist. Soc., vol. v, ed. D. W. Rannie, 1901, p. 128.

Oct. 24 (Mon.). Mr. [Richard] Smith had Chaucer's works fol. the best Edit. 1602, with a MS^t. of a Tale of Gamelyn, taken out of a MS^t. of Chaucer's Works in the University Library of Oxford, Cat. p. 274.

[*See* above, 1682, p. 256, Chiswell.]

1715. Croxall, Samuel. *The Vision, a poem,* pp. 14, 15.

> Hard by, a Turfy Mount with Flowrets spread
> Mantled in Green uprais'd its double Head:
>
> .   .   .   .
>
> High on the forky Ridge two Rev'rend Sires
> Their Voices tun'd, and struck their Golden Lyres;
> In Notes so sweet that ev'ry list'ning Ear
> Was held attent their gentle Strains to hear:
>
> .   .   .   .
>
> *Chaucer* the Parent of *Britannic* Lays
> His Brow begirt with everlasting Bays,
> All in a Kirtle of green Silk array'd
> With gleeful smile his merry Lesson play'd.
> His fellow Bard beside him *Spenser* sate
> And twitched the sounding chords in solemn State.

[The poet has first a vision of certain of the most famous of the monarchs of England, and it is significant that in the following vision the only two poets he sees are Chaucer and Spenser.]

CHAUCER CRITICISM.

1715. Elstob, Elizabeth. *The Rudiments of Grammar for the English-Saxon Tongue, first given in English : with an Apology for the study of Northern Antiquities.   Being very useful toward the understanding our ancient* English Poets, and other Writers.   By Elizabeth Elstob . . . London . . . 1715.   Preface, pp. xvi–xviii, note, xix, xxiv, xxviii–ix.

[Paraphrase of pp. xi–xiii.   An Examination of (1) whether the charge made against the Northern languages is true, that they consist of nothing but Monosyllables ; and (2) whether the copiousness and variety of Monosyllables may be always justly reputed a fault.   The answer to (1) is that the ancient Northern languages (Gothick, Saxon and Teutonick) do not wholly nor mostly consist of Monosyllables.   The answer to (2) is that if copiousness and variety of Monosyllables be a fault, it is one that might as justly be charged upon Latin and Greek—here follow examples from Greek and Latin poets. Not only so, but in modern poets we find great use of monosyllables, even in Dryden, who would have us believe he had a great aversion to them ; note Denham's lines on *Cooper's Hill,* which Dryden so admires.]

[p. xvi]   To give greater Probability to what I have said concerning *Monosyllables,* I will give some Instances, as well from such Poets as have gone before him [Dryden], as those which have succeeded him.   It will not be taken amiss by those who value the Judgment of Sir *Philip Sydney,* and that of Mr. *Dryden,* if I begin with Father *Chaucer.*

> Er it was Day, as was her won to do.

Again,

> And but I have her Mercy and her Grace,
> That I may seen her at the leste way ;
> I nam but deed there nis no more to say.

[p. xvii]   Again,

> Alas, what is this wonder Maladye :
> For heate of colde, for colde of heate I dye.

Chaucer's first Book of *Troylus,* fol. 159, b.   [ll. 419-20]

. . . .

But before, at least contemporary with *Chaucer,* we find Sir *John Gower,* not baulking *Monosyllables ;*   . .

. . . .

[p. xviii, *note*]   Besides the Purpose for which these Verses are here cited, it may not be amiss to observe from some Instances of Words contain'd in them, how necessary, at least useful, the Knowledge of the Saxon Tongue is, to the right understanding our *Old English Poets*, and other Writers. For example, ᛚᚱᚾᚾᛋᛏ, this is the same with the *Saxon* ᛚᛖᚩᚱᚩᚱᛏ, *most beloved*, or *desirable*. 𝔊𝔬𝔡𝔡𝔢𝔰 𝔣𝔬𝔩𝔨𝔢, not *God his Folk*, this has plainly the Remains of the *Saxon* Genitive Case, [&c.].

[p. xix] "Let *Lydgate*, *Chaucer*'s Scholar also be brought in for a Voucher;

> For *Chaucer* that my Master was and knew
> What did belong to writing Verse and Prose,
> Ne'er stumbled at small faults, nor yet did view
> With scornful Eye the Works and Books of those
> That in his time did write, nor yet would taunt
> At any Man, to fear him or to daunt.

Tho' the Verse is somewhat antiquated, yet the Example ought not to be despised by our modern Criticks, especially those who have any Respect for *Chaucer*.

[p. xxvi] To these let me add the Testimony of that Darling of the Muses, Mr. *Prior*, with whom all the Poets of ancient and modern Times of other Nations, or our own, might seem to have intrusted the chief Secrets, and greatest Treasures of their Art. I shall speak only concerning our own Island, where his Imitation of *Chaucer*, of *Spencer*, and of the old *Scotch Poem*, inscribed the *Nut-Brown Maid*, shew how great a Master he is. . . .

[p. xxviii] Sir, from these numerous Instances, out of the writings of our greatest and noblest Poets, it is apparent, That had the Enmity against *Monosyllables* with which there are some who make so great a Clamour, been so great in all Times, we must have been deprived of some of the best Lines, and finest Flowers, that are to be met with in the beautiful Garden of our *English* Posie [*sic*] . . . .

I speak not this, upon Confidence of any Judgment I have in *Poetry*, but according to that Skill, which is natural to the [p. xxix] Musick of a *Northern Ear*, which, if it be deficient, as I shall not be very obstinate in its Defence, I beg leave it may at least be permitted the Benefit of Mr. *Dryden*'s Apology, for the Musick of old Father *Chaucer*'s Numbers, "That there is the rude Sweetness of a *Scotch* Tune in it, which is natural and pleasing, tho' not perfect.

[All the verse quotations are in black letter.]

1715. Gay, John.   *Letter from Gay and Pope to John Caryll* [April 1715].   (Pope, Works, 1871, vol. vi, 1871, p. 227.)

Mr. Rowe's Jane Grey is to be played in Easter week, when Mrs. Oldfield is to personate a character directly opposite to female nature—for what woman ever despised sovereignty? Chaucer has a tale where a knight saves his head by discovering that it was the thing which all women most coveted.

[The first part of this letter is by Gay.]

1715. Hughes, [John].   *Works of Edmund Spenser . . . publish'd by Mr. Hughes*, six vols., vol. i, Life, pp. ii, xv, xvii, xviii (quotes Camden's account of Spenser's tomb: *see* above, p. 163).—Essay on Allegorical Poetry, pp. xxvi, xxxvii.—Remarks on the Fairy Queen, pp. lxxxvii, xciv,—Remarks on the Shepherd's Calendar, pp. ciii, cvii, Glossary cxxi, cxxv, etc.

[p. ii]   . . . Edmund Spenser, the most Eminent of our Poets till that time, unless we except *Chaucer*, who was in some respects his Master and Original. . . .

[Essay on Allegorical Poetry, p. xxvi]
[Mr. Waller says that a great misfortune which attends English Poets is that they are writing in a tongue which is changing daily. They should therefore, like wise sculptors, choose more durable material, and carve in Latin or Greek, if they would have their labours preserved.] Notwithstanding the Disadvantage he has mention'd, we have two Antient *English* Poets, *Chaucer* and *Spenser*, who may perhaps be reckon'd as Exceptions to this Remark.   These seem to have taken deep Root, like old *British* Oaks, and to flourish in defiance of all the Injuries of Time and Weather.   The former is indeed much more obsolete in his Stile than the latter; but it is owing to an extraordinary native Strength in both, that they have been able thus far to survive amidst the Changes of our Tongue, and seem rather likely, among the Curious at least, to preserve the Knowledg of our Antient Language, than to be in danger of being destroy'd with it, and bury'd under its Ruins.

Tho Spenser's Affection to his Master *Chaucer* led him in many things to copy after him, yet those who have read both will easily observe that these two Genius's were of a very different kind.   *Chaucer* excell'd in his Characters; *Spenser* in his Descriptions.   The first study'd Humour, was an excellent Satirist, and a lively but rough Painter of the Manners of that rude Age in which he liv'd. . . .

[p. xxvii]

·   ·   ·   ·   ·   ·   ·   ·   ·   ·

[Remarks on the Fairy Queen, p. xciv]   Before his [Spenser's] time, Musick seems to have been so much a Stranger to our Poetry, that, excepting the Earl of *Surry's* Lyricks, we have very few Examples of Verses that had any tolerable Cadence. In *Chaucer* there is so little of this, that many of his Lines are not even restrain'd to a certain Number of Syllables.

1715. [Oldmixon, John.] *The Life and Posthumous Works of Arthur Maynwaring, Esq.,* pp. 324-6.

[p. 326]   When I was inserting some of his Poetical Works, I should have remember'd that he was the Author of the *Court of Love,* which is annex'd to a Version of *Ovid's* Art of Love, Printed by Mr. *Tonson* his Friend. I shall repeat only a few Lines. . . . Whoever will be at the Pains to compare this *Court of Love* with the Tale in *Chaucer,* from whence 'tis taken, will be extreamly well pleas'd to see how he has improv'd it; and will find the Poem intire, with *Ovid's Art* and *Remedy of Love,* Printed for Mr. *Tonson.*

[*See* above, p. 310, 1709, Maynwaring.]

1715. Sewell, [George]. *The Life and Character of Mr. John Philips,* written by Mr. Sewell, 2nd edn. 1715, [a small pamphlet], pp. 5, 6, 32, 34; [reprinted in] The Whole Works of Mr. John Philips, 1720, pp. iv, xxxv, xxxvii. [The two last references are to Philips's monument in Westminster; *see* above, 1708, Freind, etc., p. 295-6, and below, 1823, Neale.]

[p. 5]   Nor was he less curious in observing the Force and Elegancy of his Mother Tongue, but, by the Example of his Darling *Milton,* search'd backwards into the Works of our Old *English* Poets, to furnish himself with proper, sounding, and significant Expressions, and prove the due Extent, and Compass of the *Language.* For this purpose, he carefully read over *Chaucer, Spenser;* and, afterwards, in his Writings, did not scruple to revive any Words, or Phrases, which he thought deserv'd it. . . .

17$\frac{15}{16}$. Brome, William. *Letter to Thomas Hearne,* dated Feb. 22. 17$\frac{15}{16}$, MS. Rawl. Lett. 13, f. 140, [abstract of first part in] Remarks and Collections of T. Hearne, Oxford Hist. Soc., vol. v, ed. D. W. Rannie, 1901, p. 175.

Dear Sir I received yours of Jan. y^e 6th . . . by the Bearer of this I intend to write to D^r. Terry to deliver the Books and MSS. belonging to Dr. Sloane and Mr. Bagford to you ; and shall acquaint him that your discharge shall be as obliging as one under my own hand , so I hope upon your waiting upon him they will be deliver'd to you, except the Editors of Chaucer have farther occasion for them, and then I suppose by your interposition Dr. Sloane will oblige them by a longer loan of them. . . .

17$\frac{15}{16}$. Hearne, Thomas. *Letters* (1) to William Brome (MS. Rawl. Lett. 13, f. 141), (2) to Hans Sloane (MS. Rawl. Lett. 39, f. 80), both dated Feb. 28, 17$\frac{15}{16}$, (3) to James Sotheby (MS. Rawl. Lett. 16, f. 92) dated March 1, 17$\frac{15}{16}$, (4) to Thomas Rawlinson, (MS. Rawl. Lett. 33, f. 16), dated March 13, 17$\frac{15}{16}$, [abstracts in] Remarks and Collections of T. Hearne, Oxford Hist. Soc., vol. v, ed. D. W. Rannie, 1901, pp. 178–9, 182.

[To W. Brome] Feb. 28 . . . Sir, I rec[d] yesterday D[r]. Sloane's two MSS. that were in D[r]. Terry's Hands, and have left a note of them with Him. I have sent them this day to D[r]. Sloane. At the same time D[r]. Terry deliver'd me M[r]. Bagford's Copy of Caxton's Ed. . . D[r]. Terry hath not M[r]. [Thomas] Rawlinson's Copy, at least he does not find it. I remember y[t] it was a small old MS : but I did not take down the Title, and have no other note ab[t] it then this, viz. *June* 16th (*Mond.*) 1712. *Rec[d]. of M[r]. Rawlinson a Chaucer for M[r] Urry, w[ch] I delivered to M[r]. Urry the same day.* I took no note for it of M[r]. Urry. I hope you will be able to find it. I will write ab[t] it to M[r]. Rawlinson himself, who perhaps can recover the Title. I am, Sir, . . .

[To H. Sloane] Feb. 28 . . . Hon[rd]. Sir, I have at last heard from M[r]. Brome, and yesterday D[r]. Terry delivered me your two Chaucers, viz. (1) The works of G. Chaucer Lond. 1598. in fol. mark'd P. 150. (2) Tractatus Astrologico Magicus, with a discourse written by S[r]. G. Chaucers own hand of the Astrolabe mark'd MS. 378. in 4°.—I sent them to you by this day's waggon y[t] sets up at y[e] Oxford Arms. I formerly sent you the Conclusion of y[e] Astrolabe by G. Chaucer mark'd MS. 324. in fol. so y[t] now you have all y[t] you was pleased to lend M[r]. Urry. I hope the two I now send may come safe, and I am, . . .

[To James Sotheby] Mar. 1. . . . . Tell M[r]. Bagford I have procured his Copy of Chaucer of Caxton's Ed.

[To Thomas Rawlinson] Mar. 13. . . . . Be pleased to send me the Title of the little MS. that you lent M[r]. Urry, I cannot otherwise procure it for you. I did not put it down. And I do not find y^t they are very ready to return Books unless the Titles can be given them distinctly.

17$\frac{15}{16}$. **Sloane**, Hans. *Letter to Thomas Hearne*, dated March 1, 17$\frac{15}{16}$. MS. Rawl. Lett. 9, f. 75. [abstract in] Remarks and Collections of T. Hearne, Oxford Hist. Soc., vol. v, ed. D. W. Rannie, 1901, p. 179.

S^r., I give you very many thanks for yor favours and the books [edns. of Chaucer] which I received last night and which without yor help I should have lost. I am much in yor debt on that and many other accounts and should be glad to have it in my power to shew you that I am very sincerely yor most obed^t. . . .

[1716.] **Bridges**, John. *Letter to Thomas Hearne* [*c*. June 5, 1716] (MS. Rawl. Lett. 3, f. 5) [abstract in] Remarks and Collections of T. Hearne, Oxford Hist. Soc., vol. v, ed. D. W. Rannie, 1901, p. 233.

I saw Chaucers Picture, wch Mr. Murray mentions to be in his Custody . . .

1716. **Hearne**, Thomas. *Letters* to Thomas Rawlinson, dated Mar. 30, and April 27, (MS. Rawl. Lett. 33, f. 20 and 33, f. 21) to John Murray, dated June 3, (MS. Rawl. Lett. 112, f. 71) [abstracts in] Remarks and Collections of T. Hearne, Oxford Hist. Soc., vol. v, ed. D. W. Rannie, 1901, pp. 190–1, 211, 231–2.

[To T. Rawlinson], March 30, 1716. . . . I desired you to send me the Title of the little MS. of Chaucer y^t you lent M^r. Urry.—I urge the Request again, that I may get it again. If you do not call to mind what it was it will be lost, the Books being all at Christ-Church in D^r. Terry's Hands, to whom they were delivered by M^r. Broome. I got D^r. Sloane's and M^r. Bagford's, otherwise theirs would have been lost too.

[To T. Rawlinson], Ap. 27, 1716. . . . I hope you will take care to retrieve your two Chaucers. I suppose they are in D^r. Terry's Hands. . . .

[To John Murray], June 3, 1716. I have preserved your notes about Hoccleve in one of my Books [see below, p. 344, Diary for June 26, 1716]. I long to see the MS. it self, particularly the Picture of Chaucer.

1716. Hearne, Thomas. *Extract from his Diary,* June 26, 1716, [in] Remarks and Collections of T. Hearne, Oxford Hist. Soc., vol. v, ed. D. W. Rannie, 1901, p. 241, and App. p. 382.

The Note here pasted in about Occleve I had from Mr. John Murray of London, who hath got a fine MS. of Occleve de Regimine Principis, with Chaucer's Picture done by Occleve :—

Thomas Hoccleve wrote this Book about y⁰ year of our Lord 1400, and dedicated and presented it to Henry, Duke of Monmouth. This Hoccleve was Friend and, by his own Testimony, Scholar of Geofry Chaucer & Jn⁰ Gower, whose wit and Eloquence he largely Extolls, and has depicted the Portraiture of Geofry Chavcer in yᵉ Margin of yᵉ 71 Page, with yᵉ praises of yᵉ same Chavcer. . . .

1716. Brome, William. *Letter to Thomas Hearne,* dated Sept. 19, 1716 (Rawl. 3, 130) [abstract in] Remarks and Collections of T. Hearne, Oxford Hist. Soc., vol. v, ed. D. W. Rannie, 1901, pp. 314–5.

If you are acquainted with Mʳ. Tickell of Queen's Coll. Enquire of him whether he ever lent Mʳ. Urry an old Chaucer, that if he has, I may look after the Book.

1716. *Proposals for Printing Chaucer's Works,* dated June 30, 1716, inserted before the title page of the interleaved and annotated copy of Urry's edn. of Chaucer in B. M. [pr. m. 643. m. 4].

Proposals for printing by subscription the Works of the celebrated and ancient English Poet Jeoffrey Chaucer : Carefully compar'd, not only with former Editions of Value, but with many rare and ancient MANUSCRIPTS : From the Collating of which the Text is in a great Measure restor'd and perfected ; many Errors and Corruptions that have crept in, *and continued in all the Editions hitherto printed,* are amended ; and many whole Lines, omitted in all the Printed Editions, are inserted in their proper Places.

Three entire New TALES of this Author in *Manuscript* (never yet printed) have been recovered, and will be added to this· Edition ; by which *Alterations, Amendments,* and *Additions,* this Work is in a manner become new.

This Work was at first undertaken and was very near compleated by John Urry, Student of *Christ-Church, Oxon,* and is now finish'd from his Papers by a Member of the same College. A more Useful and Copious Glossary, for the better Understanding of this Poet, than has yet been printed, will be added at the End by Anthony Hall, A.M., Fellow of *Queen's-College, Oxon.*

N.B. One third of the Monies, that shall arise from Sub-scriptions, will be Employ'd towards the finishing of *Peck-Water* Quadrangle in *Christ-Church*; so that all Subscribers to this Edition will be Benefactors to that College.

[On the back of the page of which we have given the text above, is printed the Queen's Licence to Urry (or his executors) for the sole Printing of Chaucer for 14 years from 25 July 1714 (*see* below, Appendix A., 1714), and there follows a specimen page of the Prologue to the Canterbury Tales. Timothy Thomas did the Glossary eventually, not Anthony Hall, as advertised.]

1716. Unknown. *Brown Bread and Honour, A Tale moderniz'd from an Ancient Manuscript of Chaucer.* London. Printed for John Morphew, near Stationers-Hall, 1716 (Price 3*d.*).

[There is nothing about Chaucer in the poem, which is a satire in verse, the title being founded on the Prol. to W. of Bath's Tale, ll. 143–4;

> Lat hem be breed of pured whete-seed,
> And lat us wyves hoten barly-breed.]

1717. Catcott, [Alexander Stopford]. *The Court of Love. A Vision from Chaucer.* Oxford, 1717.

[A free paraphrase in heroic couplets of the original poem, which is not by Chaucer.]

[1717. Dennis, John.] *A True Character of Mr. Pope.* The Second Edition. p. 3. [Not in first edition.]

. . . In all his Productions, he has been an *Imitator* . . . His *Pastorals* were writ in Imitation of VIRGIL . . . His *Temple of Fame*, of CHAUCER.

1717. [Fenton, Elijah.] *A Tale Devised in the pleasaunt manere of gentil Maister* JEOFFREY CHAUCER [no reference to Chaucer in the Poem] Poems on Several Occasions [by Elijah Fenton]. Printed for Bernard Lintot, 1717, p. 169. (The Works of the English Poets, by Dr. Samuel Johnson. Additional Lives by A. Chalmers, 1810, vol. x, p. 412.)

1717. Gay, John. *An Answer to the Sompner's Prologue of Chaucer In Imitation of Chaucer's Style.* [published in] Poems on Several Occasions, by Mr. John Gay, . . . London . . . 1720, vol. ii, pp. 311–5. (Poems of John Gay, Muses' Library, ed. John Underhill, 1893, vol. ii, pp. 379–81; the note on p. 378 as to date of first appearance is incorrect.)

1717. Pope, Alexander. *Eloisa to Abelard,* [in] The Works of Mr. Alexander Pope, 4°, p. 421. (Works, 1871, vol. ii, p. 241.)

> Love, free as air, at sight of human ties,
> Spreads his light wings, and in a moment flies.

<small>[The reference is to the Frankeleyn's Tale, ll. 36–88. See below, p. 489.]</small>

1717. [Sewell, George.] *Memoirs* [prefixed to] Poems of Henry Howard Earl of Surrey, pp. xv–xvi.

<small>[Sewell quotes Fenton's lines on Chaucer. *See* above, 1710–11, p. 313.]</small>

1717. Winchelsea, Anne, Countess of. *To Mr Pope, by the Right Honourable Anne, Countess of Winchelsea,* [in] The Works of Mr Alexander Pope. London. Printed for Bernard Lintot 1717. fol. sign. d. i. (Pope, Works, 1871, vol. i, p. 21.)

> Your Tales be easy, natural and gay,
> Nor all the Poet in that part display;
> Nor let the Critic, there his skill unfold,
> For *Boccace* thus, and *Chaucer* tales have told.

1718. Dart, John. *The Complaint of the Black Knight, from Chaucer,* by Mr. Dart. *Preface,* sign. a 2, a 5 *b.*

He [Chaucer] who doubtless was a gentleman indu'd with all the Accomplishments that could oblige the Learned, and the Fair; He who was finely turn'd for the Court, and excellently form'd for Love, seems now [through the obsoleteness of his language] a very unfashionable courtier and an anti- [sign.a 5] quated Lover. . . . I could wish that Gentlemen would [sign. a 5 b] unite their Endeavours to dress him intirely in a more refin'd Habit . . . that he may be fashionable to keep Company with the Ladies who otherwise are depriv'd of Conversing with the greatest Poet that *England* (or perhaps the World) ever produc'd.

<small>[There are references to Chaucer on every page of the preface. This is really Lydgate's poem, 1402–3 (*q. v.* above, p. 16), and references to Chaucer's Knight's Tale are on pp. 19–20 of this edition.]</small>

1718. Gildon, Charles. *The Complete Art of Poetry,* vol. i, pp. 67, 82.

[p. 67] [Various objections to Poetry. That it is the mother of Lies, the Nurse of Abuse] 'Tis farther urged, that *Chaucer* says, that before *Boers* [*sic for* Poets] had soften'd us, we were full of *Courage,* and given to Martial Exercises, the Pillars of *Manlike Liberty;* not lull'd asleep in *Shady Idleness,* and *Poetical Pastimes.*

.   .   .   .

[p. 82]   As for its Rise in *England,* especially in our native Tongue,
we have very blind Footsteps to trace it; *Chaucer, Gower,*
and *Lydgate,* were the first who made any tolerable Figure in
that Dress; of whom Chaucer is the only one who may justly
claim the Name of a Poet. After him, *English* Poetry was
totally neglected. . . .

[The first part of this book is an essay on Poetry, and the second part a collection of
extracts from various poets on different subjects, of the same nature as Bysshe's Art
of Poetry, 1702. In vol. ii, to face title page, Chaucer is among the list of "Authors
cited in this Book," but all quotations are from Dryden's versions.]

[1718 ?] **Prior**, Matthew. *In the same* [*i. e.* Chaucer's] *Style* [in]
Poems on several occasions by M. Prior, 1718, pp. 289-90. (Prior's
poetical works, ed. R. Brimley Johnson (Aldine edn.), 1892, vol. ii,
p. 3.)

[A poem in 4 accented rhyming couplets, with no Chaucer
reference.]

1718. **Sewell**, George. *The Proclamation of Cupid, or, a Defence of
Women, a poem from Chaucer,* by Mr. Sewell. London . . 1718
[a folio pamphlet of 20 pp.]. Sign. * a *b.,* a and a *b.*

To the Ladies.

To You, bright *British Fair,* whom she defends,
The Muse her undesigning Verse commends :
Smile, while She makes old *Chaucer* plead your Cause ;
It is no Crime to give the Dead Applause,
For never Man, nor even *Woman* yet
Made lewd Constructions on a buried *Wit.*
If Graves and Tombstones don't offend your Ears,
He has been shrouded—*full three hundred Years ;*
And now returns to shame this graceless Age,
Who Libel *Woman* from the Press, and Stage : . . .

.   .   .   .

Our Bard, who if from Picture we may trace,
Had Strength, and Vigour, and an *English* Face,
Scorn'd the Design of Nature's Gifts to spoil,
And damn his comely Person by his Stile.
He knew, whate'er might be his secret Thoughts
The Sex too well, to tell them half their Faults,

Not that he flatter'd them, and gave Pretence
To those he courted, to suspect his Sense.

    .   .   .   .   .   .

Chaucer, who shuns the Folly of Extremes,
With Wit and Truth records these common Themes;
Not wholly to the *Fair* devotes his Pen,
But wisely turns the Satyr on the Men:
Their Arts, their Stratagems at large displays,
And telling them, gives *Woman* silent Praise.

    .   .   .   .

The Preface.

[sign. a]   This Poem is generally admired by those who can taste it in the obsolete Language of the Author, which inclin'd me to believe it would not be unpleasing in a Modern Dress, the Subject being adapted to all Times, Humours, and almost every Stage of Life: . . .

Chaucer knew the State of the Case between the Sexes as well as the best Poets of any Age, and in this Piece has plainly shewn what a Master he was of Human Nature: . . .

[sign. a b]   I must not dissemble that in some Editions of *Chaucer* this Work is attributed to *Thomas Occleve* a Scholar of his, and is said to have bore [*sic*] this Title, *A Treatise of the Conversation of Men and Women in the little Island of Albion.* But this in all Probability is a mere Fiction; the Title indeed might be added by *Occleve*, but *Leland* positively ascribes *Epistolam Cupidinis* to *Chaucer*, and reckons it among his *genuine* Pieces. What makes this more probable is, that *Chaucer* refers to his *Legend of Good Women* in this Poem, and to the *Romaunt of the Rose*, which he translated from the *French* of *John de Mohun*. I know the common Story of *Occleve's* Recantation, but I believe this Authority enough to overballance that; beside that *Chaucer* in his *Praise of Woman* has much the Same Thoughts, and goes upon the same Topicks as in this *Letter* of *Cupid's*.

I cannot call this Attempt of Mine an *Imitation*, for though I have commonly had the Poet's Scheme in my Eye, yet I have very often taken the Liberty of grafting upon his Stock, where I fancied it would bear it without forcing Nature too much. As to the Design, No one ought to be offended since the *Satyr* is pretty equally dealt on each Hand; there is Severity, but the Severity of a Court-Poet; much Wit and more good Manners. This I speak of the Original . . .

1720. Jacob, Giles. *An Historical Account of the Lives and Writings of our most Considerable English Poets* [being the 2nd vol. of the] Poetical Register, 1719, pp. v, 26–30, 36, 55, 66, 93–4, 148–9, 191, 203, 277. [Opposite the title page are the pictures of Milton, Butler, Chaucer, Cowley, Waller; Chaucer's picture, in the middle, is the largest and most prominent.]

[p. v]   [Dedication to the Duke of Buckingham.]

If all the Poets, whose writings I have enumerated, . . . were yet living, they would approve my choice in Addressing to Your Grace as to the most proper Patron for a Work of this Nature: they would all jointly and unanimously trust the Decision of their Fame to Your Grace's Judgment; and *Chaucer, Spenser,* and *Milton* would stand by the Determination of the Duke of *Buckingham.*

[pp. 26–30] [Life of Chaucer.]

[The usual account of Chaucer, educated at both Universities, his Travels, position at Court, &c.] . . . His liberal Education at the Universities, and his Improvements in foreign Countries, rendered him both fit for the Court at home, and also for the greatest Employments abroad; but it does not appear that he had any other Preferment than that of Poet Laureat in the Reigns of *Henry* the Fourth and *Henry* the Fifth. This he obtained by the Interest of *John* of *Gaunt,* the Great Earl of *Lancaster* (to whom he was allied by Marriage), and Knighted upon that occasion. . . .

Some Authors, for the sweetness of his Poetry, compare him to *Stesichorus;* and as *Cethegus* was called, *Suadæ Medulla,* so *Chaucer* may be esteemed the Sinews of Eloquence, and the very Life of all Mirth and Pleasantry in Writing. He had one Excellency above all other Poets, and wherein, none, since his time, but the famous *Shakespear,* has come near him, *viz.* Such a lively Description of Persons and Things, that it seems to surpass Imagination, and you see everything before your Eyes which you only Read: And herein his *Canterbury Tales* are most valued and esteemed. [Here follow appreciations by Sir Henry Savile, Spenser, Sidney, Sir John Denham, Sir Richard Baker, Camden,

[p. 29] Leland.] He died in the year 1400 after he had lived above Seventy two Years . . .

[p. 36]   [Life of Mr. Samuel Cobb, who wrote the Miller's Tale, from Chaucer. *See* above, 1712, p. 319.]

[p. 55]   [Life of Elijah Fenton, and Works. He wrote A Tale in the manner of Chaucer. *See* above 1717, p. 345.]

[p. 66] [Life of Gower.]

[pp. 93–4] [Life of Lydgate.] . . . He justly acquired the Reputation of the best Author of the Age, wherein he lived; and if *Chaucer's* Works had greater Learning, *Lydgate's* were superior for Language. His Poetry is so pure, and so easie, that one might mistake him for a Modern writer.

[pp. 148–9] [Life of Pope. List of his Works.] *The Temple of Fame.* . . . The Hint of this Piece was taken from *Chaucer's House of Fame.*

January and May . . . from *Chaucer*. *The Wife of Bath*, from Chaucer.

[p. 191] [Life of John Skelton.] During his Restraint, either to amuse his solitude, or at the Request of the Abbot, he adorn'd the Monuments of Several great Personages in *Westminster Abbey* with Tables and Epitaphs; as those of *Sigebert* the *Saxon*, *Henry VII, Chaucer,* and others; some of which still remain, tho' most of them were destroy'd in the grand Rebellion.

[p. 203] [Life of Spenser, buried near Chaucer.]

[p. 277] [Life of N. Rowe, buried near Chaucer.]

1720. Lewis, John. *The History of the Life and Sufferings of the Reverend and Learned John Wicliffe, D.D.*, London, 1720, ch. x, pp. 175, 201.

[Chap. x, p. 175] An Account of the principal Persons who favoured Dr. *Wicliffe* and his Doctrines.

[*Leland de scriptor. Britann., p. 420*] *Geoffery Chaucer.* He is said to have been educated in *Canterbury* or *Merton* College with *John Wicliffe*, and thereupon to have commenced an accute [*sic*] Logician, a sweet Rhetorician, a pleasant Poet, a grave Philosopher, and an ingenious Mathematician, and an holy Divine. He died 1400, *æta.* 72.

[For Leland's Life *see* below, Appendix A, c. 1545.]

1720. [Sewell, George.] *A Defence of Women of* [*sic*] *the Proclamation of Cupid, a poem from Chaucer. The Preface to the Proclamation of Cupid. Preface to The Song of Troilus,* and *The Song of Troilus* [in] A New Collection of original Poems, never before printed in any Miscellany, by the Author of Sir Walter Raleigh. London, 1720, pp. 16–22, 43 *n.*, 44 *n.*, 82–5.

[The first poem here referred to, and the prefatory verses and Preface, are an exact reprint from *The Proclamation of Cupid,* 1718. *See* above, p. 347.]

[p. 82] Preface [to the Song of Troilus].

I have often wonder'd that *Chaucer*, the Father of our *English* Poetry, generally acknowledged as such, and frequently applauded for his Excellence, should be so *little read*, as appears from most of our Modern Compositions. His Fame is taken upon Credit, from the Recommendations of others; and they who speak of him, rather pay a blind Veneration to his Antiquity than his intrinsic Worth, which perhaps may bear a Competition with the Refiners of Poetry in any other Language. They who seem most to have studied him, are our incomparable *Spenser*, *Milton*, and *Dryden;* others have but mimick'd his Garb, without hitting his Air and Mien. An old Word, or Phrase or two, accidentally thrown among twenty modern and fashionable ones, have given an unjust Repute to some Imitations of *Chaucer*. In the mean time, the Boldness of his Imagery, the natural Beauty of his Similitudes, and the Delicacy of his Thoughts, are generally neglected, though his best Ornaments: They have rubb'd of his Rust for their own Use, and left the Steel in the Possession of the right Owner. Mr. *Dryden* indeed stands an exception to this Accusation, he never missing, but improving [p. 83] every noble Hint of this Author; regardless of the Expression, his view is at the Sense, the Spirit, the Figures of his Predecessor. Before ever he undertook to dress him in Modern *English*, it is plain to me, that he was an early Admirer of him, and transferr'd many of his Beauties into his own Poems; as commendable a Design, as *Virgil*'s in borrowing from *Ennius*, and *Lucretius*. I could give many instances of this; but let one general, and one particular be sufficient. The manner of reasoning in Verse, which Mr. *Dryden* so artfully introduced into his *Heroic Plays*, is entirely *Chaucer*'s, as may be seen even by this little Piece following. That he used his Images and Thoughts, be this a Testimony. In the Description of *Absalom*'s Beauty, he summs up all with this Line;

And Paradise was open'd in his Face.

Chaucer in his Cresseide, says,

That Paradise stood formed in her Eyen.

The Thought in this *Song* has been used, and diversified a hundred times since *Chaucer*'s Days; and yet he seems to have said more, and that more pathetically than any of his Imitators. It is taken from the First Book of *Troilus* and *Cresseide*; and the Reader by a Comparison may see how little Variation there is from the Original, and give his Judgment at Pleasure. I only wish that so excellent a Poet as *Chaucer* may be no longer admir'd at a Distance, but brought into the Acquaintance of the Polite World; and it it is to be hoped the *New Edition* of his Works [Urry's Chaucer, 1721] will compleat that Wish.

1720. Strype, John. *A Survey of the Cities of London and Westminster: . . . Written at first in the Year MDXCVIII. By John Stow. . . . Since Reprinted and Augmented by the Author; And afterwards by A. M., H. D. and others. Now Lastly, Corrected, Improved, and very much Enlarged: . . . By John Strype, M.A. . . . The Second Volume. . . .* London. *. . .* MDCCXX. *. . .*
A Survey of the City of Westminster. Book VI. *. . . The Monastry of St.* PETER, 31.

In the South Ile.

Galfridus Chaucer, *Poêta celeberrimus, qui primus* Anglicam *Poêsin ita illustravit, ut* Anglicus Homerus *habeatur. Obiit* 1400. *Anno vero* 1555. Nicholaus Brigham, *Musarum nomine hujus ossa transtulit, & illi novum tumulum ex marmore, his versibus inscriptis posuit :* He lyeth buried in the South Part of the Church.

> *Qui fuit* Anglorum *Vates ter maximus olim,*
> Galfridus Chaucer, *conditur hoc tumulo.*
> *Annum si quæras Domini, si tempora mortis,*
> *Ecce notæ subsunt, quæ tibi cuncta notant.*

25 Octobris, 1400.

[This epitaph is not in the edition of 1598 ; in the enlarged sixth edition of 1755, it is in vol. ii, p. 604, col. 2.]

1720. Theobald, [Lewis]. *Preface* to The Tragedy of King Richard the II. . . . altered from Shakespear, By Mr. Theobald, 1720, sign. Aa 4 *b*, Bb 1.

Our late Laureat [Dryden], and some Others before him, have seem'd to be of Opinion that our Poet [Shakespeare] took his *Troilus* and *Cressida* from *Lollius* and *Chaucer*, who borrow'd his Argument from the *Lombard*. But the Incidents and Characters of these Poems are so few, their Arguments so narrow, and confin'd, in Comparison to that Scope which our Poet takes, that I dare be positive he drew out his Scheme, and modell'd it from *Homer* himself.

1720. Unknown. *Article on* and *reprint of the Cuckow and the Night-ingale,* [in] The Free-Thinker, May 24 and May 27, 1720.   Nos. ccxxvii & ccxxviii.

I was not willing to let the present Month, the fairest in the whole Circle of the Year, pass over, without entertaining my youthful Readers of either Sex, with something suitable to the Gayety of the Season.   And yet, I should have been greatly at a Loss for a proper Entertainment, had not a Gentleman whose Knowledge of the Polite Writers in every Language is the least of his Commendations, obliged me with a Piece of fine Invention out of *Chaucer,* which is properly a very elegant *May-poem* . . . .

It is hard to say, whether the copiousness of *Chaucer's* Invention, or the Liveliness of his Imagination, is most to be admired throughout his Writings.   He flourished above Three Hundred Years ago : and yet through the Cloud of his antiquated Language, his Images still shine out with greater Brightness than those which appear in any of our succeeding Poets, if we except *Spencer,* and *Shakespear,* and *Milton.*   He was a great Master of Perspicuity and Sim-plicity, in all his Narrations ; and his Expression is always precise to the Justness of his Ideas . . . *Chaucer* is, likewise, a diligent observer of Nature, whether he deals in Realities or in Fables.

1721. The Works of Geoffrey Chaucer, compared with the Former Editions and many valuable MSS.   Out of which, Three Tales are added which were never before Printed ; By John Urry, Student of Christ-Church, Oxon, Deceased : Together with a Glossary, By a Student of the same College.   To the Whole is prefixed The Author's Life, newly written, and a Preface, giving an Account of this Edition.   London, Printed for Bernard Lintot, between the Temple Gates. 1721.

[This edition is, from the point of view of the text, the worst ever issued.   Urry altered, respelt and even added words to Chaucer's text with the greatest freedom, without giving any indication that he had done so—*see* Preface by Timothy Thomas. Urry apparently did all the work of preparing the text for the press, and then died, on March 18, 17¹⁸⁄₁₉, before the prefaces, glossary &c. were written.   The rights of printing the edition were handed over by Urry to his executor Mr. Brome and the Dean and Chapter of Christ-Church and Bernard Lintot, bookseller, and proposals to print the book by subscription were issued in 1716 [*q. v.*, p. 344].   It was not, however, published till 1721, being then completed with Preface, Glossary, etc., by Timothy Thomas, which were revised for press by William Thomas.   (*See* below for W. Thomas' annotated copy.)   Urry included in this edition two spurious Tales, which had never before been printed : viz. : The Coke's Tale of Gamelyn, pp. 36-48, and the Mery Adventure of the Pardonere and Tapstere and Tale of Beryn, one piece, pp. 594–626.   For an account of Urry, *see* extract here given from the diary

CHAUCER CRITICISM.

of Thomas Hearne, Mar. 17, 17⅟₁, pp. 331–2 above, and also the whole entry in Remarks and Collections of Thomas Hearne, Oxford Hist. Soc., vol. v, ed. D. W. Rannie, 1901, pp. 33–6. *See also* the account of Urry's will given by Hearne, May 13, 1715, *ibid.*, p. 58, also pp. 72 and 105.

For further information about Urry and the production of this edition, *see* Literary Anecdotes of the 18th century, by John Nichols, 1812, vol. i, pp. 196–9, where he says, amongst much else, "About the latter end of the year 1711, it was proposed to Mr. Urry, who was a native of Scotland, by some persons well acquainted with his qualifications (who he thought, had a right to command him) to put out a new edition of Chaucer; which he was persuaded to undertake, though much against his inclinations. This recommendation was, probably, from Dean Aldrich, who well knew the talents of his pupil." Then follows a full account of the production of the book, Urry's application for a patent, his death, and epitaph, his character, the Agreement for the printing of Chaucer (*see* under 1715), the Proposals (*see* under 1716), and the Glossary; also a reference to the copy of Urry's Chaucer annotated by T. Thomas, then in the possession of Mr. A. Chalmers (now in the British Museum, *see* below), in which Thomas says that Bishop Atterbury was the chief person who proposed to Urry to undertake an edition of Chaucer. Mr. Thomas adds, that the Bishop (then Dean of Christ-Church) "did by no means judge rightly of Mr. Urry's talents in this case; who, though in many respects a most worthy person, was not qualified for a work of this nature." *See also* Tyrwhitt, in his Appendix to the Preface to the Canterbury Tales, vol. i, 1775, pp. xix, xx and *note*. "I shall say but little of that [Urry's] edition, as a very fair and full account of it is to be seen in the modest and sensible Preface prefixed to it by Mr. Timothy Thomas, upon whom the charge of publishing Chaucer devolved, or rather was imposed, after Mr. Urry's death. The strange licence, in which Mr. Urry appears to have indulged himself, of lengthening and shortening Chaucer's words according to his own fancy, and of even adding words of his own, without giving his readers the least notice, has made the text of Chaucer in his Edition by far the worst that was ever published."

Tyrwhitt adds, in a footnote to p. xx., that he learns Timothy Thomas wrote the preface "from a MS. note in an interleaved copy of Urry's Chaucer, presented to the British Museum by Mr. *William Thomas*, a brother, as I apprehend, of Mr. T. Thomas. T. Thomas was of Christ-Church, Oxford, and died in 1757, aged LIX. ... Mr. W. Thomas has taken a great deal of unnecessary pains in collating that copy of Urry's Edit. with several MSS. The best part of the various readings serves only to correct the arbitrary innovations, which Mr. Urry had introduced into the text. He has employed himself to better purpose upon the Glossary, where he has made many emendations and additions, which may be of considerable use, if ever a new Glossary to Chaucer shall be compiled." In Tyrwhitt's Advertisement to his Chaucer Glossary, published 1778, vol. v. of the Canterbury Tales, p. ii, he acknowledges his debt to T. Thomas, saying he has "built upon his foundations, and often with his materials."]

CONTENTS : [To face title page, engraved portrait of Urry.]

[Title page, as above, with engraved picture of Chaucer's tomb.]

[An engraved oval portrait of Chaucer, written above "Geoffrey Chaucer, our Antient & Learned English Poet, died 1400, Æta. 72.", and underneath :

" Anglia Chaucerum veneratur nostra Poetam,
        Cui veneres debet patria lingua suas."

Tho. Occleve Contemporar. & discipulus ejusdem Chauceri ad viv. delin.   Geo. Vertue sculp. 1717.]

[sign. a–f2] The Life of Geoffrey Chaucer.   [By Dart, corrected by W. Thomas, *see* below, pp. 358–61.]

[sign. f 2ᵇ
–i 1ᵇ.] Testimonies of Learned Men concerning Chaucer and his
Works. [By W. Thomas.]

[Testimonies from Gower, Lidgate, Occleve, Anonymous
verses taken by Speght from a book of Stow's, Gawin Douglas,
Leland, Wm. Thynne, the publisher of Lidgate's Trojan war
1555, Roger Ascham, Sir Philip Sidney, Puttenham, Fox,
Surigonius, Camden, Spenser, Verstegan, Francis Beaumont,
Sir Henry Savil, Selden, Sir John Denham, Milton, Sprat,
Skinner, Sir Richard Baker, Peacham, Will. Winstanley,
Edw. Philips, Sir Thos. Pope Blount, Rymer, Dryden—and in
MS. added by W. Thomas, the Description of Chaucer out of
Greene's Vision c. 1592, Skelton's Phillyp Sparrow, Lilius
Gyraldus Dialogi de Poetis & Flor. 1551, p. 72, Caxton at end
of his edn. of Chaucer's Boethius, Addison, Alex. Gil, Strype,
and Hearne's Letter to Bagford.]

[sign. i 2ᵃ
–m 2ᵃ] The Preface. [By T. Thomas, revised by W. Thomas.]

[sign. m 2ᵇ–n 1ᵃ] The Contents [of the Text].

[sign. n 1ᵇ–n 2ᵃ] Eight godely Questions with their Answeres.

[sign 2nᵇ] [The Licence, dated 20 July 1714, *q.v.* below, App. A, 1714.]

[sign. B (p. 1)
–p. 626] [The text.]

A Glossary explaining the obsolete and difficult words in
Chaucer [by T. Thomas].

[sign. 8 Q³
to end] A Short Account of some of the Authors cited by Chaucer.

[Description of an interleaved and annotated copy of the
above edition bound in two volumes [ordinary copies are
in one volume], notes by T. and W. Thomas, in the British
Museum, 643. m. 4.]

[vol. i] [Inserted at the beginning an Agreement for the printing of
Chaucer, in MS., dated 1715. *See* above, pp. 333–4.]

Proposals [for printing Chaucer by subscription, two pages
printed folio, dated June 30, 1716. *See* above, pp. 344–5].

[Title page as above, with engraved picture of Chaucer's
tomb.]

[Inserted between portrait of Urry and title page, two copies
of Urry's epitaph (1714, *see* above, p. 332), one in Urry's
writing, the other a copy.]

Testimonies of Learned Men concerning Chaucer and his
Works, sign. f 2 *b.*–i 1 *b.* [MS. note "collected by W. T.
1720."]

The Preface, [MS. note "by T. T. with corrections and
additions by W. T."] sign. i 2–m 2.

[MS. leaf inserted between sign. l 1 *b* and l 2, containing a description of three MS. copies of the Canterbury Tales belonging to the Earl of Oxford.]

[On blank page before the Glossary extract in MS. from a letter from Mr. Wotton, May 5, 1722. *See* below, p. 363.]

[vol. ii] A Glossary explaining the obsolete and difficult words in Chaucer [MS. note "By Timothy Thomas"], sign. 7 U 2– 8 Q 1.

[Copious MS. notes all through by Timothy Thomas and by W. Thomas.]

1721. Bailey, Nathan. *An Universal Etymological Dictionary.*

[Occasional references to Chaucer, *e. g. Abedge.* Chatterton is known to have used Bailey's Dictionary; *see* below, *a.* 1770, p. 433.]

1721. Thomas, Timothy. *Preface and Glossary* to The Works of Chaucer . . . printed by John Urry . . . London, 1721. [MS. note in margin : "by T. T. with corrections and additions by W. T."] also copious MS. notes to edn. of Urry's Chaucer [B. M. pr. m. 643. m. 4.]

[sign. i 2] The Reader will meet with no more interruption here, than will be necessary to acquaint him in some measure with Mr. *Urry*'s Design in this Edition . . . . As for my self, I was equally a stranger to Mr. *Urry* and his Undertaking, till some time after his Death; when a Person [in a MS. note in margin 'Dr. Smalridge, then Dean of Christ Church'] whose Commands I was in all Duty bound to obey, put the Works of *Chaucer* into my hands, with his Instructions to assist in carrying on this Edition, and to prepare Matter for a *Glossary* to it. Mr. *Thomas Ainsworth* of *Christ-Church* had been employed by Mr. *Urry* in transcribing part of the Work for the Press, and was therefore thought qualified to proceed in preparing the rest for my perusal. This Gentleman likewise dyed in *August* 1719, soon after the whole Text of *Chaucer* was printed off. . . .

About the latter end of the year 1711, some Persons well acquainted with Mr. *Urry*'s Qualifications [MS. note :—'Dr. Atterbury, Dean of Ch. Ch.'] (who, he thought, had a right to command him) proposed to him to put out a new Edition of *Chaucer*; which he was perswaded to undertake, though much against his inclination : "For, though (as he says) his skill in the Northern Language spoken in the Lowlands of *Scotland* qualified him to read this Poet with more ease and pleasure than one altogether bred be-South *Trent* could do without more than common Application, yet he assures us, he had not the least thought of publishing his private Diversions.

Having thus undertaken the Work, he proposed to proceed in this Method, *viz.* to correct the Text of *Chaucer*, and add what he could find of his Works in MSS. which had not been printed; to make some Observations upon the Author, and among other things to shew where he had imitated or borrowed from the *Greek* or *Latin* Poets; to add a more copious *Glossary* than had been printed before; to write a fuller Account of his Life than had been yet published; and to acquaint the Reader in a Preface what he should have performed in this Edition. . . . .

[sign. i2b] His chief business was to make the Text more correct and compleat than before. He found it was the opinion of some learned Men that *Chaucer's* Verses originally consisted of an equal number of Feet; and he himself was perswaded that *Chaucer* made them exact Metre, and therefore he proposed in this Edition to restore him (to use his own Expression) *to his feet again*, which he thought might be performed by a careful Collation of the best printed Editions and good MSS.

He had observed that several Initial and Final Syllables in use in *Chaucer's* time, and since, had been omitted or added at pleasure in the MSS. by unskilful Transcribers, from whence the same Errors crept into the Printed Editions, whereby many Verses were rendered unjust in their Measure; so that the lameness of many of them might easily be remedied by the discreet Addition or Omission of such Syllables.

The Initial Syllables were chiefly *a, i,* and *y.* . . . The Final Syllables . . . the chiefest of which . . . was the Final *è,* which he always marked with an accent when he judged it necessary to pronounce it; . . . . Whether the assistance of this Final *è* be not here too frequently, and sometimes unnecessarily, called in, is not my business at present to enquire into. . . . [Other methods used by Urry of lengthening the words were the pronounciation of the terminations *ed* and *id* in the past tenses of verbs, &c., of *en* and *in* as terminations of verbs, nouns and adverbs, and of the [sign.k1]plural endings *es* and *is*] And in short I find it acknowledged by him, "That whenever he could by no other way help a Verse to a Foot, which he was perswaded it had when it came from the Maker's hands, but lost by the Ignorance of

Transcribers, or Negligence of Printers, he made no scruple to supply it with some Word or Syllable that serv'd for an Expletive ": But I find at the same time that he had once a design of enclosing such words in hooks thus [   ] to distinguish them from what he found justified by the authority of MSS., but how it came to pass that so just, useful and necessary a Design was not executed, I cannot satisfy the curious Reader. . . .

[Then follows a complete list and description of the various MSS. and the printed editions of Chaucer consulted.]

[For some account of T. Thomas, and appreciation of his work, see Tyrwhitt's Preface to the Canterbury Tales, vol. i, 1775, p. xx and note, also Advertisement to Glossary, vol. v, 1778, p. ii, partially reprinted here in the note to Urry's edition, p. 354 above.]

1721. Dart, John. *Life of Geoffrey Chaucer,* prefixed to Urry's edition of Chaucer's Works, 1721, [*q. v.*], sign. a 1–f. 2.

[sign. b 2] Thus beloved, esteemed and honoured, he spent his younger years in a constant attendance upon the Court, and for the most part living near it, when residing at *Woodstock,* in a square stone house near the Park Gate, still called *Chaucer's House,* That this was the chief place of his abode, appears by his frequent descriptions of the Park ; as particularly a *Park walled with green stone (note* Bl. Kn. 42), that being the first Park walled in *England,* and not many years before his time. In most of his pieces, where he designs an imaginary Scene, he certainly copies it from a real Landskape : So in his *Cuckow* and *Nightingale,* the *Morning walk* he takes was such as at this day may be traced from his House through part of the Park, and down by the Brook into the Vale under *Blenheim* Castle, as certainly as we may assert that Maples in stead of *Phylireas,* were the ornaments round the Bower ; which place he likewise describes in his Dream, as a white Castle standing upon a hill ; the Scene in that Poem being laid in *Woodstock* Park. . . .

[sign. a 2 b] When disengaged from publick Affairs, his time was entirely spent in study and reading : So agreeable to him was this exercise, that he says, he preferred it to all other sports and diversions. He lived within himself, neither desirous to hear nor busy to concern himself with the affairs of his Neighbours. His course of living was temperate and regular ; he went to rest with the Sun, and rose before it, and by that means enjoyed the pleasures of the better part of the day, his morning walk and fresh contemplations. This gave him the Advantage of describing the Morning in so lively a manner as he does everywhere in his Works : The springing Sun glows warm in his lines, and the fragrant Air blows cool in his descriptions ; we smell the sweets of the bloomy Haws, and hear the Musick of the feathered Choir, when ever we take a Forrest walk with him. The hour of the day is not easier to be discovered from the Reflexion of the Sun in *Titian*'s Paintings, than in *Chaucer*'s Morning Landskapes. 'Tis true those Descriptions are sometimes too long, and (as it is before observed) when he takes those early rambles, he almost tires his Reader with following him, and seldom knows how to get out of a Forrest, when once entered into it : But how advantageous this beautiful extravagance is, most of his Successors well know, who have very plentifully lopt off his exuberant Beauties, and placed them as the chief Ornaments of their own Writings.

His Reading was deep, and extensive, his Judgment sound, and discerning : but yet (a thing rarely found in Men of great Learning and poignant Wit) he was communicative of his Knowledge, and ready to correct or pass over the Faults of his Cotemporary Writers. He knew how to judge of, and to excuse the slips of weaker Capacities, and pitied rather than exposed the Ignorance of that Age.

In one word, he was a great Scholar, a pleasant Wit, a candid Critick, a sociable Companion, a stedfast Friend, a grave Philosopher, a temperate OEconomist and a pious Christian. He was not unacquainted with the ancient Rules of Poetry, nor did he disdain to follow them, tho' he thought it the least part of a Poet's perfections. As he had a discerning Eye, he discovered Nature in all her appearances, and stript off every disguise with which the *Gothick* Writers had cloathed her : He knew that those Dresses would change as Times altered ; but that she herself would always be the same, and that she could never fail to please in her simple attire, nor that Writer who drew her so ; and therefore despising the mean assistances of Art, he copied her close. He knew what it was to be *nimis Poeta*, and avoided it as the most dangerous extreme. His Strokes are bold, and his Colours lively ; but the first not too much laboured, nor the other too showy or glaring. There is a wild Beauty in his Works, which comes nearer the Descriptions of *Homer*, than any other that followed him : And though his Pieces have not that regular disposition as those of the *Grecians*, yet the several Parts separately compared, bear an equal value with theirs; and Mr. *Dryden*, than whom there was no better Judge of the Beauties of *Homer* and *Virgil*, positively asserts that he exceeded the latter, and stands in competition with the former. Whoever reads the *Knight's Tale*, which is the best of his Performances, being a finished Epick Poem, and examines the Characters, the Sentiments, the Diction, Disposition, and Time, will find that he was not unacquainted with the Rules of that way of Writing; but this requires an abler hand, and longer time to enlarge upon it.

That he was a true Master of Satyr, none will deny. It is true the Persons levelled against, and the Crimes exposed, would not allow of the severe Scourge *Juvenal* made use of, nor was there such a variety of Follies as *Horace* facetiously exploded : Not but that *Chaucer* had a Scene of Vice in the Court of that time, capable of supplying him with matter sufficient for the sharpest strokes of Satyr; but he was wise enough not to exasperate a Court by which he was supported . . . and having a Court to back him, he has shewn by severely lashing an ignorant and corrupt Clergy, that he could (had it been safe) have applied as severe a lash to a vicious irreligious Laity. . . .

That in the Elegiack Kind of Poetry he was a compleat Master, appears plainly by his *Complaint of the Black Knight*, the Poem called *La belle Dame sans mercy*, and several of his Songs. He was an excellent Master of Love-Poetry. . . . His *Troilus* and *Creseide* is one of the most beautiful Poems of that kind. . . .

It is thought by some that his Verses every where consist of an equal number of feet, and that if read with a right accent, are no where deficient; but those nice discerning Persons would find it difficult with all their straining and working, to spin out some of his Verses into a measure of ten Syllables. He was not altogether regardless of his Numbers; but his thoughts were more intent upon solid sense than gingle, and he tells us plainly that we must not expect regularity in all his Verses.

His Language, how unintelligible soever it may seem, is more modern than that of any of his Cotemporaries, or of those that followed him at the distance of Fifty or Sixty

[sign f. 1]

years, as *Harding, Skelton* and others; and in some places
it is to this day so smooth, concise, and beautiful, that even
Mr. *Dryden* would not attempt to alter it, but has copied
some of his Verses almost *literatim* : And *Chaucer* was the
first that adorned and amplified the *English* Tongue from the
Provençal . . .

[In the annotated copy of Urry's Chaucer in B. M. (pr. ṁ. 643. m. 4), Timothy
Thomas has written the following note at the head of Dart's Life of Chaucer: "This
Life was very uncorrectly drawn up by Mr. Dart, and corrected and enlarged by
W. T. [*i. e.* William Thomas], especially in that part which gives an accoᵗ. of the
Author's works, as will appear by the Or[iginal] with W. T.'s corrⁿˢ. reposited wᵗʰ
the Rᵗ. Honᵇˡᵉ. Edwᵈ. E. of Oxford &c. in his Library." *See also* Dart's remarks on
the way his " Life" was cut down and altered, below, p. 865.]

1721. Atterbury, Francis. *Letter* to Pope, dated Aug. 2, 1721, [printed
in] Pope's Works, 1871, vol. ix, p. 26.

I have found time to read some parts of Shakespeare, which
I was least acquainted with. I protest to you in a hundred
places I cannot construe him : I do not understand him. The
hardest part of Chaucer is more intelligible to me than some
of those scenes . . .

1721. Dart, John. *Westminster Abbey, a Poem,* 1721 [printed in]
Westmonasterium, by John Dart, 1742, vol. i, pp. xxxviii–ix.

[vol, i,
p. xxxviii]   To *Chaucer*'s Name eternal Trophies raise,
    And load the antique Stone with Wreaths of Bays;
    Father of Verse ! who in immortal Song
    First taught the Muse to speak the *English* Tongue.
    In early Time he rear'd his rev'rend Head,
    When Learning was with thickening Mists o'erspread;
    When rhyming Monks in barb'rous Numbers try
    The Lives of Saints, and Feats of Errantry;
    Above such trifling idle Tales as these
    His Muse disdain'd by vulgar Ways to please :
    On the fam'd *Græcian* Bard he fix'd his Sight.
    And saw his Beauties thro' a Cloud of Night;
    With Flight advent'rous dar'd the darksom Way,
    And gave the promise of a following Day;
    And that he might his Meaning better meet
    He made the *Mantuan* Verse a Lanthorn to his Feet
    Justly design'd, and with a steddy View
    And piercing Eye he look'd all Nature thro',
[p. xxxix]   Not thro' the gaudy Prism and painted Glass,
    But saw her plain, and drew her as she was.

His rough bold Strokes, with rude unpolish'd Pride,
Art's curious Touch and nicest Care deride :
The Warrior Tale and *Arcite*'s Love survey
And let the *Greek* and *Roman* Bards give way.

[There is no copy of the 1st edn. of this poem in the B. M.]

1721. [**Madan**, Julia.] *The Progress of Poetry*, MS. Add. 28,101, fol. 155 *b*. [first printed in] The Flower Piece. A Collection of Miscellany Poems by Several Hands, 1731, p. 134.

Here [in Britain] CHAUCER first his comic Vein display'd,
And merry Tales in homely Guise convey'd ;
Unpolish'd Beauties grac'd the artless Song,
Tho' rude the diction, yet the Sense was Strong.

[Amongst the other poets mentioned are Shakespeare, Cowley, Waller, Milton, Denham, Dryden, Congreve, Addison, Pope, etc. The MS. is dated 1721 ; the volume in which it is contained is inscribed : "A. Cowper. The family Miscellany." This poem was reprinted in The Poetical Calendar, by Francis Fawkes and William Woty, vol. iii, 1764, p. 21 ; it appeared separately in 1783, but there is no copy in the B. M., and it was also printed (without the author's name) in the Annual Register for 1772, pt. 2, p. 227. A short account of Mrs. Madan will be found in the Gentleman's Magazine, vol. liii, p. 152, 1783.]

1722. [**De la Roche**, Michel ? editor.] *Memoirs of Literature*, containing a large account of many valuable books . . . &c. 2nd edn., 1722, vol. iv, Art. 70, p. 422.

[The writer is reviewing "De Literis Inventis Libri Sex," by William Nicols, 1711 (*see* above, p. 317), and says] *Mr. Nicols* having observed, That our Modern Languages are liable to great Alterations, is afraid the Works of the best *English* Poets will not be very lasting, and that their Fate in Future Ages will be the same with that of *Chaucer* in our Days.

Nulla diu vivent quæ vulgi condita lingua

.   .   .   .

Eloquio condas, secula cuncta legent.

Mr. *Waller* expresses himself to the same Purpose in the following Verses.

[Here follow Waller's verses without the Chaucer reference. *See* above, 1668, p. 244.]

1722. Trapp, Joseph. *Prælectiones Poeticæ*, 2nd edn., p. 386. [Chaucer reference is not in 1st edn. of 1711.]

In hoc Scripti genere parum inter se sunt comparandi Veteres & Neoterici ; cum vix quidquam extet Neotericum, quod Poëmatis Heroici titulum mereatur. Novimus quidem *Angli* judicium *Drydeni* popularis nostri de Poëmate quodam

Chauceri, pulchro sane illo, & plurimum laudando; nimirum quod non modo vere Epicum sit, sed *Iliada* etiam, atque *Æneida* æquet, imo superet.

[*See* below, 1779–81, p. 458, Dr. Johnson's reference to Trapp in his Life of Dryden, where he quotes this passage.]

1722. Wotton, Rev. William, D.D.   *Letter to the Rev. Moses Williams,* dated from Bath, May 5, 1722.

I have lately at by Houres amused my self wth the new Edition of Chaucer.   The Glossary I read with great Pleasure; who ever writ it is a very able Man.   He seems to me to understand Welsh; he quotes Welsh words every now and then, & always to the purpose.   If you know who writ it, let me know; for I perceive Mr. Urry did little or nothing in it.

[This extract is copied in MS. in the writing of Timothy Thomas (the author of the Glossary) in his copy of Urry's Chaucer [B. M. pr. m. 643, m. 4], vol. ii, on the blank page before the Glossary.]

1723. Dart, John.   *Westmonasterium,* or the History and Antiquities of the Abbey Church of St. Peter's, Westminster, 2 vols., 1723, [another edn.], 1742, vol. i, pp. 82–4, 86–9.

[p. 82]   Next adjoining to Mr. *Drayton's,* and between that and *Chaucer's* Monument, is a curious Cenotaph of White-Marble . . .

[p. 83]   . . . Adjoining to this of Mr. *Philips,* is an antient Monument of grey Marble in the Wall, erected to the Memory of the Father of our *English* Poets, *Geoffrey Chaucer,* of whom I have given a large Account in his Life; printed before the last Edition of his Works; and shall therefore in this Place give only some Hints of him.

[Here follows the usual description of Chaucer's life, followed by one of his tomb.]

    . . . His stone of broad Grey Marble, as I take it, was not long since remaining; but was taken up when Mr. *Dryden's* Monument was erected, and sawn to mend the pavement . .

[p. 86]   . . . While I am speaking of *Chaucer,* give me the Liberty of one Digression, (for I think I shall not trouble you with many,) and that is to clear this great Man's Character, and at a long Distance —— my own.   It has been for many Years believ'd, that *Chaucer* was the Author of that scandalous railing Ballad, *The Ploughman's Tale,* and, I think, it has not been contested.   This, I know, makes him obnoxious to many

Men of Letters, especially those who are *Roman Catholicks*. But their Resentment will cease to appear, when I almost evidently prove to them, that this Piece came from a Quarter of less Learning, and more ill Manners; and that *Chaucer*, who was a fine Gentleman, and one who had a Value for, and was valu'd by the better Sort of the Clergy of that Time, would never have fallen so rudely foul on the whole Order, when his Practice was only to lash those who were obnoxious to the rest.   First then, we must observe, that this Tale is in none of the antient Manuscripts of *Chaucer*, not in any one I have seen, neither in that curious one of my Lord *Harley*, nor in those in the King's Library, which were borrow'd for Mr. *Urry*: But after the verse, *By this the Manciple had his Tale I ended*, &c., comes on *The Parson's Prologue* and *Tale*; whereas they have in the printed Copies thrust this in between, and, to favour the Deceit, chang'd the very Verse, and made it, *By this the Ploughman had his Tale y ended*, &c.   And, indeed, the Tale it self seems to be of a different Piece, having no Introduction; and this Ploughman seems abruptly to have fallen in with them by the way, and to be a different sort of a Creature from that *modest, quiet, good* Parishoner, that came with his Parson to them at *Southwark;* they are not more different in their Dresses, than in their Manners and Characters.   The first came upon a Horse: This Fellow is presented with a Pilgrim's Staff, a cumbersome Utensil for one that rides.   *Chaucer* has taken care to give his Farmer the Character of a quiet useful Man to others, and one that chearfully paid his Tithes; or else indeed I think he would have been strangely out, to have brought the Parson with him: But this ill-bred, saucy Fellow minds nothing but the satisfaction of Gain, having *left his Cattle in Grass up to the Chin;* and indeed we may perceive him to be a covetous [p. 87] Hog, by his railing against Tithes, the too common Cry of those sordid Wretches.   Now if, having set these two Men before you, you can still think them the same, I'll tell you the very Places they came from; and tho' I believe (with Mr. *Stow*) that they were both born at a time, yet they had very different Originals; one had to his Father our *learned*, I may safely say, *religious*, and *well-bred* Poet, (for the Obscenity of his Writings, I have sufficiently spoke of both Prose and [1] Verse, tho' the first, I think, is left out in the printed Copy of the Life:)   The other was the Son of one

[1] *Poem on Chaucer and his Writings*, Lond. 1722.

of his Name, a *hot warm Incendary,* as (pity it is, too many Creatures of the State-Faction pretending *Wickliff's* Opinions were) one *Pierse Ploughman.* And, I think, this will need no other Proof than what this Fellow says in his Tale of another of his Performances, *Of Freers I have spoken before in a making of a Creed,* &c. Now this same *Pierse Plough-man* wrote that very thing which is at the end of his Book, and call'd a *Creed of Fryers,* which I have by me : For Mr. *Fox,* who thinks *Jack Upland* must be it, or none, has mistaken a *Catechism* for a *Creed.* Mr. *Stow* is more modest, as he was more calm, and says, he had seen it in an antient Manu-script about *Chaucer's* Time, and (tho' he believes) does not positively assert it to be his. These Arguments, or to the like Purpose, I have laid down in the Life of *Chaucer,* which lately was printed before the *Christ-Church* Edition, the Copy of which was submitted to their Perusal, or some deputed by them ; and upon the Queries mark'd, I submitted to such corrections as they thought proper. After which, when the Book had been some time out, I found upon perusing it, that all these Arguments were entirely omitted, and I am barely made to assert, by my own Authority, that *Chaucer* never wrote this Piece : Yet the Alterer has made me so modest (without my knowledge, I am sure,) to refer to the Preface. Upon which, at least, I expected the ingenious Gentleman who wrote it, (and, I believe, knew nothing of what was said in the Life,) had some better Arguments for what I had said. But suddenly, to my Suprize, old Mr. *Fox* was set there to stare me in the Face, and give the Lye, by no more Authority, than what they allow'd me ; and one, who, I believe, was willing to make all the great Names he could oppose the Innovations of the Times, and whose Zeal, Passion, laborious Search, and Hurry, made him (I'm sorry to say it) guilty of too many errors. This Usage was such as, I hope, will influence the Reader to excuse my leading him out of the way. The Life was in other Places alter'd, as concerning Mr. *Packer's* Estate at *Donington,* and some few other Places, which I cannot now remember : For the Book I have never seen but upon a Bookseller's Compter, not being willing to buy it, when my old one, with my own written Notes, serv'd me as well. This Usage, I think undeserv'd, having spar'd no Pains, and was at a very extraordinary Expence to collect Records, and write as particular and full a Life as possible, of a Name I ever reverenc'd, and for a Body

of Men who have been always remark'd for a distinguishing
Taste : A Life, which I have been told by no mean Judges,
has not displeas'd.   This I here mention to vindicate my self
from those Mistakes of which I am not guilty; and this
indeed was the chief Motive to my Conclusion of a Poem
upon this Man and his Works, with which I shall likewise
close this Account of his Tomb.

> *Industrious thus to do my Master right,*
> *And save his Actions Time —— conceal'd from Night ;*
> *Long on the dusty Roll and mould'ring File,*
> *I urg'd the intricate laborious Toil ;*
> *Toil ill return'd by this ungenerous Age,*
> *Unthank'd the Labour, and defac'd the Page.*
> [p. 89] *Yet not discouraged thus, with grateful Fire,*
> *I try at Verse, and reassume the Lyre :*
> *Suspend, great Bard, this Tablet at thy Shrine,*
> *And bribe the World to Fame, by sounding thine.*

[There is no copy of the 1st edn. at the B. M. ; Westminster Abbey, a Poem, is
prefixed to the edn. of 1742 (*see* above, 1721, Dart, J., p. 361).   The "Poem on
Chaucer and his Writings, 1722," is not in the B. M. or Bodl., nor have we been able
to trace it.   The edn. of 1742 contains also a full-page engraving of Chaucer's
monument.]

1723. Pope, Alexander. *Letter [to Mrs. Judith Cowper]*, September 26,
1723, [in] Letters of the late Alexander Pope, Esq. to a Lady.
Never before Published.   Printed for J. Dodsley, 1769, Letter xii,
pp. 79, 80–82.   (Works, 1871, vol. ix, pp. 431–32, and see also
ibid. p. 430.)

[p. 80]   I could wish you tried something in the descriptive way on
any subject you please, mixed with vision and moral; like
pieces of the old provençal poets, which abound with fancy,
and are the most amusing scenes in nature.   There are
three or four of this kind in Chaucer's admirable : 'the
Flower and the Leaf' every body has been delighted with.

[p. 81]   . . . I think, one or two of the Persian tales would give one
hints for such an invention [a fairy tale]: and perhaps if the
scenes were taken from real places that are known, in order
to compliment particular gardens and buildings of a fine taste

[p. 82] (as I believe several of Chaucer descriptions do, though it is
what nobody has observed), it would add great beauty to the
whole.

1724. [Defoe, Daniel.] *The Fortunate Mistress (Roxana)*, p. 359.

That foolish young girl held us all in a Canterbury story ;
I thought she would never have done with it.

1724. Hearne, Thomas.   *Glossary* [to] Robert of Gloucester. . . .
Transcrib'd . . . by Thomas Hearne, 1724, vol. ii, p. 642.

dighte, sive dight. *deck'd, prepared, Qui pottas dightavit*
[non *dihtavit,,* ut Ed. Oxon.] *& assas jecerat* [non *jecerit,* ut
Ed. Oxon.] *extra* Polemo-Middin per Drummonde.   Hac voce
crebro utitur Chaucerus.   Vide cl. Gibsoni Notas ad Jacobi v
Christs kirk on the greene, p. 11. . . .

<small>[For Gibson, *see* below, Appendix A, 1691.]</small>

1724. Welsted, [Leonard].   A *Dissertation concerning the Perfection
of the English Language, the State of Poetry,* &c. [prefixed to]
Épistles, Odes, &c. . . . By Mr. Welsted, . . . 1724, pp. x, xii, xiii.

The vulgar Opinion therefore is a vulgar Error, *viz.* that
our Language will continue to go on from one Refinement to
another, and pass through perpetual Variations and Improvements, till in Time the *English,* we now speak, is become as
obsolete and unintelligible as that of *Chaucer,* and so on, as
long as we are a People ; this is what one of our Poets laid
down some years ago as an undoubted maxim,

And what now Chaucer is, shall Dryden be.

But whoever this Writer is [Pope, in his Essay on Criticism,
l. 483 ; *see* above, p. 311, and for other references to it *see*
above, p. 315, and below, pp. 369, 379, 383], he certainly
judg'd the Matter wrong ; it is with Languages, as it is with
Animals, Vegetables, and all other Things ; they have their
Rise, their Progress, their Maturity, and their Decay. . . .

[p. xii]   The Notion I have . . . is, that the *English* Language
[p. xiii] does, at this Day, possess all the Advantages and Excellencies, which are very many, that its Nature will admit
of. . . .

<small>[The same idea, without any mention of Chaucer's name, is expressed in Welsted's
Epistle to the Duke of Chandos, *ibid.* pp. 43–5.</small>

<small>The Growth of Learning, like the Growth of Trees,
Thrives unobserved, and springs by slow Degrees ;</small>
<small>[p. 44]   Like the famed *English* Oak, her Head she rears,
And gains Perfection thro' a Length of Years ;
The first Essays in Verse are rudely writ,
The Numbers rough, and unchastized the Wit :
Thus, BRIDGES, in thy great Forefathers' Times,
Harsh was our Language, and untuned our Rhimes ;
Great SPENCER first, in blest ELIZA's Days,
Smoothed our old Metre, and refined our Lays ;
Next manly MILTON, Prince of Poets, came,
And to our Numbers added Homer's Flame ;
Since when, in]Verse few Wonders have been wrought,
And our smooth Cadence flows devoid of Thought.</small>
<small>.   .   .   .   .</small>
<small>[p. 45]   Th' approaching Times my raptured Thought engage ;
I see arise a New *Augustean* [*sic*] Age.]</small>

[**1725** *et seq.*] O[ldys, William]. *MS. note* in annotated copy of **An account of the English Dramatick Poets**, by Gerard Langbaine, 1691 [This is Haslewood's copy with Oldys' notes, B. M., pr. m. C. 45. d. 14], to face p. 215. [*See* above, 1691, p. 262.]

[Beaumont & Fletcher. Two Noble Kinsmen.]

Note. The Story from Chaucer. Warburton says Shakespeare wrote only the first act in this Palemon and Arcite. O.

1725. Pope, Alexander. *The Works of Shakespear, Collated and Corrected by the former Editions by Mr. Pope.* Printed for J. Tonson, Preface, vol. i, pp. xi–xiii. (Works, 1871, vol. x, pp. 541-2.)

[p. xi]   We may conclude him [Shakespeare] to be no less conversant with the Ancients of his own country, from the use he has made of *Chaucer* in *Troilus* and *Cressida*, and in the *Two Noble Kinsmen. . . .*

[p. xii]   [Reference to Ben Jonson's praise of Shakespeare :] He
[p. xiii] exalts him not only above all his Contemporaries, but above *Chaucer* and *Spenser.*

1726. Sykes, James. *Letters* to Robert Harley, Earl of Oxford, [printed in] *Report on the Manuscripts of His Grace the Duke of Portland,* preserved at Welbeck Abbey, vol. vi (Historical MSS. Commission), London, 1901, p. 17.

[Sykes is ordered by his father's executors to apply for fifteen guineas, due for a picture of Chaucer. Has also pictures of Jonson, Shakspere and Milton, which he desires to give the Earl the refusal of. Receipt annexed.]

1726. Theobald, Lewis. *Shakespeare Restored*, pp. 31, 53, 85, 119, 179, 187.

[Theobald quotes Chaucer in support of his emendations in the text of Shakespeare.]

1727. [Defoe, Daniel.] *A Tour Thro' the Whole Island of Great Britain . . . By a Gentleman,* 1724-7, vol. iii, 1727, p. 81.

We had a fair View of that antient Whittl-making, Cutlering Town, called *Sheffield ;* the Antiquity, not of the Town only, but of the Trade also, is established by those famous Lines of *Geoffry Chaucer* on the Miller of *Trumpington,* which, however they vary from the print in Chaucer, as now extant, I give it you as I find it :

> *At* Trumpington, *not far from* Cambridge,
> *There dwelt a Miller upon a Bridge ;*
> *With a rizzl'd Beard, and a hooked Nose,*
> *And a* Sheffield *Whittl in his Hose.*

1727. Harte, Walter. *To a Young Lady, with Mr. Fenton's Miscellany,* and *Notes upon the Sixth Thebaid of Statius,* [in] *Poems on Several Occasions.* . . . London, Printed for Bernard Lintot, pp. 97, 98, 189–90, 195. (The Works of the English Poets, by Dr. Samuel Johnson, additional lives by A. Chalmers, 1810, vol. xvi, p. 330.) For the text of the *Notes,* see below, App. A., 1727.

> Here *Spenser's* thoughts in solemn numbers roll,
> Here lofty *Milton* seems to lift the soul.
> There sprightly *Chaucer* charms our hours away
> With stories queint, and gentle *roundelay.*
> Muse! at that name each thought of pride recall,
> Ah, think how soon the wise and glorious fall!
> . . . .

[p. 98]
> Not *Chaucer's* beauties could survive the rage
> Of wasting envy, and devouring age:
> One mingled heap of ruin now we see;
> Thus *Chaucer* is, and *Fenton* thus shall be!

[Cf. Pope, *Essay on Criticism,* 1709,
"And such as Chaucer is, shall Dryden be."
See above, pp. 310-11, 315, 367, *and* below, pp. 379, 383, 468.]

1727. Pope, Alexander. *A Tale of Chaucer, Lately found in an old Manuscript,* [in] Miscellanies in Prose and Verse, London, Printed for B. Motte, 1727. The Last Volume [vol. 4] pp. 44–5, [generally called Swift's Miscellanies] (Works, 1871, vol. iv, p. 423).

1727. Unknown. *Magna Britannia et Hibernia.* . . . *A new Survey of Great Britain wherein to the Topographical account given by Mr. Cambden* . . . *is added a more large History* . . . *of Cities, Towns* . . . vol. iv, pp. 374–5.

This town [Woodstock] . . . is not a little proud, that it is the Birth-place of our famous *English Homer, Jeffrey Chaucer.* Other Places indeed claim that Honour, as they did *Homer's,* viz.: *Newbury* in *Berkshire, Dunnington* Castle there being his Inheritance, and *London,* in which he says he was forth grown, which may rather imply his Education than Birth; but *Woodstock* has the greatest Probability on her Side; *Leland, Pitts* and *Cambden,* our greatest Antiquaries positively asserting it; and *Pitts* tells us his Father was a Knight; and since Authority much strengthens Learning, we may be thoroughly [p. 375] satisfied that here was he born, and dwelt, because Queen *Elizabeth* passed a fair Stone-house in this town, standing near
CHAUCER CRITICISM.

her Palace, unto the Tenant, by the name of *Chaucer*'s House, as 'tis called to this Day.

[There is a further reference to "Chaucer's House" on p. 374, in connection with the famous "Polysyllabical Ecchoes."]

1728. Markland, Jeremiah. *Modernisations of Canterbury Tales,* [in] The Altar of Love.

[Advertised (as "just published") in "The Velvet Coffee-woman" (Anne Rochford , 1728, as "A Collection of Love Poetry." "The Tales from Boccace to Chaucer are moderniz'd in a smooth and easy manner by Mr. Markland, of Peterhouse." The advertisement claims that Pope had "a large share in it." No copy of this book has been found. *See* below, p. 389, 1741, Ogle.]

1728-30. Pope, Alexander. [*Sayings* reported in] *Anecdotes . . . of Books and Men, collected from the Conversation of Mr. Pope . . . by the Rev. Joseph Spence.* First published with notes by Samuel Weller Singer, 1820, Section i, pp. 19-21, 23, 49, 50. [*See also* below, 1734-6, p. 377.]

[p. 19] I read Chaucer still with as much pleasure as almost any of our poets. He is a master of manners, of description, and the first tale-teller in the true and enlivened natural way.

[p. 20] There is but little that is worth reading in Gower: he wants the spirit of poetry, and the descriptiveness, that are in Chaucer.

[p. 21] Mr. Sackville . . . was the best English poet, between Chaucer's and Spenser's time.

[p. 50] [Speaking of the Letter to Sacheverel, by Addison. *See* above, p. 266.] That was not published till after his [Addison's] death, and I dare say he would not have suffered it to have been printed had he been living; for he himself used to speak of it as a poor thing. He wrote it when he was very young; and as such, gave the characters of some of our best poets in it, only by hearsay. Thus his character of Chaucer is diametrically opposite to the truth; he blames him for want of humour.

1729. Carey, H[enry]. *Epilogue intended for Mr. Cibber's new Pastoral called Love in a Riddle. To the Tune of Sally in our Alley,* [in] Poems on Several Occasions . . . The Third Edition much enlarged, p. 98. [Not in first edition.]

> We want, alas! the Voice and Gift
> Of charming SENESINI;
> Permit us then to make a shift
> With Signor CIBBERINI.

> What tho' his Lays he cannot raise
> To soft CUZZONI'S Treble,
> Like CHAUCER'S Clark our tuneful Spark
> Can squeak a sweet Quinible.

1729. Thomas, Elizabeth. *Account of John Dryden's funeral.* [printed by Malone in] Prose Works of Dryden, 1800, vol. i, pt. i, p. 362.

17$\frac{29}{30}$. Theobald, Lewis. *Letters to* [William] *Warburton,* March 6, 1729–30, March 31 and Sept. 15, 1730, [in] Illustrations of the Literary History of the 18th century, by John Nichols, 1817, vol. ii, pp. 540, 591, 608.

March 6. [Notes on Shakespeare's Troilus and Cressida] And to this old Treatise it is, [viz. The Recuyles and Sieges of Troy, printed by W. de Worde, 1503] (and not to Lollius, or Chaucer, as the Editors imagine) that our Author owes his subject, for hence only could he derive the name of Hector's horse, Galathe . . .

[See Theobald's edn. of Shakespeare's Works, 1733, vol. vii, p. 114, where this reference is given, in slightly different words, in a note. *See* below, p. 375.
J. O. Halliwell-Phillipps in his Memoranda on Shakespeare's Tragedy of Troilus and Cressida, 1880, quotes Theobald's letter of March 6, slightly altering the words.]

March 31. [Speaking of Shakespeare's use of "affects" for affections] In this he is an imitator of his two great masters, Chaucer and Spenser.

Sept. 15. [Speaking of Shakespeare's use of "gemell" in Midsummer Night's Dream "found Demetrius like a gemell."] This is so finely guessed, and gives so natural a sense where before there was none at all, that I wish heartily the word had ever been used again by Shakespeare ; or that I could meet with it either in Spenser, Chaucer, or any of the old Glossaries.

[*a.* **1730.**] **Wotyx,** W. *A Familiar Epistle from the Shades below giving an Account of the Station of the Poets* [in] The Shrubs of Parnassus . . . by J. Copywell, of Lincoln's Inn Esq., 1760, pp. 129–130 [The above poem is preceded by this note:] The three following [poems] were written many years since by —— Esq ; (lately deceased). [It is signed] Parnassus, Sept. 7, 1730. [*See* below, c. 1833, Haslewood's Collections.]

> The Poets, both Grecian and Roman of old,
> Of whom we so many fine things have been told,
> Live here in great state, are Grandees of the Court
> To whom all the Moderns most humbly resort.

Yet few find admittance, or favour with those,
So poor their appearance, so shabby their cloaths :
Some, indeed, a small pittance, or place, may obtain ;
But the rest are a sad ragged crew in the main :

.   .   .   .

Old Chaucer and Drayton I found in good plight,
And Shakespear and Spencer appear pretty tight,
They've each a small freehold, tho' troth bounded in sore,
And live not unlike to our poor Knights of Windsor.
Ben Johnson sells ale on the side o' the hill,
And Beaumont and Fletcher go halves in a mill.

1730. B.   *Letter* [signed B. and dated Cambridge June 23, 1730, in]
Memoirs of the Society of Grub Street, vol. i, no. 26, pp. 138-9,
1737.

Mr. Bavius, [*i. e.* John Martyn, M.D.] Your just warmth
for restoring the true reading in some of our English poets,
must needs be very agreeable to every lover of criticism. . . .
It would be worth your while to collate all the most ancient
editions, which are commonly the best.   Who can make
sense of the following passage concerning VENUS *in* CHAUCER'S
House of Fame B. i, as it stands in Mr. URRY's edition ?

And also on her hedde parde
Her rose garlande, white and redde
And her combe for to kembe her hedde.
Her doves, and dan Cupido.

But in that scarce and valuable edition *emprynted by Wyllyam
Caxton* the sense is clear,

𝕽ose garlondes smellyng as a mede,
𝕬nd also flying about her hede
𝕳er doves, etc.

That the passage ought to be read thus, may farther appear
by comparing it with the description of the statue of VENUS
in the *Knight's tale.*

A citriole in her right hande had she

.   .   .   .

Beforne her stoode her sonne Cupido. [ll. 1959-63.]

If your learned Society approve of this reading as I have
restored it, it will be a pleasure to

Your humble Servant B.

[The Grubstreet Journal commenced Jan. 8, 1730, and was continued till 1787.
Unfortunately the number which contained this letter has not been preserved with
the others in the Bodleian library. The Memoirs of the Society of Grubstreet are
really a reprint of the best papers which appeared in the Journal.]

1730. Unknown. *Letter* [signed " Zoilus," and dated] Trinity College,
Cambridge, Aug. 23, 1730, Sunday Afternoon, in Chappel-Time,
[in] Grub Street Journal, Sept. 3, 1730. [Inserted by J. Haslewood in his 'Collections,' vol. i, p. 204. *See* below, c. 1833.]

To Mr. Bavius, Secretary to the Grubæan Society. Sir,
Your industrious tho' feeble efforts towards Criticism, mani-
fested by some so-so emendations of Milton and Chaucer,
have prevailed upon my Knave Humanity to enrich your
Paper [by the Communication of an emendation to Butler's
Hudibras].

[c.1730. Young, Edward.] *Two Epistles to Mr.Pope. See* below, App. A.

1731. Unknown. *Letter,* [dated] March 30, [in] Gentleman's Magazine, March, 1731, vol. i, p. 118.

Another Difficulty started by the writer of the *Courant*,
is, the Fluctuation of our Language, whereby it may become
unintelligible to Posterity, as *Chaucer* and *Gower* are now.

[For an Essay in the September No. *see* below, App. A.]

1731. Unknown. *Article against Law proceedings being in English*,
[in the] Daily Courant, March 4, 1731. [*See* below, c. 1833,
Haslewood, J.]

Many Technical words, or Terms of Art, have been invented
and adapted to Legal Proceedings, which have long since
acquired fixed and settled Meanings . . . This, with the
fixed meaning of the Latin Tongue, shortens Debates, renders
Judgments intelligible . . . Whereas if the Records and
Deeds were to be in the Language in Use for the Time being,
in two or three Generations a great Part of the meaning would
be lost, as we see in *Chaucer, Gower,* and other ancient
English Poets; which although not much above Two Hundred
years old, and wrote in the best language of those Times, are
scarce intelligible at this Day.

1731. Unknown. [*A Newspaper cutting* inserted by Haslewood in his
annotated edn. of Giles Jacob's Historical Account of the Lives and
Writings of our most considerable English Poets, B. M. (pr. m. C.
45. d. 18.) to face p. 26. *See* below, c. 1833, Haslewood.]

From the PEGASUS in Grub-Street [Haslewood has added
in writing] Journal, 11 Mar. 1731.

Mr. T. D. Attorney, who wrote the *Letter to a Member of Parliament,* printed in the *Courant* of *Tuesday, Mar.* 4, is desired to consult that accurate Work of our learned Brother Mr. GILES JACOB, *The Poetical Register,* Vol. I, where he will find himself under a great mistake, in asserting that CHAUCER and GOWER are (as he expresses it) *not much above two hundred years old :* the former of whom died in 1400, and the latter in 1402.

[The Grubstreet Journal is not in the B. M., and this extract is not in the Memoirs of the Society of Grub Street, 2 vols., 1737, a collection of the best pieces from the Journal. The Courant, or The Daily Courant, is also not in the B.M.]

[a. 1732]. Herbert, Thomas, 8th Earl of Pembroke [d. 1733]. *MS. Notes* [in] The Book of Miscellanies, [printed at S. Albans].

[In a second edn. of this book, printed by Winkyn de Worde in 1529, there is] the *Nut brown maid,* suppos'd by *Chaucer,* as *Skelton* confirms, by having had a copy given him by *Lidgate* . . . Mr. *Prior* has made a paraphrase on it, and has also printed it from the old *English* but knew not that it was by *Chaucer.* [Quoted by Samuel Palmer, q.v., immediately below.]

1732. Palmer, S[amuel]. *The General History of Printing.* Book III. Of English Printing and Printers, p. 136. [Extract from MS. notes by the Earl of Pembroke in The Book of Miscellanies printed at St. Albans in the Pembroke Library [*see* last entry], pp. 342–4, 378-9. [Edns. of Chaucer's Poems and Works, by Caxton and Winkin de Worde, Robert Toy and John Stowe.]

[There is a flaw in the pagination of the B. M. copy ; pp. 313 to 336 are wrongly numbered pp. 121 to 144 ; p. 136 should be p. 328.]

1732. [Theobald, Lewis.] *A Miscellany on Taste,* by Mr. Pope, &c. [with Remarks by Lewis Theobald]. Remark b. on pp. **3, 4.**

b. *And Books for* Mead,] This worthy Gentleman [Dr. Richard Mead] has a vast and valuable Library, stor'd with all sorts of Books Foreign and Domestic . . . he may very likely have some, among so prodigious a Collection, which he has hardly deign'd a reading. But I hope Mr. *Pope's* Works are none of that Number, tho' he may well save himself the Trouble even of looking into them ; for whether Mr. *Pope* knows it or no, he can read *Homer* and *Statius,* nay, and *Chaucer* and *Shakespear,* in their Originals, without Recourse either to a rhiming Translator or a Modernizer to point him out their Meaning.

1732. Unknown. *Essays,* [in] Gentleman's Magazine. *See* below, App. A.

1733. Brome, [William.] *Letter* to Mr. [Thomas?] Rawlins, June 23, 1733, [in] Letters written by Eminent Persons, 1813, vol. ii, pt. i, pp. 95-7.

. . . I find you a very curious person (inter alia) about books, for I see your name among Mr. Hearne's subscribers; and if your acquaintance be much among the Litterati, as I suppose it is, you may do me a kindness. One Mr. Urry, student of Christ Church, was engaged to put out a new edition of Chaucer with a Glossary, &c. Before he had finished it, he dies, and leaves me executor with an intention that some of the profits arising from the impression should go towards building the new Quadrangle. The College, myself, and Mr. Lintot, the bookseller, enter into a tripartite agreement upon these terms. The College and myself to get the copy of Chaucer, with Prefaces, Indexes, Glossary, &c., for Mr. Lintot. Mr. Lintot to be at the expense of printing and paper: and the copies were to be equally divided in three parts between us. The College oblige scholars upon their entrance to take off a copy; and by their acquaintance dispose of their share. Mr. Lintot is in the way of business, and sells off his; but mine lie upon hand, so that I am like to be a great sufferer. By our articles we are not to sell a copy under the subscription price, which is, large paper fifty shillings, small paper thirty shillings, in sheets: the book is adorned with copper plates before each tale. If any friend of yours wants such a book, I can supply him at London: but by no means I would have you importunate with any person on my account. [For the Agreement, *see* above, 1715, p. 333.]

1733. Grosvenor, ——. *See* below, App. A.

1733. [Theobald, Lewis.] *The Works of Shakespeare* (Troilus and Cressida), vol. vii, pp. 4, 12, 48, 96, 114 [*See* above, letter from Theobald to Warburton, March 6, 1729-30, p. 371. For additions in the second edition, *see* below, 1740, p. 388.]

[Notes on words] Sperre *up the sons of* Troy [Prol. l. 19]. To *sperre* or *spar* . . . signifies to *shut up, defend* . . . And in this very Sense has CHAUCER used the Term in the 5th Book of his Troilus and Creseide [l. 531].

[p. 12] *Before the Sun rose, he was* harness-dight [Act I, sc. ii, l. 8]. . . . It is frequent with our Poet, from his Masters *Chaucer* and Spenser, to say *dight* for *deck'd*.

[p. 48] *He* shent *our Messengers* [Act II. sc. iii. l. 74].

The word *shent*, disgraced, shamed . . . is frequent both in *Chaucer* and *Spenser*.

[pp. 95–6] *But by the forge that* stythied Mars *his helm* [Act IV, sc. v, l. 255] . . .

A *Stithy* or *Stith* signifies an Anvil. So CHAUCER in his *Knight's Tale* [l. 2025]. . . . But I own I suspect this not to have been our Author's Word. [Theobald in the text emended the word to smithied.]

[p. 114] [Theobald refers to the Destruction of Troy printed by Caxton,] from which Book our Poet has borrow'd more Circumstances of this Play, than from *Lollius or Chaucer*.

[The Shakespeare references are to the edn. of W. G. Clark and W. A. Wright, vol. xxv, 1893.]

17$\frac{34}{35}$. **Hearne,** Thomas. *Letter to Dr. Richard Rawlinson*, March 13, 1734–5 [in] Letters written by Eminent Persons . . . 1813, vol. ii, pp. 97–8.

Dear Sir,

I thank you for the large parcel of books I received from you on Saturday last, the 15th inst. Several of them are old Chaucers', such as what you mentioned some time since. The more I look upon such old black-lettered editions, the more I wish that the late edition had been printed in the black letter, which was what my friend Mr. Urry intirely designed, as I have often heard him say, tho' the managers afterwards, for frivolous reasons, acted contrary to it. Curious men begin to esteem the old editions more than the new one, partly upon account of the letter, and partly upon account of the change that hath been made in the new edition, without giving the various lections, which would have been of great satisfaction to critical men. John Stowe was an honest man, and knowing in these affairs, and would never have taken such a liberty, and I have reason to think Mr. Urry would (what I used often to tell him to do) have accounted for the alterations with a particular nicety, had he lived to have printed the book himself. . . .

1735. Hearne, Thomas. *Appendix ad Præfationem. The Publishers Addition to the Account of Dr. Borde in Athenæ Oxon:* [in] Benedictus Abbas Petroburgensis, De Vita et Gestis Henrici II et Ricardi I [ed. T. Hearne], vol. i, pp. lv–lvi.

Robert Burton being so curious and diligent in collecting judicious and merry little pieces, 'tis no wonder, that he procured likewise Dr *Borde's right pleasant and merry history of the Mylner of Abington.* . . . 'Tis probable Dr *Borde* took the hint of this merry piece from *Chaucer's Reve's Tale,* with which it ought by such as have opportunity to be compared, to see, whether it be not, in great measure, the same.

1735. Pope, Alexander. *Note* to Letter to Henry Cromwell, [the letter dated] May 7, 1709, [in] Letters of Mr. Alexander Pope and several of his Friends. London. Printed by J. Wright, 1737, p. 43 (Works, 1871, vol. vi, p. 76).

[The letter contains an allusion to Jacob Tonson's 6th vol. of Poetical Miscellanies, and the note added by Pope in 1735 states that some of his versions of Homer and Chaucer were first printed there.]

1735. Unknown. *Essays* [in] The Gentleman's Magazine. *See* below, App. A.

[1734-36.] Pope, Alexander. *Sayings* [reported in] *Anecdotes . . . of Books and men collected from the conversation of Mr. Pope . . . by the Rev. Joseph Spence.* First Published with notes by Samuel Weller Singer, 1820, section iv, pp. 171-2.
[*See also* above 1728-30, p. 370.]

[p. 171] It is easy to mark out the general course of our poetry. Chaucer, Spenser, Milton, and Dryden are the great land marks for it.

[p. 172] Chaucer and his contemporaries, borrowed a good deal from the Provençal poets.

1736. Byrom, John. *Shorthand Journal* [for May 22, 1736, printed in] The Private Journal and Literary Remains of John Byrom . . . ed. Richard Parkinson, Chetham Soc., 1856, vol. ii, part i, pp. 48-9.

. . . Went with Taylor White to his room, where he desired me to write out of Chaucer the character of a good parson, which I did, and he desired I would put it into verse.

1736. Entick, John. *Proposals for Printing by Subscription in Two Volumes Folio the Works of that Most Learned Facetious and Ancient English Poet, Sir Geoffrey Chaucer Knt. Poet Laureat. . . . Critical, Poetical, Historical and Explanatory Notes, to render the Work both easy and pleasant to the Reader, and, by shewing his un-parellel'd Beauties, convince every judicious Englishman that this our Author is no ways inferior to the greatest Poets that have wrote in any Nation or Language, either before or after him. . . .*

The Introduction.

[p. 2, col. 1] Poetry in *England* never flourisht more than in the days of Sir GEOFFERY CHAUCER, the Riches of his Understanding flow'd like Nectar on every Word ; whose elegant stile adorn'd his happy Invention, and his Profession obtain'd for him Riches and Honours. . . . THEREFORE my present Undertaking is to rescue that famous *English* Poet, Sir GEOFFERY CHAUCER out of that Oblivion into which his *piratical* Imitators have endeavour'd to bring him. . . . [The praises of Chaucer, by Denham, Lydgate, Spenser, Wm. Thynne, Francis Beaumont, Peacham, Dryden and Sir Henry Savil, are then quoted.] [p. 4, col. 2] Therefore, as it is agreed upon by all hands that CHAUCER was accounted the Chief of the *English* POETS, not only in his Time, but continues to be so esteem'd in this Age : what shou'd discourage my Undertaking to publish his WORKS in such a modern Dress, that it may be justly said I now restore to this Age the most valuable Treasure of the *English-Poetic* Library ; so that, from the success we hope this WORK will meet with from our COUNTRYMEN, as formerly HORACE took the Liberty to speak of Himself and Works, Methinks I hear CHAUCER say :

' 'Tis finish'd ; I have rais'd a Monument,
More strong than Brass, and of a vast Extent,

. . . . . .

Which eating Show'rs, nor *North* wind's piercing Blast,
Nor whirling Time, nor Flight of Years can waste :
Whole *Chaucer* shall not die, his Songs shall save
His greatest Portion from the silent Grave.

. . . . . .

[A specimen of the Prologue then follows, with copious notes.]

1736-7. Bernard, John Peter.
   Birch, Thomas.
   Lockman, John.
   A general Dictionary ... in which a New and Accurate Translation of that of the celebrated Mr. Bayle. . . . is included [by the above] *and other Hands.* 10 vols., 1734–41 ; vol. iv, 1736, pp. 292–9 [an ordinary life, followed by eulogies from Ascham, Sidney, Beaumont, Milton, etc.] ; vol. v, 1737, p. 494 [Gower contemporary with Chaucer.]

1737. *Amatory Poetry selected from Chaucer, Lidgate, Skelton, Surrey, Wyatt, Nash, Daniel,* etc.
   [Not in B. M. or Bodl. Known from a dealer's list.]

1737. [Cooper, Elizabeth.] *The Muses Library ; or a Series of English Poetry from the Saxons, to the Reign of King Charles* II. . . . Preface, pp. viii, xi, xii, pp. 1, 7, 8, 19, 23, 24–33, 140.
[p. viii] Those, who read the ensuing Volume with Attention, will be convinc'd that Sense, and Genius have been of long standing in this Island ; and 'tis not so much the Fault of our Writers, as the Language it self, that they are not read with Pleasure at this Day. This, naturally, provokes an Enquiry,

whether 'tis in the same Vagrant Condition still; or whether
the Fame of our most admir'd Moderns, is not almost as
precarious, as that of their now obsolete Predecessors has
prov'd to be; agreable to that Line in the celebrated *Essay on
Criticism,*

> And what now *Chaucer* is, shall *Dryden* be.

[*See* above, 1709, pp. 310–11, and pp. 315, 367, 369, and below, p. 383.]

. . . .

[p. xi]   *Chaucer*, not the next Writer, [to Langland] tho' the next
extraordinary Genius, encountered the Follies of Mankind, as
well as their Vices, and blended the acutest Raillery, with
the most insinuating Humour. By his Writings, it plainly
appears that Poetry, and Politeness grew up together; and had
like to have been bury'd in his Grave. . . .

. . . .

[p. xii]   'Tis certain, very Few of these great Men are generally
known to the present Age: And tho' *Chaucer*, and *Spencer*
are ever nam'd with much Respect, not many are intimately
acquainted with their Beauties.

[p. 23]   *Chaucer*, The Morning-Star of the *English* Poetry! . .
[short account of his life]. All agree he was the first Master
of his Art among us, and that the Language, in general, is
much oblig'd to him for Copiousness, Strength and Ornament.
It would be endless, almost, to enumerate the Compliments
that have been paid to his Merit, by the Gratitude of those
Writers, who have enrich'd themselves so much by his
inestimable Legacies.—But his own Works, are his best
Monument. In those appear a real Genius, as capable of
inventing, as improving; equally suited to the Gay, and the
Sublime; soaring in high Life, and pleasant in low: . . .
[p. 24] Ever both entertaining, and instructive! All which is so well
known, 'tis, in a Manner, needless to repeat: . . . it is not a
little difficult to chuse one [a quotation] that will do him
Justice: Most of his principal Tales have been already
exhausted by the Moderns, and consequently, neither of them
would appear to Advantage in their antiquated, original
Dress . . . [The Pardoner's Prologue is then given.]

[p. 31]   [Occleve] To his Care and Affection is owing the Original
of that Print, which is now so common of *Chaucer*.

1737. Dodd, Charles. *The Church History of England from the
year* 1500 *to the year* 1688. Brussels. Printed in the year
MDCCXXXVII, vol. i, Book i, Art i, p. 61; Book ii, Art iii, p. 369.

The courtiers indeed, at this time [the reign of Edward III]
were disposed to buzz many thing[s] in the king's ear, that were
prejudicial to the Church; in which they were encouraged by
a flattering divine called *John Wickliff*, and the witty satires
of sir *Geoffrey Chaucer*, who took all occasions to lessen the
power of churchmen, and ridicule their character . . . As for
sir *Geoffrey Chaucer*, he was, according to the stile of those
days, esteemed an excellent poet, and being infected by
Wickliff, could not fail of being acceptable to the libertines of
the court.

[p. 369]   *Nicholas Brigham* . . . having a natural genius for poetry,
he sported away some of his youthful hours in that way; but
quickly laying that passion asleep, he followed the more useful
studies of law and history. However, the regard he had for
poetry, and particularly for sir *Geoffrey Chaucer's* memory,
engaged him to be at the expense of beautifying the monument of that celebrated person, in the year 1556, and removing
it to a more conspicuous place, in *Westminster* church, as we
now find it.

[*See* above, 1556, p. 94.]

1737. **Lewis,** John. *Life of Mayster Wyllyam Caxton.* p. xix. (Testimonies concerning Wylliam Caxton. Joannes Pits. 1600, *see* below,
App. A); pp. 60, 80-1, 92, 102-8, 114, 122-4.

[p. 60]   . . . Now it was but an hundred and twenty four Years
since that Translation [Trevisa's of the Polychronicon] was
made; whereas Archbishop *Parker* noted it as very strange,
that our Language should be so changed in four hundred
Years from his time, the Manuscript Book of *the Lives of the
Saints*, written about *A.D.* 1200, in old *English* Verse, now
in *Bennet* College Library, was so written, that People could
not understand it. This seems owing to the generous
Endeavours of those two great Genius's, *Chaucer* and *Gower*,
to polish and improve their Mother-tongue.

[pp. 80-1]   He [*John Gower*] was an intimate Friend and Acquaintance
of that eminent Poet *Geoffery Chaucer*, as he shews in this Book,
[Confessio Amantis] and used to submit his Lucrubrations [*sic*]
to *his* Judgment, as *Chaucer* did his Loves of *Troilus*, to the
Censure and Correction of *Gower* and *Strode*.

[p. 122]   Of all our *English* Writers, M^r. *Caxton* most admired our
Poet *Geoffrey Chaucer*. "In all his works, he sayd, he
excelled, in his opinion, all other writers in our *English*."

[Here Lewis quotes Caxton's Epilogue to the Book of Fame, *see* above, 1483, p. 61.]

Accordingly, as a Proof of the Respect which Mr. *Caxton* had for this great and worthy Man's Memory and Writings, and his Desire to preserve and perpetuate them, one of his most early Performances was his collecting and printing as many of his Works as he could get. He likewise procured, as has been hinted before, an Elegy to be made for him in *Latin* Verse, and caused two of the Verses, there being in all thirty four, to be inscribed on *Chaucer*'s Monument in *Westminster* Abby, *viz.*

> Galfridus Chaucer *vates et fama Poesis*
> *Materne, hac sacra sum tumulatus humo.*
>
> [*See* above, 1479, p. 59.]

Lastly, Mr *Caxton* desired his Readers, according to the [p. 124] Superstition of his Time, that of their charite they would pray for the said worshipful *Geffery Chaucer.*

[On pp. 102–8 are references to Caxton's edns. of Chaucer's works; on pp. 92, 114 are slight allusions to Chaucer by Lewis.]

1737. [**Morell,** Thomas.] *The Canterbury Tales of Chaucer, in the Original, from the Most Authentic Manuscripts; And as they are Turn'd into Modern Language by Mr. Dryden, Mr. Pope, and other Eminent Hands.* London, 1737, Dedication, pp. iii–vi. William Thynne's dedication to Henry VIII, pp. vii–xiv. Account of the Life of Chaucer [drawn from the Life in Urry's edn. 1721], pp. xv–xx. Preface, pp. xxi–xxxvj. Appendix, pp. 349–452. [The book only contains the general Prologue to the Tales, and the Knight's Tale. *See* below, 1771, p. 436, and 1741, p. 389, Ames.]

[Preface p. xxii]
This ancient Poet *Jeoffery Chaucer,* has now stood the Test of above 300 Years, still read, and still admired, notwithstanding he hath been so wretchedly abused, *miswrote and mismetred* by all his Editors, the last not excepted. I speak not this to derogate from the Fame of the late Mr. *Urry,* who died before he had completed his work. . . . [Quotations from Thomas's preface to Urry's edn.: that Urry was of opinion that Chaucer wrote in exact Metre, and therefore he proposed,
[p. xxiv]
'to restore him to his Feet again.'] But if Chaucer was a Cripple before Mr. *Urry restored him to his Feet,* . . . he was really born such; 'twas a natural Lameness, and no more a Blemish in *Chaucer*'s Time, than Round-Shoulders were in the Days of *Alexander* the Great. . . .

[p. xxv]
From this last Line [from the H. of Fame, l. 1098, ' 'Tho som Verse fail of a Syllable '], I conclude, that an exact

[p. xxvi] Numerosity (as Bp. *Sprat* expresses it in his Life of *Cowley*, which, by the way, runs parallel with our Author's in many Cases) was not *Chaucer*'s main Care; but that he had sometimes a greater Regard for the Sense, than the Metre: His Numbers, however, are, by no Means so rough and inharmonious as some People imagine; there is a charming Simplicity in them, and they are always musical, whether they want or exceed their Complement. . . .

[p. xxvii] As to the final E, it was anciently pronounc'd, no doubt, in feminine Adjectives, both from the *Saxon* and *French*, and in those Substantives, that from the old *Saxon* are made *English*, by changing *a* into *e*. . . . However, our Author seems to have taken the Liberty to use it or not, as it best served his Metre; But give me leave to observe, that he has never used it in any even Place, except the 2d, where it is allowable, especially if the Accent be strong upon the 4th.

> Whanné that Apryl. v. 1.
> Thatté no Drop. v. 131.

I say, that the final E, (and I believe I might say the same of the plural *es* or *is*, especially of Monosyllables, . . .) is never used in the 4th, 6th, 8th, or last Syllable of the Verse, which is a Fault that most injudiciously runs thro' Mr. *Urry*'s whole edition.

> In a Gounè. v. 393.
> And in a Glass haddè he, 699.

. . . [pp. xxviii—xxxiv, remarks on Chaucerian English and grammar].

[p. xxxv] So lively are *Chaucer*'s Descriptions, that only to read them, is to carry Life back again, as it were, 300 Years, and to join Conference with his merry Crew in their Pilgrimage to *Canterbury*. From whence we may observe, that Nature is still the same, however alter'd in her outward Dress, and the Man that, like *Chaucer* and *Shakespear*, can trace her in her most secret Recesses, will be sure, in every Age, to please.

1737. Pope, Alexander. *The Second Book of the Epistles of Horace. Imitated by Mr. Pope.* Printed for T. Cooper.—Epistle i, To Augustus, p. 3. (Works, 1871, vol. iii, p. 351.)

[l. 31]   Just in one instance, be it yet confest
Your People, Sir, are partial in the rest.
Foes to all living worth except your own,

[l. 35]   And Advocates for Folly dead and gone.

Authors, like Coins, grow dear as they grow old ;
It is the rust we value, not the gold.
Chaucer's worst ribaldry is learn'd by rote,
And beastly Skelton Heads of Houses quote.

1737. Unknown. *Quotation* [in] Notes and Queries, May 19, 1866, 3rd
S. ix, 414.

I met this passage in a book printed in 1737—" In a word
they seemed to strive who should make us yawn first. The
instant one of them had cited a passage from an Ancient
author, the other would begin a long *Canterbury* story of a
duel he had fought." Whence this expression ?   A. D.

[There follows an explanatory note in answer to the above,
very long, but without mention of the source.]

1737. Unknown. *Modernization* [in] The Gentleman's Magazine. *See*
below, App. A.

1738. Bancks, John. *Miscellaneous works in verse and prose of John
Bancks,* vol. i, Preface p. xiii. To Mr. Hogarth . . . p. 88 and
note p. 89. A Critical Epistle . . . vol. ii, p. 206.

[vol. i.,   Perhaps in CHAUCER's antient Page
p. 88]   We view the HOGARTH of his Age :
         Upon the Canvas first, like Thine,
         His deathless Characters might shine.

       .   .   .   .

[vol. ii.,   If DRYDEN must, as POPE has wrote
p. 206]   Lose all the Charms he now has got ;
         If POPE must grow like Father CHAUCER
         Niceness is Nonsense for that Cause, Sir.

[For Pope's remark on Dryden and Chaucer, *see* above, 1709, pp. 310-11, and for
other references to it, *see* above, pp. 315, 367. 369, 379.]

[1738.] Davies, Sneyd. *Letter to Timothy Thomas* [written c. Feb.
1738, printed in] Illustrations of the Literary History of the 18th
century . . . by John Nichols, vol. i, 1817, p. 522.

I cannot thank you too often for the noble Edition of
Chaucer, valuable in itself, but more so for the sake of the
expositor, and the giver.

[Nichols notes that this was Urry's Chaucer [1721], to which Thomas wrote the
Preface and Glossary.]

1738. [Oldys, William.] *The British Librarian;* pp. 86-7 *n.,* 88-9, 138,
218, 223, 309, 346-7, 356, 360.

[p. 86]   [An account of W. Webbe's Discourse of English Poetrie,
see above, 1586, p. 129.] Our end of reviving here, or reviewing
this *Discourse,* is chiefly for the sake of those Characters,

which our Author has given in it, of the antient, and more
especially the *English Poets*, from *Chaucer* and *Gower* down
to the most considerable of those who flourish'd at the Time
of this Publication; that the critical Reader may better know,
whether the Opinions held of them in those Days, and ours,
correspond. . . .

[p. 88]   [Summary of Webbe's criticism of Chaucer, *see* above, p. 129.]

[p. 138]   [Account of Hakluyt's Voyages, 1598, where there is a
mention of Chaucer, *see* above, p. 157.]

[pp. 218,
228]   [Account of Scot's Discovery of Witchcraft, 1651, with
Chaucer reference, *see* above, 1584, p. 124.]

[p. 309]   [Chaucer criticism in A Restitution of decay'd Intelligence
in Antiquities, by R. V[erstegan], 1605, *see* above, p. 176.]

[pp. 346,
360]   [Chaucer references in Weever's Ancient Funeral Monuments, 1631, *see* above, p. 204.]

1738. Unknown. *The Apotheosis of Milton. A Vision* [in] The Gentleman's Magazine, May 1738, vol. viii, p. 233.

. . . I percieved [*sic*] a Door unfold, and a venerable Figure
enter, clothed in a deep Violet-coloured Robe, with a Wand in
his Hand, and proceeding slowly to the Chair at the upper end
of the Table, where he seated himself. *That Old Man*, said
my Conductor, *whose Face you see wears the Furrows of Age,
is the Father of* English Poesy : *Notwithstanding the Solemn
Figure he makes here, if you were near enough to observe him
aright, you might perceive an Archness in his Looks, and a
certain Vivacity, that is either not to be found, or is very
aukward, in most of his Poetical Descendants.* Here my
Conductor was silent, and upon a narrow View of the old
Personage, I could easily perceive that it must be *Chaucer*.

[For the continuation in February, 1739, *see* below, App. A.]

1739. Ogle, George. *Gualtherus and Griselda :* or the Clerk of Oxford's
Tale. From Boccace, Petrarch, and Chaucer. To which are added,
A Letter to a Friend, with the Clerk of Oxford's Character, &c.
The Clerk of Oxford's Prologue from Chaucer. The Clerk of
Oxford's Conclusion, from Petrarch. The Declaration, or L'envoy
de Chaucer a les Maris de notre Temps, from Chaucer. The Words
of our Host, from Chaucer. A Letter in Latin, from Petrarch to
Boccace. By George Ogle, Esq. ; London : Printed for R. Dodsley,
at Tully's-Head, Pall-Mall. M. D. CC. XXXIX. (Price Three
Shillings.)

[p. vi]   [In his "Letter to a Friend," Ogle contends that Chaucer
[p. vii] was one of Petrarch's friends, and conjectures that] the Person
of so much Humanity, whom Petrarch mentions [in his Latin

letter of 1373 to Boccaccio about Grisild] to have seen at Padua, may be taken for our very Chaucer.

This Tale [of Griselda] . . . has already pass'd thro' the Hands of BOCCACE, PETRARCH and CHAUCER; that is, thro' the Hands of three Men of as great Genius as ever appear'd in one Age. BOCCACE may be suppos'd to have improv'd on Those He follow'd; PETRARCH most certainly improv'd on Him; and our Countryman undeniably improv'd on them Both . . . .

[p. viii] I hold Mr. DRYDEN to have been the first Who put the Merit of CHAUCER into its full and true Light, by Turning Some of the *Canterbury Tales* into our Language, as it is now refin'd, or rather as He himself refin'd it. . . .

Treating of CHAUCER (Whom He puts on a Footing of Comparison in some Instances with Ovid) He observes; that, among other Excellencies, He was perfect Master of the Manners . . . .

[p. ix] As to the Point of Characterizing, at which CHAUCER was most singularly happy; You can name no Author even of Antiquity, whether in the Comic or in the Satiric Way, equal, at least superior, to Him. Give Me Leave, only to throw together a few Touches taken from his Descriptions of the Pilgrims. [Here follow a large number of quotations in this style] . . . The *Squire*; with Locks curl'd, just *fresh* from the *Press!* . . . The Lady *Prioress*; Who *wept* if She saw a *Mouse* taken in a *Trap!* . . . To conclude, the Doctor of Physic; whose *Study* was *little* in the *Bible!* And the *Serjeant at Law*; Who *seemed* much *busier* than he *was!* All these, I say, are the Strokes of no common Genius, but of a Man perfectly conversant in the Turns and Foibles of human Nature. Observe but his Manner of Throwing Them in, and You will not think I exaggerate, if I say, these Turns of Satire, are not unworthy of PERSIUS, JUVENAL, or HORACE himself. Before I cool upon this Subject, I shall venture (as far as the Ludicrous may hold Comparison with the Serious) to rank our CHAUCER with whatever We have of greatest Perfection in this Character of Painting; I shall venture to Rank Him (making this Allowance) either with SALUST [*sic*] or CLARENDON . . . .

[p. x] For it was not to the Distinguishing of Character from Character, that the Excellence of CHAUCER was confin'd; He was equally Master of Introducing them properly on the Stage; and after having introduced them, of Supporting them agreeably to the Part They were formed to personate. In This,

He claims equal Honour with the best Comedians; there is no Admirer of PLAUTUS, TERENCE, or ARISTOPHANES, that will pretend to say, CHAUCER has not equally, thro' his *Canterbury Tales*, supported his Characters. And all must allow, that the Plan, by which He connects and unites his Tales, one with another, is well designed, and well executed. [Here Ogle gives a sketch of the plan of the *Canterbury Tales*, with long quotations.]

[A later edn. of the above appeared in 1741, 12mo, the same year as the Canterbury Tales, with the Title as above, except the place, and publisher, which are "Dublin: Printed for George Faulkner in Essex Street. 1741." The "Letter to a Friend" was reprinted in extenso in Ogle's edn. of the modernised "Canterbury Tales," 1741, *see* below, pp. 389–90.]

1739. Unknown. *Review* of John Lewis's The Life of Mayster Wyllyam Caxton, 1737, [in] The History of the Works of the Learned . . . containing Impartial Accounts and Accurate Abstracts of the Most Valuable Books published in *Great Britain and Foreign Parts*, 1739, vol. i, pp. 269–70, article xviii [reference to Chaucer's Works printed by Caxton, *see* above, 1737, Lewis, pp. 380–1].

[In 1736 "The Literary Magazine or the History of the Works of the Learned," ed. by Ephraim Chambers, and "The Present state of the Republick of Letters," ed. by Andrew Reid, were converted into "The History of the Works of the Learned."]

1739. Unknown. *The Apotheosis of Milton*, continued. *See* below, App. A.; for the first part *see* above, 1738, p. 384.

1739. Vinegar, Tim., pseud. *Letter to Captain Vinegar*, November 24, 1739, from Tim. Vinegar [in] The Champion, containing a series of papers humourous, moral . . . London, 1741, vol. i, p. 29.

. . . No one City in the Universe has produc'd so many Ornaments of polite Learning as this [London]: and when I mention the great Names of *Chaucer, Spencer, Donne, Milton* and *Cowley*, with those of Mr. *Pope*, and Mr. *Glover*, all Natives of London; no Body will presume to treat the Word Citizen, as a Term of Reproach any more.

1740. Alcæus, pseud. *Letter* [in] The Gentleman's Magazine, August 1740, vol. x, p. 404.

Sir,

As there is a very noble Edition of the Prince of our *English* Poets, in a modern Dress, preparing for the Publick, it may not be disagreeable to some of your Readers to present them with a Specimen of that Undertaking, which I hope the generous Editor will forgive me for, as it proceeds from an

Apprehension you may receive the Part I send you, more incorrect from another Quarter.

I am, Sir, yours &c., Alcæus.

[Here follows an extract from *Cambuscan*, by Ogle, *see* below, 1741, pp. 389–90.]

1740. Astrophil, pseud. *In Praise of Chaucer, Father of English Poetry* [in] The Gentleman's Magazine, Jan. 1740, vol. x, p. 31.

Long veil'd in *Gothick* mists our *Britain* lay,
Ere dawning science beam'd a cheering ray,
Dark monkish systems, and dull senseless rhymes
Swell'd the vain volumes of those ruder times:
When *Chaucer* rose, the *Phœbus* of our isle,
And bid bright art on downward ages smile;
His genius pierc'd the gloom of error through,
And truth with nature rose at once to view.
    In regal courts by princely favours grac'd
His easy muse acquir'd her skilful taste:
A universal genius she displays
In his mixt subject tun'd to various lays.
If in heroic strain he tries his art,
All *Homer*'s fire and strength his strains impart.
Is love his theme?   How soft the lays, how warm!
With *Ovid*'s sweetness all his numbers charm
His thoughts so delicate, so bright his flame,
Not juster praise we owe the *Roman* name.
What pious strains the heavenly piece adorn,
Where guilty *Magdalen* is taught to mourne.
Devotion's charms their strongest powers combine,
And with the poet equal the divine.
When he some scene of tragic woe recites,
Our pity feels the strong distress he writes;
Like *Sophocles* majestic he appears,
And claims alike our wonder and our tears.
Does he to comic wit direct his aim?
His humour crowns th' attempt with equal fame.
Meer fictions for realities we take,
So just a picture his descriptions make;
So true with life his characters agree,
What e'er is read we almost think we see.
    Such *Chaucer* was, bright mirror of his age
Tho' length of years has quite obscur'd his page;

His stile grown obsolete, his numbers rude,
Scarce read, and but with labour understood.
Yet by fam'd modern bards new minted o'er,
His standard wit has oft enrich'd their store;
Whose *Canterbury Tales* could task impart
For *Pope*'s and *Dryden*'s choice-refining art;
And in their graceful polish let us view
What wealth enrich'd the mind where first they grew.
                                        Astrophil.

[*c.* **1740 ?**] **Clarke**, William. *An Impromptu on some of the English Poets*, [first printed by John Nichols in] Literary Anecdotes of the 18th century, vol. iv, 1812, p. 376.

See the Fathers of Verse,
In their rough uncouth dress,
    Old *Chaucer* and *Gower* array'd
And that Fairy-led Muse,
Which in Spenser we lose,
    By Fashion's false power bewray'd.

[Five more verses, on Shakespeare, Fletcher, Beaumont, Ben Jonson, Milton Cowley, Butler, Waller, Dryden, Prior, Addison and Pope.]

1740. Theobald, [Lewis]. *Notes* to The Works of Shakespeare, in 8 volumes, 2nd edn. 1740, vol. i, p. 123 [" Gemell" not used by Chaucer], vi, pp. 80 [" Fumitory" written "femetere" by Chaucer], 237 [quotes glossary to Urry's Chaucer for or, = before, ere]. [For the first edition *see* above, 1733, p. 375.]

1740. Vorio, pseud. *Verses occasioned by the Translation of Chaucer in your last Magazine* [in] The Gentleman's Magazine, Sept. 1740, vol. x, p. 463. [Cambuscan, *see* above, 1740, Alcaéus, p. 387.]

Æson (says *Ovid* in his book)
Medea takes in hand to cook,
Him in a kettle first she fixes,
Then powerful charms and juices mixes,
Till warm'd all over up he sprung,
Danc'd with his daughter and was young!
Such *Chaucer* seems.—The Muse ordains
This fate should mark his endless strains:
That future bards who read his page,
Shall spread his praise from age to age,
Not by their own inferior thought,
But by restoring what he wrote!

1741. Ames, Joseph. *MS. Notes from Ames's collections for the history of printing, and a letter from him to —— [dated] London 19 Aug. [17]41.* Add. MS. 5151, ff. 21, 109, 138, 151, 258, etc.

[fol. 258] There is a Curious Edition of Chaucer now lately done by one Mr. Morell a Clergy man and member of our society, encouraged much by Mr. Harding Clark of the House of Coms., one vol. is printed of, in 8° (and I purpose to let him have the use of my MS. of Chaucer's on the *magnet* never yet printed that I know of, it is Joyn'd with that of the astrolabe) without his name.

[T. Morell's Canterbury Tales appeared in 1737, *see* above, p. 381; *see also* below, 1771, p. 436. The references on the other pages are to various printers of Chaucer's works.]

[1741 ?] Minshull, Randal. *Proposals* for Printing an exact and Ample Account of all the Books Printed by William Caxton . . . with a Vocabulary of the *Old English Words,* and an Explanation of them, which will greatly illustrate the Ancient *English* Language, as it was written in the Reign of *Edward III* and continued down to *Henry VII* Kings of *England,* contained in the Writings of *Thomas Woodstock* Duke of *Glocester, Anthony Woodville* Earl *Rivers, John Gower, Geoffry Chaucer, John Lydgate,* and other famous Persons. By R. Minshull, Library-Keeper to the Right Honourable the Earl of Oxford, deceas'd.

[These Proposals were apparently never carried into effect. On the back of a copy of the Proposals inserted in the beginning of W. Herbert's interleaved copy of Typographical Antiquities [B. M. pr. m. 824. k. 1–6] vol. I. i, there is a receipt by Minshull to Dr. [Richard] Mead for one guinea, being the first half of the subscription, dated March 1, 1741.]

1741. Betterton, Thomas.
Boyse, Samuel.
Brooke, Henry.
Cobb, Samuel.
Grosvenor, ——. (*See also* below, App. A., 1733.)
Markland, Jeremiah. (*See also* above, 1728, p. 370.)
All took part in modernising the Canterbury Tales, *q. v.* Ogle, immediately below.

1741. Ogle, George and others. *The Canterbury Tales of Chaucer,* modernis'd by several hands. [*i. e.* Betterton, Ogle, Dryden, Cobb, Pope, Markland, Grosvenor, Boyse and Brooke.] Publish'd by Mr. Ogle, 1741.

[Dart's] *Life of Chaucer,* [as published in Urry's edn. of Chaucer, 1721], vol. i, pp. iii–lx.

A Letter to a Friend, with the Poem of Gualtherus and Griselda, [by George Ogle] vol. iii, pp. v–xxviii [reprinted from Gualtherus and Griselda, 1739, *see* above, p. 384.]

[Contents.—Order of the Tales, and names of modernisers.]

[Another edn. appeared in Dublin in 1742, in 2 vols.; the names of the contributors are given on the title page (Boyse being misprinted ' Boyle '.)]

1742. Dart, John. *Westmonasterium.* *See* above, 1721, p. 361 ; 1723, p. 363.

1742. Walpole, Horace. *Letter to Sir Horace Mann*, Chelsea, July 29, 1742. (Letters of Horace Walpole, ed. Mrs. Paget Toynbee, 1903, vol. i, p. 262.)

They have given Mrs. Pulteney an admirable name, and one that is likely to stick by her—instead of Lady Bath, they call her the wife of Bath. Don't you figure her squabbling at the gate with St. Peter for a halfpenny?

[Note by Walpole] In allusion to the old ballad. [*See* above, 1700, p. 288, and below, App. A., c. 1670.]

1743. Junius, Franciscus, the younger. *Etymologicum Anglicanum.* [Continual references to Chaucer. Amongst others] ARSENICKE, sig. E.2. BALE, sig. G. WARRY, sig. H h h h h h 1b. WENDE, sig. K k k k k k 1.

1743. Unknown. *Article* and *quotation* [in] The Gentleman's Magazine. *See* below, App. A.

1744. Thomson, James. *Summer* [in] The Seasons, Printed for A.
Millar, in the Strand, 1744, p. 119, ll. 1557–1564. [These lines
are not in any of the earlier editions of "Summer." In that of
1746, which contained Thomson's final alterations, the references to
the above are pp. 115–6, ll. 1557–64. (The Seasons and the
Castle of Indolence, ed. J. Logie Robertson, Clarendon Press, 1891,
p. 108. [Also notes on pp. 303, 306.])

> Nor shall my Verse, that elder Bard forget,
> The gentle SPENSER, Fancy's pleasing Son;
> Who, like a copious River, pour'd his Song
> O'er all the Mazes of enchanted Ground:
> Nor Thee, his antient Master, laughing Sage,
> CHAUCER, whose native Manners-painting Verse
> Well-moraliz'd, shines thro' the Gothic cloud
> Of Time and Language o'er thy Genius thrown.

1744. Whitehead, William. *On Nobility. See* below, App. A., 1744.

[a. 1745.] Anstis, John. *MS. History of the Officers of Arms in the
Herald's Office.* MS. at the Coll. of Arms, vol. ii, p. 5, under
Lancaster, ch. xi, sect. 13, p. 559. (Thynne's Animadversions,
ed. F. J. Furnivall, Chaucer Soc., 1876, p. 137, also *ibid.* p. cv.)
[This is merely a reference to Francis Thynne's work on Chaucer.]

1745. Montagu, Elizabeth. *Letter to the Duchess of Portland,* July 24.
(Elizabeth Montagu, by E. J. Climenson, 1906, vol. i, pp. 155–7,
198–9.)

[p. 198]   One day this week we rode to Chaucer's Castle [Donning-
ton] where you will suppose we made some verses no doubt,
and when they showed us Chaucer's well, I desired some
Helicon, hoping thereby to write you a more poetical letter,
but the place having been, during the last Civil War, besieged,
the Muses were frightened away, and forbade this spring to
flow. . . .

1745. Thompson, William. *Sickness, a Poem in Three Books.*
London, 1745. Book I, p. 18, and Notes p. 43.

[l. 275]   Father of fancy, of descriptive verse,
    And shadowy beings, gentle Edmund, hight
    Spenser! the sweetest of the tuneful throng,
    Or recent, or of eld.

[p. 43]   [Note to above, wrongly printed ver. 267.] The date of
our English poetry may with great justice begin with *Spenser.*
It is true, *Chaucer, Gower,* and *Lydgate* were masters of
uncommon beauties, considering the age they lived in, and

have described the humours, passions &c. with great discernment. Yet none of them seem to have been half so well
acquainted with the very life and being of poetry, invention, painting, and design, as *Spenser*. *Chaucer* was the
best before him; but then he borrowed most of his poems,
either from the ancients, or from *Boccace*, *Petrarch*, or the
Provençal writers, &c. Thus his Troilus and Cressida, the
largest of his works, was taken from *Lollius*; and the Romant
of the Rose, was translated from the French of *John Noon*,
[*sic*] an Englishman, who flourished in the reign of Richard II.
and so of the rest. As for those who follow'd him, such as
Heywood, Scogan, Skelton, &c. they seem to be wholly ignorant
of either numbers, language, propriety, or even decency itself.
I must be understood to except the Earl of *Surry*, Sir *Thomas
Wiat*, Sir *Philip Sidney*, several pieces in the mirror of
magistrates, and a few parts of Mr. *G. Gascoign*'s and
Turbervill's works.

[*c.* 1745.] **Thompson**, William. *In Chaucer's Boure*, Garden Inscrip-
tions no. vii, [in] The Poetical Calendar . . . by Francis Fawkes
and William Woty, vol. viii, ed. 2, 1763, p. 103. [also in] Poetical
Works of William Thompson, ed. Park, British Poets, vol. 26, 1807.
p. 181.

In Chaucer's Boure.

Who is this thilke old bard which wonneth here?
This thilke old bard, sirs, is Dan Chaucer:
Full gentle knight was he, in very sooth,
Albee a little japepish [*sic*] in his youth.
He karoll'd deftly to his new psautry,
And eke couth tellen tales of jollity.
And sangs of solace, all the livelong day,
Soote as the ouzle or throstell in May.
Withouten words mo, a merie maker he,
Ne hopen I his permagall[1] to see.
Ne Johnny Gay, perdie, ne Matthew Prior,
In diting tales of pleasaunce couth go higher.
Here in this gardyn full of flowers gend,
Betwixt this elder-tree and fresh woodbend,
He hearkeneth the foules' assemblie,
That fro the twigs maken their melodie.
Ye pied daisies, spring neath his feet,
Who sung so sootly, "The daisy is so sweet:"

[1] His equal.

> And whilest, "benedicite," he sings,
> Ryn little beck, in silver murmurings,
> O pleasaunt poete, thyselven solace here,
> And merie be thy heart, old Dan Chaucer.

[17]46. **Rudd**, Abraham Joseph. *Two letters* from S. John's College, Oxford, dated respectively April 21 and 29, [17]46, to Mr. Ames [Joseph Ames, the bibliographer and antiquary] Wapping Street, near the Hermitage, London ; describing Caxton's first edition of the Canterbury Tales [no criticism of Chaucer. These letters are now inserted in the copy of Caxton's first edn. of the Canterbury Tales in B. M. (pr. m. 167. c. 26).]

[*See* Ames's Typographical Antiquities, 1749, p. 55.]

1746. Unknown. *Poem* [in] The Gentleman's Magazine. *See* below, App. A.

1746. Upton, John. *Critical Observations on Shakespeare,* pp. 193, 327. ["Fere" and "atwain," old words used by Chaucer.]

[*See* the enlarged edn. of 1748, below, p. 396, for many more Chaucer allusions.]

1747. Mason, William. *Musæus, a monody to the memory of Mr. Pope, in imitation of Milton's Lycidas,* pp. 8-10.

> First, sent from Cam's fair banks, like Palmer old,
> Came TITYRUS [1] slow, with head all silver'd o'er,
> And in his hand an oaken crook he bore,
> And thus in antique guise short talk did hold.
> ' Grete clerk of Fame'is house, whose excellence
> Maie wele befitt thilk place of eminence,
> Mickle of wele betide thy houres last,
> For mich gode wirkè to me don and past.
> For syn the daies whereas my lyre ben strongen,
> And deftly many a mery laie I songen,
> Old Time, which alle things don maliciously,
> Gnawen with rusty tooth continually,
> Gnattrid my lines, that they all cancrid ben,
> Till at the last thou smoothen 'hem hast again ;
> Sithence full semely gliden my rymes rude,
> As, (if fitteth thilk similitude),
> Whannè shallow brooke yrenneth hobling on,
> Ovir rough stones it maken full rough song ;
> But, them stones removen, this lite rivere
> Stealen forth by, making plesaunt murmere :
> So my sely rymes, whoso may them note,
> Thou maken everichone to ren right sote ;

[1] *i.e.* CHAUCER, a name frequently given him by Spenser. [Note by Mason.]

And in thy verse entuneth so fetisely,
That men sayen I make trewe melody,
And speaken every dele to myne honoure,
Mich wele, grete clerk, betide thy parting houre ! '
He ceas'd his homely rhyme.

[After Chaucer come Colin Clout (Spenser) and Thyrsis (Milton).]

1747. Unknown. *An Account of Barkshire or Berkshire.* [Article in] Universal Magazine, June 1747, vol. i, p. 15.

[The reference is to Chaucer's connection with Donnington Castle.]

1747. Vertue, George. *Remarks of G. Vertue's on a Letter* from Mr. G. Stovin to his Son, concerning the body of a Woman and an antique Shoe found in a Morass . . . Philosophical Transactions [of the Royal Soc.] vol. xliv, no. 484 (1747), p. 575 (*see* below, 1749, p. 400, Unknown, in The Gentleman's Magazine).

. . . *Chaucer* in his Time mentions the Use of long piked Shoes, so long as to be tied up by Strings or small Chains to their Knees.

1747. Warburton, William. *The Works of Shakespeare,* 8 vols.

[A few references in the footnotes on words and phrases.]

1747. Warton, Thomas, the elder. *Hereafter in English Metre ensueth a Paraphrase on the Holie Book entituled Leviticus Chap. xi, vers. 13 &c. Fashioned after the Maniere of Maister Geoffery Chaucer in his Assemblie of Foules:* [a poem in] Poems on Several Occasions, by the Reverend Mr. Thomas Warton . . . sometime Professor of Poetry in the University of Oxford . . . London . . . 1747.

[For a specimen of this translation, *see* below, App. A., 1747.]

1748. Stanhope, Philip Dormer, 4th Earl of Chesterfield. *Letter to his Son,* Sept. 27, o.s., 1748. Letters written by the . . . Earl of Chesterfield to his son . . . published by Mrs. Eugenia Stanhope . . . 2 vols., 1774. vol. i, pp. 341–2.

I have always observed, that the most learned people, that is those who have read the most Latin, write the worst; and that distinguishes the Latin of a Gentleman scholar, from that of a Pedant. . . . [A Pedant] will rather use *olli* than *illi*, . . . and any bad word, rather than any good one, provided he can but prove, that, strictly speaking, it is Latin; that is, that it was written by a Roman. By this rule, I
[p. 342] might now write to you in the language of Chaucer or Spenser,

and assert that I wrote English, because it was English in their days; but I should be a most affected puppy if I did so, and you would not understand three words of my letter.

[In a letter dated Mar. 2, 17$\frac{4}{5}\frac{2}{3}$, apropos of reading, Lord Chesterfield says: "A gentleman should know those which I call classical works, in every language; such as Boileau, Corneille, Racine, Molière, &c., in French; Milton, Dryden, Pope, Swift, &c., in English, and Boccacio, Tasso, and Ariosto in Italian." This is of interest as mentioning no writer earlier than Milton as an English classic.]

1748. Unknown. *Biographia Britannica*, vol. ii, pp. 1026 [account of W. Bullein, Dialogue, *see* above, 1564, p. 98], 1229, 1240-1, 1245-6 [Caxton], 1293–1308 [a long article on Chaucer]. For later volumes *see* below, App. A., 1757 and 1760.

CHAUCER (Geoffrey) the Father of our English Poets, and the first great improver and reformer of our language . . . as he justly obtained the highest admiration amongst his contemporaries, so his memory has ever since been highly honoured. [Here follow the events of his life in great detail, and a statement of the difficulties of getting at the facts about it. Sprat, Pits, Leyland, Speght, Dart, Hearne, Ashmole, Bale, and others are quoted.] . . .

[p. 1305] If we look upon him as an author, he may truly be stiled the Father of English Poetry, and perhaps the Prince of it, for except the unavoidable defects of language, his Works have still all the beauties that can be wished for or expected, in every kind of composition. He was not unacquainted with the antient rules of Poetry, nor was he incapable of writing up to them, as very clearly appears by the *Knight's Tale*, which, as Mr. Dryden very justly says, is a finished Epick Poem, but he did not always judge this exactness necessary. . . .

[p. 1307] We are not however to suppose, that with all these great qualifications ['true genius, extensive learning, and a free spirit'], Chaucer could entirely escape the fang of false criticks . . . Those who have attacked Chaucer have not presumed to question his wit, for of this perhaps no writer of our nation ever had more, neither have they disputed his poetical abilities, which certainly set his on a level with the greatest names in antiquity; nor have they dared to throw any aspersion on his learning, the extent of which is not greater than the masterly degree of propriety with which it is everywhere applied: but the point to which they object, is, his changing, debasing, or corrupting our language, by introducing

foreign words, as if the worth of all languages did not arise
from their being thus enlarged and compounded . . .

. . . .

[p. 1308]   It is however just to observe, that this reflection never made
any great impression, and that with the best and most elegant
writers in our tongue, Chaucer passes not only for a great
improver, but for the very Father and Founder of it; and it
is not a little to his honour, that amongst those who are of
this opinion we may reckon one of the soundest of our Critics
[Rymer], and one of the correctest writers in our language
[Sprat].

[*See* above, 1692, p. 265, Rymer, and 1667, p. 244, Sprat.]

1748. Upton, John. *Critical Observations on Shakespeare,* the second
edition, with Alterations and Additions. Preface, pp. xvi–xxii,
xxiv–v, xxvii, 136 note, 184 note, 185 note, 226 note, 232–3, 241
note, 253, 277 note, 297 and note, 298, 327 note, 329 note, 336
note, 346 note, 347 note, 362 note, 363, [Additional notes at end]
403–4, 410. [*See* above, 1746, p. 393, for 1st edn.]

[Preface,   There is an English author, which was much studied by
p. xvi]
[p. xvii] Shakespeare, but very superficially by Shakespeare's editors
now lying before me. 'Tis well known that the *Coke's Tale
of Gamelyn* was the original of the play called *As You Like It.*
A Midsummer Night's Dream had its origin from *The Knight's
Tale;* which I don't remember to have seen, as yet, taken
notice of. There are some passages of Chaucer's *Troilus and
Creseide* in a play of the same name by our Tragedian; and
several imitations there are likewise, very elegantly interspersed, in other plays, which some time or other may be
pointed out: at present I shall content myself with the
following in King Lear, Act III. Where the Fool thus
speaks,

" I'll speak a prophecy or ere I go."
. . . [Upton then quotes the prophecy, ending :]
[p. xix.]   " This prophecy Merlin shall make, for I live before his
time."

This Merlin is the prophet Dan Geoffrey Chaucer. Among
some verses prefixed to the prologues of the Canterbury tales
are the following, intitled

Chaucer's Prophecie.
" When faith faylith in Priest'is sawes,
And lordes hestes are holde for lawes,

> And robberie is holde purchace,
> And letcherie is holde solace;
> Then shall the lond of Albion
> Be brought to great confusion."

Shakespeare has taken this *prophecy*; but to make it more resemble the oracular responses of antiquity, and the prophetical stile, he has *artfully* involved it in a seeming confusion: 'Tis ONE prophecy consisting of two parts; the former part having a relation to what *now is*; the latter to what never *shall be*. The fool to the two lines of Chaucer, has humorously added two lines of his own, which properly can be referred only to the former part of the prophecy . . .

[p. xx]   [Upton next points out that in the expression "bold beating oaths" used by Falstaff in *The Merry Wives* II; beating is from the A.S. betan, excitare, as used by Chaucer in the Reve's Tale, v. 828—

> "He was a Markit beter at the full,"
>   [A, l. 3936.]

or in the Knight's Tale,

> "I will don sacrifice, and firis bete."

[p. xxi] Again, "alder lievest" as used by Shakespeare in Hen. VI. 2. I, has the same meaning as in Chaucer's Tr. and Cress. III. v. 240. So with overcome, meaning overcast, and Child Rowland (K. Lear III) meaning prince; as in Tale of Gamelyn, 225].

.   .   .   .

[pp. 184 n., 185 n.]   [A long note on the use of "fere" by Chaucer.]

.   .   .   .

[p. 232]   In Troilus and Cressida.   Act I.

> "They say he is a very MAN PER SE
> And stands alone."

As plausible as this reading appears, it seems to me originally to come from the corrector of the press. For our poet I imagine made use of Chaucer's expression, from whom he borrowed so many circumstances in this play. . . .

[p. 233]   "O faire Creseide the floure and A PER SE
          Of Troie and Greece."   [Test. of Creseide, v. 78.]

Douglas in his preface calls Virgil, *The* A PER SE, i. e. as the glossary explains it, an extraordinary or incomparable person, like the letter *A* by itself . . . I would therefore thus read in Shakespeare,

> "They say he is a very A PER SE
> And stands alone."

[Errors in transcription in old writers.]   In the Legende of Hypsipyle and Medæa, l. 308,

> " And of thy tongue the *infynite* graciousnesse ? "

Can it be doubted then that Chaucer wrote *yfained* or *ifained*, *i. e.* feigned, dissembled . . . ?   There is another blunder . . . in line 381 of the Prologue,

> " And *pouder Marchant*, tarte and galingale,"

[p. 404] I would read

> " And *purveigh Manchet*,"

i. e. They had a cook with them whose business 'twas to boil, &c., and to provide Manchet, &c.

[The phrases in italics are in black letter in the original.]

1748. Walpole, Horace. *Letter to George Montagu*, Strawberry Hill, Aug. 11, 1748. (Letters of Horace Walpole, ed. Mrs. Paget Toynbee, 1903, vol. ii, p. 330.)

. . . In this search [for his possible descent from the house of Vere] I have crossed upon another descent, which I am taking great pains to verify (I don't mean a pun), and that is a probability of my being descended from Chaucer, whose daughter, the Lady Alice, before her espousals with Thomas Montacute, Earl of Salisbury, and afterwards with William de la Pole, the great Duke of Suffolk . . . was married to a Sir John Philips, who I hope to find was of Picton Castle, and had children by her ; but I have not yet brought these matters to a consistency ; Mr. Chute is persuaded I shall, for he says anybody with two or three hundred years of pedigree may find themselves descended from whom they please ; and thank my stars and my good cousin the present Sir J. Philipps, I have sufficient pedigree to work upon . . .

Yours ever,
Chaucerides.

[Alice Chaucer was the daughter of Thomas Chaucer, who was probably the poet's son. *See* D. N. B. She had no children by her first husband, Sir John Philip.]

1749. Ames, Joseph. *Typographical Antiquities*, Preface [p. **3**], sign. a 4, pp. 54–58, 60–62, 66, 127–8, 130, 141, 149, 210, 221–2, 263, 296, 404.

to face sign. b 1. Specimen of Caxton's printing of Boethius. [*See* above, p. 58.]

pp. 54–8. Extracts from Canterbury Tales and Boethius by Caxton. [*See* above, pp. 58–9, 61–3.]

pp. 60–2. Book of Fame, &c., by Caxton. [*See* above, p. 61.]

p. 66. Werk of Sapience. [*See* above, pp. 16, 17.]

pp. 127–8, 130. Pynson's edns. of Chaucer. [*See* above, pp. 64, 75, 76.]

p. 141. Godfray's edn. [*See* above, p. 78.]

pp. 148–9. Rastell's Terence in Englysh. [*See* above, p. 73.]

p. 210. Thos. Petit's Chaucer. ⎫
p. 221. Robt. Toy's edn. 1546. ⎬ [*See* above, p. 86.]
p. 263. Richd. Kele's edn. ⎭

p. 296. John Kingston's edn. 1561. [*See* above, p. 96.]

p. 404. Robert Robertson's The northern mother's blessing, 1597. "Written nine years before the death of G. Chaucer." [*See* above, p. 144.]

[For additions in Herbert's 2nd edn. of Ames, *see* below, 1785, p. 477, 1786, p. 483, and 1790, p. 491, and for Dibdin's 3rd edn., 1810.]

1749. B., C. *Note* [to verses entitled] To the Memory of Mr. Pope, occasioned by reading the Monody wrote by Mr. Mason [in] The Gentleman's Magazine, vol. xix, 1749, p. 468.

Tho' the works of *Chaucer*, and *Spencer*, do justly entitle them to a place among poets of a distinguished rank, yet is it for their language, or their sentiments, that we admire them? If for the latter, which is most assuredly the case, what has any poet of these days to do with the former? . . . Those authors, at the time they wrote, appeared in all the pomp and splendor of poetry, that the language of the times would admit of; which then, perhaps, seemed as well suited to the maintenance of their genius as did the ruff of Queen *Elizabeth* to that of her person.

—Sed tempora (& lingua) mutantur.—

Instead therefore of thus meanly borrowing their dress, it would be but justice to them, and to posterity, if we generously lent them our own. Who can read those embellished tales of *Chaucer*, and the no less improved satires of Dr. *Donne* without admiring the piety, as well as the poetry of *him*, who has rescued from oblivion, what must else have perished in the ruins of an antiquated style, and given them immortality by a language, which we trust will never die?

Nottinghamshire.   C. B.

1749. C., J. *Verses* [in] The Gentleman's Magazine. *See* below, App. A.

1749. Newton, Thomas. *Paradise Lost . . . by . . . John Milton . . . with Notes. . . .* vol. i, pp. 60, 71, 340 ; vol. ii, p. 397. [All references to words or expressions used by Chaucer.]

1749. Potter, [Robert]. *A Farewell Hymne to the Country, attempted in the manner of Spenser's Epithalamion,* pp. 15, **16.**

> Oft too thy hallow'd Sonnes enthroned hie,
>   O peerlesse Poesie !
> Sounding great Thoughts my raptur'd Mind delight ;
>   He first, the glorious Child of Libertie,
> *Mæonian* MILTON, beaming heav'nly bright,
>   He who full fetously the Tale ytold,
>   The *Kentish* TITYRUS old ;
> And he above the Pride of Greatness Great,
>   Sweet COWLEY : . . .

[In the 2nd ed. of 1750 the reference to Chaucer (*i. e.* Tityrus) is identical ; but there is also a list of contents to face the title page, with the following words :] Leisure-philosophic-poetic-Praise of Milton—of Chaucer.

1749 Unknown. [*Description of a sandal,* in] *Explanation of the Figures on the half-sheet Plate* [in] The Gentleman's Magazine, vol. xix, May, 1749, p. 203.

> Fig. VIII. The form of a woman's sandal, found in digging peat at *Amcott*'s moor, in *Lincolnshire* . . . A very particular account of the discovery is given in the *Philos. Trans.,* No. 484, just published. [*See* above, 1747, Vertue, George, p. 394.] . . . *Chaucer* mentions long piked men's shoes, ty'd up at the knee by strings, or silver chains . . .

[1749. Warton, Thomas.] *The Triumph of Isis. A Poem, Occasioned by Isis, an Elegy.* London, printed for W. Owen, at *Homer's Head* near *Temple Bar,* p. 12, sign. B. 2 *b.* (The Triumph of Isis, [in] The Cabinet of Poetry, 1808, vol. vi, p. 326.)

> Ev'n now confest to my adoring eyes,
> In awful ranks thy [Oxford's] sacred sons arise :
> With ev'ry various flow'r thy temples wreath'd,
> That in thy gardens green its fragrance breath'd.
> Tuning to knightly tale his British reeds,
> Thy crowding Bards immortal CHAUCER leads :
> His hoary head o'erlooks the gazing choir,
> And beams on all around cælestial fire.

1750. Jackson, A[ndrew.] *Matrimonial Scenes; consisting of the Sea-man's Tale, the Manciple's Tale, the Character of the Wife at* [sic] *Bath, the Tale of the Wife of Bath and her Five Husbands—all modernized from Chaucer.*

> The first *refiner* of our native *lays*
> Chaunted these *tales* in Second *Richard's* days ;
> Time grudg'd his *wit,* and on his language fed,
> We rescue but the *living* from the *dead ;*
> And *what* was *sterling verse* so long ago
> Is here *new coined* to make it *current* now.

[The above title and verse are quoted in a note by John Nichols, in his Literary Anecdotes of the 18th century, vol. iii, 1812, pp. 625-6 note. The author, Andrew Jackson, was, says Nichols, well known to many dealers in old books and black letter, and kept a shop for more than 40 years in Clare Court, Drury Lane. In 1740 he published the first book of Paradise Lost in rhyme. In 1751, in conjunction with Charles Marsh, he republished, as Shakespeare's, a "Briefe conceipte touching the Commonweale of this Realme of England ; originally printed in 1581." He issued Book Catalogues (in rhyme) 1756, 57, 59. He died July 25, 1778. There is no copy of this book in either the B. M. or the Bodleian Library.]

[c. 1750 ?] Johnson, Samuel. *Extract from a catalogue* of publications projected by Johnson at different periods; [printed in] Sir John Hawkins' Life of Johnson, 1787, p. 82. (This is given also by Boswell, in his Life of Johnson 1799 (vol. iv, p. 405), who adds "From the Catalogue of intended works presented by Johnson to Mr. [Bennet] Langton, and by him to the King." See also Essays Biographical . . . illustrative of the Rambler . . . by Nathan Drake, 1809 (*q.v.* below), vol. i, pp. 159, 160. (Boswell's Johnson, ed. G. Birkbeck Hill, vol. iv, 1887, p. 381.)

Chaucer, a new edition of him, from manuscripts and old editions, with various readings, conjectures, remarks on his language, and the changes it had undergone from the earliest times to his age, and from his to the present : with notes explanatory of customs, &c., and references to Boccace, and other authours from whom he has borrowed, with an account of the liberties he has taken in telling the stories; his life, and an exact etymological glossary.

1750. Unknown. *A Panegyrick on the Ladies.* Being Chaucer's Recantation for [1] The blind eat many a fly. As it is sung at the Spring Gardens, Vaux Hall, with great applause, [in] The Student, or the Oxford and Cambridge Monthly Miscellany, vol. i, no. vi, June 30, 1750, p. 230.

> Recitative
>
> Old Chaucer once to this re-ecchoing [sic] grove
> Sung " of the sweet bewitching tricks of love ";
> But soon he found, he'd sullied his renown,
> And arm'd each charming hearer with a frown;

[1] [Footnote, p. 230.] A song moderniz'd from the old English of Chaucer.
CHAUCER CRITICISM.

Then self-condemn'd anew his lyre he strung,
And in repentant strains this recantation sung.

Air

I

Long since unto her native sky
Fled heav'n-descended Constancy;
Nought now that's stable's to be had,
The world's grown mutable and mad :
Save WOMEN—They, we must confess,
Are miracles of stedfastness,
And every witty, pretty dame
Bears for her motto—*Still the same.*

[3 more Stanzas, and Chorus.]

[The above poem was reprinted in *The London Magazine,* August, 1750, p. 376.]

[*c.* 1750.] **Unknown.** *Verses* [in] *Holkham MS.* 667, *Canterbury Tales,* imperfect. In the blank 2nd column of fol. 42 (which has its back blank too) is written in an 18th century text hand :

Poetes haue licence, tis no matter what they write
be it good or bad for both they doe recite
Old Chaucer here hath kept as even a straine
twixt good and bad that alle comend his vaine.

1751. Birch, Thomas. *The Life of Edmund Spenser,* [in] The Faerie Queen . . . with an exact collation of the two original editions, p. ii.

[Spenser], to whom we owe, not only the chief Improvement of our Poetry since the Time of CHAUCER, but likewise the forming of the genius of MILTON, etc.

1751. Lloyd, Robert. *The Progress of Envy,* written in the year 1751, stanza vi. [in] Poems, by Robert Lloyd, A.M., London, 1762, p. 209

Not far from these,[1] DAN CHAUCER, antient wight,
A lofty seat on Mount Parnassus held,
Who long had been the Muses' chief delight;
His reverend locks were silver'd o'er with eld ;
Grave was his visage, and his habit plain ;
And while he sung, fair nature he display'd,
In verse albeit uncouth, and simple strain ;
Ne mote he well be seen, so thick the shade,
Which elms and aged oaks had all around him made.

1751. Unknown. *Letter* [in] The Gentleman's Magazine. *See* below, App. A.

[1] Spenser and Milton.

1751. Upton, John. *A Letter concerning a new edition of Spenser's Faerie Queene. To Gilbert West Esq.,* pp. 9–16, 19, 22–3, 25–8, 34–5, 37–8. [The letter is signed John Upton ; it consists of some informal notes sent as a sketch of what the author might do, did he undertake to edit the Faerie Queene. A large portion of them is concerned with Spenser's debt to Chaucer ; and we print some specimens only.]

[p. 9]   . . . My province at present is to consider . . . our poet's
[p. 10]   knowledge of antiquity, and ancient books . . . What poet shall I first take in hand ? whom preferable to his *Tityrus,* 'his renowmed poet, the well of undefiled English ? ' whose footsteps with reverence *Spenser* always followed ? I could wish however that he never thought of compleating *the Squier's tale,*

> ' Or call up him that left half told
> The story of *Cambuscan* bold,' . . .

I must own that when I red *Chaucer's* tale, and the completion of it by *Spenser,* that he seemed below himself. 'Tis elegant however to imitate *Chaucer* in the introduction to the story,

> ' Whylome as antique stories tellen us,'

Which is the beginning of the *Knight's tale.* I hardly think that a story promising so fair in the beginning should be *left half told.* I rather think with *Spenser,* that *wicked Time hath defaced that famous monument :* or a negligent transcriber might have lost *Chaucer's* original copy. For as to those verses in Mr. *Selden's MS.* which perhaps influenced *Milton's* judgment, I make no doubt of their being surreptitious : and to me they seem to have been added by *Lidgate* . . . for they are exactly after his cast.

Will you acknowledge with me, that the authority of *Chaucer,* considered merely as authority, stands in the same rank with the authorities of more antient poets ? If so then *Spenser* had *Chaucer's* authority [1] for making ' *Morpheus* the "God of Slepe." He had *Chaucer* too before him, when he wrote that beautiful description, in the first book of ' *Morpheus'* house.' . . .

[p. 15]   Give me leave now to explain and correct a verse in *Chaucer,* where he is describing *the Prioresse ;* having finished her mental qualifications, he speaks of her person and dress,

> ' Full fetise was her cloke, as I was ware.' v. 157.

I can get no insight into the meaning of this verse from any

[1] *The dreme of Chaucer,* v. 136. [*The Isle of Ladies,* not by Chaucer.]

edition or glossary : I thought once that *ware* was thus written to rhime to the word *bare*, and was the same as *warne*, i.e. assured. But *Chaucer* draws the characters of the Pilgrims, and describes their particular dresses, from his own observations. I think therefore the place corrupted, and without altering a letter, and by an easy transposition, we may read,

'Full fetise was her cloke as was iware' :

i.e. Her cloak was very neat, and as handsome as was worn by any woman. . . .

I omit many expressions that *Spenser* borrows from *Chaucer*, such as, *Put in his hode an ape—well, to file his tongue—doughty dousipeers—cost him many a Jane—well mote thou the*—Sit : to become, suit, agree with . . .

[p. 16]   [Satire against the clergy in the *Ploughman's tale.*]

. . . .

[p. 25]   Let me explain a difficult passage in *Chaucer*,

'That gifte nought to praisin is
That a man gevith *malgre his.*'
Rom. of Rose [ll. 2385–6]. . .

[Upton also quotes Rom. of Rose, C. ll. 5933–4, and gives the French original in both cases.]

[p. 26]   *Chaucer* should have said *malgre him*, himself ; but the rime would not permit him, so that *his* stands for *himself* : and this is a usual liberty which the old poets took, and sometimes *Spenser* too has taken, *viz.* of risking a little false grammar rather than risk a false rime.

. . . .

I have twice at least cited *The Court of Love*, as written by *Chaucer*, but accidentally turning over the new edition of *Cave's History of the Ecclesiastical writers*, I there met with *a little History of Chaucer*, drawn up by a learned archbishop of *Canterbury* [Tenison], who tells me I am mistaken in thinking *The Court of Love* was written by *Chaucer*.

'*Sunt qui Cantabrigiæ etiam literis illum incubuisse volunt; testimonio ex* Amoris Aulâ *desumpto innixi. Verum libellum istum Chauceri non esse nos infra adnotabimus.*' And presently after 'Amoris Aula, *quæ quidem Chaucero abjudicanda videtur. In prooemio enim author ruditatem suam excusans, ait neque*

Tullii flosculos nec Virgilii poesia [poemata] *nec Galfridi (quo nomine Chaucerum designari parum est dubium) artem à se expectanda esse.'* [From H. Wharton's account of Chaucer, *see below*, App. A, c. 1687.]

Now if there were no other *Jeffry* in the world but *Jeffry Chaucer*, his Grace's criticism would have some weight: but with all submission, this *Jeffry* mentioned in the *Court of Love* was *Jeffry Vinesaufe*, or as he is called in Latin *Galfridus de Vino Salvo.* . . .

If this poem is not *Chaucer's*, by a parity of reasoning and learning, He did not write *the House of Fame*: for there . . .
[p. 27] mention is made of an 𝕰𝖓𝖌𝖑𝖎𝖘𝖍𝖊 𝕲𝖆𝖑𝖋𝖗𝖎𝖉𝖊: Nor did he write the *Story of the Cock and the Fox*, for there likewise we meet this same *Galfride* . . .

[See a letter signed 'Philologus,' in The Gentleman's Magazine, July 1790, vol. lx, p. 613, saying that he is disappointed no good life or account of Upton has been published, and that a new edition of his works would be very desirable, for he is "justly celebrated for his Canons of Criticism, Remarks upon Spenser, Observations on Shakespeare, and also for some Strictures on Chaucer."]

1752. Fawkes, Francis. *A description of May from Gawin Douglas, by Francis Fawkes.* Preface, pp. v–vi.

The following poem [*viz.* Proloug of the Description of May] . . . may also serve as an instance, that the Lowland Scotch language and the English, at that time were nearly the same. CHAUCER and DOUGLAS may be looked upon as the two bright stars that illumin'd England and Scotland, after a
[p. vi] dark interval of dulness, a long night of ignorance and superstition, and foretold the return of day and the revival of learning.

[1752.] Unknown. *Observations upon the English Language. In a Letter to a Friend.* London. Printed for Edward Withers, p. 19, note.

. . I am desirous, if possible, that we might all write with the same Certainty of Words and Purity of Phrase to which the ITALIANS first arrived and then the FRENCH. It should mortify an *Englishman* to consider that from the time of

Boccace and Petrarch the Italian hath varied very little, and
that the *English* of *Chaucer* their Co-temporary is not to be
understood without the Help of a Dictionary : but their *Goth*
and *Vandal* had the advantage to be grafted on a *Roman*
stock.

1753. [**Armstrong**, John.]   *Taste.*   *See* below, App. A.

1753. Carter, Edmund.   *The History of the County of Cambridge,* . . .
By Edmund Carter, of Cambridge.   Cambridge . . . 1753, pp. 279–
286.

In this parish [Trumpington] was formerly a water [?-mill]
on the *Cam*, (the ruins of which are still visible) chiefly noted
for the diverting copy of verses made by the incomparable
Chaucer, upon the *Miller* thereof, *viz.*

The Miller of Trumpington.

A *Tale.*

At *Trumpington*, not far from *Cambridge*, stood,
Across a pleasant stream, a *Bridge* of Wood . . .

[The whole tale is then quoted in Dryden's version, without comment.]

1753. Cibber, [Theophilus].   *The Lives of the Poets of Great Britain and
Ireland.* . . . in 4 [or rather 5] vols. . . . vol. i, pp. 1–17 ; [Life
of Chaucer, founded on Leland, Pits, Speght, and Dart], 18, 20, 21,
23, 25, 27, 30, 97 ; vol. ii, p. 53 ; vol. iii, p. 79.

[Robert Shiels, a Scotchman, was the author in whole or in part of this work. See
Boswell's *Johnson*, April 10, 1776, and the following note made by Isaac Reed in his
copy of Cibber's *Lives* (annotated by J. Haslewood, vol. i, flyleaf, British Museum,
10854. a. 1): "Mr. Rob\`. Shields wrote the greater part of these Volomes. He was
Amanuensis to Dr. S. Johnson and wrote several Poems. He dyed 27 Dec\`. 1753."
See also *Six Essays on Johnson*, by Sir Walter Raleigh, Oxford, 1910, p. 120 note.]

[p. 13]   His language, how unintelligible soever it may seem, is
almost as modern as any of his cotemporaries . . . and in some
places it is so smooth and beautiful, that Dryden would not
attempt to alter it; I shall now give some account of his
works . . . and subjoin a specimen of his poetry, [Pardoner's
Prologue], of which profession as he may justly be called the
Morning, Star, so as we descend into later times, we may see
the progress of poetry in England from its great original,
Chaucer, to its full blaze, and perfect consummation in
Dryden. . . .

[p. 18]   Langland.   It has been disputed amongst the critics
whether this poet preceded or followed Chaucer. . . .   I am
rather inclined to believe that he was cotemporary with him
. . . and my conjecture is strengthened by the consideration
of his stile which is equally unmusical and obsolete with

Chaucer's : and tho' Dryden has told us that Chaucer exceeded those who followed him at 50 or 60 years distance, in point of smoothness, yet with great submission to his judgment, I think there is some alteration even in Skelton and Harding. One cannot read the works of this author, or Chaucer, without lamenting the unhappiness of a fluctuating language, that buries in its ruins even genius itself; for like edifices of sand, every breath of time defaces it, and if the form remain, the beauty is lost.

1753. [**Colman**, George, the elder.] *Literary Offerings in the Temple of Fame: A Vision* [in] The Adventurer, No. 90, September 15, 1753, p. 118. [Reprinted in The Gentleman's Magazine, September, p. 422, signed " Crito."] (The British Essayists, ed. A. Chalmers, vol. xx, 1823. Adventurer, vol. ii, p. 294.)

[p. 116]   . . . By command of Apollo and the Muses, all who have ever made any pretensions to fame by their writings, are injoined to sacrifice upon the altar in this temple, those parts of their works, which have hitherto been preserved to their infamy, that their names many [*sic*] descend spotless and unsullied to

[p. 118] posterity. . . . I marked with particular attention the several offerings of the most eminent English Writers. CHAUCER gave up his obscenity, and then delivered his works to DRYDEN, to clear them from the rubbish that encumbered them. DRYDEN executed his task with great address . . . he not only repaired the injuries of time but threw in a thousand new graces.

1753. Unknown. *The Life of Geoffrey Chaucer, the Father of English Poetry. With a curious Print of his head,* [in] The London Magazine, September, 1753, pp. 398–400.

[The Life is followed by " An Account of Chaucer's Works," i. e. chiefly of the occasions on which they were supposed to have been written, and " A Specimen of Chaucer's Poetry," from the Pardoner's Prologue, " Lordings, quoth he . . . So that he offer good pens or grotes." This example was probably taken from Elizabeth Cooper's *Muses' Library,* 1737, *q.v. above,* p. 379.]

[**1753.**] **Unknown.** *Newspaper Cutting* of Publisher's advertisement of the Lives of the Poets by Theophilus Cibber, 1753, to come out in weekly numbers. [No name or date. In an interleaved copy of Cibber's Lives of the Poets, 1753, with MS. notes, &c. by Isaac Reed and Joseph Haslewood, (B. M. pr. m. 10854 a. 1) immediately before contents of vol. i.]

[A long and puffing account of the need there is for this work, and the excellence of its execution.] The Lives of

the Poets have been less perfectly given to the World, than
the Figure they have made in it and the Share they have in
our Admiration, naturally demand. . . . The general Error
into which Langbain, Mrs. Cooper, and all the other Biographers have fallen, is this : They have Considered the
Poets merely as such, without tracing their Connexions in
civil Life, the various Circumstances they have been in,
their Patronage, their Employments, in short . . . while
they have shewn us the Poet, they have quite neglected
the Man. . . .

   We have . . . taken in all who have had any Name as
Poets, of whatever Class : . . . We have likewise Considered
the Poets, not as they rise Alphabetically, but Chronologically,
from Chaucer, the Morning Star of English Poetry, to the
present Times : And we promise in the Course of this Work,
to make short Quotations by way of Specimen from every
Author, so that the Readers will be able to discern
the Progress of Poetry from its Origin in Chaucer to its
Consummation in Dryden.

[1753.] Unknown. *The Stage Coach containing the character of Mr.
Manley and the History of his Fellow Travellers,* vol. ii, pp. 182-3.

   Chap. v.   *A Canterbury tale is told.*

   . . . 'If you would oblige me with a detail of it [your life]
I should acknowledge it as a great favour.' 'With all my
heart, colonel,' reply'd the old gentleman, 'if you can have
the patience to attend to an old man's Canterbury tale ; for in
that city I drew my first breath.'

1754. Gemsege, Paul, [pseud. Pegge, Samuel] and Others. *Letters* [in]
The Gentleman's Magazine, 1754. *See* below, App. A.

1754. Grey, Zachary. *Critical, Historical, and Explanatory Notes on
Shakespeare,* vol. i, Preface, p. ix, Notes, pp. 19, 20, 26, 31, 35, 40-
1, 43, 45, 53, 57, 62, 91-2, 125, 128-31, 137-39, 145, 153, 155-6, 158,
163, 173, 191, 196, 231, 234-5, 252, 262, 332, 349, 365-6, 384, 386-
7, 397; vol. ii, pp. 10-12, 16, 22, 34, 37, 39, 41, 81, 104-8, 116, 118,
125, 129, 131, 133, 141-2, 170, 196, 227, 230, 266, 275, 285-6, 308,
316, 321.

[p. ix]   I have read over the works of *Chaucer, Skelton,* and *Spenser,*
and have endeavoured to point out those passages, which
Shakespeare probably borrowed from thence. . .
   [It is remarkable what a very large number of notes are
here given, compared for instance with Theobald, 1740, on
resemblances between Shakespeare and Chaucer, mostly on

similar uses of words, but also on similar expressions and references to the same proverbs [i, pp. 20, 366]; or incidents [i, pp. 35, 137]; or things [i, 365]; or persons [ii, 142]; a suggested borrowing by Shakespeare [i, 155]; possible ref. to lines in Chaucer [ii, 125]; comparison of the description of the funeral of Marcius, *Coriolanus*, act v, sc. 6, and that of Arcite in Chaucer's *Knight's Tale* [ii, 170]; note on duels, *Romeo and Juliet*, act iii, sc. 4 ; [ii, 275] 'one might imagine that duels were prohibited in Chaucer's time from Knt's Tale ' ll. 1704–13.]

1754. Warton, Thomas. *Observations on the Faerie Queene of Spenser,* pp. 36 *n.*, 40, 41 and *n.*, 42, 66, 81, 85, 87 *n.*, 88 and *n.*, 89 *n.*, 90, 91 *n.*, 96 and *n.*, 99 to 142, 175, 181 *n.*, 198–200, 203, 227–229, 233, 244–5, 253, 263, 269, 274, 283, 288–9.

[p. 141]   [Of Spenser's Imitations from Chaucer.]

I cannot dismiss this section without a wish, that this neglected author whom Spenser proposed in some measure, as the pattern of his language, and to whom he is not a little indebted for many noble strokes of poetry should be more universally and attentively studied. Chaucer seems to be regarded rather as an old poet, than as a good one, and that he wrote English verses four hundred years ago seems more frequently to be urged in his commendation, than that he wrote four hundred years ago with taste and judgment. We look upon his poems rather as venerable relics, than as finish'd patterns ; as pieces calculated rather to gratify the antiquarian than the critic. When I sate down to read Chaucer with the curiosity of knowing how the first English poet wrote, I left him with the satisfaction of having found what later and more refin'd ages could hardly equal in true humour, pathos, [p. 142] or sublimity. It must be confest that his uncouth or rather unfamiliar language has deterr'd many from perusing him ; but at the same time it must be allowed, that nothing has more contributed to his being little looked into, than the convenient opportunity of reading him with facility in modern imitations. Thus when translation (for such may imitations from Chaucer be call'd) becomes substituted as the means of attaining the knowledge of any difficult and antient author, the original not only begins to be neglected and excluded as less easy, but also to be despised as less ornamental and elegant. . . .

[p. 228]   . . . Gower and Chaucer were reputed the first English poets, because they first introduced INVENTION into our poetry; they MORALIZED THEIR SONG, and strove to render virtue more amiable, by cloathing her in the veil of fiction. Chaucer, it must be acknowledged, deserves to be rank'd as one of the first English poets, on another account; his admirable artifice in painting the manners, which none before him had ever attempted even in the most imperfect degree; and it should be remember'd to his honour, that he was the first who gave the English nation, in its own language, an idea of HUMOUR.

[*See* the second edn. of 1762, p. 423 below, where the first of the two above passages is somewhat altered and expanded.]

1754. Unknown. *Article* [in] The Monthly Review, Aug. 1754, vol. xi, pp. 118–19.

[A brief summary of sect. 5 of Warton's *Observations on . . Spenser*, which deals with Spenser's imitations of Chaucer. *See* above, p. 409.]

[1755. Grey, Zachary.] *Remarks upon a late Edition of Shakespeare. See* below, App. A. [1755].

1755. R., R. *Letter to Mr. Urban,* [in] The Gentleman's Magazine, August, 1755, vol. xxv, pp. 347–8 [on the use of "boro" or "borrowe" by Chaucer and Spenser].

1755. Rider, W. *Westminster Abbey. See* below, App. A.

1755. Johnson, Samuel. *A Dictionary of the English Language,* 1st edn. The History of the English Language, vol. i, pp. 9, 10, 11, 12, 13, 14.

[p. 9]   The history of our language is now brought to the point at which the history of our poetry is generally supposed to commence, the time of the illustrious *Geoffry Chaucer,* who may perhaps, with great justice, be stiled the first of our versifiers who wrote poetically. He does not however appear to have deserved all the praise which he has received, or all the censure that he has suffered. Dryden, who mistaking genius for learning, and in confidence of his abilities, ventured to write of what he had not examined, ascribes to *Chaucer* the first refinement of our numbers, the first production of easy and natural rhymes, and the improvement of our language, by words borrowed from the more polished languages of the Continent. *Skinner* [*see above,* 1667, p. 243] contrarily blames him in harsh terms for having vitiated his native speech by *whole cartloads of foreign words.* But he that reads the works of *Gower* will find smooth numbers and easy rhymes, of which *Chaucer* is supposed to have been the inventor, and the *French*

words, whether good or bad, of which *Chaucer* is charged as
the importer.   Some innovations he might probably make, like
others, in the infancy of our poetry, which the paucity of books
does [not] allow us to discover with particular exactness ; but
the works of *Gower* and *Lydgate* sufficiently evince that his
diction was in general like that of his contemporaries : and
some improvements he undoubtedly made by the various dispositions of his rhymes ; and by the mixture of different
numbers, in which he seems to have been happy and judicious.
I have selected several specimens both of his prose and verse ;
and among them, part of his translation of *Boetius* . . . "
[Johnson quotes also from the Astrolabe, the Prol. of the Test.
of Love, the Prol. to Canterbury Tales, the House of Fame,
and some short poems.]

[Johnson quotes very rarely from Chaucer in the body of
the Dictionary, on t' ~ principle expressed in the Preface :
" I have been cautious lest my zeal for antiquity might drive
me into times too remote, and croud my book with words now
no longer understood.   I have fixed Sidney's work for the
boundary, beyond which I make few excursions."   Thus for
" Reeve " he quotes Dryden, for " Chanticleer " Camden on
Chaucer, and for " Manciple " Betterton's *Miller of Trumpington*, rather than quote Chaucer himself.   But for " Welkin "
and " Shall " (" the faith I shall to God "), and probably for
a few other words, he quotes from Chaucer.]

1755. Unknown.   *The Praises of Isis; a poem.   By a Gentleman of
Cambridge*, p. 16.

> . . . Why loves to bend
> His lonely step to yonder aged oak,
> Deep-musing, while bright Cynthia silvers o'er
> The negro forehead of uncomely Night,
> Th' enraptur'd Bard ? . . .
>   . . . there Fame records
> Custom'd the merry Chaucer erst to frame
> His laughter-moving tale : nor, when his harp
> He tun'd to notes of louder pitch, and sung
> Of ladies passing fair, and bloody jousts,
> And warrior steeds, and valour-breathing knights
> For matchless prowess fam'd, deserv'd he not
> The laureat wreath ; for he, like Phœbus, knew
> To build in numbers apt the lofty song.—

1756. Unknown. *Some Account of the Life and Writings of Chaucer,* [in] The Universal Visiter and Memorialist for the Year 1756, Jan., pp. 9–15.

[p. 12] We come now to consider the writings of Chaucer, from which we shall find, that if not the greatest, he was, without controversy, the most universal, genius that ever was. . . . There is not a single species of poetry in which this great man has not left some specimens of his excellency.

[pp. 11–15] [Quotes Chaucer's ' Flee from the prees ' (modernised), ' O mercifull and O merciable,' and dedication of the Treatise of the Astrolabe.]

[The title-page of the volume bears the motto :]

Sounding with Moral Virtue was his Speech,

And gladly would he learn, and gladly teach.—CHAUCER.

[The frontispiece, by A. Walker, represents the Visiter writing before a row of busts of Chaucer, Spenser, Shakespeare, Waller and Dryden, and has a legend of six lines beginning :]

"To CHAUCER ! who the English Tongue designed." . .

[*The Universal Visiter* is largely by Smart. This article, which is signed **, has been attributed to Johnson, but was rejected by Boswell (*Life of Johnson*, ed. G. Birkbeck Hill, i. 306). *See* below, 1791, p. 492.]

1756. Warton, Joseph. *Essay on the Writings and Genius of Pope.* vol. i, p. 155 [quotes Pope's line "and such as Chaucer is, shall Dryden be," and Waller's "Chaucer his sense can only boast"], p. 257, [Chaucer appears to have been particularly struck with the tale of Ugolino in Dante] ; 301, [Chaucer and John of Meung] p. 303 *n.* [Chaucer translated Boetius].

[For vol. ii, which was not printed till 1782, *see* below, p. 470.]

1757. Gemsege, Paul [pseud. Pegge, Samuel]. *Letter* [in] The Gentleman's Magazine. *See* below, App. A.

1757. Thompson, William. *Preface* [to] *An Hymn to May,* [in] Poems on Several Occasions, by William Thompson, M.A., Oxford, 1757, p. 156.

[p. 156] As I profess'd myself in this *Canto* to take *Spenser* for my Model, I chose the Stanza [a 7-lined stanza with Alexandrine at end, rhyming ababccc, not used by Chaucer] ; which I think adds both a Sweetness and Solemnity at the same Time, to subjects of this rural and flowry Nature. The most descriptive of our old Poets have always used It from *Chaucer* down to *Fairfax*, and even long after him.

1757. Unknown. *Biographia Britannica,* vol. iv. *See* below, App. A., 1757.

[*a.* 1758.] **H[arris],** J[ames]. *A Fragment of Chaucer, by J. H. Esq.* [in] A Collection of Poems . . . by several hands, [ed.] R. Dodsley. 1758, vol. v, p. 296. [This is not in the earlier edition of 1748. See also The Epigrammatists, by H. P. Dodd, 2nd edn. 1875, p. 609.]

[Ten lines in the style of Chaucer.]

1728-58. Spence, Joseph. *Anecdotes . . . of Books and Men collected from the Conversation of Mr. Pope and other Eminent Persons of his Time.* First published with notes by Samuel Weller Singer, 1820. Section i, pp. 19–21, 23, 50 [*see* above, Pope, 1728–30, p. 370]. Section iv, p. 140 [note by editor quoting Chaucer reference in Pope's letter to Mrs. Judith Cowper. *See* above, Pope, 1723, p. 366], pp. 171–2 [*see* above, Pope, 1734–6, p. 377]. Section v, p. 206. Supplement, p. 336.

[p. 336] I have seen, of Mr. Pope's drawing, a grave old Chaucer, from Occleve.

[*a* 1758.] **Akenside,** Mark. *For a Statue of Chaucer at Woodstock.* [Inscriptions II. First published in R. Dodsley's] Collection of Poems, 1758, vol. vi, pp. 30–1. (Poetical works of . . . Akenside, ed. C. Cowden Clarke [1880], p. 256.)

Such was old Chaucer.   such the placid mien
Of him who first with harmony inform'd
The language of our fathers.   Here he dwelt
For many a cheerful day.   these ancient walls
Have often heard him, while his legends blithe
He sang; of love, or knighthood, or the wiles
Of homely life : through each estate and age,
The fashions and the follies of the world

[p. 31] With cunning hand portraying.   Though perchance
From Blenheim's towers, O stranger, thou art come,
Glowing with Churchill's trophies ; yet in vain
Dost thou applaud them, if thy breast be cold
To him, this other heroe ; who, in times
Dark and untaught, began with charming verse
To tame the rudeness of his native land.

1758. A., A. *Article* [in] The Gentleman's Magazine. *See* below, App. A.

1758–9. Church, Ralph. *Notes* [in] The Faerie Queene, by Edmund Spenser, a new edition, with notes critical and explanatory, by Ralph Church . . . in four volumes. . . 1758. [Vol. ii is dated 1759.]

[There are numerous references to Chaucer in the notes.]

1758. Gemsege, Paul [pseud. Pegge, Samuel]. *Letter to Mr. Urban,* [in] The Gentleman's Magazine, June 1758, vol. xxviii, pp. 261–2.

The botanists pretend to have made a new discovery, which they call by a very pretty metaphorical name, *the sleep of plants.* . . . The fact is remarkably observable in the daisy, which towards the evening always erects and brings close its petals. . . . And this observation, concerning this flower, is as old as the time of *Jeffrey Chaucer,* who in the proeme to the *Legende of good women,* has the following lines :

'There loveth no wight hartyer alyve
And whan that it is evyn I rynne belyve,

As sone as the sone ginneth to west,
To see this floure, how it *woll go to rest*,' &c.

[Prol. to Leg. of Good Women, Text B, ll. 59–62.]

.   .   .   .   .

I have a MS. of this part of the author, from whence, to spare the trouble of reporting various readings, I have transcribed the above passage *literatim*. Those who are curious may compare it, if they please, with the printed copies of *Chaucer*, since there are some variations, which I think preferrable [*sic*] to what at present are read in Mr. Urry; however there are none that concern the subject of this letter. [Quotes again twice from Chaucer.]

1758. [**Goldsmith**, Oliver.] *The Poetical Scale* [in] The Literary Magazine, Jan., 1758, p. 6.

This scale is supposed to consist of 20 degrees for each column, of which 19 may be attained in any one qualification, but the 20th was never yet attain'd to.	Genius.	Judgment.	Learning.	Versifications.
Chaucer	16	12	10	14
Spencer	18	12	14	18
Drayton	10	11	16	13
Shakespear	19	14	14	19
Johnson [Ben Jonson]	16	18	17	[?1]8
Cowley	17	17	15	17
Waller	12	12	10	16
Fairfax	12	12	14	13
Otway	17	10	10	17
Milton	18	16	17	18
Lee	16	10	10	15
Dryden	18	16	17	18
Congreve	15	16	14	14
Vanburgh [*sic*]	14	15	14	10
Steel	10	15	13	10
Addison	16	18	17	17
Prior	16	16	15	17
Swift	18	16	16	16
Pope	18	18	15	19
Thomson	16	16	14	17
Gay	14	16	14	16
Butler	17	16	14	16
Beaumont and Fletcher	14	16	16	12
Hill (Aaron)	16	12	13	17
Rowe	14	16	15	16
Farquhar	15	16	10	10
Garth	16	16	12	16
Southern	15	15	11	14
Hughes	15	16	13	16

[First attributed to Goldsmith in the Bohn edn., 1885, ed. by J. M. W. Gibbs.]

1758. [**Goldsmith,** Oliver.] "Brito." *The History of our own Language* [in] The Literary Magazine, Jan. 1758, pp. 57, 58.

Tho' Chaucer is generally look'd upon as the father of *English* poetry, yet several writers in the *North*, where, as we have already hinted, the *Anglo-Saxon* tongue prevailed in its greatest purity, preceded him in point of time, and in some respects, of excellence. *Barbour*, who was a domestic chaplain to *Robert* the first of *Scotland*, and if I mistake not, a native of the *North* of *England*, wrote his master's life in the *Anglo-Saxon* language long before *Chaucer's* days. . . .

[First recognised as Goldsmith's by J. M. W. Gibbs, the editor of Bohn's 1885 edn.]

1758. Massey, William. *Article* [in] The Gentleman's Magazine. *See* below, App. A.

1758. P., R. *Letter to Mr. Urban*, [in answer to Mr. Gemsage, *see* above, p. 413 ; in] The Gentleman's Magazine, July 1758, vol. xxviii, p. 315.

The real cause of the *somnus plantarum* was not known till experiments very lately determined it, and as to the *vigiliæ florum* it will scarcely be granted that *Chaucer* knew the physical cause, whatever use he might make of that phenomenon in a poetical way.

1758. Upton, John. *Spensers Faerie Queene. A new edition with a glossary and notes explanatory and critical, by John Upton*, 2 vols., vol. i, pp. vii–ix, xxxv–vi. The Glossary (sign. *a 2–*f 4) and the Notes (vol. ii, pp. 332–658) have references to Chaucer on practically every page; they are chiefly on Spenser's debt to Chaucer for words and phrases.

[*See* below, p. 416, 1759, Unknown.]

1758. Walpole, Horace. *A Catalogue of the Royal and Noble Authors of England*, 2 vols., vol. ii, pp. 182–3.

James I [of Scotland, wrote] . . . "Scotch Sonnets," one book. One of them, "A Lamentation while in England," is in manuscript in the Bodleian library, and praises Gower and Chaucer exceedingly.

[This must be the Selden MS. of the King's Quhair.]

1758. Williams, Sir Charles Hanbury. [*Verses*] *To Mrs. Bindon at Bath*, [in] A Collection of Poems in six volumes by several hands ("Dodsley's Miscellany"), 1758, vol. v., p. 156.

Apollo of old on Britannia did smile,
And Delphi forsook for the sake of this isle . . .
Then Chaucer and Spenser harmonious were heard,
Then Shakespear, and Milton, and Waller appear'd.

1759. Andrews, James Pettit. *Letter* [giving an account of the parish of Shaw-cum-Donnington, written by Andrews in] Answers to Berkshire Queries, [in the fourth volume of the] Bibliotheca Topographica Britannica, [which contains the Antiquities in Bedfordshire, Berkshire . . .] 1790, pp. 76, 80. [The pagination is not continuous.]

[p. 76]   The most remarkable building in the parish is the celebrated Donnington-castle, which was (for the latter part of his life) the dwelling-place of that father of English poetry, Chaucer. I have often heard and read of that oak under which he is said to have composed some of his poems, but on the strictest search, and the most careful enquiry of the oldest people, I cannot find the least remains of it ; though I think Camden says that in his time it was standing. . . .

[p. 80]   There is at the house near Donnington castle [belonging to the Packers, descendants of Jack of Newbury] an original portrait of the celebrated Chaucer : the very same from which all those prints and drawings which we have of him are taken.

[For additions to the above, *see* below, 1783, p. 475.]

1759. [Astle, Thomas.] *A Catalogue of the Harleian Collection of Manuscripts.* Preface, p. 25 ; a general description of Chaucer MSS. ; and see the Index.

[*See* below, p. 424, 1763, Unknown.]

1759. Johnson, Samuel. *The Idler*, no. 63, June 30, 1759 ; no. 69, August 11, 1759. (The Idler. Two vols., printed 1761, vol. ii, pp. 62–3, 91–2.)

[Merely passing references (1) to the fact that the improvement of the English language dates from the time of Gower and Chaucer ; (2) to Chaucer's translation of Boethius.]

1759. Lowth, R[obert]. *Letter to Joseph Warton*, [dated] Bath, April 19, 1759, [in] Biographical Memoirs of Joseph Warton, D.D., ed. John Wooll, 1806, pp. 261–2.

Pray where did you meet with William the Conqueror's Ode, and Chaucer's accompanying the Duke of Clarence to Milan, and being personally acquainted with Petrarch ? I should be glad if you could give us your authorities for such curious matters.

1759. Massey, William. *Article* [in] The Gentleman's Magazine. *See* below, App. A.

1759. [Unknown]. *An Impartial Estimate of the Reverend Mr. Upton's Notes on the Fairy Queen*, pp. 14–19.

[The author blames Upton for borrowing notes from Warton, (*q.v.* above, 1754, p. 409) among the rest those on Chaucer's influence upon Spenser.]

1759. [**Young**, Edward.] *Conjectures on Original Composition*, 2nd edn., pp. 7–8.

Moreover, if we consider life's endless evils, what can be more prudent, than to provide for consolation under them? A consolation under them the wisest of men have found in the pleasures of the pen. Witness, among many more, Thucydides, Xenophon, Tully, Ovid, Seneca, Pliny the Younger . . . And why not add to these their modern equals, *Chaucer, Rawleigh, Bacon, Milton, Clarendon?* . . .

[The first edn. (also 1759) omits Chaucer, and begins " *Rawleigh, Milton, Clarendon.*"]

[*a.* **1760.**] **Darrell**, Dr. *An Excellent Ballad. To the Tune of Chevy-Chace* [a satire on Browne Willis, who died in 1760, in] The Oxford Sausage, 1764, p. 158. (*See* Hone's *Every-Day Book*, vol. ii, p. 299.)

A stick, torn from that hallow'd Tree,
Where *Chaucer* us'd to sit,
And tell his Tales with leering Glee,
Supports his tott'ring Feet.

[**1760.**] **Gibbon**, Edward. *Outlines of the History of the World. The Fourteenth Century.* (The Miscellaneous Works of E. Gibbon, ed. John, Lord Sheffield, 1837, p. 618.)

If any barbarian on this side the Alps deserves to be remembered [in connection with literature], it is our country-man Chaucer, whose Gothic dialect often conceals natural humour and poetical imagery.

1760. Gray, Thomas. [*Letter*] *to* [*Horace*] *Walpole on ' Anecdotes of Painting,'* [dated] Cambridge, Sept. 2, 1760. (Gray's Letters, ed. D. C. Tovey, 1900–12, vol. iii, pp. 325–6, 330.)

[p. 325]   Mr. Vertue's MSS. (as I do not doubt you have experienced) will often put you on a false scent. Be assured that Occleve's portrait of Chaucer is not, nor ever was, in St. John's Library : they have a MS. of the Troilus and Cressida without illumina-tions, and no other part of his works. In the University Library, indeed, there is a large volume with most of his works on vellum, and by way of frontispiece is (pasted in) a pretty old print, taken (as it says) by Mr. Speed from Occleve's original painting in the book *De Regimine Principum*, in the middle is Chaucer, a whole length, the same countenance,

CHAUCER CRITICISM.

attitude, and dress that Vertue gives you in the two heads which he has engraved of him; the border is composed of escutcheons of arms, all the alliances of the Chaucer family, and at bottom the tomb of Thomas Chaucer and Maud Burghershe at Ewelm. The print and all the arms are neatly coloured. I only describe this because I never took notice of such a print any where else, though perhaps you may know it; for I suppose it was done for some of Speed's works. About the painting I have a great puzzle in my head between Vertue, M^r. D'Urry, and Bishop Tanner. Vertue (you know) has twice engraved Chaucer's head, once for D'Urry's edition of his works, and a second time. in the set of poets' heads. Both are done from Occleve's painting; but he never tells us where he found the painting, as he generally uses to do. D'Urry says there is a portrait of Chaucer (doubtless a whole length), for he describes his port and stature from it, in possession of George Greenwood, Esq., of Chastleton in Gloucestershire. A little after he too mentions the picture by Occleve, but whether the same or not does not appear. Tanner, in his *Bibliotheca* (Artic. Chaucer, see the notes) [*see* above, 1748, p. 395], speaks of Occleve's painting too, but names another work of his (not the *De Regim. Principum*), and adds, that it is in *the King's Library at Westminster:* if so, you will certainly find it in the Museum, and Casley's Catalogue will direct you to the place.

1760. Unknown. *Biographia Britannica,* vol. v. *See* below, App. A., 1760.

[1760–1?] Gray, Thomas. *Metrum. Observations on English Metre.* [Miscellaneous notes on metre and on early L⸱⸱glish poetry, which form part of the material intended for his projected History of Poetry. Pembroke MSS. Cambr., first printed by T. J. Mathias in 1814.] (Gray's Works, ed. E. Gosse, 1884, vol. i, pp. 325–6, 328–9, 335–6, 339, 343–4, 345 *n.*, 346–8, 353–5, 357 *n.*, 358–9. *Some Remarks on the Poems of John Lydgate*, pp. 390–1, 397, 401–2, 407.)

[p. 325] Though I would not with M^r. Urry,[1] the Editor of Chaucer, insert words and syllables, unauthorized by the oldest manuscripts, to help out what seems lame and defective in the measure of our ancient writers, yet as I see those manuscripts, and the first printed editions, so extremely inconstant in their manner of spelling one and the same word as to vary con-

---

[1] See the Preface to Urry's Chaucer. Fol.

tinually, and often in the compass of two lines, and seem to
have no fixed orthography, I cannot help thinking it probable,
that many great inequalities in the metre are owing to the
[p. 326] neglect of transcribers, or that the manner of reading made up
for the defects which appear in the writing.   Thus the *y*
which we often see prefixed to participles passive, *y*cleped,
*y*hewe, &c. is not a mere arbitrary insertion to fill up the
verse, but is the old Anglo-Saxon augment . . . which as
early as Edward the Confessor's time, began to be written
with a *y*, or an *i*. . . . [1] This syllable, though (I suppose)
then out of use in common speech, our poets inserted,
where it suited them, in verse.—[The same was the case
[p. 327] with the final syllable of verbs -in, -on, -en, -an] . . . As
then our writers inserted these initial and final letters, or
omitted them; and, where we see them written, we do not
doubt that they were meant to fill up the measure; it follows,
[p. 328] that these Poets had an ear not insensible to defects in metre;
and where the verse seems to halt, it is very probably
occasioned by the transcriber's neglect, who, seeing a word
spelt differently from the manner then customary, changed or
omitted a few letters without reflecting on the injury done to
the measure.   The case is the same with the genitive case
singular and the nominative plural of many nouns, . . . but
we now have reduced them, by our pronunciation, to an equal
number of syllables with their nominatives singular.   This
was commonly done too, I imagine, in Chaucer's and Lydgate's
time; but, in verse, they took the liberty either to follow the
old language in pronouncing the final syllable, or to sink the
[p. 329] vowel and abridge it, as was usual, according to the necessity
of their versification.   I have mentioned . . . the *e* mute,
and their use of it in words derived from the French, and I
imagine that they did the same in many words of true English
origin, which the Danes had before robbed of their final
consonant . . . Here we may easily conceive, that though
the *n* was taken away, yet the *e* continued to be pronounced
faintly, and though in time it was quite dropped in conversation, yet when the poet thought fit to make a syllable of it,

[1] . . . Chaucer seems to have been well aware of the injustice that his
copyists might chance to do to him : he says, towards the end of his Troilus,

'And for there is so great diversitie,
In English, and in writing of our tong;'
[quotes the whole passage, ll. 1793-6].

it no more offended their ears than it now offends those of a
Frenchman to hear it so pronounced, in verse.

[pp. 329-35] [Puttenham's remarks on metre.]

[p. 335]   These reflections may serve to shew us, that Puttenham,
though he lived within about one hundred and fifty years of
Chaucer's time, must have been mistaken with regard to what
the old writers called their *Riding Rhyme ;* for the Canterbury
Tales, which he gives as an example of it, are as exact in their
measure and in their pause as in the Troilus and Cresseide,
where he says, "*the metre is very grave and stately*"; and
this not only in the Knight's Tale, but in the comic Introduction and Characters . . .

. . . .

. . . I conclude, that he was misled by the change which
[p. 336] words had undergone in their accents since the days of
Chaucer, and by the seeming defects of measure which
frequently occur in the printed copies. I cannot pretend to say
what it was they called *Riding Rhyme*, but perhaps it might be
such as we see in the Northern Tale of Sir Thopas in Chaucer.

. . . .

But nothing can be more regular than this sort of stanza, the
pause always falling just in the middle of those verses which
are of eight syllables, and at the end of those of six. I
imagine that it was this very regularity which seemed so
tedious to *mine host of the Tabbarde*, as to make him interrupt
Chaucer in the middle of his story. . . .

. . . .

[p. 339] But the *Riding Rhyme* I rather take to be that which is
confined to one measure, whatever that measure be, but not
to one rhythm ; having sometimes more, sometimes fewer
syllables, and the pause hardly distinguishable, such as the
Prologue and History of Beryn, found in some MSS. of
Chaucer, and the Cook's Tale of Gamelyn, where the verses
have twelve, thirteen, or fourteen syllables, and the Cæsura on
the sixth, seventh, or eighth, as it happens. . . .

. . . .

Some Remarks on the Poems of John Lydgate.

[p. 397]   I do not pretend to set him [Lydgate] on a level with his
master, Chaucer, but he certainly comes the nearest to him of
any contemporary writer that I am acquainted with. His
choice of expression, and the smoothness of his verse, far
surpass both Gower and Occleve. . . .

. . . .

[p. 401]   It is observable that in images of horror, and in a certain terrible greatness, our author comes far behind Chaucer. . . .

.   .   .   .

[p. 402]   Lydgate seems to have been by nature of a more serious and melancholy turn of mind than Chaucer; yet one here and there meets with a stroke of satire and irony which does not want humour, and it usually falls (as was the custom of those times) either upon the women or on the clergy.

1761. [**Dalrymple,** Hugh ?] *Woodstock Park. An Elegy.* London, Wilson, 4°.

> Old Chaucer, who in rough unequal verse,
> Sung quaint allusion and facetious tale ;
> And ever as his jests he would rehearse,
> Loud peals of laughter echoed through the vale.
>
> .   .   .   .
>
> What though succeeding poets, as they [their ?] sire,
> Revere his memory and approve his wit ;
> Though Spenser's elegance and Dryden's fire
> His name to ages far remote transmit ;
> His tuneless numbers hardly now survive
> As ruins of a dark and Gothic age ;
> And all his blithesome tales their praise derive
> From Pope's immortal song and Prior's page.

[There is no copy of this pamphlet (published at one shilling) in the British Museum ; this extract is taken from Professor Lounsbury's *Studies in Chaucer*, iii, 289.]

1761. Unknown. [*Life of*] *Chaucer*, [in] A New and General Biographical Dictionary, vol. iii, pp. 172–7.

[An ordinary life, followed by quotations from Beaumont's letter to Speght, *q.v.* above, 1597, p. 145, and from Dryden, *q.v.* above, 1700, p. 271. In Tooke's edition of 1798 an enthusiastic reference to Tyrwhitt's edition is added at the end.]

1762. [**Hurd,** Richard (Bp. of Worcester).] *Letters on Chivalry and Romance*, pp. 58, 59 [Letter vii.], 106–108 [Letter xi.], 112.

[p. 58]   [Milton, in the Penseroso] extolls an *author* of one of these
[p. 59]   romances, as he had before, in general, extolled the *subject* of them ; but it is an author worthy of his praise ; not the writer of *Amadis*, or *Sir Launcelot of the Lake*, but Chaucer himself, who has left an unfinished story on the Gothic or feudal model.

' Or, call up him who left half-told
  The story of Cambuscan bold . . .
  Where more is meant than meets the eye.'

The conduct then of these two poets may incline us to think
with more respect, than is commonly done of the *Gothic
manners*, I mean as adapted to the uses of the greater poetry.

.   .   .   .

[p. 106]   . . . long before his [Ariosto's] time an immortal genius
of our own (so superior is the sense of some men to the age
[p. 107] they live in) saw as far into this matter as Ariosto's examiner.
This sagacious person was Dan Chaucer; who in a reign, that
almost realized the wonders of romantic chivalry, not only
discerned the absurdity of the old romances, but has even
ridiculed them with incomparable spirit.

His RIME OF SIR TOPAZ, in the Canterbury Tales, is a
manifest banter on these books, and may be considered as a
sort of prelude to the adventures of Don Quixot.   I call
it a *manifest banter* : For we are to observe that this was
Chaucer's own tale, and that, when in the progress of it
the good sense of the Host is made to break in upon him,
and interrupt him, Chaucer approves his disgust and, changing
his note, tells the simple instructive tale of Melibæus, *a moral*
[p. 108] *tale virtuous*, as he chuses to characterize it; to shew, what
sort of fictions were most expressive of real life, and most
proper to be put into the hands of the People.

One might further observe that the Rime of Sir Topas
itself is so managed as with infinite humour to expose the
leading impertinences of books of chivalry, and their impertin-
encies only; as may be seen by the different conduct of this
tale, from that of Cambuscan, which Spenser and Milton were
so pleased with, and which with great propriety is put into the
mouth of the SQUIRE.

But I must not anticipate the observations which you will
take a pleasure to make for yourself on these two fine parts of
the Canterbury Tales.   Enough is said to illustrate the point,
[p. 109] I am now upon, 'That these phantoms of chivalry had the
misfortune to be laughed out of countenance by men of sense,
before the substance of it had been fairly and truly represented
by any capable writer.'

[*See* the later edition of 1765, below, App. A, 1765, where Hurd expands considerably his comparison of Sir Topaz and Don Quixote. A portion of this is quoted by
Thomas Warton from the edn. of 1765 in his History of Poetry, vol. i, 1774, pp. 433–4.]

1762. Walpole, Horace. *Anecdotes of Painting in England . . . collected by the late Mr George Vertue . . . and now published . . . by Mr Horace Walpole.* Printed . . . at Strawberry Hill. vol. i, p. 30.

The painted effigies of Chaucer remained till within these few years on his tomb at Westminster; and another, says Vertue on his print of that poet, is preserved in an illuminated MS. of Thomas Occleve, painted by Occleve himself. D'Urry and Tanner both mention such a portrait, which places Occleve in the rank of one of our first painters as well as poets.

[*See* a note by James Dallaway in his edn. of Anecdotes of Painting in England, 1826, vol. i, pp. 56–7, note.]

1762. Warton, Thomas. *Observations on the Fairy Queen of Spenser, . . . second edition, corrected and enlarged . . .* 2 vols.

[The Chaucer references are very numerous, but very much the same as those in 1st edn., 1754 [*q. v.* above, p. 409]; we quote below a passage (vol. i, pp. 196–7) which in this edn. is somewhat altered and expanded, cf. with 1st edn. p. 409, above.]

[p. 196]   I cannot dismiss this Section without a wish, that this neg-
[p. 197] lected author, whom Spenser proposed as the pattern of his style, and to whom he is indebted for many noble inventions, should be more universally studied. This is at least what one might expect in an age of research and curiosity. Chaucer is regarded rather as an old, than as a good, poet. We look upon his poems as venerable relics, not as beautiful compositions; as pieces better calculated to gratify the antiquarian than the critic. He abounds not only in strokes of humour, which is commonly supposed to be his sole talent, but of pathos, and sublimity, not unworthy a more refined age. His old manners, his romantic arguments, his wildness of painting, his simplicity and antiquity of expression, transport us into some fairy region, and are all highly pleasing to the imagination. It is true that his uncouth and unfamiliar language disgusts and deters many readers: but the principal reason of his being so little known, and so seldom taken into hand, is the convenient opportunity of reading him with pleasure and facility in modern imitations. . . .

1762. Warburton, W[illiam] (Bishop of Gloucester). *Letter to Dr. Balguy,* Oct. 7, 1762 [in] Biographical Memoirs of Joseph Warton, D.D., ed. John Wooll, 1806, pp. 283–4.

When you see Mr. T. Warton, pray tell him with what new pleasure I have read his improved edition of his *Observations on the Fairy Queen* . . . if he goes on so, he will rescue antiquarian studies . . . from the contempt of certain learned

blockheads, and the stale ridicule of ignorant wits.   Above all
[p. 284] there is nothing I more wish than an edition of my favourite
Chaucer from his hand.

[*c.* **1763. Chatterton,** Thomas, borrows Speght's Chaucer.   *See* below,
      a. 1770, pp. 432–5.]

1763. [**Colman,** George (the Elder).]   *The Deuce is in Him, a farce* . . .
      Act ii, p. 31.   (The Deuce is in Him [in] The Modern British
      Drama, 1811, vol. v, p. 396).

            [Col. Tamper pretends to have lost a leg and an eye during
      the war, but is discovered.]
            [Bell] What! to come here with a Canterbury tale of a leg
      and an eye, and heaven knows what, merely to try the extent
      of his power over you!

1763. Unknown.   *Some account of the Harleian Collection of Manu-
      scripts now in the British Museum; from the Preface to the new
      Index to that Collection, most judiciously compiled by Mr. Astle*
      [in] Gentleman's Magazine, August 1763, vol. 33, pp. 374–5.

      [This series of articles begins on p. 153.   A few extracts from Astle's preface are
      given; for Astle *see* above, 1759, p. 416.]

1763. Unknown.   *Verses, occasioned by the death of Mrs. Oldfield* [in]
      The Poetical Calendar . . . Written and Selected by Francis
      Fawkes, and William Woty, 1763, vol. ii, p. 117.

            In vain, secure of deathless praise,
                  There [to Westminster] poets ashes come,
            Since obsolete grows Chaucer's phrase,
                  And moulders with his tomb.

1763. Walpole, Horace.   *List of Vertue's Works,* [in] A Catalogue of
      Engravers.

            Class 11.—Poets and Musicians.   Set of 12 poets . . .
      2 Geofry Chaucer. . . .
            Geofry Chaucer, large, in oval frame.*   Another smaller,
      verses in old character.*   A plate with five small heads of
      Chaucer, Milton, Butler, Cowley, Waller.*   [Walpole's note] †
      Those numbered are the set.   Those with an asterisk do not
      belong to it.

[*a.* **1764**].   **Thomas,** William.   *Copious MS. notes* in the interleaved copy
      of Urry's edn. of Chaucer, 1721, *q.v.,* [B. M. pr. m. 643, m. 4],
      presented to the British Museum by William Thomas, Dec. 1, 1764.

1764. [**Gough,** Richard ?] *A manuscript inscription* in black letter character, on the fly-leaf of an imperfect copy of Chaucer's Works, that once belonged to the antiquary Richard Gough.

[Printed by J. Haslewood, ' Eu. Hood', [in] Gentleman's Magazine, Aug. 1823, vol. 93, p. 109. Cutting inserted by Haslewood in his annotated copy of Winstanley's Lives of the Poets, to face p. 23 ; see below c. 1833.]

Knowe ye all wightes y^t on my leeves doe looke
Of Maister William Shenstone whylome was I ye boke
But syns to Dan Orcus nows [*sic,* for ' hows '] he is ygone
Ryzard of Englefield doeth me owne.
Thus goe I through all Regiouns :
Eft chaunge I my Mansiouns :
Ah me y^t I have loste
Some Leeves to my coste :
Yet of one enoughe remayneth
To delyghte him y^t complayneth
For Love or for Despyte
By day or by nyghte.
In ye yeere of ye Incarnacyon MCCDLXIV.—R. G.

1764. Unknown. *Account of the Life of Mr. Samuel Boyse* [in] Annual Register, vol. vii, [pt. ii.], p. 58.

He [Boyse] was employed by Mr. Ogle to translate some of Chaucer's tales into modern English, which he performed with great spirit, and received at the rate of threepence a line for his trouble. Mr. Ogle published a complete edition of that old poet's *Canterbury tales modernized ;* and Mr. Boyse's name is put to such tales as were done by him.

[*See* above, 1741, p. 389.]

1764. Unknown. *England Illustrated,* vol. ii, p. 171.

(Oxfordshire. Curiosities.) Geoffrey Chaucer, a famous English poet, is said to have been born at Woodstock, where there is a house which still retains his name.

[**1765,** or *a.*] **Dunkin,** William. *See* below, App. A.

1765. [**Heath,** Benjamin.] *A Revisal of Shakespear's Text,* pp. 80, 133, etc.

[Occasional quotations from Chaucer in support of readings.]

1765. Hurd, Richard. *Letters on Chivalry and Romance.* [For additions made in the 1765 edn., *see* below, App. A.]

1765. Johnson, Samuel. *Preface* [to] The Plays of William Shakespeare, in 8 vols., . . . to which are added Notes by Sam. Johnson. London, 1765, vol. i, sign. B 8 b, C 4, E 3.

[sign. B 8 b] The stories, which we now find only in remoter authours, were in his [Shakespeare's] time accessible and familiar. The fable of *As You Like it,* which is supposed to be copied from *Chaucer's* Gamelyn, was a little pamphlet of those times; and old Mr. *Cibber* remembered the tale of *Hamlet* in plain *English* prose, which the criticks have now to seek in *Saxo Grammaticus.*

[sign. C 4] Our author [Shakespeare] had both matter and form to provide; for except the characters of *Chaucer,* to whom I think he is not much indebted, there were no writers in *English,* and perhaps not many in other modern languages, which shewed life in its native colours.

[sign. E 3] The criticks on ancient authours have, in the exercise of their sagacity, many assistances, which the editor of *Shakespeare* is condemned to want. They are employed upon grammatical and settled languages, whose construction contributes so much to perspicuity, that *Homer* has fewer passages unintelligible than *Chaucer.*

1765. Percy, Thomas, Bp. of Dromore. *Reliques of Ancient English Poetry.* vol. i, pp. ix, 32, 123-4; vol. ii, pp. 6-7, 11, 13, 43, 164; vol. iii, pp. viii, ix, xii, xviii, xxi, xxiii, 11, 104, 209.

[Added in vol. i, p. lv, of 2nd edn., 1767] Junius interprets glees by *Musica Instrumenta,* in the following passages of Chaucer's Third Boke of Fame—

> . . . Stoden . . the castell all aboutin
> Of all maner of Mynstrales . . .
> And other harpers many one,
> And the Briton Glaskyrion.

[House of Fame, Skeat, Bk. iii, ll. 1195-7, 1205, 6.]
See below, vol. iii.

[vol i, p. 32] The Jew's daughter, a scottish ballad . . . The following ballad is probably built upon some Italian Legend, and bears a great resemblance to the Prioresse's Tale in Chaucer. . . . The conclusion of this ballad appears to be wanting; what it probably contained may be seen in Chaucer.

[pp. 123, 124] In Chaucer's Time "Plays of Miracles" [the words "in Lent" added in edn. 3, 1775] were the common resort of

idle gossips. [Note] See Prologue to Wife of Bath's Tale,
v. 558, Urry's ed. [l. 558, Skeat's edn.]

. . . .

[vol. ii,   This antique Elegy [on the Death of King Edward I] is
pp. 6, 7] extracted from the same MS. volume as the preceding article
[Richard of Almaigne]; is found with the same peculiarities
of writing and orthography; and tho' written at near the
distance of half a century contains little or no variation of
idiom : whereas the next following poem by Chaucer, [see
below,] which was probably written not more than 50 or 60
years after this, exhibits almost a new language. This seems
to countenance the opinion of some antiquaries that this great
poet made considerable innovations in his mother tongue,
and introduced many terms, and new modes of speech from
other languages.

. . . .

[p. 11]   An original Ballad by Chaucer.

This little sonnet, which hath escaped all the editors of
Chaucer's works, is now printed for the first time from an
ancient MS. in the Pepysian library, that contains many other
poems of its venerable author. The versification is of that
species, which the French call RONDEAU, very naturally
englished by our honest countrymen ROUND O. Tho' so
early adopted by them, our ancestors had not the honour of
inventing it : Chaucer picked it up, along with other better
things, among the neighbouring nations. A fondness for
laborious trifles hath always prevailed in the dawn of literature. The ancient Greek poets had their WINGS and AXES : the
great father of English poesy may therefore be pardoned one
poor solitary RONDEAU.—Dan Geofrey Chaucer died Oct. 25,
1400, aged 72.

. . . .

> youre two eyn will sle me sodenly
> I may the beaute of them not sustene.

. . . .

[p. 13]   It does honour to the good sense of this nation, that while
all Europe was captivated with the bewitching charms of
Chivalry and Romance, two of our writers in the crudest
times could see thro' the false glare that surrounded them, and
discover whatever was absurd in them both. Chaucer wrote
his Rhyme of sir Tropas [*sic*] in ridicule of the latter, and in

the following poem [The Turnament of Tottenham] we have a humourous burlesque of the former.

. . . .

[p. 48]   This little piece [A Ballet by the Earl Rivers], . . . is written in imitation of a poem of Chaucer's, that will be found in Urry's Edit., 1721, pag. 555, beginning thus,

Alone walkyng, In thought plainyng, &c.

. . . .

[p. 161-4]   [ref. to the word 'fitt' as used by Chaucer in Sir Thopas.]

. . . .

[vol. iii, p. viii]   [ref. to Chaucer's Sir Thopas; the verse naming the romances is quoted.]

They [the romances of chivalry] cannot indeed be put in competition with the nervous productions of so universal and commanding a genius as Chaucer, but they have a simplicity that makes them be read with less interruption, and be more easily understood. . . .

[p. ix]   . . . Chaucer and Spenser . . . abound with perpetual allusions to them [romances of chivalry]. . . .

[p. xii]   I shall select the Romance of Libius Disconius, as being one of those mentioned by Chaucer. . . .

[p. xvii]   I shall conclude this prolix account, with a List of such old Metrical Romances as are still extant: beginning with those mentioned by Chaucer. . . .

[p. xviii]   As for Blandamoure, no Romance with this title has been discovered; but as the word occurs in that of Libeaux, 'tis possible Chaucer's memory deceived him. . . .

[p. xxi]   Sir Isenbras . . . is quoted in Chaucer's R. of Thop. v. 6.

. . . .

[p. xxiii]   The Squyr of Lowe degre, is one of those burlesqued by Chaucer. . . .

[p. 11]   THE MARRIAGE OF SIR GAWAINE is chiefly taken from the fragment of an old ballad in the Editor's MS. which he has reason to believe more ancient than the time of CHAUCER, and what furnished that bard with his Wife of Bath's Tale.

. . . .

[Added in edn. 3, 1775, p. 43.]   See what is said concerning the hero of this song [Glasgerion], (who is celebrated by Chaucer under the name of Glaskyrion) in the Essay prefixed to Vol. I. Note H [or rather I] Pt IV. (2). [*See* above, vol. i.]

[p. 104]   [Sir Guy quoted by Chaucer.]

.   .   .   .

[p. 209]   THE FAIRIES FAREWELL. The departure of the Fairies is here
attributed to the abolition of monkery : Chaucer has, with equal
humour, assigned a cause the very reverse. [Wife of Bath's
Tale, ll. 1–16.]

1765. Unknown. *Review* of Percy's Reliques [in] The Gentleman's
Magazine, April 1765, vol. xxxv, pp. 179, 180. [Brief references.]

1766. [**Tyrwhitt,** Thomas.] *Observations and Conjectures upon some
Passages of Shakespeare,* p. 21.

[Chaucer's and Shakespeare's use of the word barbe.]

1766. Unknown. *The Life of Geoffrey Chaucer,* [an article in] British
Biography ; or an accurate and impartial account of the lives and
writings of Eminent Persons . . . vol. i, pp. 109–137.

[p. 109]   The Name of CHAUCER is peculiarly endeared to every lover
of English Poetry. His great and distinguished poetical
abilities, in an age in which polite literature . . . was little
known, . . . his admirable talent at painting manners and
characters ; and some other circumstances in which he has
been thought to resemble the immortal Grecian Poet, have
occasioned him to be frequently stiled the ENGLISH HOMER,
and the FATHER of the English Poets . . .

[p. 127]   As a Poet, our author has been deservedly considered as
one of the greatest, as well as earliest, which this nation
has produced. Allowing for those unavoidable defects which
arise from the fluctuation of language, his works have still all
the beauties which can be wished for, or expected, in every
species of composition which he attempted ; for it has been
truly said, that he excelled in all the different kinds of verse
in which he wrote. In his sonnets, or love songs, written
when he was a mere boy, there is not only fire and judgment,
but great elegance of thought, and neatness of composition . . .
As he had a discerning eye, he discovered nature in all her
appearances, and stripped off every disguise with which the
Gothic writers had clothed her . . . and . . . despising the
mean assistances of art, he copied her closely. He was an
excellent master of love poetry, having studied that passion
in all its turns and appearances ; and Mr. Dryden prefers
him upon that account to Ovid. His *Troilus and Creseide*
is one of the most beautiful poems of that kind, in which

love is curiously and naturally described, in its early appearance, its hopes and fears, its application, fruition and despair in disappointment. That in the elegiac poetry he was a great master, appears evidently by his *Complaint of the black Knight*, the poem called *La belle Dame sans mercy*, and several of his songs. And his great talents in the satirical and comic way, are strikingly evident. [Warton's remark on humour in Observations on . . . Spenser, 1754, is then quoted, followed by appreciations by Ascham, Sidney, Beaumont and Dryden.]

[A long article, partly compiled from that in the Biographia Britannica, 1747, and partly from Dart's Life prefixed to Urry's edition, 1721, with a certain number of unborrowed remarks. The Life is followed by a list of Chaucer's works, pp. 131-33, and the character of the Monk, modernised by Betterton, and the Clerk or Scholar of Oxford, modernised by Ogle, pp. 136-7.]

1767. **Farmer**, Richard. *An Essay on the learning of Shakespeare*, 1767, pp. 16, 18–19. The Second Edition, with large additions, 1767, pp. 24 *note*, 27, 32 (same references as 1st edition ; the following are new), pp. 36, 37 and *note*, 40 *note*.

[Passing references to Chaucer, except on p. 40, where the note is as follows :—]

Let me here make an observation for the benefit of the next Editor of *Chaucer*. Mr. *Urry*, probably misled by his predecessor, *Speght*, was determined, *Procrustes-like*, to *force* every line in the *Canterbury Tales* to the same Standard ; but a precise number of Syllables was not the Object of our old Poets. . . . *Chaucer* himself was persuaded, that the *Rime* might possibly be

—— ' somewhat agreáble,
Though some Verse faile in a Syllable.'

[*House of Fame*, ll. 1097-8.]

In short the attention was directed to the *Cæsural pause*, as the *Grammarians* call it ; [Farmer then quotes Gascoigne's remarks on Chaucer's metre, " Whosoever do peruse," &c., *see* above, 1575, p. 110.]

1767. **Percy**, Thomas, Bishop of Dromore. *Reliques of Ancient English Poetry*. For additions made in edn. 2, 1767, *see* above, edn. 1, 1765, p. 426].

1768. *A Catalogue of a large, valuable and curious Collection of Books* [to be sold] by Benjamin White, At Horace's Head, in Fleet Street, London, March 10th, 1768 ; pp. 29, 136.

[p. 29]   Chaucer's Works, by Speght, *wants title*, 4s.

Chaucer's Works, by Urry, with a Glossary, 11 5s, *neat*. 1721.

The same, *royal paper, new and neat,* 1l 11s 6d   1721.

[p. 136]   Chaucer's Canterbury Tales, published by Ogle, 3 vol. *sewed,* 7s 6d   1741.

The same Book, 3 vol. *bound, neat,* 10s 6d   1741.

1768. *A Catalogue of the Libraries of the Rev. Zachary Grey, LL.D. . . . Malachy Postlethwayte, Esq. . . . Thomas Cranmer, M.D. . . . and several other Persons deceased.* . . . . They will be sold, for *Ready Money,* . . . on Tuesday, March 8, 1768 ; . . . by L. Davis and C. Reymers, at their Great Room, over-against Gray's-Inn, Holborn, Printers to the Royal Society ; p. 42.

[p. 42]   Chaucer's Works by Urry, with a Glossary, *new and neat,* 1l 5s   1722.

Another Copy, *royal paper,* 1l 11s 6d   1722.

[1768. Capell, Edward.] *Introduction, Origin of Shakespeare's Fables,* [in] Mr. William Shakespeare, his Comedies, Histories and Tragedies, vol. i, p. 69.

The loves of Troilus and Cressida are celebrated by Chaucer, whose poem might perhaps induce Shakespeare to work them up into a play.

[1768.] Gray, Thomas. *Note* [in prose, added to] *The Progress of Poesy. A Pindaric Ode.* [The Ode was written in 1754, and first published in 1757 without notes, under the title :—Odes by Mr. Gray. Notes were first added in the edn. of 1768.] (The Works of Thomas Gray, ed. by Edmund Gosse, 1884, vol. i, p. 33.)

Progress of Poetry from Greece to Italy, and from Italy to England. Chaucer was not unacquainted with the writings of Dante or of Petrarch. The Earl of Surrey and Sir Tho. Wyatt had travelled in Italy, and formed their taste there : Spenser imitated the Italian writers ; Milton improved on them ; but this School expired soon after the Restoration, and a new one arose on the French model, which has subsisted ever since.

1768. Walpole, Horace. *Letter to George Montagu,* [dated] Strawberry Hill, April 15, 1768. (Letters of Horace Walpole, ed. Mrs. Paget Toynbee, vol. vii, 1904, p. 180.)

Your wit and humour will be as much lost upon them, as if you talked the dialect of Chaucer : for with all the divinity of wit, it grows out of fashion like a fardingale.

1769. Granger, J[ames]. *A Biographical History of England.* Article I, Class IX, Men of Genius and Learning, vol. i, pp. 45-7.

[After enumerating the portraits of Chaucer, Granger says] This great poet, whom antiquity and his own merit have contributed to render venerable, is said to have been the master of all the learning of his age. We see, and admire, in his works, the outlines of nature ; but the beauty of colouring, and the delicate touches, are now lost, as a great part of his language is grown obsolete. It is probable that his cotemporaries found little or no dissonance in his verses ; but they are very ill accomodated to the ears of the present age.

[In the 2nd edn. of 1775, vol. i, pp. 63–5, the remarks on Chaucer are slightly expanded, but the list of portraits remains the same.]

1769. Howard, Charles [afterwards 10th Duke of Norfolk]. *Historical Anecdotes of some of the Howard Family*, p. 27.

[Reference to Fenton's lines on Chaucer and Surrey, *see above*, Fenton, 17½?, p. 313. *See also* below, 1778, pp. 450–1, Anonymiana by Samuel Pegge (the elder), printed 1809, pp. 344–5, and above, 1717, Sewell, George, p. 346.]

1769. Hurd, Richard. *Letter to Joseph Warton*, Sept. 15, 1769, [in] Biographical Memoirs of Joseph Warton, D.D., ed. John Wooll, 1806, p. 349.

The Greek poem of Theseus is a curiosity, and may be well worth your perusing ; tho' you will scarce find it so masterly a performance as that of Chaucer or Dryden.

1769. Ruffhead, Owen. *The Life of Alexander Pope, Esq.*, p. 173.

[Reference to Chaucer's House of Fame, and Pope's adaptation of it.]

1769. Unknown. *Observations on the Rise and Progress of English Poetry* [in] Whitehall Evening Post, Jan. 7, 1769. [Taken from Thomas Warton's Observations on the Faerie Queene of Spenser, *see* above, 1754, p. 409.] A newspaper cutting inserted by J. Haslewood in his Collections for the Lives of the English Poets, vol. i, pp. 5–8, *see* below, c. 1833.

1769. Unknown. *Of the ancient and modern dresses of the English* [in] The Town and Country Magazine for Feb. 1769, vol. i, p. 60.

We are glad to avail ourselves of the assistance of Chaucer the poet, who describes the dresses in the time of Richard II.

[Here follows a reference from the Parson's Tale to the clothes of the period.]

[a. 1770. Chatterton, Thomas.] (i) *Poems, supposed to have been written at Bristol by Thomas Rowley and others* [edited under this title in 1777 by Tyrwhitt], (ii) *MS. Extracts and Notes*, [and] (iii) and (iv) *Articles*.

[Chatterton knew very little of Chaucer at first hand (*see* below, 1871, Skeat, edn. of Chatterton, vol. ii, pp. xxiv–vii) ; but he is known to have borrowed a copy of Speght's 1598 edn. (*see* above, 1598, p. 147, *sqq.* and *c.* 1763, p. 424), and with the aid of its glossary and of Kersey's *Dictionarium*

Anglo-Britannicum, 1708, and Bailey's *Universal Etymological Dictionary*, 1721 (*see* above, 1721, p. 353), to have compiled his own MS. Rowley vocabulary.

Chatterton died on 24th Aug., 1770, and the scanty references to Chaucer in his poems and prose articles, and in those of his manuscript notes which survive, are accordingly entered here under that year.

The Rowley Poems were very well edited by Tyrwhitt in 1777, with Chatterton's own notes (the Advertisement on p. xxvii states that "*the notes at the bottom of the several pages, throughout the following part of this book* [i. e. the text], *are all copied from MSS. in the handwriting of Thomas Chatterton*"). Tyrwhitt added an Appendix to edn. 3, 1778 (*see* below, p. 451), shewing that Chatterton was their author. Warton took the same view in his History of English Poetry, vol. ii, 1778 (*see* below, p. 454). In 1778 Dampier or Woodward, in 1781 Bryant, and in 1782 Milles (*see* below, pp. 456, 458, 468) and others defended the authenticity of the Poems, which was impugned by Mason or Baynes, Malone and others. *See* below, 1781–1782 passim. The Chattertonian controversy was finally summed up by W. W. Skeat in his edition of Chatterton, 1871, vol. ii, pp. xxiv–xxvii. The references to Chaucer in the controversy consist chiefly of notes on similar or dissimilar use of words in both poets, of allusions to Chatterton's having borrowed Speght, and of some unimportant remarks on Chaucer's versification. In most cases therefore the bare reference is all that is given here.]

(i) *Poems, supposed to have been written . . . by Thomas Rowley*, etc. [edited by T. Tyrwhitt, 1777], pp. 1, *n.*, 26–7.

[p. 1] Twayne lonelie shepsterres dyd abrodden [6] flie,

[Chatterton's note :] [6] abruptly, so Chaucer, Syke he abredden dyd attourne.

[p. 26] The underwritten lines were composed by JOHN LADGATE, a Priest in London, and sent to ROWLIE, as an Answer to the preceding *Songe of Ælla.*

> Ynne Norman tymes Turgotus and
>   Goode Chaucer dydd excelle,
> Thenne Stowe, the Bryghtstowe Carmelyte
>   Dydd bare awaie the belle.

[p. 27]
> Now Rowlie ynne these mokie dayes
>   Lendes owte hys sheenynge lyghtes,
> And Turgotus and Chaucer lyves
>   Ynne ev'ry lyne he wrytes.

CHAUCER CRITICISM.

(ii) *Autograph MSS. of Chatterton*, B.M. MSS. Add. 5766 B [miscellaneous MSS. containing notes and extracts for articles, as well as poems] ff. 31, 71, and 5766 C (The Rolle of Seynct Bartlemewis Priorie), ff. 3, 4, 7.

[B. fol. 31] After Chaucer had distributed Copys of the Tale of Piers Plowman, the first of his Performances, a Franciscan Friar, wrote a Satyric Mommery (the Comedy of the Age) upon him, which was acted at every Monastery in London and at Woodstock before the Court: Chaucer not a little nettled at the poignancy of the Satyre, & the popularity of it, meeting his Antagonist in the Fleet Street; beat him with his Dagger, for which he was fined two Shillings, as appears by a record of the Inner Temple where Chaucer was a Student. [Printed in The Town and Country Magazine, Jan. 1770, vol. ii, p. 16. For Chatterton's note of the reference to this anecdote in Speght, *see* below.]

[B. fol. 71] [Notes of the quotations in the Roll of Seynct Bartlemewes Priorie, (C) fol. 3b, 4, given below, also the following:

Rounde was his Face and Camisde was his Nose
Reeve's Tale.   [ed. Skeat, l. 3934.]

To Plaies of Miracles & to maryages.
Wife of Bath's Prologue.   [ed. Skeat, l. 558.]

Doe come he saied mye minstrales,
And jestours for to tellen us Tales,
    Anon yn mine armynge,
Of Romaunces that been roiale,
Of Popes and of Cardinauls,
    And eeke of Love Longing.
Rime of Sir Thopas.   [ed. Skeat, ll. 2035-40.]

With a red hatte as usen Minstrals.
Plowman's Tale.

Of all mannere of Minstrales,
And jestours that tellen tales,
Both of weeping and of Game,
And of all that longeth unto Fame.
The Third Book of Fame.   [ed. Skeat, ll. 1197-1200.]

Chaucer, when of the Inner Temple, as appears by the record, was fined two shillings for beating a Franciscan Friar in fleetstreete.   *Speght.*

[*See* above, 1598, Thynne, p. 154. For Chatterton's expanded version of the Anecdote, *see* above.]

[C. fol. 3] [Note to "Gilbertyne."] This Author is mentioned in Chaucer as a skilful Physician, his real name was Raufe de

12

MS. NOTE BY THOMAS CHATTERTON (A 1770)

MSS. Add. 5766. B. fol. 31 (British Museum)

Blondeuille, called Gilbertine or Le Gilbertine from his being of the Order of St. Gilbert.

[note to 'Mormalles'] . . . Chaucer in the Canterbury Tales writes—

[C.fol. 3 b.]   Botte great harme was yt as itte thoughte mee,
That one his shinne a Mormaul had hee,
And blacke Manger—

[*Prol.* ed. Skeat, ll. 385–7.]

[C.fol. 4]   [note to 'blacke Maingere'] . . . the Conclusion of the following Couplet of Chaucers would seem to mean something.

He galpethe and he spekethe thro' his Nose
As Hee were in the quacke or in the Pose.

[*Reve's Tale*, ed. Skeat, ll. 4151–2.]

·   ·   ·   ·   ·   ·   ·   ·

The Monkish Writer concludes with inveighing against the taste of the Age in considering broad bawtocks and large breasts beautiful ; he probably lived in Chaucer's time who has these Lines,

With bawtockes brode and breastis rounde and hie.

Reeve's Tale.   [ed. Skeat, l. 3975.]

[C.fol. 7b.]   [Note to Bradwardin] Archbishop of Canterbury in 1348 celebrated by Chaucer.

(iii) *An Account of Master William Canynge, written by Thomas Rowlie, Priest, in* 1460. [Printed in The Town and Country Magazine, Nov. 1775, p. 593 ; also in the Gentleman's Magazine, Sept. 1777, p. 427. (Poems of Chatterton, ed. W. W. Skeat, 1871, vol. ii, p. 222.)]

I gave Master Canninge my Bristow Tragedy, for which he gave me in hand twentie pounds, and did praise it more than I did think my self did deserve, for I can say in troth I was never proud of my verses since I did read Master Chaucer.

(iv) *Antiquity of Christmas Games.* (Poetical Works of Chatterton, ed. W. W. Skeat, 1871, vol. i, p. 280.)

Minstrels, jesters, and mummers, was the next class of performers : every Knight had two or three minstrels and jesters, who were maintained in his house, to entertain his family in their hours of dissipation ; these Chaucer mentions in the following passages. [Quotes the two passages, copied in the extracts above, from the Rime of Sir Thopas, and Third Book of Fame.]

[First printed by Southey, 1803, from a lost MS., an expanded version of B.M. MS. Add. 5766 C. fol. 4b–6a, which has not the Chaucer quotations.]

1770. [**Dalrymple**, Sir David (Lord Hailes).] *Notes* [to] *Ancient Scottish Poems, published from the MS. of George Bannatyne* . . . Edinburgh . . . 1770, pp. 224, 227, 254, 257, 264, 279, 284, [287, 295, 298.

[p. 227]   Every one must admit the justice of his [Dunbar's] panegyric on Chaucer, who was indeed a prodigy.

[The rest of the notes are chiefly on the similarity of words used by Chaucer and the Scotch Poets.]

[*c.* **1770.**] **Garrick**, David. [*Reading of Nun's Priest's Tale* ; cf. Angelo, Henry, *Reminiscences*, vol. i, p. 8 (*q.v.* below, 1828): " I remember being at Hampton many years before he [Garrick] left the stage, and after supper to amuse us boys, his reading Chaucer's Cock and the Fox."]

[Garrick bought his house at Hampton in 1754 and left the stage in 1776 ; Angelo was born in 1760, so that it cannot have occurred "many years" before Garrick left the stage, nor, in fact, much before 1770.]

1770. **Gray**, Thomas. *Letter to Thomas Warton,* [dated] Pembroke Hall, April 15, 1770.   Printed in The Gentleman's Magazine, Feb. 1783, vol. liii, p. 102.   (Gray's Letters, ed. D. C. Tovey, 1900–12, vol. iii, p. 278.)

[Gray is giving a sketch of his design for a History of English Poetry] Part II.   On Chaucer, who first introduced the manner of the Provençaux, improved by the Italians [,] into our Country.   His character, and merits at large.   The different kinds in which he excelled.   Gower, Occleve, Lydgate, Hawes, Gawen Douglas, Lyndesay, Bellenden, Dunbar, &c.

[This is the whole of Part II, and there are five parts in all ; dating from 1100 to Gray's own times.]

1771. **Morell**, Thomas. *Letter* [*to James West*? dated] Eton 18 [July 1771], B. M. Add. MS. 34728, West Papers, vol. ii, f. 203.

Dear Sir . . . I never ask'd you before you left the Town, whether you had receiv'd the Chaucer I left for you at your house,—or your Opinion of it,—and I cannot help acquainting you that the Remainder has lain by me, not *nine*, but forty years ready for the Press, as I found it too expensive to go on with it on my own bottom ;—But being at the Museum the other day, I observ'd a Gentleman collating Chaucer ; I took no notice of it, but it reminded me of my own former Labour, which being unwilling to lose, I intend to continue ere long, some way to reassume the Work, and hope to get the start of him, as there is one Volume already printed ;—but more of this, when I have the pleasure of seeing you.

See above, 1737, p. 381 and 1741, p. 389, Ames.

1771. **Unknown**. *Encyclopædia Britannica,* first edition, **3** vols., article *Language,* vol. ii, p. 878.

With regard to the pleasingness of sound alone, it [the

English language] was perhaps much more perfect in the days of Chaucer than at present.

[This is the sole reference to Chaucer in this first edition of the Encyclopædia. The omission of Chaucer under a separate heading is not remarkable, as no names of writers or great men are included. There is no article, for instance, on Shakespeare or Milton or Dryden. For the history of Chaucer articles in subsequent editions, *see* below, 1778, p. 452.]

1772. Barrett, William. Letter to Dr. Ducarel [dated March 7, 1772, in] The Gentleman's Magazine, June, 1786, p. 460.

It has been supposed . . . that no poetry can be produced, worthy the name of poetry, betwixt the time of Chaucer and Spenser.

1772. Ducarel, Andrew Coltee. *Letter to Mr. William Barrett*, Mar. 18, 1772, [in] Gentleman's Magazine, June, 1786, p. 461.

[Dr. Ducarel urges the printing of Rowley's poetry.] That there should no poets arise between Chaucer and Spenser is a very strange notion (especially to me who have never studied the antiquity of the old English poetry).

1772. Gough, Richard. *Letter to the Rev Michael Tyson*, [dated] Jan. 30, 1772, [printed in] Literary Anecdotes of the 18th century . . . by John Nichols, vol. viii, 1814, p. 579.

Mr. Tyrwhitt (late Clerk of the House of Commons) applies himself *totis viribus* to Chaucer in the Museum, where is a copy of Urry's edition, with infinite collations by Bishop Tanner. Mr. Tyrwhitt conceals his design from his most intimate friends; but much is suspected and expected from his leisure and application.

1772. Row, T. [pseud. Pegge, Samuel]. *Essay on Sirnames* [in] The Gentleman's Magazine, Nov., 1772, vol. xlii, p. 510.

[Derivation of Chaucer.]

1772. Unknown. *An Emblem of Wedlock. In Chaucer's Style.* [Poem in] The Gentleman's Magazine, April, 1772, vol. xlii, p. 192.

1772. Unknown. *The Progress of Poetry,* [in] Annual Register. Taken from edn. 2, 1775, vol. xv, [pt. ii], p. 227].

> Here CHAUCER first his comic verse display'd,
> And merry tales in homely guise convey'd :
> Unpolish'd beauties grace the artless song,
> Tho' rude the diction, yet the sense was strong.

1773. Grose, Francis. *The antiquities of England and Wales,* vol. i, Berkshire. Dunnington Castle [no pagination ; merely a reference to Chaucer at Donnington].

1773. Steevens, George. *Notes* [in] The Plays of William Shakespeare. (*See* below, Appendix A.)

1773. Strutt, Joseph. *The Regal and Ecclesiastical Antiquities of England,* pp. 25 [Description of Chaucer's Portrait given on Plate xxxvii], 26.

1774. Carter, Elizabeth. *Letter to Mrs. Montagu* [dated] Deal, September 3, 1774. Letters from Mrs. Elizabeth Carter to Mrs. Montagu . . . 1817, vol. ii, pp. 272-3.

As I never read Chaucer, I know nothing more of "Combuscan [sic] bold" than by his dim grandeur in Milton. Canace, the Ring, and the Wondrous Horse of Brass, always bring to my mind the famous story of Gyges, as it is related in Plato's Republic, and from him by Cicero, in the third book of his Offices.

[This is interesting, as being the solitary allusion to Chaucer in Miss Carter's letters. She was a great scholar and a voracious reader: Homer, Virgil, Plato, Aristotle, Xenophon, Plutarch, Euripides, Æschylus, Cicero, Livy, Tacitus, Longinus, Thucydides, Pliny, among the ancients; Erasmus, Ariosto, Corneille, Racine, Voltaire, Rosseau, and Spenser, Shakespeare, Milton Cowley, Locke, and Hume among moderns, are continually alluded to by her in her letters; yet not only has she not read Chaucer, but has apparently not the faintest desire to do so.]

1774. Cooke, William. *The Cuckow and the Nightingale. Modernized from Chaucer* [in] Poetical Essays on several occasions by the Rev. William Cooke, A.M. 1774, pp. 85–103.

1774. Falconer, T., *Letter* to C[harles] G[ray], dated Chester, Sept. 3, Hist. MSS. Comm., 14th Report, App. ix, p. 305.

Warton's account of English poetry is entertaining in many parts; but his extracts before the time of Chaucer were so uncouth that I would as soon attempt the Chinese . . .

[For Warton's *History of English Poetry*, vol. i, *see* below, p. 439.]

1774. [Graves, Rev. Richard.] *Note* [to] Galateo : or a Treatise on Politeness . . . from the Italian of Monsig. Giovanni de la Casa, 1774, p. 180.

[Casa says that those who carry tooth-pick cases hanging down from their necks are undoubtedly mistaken in their notions of politeness.] We see in the pictures of Chaucer (who had been much in Italy) a pen-knife, (if I mistake not) hanging in this manner.

1774. Unknown. *Tears of the Muses for the Death of Dr. Goldsmith* [under the heading] Flowers of Parnassus, [in] The Monthly Miscellany for June 1774, p. 309. [*See also* below, c. 1833, Haslewood, J., Collections for the Lives of the English Poets, vol. ii, p. 447.]

MELPOMENE.

. . . Thy [Death's] unrelenting hand
With envious haste snatch'd CHAUCER from our arms ;
And as succeeding bards rose up to view,
Thine arrows pierc'd them.—SPENCER, DRYDEN, GAY,
ROWE, SHAKESPEARE, OTWAY, and the matchless POPE :
THOMSON, with SHENSTONE and unnumber'd throngs
Of gentle bards, thy early victims fell.

1774. Unknown. *Review* of Warton's History of English Poetry, [in] The Gentleman's Magazine, Aug. and Sept. 1774, vol. xliv, pp. 372–73, 425–29.

[The part on Langland and Chaucer ends as follows :—]

If the dross of these old bards, troubadours, and minstrels, like that of Ennius in the hands of Virgil, has here received both lustre and value from the skill and taste with which they have been refined and illustrated, what may we not expect in the golden age of literature, in the æra of a Spenser and a Shakespeare, a Milton and a Dryden?

[For Warton's *History of English Poetry*, vol. i, *see* below, 1774.]

1774. Walpole, Horace. *Letter to the Rev. William Mason,* [dated] Strawberry Hill, April 7, 1774. (Letters of Horace Walpole, ed. Mrs. Paget Toynbee, 1904, vol. viii, p. 439–40.)

Well, I have read Mr. Warton's book; [the History of English Poetry, vol. i, 1774, *q.v.* immediately below] and shall I tell you what I think of it? I never saw so many entertaining particulars crowded together with so little entertainment and vivacity. The facts are overwhelmed by one another, as Johnson's sense is by words; they are all equally strong. Mr. Warton has amassed all the parts and learning of four centuries, and all the impression that remains is that those four ages had no parts or learning at all. There is not a gleam of poetry in their compositions between the Scalds and Chaucer. . . . I am sorry Mr. Warton has contracted such an affection for his materials, that he seems almost to think that not only Pope but Dryden himself have added few beauties to Chaucer.

1774. Warton, Thomas. *The History of English Poetry,* vol. i. [For vol. ii *see* below, 1778, p. 454, for vols. iii and iv *see* below, 1781, p. 464.] Dissertation i, on the origin of romantic fiction in Europe, sign. a 3 *b*, *n.*; Dissertation ii, on the introduction of learning into England, sign. f 3 *b*, *n.* ; sign. h 2, *n.* ; pp. 38, 68 *n.*, 126 *n.*, 127–8, 142, 144, 148, 164 *n.*, 165 *n.*, 169 and *n.*, 172–3 *n.*, 175, 197 and *n.*, 208 *n.*, 215 *n.*, 220 *n.*, 222 *n.*, 224 *n.*, 225 *n.*, 234–5, and *n.*, 236, 255, 278 and *n.*, 282 *n.*, 302 *n.*, 306 and *n.*, 333–4, 339, 341–468.

[vol. i, sect. xii, p. 341] [Here the account and criticism of Chaucer begins, and continues till the end of the volume, p. 468. We can only quote a few passages of special interest.]

[p. 367] [Speaking of the *Knight's Tale.*] We are surprised to find, in a poet of such antiquity, numbers so nervous and flowing : a circumstance which greatly contributed to render Dryden's paraphrase of this poem the most animated and harmonious piece of versification in the English language. . . .

[p. 396]   Pope has imitated this piece [*House of Fame*], with his
usual elegance of diction and harmony of versification.   But
in the meantime he has not only misrepresented the story, but
marred the character of the poem.   He has endeavoured to
correct it's extravagancies, by new refinements and additions
of another cast : but he did not consider, that extravagancies
are essential to a poem of such a structure, and even constitute
it's beauties.   An attempt to unite order and exactness of
imagery with a subject formed on principles so professedly
romantic and anomalous, is like giving Corinthian pillars to a
Gothic palace.   When I read Pope's elegant imitation of this
piece, I think I am walking among the modern monuments
unsuitably placed in Westminster-abbey.

.   .   .   .

[p. 435]   But Chaucer's vein of humour, although conspicuous in
the CANTERBURY TALES, is chiefly displayed in the Characters
with which they are introduced.   In these his knowledge of
the world availed him in a peculiar degree, and enabled
him to give such an accurate picture of antient manners,
as no cotemporary nation has transmitted to posterity.
It is here that we view the pursuits and employments, the
customs and diversions, of our ancestors, copied from the life,
and represented with equal truth and spirit, by a judge of
mankind, whose penetration qualified him to discern their
foibles or discriminating peculiarities ; and by an artist, who
understood that proper selection of circumstances, and those
predominant characteristics, which form a finished portrait.
We are surprised to find, in so gross and ignorant an age,
such talents for satire, and for observation on life ; qualities
which usually exert themselves at more civilised periods. . . .
These curious and valuable remains are specimens of Chaucer's
native genius, unassisted and unalloyed. . . .

.   .   .   .

[p. 457]   It is not my intention to dedicate a volume to Chaucer,
how much soever he may deserve it ; nor can it be expected,
that in a work of this general nature, I should enter into a
critical examination of all Chaucer's pieces.   Enough has
been said to prove, that in elevation, and elegance, in harmony
and perspicuity of versification, he surpasses his predecessors
in an infinite proportion : that his genius was universal,
and adapted to themes of unbounded variety : that his merit
was not less in painting familiar manners with humour and
propriety, than in moving the passions, and in representing the
beautiful or the grand objects of nature with grace and sublimity.

In a word, that he appeared with all the lustre and dignity of a true poet, in an age which compelled him to struggle with a barbarous language, and a national want of taste ; and when to write verses at all, was regarded as a singular qualification.

1775. Ash, John. *A New and Complete Dictionary of the English Language, in which . . . The Obsolete and Uncommon Words* [are] *supported by Authorities*, etc. 2 vols.

[Chaucer is freely quoted throughout ; Mason in his Supplement to Johnson, 1801 (*q.v.* below) states that Ash's chief work was that he " carried his [Johnson's] language back to the writings of Chaucer."]

1775. Atticus. *Stanzas on Poetry* [in] The Gentleman's Magazine. *See* below, App. A.

1775. Dobson, Susanna. *The Life of Petrarch*, London 1775, vol. i, pp. xvi–xvii. [The preface is dated Feb. 8, 1775.]

. . . The two famous English poets Gower and Chaucer were also contemporaries with Petrarch . . The various beauties interspersed in the works of Chaucer and particularly the masterly strokes of character we find in them, though obscured by an obsolete language and mixed with many blemishes, shew the powers of a fine imagination, great depth of knowledge, and that perfect conception of men and manners which is the surest mark of an elevated genius. The picture he has given us of those times is indeed so animated that we seem actually to converse with his characters, and are pleased to consider men like ourselves even in the nicest resemblances, under the different circumstances of an age so very remote.

1775. Unknown. *Catalogue of New Publications* [in] The Gentleman's Magazine, March, 1775, vol. xlv, p. 141.

[Tyrwhitt's Canterbury Tales.]

1775. Unknown. *Review of Mrs. Dobson's Life of Petrarch*, [in] Gentleman's Magazine, May 1775, vol. xlv, pp. 242–3.

No mention (it is observable) is made in this work of Chaucer being present at Milan, at the marriage of the Duke of Clarence, and of his being there introduced to Petrarch, as Mr. Warton has affirmed (we know not on what authority, see vol. xliv, p. 427) in his History of English Poetry. [Further remarks on this point.]

1775. Percy, Thomas, Bp. of Dromore. *Reliques of Ancient English Poetry*. [For additions made in edn. iii, *see* above, p. 426, edn. i, 1765.]

1775. Unknown. *Letter* [in] Gentleman's Magazine, Sept. 1775, vol. xlv, p. 423.

[Remarking that Warton, in his History of English Poetry, produces no authority for supposing Chaucer met Petrarch at Milan, and asking from what writer Warton took this curious anecdote.]

1775. [Editor of Gentleman's Magazine.] *Note,* by the editor, to above letter, [in] Gentleman's Magazine, Sept. 1775, vol. xlv, p. 423.

[If the writer could have given Warton's authority, we should have been much obliged to him.]

1775. Parkin, Charles. *An Essay Towards a Topographical History of the County of Norfolk* [in] an Essay Towards a Topographical History of the County of Norfolk, by Francis Blomefield, 1739 . . . and continued from vol. iii, p. 678, by the late Reverend Charles Parkin, A.M.; vol. iv, pp. 319, 320, 402. (In the edition of 1805–10, the references are vol. viii, 1808, pp. 127, 243.)

[Vol. iv, pp. 819] Gresham [manor]. Sir John Burghersh was lord of the other moiety, in right of his wife Maud, and dying in the 19 of Richard II his daughter and co-heir, Maud, brought it by marriage to Thomas Chaucer, Esq.; son of the famous poet Sir Geffrey. . . .

[p. 402] Kierdeston Manor . . . William de la Pole Earl of Suffolk and Alice, his wife, daughter and heir of Thomas Chaucer, Esq., son of the famous poet of that age. . . .

1775. [Tyrwhitt, Thomas.] **The Canterbury Tales of Chaucer. To which are added an Essay upon his Language and Versification; an Introductory Discourse; and Notes. In Four volumes, 1775.** Of Tyrwhitt's writing, vol. i contains The Preface, pp. i–v, Appendix to the Preface [containing (A) an account of former edns. of the *Canterbury Tales,* pp. vi–xxi, (B) a list of MSS. collated, or consulted, pp. xxii–iii, (C) an abstract of the historical passages of the Life of Chaucer, pp. xxiv–xxxvi]. Vol. iii, Notes on the 3rd volume, pp. 281–314. Additional notes, pp. 315–20. Vol. iv, An Essay on the language and versification of Chaucer, pp. 1–111, An Introductory Discourse to the Canterbury Tales, pp. 112–189. Notes on the Canterbury Tales [1st and 2nd vols.], pp. 190–336. [For vol. v, *see* below, 1778, p. 451.]

An Essay on the Language and Versification of Chaucer.

[vol. iv, p. 1] The Language of Chaucer has undergone two very different judgements. According to one, he is the "well of English undefiled"; according to the other, he has corrupted and deformed the English idiom by an immoderate mixture of French words. Nor do the opinions with respect to his Versification seem to have been less discordant. His con-

[p. 2] temporaries, and they who lived nearest to his time, universally extoll him as the "chief Poete of Britaine," "the flour of Poetes," etc., titles, which must be supposed to implie their admiration of his metrical skill, as well as of his other poetical

[p. 3] talents ; but the later critics, though they leave him in possession of the same sounding titles, yet are almost unanimously agreed, that he was either totally ignorant or negligent of metrical rules, and that his verses (if they may be so called) are frequently deficient, by a syllable or two, of their just measure.

It is the purpose of the following Essay to throw some light upon both these questions. Admitting the fact, that the English of Chaucer has a great mixture of French in it, I hope to shew, that this mixture (if a crime) cannot fairly be laid to his charge. I shall then proceed to state some observations upon the most material peculiarities of the Norman-Saxon, or English language, as it appears to have been in general use in the age of Chaucer; and lastly, applying these observations to the poetical parts of the Canterbury Tales, as they are faithfully printed in this edition from the

[p. 4] best Mss. which I coud procure, I shall leave it to the intelligent Reader to determine, whether Chaucer was really ignorant of the laws, or even of the graces, of Versification, and whether he was more negligent of either than the very early Poets in almost all languages are found to have been.

. . . .

[pp. 4–26 contain an account of the reasons for the great admixture of French in English in the 12th, 13th and 14th centuries.]

. . . .

[p. 26] From what has been said, I think, we may fairly conclude, that the English language must have imbibed a strong tincture of the French, long before the age of Chaucer, and consequently that he ought not to be charged as the importer of words and phrases, which he only used after the example of his predecessors and in common with his contemporaries. . . . [pp. 26–28, more proof of this.]

[pp. 28–46. Examination of the English language in the time of Chaucer. pp. 46–75. State of English poetry before Chaucer. pp. 76–111. Versification of Chaucer.]

[p. 88] In order . . . to form any judgement of the Versification of Chaucer, it is necessary that we should know the syllabical value . . . of his words, and the accentual value of

his syllables, as they were commonly pronounced in his
[p. 89] time, for without that knowledge, it is not more probable that
we should determine justly upon the exactness of his metres,
than that we should be able to cast up rightly an account
stated in coins of a former age, of whose current rates and
denominations we are totally ignorant.

. . . .

[p. 91] The great number of verses, sounding complete even to our
ears, which is to be found in all the least corrected copies of
his works, authorizes us to conclude, that he was not ignorant
of the laws of metre. Upon this conclusion it is impossible
not to ground a strong presumption, that he intended to observe
the same laws in the many other verses which seem to us
irregular; and if this was really his intention, what reason
can be assigned sufficient to account for his having failed so
grossly and repeatedly, as is generally supposed, in an opera-
tion, which every Ballad-monger in our days, man, woman, or
child, is known to perform with the most unerring exactness,
and without any extraordinary fatigue? . . .

. . . .

[p. 93] But a great number of Chaucer's verses labour under an
apparent Deficiency of a syllable, or two. In some of these
perhaps the defect may still be supplied from MSS.; but for
the greatest part I am persuaded no such assistance is to be
expected; and therefore, supposing the text in these cases to
[p. 94] be correct, it is worth considering whether the verse also may
not be made correct, by adopting in certain words a pronunciation, different indeed from modern practice, but which, we
have reason to believe, was used by the author himself.

For instance, in the Genitive case Singular and the Plural
Number of Nouns . . . there can be no doubt that such
words as, *shoures*, ver. 1. *croppes*, ver. 7. *shires*, ver. 15. *lordes*,
ver. 47, &c. were regularly pronounced as consisting of two
syllables. . . . In like manner, we may be sure that *ed*, . . .
made . . . a second syllable in the words, *perced*, ver. 2,
bathed, ver. 3, *loved*, ver. 45, *wered*, ver. 75, &c. . . .

. . . .

[p. 96] But nothing will be found of such extensive use for supplying the deficiencies of Chaucer's metre as the pronunciation of
the *e* feminine. . . . [pp. 96–102. Arguments in favour of
this having been sounded in O. & M. English].

. . . .

[p. 102]   The third kind of irregularity, to which an English verse is liable, is from the Accents being misplaced. The restoring of Chaucer's words to their just number of syllables, by the methods which have been pointed out above, will often be of signal service in restoring his accents also to their proper places . . . [In addition] I am persuaded that in his French words he most commonly laid his accent according to the French custom . . . which, as is well known, is the very reverse of our practice. Thus in ver. 3, he uses *licoúr* for *líquour* . . . &c. &c.

   In the same manner he accents the last Syllable of the [p. 104] Participle Present, as, ver. 885, 6, *weddíng—comíng* . . . if he followed this practice at the end of his verses, it is more than probable that he did the same in the middle, whenever it gave a more harmonious flow to his metre; and therefore in ver. 4. instead of *vértue*, I suppose he pronounced, *vertúe;* . . . &c. . . .

   It may be proper, however, to observe, that we are not to expect from Chaucer that regularity in the disposition of his accents, which the practice of our greatest Poets in the last [p 105] and the present century has taught us to consider as essential to harmonious versification. None of his masters, either French [p. 106] or Italian, had set him a pattern of exactness in this respect; and it is rather surprizing, that, without rule or example to guide him, he has so seldom failed to place his accents in such a manner, as to produce the cadence best suited to the nature of his verse.

   I shall conclude this long and (I fear) tedious Essay, with a Grammatical and Metrical Analysis of the first eighteen lines of the Canterbury Tales.   .   .   .   .   .
  .   .   .   .

   I. [1] *Whánne* that Ápril wíth his [2] *shoúres* [3] *sóte.*

   II. The droúghte of Márch hath [1] *pérced* to the [2] *róte,*

   I. [1] *Whanne*, Sax. Hþænne, is so seldom used as a *Dissyllable* by Chaucer, that for some time I had great doubts about the true reading of this line. I now believe that it is right, as here printed, and that the [p. 107] same word is to be pronounced as a Dissyllable in ver. 703.
       But with these relikes *whanne* that be fond.
   Thanne, a word of the same form, occurs more frequently as a *Dissyllable. See* ver. 12260, 12506, 12721, 13924, 15282.
   [2] *Shoures*, Dis. *Plural number.* . . .
   [3] *Sote.* See ver. V. [Dis.]
   II. [1] *Perced*, Dis. *Participle of the Past Time.*
   [2] *Rote;* root.

III. And ¹ *báthed* évery véine in ² *swíche* ³ *licoúr*,

IV. Of whíche ¹ *vertúe* engéndred ís the floúr;

[And so on for 18 lines, pp. 106-11.]

[The Introductory Discourse to the *Canterbury Tales*, pp. 112-189, is a short account of the general plan, and of the various tales, their origins, &c. and contains practically no criticism.]

III. ¹ *Bathed*, Dis. see II. i.
² *Swiche*, such ; from swilke, SAX.
³ *Licoúr*, Fr. has the accent upon the *last* syllable after the French mode.
IV. ¹ *Vertúe*, FR. may be accented in the same manner. There is another way of preserving the harmony of this verse, by making *whiche* (from *whilke*, SAX.) a *Dissyllable*. . . . *Vertue* may then be pronounced, as it is now, with the accent on the *first ;* the second syllable being incorporated with the first of *engendred.*

1775. Unknown. *Reviews* of Tyrwhitt's edition of the Canterbury Tales, [in] the Critical Review, the London Magazine, and the Monthly Review, *see* below, App. A., 1775.

1775-6. Strutt, Joseph. Þoŋda Anᴣel-cýnnan : *or a Compleat View of the Manners, Customs, Arms, Habits, &c. of the Inhabitants of England,* vol. ii, pp. 85-6 ; vol. iii, pp. 107, 139, 157, 173.

[vol. ii, p. 85] [Quotes Chaucer's ('the great father of the English poets') remarks on clothing in the Parson's Tale ; 'Alas! may not a man see as in our daies the sinnefull costlew array of clothing' &c. [l. 414.]

[p. 86] Quotes Hoccleve, 'the disciple of Geofry Chaucer.

[vol. iii, p. 107] Quotes from Parson's Tale, as to food : 'Also in excesse of divers meates,' &c.

[p. 139] Quotes from Prologue to Wife of Bath's Tale : 'Therefore made I my visitations.' [l. 555.]

[p. 157] Wife of Bath's prologue : 'The bacon was not fet for them, I trow,' &c. [l. 217.]

[p. 173] Chaucer exposes the priests.]

1776. Hawkins, Sir John. *A General History of the science and practice of Music,* vol. ii, pp. 79-82 and *n*, 84-88, 91, 101, 103-112, 118.

[pp. 79, 80] [Influence of Provencal poets on Chaucer, Clerk of Oxford's tale taken from Petrarch.]

[pp. 81, 82] [Quotation from Pardoner's Tale, showing that the music of "harpes, lutes and geternes" was usual in Chaucer's day in taverns.]

[pp. 84-88] [Quotations from, and Comments on the Miller's Tale, as regards music.]

[p. 91] [Ballads of Chaucer.]

[p. 101]　[The history of music necessitates a knowledge of customs and modes of living peculiar to different periods] a knowledge of these is not to be derived from history . . . and were it not for the accurate and lively representation of the manners of the old Italians, and the not less ancient English, contained in the writings of Boccacce and Chaucer, the inquisitive part of mankind would be much at a loss for the characteristics of the fourteenth century. . . . [Chaucer] has feigned an assemblage of persons of different ranks, the most various and artful that can be imagined, and with an amazing propriety has made each of them the type of a peculiar character. . . .

[p. 103]　It remains now to speak of our ancient English poet, and from that copious fund of intelligence and pleasantry the Canterbury Tales, to select such particulars as will best illustrate the subject now under consideration. [Here follows an account of the Prologue to the Canterbury Tales, with such particulars as therein relate to music, also some account of the Miller's and Reeve's Tales.]

[1776 ?] **Mortimer**, J. H. *Nine drawings illustrating the Canterbury Tales.* Engraved by J. Hogg, Sharp, E. Williams and J. K. Sherwin, and published Feb. 12, 1787, by J. R. Smith, No. 31, King Street, Covent Garden. *See* the Note by Dr. Furnivall in Notes and Queries, 6th S. II, 1880, pp. 325-6.

The drawings are as follows :—

1. Prologue.
2. Palamon and Arcite fighting.
3. Nicholas and Robin (Miller).
4. Miller of Trompington (Reve).
5. The Coke and Perkin (Coke).
6. Sompnour, Devil, and Old Woman (Frere).
7. Frere and Thomas (Sompnour).
8. January and May (Merchant).
9. Three Gamblers and Time (Pardoner).

1777. Berkenhout, John. *Biographia Literaria* : or, *A Biographical History of Literature*, vol. i, pp. 309–13, "Geoffrey Chaucer, the Father of English Poetry." References to Chaucer on pp. 314, 316–8, 380.

1777. Boyd, H[enry]. *Woodstock, The Prize Poem for the year one thousand seven hundred and seventy seven* [in] Poems ; chiefly dramatic and Lyric, by the Rev. H. Boyd, 1793, pp. 469, 472-8. [The second edn. of this collection, published 1805, is called The Woodman's Tale ; the Chaucer references in it are on pp. 267, 270-6.]

[p. 469]   Ye lonely shades where Rosamund allur'd
            Her Henry's steps from Glory's paths to stray ;
            Where in the roseate bow'r of bliss immur'd,
            Reckless, he saw his laurel'd pride decay.
            How brook'd the genius of yon solemn grove,
            His ancient haunts by lawless love profan'd ?
            Disdain'd not his pure feet those lawns to rove
            Till late the [1] lyre once more his presence gain'd.

[1] In the time of Chaucer, the father of English poetry, who was born near WOODSTOCK.

[The subject of the poem is Elizabeth's confinement at Woodstock by her sister Mary ; pp. 472–8 describe her vision of Chaucer.]

1777. [Chatterton, Thomas.] *Poems, supposed to have been written at Bristol by Thomas Rowley, and others.* [Edited by Tyrwhitt, 1777. *See* above, *a.* 1770, p. 432.]

1777. Dilly, Edward. *Letter to James Boswell*, Southill, Sept. 26, 1777, (Boswell's Life of Johnson, ed. G. Birkbeck Hill, vol. iii, 1887, p. 110 ; also quoted by R. Anderson, in his Preface to Poets of Great Britain, 1795, *q.v.* below, p. 496).

The edition of The Poets, now printing, will do honour to the English press ; and a concise account of the life of each authour, by D[r]. Johnson, will be a very valuable addition . . . [reasons for the undertaking, inaccuracy of text and small type of Bell's edn. of the Poets, then printing at Edinburgh] . . . These reasons, as well as the idea of an invasion of what we call our Literary Property, induced the London Booksellers to print an elegant and accurate edition of all the English Poets of reputation, from Chaucer to the present time.

[This scheme was not carried out. Only 53 authors were included, beginning with Cowley.]

1777. [Pegge, Samuel.] *Of the Crasis*, a Grammatical Figure, [in] The Gentleman's Magazine, Aug. 1777, vol. xlvii, p. 372.

[The use of 'nill,' 'nam,' 'nart,' etc. by Chaucer.]

1777. Unknown. *Review* of Poems, supposed to have been written . . . by Thomas Rowley, and others, in the Fifteenth Century [in] The Gentleman's Magazine, June, 1777, vol. xlvii, p. 277.

[The poems of Aella, Goddwyn and the Battle of Hastings] for pure poetry . . as well as harmony . . . may vie with the most elegant and harmonious of the moderns. And this last is certainly the most suspicious circumstance, as, with all their merit, all our other old bards, from Chaucer down to Donne, are in that particular so defective, that many of their verses are mere prose, and others hardly legible.

1777. Unknown, [pseud. Historicus]. *An Account of Chaucer. (Translated from the French)* [from] The Morning Post. [In an interleaved copy of the 'Lives of the Poets' by Theophilus Cibber, 1753, with MS. notes by Isaac Reed and Joseph Haslewood. (B.M. pr. m, 10854. a. 1.) to face p. 10. The date, Nov. 1777, is added in MS.]

An Account of CHAUCER (*Translated from the French*).

Chaucer died in the year 1400 aged 70 years, and was interred in Westminster-Abbey. He contributed greatly by his poetry in praise of the Duke of Lancaster, his brother-in-law, to obtain the crown from [*sic,* should read 'for'] him, and partook of the good and bad fortune of that monarch. His poetical works were published in London in the year 1561. We find in them tales full of pleasantry, simplicity, and licentiousness, composed after the manner of those of *Troubadours* and *Bocase.* The imagination which dictated them was sharp, chearful and fruitful, but not well regulated, and very often too obscene. His stile is disgraced by a number of obscure and unintelligible words. The English language during his time was harsh and coarse. If the wit of Chaucer was agreeable, his language was not so, and the English can scarce understand it even at this time. Chaucer has left behind him, besides his poetry, some works in prose, viz. *the Testament of Love,* and *a Treatise on* [the] *Astrolabe.* He applied himself as much to Astronomy and foreign languages ; [*sic*] as to versification, he was èven inclined to dogmatize. The opinions of Weclef making a great noise at that time Chaucer embraced them, and caused himself to be driven out of his country for some time.

Historicus.

[This is a translation of the life of Chaucer by L. M. Chaudon contributed to the Nouveau Dictionnaire historique portatif, 1770 (new edn., and probably in 1st edn., 1766), and afterwards reprinted in Feller's Dictionnaire historique, 1781, and ed. 2, 1789–94.]

1778. Brooke, Henry. *Constantia* [A modernisation of the Man of Law's Tale, in] A Collection of the Pieces formerly published by Henry Brooke, Esq., vol. i, pp. 253–379.

[First published in Ogle's Canterbury Tales, *q.v.,* above, 1741, p. 389. The text of the original tale is here printed at the foot of the pages.]

1778. [**Craven,** Elizabeth Lady.] *Prologue* [to] *The Sleep Walker.* A Comedy, . . . translated from the French [Le Somnambule, by the Comte Le Pont de Veste], . . . Strawberry Hill, sign. A2 and *b.* *See also* Annual Register, xxi (Poetry), pp. 203–204. [The Prologue and Epilogue are by Lady Craven.]

CHAUCER CRITICISM.

PROLOGUE.

. . . Last night, indeed, as thro' old Chaucer's grove [1]
In solitary mood, I chanc'd to rove,

[sig. A2 b] A rev'rend form address'd my list'ning ear,
And thus advis'd me to suppress each fear.
'Welcome, thrice welcome, to this beauteous spot,
Fam'd Donnington! this once *my* happy lot.
Chaucer my name; I, first attun'd the lyre,
And gave to British sounds poetic fire.
The praise of Berkshire, erst these woods among,
Inspir'd my lays, and cheer'd my tuneful song;
Berkshire, whose scenes might rouse a poet's thought,
Berkshire, with ev'ry pleasing beauty fraught,
Demands thy fost'ring hand, thy daily pray'r,
And let the poor and aged be thy care;
Employ thy genius, and command each friend,
Turn mirth and pleasure to some pious end!'
He ceas'd. The poet's shade dissolv'd in air,
His sage advice is deeply written here.
I joyfully obey—and this night's gain
Is to relieve the voice of want or pain . . .

[1] The piece was acted for a charitable purpose at Newberry, near which is Donnington-castle, formerly the seat of Chaucer, at the feet of which stands the seat of Mr. Andrews, called Chaucer's Grove.

1778. Duncombe, John. *An Elegy written in Canterbury Cathedral. See* below, App. A.

1778. Horne (later **Horne-Tooke**), John. *A Letter to John Dunning, Esq., by Mr. Horne:* pp. 45, 46n, 52 [quotation from Junius]. [Extracts from this letter were printed in the Annual Register, vol. xxi, pt. ii, p. 187.]

[p. 45] [Same remark on Chaucer's use of *Bot* in Urry's glossary, as in Diversions of Purley, p. 241. *See* below, 1786, p. 486.]

1778. Johnson, Samuel. *Conversation* between Johnson and Allan Ramsay, April 9, 1778 (Boswell's Life of Johnson, ed. G. Birkbeck Hill, vol. iii, 1887, p. 254).

[Johnson] . . . Our literature came to us through France. Caxton printed only two books, *Chaucer* and *Gower*, that were not translations from the French; and *Chaucer* we know took much from the Italians.

[c. 1776-1778.] Pegge, Samuel (the elder). *Anonymiana; or Ten Centuries of Observations on Various Authors and Subjects*, pp. 344-5. [The above collection was never printed by Samuel Pegge, but seems to have been written between 1766 and 1778, vide pp. v, viii. It was printed in 1809 by John Nichols; the references given are to this edition of 1809.]

[p. 344, Century viii, sec- tion xi] Mr. Fenton, speaking of Chaucer and the Earl of Surrey, says,

> " Both now are prized by few, unknown to most,
> Because the thoughts are in the language lost."

[p. 345] On which Charles Howard Esq. [afterward Duke of Norfolk] criticises, by saying, the judicious Reader " will find the Earl's language not so obscure as M^r. Fenton intimates " : but, with submission, *obscurity* is not the charge ; but *obsoleteness*, on account of which few people, he thinks, will be at the pains of reading them.

[*See also* above, 1769, p. 432, Historical Anecdotes of some of the Howard family, by Charles Howard, p. 27. For Fenton's lines on Chaucer and Surrey, *see* above, 1710–11, p. 313, Epistle to Mr. Southerne ; and for another reference to these lines by George Sewell, *see* above, 1717, p. 346.]

1778. Steevens, George. *Note* [in] The Plays of William Shake- speare, edn. 2, *see* below, App. A., 1778.

1778. Tyrwhitt, Thomas. Vol. v of *The Canterbury Tales of Chaucer*, *containing A Glossary.* [For vols. i–iv *see* above, 1775, p. 442.] Advertisement, pp. i–vi. An Account of the Works of Chaucer to which this Glossary is adapted ; and of those other Pieces which have been improperly intermixed with his in the Editions, pp. vii– xxiii. A Glossary pp. 1–284. Words and Phrases not understood, pp. 285–6. Additions and corrections to the former volumes, pp. 287–90.

1778. Payne, J[ohn]. [*Review* of] The Canterbury Tales of Chaucer, to which are added an Essay upon the Language and Versification, vol. 5 [in] The Monthly Review, vol. lix, p. 310.

1778. [Tyrwhitt, Thomas.] *Appendix* to Poems, supposed to have been written at Bristol by Thomas Rowley, and others . . . [published with edn. ·3 of the Poems] pp. 315–21 and *n*, 326, 330, 332 *n*.

[p. 321] And this leads me to the capital blunder, which runs through all these poems, and would alone be sufficient to destroy their credit ; I mean the termination of *verbs in the* [note] *singular number* in *n.*— [note]. It is not surprising that Chatterton should have been ignorant of a peculiarity of the English language, which appears to have escaped the obser- vation of a professed editor of Chaucer. Mr. Urry has very frequently lengthened *verbs in the singular number*, by adding *n* to them, without any authority, I am persuaded, even from the errors of former Editions or MSS. It might seem in- vidious to point out living writers, of acknowledged learning, who have slipped into the same mistake in their imitations of Chaucer and Spenser.

[Edn. 3 of the Poems is reviewed in the Gentleman's Magazine, June 1777. *See* above, p. 448.]

1778. Unknown. *Encyclopædia Britannica*, 2nd edition, 10 vols, 1778–83, article *Chaucer*, vol. iii, 1778, pp. 1799–1800. [For Lydgate article, *see* below, 1780.]

[The history of the Chaucer articles in the *Encyclopædia Britannica* is briefly as follows :

1st edn., 3 vols., 1771.   No Chaucer article.

2nd edn., 10 vols., 1778–83.   Chaucer and Lydgate articles first appear, (extracts from them are given below) 1778 and 1780.

3rd edn., 18 vols., 1797.⎫ These same Chaucer and Lydgate
4th   „   20 vols., 1810.⎬ articles are reprinted. They are
5th   „   20 vols., 1817.⎭ also reprinted in other Cyclo-
6th   „   has not been   pædias, such as the English Cycl.
        seen.   1802.

7th   „   21 vols., 1842.   A New Chaucer article signed 'C.C.C.' (Charles Cowden Clarke?) *see* below, 1842. The Lydgate article of 1778 is reprinted.

8th edn., 21 vols., 1853–60.   Exactly the same Chaucer article as in the 7th edn., 1842 (giving the story of Chaucer's flight and imprisonment, proved impossible by Nicolas in 1845, and with no reference to Nicolas's 'Life' published in 1845), but now signed 'D.L.' (David Laing?). A new Lydgate article, unsigned, *see* below, 1857.

9th edn., 24 vols., 1875–89.   New Chaucer amd Lydgate articles by W. Minto, *see* below, 1876, and 1883.

10th edn., 11 new vols., 1902–3.   No Chaucer article or supplement to it.

11th edn., 29 vols., 1910–11.   A sound and accurate Chaucer article by Mr. A. W. Pollard embodying all Chaucer information and discoveries up to the time of writing.

The article of 1778 is as follows :]

[p. 1799, col. 2] Chaucer (Sir Geofrey) an eminent English poet in the 14th century, born at London in 1328. [There follows the usual account of the poet's travels, studies at the Inner Temple, his posts at Court and his missions abroad.] At this period [after he had returned from Genoa and had been made comptroller of the customs] Chaucer's income was about £1000 a year; a sum which in those days might well enable him to live, as he says he did, with dignity in office, and hospitality among his friends. It was in this meridian blaze of prosperity, in perfect health of body and peace of mind, that he wrote his most humorous poems. [His connection with the duke of Lancaster; Chaucer's misfortunes caused him to write *The Testament of Love*].

[p.1800, col. 1] The duke of Lancaster at last surmounting his troubles, married lady Catharine Swynford, sister to Chaucer's wife; so that Thomas Chaucer, our poet's son, became allied to most of the nobility, and to several of the Kings of England. Now the sun began to shine upon Chaucer with an evening ray; for by the influence of the duke's marriage, he again grew to a considerable share of wealth. . . . [Henry IV assumed the crown.] The measures and grants of the late king were annulled; and Chaucer, in order to procure fresh grants of his pensions, left his retirement, and applied to court: where, though he gained a confirmation of some grants, yet the fatigue of attendance, and his great age, prevented him from enjoying them. He fell sick at London; and ended his days in the 72nd year of his age, leaving the world as though he despised it, as appears from his song of *Flie from the Prese.* The year before his death he had the happiness, if at his time of life it might be so called, to see the son of his brother-in-law (Hen. IV) seated on the throne. [Tomb in Westminster Abbey, editions of his works.]

Chaucer was not only the first, but one of the best poets which these kingdoms ever produced. He was equally great in every species of poetry which he attempted; and his poems in general possess every kind of excellence, even to a modern reader, except melody and accuracy of measure; defects which are to be attributed to the imperfect state of our language, and the infancy of the art in this kingdom at the time when he wrote. [Dryden quoted as stating that he venerated Chaucer as the Greeks did Homer, and that he is a perpetual fountain of good sense, &c.] This character Chaucer certainly deserved. He had read a great deal; and was a man of the world, and of sound judgement. He was the first English poet who wrote *poetically*, as Dr. Johnson

observes in the preface to his dictionary, and (he might have
added) who wrote like a gentleman. He had also the merit
of improving our language considerably, by the introduction
and naturalisation of words from the *Provençal*, at that time
the most polished dialect in Europe.

1778. Walpole, Horace. *Postscript to Letter to William Barrett,* [dated]
Strawberry Hill, May 23, 1778, [printed in] Gentleman's Magazine,
May, 1782, p. 250. (Letters of Horace Walpole, ed. Mrs. Paget
Toynbee, 1904, vol. x, p. 251–2.)

Vertue was even a versifier, as I have many proofs in his
MSS., and searched much after Chaucer and Lidgate, of
whom he engraved portraits.

1778. Warton, Thomas. *The History of English Poetry,* vol. ii (for
vol. i, *see* above, 1774, p. 439, for vol. iii, *see* below, 1781, p. 464),
pp. 1 and note, 2 and *n.*, 5, 11 and *n.*, 25–6, 29–31, 33–34 *n.*, 38–39 *n.*,
42 *n.*, 43–4 and *n.*, 50–2, 57, 70–2, 74–5 *n.*, 78, 80 *n.*, 83 *n.*, 85 *n.*,
123, 125 *n.*, 134–5, and *n.*, 157, 165 *n.*, 167 *n.*, 168 *n.*, 169, 173, 174,
176 *n.*, 179 *n.*, 195, 212 and *n.*, 213, 215 and *n.*, 216 *n.*, 218 and *n.*,
219, 223 *n.*, 224 and *n.*, 225 *n.*, 227 *n.*, 229 *n.*, 231 *n.*, 234 *n.*, 235 *n.*,
238 *n.*, 242, 257, 259 *n.*, 260 *n.*, 264, 266 *n.*, 271 [Dunbar's reference
to Chaucer in *Golden Terge* quoted], 273 *n.*, 279, 288 *n.*, 305 *n.*, 318,
326 *n.*, 329 *n.*, 331 *n.*, 341, 348 *n.*, 350 *n.*, 353 and *n.*, [Skelton's reference to Chaucer, also Rastell's] 354 *n.*, 355 *n.*, 387, 441.

Emendations and Additions to vol. i.   Sign. a 3 *b* *n*, b 2 *b*, c 4,
d 1, d 2, d 4 and *b*, e 1 *b* and e 2 (a long note comparing Chaucer's
and Boccaccio's treatment of Palamon and Arcite], e 2 *b*, e 3, e 4
and *b*, f 1 and *b*, f 3 and *b*, f 4 and *b*, g 1.

Emendations to vol. ii, g 2, h 1 *n*, h 3, k 1 *b*, k 2 and *b*, k 3 and *b*.

[p. 50] I close this section with an apology for Chaucer, Gower
and Occleve; who are supposed, by the severer etymologists,
to have corrupted the purity of the English language, by
affecting to introduce so many foreign words and phrases.
But if we attend only to the politics of the times, we shall
find these poets . . . much less blameable in this respect,
than the critics imagine.   [Close connection with France, also
some with Spain, during this period.] . . .

It is rational therefore, . . . to suppose, that instead of
coining new words, they only complied with the common and
fashionable modes of speech. Would Chaucer's poems have
been the delight of those courts in which he lived, had they
been filled with unintelligible pedantries? The cotemporaries
of these poets never complained of their obscurity. But
whether defensible on these principles or not, they much
improved the vernacular style by the use of this exotic
phraseology. It was thus that our primitive diction was

enlarged and enriched. The English language owes its copiousness, elegance and harmony, to these innovations. . . .
[Sect. iii, p. 51] I consider Chaucer as a genial day in an English spring. A brilliant sun enlivens the face of nature with an unusual lustre, . . . and we fondly anticipate a long continuance of gentle gales and vernal serenity. But winter returns with redoubled horrors. . . .

Most of the poets that immediately succeeded Chaucer, seem rather relapsing into barbarism, than availing themselves of those striking ornaments which his judgment and imagination had disclosed. They appear to have been insensible to his vigour of versification, and his flights of fancy. . . . His successors . . . approach him in no degree of proportion.

[1778 ? Dampier, Henry ? or Woodward, Dr., of Bath ?]. *Remarks upon the eighth section of the second volume of Mr. Warton's History of English Poetry,* pp. 8-10, 27.

[An attempt to prove the authenticity of the Rowley poems.]

[The eighth section, vol. ii, pp. 139-64, contained Warton's views on Chatterton's authorship of Rowley's poems. *See* above, 1778. Warton.]

1778. Unknown. *Review* of 1st and 2nd vols. of Thomas Warton's History of English Poetry [in] Annual Register vol. xxi, pp. 219, 228-234. [Brief references.]

1778. Unknown. *Review* of vol. ii of Thomas Warton's History of English Poetry [in] Gentleman's Magazine, May 1778, vol. xlviii, pp. 225, 227, 230. [Brief references.]

1778. Unknown. *Of Chaucer and Lydgate;* [Extracts] *from Mr. Warton's History of English Poetry;* and a *Review* of the same work (vols. 1 and 2) [in] The Annual Register for 1778, vol. xxi, pt. ii, pp. 21-3, 25, 219. [For Warton's vol. i *see* above, 1774, p. 439, for vol. ii *see* immediately above, 1778.]

1779. *An Account of the Agreement between Urry's executor, the Dean and Chapter of Ch. Ch., Oxon, and Bernard Lintot for the printing of Chaucer—(q.v.* above, 1715, p. 333)—[in] Gentleman's Magazine, Sept. 1779, vol. xlix, p. 438.

1779. Antiquarius. *Letter* [in] The Gentleman's Magazine, Jan. 1779, vol. xlix, p. 24.

[Reference to Tyrwhitt's Glossary to Chaucer.]

1779. Barrington, Daines. *Observations on the earliest Introduction of Clocks; by the Honourable Daines Barrington. In a Letter to the Honourable Mr. Justice Blackstone* [in] Annual Register for 1779, vol. xxii, pt. ii, p. 135.

Mr. B. remarks upon the following lines of Chaucer[1] when he speaks of a cock's crowing,

"Full sikerer was his crowing in his loge
As is a *clock*, or any abbey orloge,"
[Nonne Preestes Tale, ll. 4043-4.]

[1] Chaucer was born A.D. 1328, and died in 1400.

that in the 14th century, *clock* was often applied to a *bell*
which was rung at certain periods, determined by the hour,
glass or sun-dial, but that the *abbey orloge* (or clock) could not
have been uncommon when Chaucer wrote these lines.

1779. Burlington, Charles. *The Modern Universal British Traveller*,
Chap. xvii, Middlesex, p. 302.

[Westminster Abbey.] The monument of that antient poet
Geoffrey Chaucer was once a very handsome one in the Gothic
stile ; but it is now greatly defaced by time.   He was born in
1328, and died in 1400.

1779-81. Johnson, Samuel. *Lives of the English Poets,* ed. G. Birkbeck Hill, 1905, vol. i, pp. 413-14, 454-5 ; vol. iii, pp. 88, 225-6.

[p. 414] [From the Life of Dryden.] In his [Dryden's] general
precepts, which depend on the nature of things, and the
structure of the human mind, he may doubtless be safely
recommended to the confidence of the reader ; but his occasional and particular positions were sometimes interested,
sometimes negligent, and sometimes capricious.   It is not
without reason that Trapp, speaking of the praises which he
bestows on Palamon and Arcite, says, "Novimus judicium
Drydeni de poemate quodam Chauceri, pulchro sane illo, et
admodum laudando, nimirum quod non modo vere epicum sit,
sed *Iliada* etiam atque *Æneida* æquet, imo superet.   Sed
novimus eodem tempore viri illius maximi non semper accura-
tissimas esse censuras, nec ad severissimam critices normam
exactas : Illo judice id plerumque optimum est, quod nunc præ
manibus habet, et in quo nunc occupatur." [*See* above, 1722,
Trapp, J., p. 363.]

.   .   .   .

[p. 454] His [Dryden's] last work was his *Fables,* in which he gave
us the first example of a mode of writing which the Italians
call *réfacimento,* a renovation of ancient writers, by modern-
izing their language. . . . The works of Chaucer, upon which
this kind of rejuvenescence has been bestowed by **Dryden,**
require little criticism.   The tale of *The Cock* seems hardly
worth revival ; and the story of *Palamon and Arcite,* containing an action unsuitable to the times in which it is placed,
can hardly be suffered to pass without censure of the hyperbolical commendation which Dryden has given it in the general
Preface, and in a poetical Dedication, a piece where his original
fondness of remote conceits seems to have revived.

[vol. iii,
p. 88] [From the Life of Pope.] By Dryden's *Fables,* which had

then been not long published, and were much in the hands of poetical readers, he was tempted to try his own skill in giving Chaucer a more fashionable appearance, and put *January and May* and the *Prologue of the Wife of Bath*, into modern English.

.   .   .   .

He [Pope] appears to have regarded Betterton with kindness and esteem ; and after his death published, under his name, a version into modern English of Chaucer's Prologues, and one of his Tales, which, as was related by Mr. Harte, were believed to have been the performance of Pope himself by Fenton, &c.

.   .   .   .

[*See* above, *a.* 1710, Betterton, p. 312, and below, 1797, p. 499, Warton.]

[pp. 225-6] *The Temple of Fame* has, as Steele warmly declared, ' a thousand beauties.' Every part is splendid ; there is great luxuriance of ornaments ; the original vision of Chaucer was never denied to be much improved ; the allegory is very skilfully continued, the imagery is properly selected and learnedly displayed : yet, with all this comprehension of excellence, as its scene is laid in remote ages, and its sentiments, if the concluding paragraph be excepted, have little relation to general manners or common life, it never obtained much notice, but is turned silently over or mentioned with either praise or blame.

1779. Knox, Vicesimus. *On the old English Poets,* Essay xxxix [in] Essays Moral and Literary. . . The second edition, corrected and enlarged. London 1779, vol. i, pp. 292-3.
[The anonymous first edition, 1778, does not contain this essay.]

The mere antiquarian taste in poetry is certainly absurd. It is more difficult to discover the meaning of many of our old poets, disguised as it is in an obsolete and uncouth phraseology, than to read an elegant Greek or Latin author. Such study is like raking in a dung hill for pearls, and gaining one's labour only for one's pains.

Our earlier poets, whose names and works are deservedly forgotten, seem to have thought that rhyme was poetry. And even this constituent requisite they applied with extreme negligence. It was, however, good enough for its readers ; most of whom considered the mere ability of reading as a very high attainment. It has had its day, and the antiquary must not despise us, if we cannot peruse it with patience. He who delights in all such reading as is never read, may derive some pleasure from the singularity of his taste ; but he ought still

to respect the judgment of mankind, which has consigned to
oblivion the works which he admires. While he pores un-
molested on Chaucer, Gower, Lydgate and Occleve, let him
not censure our obstinacy in adhering to Homer, Virgil,
Milton, and Pope.

In perusing the antiquated pages of our English bards, we
sometimes find a passage which has comparative merit, and
which shines with the greater lustre, because it is surrounded
with deformity. While we consider the rude state of literature, the want of models, the depraved taste of readers, we are
struck with the least appearance of beauty . . . We select a
few lines from a long work, and by a little critical refinement,
prove that they are wonderfully excellent. But the candid
are ready to confess that they have not often discovered
absolute merit sufficient in degree or quantity to repay the
labour of research.

. . . Notwithstanding the incontrovertible merit of many
of our antient relics of poetry, I believe it may be doubted,
whether any one of them would be tolerated as the production
of a modern poet. As a good imitation of the ancient
manner it would find its admirers, but considered independently
as an original, it would be thought a careless, vulgar, inarti-
ficial composition. There are few who do not read Mr. Percy's
own piece, and those of other late writers, with more pleasure,
than the oldest ballad in the collection of that ingenious writer.

1779. Tytler, William. *A Dissertation on the Scottish Musick* [in
Appendix to] The History of Edinburgh, by Hugo Arnot, p. 632,
note. [This Dissertation was reprinted as a supplement to Tytler's
edition of the Poetical Remains of James I of Scotland, for which
see below, 1783, p. 475.]

Within this aera [reign of James I to end of James V]
flourished Gavin Douglas, Bishop of Dunkeld, whose excellent
translation of Virgil's Æneis may compare with Chaucer.

1779. Unknown. *Account of Abraham Cowley* [in] The Antiquarian
Repertory, a miscellany, vol. ii, 1779, p. 26 [Cowley buried near
Chaucer].

1779. Unknown. *Poem To Mr. Warton* [in] The Gentleman's Magazine.
See below, App. A.

1780. Antiquarius. *Letter* [in] The Gentleman's Magazine. *See*
below, App. A.

[c. 1780 ?] Jeffereys, James. *A series of 24 sepia and wash drawings*
[each 14½ × 11 in.] *illustrating Chaucer's Pilgrims,* mounted in
imperial folio scrapbook, with MS. title page and Chaucer's
descriptions of the characters written on blue paper, in an
eighteenth century hand.

[Jeffreys (1757–84) was a clever young artist, who, at the age of 17, obtained the Royal Academy's gold medal for the best historical picture. He was sent to Italy, where he stayed four years, but, after his return to England, he died of consumption in 1784. This series of drawings was probably intended for publication, with text as here arranged. But the work never got beyond the engraving of one subject ("the Frere"), of which a trial proof is inserted. These drawings were in Jan. 1908 in the possession of Mr. James Tregaskis, the dealer, High Holborn.]

1780. R., J. *Letter* [in] The Gentleman's Magazine. *See* below, App. A.

1780. Reed, Isaac. *Preface* [to] *Dodsley's Select Collection of Old Plays,* 1780, vol. i, p. xvii.

When Mr. Dodsley undertook the present publication, the duties of an editor of English works were not so well understood as they have been since. The collation of copies had not at that time been practised in any case that the editor is informed of, (for it is certain neither Theobald nor any other editor of Shakspeare, nor either of the gentlemen who had published Chaucer or Spenser, had any claim to praise on this account), and a knowledge of the writings of contemporary authors was still less deemed necessary.

1780. Unknown. *Encyclopaedia Britannica,* 2nd edition, 10 vols., 1778–83, vol. vi, 1780, p. 4094 [article *Language,* the same as in the 1st edn. of 1771, *q.v.* above, p. 436], p. 4323 [article *Lydgate*].

[p. 4323] [A short account of Lydgate's life and work, ending :] His language is less obsolete, and his versification much more harmonious, than the language and versification of Chaucer, who wrote about half a century before him.

[*See* the note on the Chaucer and Lydgate articles in the *Encyclopaedia Britannica,* 1778, above, p. 452.]

1781. B., W. *Reviewed* [in] The Gentleman's Magazine. *See* below, App. A.

1781. Bryant, Jacob. *Observations upon the Poems of Thomas Rowley: in which the authenticity of those Poems is ascertained,* pp. 26 *n*, 58, 61 *n*, 65, 67, 77, 84, 104–6, 123, 152 [these are all glossarial notes], 166, 284, 358, 413, 444, 450–1, 577.

1781. [Cowper, William.] *Anti-Thelyphthora, A Tale, in Verse,* p. 6. (The Life and Works of William Cowper, ed. Robert Southey, 8 vols, 1853–5, vol. v, 1854, p. 91.)

But what old Chaucer's merry page befits,
The chaster muse of modern days omits.
Suffice it then in decent terms to say,
She saw—and turn'd her rosy cheek away.

1781. H. *Letters* [in] The Gentleman's Magazine. *See* below, App. A.

1781. Harris, James. *Philological Inquiries. See* below, App. A.

1781. Henry, Robert. *The History of Great Britain, from the First Invasion of it by the Romans under Julius Cæsar, Written on a New Plan,* vol. iv [A.D. 1216–1399], pp. 467, 469–471, 510-11, 522, 524, 584, 589–90, 595, 597-8, 605-6. [For a reference in vol. v, 1785, *see* below, App. A., 1785.]

[p. 467] Poetasters abound in every age; but real and great poets, who do honour to their country, and merit a place in its history, are commonly very few. Of such excellent poets, who were also men of uncommon worth and learning, I know only three, viz. John Gower, Geoffrey Chaucer, and John Barbour, who flourished in Britain in the present period [1216–1399]. . . . . . .

[p. 469] Geoffrey Chaucer, the contemporary and intimate Geoffrey friend of Gower, was born in London about A.D. Chaucer. 1328 . . . [This imaginary date is followed by other like details from the Life in Urry's Chaucer 1721, Bale, Leland, *Biographia Britannica*, and Thomas Usk's *Testament of Love*, (treated as Chaucer's). Chaucer's *Conclusions of the Astrolabe* are called "A work which discovers an extensive knowledge in astronomy, with an admirable faculty of communicating that knowledge to a child only ten years of age." The account of the poet winds up with the following :]

[p. 471] Whoever reads the works of Chaucer with attention, will be surprised at the variety and extent of his learning, as well as charmed with the fertility of his invention, the sweetness of his numbers, (for the times in which he lived), and all the other marks of a great and cultivated genius. The writer of his life prefixed to Mr. Urry's edition of his works, hath given him the following character, and produced sufficient evidence that he deserved it : "In one word, he was a great scholar, a pleasant wit, a candid critic, a sociable companion, a stedfast friend, a grave philosopher, a temperate œconomist, and a pious Christian." Should such a man ever be forgotten?

. . . .

[p. 510] When Chaucer was roused from his famous poetical dream, he expresses his surprise, that all the gay objects which he had seen in his sleep were vanished, and he saw nothing,

> Save on the wals old portraiture
> Of horsmen, haukes, and houndis,
> And hart dire all full of woundis. [1]

This, I am persuaded, is a real description of the poet's bed-chamber. In the same poem, Chaucer describes a church-window :

> ———— richly ypeint
> With lives of many divers seint.

. . . . . .

---

[1] Chaucer's Works, by Urry, p. 587, col. 1. ["Chaucer's Dream" (*The Isle of Ladies*, not by Chaucer), ll. 2168–70.]

[p. 511] It is said of the squire, or knight's son, in Chaucer,

> Songis he could make, and well endite,
> Just, and eke daunce, and well portraie and write.[1]

. . . .

[p. 522.] It is remarkable, that though Barbour was a Scotsman, his language is rather more intelligible to a modern English reader than that of any other poet of the fourteenth century, his great contemporary Chaucer himself not excepted.

Chaucer and Gower.   At the same time flourished the two princes of ancient English poets, the great improvers of their art, and polishers of the language of their country, Jeoffrey Chaucer and John Gower, whose personal histories have been briefly related. The shortest analysis that could be given of the numerous works of these two venerable bards would swell this section far beyond its due proportion ; it is therefore hoped that the reader will be satisfied with the following characters of their poetical talents, drawn by the hand of one of the most ingenious and intelligent critics of the present age, who appears to have studied their works with great attention. [Henry then quotes from ' Mr. Warton's History of English Poetry, v. i, p. 457,' last paragraph of the extract on Chaucer, *q. v.* above, pp. 440–1, " Enough hath been said to prove . . . a singular qualification " ; and adds from the same work, vol. ii (1778), p. 1, a short bit on Gower, " If Chaucer had not existed . . . to establish an English style."]

. . . .

[p. 524] Among the accomplishments of Chaucer's parish-clerk we are told,

> In twenty manir couth he trip and daunce

. . . .

> And as well couth he play on a giterne.[2]

Chaucer's miller was also a musician ; but on a more vulgar instrument.

> A bagge pipe well couth he blowe and sowne,
> And therewithal brought he us out of towne.[3]

. . . .

[p. 584] Besides this, Chaucer, Gower, Wickliff, and several others, composed voluminous works, both of prose and verse, in English ; and being men of learning, well acquainted with

---

[1] Chaucer's Works, p. 2. [ed. Skeat, Prol. ll. 95–6.]
[2] Chaucer, p. 26. [ed. Skeat, Miller's Tale, ll. 3328–33.]
[3] Ibid., p. 5. [ed. Skeat, Prol., ll. 565-6.]

French and Latin, and some of them with Greek and Italian, they borrowed many words and idioms from those languages, with which they adorned and enriched their own. By these means, the Anglo-Saxon tongue was greatly changed before the end of this period, and the language of the best writers approached much nearer to modern English than that of Robert of Gloucester, and others who flourished in the thirteenth century.

. . . .

[p. 589] Geoffrey Chaucer's account of the dresses of his age is not more favourable. "Alas! may not a man si as in our daies the sinnefull costlewe arraie of clothing. . .'[1]

[p. 590] Some other parts of this description are too indelicate to be admitted into this work. . . .

Chaucer's spruce parish-clerk Absolom

Had Paul 'is windows corven on his shose [2]

These shoes were called *crackowes;* and continued in fashion about three centuries . . .

. . . .

[p. 595] The cook in the Canterbury Tales was no mean proficient in his profession.

A coke thei haddè with them for the nones,

. . . .

For blank-manger, that made he with the best.[3]

Chaucer, in the Parson's Tale, complains of the too laboured and artificial cookery of those times : "Pride of the table [p. 596] apereth also full ofte . . . so that it is abusion to think."[4]

. . . .

[p. 597] In our present period, people of all ranks made only two stated meals a-day, dinner and supper, the former in the fore- [p. 598] noon, the latter in the evening. . . . These two meals, and the times at which they were taken, are mentioned in the following lines of Chaucer.

For every day, when Beryn rose, unwash he wold dyne,
And draw hym to his feléship, as even as a lyne,
And then come home, and ete and soop, and sclepe al nyht.[5]

The following lines contain an enumeration of some of the spices known and used in this period.

[1] Chaucer's Works, by Urry, p. 198. [ed. Skeat, Parson's Tale, 415–30.]
[2] Chaucer's Works, p. 26. [ed. Skeat, Miller's Tale, l. 3318.]
[3] Chaucer's Works, p. 4. [ed. Skeat, Prol., ll. 379–87.]
[4] Chaucer's Works, p. 198. [ed. Skeat, Parson's Tale, l. 445.]
[5] Chaucer's Works, p. 603, col. 1. [ed. Furnivall and Stone, 1887, Chaucer Society, ll. 1069–71 ; the Tale of Beryn is not by Chaucer.]

> There was ike wexing many a spice,
> As clowe, gilofre, and licorice,
> Gingiber, and grein de Paris,
> Canell at setewale of pris,
> And many a spice delitable
> To eten whan man rise fro table.[1]

. . . .

[p. 605]   Many of Chaucer's Canterbury Tales are in the facetious strain, and are therefore called comedies; some of them are mournful stories, and are called tragedies.   He gives this last name to his poem of Troilus and Creside.

[p. 606]   Go, litil boke, go, litil tragedie . . .

. . . .

> So sende me might to make some comedie.[2]

Tragedy is thus described by Chaucer's monk in the prologue to his tale,

> Tragidy is to tell a certain story,

. . . .

> Lo! this ought enough you for to suffice.[3]

Tragetours   Tragetours, . . . or jugglers, contributed to the amusement
or jugglers. of those who could afford to pay them for their exhibitions, which tended to excite surprise and admiration, by certain tricks and appearances which imposed upon the senses of the spectators.   Several of these exhibitions are described by Chaucer, of which it will be sufficient to produce an example,

> For I am sikir there be sciences,

. . . .

[p. 607]   Thus semid it to every mann'is sight.[4]

[1] Chaucer's Works, p. 224, col. 2. [ed. Skeat, Romaunt of the Rose, ll. 1367–72.]
[2] Chaucer's Works, p. 332. [ed. Skeat, Troilus, ll. 1786–8.]
[3] Chaucer's Works, p. 161. [ed. Skeat, Monk's Prol., ll. 3163–72.]
[4] [Ed. Skeat, Frankleyn's Tale, ll. 1139–51.]

1781. [**Malone**, Edmond.]   *Remarks on two new publications on Rowley's Poems, arguments of Dr. Milles and Mr. Bryant refuted,* [in] the Gentleman's Magazine, Dec. 1781, vol. li, pp. 555–6, 558, 610.

[These Remarks, signed Misopiclerus, were republished anonymously in 1782 with the title Cursory Observations on the Poems attributed to Thomas Rowley, with some Remarks on the Commentaries . . . by Dr. Jeremiah Milles . . . and Jacob Bryant . . . the second edition, revised and augmented. There are no new Chaucer references in the later edn. *See* below, 1782, Greene, E. B., p. 466, also a 'Critique' by 'Q' in The Gentleman's Magazine, Jan. 1782, p. 14.]

1781. Pinkerton, John.   *Rimes,* p. 131.   *See* below, App. A.

1781. Scrutator.   *Letter* [in] The Gentleman's Magazine.   *See* below, App. A.

1781. Unknown. *The World as it goes: Exemplified in the Characters of Nations, States. . . . Selected from the most distinguished English Poets from Chaucer to Churchill; and all the Characters applied.*

[In spite of this title there are no extracts from Chaucer in the book.]

1781. Walpole, Horace. *Letter to the Rev. William Mason,* [dated] Strawberry Hill, Nov. 13, 1781. (Letters of H. Walpole, ed. Mrs. Paget Toynbee, 1904, vol. xii, p. 92.)

I am too, though a Goth, so modern a Goth that I hate the black letter, and I love Chaucer better in Dryden and Baskerville than in his own language and dress.

[Mason had offered Walpole a black-letter Chaucer of the first edition for one guinea.]

1781. Warton, Thomas. *The History of English Poetry,* vol. iii. [For vol. i, *see* above, 1774, p. 439, for vol. ii, *see* above, 1778, p. 454.] A Dissertation on the Gesta Romanorum, pp. iii, vi and *n.*, xv, xxxiv *n.*, xxxviii, xxxix *n.*, xl, xlvii, xlviii *n.*, lvi, lix and *n.*, lxv, lxvi, lxix, lxx, lxxiv, lxxxi, lxxxiii, lxxxiv, xciii, xciv, 12 and *n.*, 14 *n.*, 25 [quotation from Ascham's Scholemaster. *See* above, 1563–8, p. 97], 35 [Wyatt's allusion to Sir Thopas and Knight's Tale. *See* above, 1542, p. 84], 41, 56–7, 76, 81 [Ashby's reference. *See* above, 1470, p. 54], 93 *n.*, 103 and *n.*, 128 *n.*, 148 *n.*, 151 *n.*, 203, 219, 276 [Ed. Bolton's reference. *See* above, 1618, p. 192] 311, 327, 335 [Wilson's reference in his Rhetoric. *See* above, 1553, p. 91], 336 *n.* [Puttenham's reference. *See* above, 1584, p. 125], 353 and *n.*, 354 and *n.* [reputation of Chaucer in 16th century], 415 [Ascham's reference. *See* above, 1563–8, p. 97], 426 *n.* [Gabriel Harvey in Gratulationes Valdinenses. *See* above, 1578, p. 115] 436 [Dekker's reference. *See* above, 1607, p. 178] 451 [B. Googe's reference. *See* above, 1569, p. 103] 464. Fragment of vol. iv at end of vol. iii, pp. 44 *n.*, 45 *n.*

1781. Unknown. *Review* of vol. iii of Thomas Warton's History of English Poetry [in] Annual Register, vol. xxiv, 1781, pt. ii, pp. 193–4. Also in The Gentleman's Magazine, April 1781, p. 181. [Brief references.]

1782. The Poetical Works of Geoff. Chaucer, in 14 volumes. The Miscellaneous Pieces from Urry's Edition, 1721; The Canterbury Tales from Tyrwhitt's Edition, 1775; Edinburgh, at the Apollo Press, by the Martins, 1782; [in John] Bell's Edition of the Poets of Great Britain, complete from Chaucer to Churchill, 109 vols., Edinburgh, 1782–83, 12°.

Vol. i, general title page to Chaucer's works, with testimonies from Gower, Lydgate, Occleve, Douglas, Dunbar. Title page to vol. i, testimonies from [Canterbury] Tales, Spenser, Denham, Akenside. The Life of Chaucer [the same as that in Biographia Britannica, *q.v.* above, 1747, p. 395], pp. vii–lxv. Abstract of hist. passages in life of Chaucer from Tyrwhitt's edn., 1775, pp. lxvi–lxxvi. Tyrwhitt's preface to the Canterbury Tales, pp. lxxvii–lxxx. Appendix to ditto, pp. lxxxi–xciii. Tyrwhitt's essay on the language and versification of Chaucer, pp. xciv–clxx. Tyrwhitt's Introductory Discourse to the Canterbury Tales, pp. clxxi–ccxxii. Tyrwhitt's List of MSS., pp. cxxiii–iv. Extract from T. Thomas's

Preface to Urry's edn., pp. ccxxv–xxxvi. Thynne's Epistle dedicatory to Henry VIII, pp. ccxxxvii–xlii. Verses to the King's most noble Grace, &c., pp. ccxliii–v. Eight goodly Questions, pp. ccxlv–vii. Chaucer's Prophecie, pp. ccxlvii. The Reader to G. Chaucer, prefaced to Speght's edn., 1602, p. ccxlviii. Upon the picture of Chaucer, from Speght's edn., p. ccxlix. Vol. xiii, Testimonies of learned men concerning Chaucer and his works [50 extracts, from Occleve to Hayley], pp. 166–200. Vol. xiv. Tyrwhitt's Glossary, with his prefatory remarks.

[For letter from Tyrwhitt on this edn., *see* below, 1783, p. 473.]

1782. [**Baynes**, John?] *An Archæological Epistle to the reverend . . . Jeremiah Milles . . . editor of a superb edition of the poems of Thomas Rowley, priest,* 1782, p. 13.

Tyrwhytte, thoughe clergyonned in Geoffroie's leare,[a]

Yette scalle yat leare stonde thee in drybblet stedde.[b]

Geoffroie wythe Rowley how maiest thoue comphere?[c]

Rowley hanne mottes,[d] yat ne manne ever redde,

Ne couthe bewryenne,[e] inne anie syngle tyme,

Yet reynneythe[f] echeone mole,[g] in newe & swotie ryme.[h]

[a] Well-instructed in Chaucer's language.   [b] Little stead.   [c] Compare.   [d] Words.   [e] Express, or speak in any single æra of our language.   [f] Runneth or floweth.   [g] Soft.   [h] In modern and sweet versification.

[This poem is generally attributed to Baynes, though he denied its authorship. Joseph Haslewood (amongst others) attributed it to William Mason, in a MS. note of his appended to the review of the Epistle which appeared in the Critical Review for July 1782 (vol. 54, pp. 19–24). The B. M. press mark of Haslewood's MS. Notes and Extracts on Chatterton is C. 39 f. 12. For Milles, *see* below, p. 468.]

1782. **Burney,** Charles. *A General History of Music.* . . . vol. ii, pp. 368–69, 371–82 and note.

[p. 371]   The most ancient of our poets perhaps that can be read with pleasure, is CHAUCER, . . .

[p. 372]   Indeed he was so superior to Gower, Lydgate, Occleve, and all his cotemporaries, and even successors, as low down as Spenser, for language, clearness, and versification, that his equal is not to be found; and for wit, humour, and other poetical excellencies, perhaps not till a much later period. . . .

[pp. 373–82] [Dr. Burney goes through Chaucer's works from the point of view of the musical references.]

1782. **Callander,** John.   *Two ancient Scottish poems ; the Gaberlunzie-man, and Christ's Kirk on the Green, with notes . . .* by John Callander, pp. 25, 39, 51, 57, etc.

[The references to Chaucer are unimportant; they occur in the philological notes which occupy the greater portion of the book.]

1782. [**Dodsley,** James?] *Note* [in] A Collection of Poems (" Dodsley's Miscellany "), vol. iv, 1782, pp. 6, 7, [on the parallel between Gray's

Even in our Ashes live their wonted Fires

and Chaucer's Reve's Prologue, v. 3880, quoting Tyrwhitt and William Mason.]

CHAUCER CRITICISM.

1782. [**Greene,** Edward Burnaby.] *Strictures upon a pamphlet intitled Cursory Observations on the Poems attributed to Rowley* [by E. Malone.] . . . *with a Postscript on Mr. Thomas Warton's Enquiry into the same subject.* sign. B 1, pp. 5, 19 [comments on Chaucer's rhymes] 26, 50, 52, 55-6, 60-2, 65.

[sign. B 1]
To the lernede DEANE PERCY :

Greteynge.

     PERCY, of Poetes olde, wythe balade clere
       Whose precious stories hertes of fere to thawe
     Full marvayleouslie flowe wythe Pitie's tere,
       Or bende stoute Chivalrie to Cupyde's law,
     Thie skylle hathe fetelie wove, great Clerke of fame,
       The guerdon swete to sente, ere CHAUCER's tale
     Stepede in nature's dewe han rered hys name,
       Tyl SPENCER dreste his Allegorycke vayle ;

  •   •   •   •   •   •   •

                              Edward Burnaby Greene.

[This sonnet is quoted in The Gentleman's Magazine, July 1782, vol. lii, p. 342. *See* above, 1781, Malone, p. 463, and below, 1782, Warton, p. 472.]

1782. **Hayley,** William. *An Essay on Epic Poetry in Five Epistles to the Revd. Mr. Mason, with Notes.* Epistle III, p. 63.
     See, on a party-colour'd steed of fire,
     With Humour at his side, his trusty Squire,
     Gay CHAUCER leads—in form a Knight of old,
     And his strong armour is of steel and gold ;
     But o'er it age a cruel rust has spread,
     And made the brilliant metals dark as lead.
     Now gentle SPENSER, Fancy's fav'rite Bard
     Awakes my wonder and my fond regard ;
[Reviewed, mentioning Chaucer reference, in The Gentleman's Magazine, July 1782, vol. lii, p. 345.]

[**1782.** **Hickford,** Rayner, and **Fell,** John.] *Observations on the Poems attributed to Rowley tending to prove that they were really written by him and other ancient authors* [by Hickford], *To which are added Remarks on the Appendix of the Editor of Rowley's Poems,* p. 30. [The remarks are by Fell; bound up together but with separate pagination and with a separate title page as well as above. The references to Chaucer occur on nearly every one of the thirty-five pages of the latter tract.]

1782. [**Mathias,** Thomas James.] *Rowley and Chatterton in the Shades, or Nugœ antiquœ et novœ, a new Elysian interlude,* pp. 34-7.

[Rowley and Chatterton are present]
Enter Pierce Plowman, Chaucer, Lydgate, and Spenser.

PIERCE PLOWMAN.

.   .   .   .

[p. 35] We have reasoned right oft in these shady solitudes,
Then answer me in accentes shrewd and artful,
For thou hast painted with a powerful pencil,
And given harmony and high-bearing to words,
Good Maister Chaucere.

CHAUCER.

Grete Plowman, if aright thy wordes I rede,
In mannis truthe thou haste but smallè crede :
I too have dwelte in many sondry londes,
And wandered farre and wide to distaunt strondes ;
I marked their manners and eache divers geste,
Their smoothè glozings, rare deceits at beste ;
Those tongues right sote who trusts, must nedès falle,
Their sugre tempred is with mickle galle.
Come then thou heavenlie gift, dread Poesie ;
With soundis fulle of pleasaunt minstrelsie ;
Come forth, but with a rightè bold semblaunce,
And vice will shrinkè with his high portaunce :
Let notes of sweetest modulation
Rise in our lines with exultation,
This be the praise and wirkè of my honde,
Fadre of polished verse in fair Englonde.

    [Lydgate announces that]
. . . a wondrous Boy has touched *our* stringes,
And veiled in termès straunge his nobile thought
[p. 36]   Whereof enmarvailled all Englonde ringes . .
[And Spenser rejoices to hear it]

CHAUCER.

Come broder-bards, among these swotie greves,[1]
While Zephyrus blowes pleasaunce through the leves.
[p. 37] Let us retire and holden mickle speeche,
If that our ken may this reportè reche,
And so that hendy Boy with poets olde
For his gode wirkè be sithence enrolde.

                    [Exeunt Pierce Plowman, etc.

CHATTERTON.

    Brave poets these ; I am always ravished with their antique
melody ; but I have given their modes a continued cadence
which justly surprizes the world. . . .

[1] sweet groves.

[This satire is reviewed in The Critical Review for July 1782, vol. liv ; there is a Chaucer reference on p. 27.]

1782. [**Maty**, Henry ?] *Short sketch of the Chattertonian Controversy from the Works of Mr. Tyrwhitt, Milles, Bryant, etc.* [in] The New Review for April 1782, ed. by Henry Maty, vol i, p. 221.

[A reference to Tyrwhitt's evidence as to Chatterton's mis-use, through ignorance, of Chaucerian words.]

1782. **Milles**, Jeremiah (Dean of Exeter). *Poems, supposed to have been written at Bristol in the fifteenth century by Thomas Rowley, Priest, with a Commentary in which the antiquity of them is considered and defended.* Preliminary Dissertation, pp. 5, 17, 19, 26, 28, 30–2. The Notes to the text have numerous Chaucer references, and these occur also on nearly every page of the additional evidence, and answer to the Appendix at the close of the book.

[*See* above, 1778, p. 451, Tyrwhitt, Appendix. This book was reviewed by Malone in the Gentleman's Magazine, Dec. 1781. *See* above, p. 463.]

1782. **N.**   *Letter* [in] The Gentleman's Magazine, Oct. 1782, p. 471.

[Chaucer's use of ' Hosen.']

1782. [**Ritson**, Joseph.] *Observations on the three first volumes of the History of English Poetry* [by Thomas Warton], *in a familiar letter to the author*, pp. 10–15, 33, 48 and *note*.

[A pamphlet pointing out mistakes and plagiarisms in Warton's History, and abusing him roundly.]

[p. 48]   Of all men living, the learned and intelligent editor of THE CANTERBURY TALES [i. e. Tyrwhitt] is the best able to afford you the requisite help . . . His publication of Chaucer is the most erudite, curious and valuable performance that (excepting only that mine of literary treasure Dr. Hickeses Thesaurus . . .) has yet appeared in this country. I do not, however, mean to pronounce it entirely faultless : It undoubt-edly contains some mistakes [1] . . .

[1] Such as his supposing Chaucer's lines to contain eleven syllables ; an idea as just as that 3 and 3 make 7 :—his adopting and misspelling certain words contrary to the evidence of all the MSS. he consulted :— a few erroneous notions with respect to Chaucer's language . . . with some others, perhaps, of still less consequence. . . .

[The above ' Observations ' are reviewed, with remarks on Occleve's lines to Chaucer, in The Gentleman's Magazine, Nov. 1782, p. 532.]

1782. [**Rogers**, Charles.] *The Inferno of Dante Translated*, Canto xxxiii, l. 88, p. 128, *n.*

[Chaucer in his Monk's Tale tells the story of "Hugelin of Pise."]

1782. **Scrutator.**   *Letter* [in] The Gentleman's Magazine, Aug. 1782, p. 367.

[W. Harte's line is borrowed from Pope, *see* above, 1727 p. 369.]

1782. Tyrwhitt, Thomas. *A Vindication of the Appendix to the Poems, called Rowley's, in reply to the answers of the Dean of Exeter, Jacob Bryant, Esquire, and a third anonymous writer;* . . . pp. 7, 8, 17 n., 22, 27, 32, 36, 37, 42, 43, 46, 47, 51, 52, 53, 55, 56 n. 57 n., 58 n., 59, 61, 67–75, 79, 84, 86 n., 87 n., 88, 154 n. [Chatterton's knowledge of Chaucer], 161, 163, 166, 169 n. 171, 173, 175, 176, 179–182, 184, 185, 205.

[Walpole refers to Tyrwhitt's *Vindication* in a letter of this year; *see* below, p. 469. For Milles, *see* above, 1782, for Bryant above, 1781, p. 459, for the anonymous writer (Hickford and Fell) above, p. 466, for Tyrwhitt above, 1788, p. 451.]

1782. Unknown. *Poem* [in] The Gentleman's Magazine. *See* below, App. A.

1782. Unknown. *[Extract from]* Address to Poetry ; an Extract from an Essay on Epic Poetry, by William Hayley, Esq., [in] Annual Register, vol. xxv, 1782, p. 191. *[See* above, p. 466.]

1782. Unknown. *Review* of Poems supposed to be by Rowley, . . . by Jeremiah Milles [in] The Critical Review for June 1782, vol. liii, pp. 410, 415 ; also July 1782, vol. liv, p. 3.

1782. Unknown. *Review* of Observations on the Poems of Thomas Rowley by Jacob Bryant [in] The Critical Review for Aug. 1782, vol. liv, pp. 88, 91–2.

[For Bryant, *see* above, p. 459.]

1782. Unknown. *Review* of a Vindication of the Appendix to the Poems called Rowley's, by Thomas Tyrwhitt [in] The Critical Review for Sept. 1782, vol. liv, pp. 189–91.

[1782.] Unknown. *An Examination of the Poems attributed to Thomas Rowley and William Canynge, with a Defence of the opinion of Mr. Warton,* Sherborne, pp. 9, 15–17.

1782. Walpole, Horace. *Letter to Earl Harcourt,* [dated] Strawberry Hill, Sept. 7, 1782. (Letters of Horace Walpole, ed. Mrs. Paget Toynbee, 1904, vol. xii, p. 328.)

Has your Lordship seen Mr. Tyrwhitt's book in answer to Mr. Bryant and Dr. Archimage? It is as good as arguments and proofs can be after what is much better, wit and ridicule. As Mr. Mason is absorbed in *Fresnoy* and Associations, I conclude he does not condescend to look at such trifles as *Archæologic Epistles,* and dissertations on the language of Chaucer.

[Dr. Archimage was Dr. Milles, Dean of Exeter, *see* above, 1782, Milles, p. 468. For the *Archæological Epistle, see* above, 1782, Baynes, p. 465.]

1782. Warton, Joseph. *An Essay on the Genius and Writings of Pope,* in two vols. Fourth edition corrected : vol. i, sect. vii, pp. 348–57, 378 *note,* 412–14 ; vol. ii, sect. viii, pp. 7–12, **30.**

[Warton published the 1st vol. in 1756, *q.v.* above, p. 412, but the 2nd vol. did not appear till 1782. The Chaucer references down to end of sect. vi are identical in the edns. of 1756 and 1782, therefore under this latter date only the new references are given from sect. vii onwards. The most important part of Warton's Chaucer criticism is here reprinted, but not quite in full.]

[vol. i, p. 348] Of the TEMPLE of FAME, from CHAUCER.

[p. 349]   . . . It was to the *Italians* we owed anything that could be called poetry : from whom Chaucer, imitated by POPE in this vision, copied largely, . . . and to which Italians he is perpetually owning his obligations, particularly to Boccace and Petrarch. . . .

[p. 351]   But whatever Chaucer might copy from the Italians, yet the artful and entertaining plan of his Canterbury Tales, was purely original and his own. This admirable piece, even exclusive of its poetry, is highly valuable, as it preserves to us the liveliest and exactest picture of the manners, customs, characters, and habits of our forefathers, whom he has brought before our eyes acting as on a stage, suitably to their different [p. 352] orders and employments.   With these portraits the driest must be delighted ; by this plan, he has more judiciously connected these stories which the guests relate, than Boccace has done his novels : whom he has imitated, if not excelled, in the variety of the subjects of his tales.   It is a common mistake, that Chaucer's excellence lay in his manner of treating light and ridiculous subjects ; for whoever will attentively consider the noble poem of Palamon and Arcite, will be convinced that he equally excels in the pathetic and the sublime. It has been but lately proved that the Palamon and Arcite of Chaucer, is taken from the Theseida of Boccace . . . I cannot forbear expressing my surprise, that the circumstance of Chaucer's borrowing this tale should have remained so long unobserved, when it is so plainly and positively mentioned in [p. 353] a book so very common, as the Memoirs of *Niceron* [1736].

.   .   .   .

[p. 355]   . . . The French are perpetually boasting, that they have been our masters in many of the polite arts, and made earlier improvements in literature.   But it may be asked, what cotemporary poet can they name to stand in competition with Chaucer, except William de Loris ? . . . I can find none of this age, but barren chroniclers, and harsh romancers in rhime, without the elegance, elevation, invention, or harmony of Chaucer . . .

.   .   .   .

[p. 356] THE HOUSE OF FAME, as Chaucer entitled his piece, gave the hint, as we observed, of the poem before us, though the design is in truth improved and heightened by the masterly hand of POPE. . . .

.   .   .   .

[vol ii, p. 7] THE WIFE OF BATH, is the other piece of Chaucer which POPE selected to imitate :   One cannot but wonder at his choice, which perhaps nothing but his youth could excuse. . . . Chaucer afforded him many subjects of a more serious and sublime species ; and it were to be wished, POPE had exercised his pencil on the pathetic story of the patience of Grisilda, or Troilus and Cressida, or the complaint of the black knight ; or, above all, on Cambuscan and Canace.   From the accidental circumstance of Dryden and POPE's having copied the gay and ludicrous parts of Chaucer, the common notion [p. 8] seems to have arisen, that Chaucer's vein of poetry was chiefly turned to the light and the ridiculous.[1]   But they who look into Chaucer, will soon be convinced of this prevailing prejudice, and will find his comic vein, like that of Shakespear, to be only like one of mercury, imperceptibly mingled with a mine of gold.

CHAUCER is highly extolled by Dryden in the spirited and pleasing preface to his Fables . . . [here Warton quotes Dryden, *q.v.* above, 1700, pp. 272–85.]

[In this year also appeared vol. ii, which had been in print for over twenty years (*see* Preface). It was issued with the 3rd edn. of vol. i, and begins with section viii; the Chaucer references are pp. 3–8, 29, 60–2, 69–75, 92, 318. On p. 6 (corresponding to p. 352 above) the reference to Niceron is omitted, but the following is given :]

I have lately met with an elegy in Joannes Secundus occasioned by this Story ; it is in his third book, and is thus intitled :[2] 'In Historiam de rebus a Theseo gestis duorumque rivalium certamine, Gallicis numeris ab illustri quadam Matrona suavissime conscriptam.'   Perhaps this compliment was addressed to Madame de Scudery, who is said to have translated Chaucer into modern French.   [*See* above, p. 282.]

---

[1] [Note by Warton.] Cowley is said to have despised Chaucer. I am not surprized at this strange judgment. Cowley was indisputably a Genius, but his taste was perverted and narrowed by a love of witticisms. [*See* above, 1700, Dryden, p. 280, below, 1795, D'Israeli, p. 496, and Cowley, App. A., *n.a.* 1667.]
[2] Eleg. 15.

1782. Unknown. *Reviews* [principally long quotations] of Warton's Essay on the Genius and Writings of Pope, [in] Annual Register, Account of Books, vol. xxv, 1782, pp ʳ11, 212. Also in The Gentleman's Magazine May 1782, vol. lii, ɹp. 236, 239.

[Brief references.]

1782. Warton, Thomas. *An Enquiry into the authenticity of the poems attributed to Thomas Rowley. In which the arguments of the Dean of Exeter* [Jeremiah Milles] *and Mr. Bryant, are examined,* pp. 7, 19, 21, 34, 35, 38, 39, 42, 49, 50, 53, 54, 56, 60, 110.

[Warton is quoted by Robert Fellowes ; *see* below, 1799, p. 501. For Milles and Bryant, *see* above, p. 468 and p. 459 respectively.]

1782. Unknown. *Review* of [Warton's] Enquiry into the Authenticity of the Poems attributed to Thomas Rowley, [in] Gentleman's Magazine, March, pp. 129–30, April, vol. lii, pp. 195–7.

1782. Unknown. *Review* of Warton's Enquiry into the Authenticity of the Poems attributed to Thomas Rowley, [in] The Critical Review for August 1782, vol. liv, pp. 98, 101.

[p. 98]   His [Chatterton's] knowledge of the Language and Phrases of our elder poets has been attained by a laborious search through the rubbish of Occleve, and the richer ore of Gower and Chaucer.

1783. Barry, James. *Account of a series of Pictures . . . at the Adelphi,* pp. 134–5.

. . . In the centre sits Homer, on his right Milton and Shakespeare, Spencer and Chaucer are next. . . .

[This is No. vi (Elysium) of the series painted by Barry, between 1777 and 1783, on the walls of the Society of Arts.]

1783. Beattie, James. *Dissertations moral and critical.* The Theory of Language, pp. 252, 261, On Fable and Romance, p. 559.

[p. 252]   [Quotes Wallis, who says in his grammar] that some old people in his time retained so much of Chaucer's pronunciation, as to say *housé* and *horsé,* articulating in these and the like words the final *e,* which is now invariably mute.

[p. 261]   [Final *e* pronounced in age of Chaucer.]

[p. 559]   The fourteenth century produced also the illustrious Geoffry Chaucer ; who, though not the first who wrote in English, is the first of our great authors, and may be truly called the father of our language and literature. His writings are chiefly translations, or imitations of the Provensal [*sic*] and Italian writers then known. But he has imitated and translated with the greatest latitude, and added many fine strokes of character, humour and description, so that we ought to consider him as an original; since he does in fact exhibit, especially in his Canterbury Tales, a more natural picture of the English manners of that age, than is to be met with in any other writer. He did not, however, fix the English tongue, as his contemporaries Petrarch and Boccaccio had fixed the Italian. Many of his words soon fell into disuse : and his language at present is not well understood, except by those who have taken some pains to study it. . . .

1783. Hoole, John. *Preface* [to] Orlando Furioso : translated . . . by John Hoole ; vol. i, p. lii ; vol. ii, p. 6 *n.*

[vol. i, p. lii] The genius of our heroic verse admits of a great variety ; and we have examples of very different species of writing, in the works of Dryden and Pope, from the sublime style of Homer and Virgil, to the familiar narratives of Boccace and Chaucer.

1783. Matthias, Thomas James. *An Essay on the evidence, external and internal, relating to the Poems attributed to Thomas Rowley, containing a general view of the whole controversy,* pp. 47, 62, 66, 68, 74, 76, 113.

1783. Pinkerton, John. *Letter to John Nichols,* [dated] Oct. 3, 1783, [printed in] Illustrations of the Literary History of the 18th century . . . by John Nichols, vol. v, 1828, p. 674.

My dear Sir,

You know well that there was no edition of Cowley for fifty years till your friend Dr. Hurd published his Select Works, which have passed through four editions already. I hope like success would attend the Select Works of Geoffrey Chaucer ; and submit this to you that you may consider if it is worth your while to try. Lose you cannot in my opinion, for every purchaser of Johnson's Poets would buy the book to complete their sets ; and I am much mistaken if the work would not be very popular, and your gain very considerable ; but you are the only judge.

My love of Chaucer has induced me to dwell on the subject *con amore*, and I doubt not but you will ponder well ere you pronounce on a design so important to English literature and antiquity, of which you are no mean proficient.

I ever am, dear Sir

1783. [Ritson, Joseph.] *Remarks . . . on . . . the last edition of Shakespeare, see* below, App. A., 1783.

1783. S., D. *Criticisms of Warton's ' History,'* [in] The Gentleman's
Magazine. *See* below, App. A.

1783. Tyrwhitt, Thomas. *A letter to a Friend, upon the late Edition of
Chaucer, by J. Bell,* [dated] Welbeck Street, June 12, 1783, [printed
in] Gentleman's Magazine, June 1783, vol. 53, pp. 461–2.
[For Bell's Chaucer, *see* above, 1782, p. 464.]

Dear Sir,

I am much obliged to you for your intelligence concerning
the late edition of Chaucer. I find it true in all particulars.
Your alarm however for my property, as you call it, is ground-
less. As I have not entered my book at Stationers-Hall, I
have, it seems, no legal property in it. But if I had, would
you advise me to go to law for a property unattended by any
profit? A certain philosopher, when his gouty shoes were
stolen, only wished, that they might fit the thief as well as
they fitted himself; and for my own part I shall be contented,
if my book shall prove just as lucrative to Mr. Bell, as it has
been to me.

At the same time I do not pretend to be without all feeling
for my own personal injury, as well as for the pernicious
tendency of the example. If a book may be thus reprinted,
with all its imperfections, whenever a hungry bookseller
thinks that he can make a penny of it, without allowing the
author an opportunity of rectifying mistakes, supplying deficiencies, &c., we must give up, I fear, all expectation of ever
seeing a really accurate work. In the present instance, I have
not only been precluded (as far as Mr. Bell can preclude me)
from the usual opportunity of lessening the faults of my book,
but several errors, which I had actually pointed out for correction, have either been left unamended, or have been
amended in such a blundering manner as to require still
further correction. [Tyrwhitt further points out that the
type, especially that of the Notes, is too small, and that the
publication was probably intended solely for the use of young
people. That this is so] . . . is further evident from Mr.
Bell's having printed the greatest part of Chaucer's works
from Urry's edition; in which (as you know very well) there
is scarce a line as the author wrote it. Having given them a
picture at the beginning of each volume, he seems to have
thought (and perhaps with reason) that they would be
perfectly unconcerned about everything else.

But leaving Mr. Bell and his edition to their respective
fates, I must add a few words upon what is the principal

object of this letter.   The assured manner in which my name
is used may lead people to imagine that I have been at least
consenting to this republication of my book; and therefore
I beg the favour of you, and all my other friends, to take
every opportunity (the more public the better) of declaring for
me, that the whole transaction has passed without my consent,
approbation, or knowledge.

I am, &c.,
T. TYRWHITT.

1783. [**Tytler**, William.]   *Poetical remains of James the First* [ed. by
W. Tytler].   Dissertation on the Life and Writings of King James
I, pp. 47–52.   Notes on the King's Quair, pp. 57, 82, 83, 85–88, 93,
117, 118, 155, 161.   [See also art. by Henry Wood, on Chaucer's
influence upon King James, in Anglia, 1880, vol. iii, pp. 223–265.]

[p. 49]   Chaucer, the father of English poetry, as he may be stiled
the first, so he is the best poet of his time.   His universal
genius has comprehended, in his Canterbury Tales, the various
manners and humours of every rank of men in his age and
country . . . And he has shewn the extent of his genius and
learning in almost every species of poetry from his heroic
poem of Palamon and Arcite to his ballads.   Having said this
in preference of Chaucer, I may, however, be allowed to
compare the episode of the *Court of Venus*, in the following
poem of James [*The King's Quair*] with the *Court of Love* of
Chaucer; in which view, . . . our poet [James] will lose
nothing by the comparison, particularly in the pourtraiture of
the mistress of each poet. . . .

[p. 50]   To such as one not versant in the old poets, Chaucer, Gower,
[p. 51]   &c., the numbers of the verses will often appear to be unequal,
as the apostrophe's, signs of contraction, elisions, and marks
for the division of the syllables for the sake of the verse,
which were used by the old poets, are now lost. . . .

What Waller says, in his elegant verses on Chaucer, . . .
may, with equal force, be applied to the poetical remains of
King James I. of Scotland: [quotes Waller's lines, " Poets,
that lasting marble seek," *see* above, p. 244].

1783. Unknown.   *Remarks* [on J. P. Andrews' Letter giving an account
of the Parish of Shaw-cum-Donnington, 1759, in] Answers to
Berkshire Queries in the fourth volume of Bibliotheca Topographica Britannica, which contains Antiquities in Bedfordshire and Berkshire, 1790, pp. *82–3. [The pagination is not
continuous.]

[p. *82]   Mr. Grove published a plan of this [Donnington] castle,
with a front view of the gate, engraved by Adam Smith, from

a very accurate plan and drawing made on purpose with much care and labour, and such as was wished for by the author of Chaucer's life prefixt to Urry's edition. . . .

[p.*83]   The portrait of Chaucer is now removed to Bucklebury, the seat of Henry Winchcombe Hartley, esq.

[For Andrews' Letter *see* above, 1759, p. 416. A note on p. * 81 states that these remarks are additions made by a correspondent twenty-four years later.]

1783. Unknown. *Article* on The Legend of Saint Cecilia [in] The Gentleman's Magazine, Aug., p. 635.

[Quotation from the Second Nonnes Tale.]

1783. V., B. *Account of Lichfield Cathedral* [in] The Gentleman's Magazine, Feb., vol. liii, p. 120.

[The library contains] a Folio—illuminated Chaucer, fairly written.

1783. J., W. *Reply* to H. T. W.'s letter, immediately below. *See* below, App. A.

1783. W., T. H. *Letter* [in] The Gentleman's Magazine.

1783. [Waldron, Francis Godolphin.] *The Sad Shepherd . . . written by Ben Jonson . . . with a Continuation, Notes and an Appendix,* [by F. G. Waldron] pp. 29, 41, notes. Supplemental notes, pp. 123–4, 128. Appendix, p. 189 [extract from Bulleyn's Dialogue. *See* above, 1564, p. 98.]

1784. Astle, Thomas. *The Origin and Progress of Writing,* p. xvi.

[In a list of eminent writers who prevented the lamp of learning from being entirely extinguished, Chaucer is mentioned, and a short account of him is given.]

1784. Eugenio; W., R., and **Unknown.** *Letters* and *Remarks* [in] The Gentleman's Magazine. *See* below, App. A.

1784. [Kippis, Andrew ?] *Supplementary article* [signed K] in the notes to the account of Chaucer in Biographia Britannica, second edition [corrected and enlarged] by Andrew Kippis [and others], vol. iii, pp. 466–82.

[The whole article on Chaucer, pp. 450–82, is reprinted verbatim from that in the 1st edn. of 1747, *q.v.*, but in addition there is a very long supplementary note giving the latest criticism on Chaucer, including the whole of Tyrwhitt's Essay on the Language and Versification of Chaucer, 1775, without his notes—also long extracts from Warton's History of English Poetry, 1774.]

[c. **1785 ?] Bell,** William. *See* below, p. 480, **Unknown.**

1785. D, J. ; E, N. ; **E,** S. ; **Unknown; W,** T, H. *Articles* and *Reviews* in The Gentleman's Magazine. *See* below, App. A.

1785. Herbert, William. *Typographical Antiquities . . . begun by the late Joseph Ames . . . considerably augmented . . . by William Herbert . . .* in 3 volumes, 1785–90, vol. i, pp. 18 n, 72–76, 79–83, 89, 123, 276–79, 281–82, 319–21, 415, 416, 420, 557, 558, 592, 593.

[Joseph Ames, the antiquary, published his Typographical Antiquities, in one vol. in 1749 (*q.v.* above, p. 398), and this was re-edited and very much enlarged, in 3 vols, 1785–90, by William Herbert. All the Chaucer references in this later edn. are given, with a note as to those already written by Ames. For vol. ii, *see* below, 1786, p. 483, for vol. iii, 1790, p. 491 ; for fuller and more correct information, see Typographical Antiquities . . . greatly enlarged by Thomas Frognall Dibdin, 4 vols, 1810–19, unfinished.]

[A specimen of Caxton's Boethius immediately before sign B1 given by Ames.]

[p. 18 note] [Pynson is mistaken in attributing the "Moral Proverbs" to Chaucer, see Caxton.]

[p. 72] [Description of Caxton's edns. of Chaucer's Canterbury tales. Ames's notes, pp. 54–8, are slightly enlarged.] Mr. Caxton printed two editions of these Tales, and both without date, for anything at present known to the contrary.

A copy of the first edition is now in the King's library, and has this MS. anecdote annexed ; "This first edition of Chaucer, printed by Caxton, is the only perfect one known in England.[1] The Earls of Pembroke and Oxford told me, after the utmost inquiry, that they never could see one. Some fragments are in the hands of Sir Peter Thompson, late Mr. Ames's, Mr. Ratcliff, and at St. John's Coll. Oxford ; but united will not make a perfect copy. J. West." I make no doubt but that this copy had been accordingly collated, and the work found perfect ; for as it has no catchwords, signatures, or numbers to the leaves, its being perfect or not could only be known by that means ; but on the leaves being told, there are found 372, including a blank leaf at the end . . . [Description of the edn. here follows, and Caxton's "Prohemye" also Chaucer's "Retraction" and the end of "Boecius" and the first and last lines of the epitaph on Chaucer by Surigo, pp. 73–76.]

[pp. 79, 83] [Description of a collection of Chaucer's and Lydgate's poems printed by Caxton in the Public Library at Cambridge. Ames describes Book of Fame and Troilus, pp. 60–2, but the notes are considerably enlarged by Herbert.]

[p. 89] [Extract from "The Werk of Sapience" printed by Caxton, with Chaucer reference given by Ames, p. 66.]

[p. 123] Chaucer's Canterbury Tales. Collected by William Caxton,

---

[1] Mr. Tyrwhitt mentions another copy seemingly complete in Merton Coll. library, Canterb. Tales, vol. i, p. 6, note a.

and printed by Wynken de Worde at Westmestre.   **1495.**
See Mr. Tyrwhit's [*sic*] Preface, pag. viii.

[p. 276]   [Description of a copy of Deguilleville's "Pylgrimage of
perfection," 1526, printed by Pynson, with 'Chaucer's prophecy' in 16th century handwriting on front leaf.]

[pp. 277-9] [Description of Pynson's edn. of Chaucer's Works, 1526.]

[pp. 281-2] [Description of Caxton's edn. of the Canterbury Tales,
printed by Pynson, c. 1492.   A few words on this is given by
Ames, pp. 127-8, and he prints Caxton's "prohemie" here.]

[pp. 319-21][Description of W. Thynne's edn. of Chaucer's Works, printed
by T. Godfray, 1532.   Discussion as to whether an edn. [in
Harleian Libr.] mentioned by Timothy Thomas in his preface
to Urry's Chaucer [1721] is the same as this edn. by Godfray,
or if not, what edn. it was.   This edn. is just mentioned by
Ames, p. 141, but all the notes are added by Herbert]

[p. 343-4] [Rastell's Terence in Englysh.   Allusion to Chaucer, given by
Ames, pp. 148-9.]

[p. 415]   [Description of W. Thynne's 2nd edn. of Chaucer's Works,
1542.]   Prynted by John Reynes dwellyinge at the synge [*sic*]
of saynte George in Pauls Churche-yarde, 1542 . . . The preface
to Urry's Chaucer mentions it being printed this year by
William Bonham ; and by the description of the cut [for
Knight's and Squire's tales] there, the printing this edition
seems to have been a joint affair between him and
Reynes.

[p. 416]   [Mention of Chaucer's Works printed by Thomas Berthelet.]

[p. 420]   [Description of Berthelet's edn. of Gower's Confessio
Amantis, 1532, with a quotation from Berthelet's testimony
to Chaucer in his address to the Reader ; *see* p. 77,
above.]

[p. 557]   [Description of the reprint of Thynne's 2nd edn. of Chaucer's
Works, 1545 or 1550, printed by Thomas Petit, *see* above,
p. 86.   This is mentioned by Ames, p. 210.]

[p. 588]   [Reference to same edn. as above, only printed by Robert
Toy, mentioned by Ames, p. 221.]

[pp. 592, 593] [Chaucer's Works, printed by W. Bonham, 1542, and 1545 or
1550.]

1785. Heron, Robert, *pseud.* [**Pinkerton,** John]. *Letters of Literature
by Robert Heron Esq.*   Letter xiv, p. 75, xxv, p. 160, xxvi, p. 166,
xxxiv, p. 244, 263, 272, xxxviii, p. 309, xxxix p. 319.

[p. 244]   Now I will hazard a bold opinion, namely, that our

language is now infinitely more barbarous, in all respects, than
it was in the days of Chaucer. For melody there is no
comparison; the *é* always pronounced, as in *spoké, shaké,* &c.
was alone sufficient to render it much more melodious.

[p. 272]   Who of us knows how Chaucer pronounced English?

[p. 309]   *Nice* occurs often in Chaucer, and in the Tale of Beryn, for
foolish.

1785. R[eeve], C[lara]. *The Progress of Romance . . . by C. R. Author
of the English Baron . . .* vol. 1, pp. 49, 50 [Extract from The
Romance of the Rose], 53, 55, 86.

[p. 86]   Chaucer's *Canterbury Tales* would tell equally well in verse
or prose . . . Permit me to remark that *Dryden's* elegant,
rich, and harmonious numbers, have preserved this [The
Knight's Tale], and many other of *Chaucer's* works, from sinking into oblivion, and he has given the old Bard a share of his
own immortality.

1785. Sterling, [Joseph]. *Cambuscan, or the Squire's Tale of Chaucer,
modernized by Mr. Boyse; continued from Spencer's Fairy Queen,
by Mr. Ogle; and concluded by Mr. Sterling,* Dublin, 1785, p. 3,
sonnet, p. 4, and Advertisement by Sterling.

[Prefatory] Sonnet.

What Chaucer sung in Woodstock's rural bow'rs,
Was marr'd by death, or Time's unsparing hand;

.   .   .   .

[p. 4]   [Advertisement.] The ingenious Mr. Warton, in the first
volume and fifteenth section of his History of English Poetry,
speaks of the story of CAMBUSCAN in terms of the highest
respect. He says, that after the KNIGHT'S TALE, it is the
noblest of the productions of Chaucer: He proves that it is
an Arabian fiction, engrafted on Gothic chivalry. This Poem
was continued by Spenser, and admired by Milton. It has
been considerably improved by M^r. BOYSE, the Modernizer.
The Concluder feels his poetic powers far inferior to those of
CHAUCER and SPENSER; but as he endeavours to amuse, hopes
for the indulgence of the Public.

1785. Unknown. *The New Oxford Guide. . . .* To which is added a
Tour to Blenheim . . . Nuneham. . . . By a Gentleman of Oxford.
7th edn. p. 131; and 8th edn. [1789?] p. 130.

A Tour to Nuneham.   The Flower Garden.   . . .   Fronting
the Gate is a Bust of FLORA on a Term ;
          Here springs the Violet all newe

.   .   .   .

          That castin up ful gode favoure.
                                        CHAUCER [R. of Rose, ll. 1431–8.]

[The extract is given from the 8th edn., as we have been unable to see the 7th,
and it does not appear in the 1st or the 6th.]

1785. Unknown. *The wife of Beith, by Chaucer . . . a new edition,*
1785. *See* above, 1700, p. 288, and below, App. A. [1670 ?].

[c. **1785 ?**] **Unknown** [possibly William **Bell**, of Ulcomb, Kent, whose
     bookplate is in the volume].   *MS. Notes* in a copy of Fables,
     Ancient and Modern, translated into Verse, from Homer, Ovid,
     Boccace, and Chaucer . . . by Mr. Dryden, 1700. [B.M. 11631.
     i. 12.]

[These notes are principally numerous corrections of the text, with a view,
apparently, to issuing a new edition of Dryden's Fables. The following note, the
first of several, is on the verso of the title page. " Imagining it in my Power
to improve Dryden's Fables (so called) which I deem at least equal to any of his
works, by elevating the unequal Parts to a level, I have employed some leisure
hours in that Task ; thinking it a pity such Jewels should want perfection." Of
the notes mentioning Chaucer only a selection is given below.]

[Note at foot of p. 7 to] "Thus Year by Year they pass
and Day by Day."

Year by year, and day by day was an anticlimax of
Chaucer ; in whom it seems remarkable that his rhymes are
carried from one paragraph to another.

[Note at foot of p. 14 to] "And wish'd that ev'ry Look
might be the last."   Chaucer wanted judgment.   This I have
pointed out in regard to Theseus : and Palamon and Arcite
are drawn ferocious instead of generous, & the latter without
candour or justice, and impious withal.

[Note at foot of p. 63 to]

     ' For this Advantage Age from Youth has won,
          As not to be outridden, though outrun.'

This is truly Chaucerian.   Chaucer was as fond of his
jests and dashes of satire as Cowley of his wit [and] puns, and
the Knight's Tale is of a mixt nature like the Fairy Queen
and the Davideis, yet the three poems are moreover all
different from one another.

Note [at foot of p. 80] to

     "Why would'st thou go, with one Consent they cry,
          When thou hadst Gold enough, and *Emily* ! "

"This is copied from Chaucer, and a miserable jest it is: though it is not always easy to say whether he meant a burlesque, or jest, or whether the homeliness and uncouthness of the language to us, gives it such a cast. Be it as it may, Dryden's interlaying satirical pleasantries, hitting exactly the manner of Chaucer, is deserving of observation, and perhaps of praise.

[Note at foot of p. 84 to] "With nameless Nymphs that liv'd in ev'ry Tree." Chaucer discovers here and there a strong inclination to spoil this Poem with burlesque, as well as with jocoseness. He puts us in mind of Charles 2. who could hardly sustain his gravity long enough even to make a speech from the throne.

[Note at foot of p. 90 and head of p. 91, at end of the Knight's Tale.]

Dryden's modernization of the *Knight's Tale*, and other works of Chaucer, being properly but imitations, quotations are made from them by writers, as Dryden's own productions: and perhaps it might be replied to an allegation of injustice therein, that Chaucer himself is but a translator, or imitator. Indeed Dryden has greatly improved and adorned the Knight's Tale, by an expansion of 2159 lines into 2446. . .

[Note on verso of the half-title to The Cock and the Fox, to face p. 222.]

The Cock and the Fox is so foolish, if not worse, that I omit it entirely notwithstanding it has some good lines. It adds little to Chaucer's Reputation that he was the original Author of it.

[Note, p. 223, above the beginning of The Cock and the Fox.]
The Printer is desired to omit this Tale.

[The tale is then all scratched out.]

[Note on verso of the half-title to The Flower and the Leaf, to face p. 383.]

The Flower and the Leaf modernized from Chaucer is so beautiful that I have more closely attended to revising it than some of the others.

[Note at foot of p. 480 to] "There haunts not any Incubus, but He." Keen indeed! This was Chaucer's. It is not to be doubted but that with his wit, learning, and penetration, he was a favourer of the reformists.

[A few slips of the pen have been corrected in transcribing the above notes.]

1785. [**Darby,** Samuel.]   *A letter to the Rev. Mr. T. Warton on his late edition of Milton's Juvenile Poems,* p. 10.

[Reference to Warton's note, p. 225, on Chaucer's use of the word "boult." *See* below, 1785, Warton, T.]

1785. **Walpole,** Horace.   *Letter to John Pinkerton,* [dated] June 22, 1785.   (Letters of Horace Walpole, ed. Mrs. Paget Toynbee, 1905, vol. xiii, p. 275.)

With regard to adding *a* or *o* to final consonants, consider, Sir, should the usage be adopted, what havoc it would make! All our poetry would be defective in metre, or would become at once as obsolete as Chaucer; and could we promise ourselves that, though we should acquire better harmony and more rhymes, we should have a new crop of poets, to replace Milton, Dryden, Gray, and, I am sorry you will not allow me to add, Pope!

1785. **Warton,** Thomas.   *Poems upon several occasions by John Milton . . . with notes by Thomas Warton,* pp. 9, 24, 49, 81–2, 225, etc.

[These are only a few of the frequent references to Chaucer in the notes; they are mainly philological. That on p. 225 is referred to by Darby. *See* above, 1785.]

[p. 81]   [*Or call up him that left half told The story of Cambuscan bold,* &c.]

Hence it appears, that Milton, among Chaucer's pieces, was [p. 82] most struck with his Squier's Tale.   It best suited our author's predilection for romantic poetry.   Chaucer is here ranked with the sublime poets: his comic vein is forgotten and overlooked.

[*And if aught else great bards beside . . .*]   From Chaucer, the father of English poetry, and who is here distinguished by a story remarkable for the wildness of its invention, our author seems to make a very pertinent and natural transition to Spenser. . . .

1785. **Worfat,** William de, *pseud.* [**Hutton,** William].   *A Bran New Wark by William de Worfat, containing a true Calendar of his Thoughts Concerning good Nebberhood.   Naw first printed fra his M.S. for the use of the hamlet of Woodland.*   Kendal: Printed by W. Pennington, 1785 (ed. W. W. Skeat in Specimens of English Dialects, English Dialect Soc., 1879, p. 195).

[p. 195, l. 260]   Withaut this binding quality o aur righteousness is as filthy rags; dea I say filthy? yea the Holy Spirit in abhorrence of sic sort of conduct, seems to mak use of words purposely braade.

See *Esaiah* 6. 5.   *Qu.* Might not the translator have conveyed to us the sense of the sacred writer by a more delicate expression ? I have often asked myself this, on reading other parts of Scripture—I know with *Chaucer* that

> " Braade words er good, whilst good folks use them
> They er only bad, when bad folks abuse them,"

And again

> " Christ spake himself full braade in holy writ,
> And weel I wat, no villainy is it. "
>
> [C. T. Prol., ed. Skeat, ll. 741-2.]

[There are only two or three copies of this first edn. extant. The best is in King's College, London, used by Skeat. No copy of this edn. is in B. M. On p. 212 will be found the editor's comment on the Chaucer reference . . . The former quotation is plainly nothing but a poor paraphrase of the same two lines, and can hardly (I think) be found in Chaucer himself.]

1786. Beatniffe, Richard. *The Norfolk Tour, or Traveller's Pocket Companion* . . . 4th edition, p. 170. [Not in former editions. The author's name does not appear on the title-page, but at the foot of the preface.]

[A short account of Nicholas of Lynne, mentioning that] Chaucer had a great esteem for him, stiling him *Frere* Nicholas Linn, a Rev. Clerke.

1786. Billam, John. *Letter to William Herbert,* [dated] Aug. 4, 1786, [with an account of Wynkyn de Worde's edn. of the Assemble of Foules, 1530, and quoting Robert Copland's lines (*q.v.* above, 1530, p. 76), in] J. Ames's Typographical Antiquities, ed. William Herbert and T. F. Dibdin, vol. ii, pp. 278-80 [*see below*, 1812].

1786-96. [Gough, Richard.] *Sepulchral Monuments in Great Britain,* vol. i, pt. i, (1786), pp. clvii, clix–clxiv, clxvii–viii, clxxvii, clxxxi, clxxxvi, clxxxviii–ix, cxci, 35 ; vol. ii, pt. ii, (1796), pp. 1–3, 106–8.

[The references to Chaucer in the Introduction consist of numerous extracts from his works, more particularly the Canterbury Tales, illustrative of the dress of his age ; those in vol. ii, pp. 1–3, are to his monument in Westminster Abbey, and to the various engravings of his portraits, and they contain also a few words on his life ; pp. 106–8 refer to the tomb of Sir Thomas Chaucer at Ewelme, and to his connection with the poet.]

1786. Herbert, William. *Typographical Antiquities . . . begun by the late Joseph Ames . . . considerably augmented . . . by William Herbert . . .* in 3 volumes, 1785–90, vol. ii, 1786, pp. 686 *n.*, 691 *n.*, 738, 747 (Rd. Kele's reprint of Thynne's 2nd edn. of Chaucer's works [1545 or 1550], mentioned by Ames, p. 263), 780 and 835 [Chaucer's works, with the Siege of Thebes 1561, mentioned by Ames, p. 296], 1152 [Speght's edn. of Chaucer, "impensis Geo. Bishop, . . 1598."], 1236. ["The Northern Mother's Blessing," *see* also Ames, p. 404], 1287, 1304.

[For vol. i, *see* above, 1785, p. 477, for vol. iii, below, 1790, p. 491 for Ames, above, 1749, p. 398, for Dibdin's enlarged but unfinished edn., below, 1810.]

1786. Pinkerton, John. *Ancient Scotish Poems*, vol. i, Preface, pp.
viii–xi, xvi, xviii. An Essay on the Origin of Scottish Poetry, pp.
lxi, lxvi, lxviii, lxx, lxxii. A List of all the Scotish Poets, pp.
lxxxii, lxxxix, xc, xciv, cxii. Vol. ii, Notes, pp. 367, 378, 380, 382–4,
397–8, 400, 412, 414, 416, 422–3, 425 *n.* Appendix, pp. 451, 482.
Additions and Corrections, 542.

[p. xi]   These Tales [The Twa Mariit Wemen and the Wedo, and
The Freirs of Berwik] place Dunbar in quite a new and more
important light; for it is believed they will be as much preferred to his Goldin Terge, and Thistle and Rose, tho these
pieces have an elegance and opulence which Chaucer nowhere
attains, as Chaucer's Tales are to his allegorical poems. Dunbar,
having a genius at least equal to Chaucer, and perhaps more
original; and having the advantage of living a whole century
after him, when the language was more rich and expressive;
it is no wonder that he should excell that venerable poet in
every point, but in the length of his pieces, a most dispensable
quality.

.   .   .   .

[p. xviii]   The old Scotish poets ought to be regarded in the same light
as Chaucer and the old English ones; and who suspects that
the perusal of the latter can injure the purity of English conversation, or writing? . . .   As long as Chaucer is read therefore, and he will be read till the English language perishes,
so long may we hope for equal attention to Barbour and
Dunbar.

.   .   .   .

[p. lxx]   And perhaps, if the mixture of French words with English
was a fault, Lermont, and not Chaucer, ought to bear the blame;
tho there be no doubt but that Lermont and Chaucer only
used the language of the politest people of the period.

.   .   .   .

[p. lxxii]   Mr. Tyrwhitt, in a note to his Life of Chaucer, says,
'Chaucer's reputation was as well established in Scotland as in
England: and I will take upon me to say, that he was as
much the father of poetry in that country, as in this.' This is
quite a mistake. Chaucer was in the highest admiration in
Scotland, as he justly deserved: but not one Scotish poet
has imitated him: or is in the least indebted to him. I wish
the Scotish writers had owned him as father of their poetry
with all my heart: but not a trace of this can be found.
They praise him; but never imitate either his language,

stanza, manner, or sentiments. . . . If Mr. Tyrwhitt will point out one imitation of the slightest passage of Chaucer in any Scotish poet whatever, it will operate to his purpose; but I know from certain knowledge that he cannot; so must refuse my assent to his opinion.

. . . .

[p. xciv] The Historian of English Poetry [T. Warton, History of English Poetry, vol. ii, 1778, p. 257. *See* above, p. 454] . . . says 'the Scotish writers have adorned the present period with a degree of sentiment, and spirit, a command of phraseology, and a fertility of imagination not to be found in any English poet since Chaucer and Lydgate.' He might safely have added, 'not even in Chaucer, or Lydgate.'

. . . .

[Notes, vol. ii, p. 382] The number of syllables was never attended to by the Gothic or the Saxon poets, save in stanza. . . . This was also the practice of our oldest English poets, and if they who fight for the regularity of Chaucer's couplet-measure had but read the *Geste of King Horn* . . . they would have dropt the idea at once.

. . . .

[p. 398] There is no passage in Chaucer so exquisite as his full description of the Carpenter's Wife in *The Miller's Tale.*

. . . .

[p. 400] *The Millere's Tale,* a poem which deserves to be called the master piece of Chaucer.

[p. 482] There are 12 English poems . . . I doubt if any one of these, ascribed to Chaucer, be in the common editions of his works, but he was lord of the manor of poetry for a long time, and all stray cattle went to him.

1786. R., B. ; Unknown; W., C. ; W., T., H. *Letters* and *Notes* [in] The Gentleman's Magazine. *See* below, App. A.

1786. Seward, Anna. *Letter to George Hardinge, Esq.,* [dated] Lichfield, Oct. 27, 1786. (Letters of Anna Seward, Edinburgh, 1811, vol. i, p. 206.)

The author [Hayley, in his Essay on Epic Poetry; *see* above, 1782, p. 466] did not mean that time had made the frolic compositions of Chaucer *heavy* as lead—he uses the word, but says "dark as lead." Time, rendering their language obsolete, may well be allowed to have made that metal dim, or dark as lead, that once was brilliant as steel and gold.

1786. Tooke, John Horne. Επεα Πτεροεντα *or the Diversions of Purley,* pp. 186 *n.,* 197–9, 216–19 *nn.,* 230 *n.,* 241 [reference to *Bot* in Glossary to Urry's Chaucer], 242, 244 *n.,* 257 [reference to Junius, who quotes Chaucer], 259, 260, 284 *n.,* 349 *n.,* 394–5, 439, 458 and *n.,* 463–4, 467, 469, 471–2, 484–5, 497–9, 500–2, 506–8, 518. [These are merely passing references, largely in the form of footnotes.] *MS. notes,* pp. 197, 198, 224, 225, 228, interleaved p. of MS. to face pp. 230–1, 232, 245, 261, 266, 267, 274, 275, 306, 374, 462, 463, 464, 465, 467, 468, 471, 472, 473, 485, 494, 496, 497, 498, 499, 500, 501, 509, 511, 517, 519; also two leaves of MS. notes at the end of the book.]

[This copy of the 1st edition (B. M. pr. m. C. 60. i. 15) has been corrected by the author for the 2nd edition, 1797, in which most of the MS. notes were subsequently embodied. These additions are principally extracts from the older poets, more especially Chaucer. *See also* below, 1790, Cassander, p. 491.]

1787. A., J. ; **Search**, T. ; **Unknown ; W.**, T. H. *Letters* and *article* [in] The Gentleman's Magazine. *See* below, App. A.

1787. Headley, Henry. *Select Beauties of Ancient English Poetry, with Remarks by Henry Headley, A.B.,* vol. i, Preface, p. x.

. . . I have avoided, as much as possible touching those who have already justly obtained the distinction of being denominated our Older Classics,[1] who, though not universally either read or understood (as must ever be the case with the best elder writers in every country), are notwithstanding familiar to us in conversation, and constantly appealed to in controverted points of poetical taste : these I have studiously avoided, and confined myself in the general, to some of the better parts of the unfortunate few who still remain unpopular. . . .

[1] As Chaucer, Shakspeare, Jonson, Milton.

[The poets quoted from are : Tho. May, Phineas and Giles Fletcher, Richard Niccols, William Browne, Thomas Sackville, Lord Buckhurst, Michael Drayton, Richard Crashawe, Samuel Daniel, George Gascoigne, William Warner, Sir John Beaumont, William King, Robert Southwell, Francis Quarles, Sir John Davies, William Habington, Sir Henry Wotton, E. Kinwelmershe, George Herbert, Sir Thomas Wyatt, Richard Lovelace, Thomas Carew, Dr. Richard Corbet, William Drummond, James Graham Lord Montrose, Sir William Davenant, Henry Howard Earl of Surrey, Q. Elizabeth, " M. Yloop," Sir Walter Raleigh.]

1787. Unknown. *Genealogical note* on a copy of a letter written by William de la Pole, Duke of Suffolk, d. 1450, to his son, John de la Pole, [in] Annual Register for 1787, vol. xxix, pt. ii, p. 96 *n.* [Mentions Alice, grand-daughter of Geoffrey Chaucer.]

1787. Warton, Thomas. *Ode on His Majesty's birthday. June 4, 1787.* Stanzas 1 and 4, [in] The Poems on Various Subjects of Thomas Warton, . . . Now first collected . . . 1791, pp. 241, 244.

[stanza i]　The noblest Bards of Albion's choir
　　Have struck of old this festal lyre.
　　Ere Science, struggling oft in vain,
　　Had dar'd to break her Gothic chain,
　Victorious Edward gave the vernal bough
　Of Britain's bay to bloom on Chaucer's brow :
　Fir'd with the gift, he chang'd to sounds sublime
　His Norman minstrelsy's discordant chime ;
　　In tones majestic hence he told
　　The banquet of Cambuscan bold ;
　　And oft he sung (howe'er the rhyme
　　Has moulder'd to the touch of time)
　　His martial master's knightly board
　　And Arthur's ancient rites restor'd ;
　The prince in sable steel that sternly frown'd,
　And Gallia's captive king, and Cressy's wreath renown'd.

[stanza iv]　Had these blest Bards been call'd, to pay
　　The vows of this auspicious day,
　　Each had confess'd a fairer throne,
　　A mightier sovereign than his own !
　Chaucer had bade his hero-monarch yield
　The martial fame of Cressy's well-fought field
　To peaceful prowess, and the conquests calm,
　That braid the sceptre with the patriot's palm . . .

1788. Belzebub. *Letters on Education* [in] The Gentleman's Magazine, May 1788, p. 391. *See* below, App. A.

1789. Diplom. [and others]. *Letters* [in] The Gentleman's Magazine, June, Sept., Nov., 1789. *See* below, App. A.

1789. Gregory, G[eorge]. *The Life of Thomas Chatterton . . . with a concise view of the controversy concerning Rowley's Poems*, pp. 44, 149, 175, 195.

[This was first published in A. Kippis's Biographia Britannica, vol. iv, 1789, pp. 573–619. The Chaucer references are pp. 579, 600, 605, 609.]

1789. N., B. ? *Verse* [with a letter, signed B. N., and dated Nottingham Jan. 1789 in] The Literary Museum, ed. by Francis Godolphin Waldron, 1792. [Each extract has a separate pagination ; *see* list of contents.]

Onne mie Maister LYDGATE, *his travellynge ynnto Fraunce*
Written three hundred and sixty years since.

　　Maister of Poettes, venerable,
　　Ryghte worthye, honourable,

　　　·　　·　　·　　·　　·　　·

Myror of deauratte Eloquence,
Sythennes dygne Mayster Chaucere,
Eke Ennglonndes Poette Dan Gowere,
And Occleue are gone fro us,
Poettes hertedde as Vergilius . . .

[Note by Waldron.] Whether this Poem was written by a *Rowley* or a *Chatterton* I will not presume to say ; I only take the liberty to say that the MS. from which it was printed has a few inaccuracies, which denote it to have been a transcript. . .

1789. [**Neve**, Philip.] *Cursory Remarks on some of the Ancient English Poets,* pp. 1–9, [account of Chaucer] pp. 10, 22, 61, 62, 128.

[p. 2] The *general Prologue* is justly the most celebrated part of *Chaucer*'s works. The acuteness of his observation, his judgment, and discrimination of character are there alike con-
[p. 3] spicuous. Nor is it wonderful that a mind, possessing much native humour, and enriched by long experience and extensive information, should exhibit characters such as are there to be found, with striking resemblance to nature and living manners.

Chaucer, for the time when he wrote, was a very learned, and a very powerful master in his art. When he began his *Canterbury Tales*, English could scarcely be called the predominant language of the country. . . . To enrich his English style, therefore, he consulted the best foreign sources. . . .

[p. 5] Against his diction, his uncouth and obsolete terms (as they are called), the general prejudice is unreasonably strong. *Chaucer* is not now what he was, before the year 1775. In that year, Mr *Tyrwhitt*, a gentleman who can never be named, without respect and gratitude, by any scholar, or reader of *Chaucer*, published the *Canterbury Tales* with a Glossary,
[p. 6] Notes, and Illustrations, executed with method, acumen and perspicuity, no where exceeded, among all the commentators on books. In this edition, the text is published in its original purity ; and a reader, to go through with it, has only to consult his faithful guide the editor; who will equally amuse and instruct him, on the pilgrimage. Of corruptions in the text of *Chaucer*, every page, sentence, almost every line would afford example, before the publication of this edition. To take the instance, which offers itself most readily to those, who have not at hand the different editions of *Chaucer* to compare ; that couplet of *Pope*, in his Epistle of *Eloisa to Abelard*,

> Love, free as air, at sight of human ties,
> Spreads his light wings, and in a moment flies—

is taken from Chaucer's *Frankeleines Tale,*

> Love wol not be *constreined* by maistrie.
> Whan maistrie cometh, the *God* of Love anon
> *Beteth* his winges, and, *farewel,* he is gon.

Bishop *Warburton,* in his notes on *Pope,* has quoted these
[p. 7] lines of *Chaucer,* from that vile edition, published by Mr.
Urry ; and they stand,

> Love will not be *confin'd* by maisterie ;
> When maisterie comes, the *Lord* of Love anon
> *Flutters* his wings, and *forthwith* is he gone :—

by which it is seen, that, in three lines, are four words, which
do not belong to *Chaucer.*

[p. 8]   [The writer next compares Chaucer to Dryden, and quotes
the description of morning from the *Knight's Tale* as given
by Chaucer and Dryden respectively, stating that in point
of harmony Chaucer excels.]

1789. P., R. O. *Particular Circumstances which connects us with past
Ages* [in] The Gentleman's Magazine, Feb. 1789, vol. lix, p. 116.

[We] are not altogether strangers to Chaucer, Lydgate and
Gower in the fourteenth [century].

1789. Powell, [?] *Preface* [to] Lille, James de, Translation from the
French of his Garden, or the Art of Laying out groundes, by
Powell, 1789. 12mo. **4**s.

[The amateur in landscape] will admire, but without regret,
the few faint touches etched by HOMER, and by VIRGIL : . . .
he will warm and enrich his imagination with the brilliant
enchantments of TASSO and ARIOSTO, with the fond fancies
of CHAUCER and SPENSER, with the Paradise of MILTON ; he
will correct his judgement with the critical lessons of BACON,
of TEMPLE, and of POPE, with the various designs of WATELET
and MOREL, with the chaste touches of MASON, and the judicious
illustrations of BURGH.   Thus, with a mind taught to admire,
and willing to imitate the fair forms of genuine nature, he
will ever follow, obedient to the ' Genius of the Place,' and, as
situation may suggest, either walk with the cautious KENT, or
tread the fairy footsteps of BROWN.

[Dr. N. Drake, in *Noontide Leisure,* 1824, vol. i, p. 111, publishes an extract from
the prefatory address by the translator of the Abbé de Lille's *Les Jardins.* He gives
the date as 1789, but not the exact title of the work ; the above title is taken from
Watt, *Bibliotheca Britannica,* 1824, under Lille, and must refer to the same work.
We have been unable to find a reference to the book itself in any catalogue.]

1789. Shaw, Stebbing. *A Tour to the West of England in 1788*, pp. 90–93. (Reprinted in 1808 in Pinkerton's Collections of Voyages and Travels, vol. ii, p. 195.)

[A description of Woodstock, taken almost verbatim from Dart's Life of Chaucer, prefaced to Urry's edn. 1721, *q.v.* above, p. 358.]

1789. Seward, Anna. *Letter to Mr Weston*, [dated] Lichfield, Jan. 7, 1789. (Letters of Anna Seward, Edinburgh, 1811, vol. ii, p. 211.)

Have you reflected, that the most brilliant and celebrated of Dryden's works (his noble Ode excepted) are paraphrastic translations from Chaucer, &c.   Neither he nor Pope have one original poem so rich in poetic invention . . . as Hayley's Triumphs of Temper.

[In a letter to the Rev. T. S. Whalley, April 16, 1799 (Letters, vol. v, p. 216), Miss Seward makes practically the same remark as above.]

1789. Seward, Anna. *Article* [in] The Gentleman's Magazine. *See* below, App. A.

1789. Waldron, Francis Godolphin. *Prefatory note* [to a reprint of] The Period of Mourning . . . by Henry Peacham . . . 1613 [in] The Literary Museum. [Each reprint has separate pagination ; *see* list of contents.]

To reprint the writings of *Chaucer, Spenser, Shakespeare,* or *Milton*, now entitles an editor to no other praise than that which results from a careful collation of ancient copies, and an intelligent illustration of the text.   To revive the almost forgotten lines of their minor contemporaries, as it is an arduous, is (it is presumed) not an immeritorious task. . . .

1789. Walpole, Horace. *Letter to Miss Mary and Miss Agnes Berry*, [dated] Strawberry Hill, Sept. 4, 1789. (Letters of Horace Walpole, ed. Mrs. Paget Toynbee, vol. xiv, p. 201.)

As Spenser says,

> A semely man our hostè is withal
> To ben a marshal in a lordis hall.

[The lines are not by Spenser, but are incorrectly quoted from Chaucer's Prologue to the C. Tales, ll. 751-2.]

1790. Cassander I, *pseud.* [i. e. **Bruckner**, John.] *Criticisms on the Diversions of Purley, in a letter to Horne Tooke, Esq.*, p. 55.

In your next article [1] you represent *Bot* and *But* as having been originally, that is in the Anglo-Saxon, two words very

[1] p. 232 [of the Diversions of Purley].

different in origin, as well as signification.   Would you be so
obliging, Sir, as to let us know, in what Anglo-Saxon author
one is likely ɩo see this nice distinction observed . . . you
quote, indeed, Chaucer and Gawin Douglas . . . But on what
ground can [the latter] be called, I will not say an original,
but an Anglo-Saxon writer?   I apprehend, that neither he,
nor Chaucer who lived an hundred years before him will pass
for one of the number among those who consider how much
the language had been vitiated at the time they lived by the
importation of foreign words.[1]

[1] See Johnson's Preface, Art. Chaucer.

[Cf. 1786, Tooke, Diversions of Purley, p. 486 above.]

1790. 'Climax.' *Letter* [on Chaucer's use of 'han' in] The Gentleman's
Magazine, Aug. 1790, p. 692.

1790. Herbert, William.   *Typographical Antiquities . . . begun by the
late Joseph Ames . . . considerably augmented . . . by William
Herbert,* in 3 volumes, 1785–90, vol. iii, 1790, pp. 1356 [Greene's
Vision, 1592, Description of Chaucer quoted, p. 137, above]; 1776
[Troilus and Cressida, printed by W. de Worde, 1517, Colophon
quoted, *see* p. 72 above]; 1777 [The assemble of foules, printed by
R. Copland, 1530, *see* p. 76 above]; 1784, 1816.   [For vol. i *see*
above, 1785, p. 477, for vol. ii, above, 1786, p. 483, for Ames,
above, 1749, p. 398, for Dibdin's enlarged edn., below, 1810.]

1790. Malone, Edmond.   *Notes* [in] The Plays and Poems of William
Shakespeare.   *See* below, Appendix A.

1790. 'Philologus.' *Letter* [in] The Gentleman's Magazine, July,
1790.   *See* above, p. 405.

1790. [Ritson, Joseph.]   *Ancient Songs from the time of King
Henry the Third to the Revolution,* Introduction, pp. xv *n.*, xix,
xxxi–iii, xxxvi *n.* 10, xli–vii, 2.

[p. xxxi]   The venerable father of English poetry had in his time
  penned "many a song and many a lecherous lay," of which
  we have infinitely more reason to regret the loss, than he had
  in his old age to repent the composition.   His larger works,
  and above all the inimitable Canterbury Tales, afford us
[p.xxxii]numerous particulars relative to the state of vocal melody in
  that age . . .

[1790 ?] Unknown. *The Good and Bad Priests.*   Fowler, Printer,
Silver Street, Salisbury.   [A single sheet.]   The Good Priest.
From Chaucer's *Canterbury* Tales [part of Dryden's Character of a
good Parson].   The Bad Priest, a modern character.

1790. White, James. *The Adventures of John of Gaunt, Duke of Lancaster,* 2 vols. 12°.

[Chaucer appears as a character. The manuscript (says the introduction) was compiled in Latin :] by friar Hildebrand, a Cistercian, at the desire, and under the auspices of Geoffrey Chaucer, that pleasant poet, for the use of his neighbour the lord abbot of Reading ; and was discovered by White, when wandering thro' the ruins of an ancient castle, well known to have been a residence of Geoffrey Chaucer, and turned into English by him.

[See an account of this by Wilbur L. Cross in *Anglia*, vol. xxv, p. 251.]

1791. Boswell, James. *The Life of Samuel Johnson, LL.D.,* by James Boswell, 1791 (ed. G. Birkbeck Hill, 1887, vol. i, p. 306).

Christopher Smart . . . was one of the stated undertakers of this miscellany [The Universal Visiter], and it was to assist him that Johnson sometimes employed his pen. All the essays marked with two *asterisks* have been ascribed to him, but I am confident, from internal evidence, that of these, neither 'The Life of Chaucer,' 'Reflections on the State of Portugal,' nor an 'Essay on Architecture,' were written by him. [*See* above, 1756, Unknown, p. 412.]

1791. C., H. *Letter* [in] The Gentleman's Magazine, Dec. 1791, p. 1119.

[Chaucer's use of ' moison.']

1791. [Huddesford, George.] *Salmagundi,* p. 143. *See* below, App. A.

1791. Lodge, Edmund. *Illustrations of British History,* etc., 3 vols. 1791, vol. iii, p. 171.

[A reference, in a note, to Chaucer's connection with Donnington.]

[This note is referred to in John Nichols' *Progresses of King James*, I, 258, note.]

1791. [Smith, John Thomas.] *Antiquities of London* [engraved plates, without pagination or signatures ; pages have been added in pencil] p. 27.

[A Picture of John Stowe] From his Monument in the church of St. Andrew, Undershaft . . . our Author Stowe, had a principal hand in two improved Editions of Chaucers works, published in this reign. . . .

1791. Unknown. *Imitation of Chaucer* [in] The Bee. *See* below, App. A.

1791. Unknown. [*Review* of] The Miller's Tale : from Chaucer [in] The Monthly Review, 1791, vol. vi, pp. 456-7.

[This is otherwise unknown ; it can hardly be by Lipscomb, who omitted the Miller's Tale from his Canterbury Tales.]

1792. G., D. R. H. ; **Mercier,** R. E. ; **Tyson,** [M.]; **Sigla ; Unknown.** *Letters, article* and *review* [in] The Gentleman's Magazine. *See* below, App. A.

1792. Lipscomb, William.	*The Pardoner's Tale . . . modernized from Chaucer.*

[This separate edition of the Pardoner's Tale is known from the notice in The Monthly Review, *q.v.* immediately below. For Lipscomb's complete Modernization of the Canterbury Tales, *see* below, 1795, p. 496.]

1792. Unknown. *Review* of The Pardoner's Tale, from Chaucer. By the Rev. Wm. Lipscomb [in] The Monthly Review, vol. ix, p. 456.

[A brief notice, postponing a full review until the whole Canterbury Tales should appear. *See* below, 1795, p. 496.]

1792. "M——s." *Letter* [in] Gentleman's Magazine, June 1792, vol. lxii, p. 532, col. ii.

Ch. Ch. Oxf., June 14.

Mr. Urban,

Every one who visits Woodstock Park and Blenheim must feel indignant at that false taste which removed, as an unpleasing object, the ruins of the antient palace of our kings, and the habitation of the Black Prince. There are, however, still existing some remains of the house of Chaucer, which is now made use of as a malt-house, and if there is no drawing of it, I wish some friendly hand would rescue so venerable an object from oblivion. In the Picture Gallery at Oxford there is a portrait of our old Bard with the date of 1400 on it, the year in which he died. May not this be the work of Thomas Occlive, who (as is said in D'Urry's [*sic*] edition] "lived in his life, and was his scholar?" The manner, however, appears to be better than might be expected from that age,[1] and the painting is in good preservation. I have not Tyrwhitt's edition to refer to.

M——s.

[1] [*Note.*] Since I wrote the above, I am induced almost to relinquish my opinion from the silence of Lord Orford, with respect to this portrait, in his Anecdotes of Painting, vol. I, p. 52.

[In the Gentleman's Magazine for July 1792, vol. xxxii, p. 624, is an article, signed D. H., in which the above is commented on : 'The portraits by Chaucer are all very much alike, and may have been copied from that by Occleve.']

1792. **Seward,** Anna. *Letter to Henry Cary, Esq., of Christ Church,*
[dated] May 29, 1792. (Letters of Anna Seward, Edinburgh, 1811,
vol. iii, pp. 140, 141.)

Your assertion that Chaucer, Spenser, and Milton are the
greatest poets of this country, may be controverted. Chaucer
had certainly genius; but beneath the rust of his obsolete,
coarse, and inharmonious diction, there is no ascertaining its
degree.

1792. **T.,** I. *Letter* [in] Gentleman's Magazine, [dated] Harewood, June
1792, vol. lxii, p. 614.

N.B. The inclosed head of Chaucer (*fig.* 4) has been in my
possession many years; I believe it (though a hasty performance) to be a good likeness of that eminent poet, and hope it
will find a place in your excellent Miscellany.

[Under the print of Chaucer, to face p. 612, is the lettering : ' Chaucer, from an
antient Illumination by his Disciple Hoccleve ; in the Collection of the Rev^d. M^r.
[Michael] Tyson.']

1793. [**Anderson,** Robert ?] *The Life of Chaucer* [prefixed to his Poems
in] The Poets of Great Britain (Anderson's Poets), 1795. [1793 is
the date on title-page of Chaucer's Works. For Anderson's general
preface to the series, *see* below, 1795, p. 496.]

1793. **Bromley,** Henry. *A Catalogue of engraved British Portraits,*
p. 18.

Literary Persons.

	Painter or Designer.	Engraver or Printseller.
. . . .		
Geoffrey CHAUCER, Poet. Ob. 1400, æt. 72.		
—— in the public library, at Ox-		
ford . . . *sm. mez.*		(Faber.)
—— in Birch's " Lives " .		J. Houbraken.
—— wh. len. with his genealogy,		
prefixed to his " Works,"		
by Speght, 1598 *l. fol.*		J. S(peght.)
—— in the set of *Poets* . *l. fol.*	T. Occleve.	G. Vertue.
—— square . . . *l. fol.*	Id.	Id.
—— prefixed to his " Canterbury		
Tales," 1727 . *8vo.*		Id.
—— oval, with Milton, Butler,		
Cowley and Walter[*sic*] *8vo.*		Id.
—— in an oval of palms *4to mez.*		
—— with Spencer, Shakespeare,		
and Jonson . *mez.*		

[1793.] Ritson, Joseph. *Letter to Mr. Robert Harrison* [dated] 7th Oct.
2d year of the French republic [in] The Letters of Joseph Ritson,
[ed. . . . by his nephew, Joseph Frank], 1833, vol. ii, p. 29.

The words *haberdasher* and *beshrew* still baffle all my etymological researches.   The former is used by Chaucer, so that I
entirely abandon the cry of Frankfort Fair : *Hebt u das herr !*

1794. Alves, Robert. *Sketches of a History of Literature: containing
Lives and Characters of the most eminent writers in different
languages, ancient and modern, and critical remarks on their
works* . . . Edinburgh . . . 1794, pp. 63, 112, 113.

[p. 112]   . . . He [Chaucer] was the author of the Canterbury
Tales, and other works of excellent humour.   But he had
an equal turn for the higher species of poetry ; being a sun
of literature, a genius of the first rank, capable of various
exertions, and justly entitled the father of English verse ; for
though his numbers are rude, and his style now obsolete, we
may still discern that his sense is strong, and his wit genuine.

1794. [Mathias, Thomas James.]   *The Pursuits of Literature, or What
you will : A Satirical Poem in Dialogue*, pp. 26, 28–9 *n.*, 37.

[p. 26]   Hold ! cries Tom Payne, that *margin* let me measure,
And rate the separate value of each treasure :
Eager they gaze—Well, Sirs, the feat is done ;
Cracherode's *Poëtæ Principes* have won :
In silent exultation down he sits,
'Mong well be-Chaucer'd Winkyn-Wordian wits.

> .   .   .   .

[p. 37]   The sage *Ichnobates* [1] see Tyrwhitt limp ;

[1] *Ichnobates* means a dog who *tracks* out the game before him.   No
one was more diligent than this dog, yet he frequently went upon a
wrong scent ; but would never suffer the huntsman to call him off,
especially in the neighbourhood of *Canterbury* and *Bristol* [i. e. Chaucer
and Chatterton]. . . . If I were again to metamorphose these hounds
into men, I should lament the application of Mr. Tyrwhitt's learning
and sagacity.

[For the reference on p. 29, *see* below, App. A., 1794.]

1794. P., B. ; **Unknown.**   *Notes* and *reviews* [in] The Gentleman's
Magazine.   *See* below, App. A.

1794. [Penn, John.]   *The Squire's Tale, a fragment from Chaucer,*
[printed in] Poems, London, 1794, sign. B 4–E 1b.

[The poem is headed by the extract from Milton's Il Penseroso,

> ' Call up him that left half told
>   The story of Cambuscan bold ' . . .

and begins :]

Part I.

In Sarra's city once, in Tartary, reign'd
A King who was with Russia's tribes maintain'd ;
By which there fell in arms, of splendid fame,
Full many a Knight,' . . .

[This is a pamphlet containing three poems only, each of which has separate pagination ; on the title page is the following note in a late 18th or early 19th century hand : "This Pamphlet was printed at the private press of the Author John Penn Esq at Stoke Park near Windsor." It is quite different from Ogle's version, which is in stanzas, while this is in heroic couplets.]

1795. Anderson, Robert. *Preface* to A Complete Edition of the Poets of Great Britain, vol. i, pp. 2–5.

[Contains some account of previous Collections of British Poets, and remarks on Chaucer having been excluded from Johnson's Poets, although the original intention was to include him ; *see* above, 1777, Dilly, Edward, p. 448. The Chaucer was printed in 1793, *see* above, p. 494.]

1795. D'Israeli, Isaac. *An Essay on the Manners and Genius of the Literary Character*, p. 117.

The witty Cowley despised the natural Chaucer.

[The reference is to Dryden's preface to his Fables ; *see* above, 1700, p. 280, and 1782, Warton, p. 471.]

1795. [Lipscomb, William.] *The Canterbury Tales of Chaucer ; completed in a modern Version. In three volumes.* 1795. Preface, pp. v–x, Postscript, p. xi, both by Lipscomb, Life of Chaucer, pp. 1–68 [Lipscomb says this Life is by Tyrwhitt, which is incorrect. It is the Life which appears in the Biographia Britannica, 1748 [*q.v.* above, p. 395] in which year Tyrwhitt was aged 17.] Introductory Discourse by Tyrwhitt, pp. 69–137. The versions of Ogle, Betterton, Dryden, Pope, Brooke, Markland, Grosvenor and Boyse, from Ogle's edn. 1741, are reprinted in vols. i and ii, and Lipscomb's own modernizations, with Boyse's Squire's Tale, follow in vol. iii. He also prints some of Tyrwhitt's notes to the tales. For Lipscomb's previous publication of the Pardoner's Tale, *see* above, 1792, p. 492.

[Preface, vol. i, p. v.] The following collection of the Canterbury Tales, now first completed in a modern version, is offered to the public under the reasonable confidence, that the improved taste in poetry, and the extended cultivation of that, in common with all the other elegant arts, which so strongly characterizes the present day, will make lovers of verse look up to the old Bard, the Father of English poetry, with a veneration proportioned to the improvements they have made in it. . . . By a fatality almost unexampled, the venerable subject of these [p. vi] pages has found the *Temple of Fame* . . . crumble from around his shrine : the materials with which it was built

were of too perishable a nature to support the pretensions
he so justly makes to immortality ; in a word, the language,
in which he wrote, hath decayed from under him . . .

1795. Unknown. *Review* of Lipscomb's Canterbury Tales of Chaucer
completed in a modern version, [in] The Monthly Review, vol.
xviii, pp. 354–5.

[After praising Tyrwhitt's Canterbury Tales, and desider-
ating a similar edition of Chaucer's other works, the reviewer
notices Lipscomb's omission of the Miller's and Reeve's Tales.]

1795. Unknown. *Review* of Lipscomb's edition of The Canterbury
Tales of Chaucer, completed in a modern version, [in] The British
Critic, April 1795, pp. 372–8.

[p. 37]   . . . It remained for him (Mr. L.) to complete the task
(of modernisation) ; and to remove the rust of antiquity from
all the parts of this irregular drama, which had hitherto been
left untried by the pen of innovation.

.   .   .   .

The Tales, which are now for the first time exhibited in
modern dress, are certainly . . . far inferior in point of interest and excellence to those which arrested the attention and
employed the genius of former dillettanti.   Under these dis-
couragements, we think Mr. L. has executed a difficult task
well ; . . . His versification is, in general, harmonious, . . .
his language is grammatically pure ; and the ear of Swift himself was not more chaste, with respect to accuracy of rhyme.

To the acute and learned Tyrwhitt, Mr. Lipscomb is under
the greatest obligations.   The whole of the Prolegomena, the
Life of Chaucer, and the few but ingenious notes, . . . are
all the productions of this accomplished scholar . . .

.   .   .   .

We are sure that whenever the shade of the old bard shall
welcome Mr. L. to the elysium of poets, he will greet him
with affectionate cordiality, and acknowledge the fidelity and
success with which he has presented him to his modern
countrymen.

1795. Sciolus ; Unknown ; Z. , K. ; *Letters* and *reviews* [in] The
Gentleman's Magazine.   *See* below, App. A.

1795. Unknown. *A Fortnight's Ramble through London*, p. 83.

The landlady, with the politest address she was mistress
of, very cordially invited him into the bar, and he found

means to entertain her with several Canterbury tales, and cock and bull stories, about his spouse, and her relations, who were all immensely oppulent [*sic*] people.

1796. Burke, Edmund. *Letter to Mr. Malone,* [dated 8 April, 1796, in] A Biographical Memoir of Edmond Malone [by James Boswell, in] The Plays and Poems of William Shakespeare, 1821, vol. i, p. lxviii.

You have . . . given us a very interesting History of our Language, during that important period in which, after being refined by Chaucer, it fell into the rudeness of civil confusion.

1796. [Gough, Richard.] *Sepulchral Monuments in Great Britain,* vol. ii, pt. ii, 1796. *See* above, 1786, p. 483.

1796. [Mason, George.] Preface, Glossary and *Notes* [to] *Poems by Thomas Hoccleve . . . selected from a MS. in the possession of George Mason* ; pp. 2, 8, 9, 17, 18, 20–1, 25 ; Notes 27, 36–9, 42, 47, 52, 62, 78, 80 ; Glossary, 89, 92, 105, 108–9. [Passing references to Chaucer.]

1796. Meen, Henry. *Letter to Dr. Thomas Percy* [dated] Aug. 6, 1796, [printed in] Illustrations of the Literary History of the 18th century . . . by John Bowyer Nichols, vol. vii, 1848, pp. 39–40.

[Remarks on "quappe" used by Chaucer.]

1796. Ritson, Joseph. *Letter to Mr. [Robert] Harrison* [dated] 15th August, 1796 [in] The Letters of Joseph Ritson, [ed. by . . . his nephew, Joseph Frank] 1833, vol. ii, p. 129.

And first as to the word

Harow

which you have so frequently met with : as for instance, in

Chaucer : "Thai crieden, out ! *harow* and wala wa ! "

1796. Steevens, George. *Letter to Dr. Thomas Percy,* [dated] Oct. 24, 1796, [printed in] Illustrations of the Literary History of the 18th century . . . by John Bowyer Nichols . . . vol. vii, 1848, pp. 5–7.

[p. 5]   I . . . take the liberty of pointing out a passage in our late friend Mr. Tyrwhitt's edition of Chaucer, that seems to encourage an idea that there has been blank verse, by a century at least, more ancient than any you have ascertained. . . . 'The Tale of Melibeus.' Mr. Thomas has observed that 'this Tale seems to have been written in *blank verse.*

[p. 6]   MSS. notes upon Chaucer, ed. Urry, in Brit. Mus. [*See* above, 1721, p. 353.] It is certain that in the former part of it we find a number of blank verses intermixed, in a much greater proportion than in any of our author's other prose writings. But this poetical style is not, I think, remarkable, beyond the first four or five pages.

· · · · · · · · · ·

[p. 7]   Mr. Thomas's remark on the *metrical* turn of the Melibeus may be countenanced, perhaps, in some degree, by the following article in Du Fresnoy's Bibliotheque, vol. ii, p. 248. 'Le roman de Melibée, &c. *en vers,* in fol. manuscrit, et in 4. dans la Bibliotheque Seguier.'

Some such MS. might have been Chaucer's original. He might have commenced his imitation in verse; and when he changed his design might have been too lazy to obliterate the vestiges of his first resolution.

1796. Unknown. *The Squire's Tale, imitated from Chaucer* [in] The Monthly Magazine, suppl. No. to vol. ii, pp. 987–92.

1796. Unknown. *Reviews* [in] The Gentleman's Magazine. *See* below, App. A.

1796. Waldron, Francis Godolphin. *Advertisement and Introductory Extracts* [in] *The Loves of Troilus and Creseid written by Chaucer with a Commentary by Sir Francis Kinaston. Never before published. Printed for and sold by F. G. Waldron.* [The advertisement is signed F. G. W. and dated Dec. 1, 1795. The references to Chaucer are continuous on every page, including numerous extracts from various authors. Waldron bought Kynaston's Latin MS. which included the translation of the whole work and a Latin commentary. He only published the first twelve stanzas of the first book and the commentary on them, though he had intended to complete the whole work. *See* p. 207, above, 1635, Kynaston.]

1797. J., J., H. *Letter* [in] The Gentleman's Magazine. *See* below, App. A.

1797. Lamb, Charles. *Letter to Coleridge,* [dated by mistake?] Jan. 5, 1797, [begun Sunday, Feb. 5, 1797]. (The Works of Charles and Mary Lamb, ed. E. V. Lucas, 1905, vol. vi, p. 90.)

Your dream, down to that exquisite line—"I can't tell half his adventures," is a most happy resemblance of Chaucer. The remainder is so so. The best line, I think, is, "He belong'd, I believe, to the witch Melancholy."

[The poem of Coleridge's here referred to as the "Dream," is that afterwards called "The Raven, a Christmas Tale, told by a school-boy to his little brothers and sisters," first printed in the Morning Post of Mar. 10, 1798. See letter to Godwin, Nov. 10, 1803.]

1797-8. Lee, Harriet and Sophia. *Canterbury Tales,* 2 vols. (vol. ii, 1798, by Sophia Lee).

[No connection with Chaucer beyond the title.]

1797. Ritson, Joseph.   *Letter to Mr. Robert Harrison,* [dated] 26 January, 1797, [in] The Letters of Joseph Ritson, [ed. by . . . his nephew, J. Frank,] 1883, vol. ii, pp. 144–5.

[On the use of "self" and "selves."]   You will see what Wallis, Lowth and Johnson, say on this subject; and may consult Tyrwhitt, if you have his *Chaucer,* on the other side.

1797. Unknown.   *Review* [of] The Loves of Troilus and Cresseid. written by Chaucer ; with a Commentary, by Sir Francis Kinaston, never before published, [in] The British Critic, Nov., 1797, p. 549. [*See* above, 1796, Waldron, p. 499.]

1797. Warton, Joseph.   *The Works of Alexander Pope, Esq. . . . With Notes and Illustrations by Joseph Warton, D.D. and others,* vol. i [Life of Pope], pp. xiii, xvii, lxiii ; vol. ii, pp. 51, 57–60, 102 [Translations, Temple of Fame], 107–8 [January and May]. Throughout this poem Warton inserts long extracts from Chaucer in the notes, pp. 109–118, 147–8, 165–6 [Wife of Bath]; vol. iv, p. 150 [Imitations of Horace].

[vol. ii, p. 166]   Mr. Harte assured me, that he was convinced by some circumstances which Fenton his friend communicated to him, that Pope wrote the characters that make the introduction to the Canterbury Tales, published under the name of Betterton.

[*See* above, n.a. 1710, Betterton, p. 312, and Johnson, 1779–81, p. 457.]

1798. The Canterbury Tales of Chaucer . . . by the late Thomas Tyrwhitt, Esq., F.R.S., 2nd edn. Oxford, Clarendon Press, 1798. [A reprint, in two large quarto vols., of Tyrwhitt's Canterbury Tales, 1775 (*q.v.* above, p. 442), with a few emendations and additions from MS. notes made by Tyrwhitt in his own copy of the first edn.]

[**1798**? **Haworth**, Dr.]   *MS. notes* [on words], pencilled in a copy of The Canterbury Tales of Chaucer, 2nd edition, ed. T. Tyrwhitt, Clarendon Press, 1798 [B. M. 11626. h. 2, 3].

1798. Jaques.   *See* below, Appendix A, 1798.

1798. Seward, Anna.   *Letter to Mr.* [*John*] *Saville,* [dated] Lichfield, June 15, 1798. (Letters of Anna Seward, Edinburgh, 1801, vol. v, pp. 116–123.)

[Practically the whole letter is devoted to comments on "Urry's Life of Chaucer," (i. e. Dart's Life of Chaucer, in Urry's edn., 1721), which Miss Seward had just been reading.

1798. Seward, Anna.   *Letter to the Rev. H. J. Todd, on receiving his edition of Milton's Comus,* [dated] Lichfield, Oct. 19, 1798. (Letters, vol. v, p. 159.)]

The utter want of harmonious flow in the numbers, which characterize our verse from Chaucer's time till Spenser's. . .

1798-1805. Tooke, John Horne. Επεα Πτεροεντα . . . Second edition. *See* first edition, above, 1786, p. 486.

1798. Unknown. [in] The British Critic, July, 1798, pp. 2–3. *Review* [of] [Gough's Sepulchral Monuments in Great Britain. Part II. Containing the Fifteenth Century]. [*See* above, 1786–96, p. 483.]

[Description of Chaucer's monument in Westminster Abbey quoted, followed by quotations referring to Chaucer's life.]

1798. Unknown ; Wiccamicus. *Review* and *Letter* [in] The Gentleman's Magazine. *See* below, App. A.

1798. Walpole, Horace. *A Catalogue of the Royal and Noble Authors of England,* [in] The Works of Horatio Walpole, 5 vols, vol. i, p. 564.

Chaucer had enriched rather than purified our language.

[The Appendix, in which this occurs, was added in this edition from Walpole's notes.]

1799. Adams, James. *The Pronunciation of the English Language vindicated from imputed anomaly and caprice,* p. 149.
[Barbour contemporary with Chaucer.]

1799. Fellowes, Robert. *Some account of Thomas Chatterton* [in] The Monthly Mirror, Sept. 1799, vol. viii, p. 146.

Mr. Warton has observed that Chaucer is like a genial day in an English spring ; but Chatterton appears to resemble a meteor seen in a summer sky, which passes away too soon for all its deviations to be noted, or all its lustre ascertained. [*See* above, 1782, Warton, p. 472.]

1799. Gilpin, John, and others. *Letter* and *Articles* [in] The Gentleman's Magazine. *See* below, App. A.

1799. M[anners, Catherine Rebecca], Lady. *Review of Poetry, Ancient and Modern. A Poem. By Lady M* * * * * * *

As amid the gloom of night,
When no star emits its light,
Swift the meteor's sudden ray
Gleams a momentary day ;
Thus gay Chaucer's mirthful rhymes
Glitter'd amid barb'rous times.

1799. Ritson, Joseph. *Letter to the Editor,* [Joseph Frank, dated] 8th October, 1799, [in] The Letters of Joseph Ritson, 1833, vol. ii, p. 188.

Egerton allows 1*l.* 7*s.* for Tyrwhitts Chaucer.

1799. Strutt, Joseph. *A complete view of the Dress and Habits of the people of England,* 1796, [vol. ii, 1799]. Vol. ii, pp. 128 *n.*, 129 *n.*, 132–4, 140 *n.*, 155 *n.*, 157, 167–170 *n.*, 172–3 *n.*, 176–7 *n.*, 191 *n.*, 251–2, 274, 277–285, 287–9, 292, 304 *n.*, 318, 320–1, 326, 332–3, 336–7, 348–350, 354 *n.*, 355, 357, 361, 363, 365–7, 370-4, 376-8.

[Chap. iv, p. 277] The Dresses of the several Personages described in Chaucer's Canterbury Tales briefly considered. . . . [pp. 277–285 devoted to this.]

The different characters exhibited by Chaucer, in his Canterbury Tales, are drawn with a masterly hand : they are, undoubtedly, pictures of real life, and throw great light upon the manners and customs of the age in which the Poet flourished. . . .

[Chap. vi, p. 318] It seems to have been almost as fashionable, in the days of Chaucer, to make occasional visits to the tomb of some favourite saint; as it now is to frequent the different watering places. The Poet calls his journey to Canterbury a *pilgrimage;* but surely, his description of this journey little justifies the appellation; and the generality of the stories introduced by the pious fraternity have not even a distant reference to religion; on the contrary, several of them are deficient in morality, and some few outrageous to common decency. It was evidently his intention to hold up these idle vagrancies to ridicule.

[*a.* **1800.**] **Pegge,** Samuel (the younger). *Anecdotes of the English Language,* 1803. [Published after the author's death, in 1800, written probably between 1780 and 1800.] pp. 21, 26, 27 and *n.*, 38, 70 *n.*, 81 and *n.*, 82–4, 96, 112 and *n.*, 116, 118 *n.*, 129, 130 and *n.*, 134, 135 *n.*, 142, 174 and *n.*, 198, 200 and *n.*, 201, 205, 224, 235 and *n.*, 236 *n.*, 241, 268, 274, 281.

[p. 38] It is no very easy matter to read and understand Chaucer, and the Poets of that age, currently in their old-fashioned spelling (apart from their obsolete words), even when translated, as I may term it, into modern types; and much less so in their ancient garb of the Gothick or black letter, till their language becomes familiarized by habit. I conceive farther, that the antiquated French tongue would be still more unintelligible to a Frenchman of the present age. . . .

1800. [**Brydges,** Sir Samuel Egerton.] *See* below, App. A.

1800. Howard, Frederick, 5th Earl of Carlisle. *Prologue* to *The Father's Revenge, a Tragedy : with other Poems,* sign. A 1. [This is not in the earlier edn. of 1783.]

PROLOGUE.

In ancient times, when Edward's conquering son,
O'er prostrate France his glorious course had run ;
'Midst clashing arms, and 'midst the din of war,
Meek Science follow'd not the Victor's car.
Though Gower and Chaucer knelt before her shrine,
And woo'd, on British ground, the tuneful Nine,
Yet she, to climes congenial to her soul,
Fled from our chilling blasts, and northern pole.

1800. [**Malone**, Edmond.] [*Preface* and *Additions to*] Theatrum
Poetarum Anglicanorum . . . by Edward Phillips . . . first
published in 1675, and now enlarged by additions to every article
from subsequent biographers and critics, pp. xlvii, xlviii, lvi, lix,
2, 3, 7–12, 13, 15, 16, 20–3, 25, 28, 35, 39, 178. [Many of these
are little more than quotations from Warton's Hist. of Eng. Poetry.]

[p. xlvii]   Chaucer, whose genius still shines brightly through all the
obscurities of four centuries, must have been as superior to
his cotemporaries in judgment as he was in fancy. In
rudeness, in barbarism, in grossness and flatness of imagery
and sentiments he is as much exceeded by them, as he totally
[p. xlviii] flies away from them in beauties. Such is the mighty flame,
so prophetic is the eye of genius, that he anticipated the
polish of nearly two hundred years. Perhaps, the native
powers and the rareness of genius can by no instance be so
unanswerably illustrated as by the character of Chaucer.

1800. **Malone**, Edmond. *The Critical and Miscellaneous Prose Works
of John Dryden*, 2 vols. ; vol. i, pt. i., [Life of Dryden], pp. 256,
257, 318, 319, 328, 362, 375–6, 377–8 note, 382 note, 557.

[p. 256]   . . . Such is the Golden Legend of Jacobus Januensis ; the
foundation of Chaucer's Second Nonnes Tale, which he has
inserted among his other Canterbury Tales, but appears to
have originally intended for a distinct work [footnote on
Tyrwhitt's observations on this point].

[p. 257]   [Footnote on St. Cecilia as inventress of the organ, and
quotation of Second N. T., 134–5.]

[p. 318]   That in the middle of the year 1698, he [Dryden] began
to modernize Chaucer, may be collected from a letter to
Mr. Pepys . . . from which we learn that "the Character
of a Good Parson" was introduced into this work on his
suggestion. . . . When he resolved to give rejuvenescence to

the venerable father of English poetry, he brought to his task only such a knowledge of his author, as would enable him to clothe Chaucer's meaning with the rich trappings of his own mellifluous verse. In this neglect of archaiologick lore he was by no means singular; for to the great mass of English readers at that time there is good reason for believing that this ancient bard was nearly as difficult to be understood, as if his works had been written in a foreign language.

1800. Mason, George. *Supplement to Johnson's English Dictionary,* London, 1801, p. iv.

Ash also by the help of glossaries carries his [*Johnson's*] language back to the writings of Chaucer. [*See* above, p. 441, 1775, Ash.]

1800. Trinitarius. *Letter* to the editor [in] The Gentleman's Magazine, April 1800, vol. lxx, pp, 1263–4.

[The writer encloses Chaucer's 'Character of the Parsone' newly modernised.]

1800. Tytler, Alexander Fraser (Lord Woodhouselee). *Poems of Allan Ramsay,* pp. lxxxi, *n.*, cviii.

[p. lxxxi *n.* : reference to language of Chaucer compared with Spenser. p. cviii, Ramsay's " Monk and Miller's Wife " compared with humorous work of Chaucer and Boccaccio.]

1800. Unknown. *Version,* partly modernised, of Chaucer's Character of the Parson, by " Trinitarius " (i. e. a member of Trinity College, Oxford, cf. the Oct. No., p. 943) [in] The Gentleman's Magazine, vol. lxx, pp. 1263–4.

1800. Unknown. *Letter* [in] The Gentleman's Magazine, April 1800, vol. lxx, p. 336. *See* below, App. A.

1800. Warton, Thomas. *Essays on Gothic Architecture,* p. 7.

[Warton quotes from] an old poem called *Pierce the Plowman's Creede,* written perhaps before Chaucer's [*Hous of Fame*].
[He also quotes from the *Hous of Fame.*]

1800. Wordsworth, William. *Lyrical Ballads, with other Poems.* (Preface, p. xii *n.* The Prose Works of William Wordsworth, ed. W. Knight, 2 vols., 1896, vol. i, p. 49 *n.*)

It is worth while here to observe, that the affecting parts of Chaucer are almost always expressed in language pure and universally intelligible even to this day.—W. W., 1800.

[This preface did not appear in the first edition of 1798.]

END OF VOL. I.

CAMBRIDGE: PRINTED BY W. LEWIS AT THE UNIVERSITY PRESS
FROM STEREOTYPE PLATES SUPPLIED